Mindfulness

HBR EMOTIONAL INTELLIGENCE SERIES

MW01031298

HBR Emotional Intelligence Series

How to be human at work

The HBR Emotional Intelligence Series features smart, essential reading on the human side of professional life from the pages of *Harvard Business Review*.

Empathy

Happiness

Mindfulness

Resilience

Other books on emotional intelligence from *Harvard Business Review*:

HBR's 10 Must Reads on Emotional Intelligence

HBR Guide to Emotional Intelligence

Mindfulness

HBR EMOTIONAL INTELLIGENCE SERIES

Harvard Business Review Press

Boston, Massachusetts

HBR Press Quantity Sales Discounts

Harvard Business Review Press titles are available at significant quantity discounts when purchased in bulk for client gifts, sales promotions, and premiums. Special editions, including books with corporate logos, customized covers, and letters from the company printed in the front matter, as well as excerpts of existing books, can also be created in large quantities for special needs. For details and discount information for both print and ebook formats, contact booksales@harvardbusiness.org, tel. 800-988-0886, or www.hbr.org/bulksales.

Copyright 2017
Harvard Business School Publishing Corporation
All rights reserved
Printed in the United States of America

20 19 18 17 16

No part of this publication may be reproduced, stored in or introduced into a retrieval system, or transmitted, in any form, or by any means (electronic, mechanical, photocopying, recording, or otherwise), without the prior permission of the publisher. Requests for permission should be directed to permissions@hbsp.harvard.edu, or mailed to Permissions, Harvard Business School Publishing, 60 Harvard Way, Boston, Massachusetts 02163.

The web addresses referenced in this book were live and correct at the time of the book's publication but may be subject to change.

Library of Congress Cataloging-in-Publication Data

Title: Mindfulness.
Other titles: HBR emotional intelligence series.
Description: Boston, Massachusetts : Harvard Business Review Press, [2017] | Series: HBR emotional intelligence series
Identifiers: LCCN 2016056277 | ISBN 9781633693197 (pbk. : alk. paper)
Subjects: LCSH: Mindfulness (Psychology) | Mindfulness-based cognitive therapy.
Classification: LCC BF637.M56 M56 2017 | DDC 152.4—dc23 LC record available at https://lccn.loc.gov/2016056277

ISBN: 978-1-63369-319-7
eISBN: 978-1-63369-320-3

The paper used in this publication meets the requirements of the American National Standard for Permanence of Paper for Publications and Documents in Libraries and Archives Z39.48-1992.

Contents

Contents

Mindfulness

HBR EMOTIONAL INTELLIGENCE SERIES

1

Mindfulness in the Age of Complexity

An interview with Ellen Langer by Alison Beard

O ver nearly four decades, Ellen Langer's research on mindfulness has greatly influenced thinking across a range of fields, from behavioral economics to positive psychology. It reveals that by paying attention to what's going on around us, instead of operating on autopilot, we can reduce stress, unlock creativity, and boost performance. Her "counterclockwise" experiments, for example, demonstrated that elderly men could improve their health by simply acting as if it were 20 years earlier. In this interview with senior editor Alison Beard, Langer applies her thinking to leadership and management in an age of increasing chaos.

HBR: *Let's start with the basics. What, exactly, is mindfulness? How do you define it?*

Langer: Mindfulness is the process of actively noticing new things. When you do that, it puts you in the present. It makes you more sensitive to context and perspective. It's the essence of engagement. And it's energy-begetting, not energy-consuming. The mistake most people make is to assume it's stressful and exhausting—all this thinking. But what's stressful is all the mindless negative evaluations we make and the worry that we'll find problems and not be able to solve them.

We all seek stability. We want to hold things still, thinking that if we do, we can control them. But since everything is always changing, that doesn't work. Actually, it causes you to lose control.

Take work processes. When people say, "This is the way to do it," that's not true. There are always many ways, and the way you choose should

4

depend on the current context. You can't solve today's problems with yesterday's solutions. So when someone says, "Learn this so it's second nature," let a bell go off in your head, because that means mindlessness. The rules you were given were the rules that worked for the person who created them, and the more different you are from that person, the worse they're going to work for you. When you're mindful, rules, routines, and goals guide you; they don't govern you.

What are some of the specific benefits of being more mindful, according to your research?

Better performance, for one. We did a study with symphony musicians, who, it turns out, are bored to death. They're playing the same pieces over and over again, and yet it's a high-status job that they can't easily walk away from. So we had groups of them perform. Some were told to replicate a previous performance they'd liked—that is, to play pretty mindlessly. Others were told to make their individual performance new in subtle ways—to play mindfully. Remember: This wasn't jazz, so the changes were very subtle indeed. But when we played recordings of the symphonies for people who knew nothing about the study, they overwhelmingly preferred the mindfully played pieces. So here we had a group performance where everybody was doing their own thing, and it was better. There's this view that if you let everyone do their own thing, chaos will reign. When people are doing their own thing in a rebellious way, yes, it might. But if everyone is working in the same context and is fully present, there's no reason why you shouldn't get a superior coordinated performance.

There are many other advantages to mindfulness. It's easier to pay attention. You remember more of what you've done. You're more creative. You're able to take advantage of opportunities when they present themselves. You avert the danger not yet arisen. You like people better, and people like you better, because you're less evaluative. You're more charismatic.

The idea of procrastination and regret can go away, because if you know why you're doing something, you don't take yourself to task for not doing something else. If you're fully present when you decide to prioritize this task or work at this firm or create this product or pursue this strategy, why would you regret it?

I've been studying this for nearly 40 years, and for almost any measure, we find that mindfulness generates a more positive result. That makes sense when you realize it's a superordinate variable. No matter what you're doing—eating a sandwich, doing an interview, working on some gizmo, writing a report—you're doing it mindfully or mindlessly. When it's the former, it leaves an imprint on what you do. At the very highest levels of any field—

Fortune 50 CEOs, the most impressive artists and musicians, the top athletes, the best teachers and mechanics—you'll find mindful people, because that's the only way to get there.

How have you shown a link between mindfulness and innovation?

With Gabriel Hammond, a graduate student, I ran a study where we asked participants to come up with new uses for products that had failed. We primed one group for mindlessness by telling them how the product had fallen short of its original intended use—to cite a famous example from 3M, a failed glue. We primed the other for mindfulness by simply describing the product's properties— a substance that adheres for only a short amount of time. Of course, the most creative ideas for new uses came from the second group.

I'm an artist as well as a researcher, writer, and consultant—each activity informs the others for me—and I got the idea to study mindfulness and mistakes when I was painting. I looked up and saw I was using ocher when I'd meant to use magenta, so I started trying to fix it. But then I realized I'd made the decision to use magenta only seconds before. People do this all the time. You start with uncertainty, you make a decision, and if you make a mistake, it's a calamity. But the path you were following was just a decision. You can change it at any time, and maybe an alternative will turn out better. When you're mindful, mistakes become friends.

How does being mindful make someone more charismatic?

We've shown this in a few studies. An early one was with magazine salespeople: The mindful ones sold more and were rated as more likable by buyers. More recently, we've looked at the bind that women executives face: If they act in strong, stereotypically masculine ways, they're seen as bitchy, but if they act feminine, they're seen as weak and not leadership material. So we asked two groups of women to give persuasive speeches. One group was told to act masculine, the other to act feminine. Then half of each group was instructed to give their speech mindfully, and we found that audiences preferred the mindful speakers, regardless of what gender role they were playing out.

And mindfulness also makes you less judgmental about others?

Yes. We all have a tendency to mindlessly pigeonhole people: He's rigid. She's impulsive. But when you freeze someone in that way, you don't get the chance to enjoy a relationship with them or use their talents. Mindfulness helps you to appreciate why people behave the way they do. It makes sense to them at the time, or else they wouldn't do it.

We did a study in which we asked people to rate their own character traits—the things they would most like to change and the things they most valued about themselves—and we found a big irony. The traits that people valued tended to be positive versions of the ones they wanted to change. So the reason I personally can't stop being impulsive is that I value being spontaneous. That means if you want to change my behavior, you'll have to persuade me not to like spontaneity. But chances are that when you see me from this proper perspective— spontaneous rather than impulsive—you won't want to change me.

Mindful management

What else can managers do to be more mindful?

One tactic is to imagine that your thoughts are totally transparent. If they were, you wouldn't think awful things about other people. You'd find a way to understand their perspective.

And when you're upset about something—maybe someone turned in an assignment late or didn't do it the way you wanted—ask yourself, "Is it a tragedy or an inconvenience?" It's probably the latter. Most of the things that get us upset are.

I also tell people to think about work/life *integration*, not balance. "Balance" suggests that the two are opposite and have nothing in common. But that's not true. They're both mostly about people. There are stresses in both. There are schedules to be met. If you keep them separate, you don't learn to transfer what you do successfully in one domain to the other. When we're mindful, we realize that categories are person constructed and don't limit us.

Remember, too, that stress is not a function of events; it's a function of the view you take of events. You think a particular thing is going to happen and that when it does, it's going to be awful. But prediction is an illusion. We can't know what's going to happen. So give yourself five reasons you won't lose the job. Then think of five reasons why, if you did, it would be an advantage—new opportunities, more time with family, et cetera. Now you've gone from thinking it's definitely going to happen to thinking maybe it will and even if it does, you'll be OK.

If you feel overwhelmed by your responsibilities, use the same approach. Question the belief that you're the only one who can do it, that there's only one way to do it, and that the company will collapse if you don't do it. When you open your views to be mindful, the stress just dissipates.

Mindfulness helps you realize that there are no positive or negative outcomes. There's A, B, C, D, and more, each with its challenges and opportunities.

Give me some scenarios, and I'll explain how mindfulness helps.

I'm the leader of a team in dissent. People are arguing vehemently for different strategies, and I have to decide on one.

There's an old story about two people coming before a judge. One guy tells his side of the story, and the judge says, "That's right." The other guy tells his side of the story, and the judge says, "That's right." They say, "We can't both be right." And the judge says, "That's right." We have this mindless notion to settle disputes with a choice between this way or that way, or a compromise. But win-win solutions can almost always be sought. Instead of letting people lock into their positions, go back and open it up. Have opponents play the debate from the other side so that they realize there are good arguments either way. Then find a way for both of them to be right.

I'm an executive with lots of commitments who's facing a personal crisis.

If I couldn't do this interview because I was having a problem at home, I would say, "Alison, I hope you'll forgive me, but my mind is elsewhere right now because I'm having this crisis." And you might say, "Oh, no, I had a crisis last week. It's OK. I understand." And then, when the crisis was over, we could come back to what we were doing, but with a whole new relationship, which would set us up for all sorts of good things in the future.

I'm a boss giving a review to an underperforming employee.

Make clear that the evaluation is *your* perspective, not a universal one, which opens up the dialogue. Let's say a student or a worker adds one and one and gets one. The teacher or employer can just say "Wrong," or he can try to figure out how the person got to one. Then the worker says, "If you add one wad of chewing gum to another wad, one plus one equals one." Now the boss has learned something.

As a leader, you can walk around as if you're God and get everybody to quiver. But then you're not going to learn anything, because they're not going to tell you, and you're going to be lonely and unhappy. It doesn't have to be lonely at the top. You can be there and be open.

How do you create a more mindful organization?

When I'm doing consulting work with companies, I usually start by showing everyone how mindless they are and what they're missing as a result. You can be mindless only if two conditions are met: You've found the very best way of doing things, and nothing changes. Of course, those conditions can't be met. So if you're going to work, you should be there and notice things. Then I explain that there are alternative ways of getting anywhere, and in fact, you can't even be sure that the destination you've chosen is ultimately where you'll want to be. Everything looks different from different perspectives.

I tell leaders they should make not knowing OK—I don't know, you don't know, nobody knows—rather than acting like they know, so everyone else pretends *they* know, which leads to all sorts of discomfort and anxiety. Eliminate zero-accident policies. If you have a zero-accident policy, you're going to have a maximum-lying policy. Get people to ask, "Why? What are the benefits of doing it this way versus another way?" When you do that, everyone relaxes a little, and you're all better able to see and take advantage of opportunities.

I was working with a nursing home years ago, and a nurse walked in, complaining that one of the residents didn't want to go to the dining room. She wanted to stay in her room and eat peanut butter. So I butted in and said, "What's wrong with that?" Her answer was "What if everybody wants to do it?" And I said, "Well, if everybody did it, you'd save a lot of money on food. But, more seriously, it would tell you something about how the food is being prepared or served. If it's only one person occasionally, what's the big deal? If it happens all the time, there's an opportunity here."

I imagine you don't like checklists?

The first time you go through a checklist, it's fine. But after that, most people tend to do it mindlessly. So in aviation you have flaps up, throttle open, anti-ice off. But if snow is coming and the anti-ice is off, the plane crashes.

Checklists aren't bad if they require qualitative information to be obtained in that moment. For example, "Please note the weather conditions. Based on these conditions, should the anti-ice be on or off?" or "How is the patient's skin color different from yesterday?" If you ask questions that encourage mindfulness, you bring people into the present and you're more likely to avoid an accident.

Mindful, qualitative comments help in interpersonal relationships, too, by the way. If you're giving a compliment, "You look great" is not nearly as effective as something like "Your eyes are sparkling today." To say that, you have to be there, and people will recognize and appreciate it.

Mindfulness and focus

The business environment has changed a lot since you began studying mindfulness. It's more complex and uncertain. We have new data and analysis coming at us all the time. So mindfulness becomes more important for navigating the chaos—but the chaos makes it a lot harder to be mindful.

I think chaos is a perception. People say that there's too much information, and I would say that there's no more information now than there was before. The difference is that people believe they have to know it—that the more information they have, the better the product is going to be and the more money the company is going to make. I don't think it depends as much on the amount of information someone has as on the way it's taken in. And that needs to be mindfully.

How has technology changed our ability to be mindful? Is it a help or a hindrance?

Again, one can bring mindfulness to anything. We've studied multitasking and found that if you're open and keep the boundaries loose, it can be an advantage. The information from one thing can help you with another. I think what we should do is learn from the way technology is fun and compelling and build that into our work.

HBR recently published an article on the importance of focus in which the author, Daniel Goleman, talks about the need for both exploration and exploitation. How do you balance mindfulness—constantly looking for the new—with the ability to buckle down and get things done?

Vigilance, or very focused attention, is probably mindless. If I'm racing through the woods on horseback, watching the branches so that I don't get hit in the face, I might miss the boulder on the ground, so then my horse stumbles and I'm thrown off. But I don't think that's what Dan means by focus. What you want is a soft openness—to be attentive to the things you're doing but not single-minded, because then you're missing other opportunities.

We hear the management community talking more about mindfulness now. When did you realize that the ideas you've been studying for decades had become mainstream?

I was at a party, and two different people came up to me and said, "Your mindfulness is everywhere."

Of course, I just saw a new film that starts with someone going around Harvard Square asking people what mindfulness is, and nobody knows. So there's still a lot of work to do.

What are you working on next?

The Langer Mindfulness Institute works in three arenas: health, aging, and the workplace. In health we want to see just how far we can push the mind-body notion. Years ago we did studies on chambermaids (who lost weight after being told their work was exercise) and vision (where people did better on eye tests that had them work up from large letters at the bottom to small ones at the top, creating the expectation that they would be able to read them). Now we're trying a mindfulness cure on many diseases that people think are uncontrollable to see if we can at least ameliorate the symptoms. We're also doing counterclockwise retreats around the world, starting in San Miguel de Allende, Mexico, using research-proven techniques to help people live boldly. And we're doing conferences and consulting on work/life integration, mindful leadership and strategy processes, stress reduction, and innovation, with companies such as Thorlo and Santander and NGOs such as CARE and Vermont's Energy Action Network.

I'm told that I drive my students crazy because I'm always coming up with new ideas. I'm thinking about maybe a mindfulness camp for children. One exercise might be to take a group of 20 kids and keep dividing them into subsets—male/female, younger/older, dark hair/light hair, wearing black/not wearing black—until they realize that everyone is unique. As I've said for 30 years, the best way to decrease prejudice is to increase discrimination. We would also play games and midway through mix up the teams. Or maybe we'd give each child a chance to rewrite the rules of the game, so it becomes clear that performance is only a reflection of one's ability under certain circumstances.

You know, if they allowed three serves in tennis, I would be a much better player.

What's the one thing about mindfulness you'd like every executive to remember?

It's going to sound corny, but I believe it fully: Life consists only of moments, nothing more than that. So if you make the moment matter, it all matters. You can be mindful, you can be mindless. You can win, you can lose. The worst case is to be mindless and lose. So when you're doing anything, be mindful, notice new things, make it meaningful to you, and you'll prosper.

ELLEN LANGER, PHD, is a professor of psychology at Harvard University and founder of the Langer Mindfulness Institute. ALISON BEARD is a senior editor at *Harvard Business Review*.

Reprinted from *Harvard Business Review*, March 2014 (product #R1403D).

2

Mindfulness Can Literally Change Your Brain

By Christina Congleton, Britta K. Hölzel,
and Sara W. Lazar

The business world is abuzz with mindfulness. But perhaps you haven't heard that the hype is backed by hard science. Recent research provides strong evidence that practicing nonjudgmental, present-moment awareness (aka mindfulness) changes the brain, and it does so in ways that anyone working in today's complex business environment—and certainly every leader—should know about.[1]

We contributed to this research in 2011 with a study on participants who completed an eight-week mindfulness program.[2] We observed significant increases in the density of their gray matter. In the years since, neuroscience laboratories from around the world have also investigated ways in which meditation, one key way to practice mindfulness, changes the brain. This year, a team of scientists from the University of British Columbia and the Chemnitz University of Technology were able to pool data from more than 20 studies to determine which areas of the brain are consistently affected.[3] They identified at least eight different regions. Here we will focus on two that we believe to be of particular interest to business professionals.

The first is the anterior cingulate cortex (ACC), a structure located deep inside the forehead, behind the brain's frontal lobe. The ACC is associated with self-regulation, meaning the ability to purposefully direct attention and behavior, suppress inappropriate knee-jerk responses, and switch strategies flexibly.[4] People with damage to the ACC show impulsivity and unchecked aggression, and those with impaired connections between this and other brain regions perform poorly on tests of mental flexibility:

They hold onto ineffective problem-solving strategies rather than adapting their behavior.[5] Meditators, on the other hand, demonstrate superior performance on tests of self-regulation, resisting distractions and making correct answers more often than non-meditators.[6] They also show more activity in the ACC than nonmeditators.[7] In addition to self-regulation, the ACC is associated with learning from past experience to support optimal decision making.[8] Scientists point out that the ACC may be particularly important in the face of uncertain and fast-changing conditions.

The second brain region we want to highlight is the hippocampus, a region that showed increased amounts of gray matter in the brains of our 2011 mindfulness program participants. This seahorse-shaped area is buried inside the temple on each side of the brain and is part of the limbic system, a set of inner structures associated with emotion and memory. It is covered in receptors for the stress hormone cortisol, and studies have shown that it can be damaged by chronic stress, contributing to a harmful spiral in the body.[9] Indeed, people with stress-related disorders like depression and PTSD tend to have a smaller hippocampus.[10] All of this points to the importance of this brain area in resilience—another key skill in the current high-demand business world.

These findings are just the beginning of the story. Neuroscientists have also shown that practicing mindfulness affects brain areas related to perception, body awareness, pain tolerance, emotion regulation, introspection, complex thinking, and sense of self. While more research is needed to document these changes over time and to understand underlying mechanisms, the converging evidence is compelling.

Mindfulness should no longer be considered a "nice to have" for executives. It's a "must have": a way to keep our brains healthy, to support self-regulation and effective decision-making capabilities, and to protect ourselves from toxic stress. It can be integrated into one's religious or spiritual life or practiced as a form of secular mental training. When we take a seat, take a breath, and commit to being mindful—particularly when we gather with others who are doing the same—we have the potential to be changed.

CHRISTINA CONGLETON is a leadership and change consultant at Axon Leadership and has researched stress and the brain at Massachusetts General Hospital and the University of Denver. She holds a master's in human development and psychology from Harvard University. BRITTA K. HÖLZEL conducts MRI research to investigate the neural mechanisms of mindfulness practice. Previously a research fellow at Massachusetts General Hospital and Harvard Medical School, she currently works at the Technical University Munich. She holds a doctorate in psychology from Giessen University in Germany. SARA W. LAZAR is an associate researcher in the psychiatry department at Massachusetts General Hospital and an assistant professor in psychology at Harvard Medical School. The focus of her research is to elucidate the neural mechanisms underlying the beneficial effects of yoga and meditation, both in clinical settings and in healthy individuals.

Notes

1. S. N. Banhoo, "How Meditation May Change the Brain," *New York Times*, January 28, 2011.

2. B. K. Hölzel et al., "Mindfulness Practice Leads to Increases in Regional Brain Gray Matter Density," *Psychiatry Research* 191, no. 1 (January 30, 2011): 36–43.

3. K. C. Fox et al., "Is Meditation Associated with Altered Brain Structure? A Systematic Review and Meta-Analysis of Morphometric Neuroimaging in Meditation Practitioners," *Neuroscience and Biobehavioral Reviews* 43 (June 2014): 48–73.

4. M. Posner et al., "The Anterior Cingulate Gyrus and the Mechanism of Self-Regulation," *Cognitive, Affective, & Behavioral Neuroscience* 7, no. 4 (December 2007): 391–395.

5. O. Devinsky et al., "Contributions of Anterior Cingulate Cortex to Behavior," *Brain* 118, part 1 (February 1995): 279–306; and A. M. Hogan et al., "Impact of Frontal White Matter Lesions on Performance Monitoring: ERP Evidence for Cortical Disconnection," *Brain* 129, part 8 (August 2006): 2177–2188.

6. P. A. van den Hurk et al., "Greater Efficiency in Attentional Processing Related to Mindfulness Meditation," *Quarterly Journal of Experimental Psychology* 63, no. 6 (June 2010): 1168–1180.

7. B. K. Hölzel et al., "Differential Engagement of Anterior Cingulate and Adjacent Medial Frontal Cortex in Adept Meditators and Non-meditators," *Neuroscience Letters* 421, no. 1 (June 21): 16–21.

8. S. W. Kennerley et al., "Optimal Decision Making and the Anterior Cingulate Cortex," *Nature Neuroscience* 9 (June 18, 2006): 940–947.

9. B. S. McEwen and P. J. Gianaros. "Stress- and Allostasis-Induced Brain Plasticity," *Annual Review of Medicine* 62 (February 2011): 431–445.

10. Y. I. Sheline, "Neuroimaging Studies of Mood Disorder Effects on the Brain." *Biological Psychiatry* 54, no. 3 (August 1, 2003): 338–352; and T. V. Gurvits et al., "Magnetic Resonance Imaging Study of Hippocampal Volume in Chronic, Combat-Related Posttraumatic Stress Disorder," *Biological Psychiatry* 40, no. 11 (December 1, 1996): 1091–1099.

Adapted from content posted on hbr.org on
January 8, 2015 (#H01T5A).

3

How to Practice Mindfulness Throughout Your Work Day

By Rasmus Hougaard and Jacqueline Carter

You probably know the feeling all too well: You arrive at the office with a clear plan for the day, and then, in what feels like just a moment, you find yourself on your way back home. Nine or ten hours have passed but you've accomplished only a few of your priorities. And, most likely, you can't even remember exactly what you did all day. If this sounds familiar, don't worry: You're not alone. Research shows that people spend nearly 47% of their waking hours thinking about something other than what they're doing.[1] In other words, many of us operate on autopilot.

Add to this that we have entered what many people are calling the "attention economy." In the attention economy, the ability to maintain focus and concentration is every bit as important as technical or management skills. And because leaders must be able to absorb and synthesize a growing flood of information in order to make good decisions, they're hit particularly hard by this emerging trend.

The good news is you can train your brain to focus better by incorporating mindfulness exercises throughout your day. Based on our experience with thousands of leaders in more than 250 organizations, here are some guidelines for becoming a more focused and mindful leader.

First, start off your day right. Researchers have found that we release the most stress hormones within minutes after waking.[2] Why? Because thinking of the day ahead triggers our fight-or-flight instinct and releases cortisol into our blood. Instead, try this: When you wake up, spend two minutes in your bed simply noticing your breath. As thoughts about the day pop into your mind, let them go and return to your breath.

Next, when you get to the office, take 10 minutes at your desk or in your car to boost your brain with the following short mindfulness practice before you dive into activity. Close your eyes, relax, and sit upright. Place your full focus on your breath. Simply maintain an ongoing flow of attention on the experience of your breathing: Inhale, exhale; inhale, exhale. To help your focus stay on your breathing, count silently at each exhalation. Any time you find your mind distracted, simply release the distraction by returning your focus to your breath. Most important, allow yourself to enjoy these minutes. Throughout the rest of the day, other people and competing urgencies will fight for your attention. But for these 10 minutes, your attention is all your own.

Once you finish this practice and get ready to start working, mindfulness can help increase your effectiveness. Two skills define a mindful mind: *focus* and *awareness*. Focus is the ability to concentrate on what you're doing in the moment, while awareness is the ability to recognize and release unnecessary distractions as they arise. Understand that mindfulness is not just a sedentary practice; it is about developing a sharp, clear mind. And mindfulness in action is a great alternative to the illusory practice of multitasking. Mindful working means applying focus and awareness to everything you do from the moment you enter the office. Focus on the task at hand, and recognize and release internal and external distractions as they arise. In this way, mindfulness helps increase effectiveness, decrease mistakes, and even enhance creativity.

To better understand the power of focus and awareness, consider an affliction that touches nearly all of us: email addiction. Emails have a way of seducing our attention and redirecting it to lower-priority tasks because completing small, quickly accomplished tasks releases dopamine, a pleasurable hormone, in our brains. This release makes us addicted to email and compromises our concentration. Instead, apply mindfulness when opening your inbox. *Focus* on what is important and maintain *awareness* of what is merely noise. To get a better start to your day, avoid checking your email first thing in the morning. Doing so will help you sidestep an onslaught of distractions and short-term problems during a time of day that holds the potential for exceptional focus and creativity.

As the day moves on and the inevitable back-to-back meetings start, mindfulness can help you lead shorter, more effective meetings. To avoid entering a meeting with a wandering mind, take two minutes to practice mindfulness, which you can do en route. Even better, let the first two minutes of the meeting be silent, allowing everybody to arrive both physically and mentally. Then, if possible, end the meeting five minutes before the hour to allow all participants a mindful transition to their next appointment.

As the day progresses and your brain starts to tire, mindfulness can help you stay sharp and avoid poor decisions. After lunch, set a timer on your phone to ring every hour. When the timer rings, cease your current activity and do one minute of mindfulness practice. These mindful performance breaks will help keep you from resorting to autopilot and lapsing into action addiction.

Finally, as the day comes to an end and you start your commute home, apply mindfulness. For at least 10 minutes of the commute, turn off your phone, shut off the radio, and simply be. Let go of any thoughts that arise. Attend to your breath. Doing so will allow you to let go of the stresses of the day so you can return home and be fully present with your family.

Mindfulness is not about living life in slow motion. It's about enhancing focus and awareness both in work and in life. It's about stripping away distractions and staying on track with both individual and organizational, goals. Take control of your own mindfulness: Test these tips for 14 days, and see what they do for you.

RASMUS HOUGAARD is the founder and managing director of The Potential Project, a leading global provider of corporate-based mindfulness solutions. He is a coauthor with Jacqueline Carter of *One Second Ahead: Enhance Your Performance at Work with Mindfulness*. **JACQUELINE CARTER** is a partner with The Potential Project and has worked with leaders around the globe, including executives from Sony, American Express, RBC, and KPMG.

Notes

1. S. Bradt, "Wandering Mind Not a Happy Mind," *Harvard Gazette*, November 11, 2010.
2. J. C. Pruessner et al., "Free Cortisol Levels After Awakening: A Reliable Biological Marker for the Assessment of Adrenocortical Activity," *Life Sciences* 61, no. 26 (November 1997): 2539–2549.

Adapted from content posted on hbr.org on
March 4, 2016 (#H02OTU).

4

Resilience for the Rest of Us

By Daniel Goleman

There are two ways to become more resilient: one by talking to yourself, the other by retraining your brain.

If you've suffered a major failure, take the sage advice given by psychologist Martin Seligman in the HBR article "Building Resilience" (April 2011). Talk to yourself. Give yourself a cognitive intervention, and counter defeatist thinking with an optimistic attitude. Challenge your downbeat thinking, and replace it with a positive outlook.

Fortunately, major failures come along rarely in life.

But what about bouncing back from the more frequent annoying screwups, minor setbacks, and irritating upsets that are routine in any leader's life? Resilience is, again, the answer—but with a different flavor. You need to retrain your brain.

The brain has a very different mechanism for bouncing back from the cumulative toll of daily hassles. And with a little effort, you can upgrade its ability to snap back from life's downers.

Whenever we get so upset that we say or do something we later regret (and who doesn't now and then?), that's a sure sign that our amygdala—the brain's radar for danger and the trigger for the fight-or-flight response—has hijacked the brain's executive centers in the prefrontal cortex. The neural key to resilience lies in how quickly we recover from that hijacked state.

The circuitry that brings us back to full energy and focus after an amygdala hijack concentrates in the left side of our prefrontal area, says Richard Davidson, a neuroscientist at the University of Wisconsin. He's also found that when we're distressed, there's heightened activity on the right side of the prefrontal area. Each of us has a characteristic level of left/right activity that predicts our daily mood range—if we're tilted to the right, more upsets; if to the left, we're quicker to recover from distress of all kinds.

To tackle this in the workplace, Davidson teamed with the CEO of a high-pressure, 24/7, biotech startup and meditation expert Jon Kabat-Zinn of the University of Massachusetts Medical School. Kabat-Zinn offered the employees at the biotech outfit instruction in mindfulness, an attention-training method that teaches the brain to register anything happening in the present moment with full focus— but without reacting.

The instructions are simple:

1. Find a quiet, private place where you can be undistracted for a few minutes. For instance, close your office door and mute your phone.

2. Sit comfortably, with your back straight but relaxed.

3. Focus your awareness on your breath, staying attentive to the sensations of the inhalation and exhalation, and start again on the next breath.

4. Do not judge your breathing or try to change it in any way.

5. See anything else that comes to mind as a distraction—thoughts, sounds, whatever. Let them go and return your attention to your breath.

After eight weeks and an average of 30 minutes a day practicing mindfulness, the employees had shifted their ratio from tilted toward the stressed-out right side to leaning toward the resilient left side. What's more, they said they remembered what they loved about their work: They got in touch with what had brought them energy in the first place.

To get the full benefit of mindfulness, a daily practice of 20 to 30 minutes works best. Think of it like a mental exercise routine. It can be very helpful to have guided instructions, but the key is to find a slot for the practice in your daily routine. (There are even instructions for using a long drive as your practice session.)

Mindfulness has steadily been gaining credence among hard-nosed executives. There are centers where mindfulness instruction has been tailored to businesspeople, from tony resorts like Miraval Resort in Arizona to programs in mindful leadership at the University of Massachusetts Medical School. Google University has been offering a course in mindfulness to employees for years.

Might you benefit from tuning up your brain's resilience circuitry by learning to practice mindfulness? Among high-performing executives, the effects of stress can be subtle. My colleagues Richard Boyatzis and Annie McKee suggest as a rough diagnostic of leadership stress asking yourself, "Do I have a vague sense of unease, restlessness, or the feeling that life

is not great (a higher standard than 'good enough')?"
A bit of mindfulness might put your mind at ease.

DANIEL GOLEMAN is a codirector of the Consortium for Research on Emotional Intelligence in Organizations at Rutgers University, coauthor of *Primal Leadership: Leading with Emotional Intelligence* (Harvard Business Review Press, 2013), and author of *The Brain and Emotional Intelligence: New Insights*.

Adapted from content posted on hbr.org on
March 4, 2016.

5

Emotional Agility

*How Effective Leaders Manage
Their Thoughts and Feelings*

By Susan David and Christina Congleton

Sixteen thousand—that's how many words we speak, on average, each day. So imagine how many unspoken ones course through our minds. Most of them are not facts but evaluations and judgments entwined with emotions—some positive and helpful (*I've worked hard and I can ace this presentation; This issue is worth speaking up about; The new VP seems approachable*), others negative and less so (*He's purposely ignoring me; I'm going to make a fool of myself; I'm a fake*).

The prevailing wisdom says that difficult thoughts and feelings have no place at the office: Executives, and particularly leaders, should be either stoic or cheerful; they must project confidence and damp down any negativity bubbling up inside them. But that goes against basic biology. All healthy human beings have an inner stream of thoughts and feelings that include criticism, doubt, and fear. That's just our minds doing the job they were designed to do: trying to anticipate and solve problems and avoid potential pitfalls.

In our people-strategy consulting practice advising companies around the world, we see leaders stumble not because they *have* undesirable thoughts and feelings—that's inevitable—but because they get *hooked* by them, like fish caught on a line. This happens in one of two ways. They buy into the thoughts, treating them like facts (*It was the same in my last job . . . I've been a failure my whole career*), and avoid situations that evoke them (*I'm not going to take on that new challenge*). Or, usually at the behest of their supporters, they challenge the existence of the thoughts and try to rationalize them away (*I shouldn't have thoughts like this . . . I know I'm not a total fail-ure*), and perhaps force themselves into similar situations, even when those go against their core values and goals (*Take on that new assignment—you've got to get over this*). In either case, they are paying too much attention to their internal chatter and allowing it to sap important cognitive resources that could be put to better use.

This is a common problem, often perpetuated by popular self-management strategies. We regularly see executives with recurring emotional challenges at work—anxiety about priorities, jealousy of others' success, fear of rejection, distress over perceived slights—who have devised techniques to "fix" them: positive affirmations, prioritized to-do lists, immersion in certain tasks. But when we ask how long the challenges have persisted, the answer might be 10 years, 20 years, or since childhood.

Clearly, those techniques don't work—in fact, ample research shows that attempting to minimize or ignore thoughts and emotions serves only to amplify them. In a famous study led by the late Daniel Wegner, a Harvard professor, participants who were told to avoid thinking about white bears had trouble doing so; later, when the ban was lifted, they thought about white bears much more than the control group did. Anyone who has dreamed of chocolate cake and french fries while following a strict diet understands this phenomenon.

Effective leaders don't buy into *or* try to suppress their inner experiences. Instead they approach them in a mindful, values-driven, and productive way—developing what we call *emotional agility.* In our complex, fast-changing knowledge economy, this ability to manage one's thoughts and feelings is essential to business success. Numerous studies, from the University of London professor Frank Bond and others, show that emotional agility can help people alleviate stress, reduce errors, become more innovative, and improve job performance.

We've worked with leaders in various industries to build this critical skill, and here we offer four practices—adapted from Acceptance and Commitment Therapy (ACT), originally developed by the University of Nevada psychologist Steven C. Hayes— that are designed to help you do the same: Recognize your patterns; label your thoughts and emotions; accept them; and act on your values.

Fish on a line

Let's start with two case studies. Cynthia is a senior corporate lawyer with two young children. She used to feel intense guilt about missed opportunities— both at the office, where her peers worked 80 hours a week while she worked 50, and at home, where she was often too distracted or tired to fully engage with her husband and children. One nagging voice in her head told her she'd have to be a better employee or risk career failure; another told her to be a better mother or risk neglecting her family. Cynthia wished that at least one of the voices would shut up. But neither would, and in response she failed to put up her hand for exciting new prospects at the office and compulsively checked messages on her phone during family dinners.

Jeffrey, a rising-star executive at a leading consumer goods company, had a different problem. Intelligent, talented, and ambitious, he was often angry— at bosses who disregarded his views, subordinates who didn't follow orders, or colleagues who didn't pull their weight. He had lost his temper several times at work and been warned to get it under control. But when he tried, he felt that he was shutting off a core part of his personality, and he became even angrier and more upset.

These smart, successful leaders were hooked by their negative thoughts and emotions. Cynthia was absorbed by guilt; Jeffrey was exploding with anger.

Cynthia told the voices to go away; Jeffrey bottled his frustration. Both were trying to avoid the discomfort they felt. They were being controlled by their inner experience, attempting to control it, or switching between the two.

Getting unhooked

Fortunately, both Cynthia and Jeffrey realized that they couldn't go on—at least not successfully and happily—without more-effective inner strategies. We coached them to adopt the four practices:

Recognize your patterns

The first step in developing emotional agility is to notice when you've been hooked by your thoughts and feelings. That's hard to do, but there are certain tell-tale signs. One is that your thinking becomes rigid and repetitive. For example, Cynthia began to see that her self-recriminations played like a broken record, repeating the same messages over and over again. Another is that the story your mind is telling seems old, like a rerun of some past experience. Jeffrey noticed that his attitude toward certain colleagues (*He's incompetent; There's no way I'm letting anyone speak to me like that*) was quite familiar. In fact, he had experienced something similar in his previous job—and in the one before that. The source of trouble was not just Jeffrey's environment but his own patterns of thought and feeling. You have to realize that you're stuck before you can initiate change.

Label your thoughts and emotions

When you're hooked, the attention you give your thoughts and feelings crowds your mind; there's no room to examine them. One strategy that may help you consider your situation more objectively is the simple act of labeling. Just as you call a spade a spade, call a thought a thought and an emotion an emotion. *I'm not doing enough at work or at home* becomes *I'm having the thought that I'm not doing enough at work or at home.* Similarly, *My coworker is wrong—he makes me so angry* becomes *I'm having the thought that my coworker is wrong, and I'm feeling anger.* Labeling allows you to see your thoughts and feelings for what they are: transient sources of data that may or may not prove helpful. Humans are psychologically able to take this helicopter view of private experiences, and mounting scientific evidence shows that simple, straightforward mindfulness practice like this not only improves behavior and well-being but also promotes beneficial biological changes in the brain and at the cellular level. As Cynthia started to slow down and label her thoughts, the criticisms that had once pressed in on her like a dense fog became more like clouds passing through a blue sky.

Accept them

The opposite of control is acceptance: not acting on every thought or resigning yourself to negativity but responding to your ideas and emotions with an open attitude, paying attention to them and letting yourself experience them. Take 10 deep breaths, and notice what's happening in the moment. This can bring relief, but it won't necessarily make you feel good. In fact, you may realize just how upset you really are. The important thing is to show yourself (and others) some compassion and examine the reality of the situation. What's going on—both internally and externally? When Jeffrey acknowledged and made room for his feelings of frustration and anger rather than rejecting them, quashing them, or taking them out on others, he began to notice their energetic quality. They were a signal that something important was at stake and that he needed to take productive action. Instead of yelling at people, he could make a clear request of a colleague or move swiftly on a pressing issue. The more Jeffrey accepted his anger and brought his curiosity to it, the more it seemed to support rather than undermine his leadership.

Act on your values

When you unhook yourself from your difficult thoughts and emotions, you expand your choices. You can decide to act in a way that aligns with your values. We encourage leaders to focus on the concept of *workability*: Is your response going to serve you and your organization in the long term as well as the short term? Will it help you steer others in a direction that furthers your collective purpose? Are you taking a step toward being the leader you most want to be and living the life you most want to live? The mind's thought stream flows endlessly, and emotions change like the weather, but values can be called on at any time, in any situation.

WHAT ARE YOUR VALUES?

This list is drawn from the Personal Values Card Sort (2001), developed by W. R. Miller, J. C'de Baca, D. B. Matthews, and P. L. Wilbourne, of the University of New Mexico. You can use it to quickly identify the values you hold that might inform a challenging situation at work. When you next make a decision, ask yourself whether it is consistent with these values.

Accuracy	Duty	Justice	Realism
Achievement	Family	Knowledge	Responsibility
Authority	Forgiveness	Leisure	Risk
Autonomy	Friendship	Mastery	Safety
Caring	Fun	Moderation	Self-knowledge
Challenge	Generosity	Nonconformity	Service
Comfort	Genuineness	Openness	Simplicity
Compassion	Growth	Order	Stability
Contribution	Health	Passion	Tolerance
Cooperation	Helpfulness	Popularity	Tradition
Courtesy	Honesty	Power	Wealth
Creativity	Humility	Purpose	
Dependability	Humor	Rationality	

When Cynthia considered her values, she recognized how deeply committed she was to both her family and her work. She loved being with her children, but she also cared passionately about the pursuit of justice. Unhooked from her distracting and discouraging feelings of guilt, she resolved to be guided by her principles. She recognized how important it was to get home for dinner with her family every evening and to resist work interruptions during that time. But she also undertook to make a number of important business trips, some of which coincided with school events that she would have preferred to attend. Confident that her values—not solely her emotions—were guiding her, Cynthia finally found peace and fulfillment.

It's impossible to block out difficult thoughts and emotions. Effective leaders are mindful of their inner experiences but not caught in them. They know how to free up their internal resources and commit to actions that align with their values. Developing emotional agility is no quick fix. Even those who, like Cynthia and Jeffrey, regularly practice the steps we've outlined here will often find themselves hooked. But over time, leaders who become increasingly adept at it are the ones most likely to thrive.

SUSAN DAVID is the CEO of Evidence Based Psychology, a cofounder of the Institute of Coaching, and an instructor in psychology at Harvard University. CHRISTINA CONGLETON is a leadership and change consultant at Axon Leadership and has researched stress and the brain at Massachusetts General Hospital and the University of Denver. She holds a master's in human development and psychology from Harvard University.

Reprinted from *Harvard Business Review*, November 2013 (product #R1311L).

6

Don't Let Power Corrupt You

By Dacher Keltner

n the behavioral research I've conducted over the past 20 years, I've uncovered a disturbing pattern: While people usually gain power through traits and actions that advance the interests of others, such as empathy, collaboration, openness, fairness, and sharing, when they start to feel powerful or enjoy a position of privilege, those qualities begin to fade. The powerful are more likely than other people to engage in rude, selfish, and unethical behavior. The 19th-century historian and politician Lord Acton got it right: Power *does* tend to corrupt.

I call this phenomenon "the power paradox," and I've studied it in numerous settings: colleges, the U.S.

Senate, pro sports teams, and a variety of other professional workplaces. In each I've observed that people rise on the basis of their good qualities, but their behavior grows increasingly worse as they move up the ladder. This shift can happen surprisingly quickly. In one of my experiments, known as "the cookie monster" study, I brought people into a lab in groups of three, randomly assigned one to a position of leadership, and then gave them a group writing task. A half hour into their work, I placed a plate of freshly baked cookies—one for each team member, plus an extra—in front of everyone. In all groups each person took one and, out of politeness, left the extra cookie. The question was: Who would take a second treat, knowing that it would deprive others of the same? It was nearly always the person who'd been named the leader. In addition, the leaders were more likely to eat with their mouths open, lips smacking, and crumbs falling onto their clothes.

Studies show that wealth and credentials can have a similar effect. In another experiment, Paul Piff of UC Irvine and I found that whereas drivers of the least expensive vehicles—Dodge Colts, Plymouth Satellites—*always* ceded the right-of-way to pedestrians in a crosswalk, people driving luxury cars such as BMWs and Mercedes yielded only 54% of the time; nearly half the time they ignored the pedestrian and the law. Surveys of employees in 27 countries have revealed that wealthy individuals are more likely to say it's acceptable to engage in unethical behavior, such as taking bribes or cheating on taxes. And recent research led by Danny Miller at HEC Montréal demonstrated that CEOs with MBAs are more likely than those without MBAs to engage in self-serving behavior that increases their personal compensation but causes their companies' value to decline.

These findings suggest that iconic abuses of power —Jeffrey Skilling's fraudulent accounting at Enron,

Tyco CEO Dennis Kozlowski's illegal bonuses, Silvio Berlusconi's bunga bunga parties, Leona Helmsley's tax evasion—are extreme examples of the kinds of misbehavior to which all leaders, at any level, are susceptible. Studies show that people in positions of corporate power are three times as likely as those at the lower rungs of the ladder to interrupt coworkers, multitask during meetings, raise their voices, and say insulting things at the office. And people who've just moved into senior roles are particularly vulnerable to losing their virtues, my research and other studies indicate.

The consequences can be far-reaching. The abuse of power ultimately tarnishes the reputations of executives, undermining their opportunities for influence. It also creates stress and anxiety among their colleagues, diminishing rigor and creativity in the group and dragging down team members' engagement and performance. In a recent poll of 800 managers and employees in 17 industries, about half the respondents who reported being treated rudely at work said they deliberately decreased their effort or lowered the quality of their work in response.

So how can you avoid succumbing to the power paradox? Through awareness and action.

A need for reflection

A first step is developing greater self-awareness. When you take on a senior role, you need to be attentive to the feelings that accompany your newfound power and to any changes in your behavior. My research has shown that power puts us into something like a manic state, making us feel expansive, energized, omnipotent, hungry for rewards, and immune to risk—which opens us up to rash, rude, and unethical actions. But new studies in neuroscience find that simply by reflecting on those thoughts and emotions—"Hey, I'm feeling as if I should rule the world right now"—we can engage regions of our frontal lobes that help us keep our worst impulses in check. When we recognize and label feelings of joy and confidence, we're less likely to make irrational decisions inspired by them. When we acknowledge feelings of frustration (perhaps because subordinates aren't behaving the way we want), we're less likely to respond in adversarial or confrontational ways.

You can build this kind of self-awareness through everyday mindfulness practices. One approach starts with sitting in a comfortable and quiet place, breathing deeply, and concentrating on the feeling of inhaling and exhaling, physical sensations, or sounds or sights in your environment. Studies show that spending just a few minutes a day on such exercises gives people greater focus and calm, and for that reason techniques for them are now taught in training programs at companies like Google, Facebook, Aetna, General Mills, Ford, and Goldman Sachs.

It's also important to reflect on your demeanor and actions. Are you interrupting people? Do you check your phone when others are talking? Have you told a joke or story that embarrassed or humiliated someone else? Do you swear at the office? Have you ever taken sole credit for a group effort? Do you forget colleagues' names? Are you spending a lot more money than in the past or taking unusual physical risks?

If you answered yes to at least a few of these questions, take it as an early warning sign that you're being tempted into problematic, arrogant displays of power. What may seem innocuous to you probably doesn't to your subordinates. Consider a story I recently heard about a needlessly hierarchical lunch delivery protocol on a cable television writing team. Each day when the team's sandwiches arrived, they were doled out to the writers in order of seniority. In failing to correct this behavior, the group's leaders were almost certainly diminishing its collaborative and creative potential. For a contrast, consider U.S. military mess halls, where the practice is the reverse, as the ethnographer and author Simon Sinek notes in the title of his most recent book, *Leaders Eat Last*. Officers adhere to the policy not to cede authority but to show respect for their troops.

Practicing graciousness

Whether you've already begun to succumb to the power paradox or not, you must work to remember and repeat the virtuous behaviors that helped you rise in the first place. When teaching executives and others in positions of power, I focus on three essential practices—empathy, gratitude, and generosity—that have been shown to sustain benevolent leadership, even in the most cutthroat environments.

For example, Leanne ten Brinke, Chris Liu, Sameer Srivastava, and I found that U.S. senators who used empathetic facial expressions and tones of voice when speaking to the floor got more bills passed than those who used domineering, threatening gestures and tones in their speeches. Research by Anita Woolley of Carnegie Mellon and Thomas Malone of MIT has likewise shown that when teammates subtly signal understanding, engagement, interest, and concern for one another, the team is more effective at tackling hard analytical problems.

Small expressions of gratitude also yield positive results. Studies show that romantic partners who acknowledge each other's value in casual conversation are less likely to break up, that students who receive a pat on the back from their teachers are more likely to take on difficult problems, and that people who express appreciation to others in a newly formed group feel stronger ties to the group months later. Adam Grant of Wharton has found that when managers take the time to thank their employees, those workers are more engaged and productive. And my own research on NBA teams with Michael Kraus of Yale University shows that players who physically display their appreciation—through head raps, bear hugs, and hip and chest bumps—inspire their team-mates to play better and win nearly two more games per season (which is both statistically significant and often the difference between making the play-offs and not).

Simple acts of generosity can be equally power-ful. Studies show that individuals who share with others in a group—for example, by contributing new ideas or directly assisting on projects not their own—are deemed more worthy of respect and influ-ence and more suitable for leadership. Mike Norton at Harvard Business School has found that when organizations provide an opportunity to donate to charities at work, employees feel more satisfied and productive.

It might seem difficult to constantly follow the ethics of "good power" when you're the boss and responsible for making sure things get done. Not so. Your capacity for empathy, gratitude, and generosity can be cultivated by engaging in simple social behaviors whenever the opportunity presents itself: a team meeting, a client pitch or negotiation, a 360-degree feedback session. Here are a few suggestions.

To practice empathy:

- Ask a great question or two in every interaction, and paraphrase important points that others make.

- Listen with gusto. Orient your body and eyes toward the person speaking, and convey interest and engagement vocally.

- When someone comes to you with a problem, signal concern with phrases such as "I'm sorry" and "That's really tough." Avoid rushing to judgment and advice.

- Before meetings, take a moment to think about the person you'll be with and what is happening in his or her life.

Arturo Bejar, Facebook's director of engineering, is one executive I've seen make empathy a priority as he guides his teams of designers, coders, data specialists, and writers. Watching him at work, I've noticed that his meetings all tend to be structured around a cascade of open-ended questions and that he never fails to listen thoughtfully. He leans toward whoever is speaking and carefully writes down everyone's ideas on a notepad. These small expressions of empathy signal to his team that he understands their concerns and wants them to succeed together.

To practice gratitude:

- Make thoughtful thank-yous a part of how you communicate with others.

- Send colleagues specific and timely emails or notes of appreciation for jobs done well.

- Publicly acknowledge the value that each person contributes to your team, including the support staff.

- Use the right kind of touch—pats on the back, fist bumps, or high fives—to celebrate successes.

When Douglas Conant was CEO of the Campbell Soup Company, he emphasized a culture of gratitude across the organization. Each day he and his executive assistants would spend up to an hour scanning his email and the company intranet for news of employees who were "making a difference." Conant would then personally thank them—everyone from senior executives to maintenance people—for their contributions, usually with handwritten notes. He estimates that he wrote at least 10 a day, for a total of about 30,000 during his decade-long tenure, and says he would often find them pinned up in employees' workspaces. Leaders I've taught have shared other tactics: giving small gifts to employees, taking them out to nice lunches or dinners, hosting employee-of-the-month celebrations, and setting up real or virtual "gratitude walls," on which coworkers can thank one another for specific contributions.

To practice generosity:

- Seek opportunities to spend a little one-on-one time with the people you lead.

- Delegate some important and high-profile responsibilities.

- Give praise generously.

- Share the limelight. Give credit to all who contribute to the success of your team and your organization.

Pixar director Pete Docter is a master of this last practice. When I first started working with him on the movie *Inside Out*, I was curious about a cinematic marvel he'd created five years before: the montage at the start of the film *Up*, which shows the protagonist, Carl, meeting and falling in love with a girl, Ellie; enjoying a long married life with her; and then watching her succumb to illness. When I asked how he'd accomplished it, his answer was an exhaustive list of the 250 writers, animators, actors, story artists, designers, sculptors, editors, programmers, and computer modelers who had worked on it with him. When people ask about the box-office success of *Inside Out*, he gives a similar response. Another Facebook executive I've worked with, product manager Kelly Winters, shares credit in a similar way. When she does PowerPoint presentations or talks to reporters about the success of her Compassion team, she always lists or talks about the data analysts, engineers, and content specialists who made it happen.

You can outsmart the power paradox by practicing the ethics of empathy, gratitude, and generosity. It will bring out the best work and collaborative spirit of those around you. And you, too, will benefit, with a burnished reputation, long-lasting leadership, and the dopamine-rich delights of advancing the interests of others.

DACHER KELTNER is a professor of psychology at the University of California, Berkeley, and the faculty director of the Greater Good Science Center.

Reprinted from *Harvard Business Review*,
October 2016 (product #R1610K).

7

Mindfulness for People Who Are Too Busy to Meditate

By Maria Gonzalez

indfulness has become almost a buzzword. But what is it, really? Quite simply, mindfulness is being present and aware, moment by moment, regardless of circumstances.

For instance, researchers have found that practicing mindfulness can reprogram the brain to be more rational and less emotional. When faced with a decision, meditators who practiced mindfulness showed increased activity in the posterior insula of the brain, an area linked to rational decision making. This allowed them to make decisions based more on fact than emotion. This is good news since other research has found that reasoning is actually suffused with emotion—the two are inseparable. What's more, our positive and negative feelings about people, things, and ideas arise much more rapidly than our conscious thoughts—in a matter of milliseconds. We push threatening information away and hold friendly information close. We apply fight-or-flight reflexes not only to predators, but also to data itself.

There are specific techniques that you can practice to help you reap the benefits of mindfulness. You may have heard about a mindfulness-enhancing technique where you meditate for a period of time before going about the rest of your day. This is definitely valuable. But I prefer practicing mindfulness all day, in every circumstance. In essence, you start living all of life mindfully, and over time there is no distinction between your formal mindfulness practice and making a presentation, negotiating a deal, driving your car, working out, or playing a round of golf.

Try a technique I call "micro meditations." These are meditations that can be done several times a day for one to three minutes at a time. Periodically throughout the day, become aware of your breath. It could be when you feel yourself getting stressed or overwhelmed, with too much to do and too little time, or perhaps when you notice yourself becoming increasingly distracted and agitated.

First, notice the quality of your breathing. Is it shallow or deep? Are you holding your breath and in so doing perhaps also holding your stomach? Are you hunching your shoulders?

Next, start breathing so that you are bringing the breath into the belly. Do not strain. If this feels too unnatural, then try bringing the breath down into the lower chest. If the mind wanders, gently come back to the breath—without judging yourself for momentarily losing focus.

You will notice that by regularly practicing this micro meditation you will become more aware and calmer. You'll find yourself to be increasingly mindful, calm, and focused. It's helpful to create reminders for yourself to practice these meditations throughout the day. You can do them two to four times a day, every hour, before you go to a meeting, or whenever you feel like multitasking is eroding your concentration—whatever is feasible and feels right to you. Micro meditations can put you back on track and help you develop your mindfulness muscle.

A second technique I use is one I call "mindfulness in action." Instead of adding a new routine to your day, just experience your day a little differently by paying attention in a particular way, for seconds at a time.

For instance, if you've ever been in a meeting and suddenly noticed that you missed what was just said because you were "somewhere else" for the last few minutes, chances are you weren't being mindful. Maybe you were thinking about your next meeting, everything on your to do list, or an incoming text. Or perhaps you just zoned out. This is incredibly common. Unfortunately, not being present in this way can cause misunderstandings, missed opportunities, and wasted time.

The next time you're in a meeting, try to do nothing but *listen* for seconds at a time. This is harder than it sounds, but with practice you will be able to listen continuously, without a break in concentration. Whenever you notice that your mind has wandered, come right back to listening to the voice of the person who is speaking. You may have to redirect your attention dozens of times in a single meeting—it's extremely common. Always bring yourself back gently and with patience. You are training the mind to be right here, right now.

These techniques can, as I've said, rewire the brain. As a result, three critical things happen. First, your ability to concentrate increases. Second, you see things with increasing clarity, which improves your judgment. And third, you develop equanimity. Equanimity enables you to reduce your physiological and emotional stress and enhances the likelihood that you will be able to find creative solutions to problems.

Practicing mindfulness—and reaping its benefits— doesn't have to be a big time commitment or require special training. You can start right now—in this moment.

MARIA GONZALEZ is the founder and president of Argonauta Consulting. Her most recent book is *Mindful Leadership: The 9 Ways to Self-Awareness, Transforming Yourself, and Inspiring Others.* She has recently launched the Mindful Leadership app.

Adapted from content posted on hbr.org on
March 31, 2014 (product #H00QLQ).

8

Is Something Lost When We Use Mindfulness as a Productivity Tool?

By Charlotte Lieberman

came to mindfulness as a healing practice after overcoming an addiction to the drug Adderall during my junior year of college. I found myself in this situation because I thought that using Adderall to help me focus was no big deal—an attitude shared by 81% of students nationwide.[1]

Adderall simply seemed like an innocuous shortcut to getting things done efficiently and effortlessly. I still remember the rush I felt my first night on Adderall: I completed every page of assigned Faulkner reading (not easy), started and finished a paper several weeks before the due date (because why not?), Swiffered my room (twice), and answered all of my unread emails (even the irrelevant ones). It's also worth noting that I had forgotten to eat all night and somehow found myself still awake at 4 a.m., my jaw clenched and my stomach rumbling. Sleep was nowhere in sight.

What I saw initially as a shortcut to more focus and productivity ultimately turned out instead to be a long detour toward self-destruction. Rather than thinking of focus as the by-product of my own power and capability, I looked outside of myself, thinking that a pill would solve my problems.

Long story short, I eventually came to grips with my problem, got off the drug, and found an antidote to my crippling self-doubt: meditation—particularly, mindfulness (or Vipassana) meditation.

So to me, it's somewhat ironic that mindfulness has taken the media by storm precisely because of its scientifically proven benefits for focus and productivity.[2]

And it's not just because I came to mindfulness as a way of healing from the fallout of the amount of pressure I put on myself to be productive. While mindfulness is not a little blue pill, it's starting to be thought of as a kind of shortcut to focus and productivity, not unlike a morning coffee. A wisdom tradition associated with personal growth and insight is now being absorbed by our culture as a tool for career development and efficiency. But should mindfulness really be used to attain a particular goal? Is it OK to think of a practice that's all about "being" as just another tool for "doing"?

Companies seem to think so. Given the mindfulness buzz, it's no surprise that corporate mindfulness programs are proliferating across the country. Google offers "Search Inside Yourself" classes that teach mindfulness meditation at work. As celebrated in the recent book *Mindful Work* by David Gelles, corporations like Goldman Sachs, HBO, Deutsche Bank, Target, and Bank of America tout the productivity-related benefits of meditation to their employees.

The world of professional athletics—most recently the NFL—too has drawn attention to the achievement-oriented underpinnings of the main-stream mindfulness movement. The 2015 *Wall Street Journal* article that explored the Seattle Seahawks' success in the 2014 Super Bowl explained that the team's secret weapon was its willingness to work with a sports psychologist who teaches mindfulness. Sea-hawks assistant head coach Tom Cable went so far as to describe the team as "incredibly mindful."

This article was written in January, a month before the Seahawks lost the 2015 Super Bowl. In the wake of their defeat, I heard several conversations among acquaintances and family members (all of whom were sports fans and were nonmeditating but aware of meditation) in which they expressed skepticism about the power of meditation for focus and success. I mean, how much can we embrace mindfulness as a tool for success if a team famous for meditating lost the Super Bowl?

Still a lot, I think. And I'm fine stopping here to admit (if you haven't already concluded yourself) that the commodification of mindfulness as a productivity tool leaves me with a strange taste in my mouth. Above all, I am resistant to the teleological attitude toward meditation: that it's a "tool" designed for a particular purpose, contingent on "results."

And yet asserting this skepticism brings me back to a conversation I had with my vegan cousin a few years ago. He is a PhD student in biological anthropology, an animal activist, and a longtime vegan. When I asked him if he was irked by all the celebrities going vegan to lose weight, he shook his head vigorously. "I'd rather have people do the right thing for the wrong reason than not do the right thing at all," he explained (the "right" thing here being veganism).

This philosophy seems applicable to the mindfulness craze (aka "McMindfulness") too. I'm happy more people are getting the myriad benefits of meditation. I am glad that you're no longer thought of as a patchouli-scented hippie if you're an avid meditator. If corporate mindfulness programs mean that employee self-care is more valued in the workplace, then so be it.

But I also think there's room to consider an alternative way of talking about meditation, especially when it comes to how we relate to our work.

Looking at mindfulness as a tool for accomplishing what we need to get done keeps us trapped in a future-oriented mindset, rather than encouraging us to dilate the present moment. Of course, this doesn't invalidate the neuroscience; mindfulness helps us get more stuff done. But what about allowing mindfulness to just be? To have the effects it is going to have, without attaching a marketing pitch to this ancient practice?

Psychologist Kristin Neff is renowned for coining the term "self-compassion." In particular, Neff has asserted that the first component of self-compassion is kindness, the ability to shrug off those times when we "let ourselves down," when we don't get to check off everything from our to do lists. The other two components of self-compassion are awareness and mindfulness. The goal is not to get more done but to understand that we are enough—and that our worth is not contingent on what we get done. (Although studies have shown that self-forgiveness actually helps us procrastinate less.[3])

I'm not an idealist. I'm not saying everyone should start "Om-ing," devoting themselves solely to self-compassion, and forgetting all about their to do lists. But I am saying that compassion, and self-compassion, ought to move into the foreground as we talk about mindfulness—even in corporate mindfulness programs.

There's no shame in wanting to be productive at work. But there's also no shame in being able to cut yourself some slack, to extend yourself some love during those times at work when things don't feel so great.

CHARLOTTE LIEBERMAN is a New York–based writer and editor.

Notes

1. A. D. DeSantis and A. C. Hane, "'Adderall Is Definitely Not a Drug': Justifications for the Illegal Use of ADHD Stimulants," *Substance Use and Misuse* 45, no. 1–2 (2010): 31–46.
2. D. M. Levy et al., "The Effects of Mindfulness Meditation Training on Multitasking in a High-Stress Information Environment," Graphics Interface Conference, 2012.
3. M. J. A. Wohl et al., "I Forgive Myself, Now I Can Study: How Self-Forgiveness for Procrastinating Can Reduce Future Procrastination," *Personality and Individual Differences* 48 (2010): 803–808.

Adapted from content posted on hbr.org on August 25, 2015 (product #H02AJ1).

9

There Are Risks to Mindfulness at Work

By David Brendel

Mindfulness is close to taking on cult status in the business world. But as with any rapidly growing movement—regardless of its potential benefits—there is good reason here for caution.

Championed for many years by pioneering researchers such as Ellen Langer and Jon Kabat-Zinn, mindfulness is a mental orientation and set of strategies for focusing one's mind on here-and-now experiences, such as abdominal muscle movements during respiration or the chirping of birds outside one's window. It is rooted in ancient Eastern philosophies, such as Taoism and Buddhism. Contemporary empirical research demonstrates its benefits for reducing anxiety and mental stress.[1] A recent study suggested that it might cut the risk of stroke and heart attack as well.

Mindful meditation and related practices are now widely accepted. For example, the *New Republic* published an article entitled "How 2014 Became the Year of Mindfulness." Mindfulness has also recently been featured on CBS's *60 Minutes* and been lauded by the *Huffington Post*. Dan Harris, a well-known ABC News correspondent, has published a best-selling book called *Ten Percent Happier*, which describes his journey to discovering mindful meditation as an optimal way to manage his very publicly shared anxiety disorder. There is increasing interest in how mindfulness can be applied in clinical medicine and psychology, and some large insurance companies are even beginning to consider providing coverage for mindfulness strategies for certain patients.

As an executive coach and physician, I often sing the praises of mindfulness practices and recommend them to clients to manage stress, avoid burnout, enhance leadership capacity, and steady the mind when in the midst of making important business decisions, career transitions, and personal life changes. Drawing on concepts from Eastern philosophies and research evidence from contemporary neuroscience, I help some clients employ controlled breathing and similar strategies in our sessions and in their everyday lives.[2] I also refer clients to trusted colleagues who teach yoga and mindful meditation in greater depth than I can provide in my coaching sessions.

But my growing knowledge of (and enthusiasm for) mindfulness is now tempered by a concern about its potential excesses and the risk that it may be crowding out other equally important models and strategies for managing stress, achieving peak performance, and reaching professional and personal fulfillment. At times, it appears that we are witnessing the development of a "cult of mindfulness" that, if not appropriately recognized and moderated, may result in an unfortunate backlash against it. Here are a couple of my concerns.

The avoidance risk

Some people use mindfulness strategies to avoid critical thinking tasks. I've worked with clients who, instead of rationally thinking through a career challenge or ethical dilemma, prefer to disconnect from their challenges and retreat into a meditative mindset. The issue here is that some problems require more thinking, not less. Sometimes stress is a signal that we need to consider our circumstances through greater self-reflective thought, not a "mindful" retreat to focused breathing or other immediate sensory experiences. Mindfulness strategies can prime the mind for sounder rational thinking—but the former clearly should not displace the latter. One of my clients spent so much time meditating and "mindfully" accepting her life "on its own terms" that she failed to confront underperforming workers (and discipline or fire the worst offenders) in her company. After periods of meditating, she struggled to return to focused, task-oriented thinking. She required significant reminders and reassurance from me that embracing Buddhist meditation does not entail tolerating substandard performance from her employees. Mindful meditation should always be used in the service of enhancing, not displacing, people's rational and analytical thought processes about their careers and personal lives.

The groupthink risk

As mindfulness practices enter mainstream American life, some organizations and companies are admirably encouraging their people to make use of them in the workplace.[3] But I'm aware of situations where this new orientation has gone too far. In one case, the director of a business unit in a financial services corporation required his direct reports to participate several times per week in a 10- to 15-minute mindfulness session that involved controlled breathing and guided imagery. Many participants came to dread the exercise. Some of them felt extremely awkward and uncomfortable, believing that mindfulness practices should be done in private. The very exercise that was supposed to reduce their work-related stress actually had increased it. The practice continued for weeks until several members of the group finally gathered the courage to tell the group leader that they would strongly prefer the daily exercises be optional, with impunity for nonparticipants. Mindfulness is rooted in a philosophy and psychology of self-efficacy and proactive self-care. Imposing it on people in a top-down manner degrades the practice and the people who might benefit from using it of their own volition.

That mindfulness has emerged as a major cultural phenomenon on the contemporary American scene and in the business world in particular can be good news for people dealing with stress, burnout, and other realities of the modern workplace. But mindfulness practices need to be incorporated as one among many self-chosen strategies for people aiming to cope with stress, think effectively, make sound decisions, and achieve fulfillment. Mindfulness practices should be used to enhance our rational and ethical thinking processes, not limit or displace them. And mindfulness practices should never be imposed on people, especially in the workplace. At its very core, mindfulness will be a huge step forward for Western culture if it stays focused on creating opportunities for individuals to discover their own personalized strategies for taming anxieties, managing stress, optimizing work performance, and reaching happiness and fulfillment.

DAVID BRENDEL is an executive coach, leadership development specialist, and psychiatrist based in Boston. He is founder and director of Leading Minds Executive Coaching and a cofounder of Strategy of Mind, a leadership development and coaching company.

Notes

1. J. Corliss, "Mindfulness Meditation May Ease Anxiety, Mental Stress," *Harvard Health Blog*, January 8, 2014.
2. M. Baime, "This Is Your Brain on Mindfulness," *Shambhala Sun*, July 2011, 44–84; and "Relaxation Techniques: Breath Control Helps Quell Errant Stress Response," *Harvard Health Publications*, January 2015.
3. A. Huffington, "Mindfulness, Meditation, Wellness and Their Connection to Corporate America's Bottom Line," *Huffington Post*, March 18, 2013.

Adapted from content posted on hbr.org on
February 11, 2015 (product #H01VIF).

Index

How to be human at work.

HBR's Emotional Intelligence Series features smart, essential reading on the human side of professional life from the pages of *Harvard Business Review*. Each book in the series offers uplifting stories, practical advice, and research from leading experts on how to tend to our emotional well-being at work.

Harvard Business Review Emotional Intelligence Series

Available in paperback or ebook format. The specially priced six-volume set includes:

- Mindfulness
- Resilience
- Influence and Persuasion

- Authentic Leadership
- Happiness
- Empathy

HBR.ORG

Buy for your team, clients, or event.
Visit hbr.org/bulksales for quantity discount rates.

Resilience

HBR EMOTIONAL INTELLIGENCE SERIES

HBR Emotional Intelligence Series

How to be human at work

The HBR Emotional Intelligence Series features smart, essential reading on the human side of professional life from the pages of *Harvard Business Review*.

Empathy

Happiness

Mindfulness

Resilience

Other books on emotional intelligence from *Harvard Business Review*:

HBR's 10 Must Reads on Emotional Intelligence

HBR Guide to Emotional Intelligence

Resilience

HBR EMOTIONAL INTELLIGENCE SERIES

Harvard Business Review Press

Boston, Massachusetts

HBR Press Quantity Sales Discounts

Harvard Business Review Press titles are available at significant quantity discounts when purchased in bulk for client gifts, sales promotions, and premiums. Special editions, including books with corporate logos, customized covers, and letters from the company printed in the front matter, as well as excerpts of existing books, can also be created in large quantities for special needs. For details and discount information for both print and ebook formats, contact booksales@harvardbusiness.org, tel. 800-988-0886, or www.hbr.org/bulksales.

Copyright 2017 Harvard Business School Publishing Corporation
All rights reserved
Printed in the United States of America

28 27 26 25 24 23 22 21 20 19

No part of this publication may be reproduced, stored in or introduced into a retrieval system, or transmitted, in any form, or by any means (electronic, mechanical, photocopying, recording, or otherwise), without the prior permission of the publisher. Requests for permission should be directed to permissions@hbsp.harvard.edu, or mailed to Permissions, Harvard Business School Publishing, 60 Harvard Way, Boston, Massachusetts 02163.

The web addresses referenced in this book were live and correct at the time of the book's publication but may be subject to change.

Library of Congress Cataloging-in-Publication Data

Title: Resilience.
Other titles: HBR emotional intelligence series.
Description: Boston, Massachusetts : Harvard Business Review Press, [2017] | Series: HBR emotional intelligence series
Identifiers: LCCN 2016056296 | ISBN 9781633693234 (pbk. : alk. paper)
Subjects: LCSH: Resilience (Personality trait) | Management.
Classification: LCC BF698.35.R47 R462 2017 | DDC 155.2/4—dc23 LC record available at https://lccn.loc.gov/2016056296

ISBN: 978-1-63369-323-4
eISBN: 978-1-63369-324-1

The paper used in this publication meets the requirements of the American National Standard for Permanence of Paper for Publications and Documents in Libraries and Archives Z39.48-1992.

Contents

Contents

Resilience

1

How Resilience Works

By Diane Coutu

When I began my career in journalism—I was a reporter at a national magazine in those days—there was a man I'll call Claus Schmidt. He was in his mid-fifties, and to my impressionable eyes, he was the quintessential newsman: cynical at times, but unrelentingly curious and full of life, and often hilariously funny in a sandpaper-dry kind of way. He churned out hard-hitting cover stories and features with a speed and elegance I could only dream of. It always astounded me that he was never promoted to managing editor.

But people who knew Claus better than I did thought of him not just as a great newsman but as a quintessential survivor, someone who had endured in an environment often hostile to talent. He had lived through at least three major changes in the magazine's leadership, losing most of his best friends and colleagues on the way. At home, two of his children succumbed to incurable illnesses, and a third was killed in a traffic accident. Despite all this—or maybe because of it—he milled around the newsroom day after day, mentoring the cub reporters, talking about the novels he was writing—always looking forward to what the future held for him.

Why do some people suffer real hardships and not falter? Claus Schmidt could have reacted very differently. We've all seen that happen: One person cannot seem to get the confidence back after a layoff; another, persistently depressed, takes a few years off from life after her divorce. The question we would all like answered is, Why? What exactly is that quality of resilience that carries people through life?

It's a question that has fascinated me ever since I first learned of the Holocaust survivors in elementary school. In college, and later in my studies as an affiliate scholar at the Boston Psychoanalytic Society and Institute, I returned to the subject. For the past several months, however, I have looked on it with a new urgency, for it seems to me that the terrorism, war, and recession of recent months have made understanding resilience more important than ever. I have considered both the nature of individual resilience and what makes some organizations as a whole more resilient than others. Why do some people and some companies buckle under pressure? And what makes others bend and ultimately bounce back?

My exploration has taught me much about resilience, although it's a subject none of us will ever understand fully. Indeed, resilience is one of the great puzzles of human nature, like creativity or the religious instinct. But in sifting through psychological research and in reflecting on the many stories of resilience I've heard, I have seen a little more deeply into the hearts and minds of people like

Claus Schmidt and, in doing so, looked more deeply into the human psyche as well.

The buzz about resilience

Resilience is a hot topic in business these days. Not long ago, I was talking to a senior partner at a respected consulting firm about how to land the very best MBAs—the name of the game in that particular industry. The partner, Daniel Savageau (not his real name), ticked off a long list of qualities his firm sought in its hires: intelligence, ambition, integrity, analytic ability, and so on. "What about resilience?" I asked. "Well, that's very popular right now," he said. "It's the new buzzword. Candidates even tell us they're resilient; they volunteer the information. But frankly, they're just too young to know that about themselves. Resilience is something you realize you have *after* the fact."

"But if you could, would you test for it?" I asked. "Does it matter in business?"

Savageau paused. He's a man in his late forties and a success personally and professionally. Yet it hadn't been a smooth ride to the top. He'd started his life as a poor French Canadian in Woonsocket, Rhode Island, and had lost his father at six. He lucked into a football scholarship but was kicked out of Boston University twice for drinking. He turned his life around in his twenties, married, divorced, remarried, and raised five children. Along the way, he made and lost two fortunes before helping to found the consulting firm he now runs. "Yes, it does matter," he said at last. "In fact, it probably matters more than any of the usual things we look for." In the course of reporting this article, I heard the same assertion time and again. As Dean Becker, the president and CEO of Adaptiv Learning Systems, a four-year-old company in King of Prussia, Pennsylvania, that develops and delivers programs about resilience training, puts it: "More than education, more than experience, more than training, a person's level of resilience will determine who succeeds and who fails. That's true in the cancer ward, it's true in the Olympics, and it's true in the boardroom."

Academic research into resilience started about 40 years ago with pioneering studies by Norman Garmezy, now a professor emeritus at the University of Minnesota in Minneapolis. After studying why many children of schizophrenic parents did not suffer psychological illness as a result of growing up with them, he concluded that a certain quality of resilience played a greater role in mental health than anyone had previously suspected.

Today, theories abound about what makes resilience. Looking at Holocaust victims, Maurice Vanderpol, a former president of the Boston Psychoanalytic Society and Institute, found that many of the healthy survivors of concentration camps had what he calls a "plastic shield." The shield was comprised of several factors, including a sense of humor. Often the humor was black, but nonetheless it provided a critical sense of perspective. Other core characteristics that helped included the ability to form attachments to others and the possession of an inner psychological space that protected the survivors from the intrusions of abusive others. Research about other groups uncovered different qualities associated with resilience. The Search Institute, a Minneapolis-based nonprofit organization that focuses on resilience and youth, found that the more resilient kids have an uncanny ability to get adults to help them out. Still other research showed that resilient inner-city youth often have talents such as athletic abilities that attract others to them.

Many of the early theories about resilience stressed the role of genetics. Some people are just born resilient, so the arguments went. There's some truth to that, of course, but an increasing body of empirical evidence shows that resilience—whether in children, survivors of concentration camps, or businesses back from the brink—can be learned. For example, George Vaillant, the director of the Study of Adult Development at Harvard Medical School in Boston, observes that within various groups studied during a 60-year period, some people became markedly more resilient over their lifetimes. Other psychologists claim that unresilient people more easily develop resiliency skills than those with head starts.

Most of the resilience theories I encountered in my research make good common sense. But I also observed that almost all the theories overlap in three ways. Resilient people, they posit, possess three characteristics: a staunch acceptance of reality; a deep belief, often buttressed by strongly held values, that life is meaningful; and an uncanny ability to improvise. You can bounce back from hardship with just one or two of these qualities, but you will only be truly resilient with all three. These three characteristics hold true for resilient organizations as well. Let's take a look at each of them in turn.

Facing down reality

A common belief about resilience is that it stems from an optimistic nature. That's true but only as long as such optimism doesn't distort your sense of reality. In extremely adverse situations, rose-colored thinking can actually spell disaster. This point was made poignantly to me by management researcher and writer Jim Collins, who happened upon this concept while researching *Good to Great*, his book on how companies transform themselves out of mediocrity. Collins had a hunch (an exactly wrong hunch) that resilient companies were filled with optimistic people. He tried out that idea on Admiral Jim Stockdale, who was held prisoner and tortured by the Vietcong for eight years.

Collins recalls: "I asked Stockdale: 'Who didn't make it out of the camps?' And he said, 'Oh, that's easy. It was the optimists. They were the ones who said we were going to be out by Christmas. And then they said we'd be out by Easter and then out by Fourth of July and out by Thanksgiving, and then it was Christmas again.' Then Stockdale turned to me and said, 'You know, I think they all died of broken hearts.'"

In the business world, Collins found the same unblinking attitude shared by executives at all the most successful companies he studied. Like Stockdale, resilient people have very sober and down-to-earth views of those parts of reality that matter for survival. That's not to say that optimism doesn't have its place: In turning around a demoralized sales force, for instance, conjuring a sense of possibility can be a very powerful tool. But for bigger challenges, a cool, almost pessimistic, sense of reality is far more important.

Perhaps you're asking yourself, "Do I truly understand—and accept—the reality of my situation? Does my organization?" Those are good questions, particularly because research suggests most people slip into denial as a coping mechanism. Facing reality, really facing it, is grueling work. Indeed, it can be unpleasant and often emotionally wrenching. Consider the following story of organizational resilience, and see what it means to confront reality.

Prior to September 11, 2001, Morgan Stanley, the famous investment bank, was the largest tenant in the World Trade Center. The company had some 2,700 employees working in the south tower on 22 floors between the 43rd and the 74th. On that horrible day, the first plane hit the north tower at 8:46 a.m. and Morgan Stanley started evacuating just one minute later, at 8:47 a.m. When the second plane crashed into the south tower 15 minutes after that, Morgan Stanley's offices were largely empty. All told, the company lost only seven employees despite receiving an almost direct hit.

Of course, the organization was just plain lucky to be in the second tower. Cantor Fitzgerald, whose offices were hit in the first attack, couldn't have done anything to save its employees. Still, it was Morgan Stanley's hard-nosed realism that enabled the company to benefit from its luck. Soon after the 1993 attack on the World Trade Center, senior management recognized that working in such a symbolic center of U.S. commercial power made the company vulnerable to attention from terrorists and possible attack.

With this grim realization, Morgan Stanley launched a program of preparedness at the micro level. Few companies take their fire drills seriously. Not so Morgan Stanley, whose VP of security for the Individual Investor Group, Rick Rescorla, brought a military discipline to the job. Rescorla, himself a highly resilient, decorated Vietnam vet, made sure that people were fully drilled about what to do in a catastrophe. When disaster struck on September 11, Rescorla was on a bullhorn telling Morgan Stanley employees to stay calm and follow their well-practiced drill, even though some building supervisors were telling occupants that all was well. Sadly, Rescorla himself, whose life story has been widely covered in recent months, was one of the seven who didn't make it out.

"When you're in financial services where so much depends on technology, contingency planning is a major part of your business," says President and COO Robert G. Scott. But Morgan Stanley was prepared for the very toughest reality. It had not just one but three recovery sites where employees could congregate and business could take place if work locales were ever disrupted. "Multiple backup sites seemed like an incredible extravagance on September 10," concedes Scott. "But on September 12, they seemed like genius."

Maybe it was genius; it was undoubtedly resilience at work. The fact is, when we truly stare down reality, we prepare ourselves to act in ways that allow us to endure and survive extraordinary hardship. We train ourselves how to survive before the fact.

The search for meaning

The ability to see reality is closely linked to the second building block of resilience, the propensity to make meaning of terrible times. We all know people who, under duress, throw up their hands and cry, "How can this be happening to me?" Such people see themselves as victims, and living through hardship carries no lessons for them. But resilient people devise constructs about their suffering to create some sort of meaning for themselves and others.

I have a friend I'll call Jackie Oiseaux who suffered repeated psychoses over a 10-year period due to an undiagnosed bipolar disorder. Today, she holds down a big job in one of the top publishing companies in the country, has a family, and is a prominent member of her church community. When people ask her how she bounced back from her crises, she runs her hands through her hair. "People sometimes say, 'Why me?' But I've always said, 'Why *not* me?' True, I lost many things during my illness," she says, "but I found many more—incredible friends who saw me through the bleakest times and who will give meaning to my life forever."

This dynamic of meaning making is, most researchers agree, the way resilient people build bridges from present-day hardships to a fuller, better-constructed future. Those bridges make the present manageable, for lack of a better word, removing the sense that the present is overwhelming. This concept was beautifully articulated by Viktor E. Frankl, an Austrian psychiatrist and an Auschwitz survivor. In the midst of staggering suffering, Frankl invented "meaning therapy," a humanistic therapy technique that helps individuals make the kinds of decisions that will create significance in their lives.

In his book *Man's Search for Meaning*, Frankl described the pivotal moment in the camp when he developed meaning therapy. He was on his way to work one day, worrying whether he should trade his last cigarette for a bowl of soup. He wondered how he was going to work with a new foreman whom he knew to be particularly sadistic. Suddenly, he was disgusted by just how trivial and meaningless his life had become. He realized that to survive, he had to find some purpose. Frankl did so by imagining himself giving a lecture after the war on the psychology of the concentration camp, to help outsiders understand what he had been through. Although he wasn't even sure he would survive, Frankl created some concrete goals for himself. In doing so, he succeeded in rising above the sufferings of the moment. As he put it in his book: "We must never forget that we may also find meaning in life even when confronted with a hopeless situation, when facing a fate that cannot be changed."

Frankl's theory underlies most resilience coaching in business. Indeed, I was struck by how often businesspeople referred to his work. "Resilience training—what we call hardiness—is a way for us to help people construct meaning in their everyday lives," explains Salvatore R. Maddi, a University of California, Irvine psychology professor and the director of the Hardiness Institute in Newport Beach, California. "When people realize the power of resilience training, they often say, 'Doc, is this what psychotherapy is?' But psychotherapy is for people whose lives have fallen apart badly and need repair. We see our work as showing people life skills and attitudes. Maybe those things should be taught at home, maybe they should be taught in schools, but they're not. So we end up doing it in business."

Yet the challenge confronting resilience trainers is often more difficult than we might imagine. Meaning can be elusive, and just because you found it once doesn't mean you'll keep it or find it again. Consider Aleksandr Solzhenitsyn, who survived the war against the Nazis, imprisonment in the gulag, and cancer. Yet when he moved to a farm in peaceful, safe Vermont, he could not cope with the "infantile West." He was unable to discern any real meaning in what he felt to be the destructive and irresponsible freedom of the West. Upset by his critics, he withdrew into his farmhouse, behind a locked fence, seldom to be seen in public. In 1994, a bitter man, Solzhenitsyn moved back to Russia.

Since finding meaning in one's environment is such an important aspect of resilience, it should come as no surprise that the most successful organizations and people possess strong value systems. Strong values infuse an environment with meaning because they offer ways to interpret and shape events. While it's popular these days to ridicule values, it's surely no coincidence that the most resilient organization in the world has been the Catholic Church, which has survived wars, corruption, and schism for more than 2,000 years, thanks largely to its immutable set of values. Businesses that survive also have their creeds, which give them purposes beyond just making money. Strikingly, many companies describe their value systems in religious terms. Pharmaceutical giant Johnson & Johnson, for instance, calls its value system, set out in a document given to every new employee at orientation, the Credo. Parcel company UPS talks constantly about its Noble Purpose.

Value systems at resilient companies change very little over the years and are used as scaffolding in times of trouble. UPS Chairman and CEO Mike Eskew believes that the Noble Purpose helped the company to rally after the agonizing strike in 1997. Says Eskew: "It was a hugely difficult time, like a family feud. Everyone had close friends on both sides of the fence, and it was tough for us to pick sides. But what saved us was our Noble Purpose. Whatever side people were on, they all shared a common set of values. Those values are core to us and never change; they frame most of our important decisions. Our strategy and our mission may change, but our values never do."

The religious connotations of words like "credo," "values," and "noble purpose," however, should not be confused with the actual content of the values. Companies can hold ethically questionable values and still be very resilient. Consider Phillip Morris, which has demonstrated impressive resilience in the face of increasing unpopularity. As Jim Collins points out, Phillip Morris has very strong values, although we might not agree with them—for instance, the value of "adult choice." But there's no doubt that Phillip Morris executives believe strongly in its values, and the strength of their beliefs sets the company apart from most of the other tobacco companies. In this context, it is worth noting that resilience is neither ethically good nor bad. It is merely the skill and the capacity to be robust under conditions of enormous stress and change. As Viktor Frankl wrote: "On the average, only those prisoners could keep alive who, after years of trekking from camp to camp, had lost all scruples in their fight for existence; they were prepared to use every means, honest and otherwise, even brutal . . . in order to save themselves. We who have come back . . . we know: The best of us did not return."

Values, positive or negative, are actually more important for organizational resilience than having resilient people on the payroll. If resilient employees are all interpreting reality in different ways, their decisions and actions may well conflict, calling into doubt the survival of their organization. And as the weakness of an organization becomes apparent, highly resilient individuals are more likely to jettison the organization than to imperil their own survival.

Ritualized ingenuity

The third building block of resilience is the ability to make do with whatever is at hand. Psychologists follow the lead of French anthropologist Claude Levi-Strauss in calling this skill bricolage.[1] Intriguingly, the roots of that word are closely tied to the concept of resilience, which literally means "bouncing back." Says Levi-Strauss: "In its old sense, the verb *bricoler* . . . was always used with reference to some extraneous movement: a ball rebounding, a dog straying, or a horse swerving from its direct course to avoid an obstacle."

Bricolage in the modern sense can be defined as a kind of inventiveness, an ability to improvise a solution to a problem without proper or obvious tools or materials. Bricoleurs are always tinkering—building radios from household effects or fixing their own cars. They make the most of what they have, putting objects to unfamiliar uses. In the concentration camps, for example, resilient inmates knew to pocket pieces of string or wire whenever they found them. The string or wire might later become useful—to fix a pair of shoes, perhaps, which in freezing conditions might make the difference between life and death.

When situations unravel, bricoleurs muddle through, imagining possibilities where others are confounded. I have two friends, whom I'll call Paul Shields and Mike Andrews, who were roommates throughout their college years. To no one's surprise, when they graduated, they set up a business together selling educational materials to schools, businesses, and consulting firms. At first, the company was a great success, making both founders paper millionaires. But the recession of the early 1990s hit the company hard, and many core clients fell away. At the same time, Paul experienced a bitter divorce and a depression that made it impossible for him to work. Mike offered to buy Paul out but was instead slapped with a lawsuit claiming that Mike was trying to steal the business. At this point, a less resilient person might have just walked away from the mess. Not Mike. As the case wound through the courts, he kept the company going any way he could—constantly morphing the business until he found a model that worked: going into joint ventures to sell English-language training materials to Russian and Chinese companies. Later, he branched off into publishing newsletters for clients. At one point, he was even writing video scripts for his competitors. Thanks to all this bricolage, by the time the lawsuit was settled in his favor, Mike had an entirely different, and much more solid, business than the one he had started with.

Bricolage can be practiced on a higher level as well. Richard Feynman, winner of the 1965 Nobel Prize in physics, exemplified what I like to think of as intellectual bricolage. Out of pure curiosity, Feynman made himself an expert on cracking safes, not only looking at the mechanics of safecracking but also cobbling together psychological insights about people who used safes and set the locks. He cracked many of the safes at Los Alamos, for instance, because he guessed that theoretical physicists would not set the locks with random code numbers they might forget but would instead use a sequence with mathematical significance. It turned out that the three safes containing all the secrets to the atomic bomb were set to the same mathematical constant, e, whose first six digits are 2.71828.

Resilient organizations are stuffed with bricoleurs, though not all of them, of course, are Richard Feynmans. Indeed, companies that survive regard improvisation as a core skill. Consider UPS, which empowers its drivers to do whatever it takes to deliver packages on time. Says CEO Eskew: "We tell our employees to get the job done. If that means they need to improvise, they improvise. Otherwise we just couldn't do what we do every day. Just think what can go wrong: a busted traffic light, a flat tire, a bridge washed out. If a snowstorm hits Louisville tonight, a group of people will sit together and discuss how to handle the problem. Nobody tells them to do that. They come together because it's our tradition to do so."

That tradition meant that the company was delivering parcels in southeast Florida just one day after Hurricane Andrew devastated the region in 1992, causing billions of dollars in damage. Many people were living in their cars because their homes had been destroyed, yet UPS drivers and managers sorted packages at a diversion site and made deliveries even to those who were stranded in their cars. It was largely UPS's improvisational skills that enabled it to keep functioning after the catastrophic hit. And the fact that the company continued on gave others a sense of purpose or meaning amid the chaos.

Improvisation of the sort practiced by UPS, however, is a far cry from unbridled creativity. Indeed, much like the military, UPS lives on rules and regulations. As Eskew says: "Drivers always put their keys in the same place. They close the doors the same way. They wear their uniforms the same way. We are a company of precision." He believes that although they may seem stifling, UPS's rules were what allowed the company to bounce back immediately after Hurricane Andrew, for they enabled people to focus on the one or two fixes they needed to make in order to keep going.

Eskew's opinion is echoed by Karl E. Weick, a professor of organizational behavior at the University of Michigan Business School in Ann Arbor and one of the most respected thinkers on organizational psychology. "There is good evidence that when people are put under pressure, they regress to their most habituated ways of responding," Weick has written. "What we do not expect under life-threatening pressure is creativity." In other words, the rules and regulations that make some companies appear less creative may actually make them more resilient in times of real turbulence.

———————————

Claus Schmidt, the newsman I mentioned earlier, died about five years ago, but I'm not sure I could have interviewed him about his own resilience even if he were alive. It would have felt strange, I think, to ask him, "Claus, did you really face down reality? Did you make meaning out of your hardships? Did you improvise your recovery after each professional and personal disaster?" He may not have been able to answer. In my experience, resilient people don't often describe themselves that way. They shrug off their survival stories and very often assign them to luck.

Obviously, luck does have a lot to do with surviving. It was luck that Morgan Stanley was situated in the south tower and could put its preparedness training to work. But being lucky is not the same as being resilient. Resilience is a reflex—a way of facing and understanding the world—that is deeply etched into a person's mind and soul. Resilient people and companies face reality with staunchness, make meaning of hardship instead of crying out in despair, and improvise solutions from thin air. Others do not. This is the nature of resilience, and we will never completely understand it.

DIANE L. COUTU is a former senior editor at HBR specializing in psychology and business.

Note

1. See, e.g., Karl E. Weick, "The Collapse of Sense-making in Organizations: The Mann Gulch Disaster," *Administrative Science Quarterly*, December 1993.

Reprinted from *Harvard Business Review*,
May 2002 (product #R0205B).

2

Resilience for the Rest of Us

By Daniel Goleman

There are two ways to become more resilient: one by talking to yourself, the other by retraining your brain.

If you've suffered a major failure, take the sage advice given by psychologist Martin Seligman in the HBR article "Building Resilience" (April 2011). Talk to yourself. Give yourself a cognitive intervention, and counter defeatist thinking with an optimistic attitude. Challenge your downbeat thinking, and replace it with a positive outlook.

Fortunately, major failures come along rarely in life.

But what about bouncing back from the more frequent annoying screwups, minor setbacks, and irritating upsets that are routine in any leader's life? Resilience is, again, the answer—but with a different flavor. You need to retrain your brain.

The brain has a very different mechanism for bouncing back from the cumulative toll of daily hassles. And with a little effort, you can upgrade its ability to snap back from life's downers.

Whenever we get so upset that we say or do something we later regret (and who doesn't now and then?), that's a sure sign that our amygdala—the brain's radar for danger and the trigger for the fight-or-flight response—has hijacked the brain's executive centers in the prefrontal cortex. The neural key to resilience lies in how quickly we recover from that hijacked state.

The circuitry that brings us back to full energy and focus after an amygdala hijack concentrates in the left side of our prefrontal area, says Richard Davidson, a neuroscientist at the University of Wisconsin. He's also found that when we're distressed, there's heightened activity on the right side of the prefrontal area. Each of us has a characteristic level of left/right activity that predicts our daily mood range—if we're tilted to the right, more upsets; if to the left, we're quicker to recover from distress of all kinds.

To tackle this in the workplace, Davidson teamed with the CEO of a high-pressure, 24/7, biotech startup and meditation expert Jon Kabat-Zinn of the University of Massachusetts Medical School. Kabat-Zinn offered the employees at the biotech outfit instruction in mindfulness, an attention-training method that teaches the brain to register anything happening in the present moment with full focus—but without reacting.

The instructions are simple:

1. Find a quiet, private place where you can be undistracted for a few minutes. For instance, close your office door and mute your phone.

2. Sit comfortably, with your back straight but relaxed.

3. Focus your awareness on your breath, staying attentive to the sensations of the inhalation and exhalation, and start again on the next breath.

4. Do not judge your breathing or try to change it in any way.

5. See anything else that comes to mind as a distraction—thoughts, sounds, whatever. Let them go and return your attention to your breath.

After eight weeks and an average of 30 minutes a day practicing mindfulness, the employees had shifted their ratio from tilted toward the stressed-out right side to leaning toward the resilient left side. What's more, they said they remembered what they loved about their work: They got in touch with what had brought them energy in the first place.

To get the full benefit of mindfulness, a daily practice of 20 to 30 minutes works best. Think of it like a mental exercise routine. It can be very helpful to have guided instructions, but the key is to find a slot for the practice in your daily routine. (There are even instructions for using a long drive as your practice session.)

Mindfulness has steadily been gaining credence among hard-nosed executives. There are centers where mindfulness instruction has been tailored to businesspeople, from tony resorts like Miraval Resort in Arizona to programs in mindful leadership at the University of Massachusetts Medical School. Google University has been offering a course in mindfulness to employees for years.

Might you benefit from tuning up your brain's resilience circuitry by learning to practice mindfulness? Among high-performing executives, the effects of stress can be subtle. My colleagues Richard Boyatzis and Annie McKee suggest as a rough diagnostic of leadership stress asking yourself, "Do I have a vague sense of unease, restlessness, or the feeling that life is not great (a higher standard than 'good enough')?" A bit of mindfulness might put your mind at ease.

DANIEL GOLEMAN is a codirector of the Consortium for Research on Emotional Intelligence in Organizations at Rutgers University, coauthor of *Primal Leadership: Leading with Emotional Intelligence* (Harvard Business Review Press, 2013), and author of *The Brain and Emotional Intelligence: New Insights.*

Adapted from content posted on hbr.org
on March 4, 2016.

3

How to Evaluate, Manage, and Strengthen Your Resilience

By David Kopans

Think back to your last off-site meeting. You and the rest of your team likely poured over reports and spreadsheets, facts and figures. Strewn about the table were probably the tools of your trade: reams of data, balance sheets, and P&Ls. Managers understand that clear-eyed analysis—both quantitative and qualitative—is the key to building a resilient business. And yet when it comes to measuring and strengthening our own ability to adapt, grow, and prosper, rarely do we apply the same methodical approach.

But we should. Based on my own experience starting, building, and growing companies, as well as upon decades of research showing the underlying components of personal resilience, I've discovered a few fundamental things you can do to actually evaluate, manage, and strengthen your own resilience in the same way that you would increase the resiliency of your company:

Build up your positivity currency. We can't just print resilience the way countries print money. Individuals must use what I call a "positivity currency" approach that is grounded in actual positive interactions, events, and memories—factors that are known to boost resilience. This currency is only "printed" and stored as assets when we focus on positive things and express gratitude for them. Why? Because maintaining a positive outlook and regularly expressing gratitude are the bullion bars that have real value in backstopping and building resilience.

Research by Robert Emmons of UC Davis, Michael McCullough of the University of Miami, and others clearly shows that they are among the most reliable methods for increasing personal happiness and life satisfaction.[1] Creating such positivity currency can decrease anxiety, reduce symptoms of illness, and improve the quality of your sleep. All of which, of course, lead to greater personal resilience.

Keep records. None of the tools we use to evaluate companies work very well without good record keeping. That's also true when it comes to building individual resilience. When you commit positive interactions, events, and memories to the written word, they register higher value than other non-written forms of positivity currency-based activity, according to research by positive psychology expert Martin Seligman of the University of Pennsylvania.[2] Record your positive currency transactions (by jotting them down in a leather bound journal or a digital equivalent). The data points you record could be as simple as keeping a written tally by category (such as family, friends, or work) in a paper notebook, entering the information into a spreadsheet, or assigning hashtags to items in a digital gratitude journal.

Create a bull market. Financial markets boom when increasing numbers of investors want in. Likewise, our own resilience grows when we encourage positivity buyers to enter the market. It's not a difficult task; positivity is socially contagious. In the research behind their book *Connected: The Surprising Power of Our Social Networks and How They Shape Our Lives*, Harvard's Nicholas Christakis and the University of California, San Diego's James Fowler detail how happiness depends not just on our own choices and actions, but also on those of people who are two or even three degrees removed from us. What this means is by being more positive ourselves, we encourage others to do the same, and this in turn creates a virtuous "reverse run on the bank" positive feedback loop, and our own resilience is increased and strengthened by the actions of others.

Take a portfolio approach. Resilient businesses diversify risk. Accordingly, resilient individuals diversify their positivity currency. They look to increase their overall resilience by evaluating what it is that provides the highest returns across their entire "life portfolio" and then investing more in those areas. Most frequently, these high-return assets come from our lives outside of the office. Indeed, while we may spend the majority of waking hours at work, our job should not be central to our overall positive outlook. In a 2015 report entitled "The Happiness Study" from Blackhawk Engagement Solutions, respondents ranked their jobs eighth out of a list of 12 contributors to overall happiness. Ranking in the top spots were family, friends, health, hobbies, and community.[3] It follows that by generating more positivity currency in those areas, you will increase the ability to bring your best self to work.

Report regularly. Finally, just as regular review of a company's financials is important to building a resilient business, building individual resilience requires regular review of positivity currency data. This review not only enables you to glean insights and take corrective actions, but also to boost your resilience by simply increasing your exposure to positive interactions and expressions of gratitude. As suggested in a famous 2014 experiment conducted by Facebook's data scientists and published in the Proceedings of the National Academy of Sciences of the United States of America, if your news feed skews positive, so will you.[4]

Even if you don't analyze your positivity currency data deeply like a Wall Street quant, just exposing yourself to it on a regular basis will make you more resilient. So find a regular time to celebrate and reflect on your positivity currency (I do it while I wait for my morning coffee). Make it a habit, and your level of resilience—and that of your friends, family, and coworkers—will rise.

DAVID KOPANS is the founder and CEO of PF Loop, a company that aims to make positive change in the world through software applications and digital services grounded in positive psychology research.

Notes

1. R. Emmons, "Why Gratitude Is Good," *Greater Good*, November 16, 2010, http://greatergood.berkeley.edu/article/item/why_gratitude_is_good; and "Why Practice Gratitude," *Greater Good*, October 31, 2016, http://greatergood.berkeley.edu/topic/gratitude/definition#why_practice.
2. M. E. Seligman et al., "Positive Psychology Progress: Empirical Validation of Interventions," *American Psychologist* 60, no. 5 (July–August 2005): 410–421.
3. "The Happiness Study: An Employee Rewards and Recognition Study," Blackhawk Engagement Solutions,

June 2, 2105, www.bhengagement.com/report/
employee-happiness-study/.

4. A. D. I. Kramer et al., "Experimental Evidence of Massive-
Scale Emotional Contagion Through Social Networks,"
*Proceedings of the National Academy of Sciences of the
United States of America* 111, no. 24 (2014): 8788–8790.

Adapted from content posted on hbr.org on
June 14, 2016 (product # H02XDP).

4

Find the Coaching in Criticism

By Sheila Heen and Douglas Stone

F eedback is crucial. That's obvious: It improves performance, develops talent, aligns expectations, solves problems, guides promotion and pay, and boosts the bottom line.

But it's equally obvious that in many organizations, feedback doesn't work. A glance at the stats tells the story: Only 36% of managers complete appraisals thoroughly and on time. In one recent survey, 55% of employees said their most recent performance review had been unfair or inaccurate, and one in four said they dread such evaluations more than anything else in their working lives. When senior HR executives were asked about their biggest performance management challenge, 63% cited managers' inability or unwillingness to have difficult feedback discussions. Coaching and mentoring? Uneven at best.

Most companies try to address these problems by training leaders to give feedback more effectively and more often. That's fine as far as it goes; everyone benefits when managers are better communicators. But improving the skills of the feedback giver won't accomplish much if the receiver isn't able to absorb what is said. It is the receiver who controls whether feedback is let in or kept out, who has to make sense of what he or she is hearing, and who decides whether or not to change. People need to stop treating feedback only as something that must be pushed and instead improve their ability to pull.

For the past 20 years we've coached executives on difficult conversations, and we've found that almost everyone, from new hires to C-suite veterans, struggles with receiving feedback. A critical performance review, a well-intended suggestion, or an oblique comment that may or may not even be feedback

("Well, your presentation was certainly interesting") can spark an emotional reaction, inject tension into the relationship, and bring communication to a halt. But there's good news, too: The skills needed to receive feedback well are distinct and learnable. They include being able to identify and manage the emotions triggered by the feedback and extract value from criticism even when it's poorly delivered.

Why feedback doesn't register

What makes receiving feedback so hard? The process strikes at the tension between two core human needs—the need to learn and grow, and the need to be accepted just the way you are. As a result, even a seemingly benign suggestion can leave you feeling angry, anxious, badly treated, or profoundly threatened. A hedge such as "Don't take this personally" does nothing to soften the blow.

Getting better at receiving feedback starts with understanding and managing those feelings. You might think there are a thousand ways in which feedback can push your buttons, but in fact there are only three.

Truth triggers are set off by the content of the feedback. When assessments or advice seem off base, unhelpful, or simply untrue, you feel indignant, wronged, and exasperated.

Relationship triggers are tripped by the person providing the feedback. Exchanges are often colored by what you believe about the giver (He's got no credibility on this topic!) and how you feel about your previous interactions (After all I've done for you, I get this petty criticism?). So you might reject coaching that you would accept on its merits if it came from someone else.

Identity triggers are all about your relationship with yourself. Whether the feedback is right or wrong, wise or witless, it can be devastating if it causes your sense of who you are to come undone. In such moments you'll struggle with feeling overwhelmed, defensive, or off balance.

All these responses are natural and reasonable; in some cases they are unavoidable. The solution isn't to pretend you don't have them. It's to recognize what's happening and learn how to derive benefit from feedback even when it sets off one or more of your triggers.

Six steps to becoming a better receiver

Taking feedback well is a process of sorting and filtering. You need to understand the other person's point of view, try on ideas that may at first seem a poor fit, and experiment with different ways of doing things. You also need to discard or shelve critiques that are genuinely misdirected or are not helpful right away.

But it's nearly impossible to do any of those things from inside a triggered response. Instead of ushering you into a nuanced conversation that will help you learn, your triggers prime you to reject, counterattack, or withdraw.

The six steps below will keep you from throwing valuable feedback onto the discard pile or—just as damaging—accepting and acting on comments that you would be better off disregarding. They are presented as advice to the receiver. But, of course, understanding the challenges of receiving feedback helps the giver be more effective, too.

1. Know your tendencies

You've been getting feedback all your life, so there are no doubt patterns in how you respond. Do you defend yourself on the facts ("This is plain wrong"), argue about the method of delivery ("You're really doing this by email?"), or strike back ("You, of all people?")? Do you smile on the outside but seethe on the inside? Do you get teary or filled with righteous indignation? And what role does the passage of time play? Do you tend to reject feedback in the moment and then step back and consider it over time? Do you accept it all immediately but later decide it's not valid? Do you agree with it intellectually but have trouble changing your behavior?

When Michael, an advertising executive, hears his boss make an offhand joke about his lack of professionalism, it hits him like a sledgehammer. "I'm flooded with shame," he told us, "and all my failings rush to mind, as if I'm Googling 'things wrong with me' and getting 1.2 million hits, with sponsored ads from my father and my ex. In this state it's hard to see the feedback at 'actual size.'" But now that Michael understands his standard operating procedure, he's able to make better choices about where to go from there: "I can reassure myself that I'm exaggerating, and usually after I sleep on it, I'm in a better place to figure out whether there's something I can learn."

2. Disentangle the "what" from the "who"

If the feedback is on target and the advice is wise, it shouldn't matter who delivers it. But it does. When a relationship trigger is activated, entwining the content of comments with your feelings about the giver (or about how, when, or where she delivered the comments), learning is short-circuited. To keep that from happening, you have to work to separate the message from the messenger, and then consider both.

Janet, a chemist and a team leader at a pharmaceutical company, received glowing comments from her peers and superiors during her 360-degree review but was surprised by the negative feedback she got from her direct reports. She immediately concluded that the problem was theirs: "I have high standards, and some of them can't handle that," she remembers thinking. "They aren't used to someone holding their feet to the fire." In this way, she changed the subject from her management style to her subordinates' competence, preventing her from learning something important about the impact she had on others.

Eventually the penny dropped, Janet says. "I came to see that whether it was their performance problem or my leadership problem, those were not mutually exclusive issues, and both were worth solving." She was able to disentangle the issues and talk to her team about both. Wisely, she began the conversation with their feedback to her, asking, "What am I doing that's making things tough? What would improve the situation?"

3. Sort toward coaching

Some feedback is evaluative ("Your rating is a 4"); some is coaching ("Here's how you can improve").

Everyone needs both. Evaluations tell you where you stand, what to expect, and what is expected of you. Coaching allows you to learn and improve and helps you play at a higher level.

It's not always easy to distinguish one from the other. When a board member phoned James to suggest that he start the next quarter's CFO presentation with analyst predictions rather than internal projections, was that intended as a helpful suggestion, or was it a veiled criticism of his usual approach? When in doubt, people tend to assume the worst and to put even well-intentioned coaching into the evaluation bin. Feeling judged is likely to set off your identity triggers, and the resulting anxiety can drown out the opportunity to learn. So whenever possible, sort toward coaching. Work to hear feedback as potentially valuable advice from a fresh perspective rather than as an indictment of how you've done things in the past. When James took that approach, "the suggestion became less emotionally loaded," he says. "I decided to hear it as simply an indication of how that board member might more easily digest quarterly information."

4. Unpack the feedback

Often it's not immediately clear whether feedback is valid and useful. So before you accept or reject it, do some analysis to better understand it.

Here's a hypothetical example. Kara, who's in sales, is told by Johann, an experienced colleague, that she needs to "be more assertive." Her reaction might be to reject his advice ("I think I'm pretty assertive already"). Or she might acquiesce ("I really do need to step it up"). But before she decides what to do, she needs to understand what he really means. Does he think she should speak up more often, or just with greater conviction? Should she smile more or less? Have the confidence to admit she doesn't know something or the confidence to pretend she does?

Even the simple advice to "be more assertive" comes from a complex set of observations and judgments that Johann has made while watching Kara in meetings and with customers. Kara needs to dig into the general suggestion and find out what in particular prompted it. What did Johann see her do or fail to do? What did he expect, and what is he worried about? In other words, where is the feedback coming from?

Kara also needs to know where the feedback is going—exactly what Johann wants her to do differently and why. After a clarifying discussion, she might agree that she is less assertive than others on the sales floor but disagree with the idea that she should change. If all her sales heroes are quiet, humble, and deeply curious about customers' needs, Kara's view of what it means to be good at sales might look and sound very different from Johann's *Glengarry Glen Ross* ideal.

When you set aside snap judgments and take time to explore where feedback is coming from and where it's going, you can enter into a rich, informative conversation about perceived best practices—whether you decide to take the advice or not.

5. Ask for just one thing

Feedback is less likely to set off your emotional triggers if you request it and direct it. So don't wait until your annual performance review. Find opportunities to get bite-size pieces of coaching from a variety of people throughout the year. Don't invite criticism with a big, unfocused question like "Do you have any feedback for me?" Make the process more manageable by asking a colleague, a boss, or a direct report, "What's one thing you see me doing (or failing to do) that holds me back?" That person may name the first behavior that comes to mind or the most important one on his or her list. Either way, you'll get concrete information and can tease out more specifics at your own pace.

Roberto, a fund manager at a financial services firm, found his 360-degree review process overwhelming and confusing. "Eighteen pages of charts and graphs and no ability to have follow-up conversations to clarify the feedback was frustrating," he says, adding that it also left him feeling awkward around his colleagues.

Now Roberto taps two or three people each quarter to ask for one thing he might work on. "They don't offer the same things, but over time I hear themes, and that gives me a good sense of where my growth edge lies," he says. "And I have really good conversations—with my boss, with my team, even with peers where there's some friction in the relationship. They're happy to tell me one thing to change, and often they're right. It does help us work more smoothly together."

Research has shown that those who explicitly seek critical feedback (that is, who are not just fishing for praise) tend to get higher performance ratings. Why?

Mainly, we think, because someone who's asking for coaching is more likely to take what is said to heart and genuinely improve. But also because when you ask for feedback, you not only find out how others see you, you also *influence* how they see you. Soliciting constructive criticism communicates humility, respect, passion for excellence, and confidence, all in one go.

6. Engage in small experiments

After you've worked to solicit and understand feedback, it may still be hard to discern which bits of advice will help you and which ones won't. We suggest designing small experiments to find out. Even though you may doubt that a suggestion will be useful, if the downside risk is small and the upside potential is large, it's worth a try. James, the CFO we discussed earlier, decided to take the board member's advice for the next presentation and see what happened. Some directors were pleased with the change, but the shift in format prompted others to offer suggestions of their own. Today James reverse-engineers his presentations to meet board members' current top-of-mind concerns. He sends out an email a week beforehand asking for any burning questions and either front-loads his talk with answers to them or signals at the start that he will get to them later on. "It's a little more challenging to prepare for but actually much easier to give," he says. "I spend less time fielding unexpected questions, which was the hardest part of the job."

That's an example worth following. When someone gives you advice, test it out. If it works, great. If it doesn't, you can try again, tweak your approach, or decide to end the experiment. Criticism is never easy to take. Even when you know that it's essential to your development and you trust that the person delivering it wants you to succeed, it can activate psychological triggers. You might feel misjudged, ill-used, and sometimes threatened to your very core.

Your growth depends on your ability to pull value from criticism in spite of your natural responses and on your willingness to seek out even more advice and coaching from bosses, peers, and subordinates. They may be good or bad at providing it, or they may have little time for it—but you are the most important factor in your own development. If you're determined to learn from whatever feedback you get, no one can stop you.

SHEILA HEEN and DOUGLAS STONE are cofounders of Triad Consulting Group and teach negotiation at Harvard Law School. They are coauthors of *Thanks for the Feedback: The Science and Art of Receiving Feedback Well*, from which this article is adapted.

Reprinted from *Harvard Business Review*, January–February 2014 (product #R1401K).

5

Firing Back

How Great Leaders Rebound
After Career Disasters

By Jeffrey A. Sonnenfeld and Andrew J. Ward

Among the tests of a leader, few are more challenging—and more painful—than recovering from a career catastrophe, whether it is caused by natural disaster, illness, misconduct, slipups, or unjust conspiratorial overthrow. But real leaders don't cave in. Defeat energizes them to rejoin the fray with greater determination and vigor.

Take the case of Jamie Dimon, who was fired as president of Citigroup but now is CEO of JPMorgan Chase. Or look at Vanguard founder Jack Bogle, who was removed from his position as president of Wellington Management but then went on to create the index fund and become a leading voice for governance reform. Similarly, there's former Coca-Cola president Steve Heyer, who was surprisingly passed over for the CEO position at Coke but then was quickly named head of Starwood Hotels. Most colorful, perhaps, is Donald Trump, who recovered from two rounds of financial distress in his casino business and is admired today both as a hugely successful estate developer and as a producer and star of popular reality TV shows—and of course ran successfully for President of the United States.

These stories are still the exception rather than the rule. F. Scott Fitzgerald's famous observation that there are no second acts in American lives casts an especially dark shadow over the derailed careers of business leaders. In our research—analyzing more than 450 CEO successions between 1988 and 1992 at large, publicly traded companies—we found that only 35% of ousted CEOs returned to an active executive role within two years of departure; 22% stepped back and took only advisory roles, generally counseling smaller organizations or sitting on boards.

But 43% effectively ended their careers and went into retirement.

What prevents a deposed leader from coming back? Leaders who cannot recover have a tendency to blame themselves and are often tempted to dwell on the past rather than look to the future. They secretly hold themselves responsible for their career setback, whether they were or not, and get caught in a psychological web of their own making, unable to move beyond the position they no longer hold. This dynamic is usually reinforced by well-meaning colleagues and even by family and friends, who may try to lay blame in an attempt to make sense of the chaos surrounding the disaster. Sadly, their advice can often be more damaging than helpful.

In every culture, the ability to transcend life's adversity is an essential feature of becoming a great leader. In his influential 1949 book, *The Hero with a Thousand Faces*, anthropologist Joseph Campbell showed us that the various stories of great leaders around the world, in every culture and every era, are all essentially the same story—the "hero myth." This myth is embodied in the life stages of such universal archetypes as Moses, Jesus, Muhammad, Buddha, Aeneas, Odysseus, and the Aztecs' Tezcatlipoca. Transformational leaders follow a path that entails a call to greatness, early successes (involving tough choices), ongoing trials, profound setbacks, and, ultimately, triumph as they reintegrate into society. If Campbell were writing today, he might want to include business leaders in his study, as they must confront similar trials on their way to greatness.

This article is intended to help leaders—or anyone suffering from an unexpected setback—examine their often abrupt fall from grace and to give them a process through which they can recover, and even exceed their past accomplishments. From our 22 years of interviews with 300 fired CEOs and other derailed professionals, our scholarly study of leadership, our consulting assignments, and our own searing personal experiences, we are convinced that leaders can triumph over tragedy, provided they take conscious steps to do so. For a start, they must carefully *decide how to fight back*. Once this crucial decision has been taken, they must *recruit others into battle*. They must then *take steps to recover their heroic status*, in the process proving to themselves and others that they have the *mettle* necessary to *rediscover their heroic mission*.

Few people exemplify this journey better than President Jimmy Carter. After his devastating 1980 reelection loss to Ronald Reagan, Carter was emotionally fatigued. As he told us sometime later, "I returned to Plains, Georgia, completely exhausted, slept for almost 24 hours, and then awoke to an altogether new, unwanted, and potentially empty life." While proud of his achievements—his success in deregulating energy, for example, his efforts to promote global human rights, and his ability to broker peace between Israel and Egypt through the Camp David Accords—post election, Carter needed to move past his sense of frustration and rejection, particularly his failure to secure the timely release of the American hostages in Iran.

Despite his pain and humiliation, Carter did not retreat into anger or self-pity. He realized that his global prominence gave him a forum to fight to restore his influential role in world events. Accordingly, he recruited others into battle by enlisting the enthusiastic support of his wife, Rosalynn, several members of his administration, academic researchers in the sciences and social sciences, world leaders, and financial backers to build the Carter Center. He proved his mettle by refusing to remove himself from the fray. Indeed, he continued to involve himself in international conflict mediation in Ethiopia and Eritrea, Liberia, Haiti, Bosnia, and Venezuela, demonstrating in the process that he was not a has-been. He regained his heroic stature when he was awarded the Nobel Peace Prize in 2002 "for his decades of untiring effort to find peaceful solutions to international conflicts, to advance democracy and human rights, and to promote economic and social development." And he has rediscovered his heroic mission by using the Carter Center to continue his drive to advance human rights and alleviate needless suffering.

Let us look now at how some great business leaders have followed the same path to recover from their own disastrous career setbacks.

Decide how to fight back

The first decision you will face in responding to a career disaster is the question of whether to confront the situation that brought you down—with an exhausting, expensive, and perhaps embarrassing battle—or to try to put it behind you as quickly as possible, in the hope that no one will notice or remember for long. In some cases, it's best to avoid direct and immediate confrontation. Home Depot cofounder Bernie Marcus, for example, decided to sidestep the quicksand of litigation against Sandy Sigoloff, the conglomerateur who fired Marcus from Handy Dan

Home Improvement. Marcus made his battleground the marketplace rather than the courtroom. Thanks to this strategy, he was free to set the historic course for the Home Depot, which now under his successor is approaching $100 billion in sales, with several hundred thousand employees.

Other comeback kids also began with a graceful retreat. Jamie Dimon was sacked as president of Citigroup by then chairman Sandy Weill following 16 years of partnership in building the institution. When he spoke to us and to others, he did not dwell on his disappointment or sense of injustice. Monica Langley in her 2003 book *Tearing Down the Walls* describes what happened when Weill asked Dimon to resign. Dimon was shocked but replied, "You've obviously thought this through, and there's nothing I can do." As he scanned the already-prepared press release, Dimon saw that the board agreed with Weill. The firm offered Dimon a generous, nonrestrictive severance package, so a battle with Weill seemed pointless. While he was unemployed, Dimon read biographies of great national leaders who had truly suffered. He also took up boxing—another way, perhaps, of dealing with the stress and pain. After a year of this, Dimon decided he needed closure, so he invited Weill to lunch at the Four Seasons to thank him. As Dimon recounts in Harvey Mackay's 2004 book, *We Got Fired!*: "I had mellowed by then. Sandy wasn't going to call me. . . . I knew I was ready to say thank you for what he did for me. I also knew he and I should talk about what happened. I wanted to get this event behind me so I could move on. Part of me said I had spent sixteen years with him. Twelve or thirteen were pretty good. You can't just look at one side and not the other. I made my own mistakes; I acknowledged I was partly to blame. Whether I was 40 percent or 60 percent to blame really didn't matter. I felt very good about my meeting with him." In this way, Dimon was able to turn his ouster into an event that yielded both helpful perspective and reassuring resolution. (See the sidebar "Getting Beyond Rage and Denial.")

GETTING BEYOND RAGE AND DENIAL

One of the most important steps on the route to recovery is to confront and acknowledge failure. This can be as simple as understanding the Machiavellian politics of others. So as you set about rebuilding your career, make sure you:

- *Remember that failure is a beginning, not an end.* Comeback is always possible.

- *Look to the future.* Preemptive actions are often more effective than reactive ones—even if they only take the form of standing back and reflecting on what to do next.

About six months after that lunch, in March 2000, Dimon became CEO of Bank One, a huge Chicago bank that survived the merger of First Chicago and the original Banc One. That year, Bank One posted a loss of $511 million. Three years later, under Dimon's

- *Help people deal with your failure.* Even close friends may avoid you because they don't know what to say or do. Let them know that you are ready for assistance and what kind of aid would be most useful.

- *Know your narrative.* Reputation building involves telling and retelling your story to get your account of events out there and to explain your downfall. Be consistent.

leadership, Bank One was earning record profits of $3.5 billion, and its stock price had soared 85%. Adding to the sweetness of vindication, the following year Bank One merged with JPMorgan Chase, an institution with which Weill had long wanted Citigroup to merge. Dimon became CEO of the new company and is now widely regarded as one of the most influential financial executives in the world.

Of course, it's not always a good decision to sit on the sidelines and presume that justice will prevail. The highly respected Nick Nicholas, outmaneuvered as CEO of Time Warner by his skilled rival Gerald Levin, never challenged his old firm. He went off to Vail to ski at the time, awaiting a call back to service, soon becoming a very successful investor in new businesses, a professor, and a board director. But he never regained his role as the leader of a great public enterprise. Other deposed CEOs, such as Ford's Jacques Nasser, Hewlett-Packard's Carly Fiorina, IBM's John Akers, United Air Lines' Richard Ferris, and Apple's John Sculley have similarly failed to return to lead major public firms. They were considered brilliant leaders by many and were never accused of plundering the shareholders' wealth, like some rogue CEOs of recent years. But they never fought back, and they disappeared from the corner office.

The key determinant in the fight-or-flight question is the damage (or potential damage) incurred to the leader's reputation—the most important resource of all leaders. While departed CEOs and other leaders may have enough other resources and experience to rebound, it is their reputation that will make the difference between successful career recovery and failure.

Fights that will result only in a Pyrrhic victory are best avoided. Battles of pure revenge can resemble Shakespearean tragedies, where all parties lose. Hewlett-Packard board member Tom Perkins, for example, in trying to defend his friend and fellow director George Keyworth from allegations of leaking confidential board discussions, not only brought down HP chairman Patricia Dunn but also caused his friend far greater humiliation, forcing him off the board as well. A leader must consider whether fighting the allegations will exacerbate the damage by making the accusations more public.

When, however, the allegations are not only sufficient to cause a catastrophic career setback but would also block a career comeback, then leaders need to fight back. Consider former Israeli prime minister Ariel Sharon. He was a triumphant commander on the Egyptian front in the Six Day War of 1967. Fifteen years later, as minister of defense, Sharon initiated an attack on the Palestine Liberation Organization in Lebanon. Christian militias seized the opportunity to massacre hundreds of Palestinians in acts of revenge against the PLO in the Israeli-controlled Sabra and Shatila refugee camps.

In a February 21, 1983, cover story, *Time* magazine reported that these massacres were the result of a plot between Sharon and the militias to avenge the killing of Lebanon's Christian president Bashir Gemayel. Sharon sued *Time* in Israel and in New York in lengthy litigation. In both places, juries found *Time*'s accusations to be false and defamatory. The magazine settled and apologized. "It was a very long and hard struggle and was worth it," Sharon said publically at the time. "I came here to prove that *Time* magazine lied: We were able to prove that *Time* did lie."

A ferocious warrior, Sharon took on this carefully calculated battle for his reputation and executed it with focus and determination. He knew that if he did not vigorously defend himself, no one else would be able to help him. Sharon could not have regained his honor and returned to public office if he had not challenged these false charges and then moved on with his life.

Recruit others into battle

Whether you fight or tactically retreat for a while, it is essential to engage others right from the start to join your battle to put your career back on track. Friends and acquaintances play an instrumental role in providing support and advice in the process of recovery.

Those who really care for you can help you gain perspective on the good and bad choices you have made. You are also more likely to make yourself vulnerable with those you trust. Without such vulnerability, you cannot hope to achieve the candid, self-critical perspective you will need to learn from your experience. Still, although family and friends can provide invaluable personal support, they may be less effective when it comes to practical career assistance. Research has shown that slight acquaintances are actually more helpful than close friends in steering you toward opportunities for new positions in other organizations.

In an acclaimed study, Stanford University's Mark Granovetter discovered that of those individuals who landed jobs through personal contacts, only 16.7% found them through people they saw at least twice a week; 55.6% found positions through acquaintances seen at least once a year. But 27.8% of job candidates found work through distant acquaintances, whom they saw less than once a year—old college friends, former workmates, or people known through professional associations. In other words, more job contacts will come to you through people you see less than once a year than from people you see twice or more a week. That's because close friends share the same networks as you do, whereas acquaintances are more likely to introduce you to new people and contacts. Indeed, through the power of acquaintance networks, you can reach almost anyone within a few steps. Thus, distant acquaintances that don't appear to have any connection to you may prove key to your recovery when you are trying to get back on your feet.

But it's not enough to have a wide network of acquaintances. The quality of the connections, even the more distant ones, matters as well. That was the case for Home Depot's Bernie Marcus. Marcus was devastated when he was fired as CEO of Handy Dan on what he felt were trumped-up charges made by Sandy Sigoloff, the threatened boss of the parent company, Daylin. "There was a lot of self-pity on my part," Marcus told us. "I was drowning in my sorrow, going several nights at a time without sleeping. For the first time in my adult life, instead of building, I was more concerned with surviving."

Marcus, however, had an unexpected resource. Whether they were close friends and colleagues with whom he worked or acquaintances he dealt with on a casual basis, Marcus treated others with uncommon honesty, respect, and trust. This consideration was reciprocated by people in his network when he needed help; it was one of his less frequent acquaintances, Rip Fleming at Security Pacific National Bank, who made it possible for Marcus to launch Home Depot.

Marcus had raised $2 million in seed money for the Home Depot venture, but that was not enough to get his new company off the ground. He applied to several banks for a line of credit but was turned down every time. Eventually, he knocked at Fleming's door at Security Pacific National. Both Marcus and Fleming believed that the relationship between banker and client should amount to more than just the business transactions they conducted. Consequently, Fleming had become an adviser to Marcus at Handy Dan. Despite these strong professional ties, though, Fleming was initially reluctant to issue a line of credit until Marcus flew out to Los Angeles and sold Fleming on the idea. In the end, Security Pacific National provided a $3.5 million line of credit, which enabled Home Depot to get up and running. Unbeknownst to Marcus, the proposal was repeatedly turned down by the bank's loan committee and was approved only when Fleming marched into the president's office with his resignation letter in hand.

How you build relationships has a huge impact on your prospects for career recovery. Marcus had a way of building relatively strong relationships even in circumstances when most people would settle for weak acquaintanceships. This capacity for affiliation is a litmus test of a leader's ability to bounce back. People who can create connections are much more likely to engender the kind of help they need when fate turns against them.

Recover your heroic status

It's not enough for you to recruit others to advance your career. To launch your comeback, you must actually *do* things to win back the support of a wider audience. To manage this, you must regain what we call your heroic status.

The great leader has a heroic persona that confers a larger-than-life presence. You can achieve this status by developing a personal dream that you offer as a public possession. If your dream is accepted, you achieve renown. If for whatever reason your public vision is ultimately discarded, you suffer the loss of both your private dream and your public identity. After a career disaster, you can rebound only if you are able to rebuild your heroic stature—that is, the public reputation with which you were previously perceived. An intrinsic part of recovering this heroic status involves getting your story out. This calls for a public campaign to educate and inform.

When a CEO is fired, the true causes for the dismissal are often deliberately hidden, as the board seeks to protect the reputation of the firm and itself. The organization often engages in elaborate face-saving activities to disguise the real nature of the exit. Euphemistically, the press reports that the CEO resigned "for personal reasons" or "to spend more time with family." In our interviews with dismissed CEOs, we found that their greatest frustration stemmed from not being able to rebuild their heroic stature by telling their side of the story. We have interviewed several people who had seven-figure separation agreements that were contingent on their toeing the party line when they left. That's a problem when CEOs are publicly sacrificed even though they are not guilty of the accusations that led to their ouster. In such cases, CEOs' inability to challenge and set the record straight can lead to destructive speculation in the press, which can damage their reputations so much that it becomes all but impossible to recover.

Popular wisdom holds that a deposed leader should sign the nondisparagement agreement, accept the noncompete clause, take the money, and run. Our strong belief is that such agreements are a mistake. In the end, your cash will disappear, and you won't be able to get your story out. If you agree not to speak out, be prepared to be unemployed for a number of years.

A lesser-known player in the Enron saga, Daniel Scotto, comes to mind. Scotto was the financial analyst who headed up the research department for the large global investment bank Paribas. Early on, Scotto said that Enron was losing money in all its mainstream businesses and that it was only through offshore finagling that the company was creating the image of profitability. Paribas, which was underwriting a large part of the debt, asked Scotto to recant. When he wouldn't, Paribas put him on an imposed medical leave for three weeks and then fired him. He was forced to sign a nondisparagement agreement that hurt his ability to get his story out. Scotto has been unemployed for five years.

Martha Stewart is the best reminder that it doesn't have to be that way. As the most public example in recent times of a CEO who got her story out, Stewart is a model for how to regain your heroic status. She did it by carefully orchestrating a multitiered campaign to restore her reputation.

The day after she was indicted for obstruction of justice in the federal government's insider-trading investigation of ImClone stock, Stewart took out a full-page advertisement in *USA Today* and the *New York Times* and launched a new website, marthatalks.com. In an open letter to her public, Stewart clearly proclaimed her innocence and her intention to clear her name. She understood intuitively that when a hero stumbles, constituents have to reconcile two conflicting images of the person—the larger-than-life presence the hero once commanded and the hero's new fallen state. In her letter, Stewart managed to eliminate the confusion by making sure that people knew her side of the story. She openly denied any charges of insider trading and hammered home the unreliability of the three witnesses upon which the government based its case. Stewart very proactively helped others continue to believe in her heroic status.

Stewart's open letter was supported by a statement on her website by her attorneys, Robert G. Morvillo and John J. Tigue Jr., who challenged the media to investigate why the government waited nearly a year and a half to file the charges. "Is it because she is a woman who has successfully competed in a man's business world by virtue of her talent, hard work, and demanding standards?" they asked.

With the aid of her attorneys, Stewart ingeniously—and successfully—portrayed herself as a David struggling in a just and valiant quest against the Goliath of government. Her fans, far from abandoning a fallen star, rallied around her. The astounding strength of this sentiment is measured in the stock price of Martha Stewart Living Omnimedia. Even at the midpoint of Stewart's prison sentence, the stock had not merely rebounded—it was 50% higher than before anybody had heard of ImClone and the ill-fated stock transaction. Upon her release from prison, the share price neared an all-time high, ad revenue at her magazines picked up, and she launched two national network TV shows. The more Stewart got her story out, the more loyal her public became.

Stewart managed to provide a reassuring account of what really happened in her case. But what if you can't? What if you have truly stumbled? If you cannot refute the facts of your dismissal because they are so condemning, show authentic remorse. The public is often enormously forgiving of genuine contrition and atonement.

Prove your mettle

Protecting your reputation by knowing how to fight unjust accusations and bringing others on board are both essential precursors to relaunching a career in the aftermath of catastrophe. Ultimately, however, you will recover fully only when you take on that next role or start a new organization. When you show that you can still perform at a credible or superior level, others will begin to think of you as having the mettle to triumph over your career calamity. (See the sidebar "How to Come Back.")

Showing mettle is not easy. Fallen leaders face many barriers on the path to recovery, not least of which are doubts in their own ability to get back to the top. As one fired CEO told us, "I'd never sit here and say, 'Geez, all I have to do is just replicate and do it again.' The chances of doing it again are pretty small." Yet leaders who rebound are unfailingly those who get over this doubt about their ability to do it

HOW TO COME BACK

Our interviews with some 300 derailed CEOs and other professionals, as well as our scholarly leadership research, consulting assignments, and personal experiences, have brought to light five key steps for rebounding from career disaster. Anyone trying to recover from a catastrophic setback can use these steps to match, or even exceed, their past accomplishments.

- *Decide how to fight back.* Pyrrhic victories will hurt you by calling attention to the accusations leveled against you. But when your reputation is unfairly damaged, you must take quick action.

- *Recruit others into battle.* Friends and family can provide comfort and, perhaps, some perspective in your hour of need. But acquaintances may be more important in landing that next job.

(Continued)

- *Recover your heroic status.* Deposed leaders are often advised to sign nondisparagement agreements. Don't do it. Engage instead in a multitiered campaign to clear your reputation and restore your stature.

- *Prove your mettle.* After suffering career disaster, you will probably have doubts about your ability to get back to the top. You must overcome that insecurity and in the process find the courage to prove to others—and yourself—that you have not lost your magic touch.

- *Rediscover your heroic mission.* It is the single-minded pursuit of a lasting legacy that sets great leaders apart. To recover from a disastrous setback, find a new heroic mission that renews your passion and creates new meaning in your life.

again. Even when forced from familiar arenas into totally new fields, some leaders remain unafraid of trying new ventures. This capacity to bounce back from adversity—to prove your inner strength once more by overcoming your shattered confidence—is critical to earning lasting greatness.

Take Mickey Drexler. When Gap founder Donald Fisher poached Drexler away from Ann Taylor in 1983, the Gap was struggling to compete, since it sold the same brands of clothing as everyone else and was caught in a pricing game. Drexler expanded the retailer beyond the core Gap stores to brand extension such as GapKids, babyGap, and GapBody, as well as introducing other complementary brands, including Banana Republic and Old Navy. Between the time he arrived in 1983 and 2000, Gap's sales increased from $480 million to $13.7 billion, and its stock rose 169-fold.

Then things began to go awry. Drexler was accused of having lost his touch as a prescient merchant; suspicion arose in the minds of analysts and in the media that the goods had become too trendy. Although some people have suggested that the real problem was that Fisher's brother had built too many stores too close to one another, Drexler was blamed for the slump, as same-store sales dropped every quarter for two years, and the stock plummeted 75%. On May 21, 2002, Drexler presented the upcoming season's merchandise to the board, confident that he had a great selling line for the fall. It wasn't enough for the directors, and the next morning Fisher fired him, believing that the company was now too large for Drexler's hands-on management style.

Drexler was by this time independently wealthy, but he was nonetheless determined to prove that the failures of the previous two years were not primarily his fault and did not reflect his abilities. He knew that the only way to restore his belief in himself, as well as other people's confidence in him, was to return to a role in which he could once again demonstrate his expertise. He turned down a multimillion-dollar severance package from Gap because it contained a noncompete clause. After he explored a few other avenues, opportunity came knocking in the guise of struggling fashion retailer J.Crew.

With only about 200 stores, J.Crew was a small fraction of the Gap's size and consequently much more amenable to Drexler's hands-on style, giving him a greater opportunity to make an impact. Drexler invested $10 million of his own money to buy a 22% stake in the company from the retailer's private owner, the investment firm Texas Pacific. He took a salary that was less than a tenth of what he had earned at his former employer. "You've no idea how much it's costing me to run this company," he joked in a *New York* magazine article shortly after taking over.

The results more than proved that Drexler still had the right stuff. J.Crew rebounded from a $30 million operating loss in 2003 to an operating profit of over $37 million in 2004. Same-store sales per square foot, one of the key metrics in retailing, rose 18% from $338 to $400, while at his old employer, sales per square foot dropped 3%. By the summer of 2006,

Drexler had increased both sales and profits by 20% and launched a wildly embraced IPO to take J.Crew public. The media celebrated his recovery and acknowledged his obvious talent.

For Drexler, as for others, the comeback required him to prove his worth in a situation that was perceived to be enormously difficult. Start-ups or turnarounds are common contexts in which fallen leaders can recover grace. It is in these demanding situations that leaders find the mettle to prove to themselves and to others that they have not lost their magic touch and that no obstacle is too great to overcome in their quest for return.

Rediscover your heroic mission

Most great leaders want to build a legacy that will last beyond their lifetime. This does not mean having their names etched on an ivy-clad university ediface but rather advancing society by building and leading an organization. This is what we call the leader's heroic mission.

Most of the leaders we have profiled in this article were deeply engaged in building a lasting legacy even before they suffered their career setbacks. It is the loss of this mission that really raises a derailment to catastrophic proportions in the leader's own mind, since it puts at risk a lifetime of achievement. On the day Steve Jobs was fired from Apple in 1985, for example, his friend Mike Murray was so concerned about Jobs's reaction that he went over to Jobs's house and sat with him for hours until Murray was convinced that Jobs would not commit suicide.

Jobs did not wallow in despair for long. A week after his ouster from Apple, he flew to Europe and, after a few days in Paris, headed for the Tuscan hills of northern Italy, where he bought a bicycle and a sleeping bag and camped out under the stars, contemplating what he would do next. From Italy, he went to Sweden and then to Russia before returning home. Once back in California, with his passion and ambition renewed, Jobs set about re-creating himself as a force in the IT world. He went on to found another computer company, NeXT, which Apple purchased in 1996 for $400 million, at which point Jobs returned to Apple and at the same time became the driving force behind the hugely successful computer-graphics studio Pixar. Once back at Apple, Jobs revived and reenergized the company with breakthrough, high-design products, such as the iMac, iBook, and iPod, and took the company into emerging businesses, such as iTunes.

Like Martha Stewart, Steve Jobs was able to recapture his original heroic mission. Other deposed leaders, however, must truly start again because the door to their familiar field is firmly closed, and they must seek new opportunities and create a totally new heroic mission.

That's what Drexel Burnham Lambert financier Michael Milken, the imaginative "king of the junk bonds," had to do. Milken's life was almost the incarnation of the American dream. Born on the Fourth of July, Milken had become a billionaire by his mid-forties and one of the most influential financiers in the world. Then it all came tumbling down. He was charged with a 98-count criminal indictment, and a massive civil case was brought against him by the SEC for insider trading, stock parking, price manipulation, racketeering, and defrauding customers, among other crimes. He ended up pleading guilty to six relatively minor counts. In November 1990, he was sentenced to 10 years in prison, agreed to pay $600 million at the time, and ended up paying a further $42 million over a probation violation. After serving 22 months, Milken was released early for cooperating with other inquiries. But he was barred from the securities industry for life.

A week later, Milken was diagnosed with prostate cancer and was told he had 12 to 18 months to live. He immediately turned his maniacal zeal into a new heroic mission to conquer this disease. Through aggressive treatment and his own dietary research, he survived to build a huge foundation supporting research to battle prostate cancer. He also created an economic research institute that attracts the world's top scientific, political, religious, and business leaders. Milken still argues that he was wrongly accused. Others may disagree, but few would doubt that he has earned restitution. The public has come to accept that he has paid for his crimes, and there has even been some reconsideration of their actual severity.

It is the single-minded, passionate pursuit of a heroic mission that sets leaders like Steve Jobs and Michael Milken and Jimmy Carter apart from the general population, and it is what attracts and motivates followers to join them. In the worst of cases, to have that life purpose ripped from you and to be prohibited from its further pursuit can leave an unbearable void and doubts as to your reason for being. Finding a new mission to replace your lifelong purpose can be a great struggle, but one that is necessary if you are to recover.

The tragedies and triumphant comebacks of the leaders we have profiled in this article can seem remote, bordering on the mythological, perhaps. But their stories point to important lessons about recovering from career catastrophe. Stunning comeback is possible in all industries, though the challenges vary according to the leadership norms of each field's culture. For example, clergy ensnarled in publicized sex scandals will probably see their careers dissolve, whereas entertainment figures may not only recover but actually benefit from notoriety. Where one profession values trust, another values celebrity. Thus, recovery plans must be adapted to the cultures of different industries.

Whatever the arena in which your recovery takes shape, the important thing to remember is that we all have choices in life, even in defeat. We can lose our health, our loved ones, our jobs, but much can be saved. No one can truly define success and failure for us—only we can define that for ourselves. No one can take away our dignity unless we surrender it. No one can take away our hope and pride unless we relinquish them. No one can steal our creativity, imagination, and skills unless we stop thinking. No one can stop us from rebounding unless we give up.

JEFFREY A. SONNENFELD is the senior associate dean for executive programs, the Lester Crown Professor of Management Practice at the Yale School of Management, and the president of the Executive Leadership Institute at Yale University in New Haven, Connecticut. ANDREW J. WARD is an assistant professor of management at the University of Georgia in Athens, Georgia. This article is drawn from their book of the same title (Harvard Business School Press, 2007).

Reprinted from *Harvard Business Review,*
February 2007 (product #R0701G).

6

Resilience Is About How You Recharge, Not How You Endure

By Shawn Achor and Michelle Gielan

As constant travelers and parents of a 2-year-old, we sometimes fantasize about how much work we can do when one of us gets on a plane, undistracted by phones, friends, and *Finding Nemo*. We race to get all our ground work done: packing, going through TSA, doing a last-minute work call, calling each other, boarding the plane. Then, when we try to have that amazing in-flight work session, we get nothing done. Even worse, after refreshing our email or reading the same studies over and over, we are too exhausted when we land to soldier on with the emails that have inevitably still piled up.

Why should flying deplete us? We're just sitting there doing nothing. Why can't we be tougher—more resilient and determined in our work—so we can accomplish all of the goals we set for ourselves? Through our current research, we have come to realize that the problem is not our hectic schedule or the plane travel itself; the problem comes from a misunderstanding of what it means to be resilient and the resulting impact of overworking.

We often take a militaristic, "tough" approach to resilience and grit. We imagine a marine slogging through the mud, a boxer going one more round, or a football player picking himself up off the turf for one more play. We believe that the longer we tough it out, the tougher we are, and therefore the more successful we will be. However, this entire conception is scientifically inaccurate.

The very lack of a recovery period is dramatically holding back our collective ability to be resilient and successful. Research has found that there is a direct correlation between lack of recovery and increased incidence of health and safety problems.[1] And lack of recovery—whether by disrupting sleep with thoughts of work or having continuous cognitive arousal by watching our phones—is costing our companies $62 billion a year (that's billion, not million) in lost productivity.[2]

And just because work stops, it doesn't mean we are recovering. We "stop" work sometimes at 5 p.m., but then we spend the night wrestling with solutions to work problems, talking about our work over dinner, and falling asleep thinking about how much work we'll do tomorrow. In a study released last month, researchers from Norway found that 7.8% of Norwegians have become workaholics.[3] The scientists cite a definition of "workaholism" as "being overly concerned about work, driven by an uncontrollable work motivation, and investing so much time and effort to work that it impairs other important life areas."[4]

We believe that this definition applies to the majority of American workers (including those who read HBR), and this prompted us to begin a study of workaholism in the United States. Our study will use a large corporate data set from a major medical company to examine how technology extends our working hours and thus interferes with necessary cognitive recovery. We believe this is resulting in huge health care costs and high turnover rates for employers.

Misconceptions about resilience is often bred from an early age. Parents trying to teach their children resilience might celebrate a high school student staying up until 3 a.m. to finish a science fair project. What a distortion of resilience! A resilient child is a well-rested one. When an exhausted student goes to school, he risks hurting everyone on the road with his impaired driving, he doesn't have the cognitive resources to do well on his English test, he has lower self-control with his friends, and at home, he is moody with his parents. Overwork and exhaustion are the opposite of resilience. And the bad habits we learn when we're young only magnify when we hit the workforce.

In her excellent book *The Sleep Revolution*, Arianna Huffington wrote, "We sacrifice sleep in the name of productivity, but ironically our loss of sleep, despite the extra hours we spend at work, adds up to 11 days of lost productivity per year per worker, or about $2,280."

The key to resilience is trying really hard, then stopping, recovering, and then trying again. This conclusion is based on biology. Homeostasis is a fundamental biological concept describing the ability of the brain to continuously restore and sustain well-being.[5] Positive neuroscientist Brent Furl from Texas A&M University coined the term "homeostatic value" to describe the value that certain actions have for creating equilibrium, and thus well-being, in the body. When the body is out of alignment from overworking, we waste vast mental and physical resources trying to return to balance before we can move forward.

As *Power of Full Engagement* authors Jim Loehr and Tony Schwartz have written, if you have too much time in the performance zone, you need more time in the recovery zone; otherwise you risk burnout. Mustering your resources to "try hard" requires burning energy in order to overcome your currently low arousal level. This is called "upregulation." It also exacerbates exhaustion. Thus, the more imbalanced we become due to overworking, the more value there is in activities that allow us to return to a state of balance. The value of a recovery period rises in proportion to the amount of work required of us.

So how do we recover and build resilience? Most people assume that if you stop doing a task like answering emails or writing a paper that your brain will naturally recover, that when you start again later in the day or the next morning, you'll have your energy back. But surely everyone reading this has had times when they lie in bed for hours, unable to fall asleep because their brain is thinking about work. If you lie in bed for eight hours, you may have rested, but you can still feel exhausted the next day. That's because rest and recovery are not the same thing. Stopping does not equal recovering.

If you're trying to build resilience at work, you need adequate internal and external recovery periods. As researchers Fred R. H. Zijlstra, Mark Cropley, and Leif W. Rydstedt write in their 2014 paper: "Internal recovery refers to the shorter periods of relaxation that take place within the frames of the workday or the work setting in the form of short scheduled or unscheduled breaks, by shifting attention or changing to other work tasks when the mental or physical resources required for the initial task are temporarily depleted or exhausted. External recovery refers to actions that take place outside of work—e.g. in the free time between the workdays, and during weekends, holidays or vacations."[6] If after work you lie around on your bed and get riled up by political commentary on your phone or get stressed thinking about decisions about how to renovate your home, your brain has not received a break from high mental arousal states. Our brains need a rest as much as our bodies do.

If you really want to build resilience, you can start by strategically stopping. Give yourself the resources to be tough by creating internal and external recovery periods. In her upcoming book *The Future of Happiness*, based on her work at Yale Business School, Amy Blankson describes how to strategically stop during the day by using technology to control overworking.[7] She suggests downloading the Instant or Moment apps to see how many times you turn on your phone each day. The average person turns on their phone 150 times every day.[8] If every distraction took only one minute (which would be seriously optimistic), that would account for 2.5 hours of every day.

You can use apps like Offtime or Unplugged to create tech free zones by strategically scheduling automatic airplane modes. In addition, you can take a cognitive break every 90 minutes to recharge your batteries. Try to not have lunch at your desk, but instead spend time outside or with your friends—not talking about work. Take all of your paid time off, which not only gives you recovery periods but raises your productivity and the likelihood of promotion.[9]

As for us, we've started using our plane time as a work-free zone and thus as time to dip into the recovery phase. The results have been fantastic. We are usually tired already by the time we get on a plane, and the cramped space and spotty internet connection make work more challenging. Now, instead of swimming upstream, we relax, meditate, sleep, watch movies, journal, or listen to entertaining podcasts. And when we get off the plane, instead of being depleted, we feel rejuvenated and ready to return to the performance zone.

SHAWN ACHOR is the *New York Times* best-selling author of *The Happiness Advantage* and *Before Happiness*, and a popular TED talk, "The Happy Secret to Better Work." He has lectured or researched at over a third of the *Fortune* 100 companies and in 50 countries, as well as for the NFL, Pentagon, and White House. Shawn is leading a series of courses on "21 Days to Inspire Positive Change" with the Oprah Winfrey Network. MICHELLE GIELAN, a national CBS News anchor turned University of Pennsylvania positive psychology researcher, is now the best-selling author of *Broadcasting Happiness*. She is partnering with Arianna Huffington to research how transformative stories fuel success.

Notes

1. J. K. Sluiter, "The Influence of Work Characteristics on the Need for Recovery and Experienced Health: A Study on Coach Drivers," *Ergonomics* 42, no. 4 (1999): 573–583.
2. American Academy of Sleep Medicine, "Insomnia Costing U.S. Workforce $63.2 Billion a Year in Lost Productivity," *ScienceDaily*, September 2, 2011.
3. C. S. Andreassen et al., "The Relationships Between Workaholism and Symptoms of Psychiatric Disorders: A Large-Scale Cross-Sectional Study," *PLoS One* 11, no. 5 (2016).
4. C. S. Andreassen et al., "Psychometric Assessment of Workaholism Measures," *Journal of Managerial Psychology* 29, no. 1 (2014): 7–24.
5. "What Is Homeostasis?" *Scientific American*, January 3, 2000.

6. F. R. H. Zijlstra et al., "From Recovery to Regulation: An Attempt to Reconceptualize 'Recovery from Work'" (special issue paper, John Wily & Sons, 2014), 244.
7. A. Blankson, *The Future of Happiness* (Dallas, Texas: BenBella Books, forthcoming 2017).
8. J. Stern, "Cellphone Users Check Phones 150x/Day and Other Internet Fun Facts," *Good Morning America*, May 29, 2013.
9. S. Achor, "Are the People Who Take Vacations the Ones Who Get Promoted?" *Harvard Business Review* online, June 12, 2015.

Adapted from content posted on hbr.org,
June 24, 2016 (product #H02Z3O).

Index

Engage with HBR content the way you want, on any device.

With HBR's new subscription plans, you can access world-renowned **case studies** from Harvard Business School and receive **four free eBooks**. Download and customize prebuilt **slide decks and graphics** from our **Visual Library**. With HBR's archive, top 50 best-selling articles, and five new articles every day, HBR is more than just a magazine.

Subscribe Today
hbr.org/success

Harvard Business Review

Invaluable insights
always at your fingertips

With an All-Access subscription to
Harvard Business Review, you'll get
so much more than a magazine.

Exclusive online content and tools
you can put to use today

My Library, your personal workspace for sharing,
saving, and organizing HBR.org articles and tools

Unlimited access to more than 4,000 articles in the
Harvard Business Review archive

Subscribe today at hbr.org/subnow

The most important management ideas all in one place.

We hope you enjoyed this book from *Harvard Business Review*. For the best ideas HBR has to offer turn to HBR's 10 Must Reads Boxed Set. From books on leadership and strategy to managing yourself and others, this 6-book collection delivers articles on the most essential business topics to help you succeed.

HBR's 10 Must Reads Series

The definitive collection of ideas and best practices on our most sought-after topics from the best minds in business.

- Change Management
- Collaboration
- Communication
- Emotional Intelligence
- Innovation
- Leadership
- Making Smart Decisions
- Managing Across Cultures
- Managing People
- Managing Yourself
- Strategic Marketing
- Strategy
- Teams
- The Essentials

hbr.org/mustreads

Buy for your team, clients, or event.
Visit hbr.org/bulksales for quantity discount rates.

Influence and Persuasion

HBR EMOTIONAL INTELLIGENCE SERIES

HBR Emotional Intelligence Series

How to be human at work

The HBR Emotional Intelligence Series features smart, essential reading on the human side of professional life from the pages of *Harvard Business Review*.

Authentic Leadership

Empathy

Happiness

Influence and Persuasion

Mindfulness

Resilience

Other books on emotional intelligence from *Harvard Business Review*:

HBR's 10 Must Reads on Emotional Intelligence

HBR Guide to Emotional Intelligence

Influence and Persuasion

HBR EMOTIONAL INTELLIGENCE SERIES

Harvard Business Review Press

Boston, Massachusetts

HBR Press Quantity Sales Discounts

Harvard Business Review Press titles are available at significant quantity discounts when purchased in bulk for client gifts, sales promotions, and premiums. Special editions, including books with corporate logos, customized covers, and letters from the company or CEO printed in the front matter, as well as excerpts of existing books, can also be created in large quantities for special needs.

For details and discount information for both print and ebook formats, contact booksales@harvardbusiness.org, tel. 800-988-0886, or www.hbr.org/bulksales.

Copyright 2018 Harvard Business School Publishing Corporation
All rights reserved
Printed in the United States of America

23 22 21 20 19 18 17 16

No part of this publication may be reproduced, stored in or introduced into a retrieval system, or transmitted, in any form, or by any means (electronic, mechanical, photocopying, recording, or otherwise), without the prior permission of the publisher. Requests for permission should be directed to permissions@hbsp.harvard.edu, or mailed to Permissions, Harvard Business School Publishing, 60 Harvard Way, Boston, Massachusetts 02163.

The web addresses referenced in this book were live and correct at the time of the book's publication but may be subject to change.

Library of Congress cataloging information is forthcoming

ISBN 978-1-63369-393-7
eISBN 978-1-63369-394-4

The paper used in this publication meets the requirements of the American National Standard for Permanence of Paper for Publications and Documents in Libraries and Archives Z39.48-1992.

Contents

Contents

Influence and
Persuasion

HBR EMOTIONAL INTELLIGENCE SERIES

1

Understand the Four Components of Influence

By Nick Morgan

We've all encountered people who say less but what they say matters more; people who know how to use silence to dominate an exchange. So having influence means more than just doing all the talking; it's about taking charge and understanding the roles that positional power, emotion, expertise, and nonverbal signals play. These four aspects of influence are essential to master if you want to succeed as a leader.

Take *positional power*. If you have it, influence becomes a relatively simple proposition. People with power over others tend to talk more, to interrupt more, and to guide the conversation more, by picking the topics, for example.

If you don't have the positional power in a particular situation, then, expect to talk less, interrupt less, and choose the topics of conversation less. After all, exercising their right to talk more about the subjects they care for is one of the ways that people with positional power demonstrate it.

What do you do if you want to challenge the positional authority? Perhaps you have a product, or an idea, or a company you want to sell, and you have the ear of someone who can buy it. How do you get control in that kind of situation?

The second aspect of influence is *emotion*, and using it is one way to counteract positional power and generally to dominate a conversation. When the other side has the power and you have the emotion, something closer to parity is possible. Indeed, passion can sweep away authority, when it's well supported and the speaker is well prepared. We've all witnessed that happen when a young unknown performer disarms and woos the judges, devastating the competition, in one of those talent competitions. The purity and power of the emotion in the performance is enough to silence—and enlist—the judges despite their positional authority. Indeed, the impassioned speech, the plea for clemency, the summation to the jury that brings them to tears and wins the case for the defendant—this is the stuff of Hollywood climaxes.

Passion often links with *expertise*, the third aspect of influence. And indeed, you can dominate the conversation, beating out positional power, if you have both passion and expertise. The diffident expert's voice is sometimes lost in the clamor of people wanting to be heard. So expertise without passion is not always effective, but if it's patient, it can be the last person standing in a debate and thereby get its turn.

The final aspect of influence is the subtlest of the four and as such rarely can trump either positional authority or passion. But in rare instances, artfully manipulated, I have seen it prevail. What is it? It is the mastery of the dance of human interaction.

We have very little conscious awareness of this aspect of influence, but we are all participants in it with more or less expertise. We learn at a very early age that conversation is a pas de deux, a game that two (or more) people play that involves breathing, winking, nodding, eye contact, head tilts, hand gestures, and a whole series of subtle nonverbal signals that help both parties communicate with each other.

Indeed, conversation is much less functional without these *nonverbal signals*. That's why phone conversations are nowhere near as satisfying as in-person encounters and why conference calls inevitably involve lots more interruptions, miscues, and cross talking. We're not getting the signals we're used to getting to help us know when the other person is ready to hand the conversational baton on to us, and vice versa.

Can you manage influence only using this fourth aspect? I have seen it done in certain situations, but the other three aspects will usually trump this one. Nonetheless, I once watched a senior executive effortlessly dominate a roomful of people who were ostensibly equal—a group of researchers gathered from around the world to discuss the future of IT. Within a few minutes, everyone in the room was unconsciously deferring to this executive, even though he had no positional power and was not particularly passionate about the subject. His mastery of the subtle signals of conversational cuing was profound, and soon he had everyone dancing to his verbal beat. It was beautiful to watch; he showed complete conversational mastery in action.

Influence, then, is a measure of how much skin the participants have in the game, and most of us are unconscious experts at measuring it. To wield it, you need to have the edge in at least one of its four aspects—and preferably more than one.

NICK MORGAN is an author, speaker, coach, and the president and founder of Public Words, a communications consulting firm.

Excerpted from the author's book *Power Cues: The Subtle Science of Leading Groups, Persuading Others, and Maximizing Your Personal Impact* (product #11710), Harvard Business Review Press, 2014.

2

Harnessing the Science of Persuasion

By Robert Cialdini

lucky few have it; most of us do not. A handful of gifted "naturals" simply know how to capture an audience, sway the undecided, and convert the opposition. Watching these masters of persuasion work their magic is at once impressive and frustrating. What's impressive is not just the easy way they use charisma and eloquence to convince others to do as they ask. It's also how eager those others are to do what's requested of them, as if the persuasion itself were a favor they couldn't wait to repay.

The frustrating part of the experience is that these born persuaders are often unable to account for their remarkable skill or pass it on to others. Their way with people is an art, and artists as a rule are far better at doing than at explaining. Most of them can't offer much help to those of us who possess no more than the ordinary quotient of charisma and eloquence but who still have to wrestle with leadership's fundamental challenge: getting things done through others. That challenge is painfully familiar to corporate executives, who every day have to figure out how to motivate and direct a highly individualistic work force. Playing the "Because I'm the boss" card is out. Even if it weren't demeaning and demoralizing for all concerned, it would be out of place in a world where cross-functional teams, joint ventures, and intercompany partnerships have blurred the lines of authority. In such an environment, persuasion skills exert far greater influence over others' behavior than formal power structures do.

Which brings us back to where we started. Persuasion skills may be more necessary than ever, but how can executives acquire them if the most talented practitioners can't pass them along? By looking to science. For the past five decades, behavioral scientists have conducted experiments that shed considerable light on the way certain interactions lead people to concede, comply, or change. This research shows that persuasion works by appealing to a limited set of deeply rooted human drives and needs, and it does so in predictable ways. Persuasion, in other words, is governed by basic principles that can be taught, learned, and applied. By mastering these principles, executives can bring scientific rigor to the business of securing consensus, cutting deals, and winning concessions. In the pages that follow, I describe six fundamental principles of persuasion and suggest a few ways that executives can apply them in their own organizations.

The principle of liking: People like those who like them.

The application: Uncover real similarities and offer genuine praise.

The retailing phenomenon known as the Tupperware party is a vivid illustration of this principle in action. The demonstration party for Tupperware products is hosted by an individual, almost always a woman, who invites to her home an array of friends, neighbors, and relatives. The guests' affection for their hostess predisposes them to buy from her, a dynamic that was confirmed by a 1990 study of purchase decisions made at demonstration parties. The researchers, Jonathan Frenzen and Harry Davis, writing in the *Journal of Consumer Research*, found that the guests' fondness for their hostess weighed twice as heavily in their purchase decisions as their regard for the products they bought. So when guests at a Tupperware party buy something, they aren't just buying to please themselves. They're buying to please their hostess as well.

What's true at Tupperware parties is true for business in general: If you want to influence people, win friends. How? Controlled research has identified several factors that reliably increase liking, but two stand out as especially compelling—similarity and praise. Similarity literally draws people together. In one experiment, reported in a 1968 article in the *Journal of Personality*, participants stood physically closer to one another after learning that they shared political beliefs and social values. And in a 1963 article in *American Behavioral Scientists*, researcher F. B. Evans used demographic data from insurance company records to demonstrate that prospects were more willing to purchase a policy from a salesperson who was akin to them in age, religion, politics, or even cigarette-smoking habits.

Managers can use similarities to create bonds with a recent hire, the head of another department, or even a new boss. Informal conversations during the workday create an ideal opportunity to discover at least one common area of enjoyment, be it a hobby, a college basketball team, or reruns of *Seinfeld*. The important thing is to establish the bond early because it creates a presumption of goodwill and trustworthiness in every subsequent encounter. It's much easier to build support for a new project when the people you're trying to persuade are already inclined in your favor.

Praise, the other reliable generator of affection, both charms and disarms. Sometimes the praise doesn't even have to be merited. Researchers at the University of North Carolina writing in the *Journal of Experimental Social Psychology* found that men felt the greatest regard for an individual who flattered them unstintingly even if the comments were untrue. And in their book *Interpersonal Attraction* (Addison-Wesley, 1978), Ellen Berscheid and Elaine

Hatfield Walster presented experimental data show-ing that positive remarks about another person's traits, attitude, or performance reliably generates lik-ing in return, as well as willing compliance with the wishes of the person offering the praise.

Along with cultivating a fruitful relationship, adroit managers can also use praise to repair one that's dam-aged or unproductive. Imagine you're the manager of a good-sized unit within your organization. Your work frequently brings you into contact with another man-ager—call him Dan—whom you have come to dislike. No matter how much you do for him, it's not enough. Worse, he never seems to believe that you're doing the best you can for him. Resenting his attitude and his obvious lack of trust in your abilities and in your good faith, you don't spend as much time with him as you know you should; in consequence, the performance of both his unit and yours is deteriorating.

The research on praise points toward a strategy for fixing the relationship. It may be hard to find, but there has to be something about Dan you can sincerely admire, whether it's his concern for the people in his department, his devotion to his family, or simply his work ethic. In your next encounter with him, make an appreciative comment about that trait. Make it clear that in this case at least, you value what he values. I predict that Dan will relax his relentless negativity and give you an opening to convince him of your competence and good intentions.

The principle of reciprocity: People repay in kind.

The application: Give what you want to receive.

Praise is likely to have a warming and softening effect on Dan because, ornery as he is, he is still human and subject to the universal human tendency to treat people the way they treat him. If you have ever caught yourself smiling at a coworker just because he or she smiled first, you know how this principle works.

Charities rely on reciprocity to help them raise funds. For years, for instance, the Disabled American Veterans organization, using only a well-crafted fund-raising letter, garnered a very respectable 18% rate of response to its appeals. But when the group started enclosing a small gift in the envelope, the response rate nearly doubled to 35%. The gift—personalized address labels—was extremely modest, but it wasn't what prospective donors received that made the difference. It was that they had gotten anything at all.

What works in that letter works at the office, too. It's more than an effusion of seasonal spirit, of course, that impels suppliers to shower gifts on purchasing departments at holiday time. In 1996, purchasing managers admitted to an interviewer from *Inc.* magazine that after having accepted a gift from a supplier, they were willing to purchase products and services they would have otherwise declined. Gifts also have a startling effect on retention. I have encouraged readers of my book to send me examples of the principles of influence at work in their own lives. One reader, an employee of the State of Oregon, sent a letter in which she offered these reasons for her commitment to her supervisor:

He gives me and my son gifts for Christmas and gives me presents on my birthday. There is no promotion for the type of job I have, and my only choice for one is to move to another department. But I find myself resisting trying to move. My boss is reaching retirement age, and I am thinking I will be able to move out after he retires . . . [F]or now, I feel obligated to stay since he has been so nice to me.

Ultimately, though, gift giving is one of the cruder applications of the rule of reciprocity. In its more sophisticated uses, it confers a genuine first-mover advantage on any manager who is trying to foster positive attitudes and productive personal relationships in the office: Managers can elicit the desired behavior from coworkers and employees by displaying it first. Whether it's a sense of trust, a spirit of cooperation, or a pleasant demeanor, leaders should model the behavior they want to see from others.

The same holds true for managers faced with issues of information delivery and resource allocation. If you lend a member of your staff to a colleague who is shorthanded and staring at a fast-approaching deadline, you will significantly increase your chances of getting help when you need it. Your odds will improve even more if you say, when your colleague thanks you for the assistance, something like, "Sure, glad to help. I know how important it is for me to count on your help when I need it."

The principle of social proof:
People follow the lead of similar others.

*The application: Use peer power
whenever it's available.*

Social creatures that they are, human beings rely heavily on the people around them for cues on how to think, feel, and act. We know this intuitively, but intuition has also been confirmed by experiments, such as the one first described in 1982 in the *Journal of Applied Psychology*. A group of researchers went door-to-door in Columbia, South Carolina, soliciting donations for a charity campaign and displaying a list of neighborhood residents who had already donated to the cause. The researchers found that the longer the donor list was, the more likely those solicited would be to donate as well.

To the people being solicited, the friends' and neighbors' names on the list were a form of social evidence about how they should respond. But the evidence would not have been nearly as compelling had the names been those of random strangers. In an experiment from the 1960s, first described in the *Journal of Personality and Social Psychology*, residents of New York City were asked to return a lost wallet to its owner. They were highly likely to attempt to return the wallet when they learned that another New Yorker had previously attempted to do so. But learning that someone from a foreign country had tried to return the wallet didn't sway their decision one way or the other.

The lesson for executives from these two experiments is that persuasion can be extremely effective when it comes from peers. The science supports what most sales professionals already know: Testimonials from satisfied customers work best when the satisfied customer and the prospective customer share similar circumstances. That lesson can help a manager faced with the task of selling a new corporate initiative.

Imagine that you're trying to streamline your department's work processes. A group of veteran employees is resisting. Rather than try to convince the employees of the move's merits yourself, ask an old-timer who supports the initiative to speak up for it at a team meeting. The compatriot's testimony stands a much better chance of convincing the group than yet another speech from the boss. Stated simply, influence is often best exerted horizontally rather than vertically.

The principle of consistency: People align with their clear commitments.

The application: Make their commitments active, public, and voluntary.

Liking is a powerful force, but the work of persuasion involves more than simply making people feel warmly toward you, your idea, or your product. People need not only to like you but to feel committed to what you want them to do. Good turns are one reliable way to make people feel obligated to you. Another is to win a public commitment from them.

My own research has demonstrated that most people, once they take a stand or go on record in favor of a position, prefer to stick to it. Other studies reinforce that finding and go on to show how even a small, seemingly trivial commitment can have a powerful effect on future actions. Israeli researchers writing in 1983 in the *Personality and Social Psychology Bulletin* recounted how they asked half the residents of a large apartment complex to sign a petition favoring the establishment of a recreation center for the handicapped. The cause was good and the request was small, so almost everyone who was asked agreed to sign. Two weeks later, on National Collection Day for the Handicapped, all residents of the complex were approached at home and asked to give to the cause.

A little more than half of those who were not asked to sign the petition made a contribution. But an astounding 92% of those who did sign donated money. The residents of the apartment complex felt obligated to live up to their commitments because those commitments were active, public, and voluntary. These three features are worth considering separately.

There's strong empirical evidence to show that a choice made actively—one that's spoken out loud or written down or otherwise made explicit—is considerably more likely to direct someone's future conduct than the same choice left unspoken. Writing in 1996 in the *Personality and Social Psychology Bulletin*, Delia Cioffi and Randy Garner described an experiment in which college students in one group were asked to fill out a printed form saying they wished to volunteer for an AIDS education project in the public schools. Students in another group volunteered for the same project by leaving blank a form stating that they didn't want to participate. A few days later, when the volunteers reported for duty, 74% of those who showed up were students from the group that signaled their commitment by filling out the form.

The implications are clear for a manager who wants to persuade a subordinate to follow some particular course of action: Get it in writing. Let's suppose you want your employee to submit reports in a more timely fashion. Once you believe you've won agreement, ask him to summarize the decision in a memo and send it to you. By doing so, you'll have greatly increased the odds that he'll fulfill the commitment because, as a rule, people live up to what they have written down.

Research into the social dimensions of commitment suggests that written statements become even more powerful when they're made public. In a classic experiment, described in 1955 in the *Journal of Abnormal and Social Psychology*, college students were asked to estimate the length of lines projected on a screen. Some students were asked to write down their choices on a piece of paper, sign it, and hand the paper to the experimenter. Others wrote their choices on an erasable slate, then erased the slate immediately. Still others were instructed to keep their decisions to themselves.

The experimenters then presented all three groups with evidence that their initial choices may have been wrong. Those who had merely kept their decisions in their heads were the most likely to reconsider their original estimates. More loyal to their first guesses were the students in the group that had written them down and immediately erased them. But by a wide margin, the ones most reluctant to shift from their original choices were those who had signed and handed them to the researcher.

This experiment highlights how much most people wish to appear consistent to others. Consider again the matter of the employee who has been submitting late reports. Recognizing the power of this desire, you should, once you've successfully convinced him of the need to be more timely, reinforce the commitment by making sure it gets a public airing. One way to do that would be to send the employee an email that reads, "I think your plan is just what we need. I showed it to Diane in manufacturing and Phil in shipping, and they thought it was right on target, too." Whatever way such commitments are formalized, they should never be like the New Year's resolutions people privately make and then abandon with no one the wiser. They should be publicly made and visibly posted.

More than 300 years ago, Samuel Butler wrote a couplet that explains succinctly why commitments must be voluntary to be lasting and effective: "He that complies against his will/Is of his own opinion still." If an undertaking is forced, coerced, or imposed from the outside, it's not a commitment; it's an unwelcome burden. Think how you would react if your boss pressured you to donate to the campaign of a political candidate. Would that make you more apt to opt for that candidate in the privacy of a voting booth? Not likely. In fact, in their 1981 book *Psychological Reactance* (Academic Press), Sharon S. Brehm and Jack W. Brehm present data that suggest you'd vote the opposite way just to express your resentment of the boss's coercion.

This kind of backlash can occur in the office, too. Let's return again to that tardy employee. If you want to produce an enduring change in his behavior, you should avoid using threats or pressure tactics to gain his compliance. He'd likely view any change in his behavior as the result of intimidation rather than a personal commitment to change. A better approach would be to identify something that the employee genuinely values in the workplace—high-quality workmanship, perhaps, or team spirit—and then describe how timely reports are consistent with those values. That gives the employee reasons for improvement that he can own. And because he owns them, they'll continue to guide his behavior even when you're not watching.

The principle of authority: People defer to experts.

The application: Expose your expertise; don't assume it's self-evident.

Two thousand years ago, the Roman poet Virgil offered this simple counsel to those seeking to choose correctly: "Believe an expert." That may or may not be good advice, but as a description of what people actually do, it can't be beaten. For instance, when the news media present an acknowledged expert's views on a topic, the effect on public opinion is dramatic. A single expert-opinion news story in the *New York Times* is associated with a 2% shift in public opinion nationwide, according to a 1993 study described in the *Public Opinion Quarterly*. And researchers writing in the *American Political Science Review* in 1987 found that when the expert's view was aired on national television, public opinion shifted as much as 4%. A cynic might argue that these findings only illustrate the docile submissiveness of the public. But a fairer explanation is that, amid the teeming complexity of contemporary life, a well-selected expert offers a valuable and efficient shortcut to good decisions. Indeed, some questions, be they legal, financial, medical, or technological, require so much specialized knowledge to answer, we have no choice but to rely on experts.

Since there's good reason to defer to experts, executives should take pains to ensure that they establish their own expertise before they attempt to exert influence. Surprisingly often, people mistakenly assume that others recognize and appreciate their experience. That's what happened at a hospital where some colleagues and I were consulting. The physical therapy staffers were frustrated because so many of their stroke patients abandoned their exercise routines as soon as they left the hospital. No matter how often the staff emphasized the importance of regular home exercise—it is, in fact, crucial to the process of regaining independent function—the message just didn't sink in.

Interviews with some of the patients helped us pinpoint the problem. They were familiar with the background and training of their physicians, but the patients knew little about the credentials of the physical therapists who were urging them to exercise. It was a simple matter to remedy that lack of information: We merely asked the therapy director to display all the awards, diplomas, and certifications of her staff on the walls of the therapy rooms. The result was startling: Exercise compliance jumped 34% and has never dropped since.

What we found immensely gratifying was not just how much we increased compliance, but how. We didn't fool or browbeat any of the patients. We *informed* them into compliance. Nothing had to be invented; no time or resources had to be spent in the process. The staff's expertise was real—all we had to do was make it more visible.

The task for managers who want to establish their claims to expertise is somewhat more difficult. They can't simply nail their diplomas to the wall and wait for everyone to notice. A little subtlety is called for. Outside the United States, it is customary for people to spend time interacting socially before getting down to business for the first time. Frequently they gather for dinner the night before their meeting or negotiation. These get-togethers can make discussions easier and help blunt disagreements—remember the findings about liking and similarity—and they can also provide an opportunity to establish expertise. Perhaps it's a matter of telling an anecdote about successfully solving a problem similar to the one that's on the agenda at the next day's meeting. Or perhaps dinner is the time to describe years spent mastering a complex discipline—not in a boastful way but as part of the ordinary give-and-take of conversation.

Granted, there's not always time for lengthy introductory sessions. But even in the course of the

PERSUASION EXPERTS, SAFE AT LAST

Thanks to several decades of rigorous empirical research by behavioral scientists, our understanding of the how and why of persuasion has never been broader, deeper, or more detailed. But these scientists aren't the first students of the subject. The history of persuasion studies is an ancient and honorable one, and it has generated a long roster of heroes and martyrs.

A renowned student of social influence, William McGuire, contends in a chapter of the *Handbook of Social Psychology*, 3rd edition (Oxford University Press, 1985), that scattered among the more than four millennia of recorded Western history are four centuries in which the study of persuasion flourished as a craft. The first was the Periclean Age of ancient Athens, the second occurred during the years of the

(Continued)

PERSUASION EXPERTS, SAFE AT LAST

Roman Republic, the next appeared in the time of the European Renaissance, and the last extended over the hundred years that have just ended, which witnessed the advent of large-scale advertising, information, and mass media campaigns. Each of the three previous centuries of systematic persuasion study was marked by a flowering of human achievement that was suddenly cut short when political authorities had the masters of persuasion killed. The philosopher Socrates is probably the best known of the persuasion experts to run afoul of the powers that be.

Information about the persuasion process is a threat because it creates a base of power entirely separate from the one controlled by political authorities. Faced with a rival source of influence, rulers in previous centuries had few qualms about eliminating those rare individuals who truly understood how to marshal forces that heads of state have never been able to monopolize, such as cleverly crafted language, strategically placed information, and, most important, psychological insight.

It would perhaps be expressing too much faith in human nature to claim that persuasion experts no longer face a threat from those who wield political power. But because the truth about persuasion is no longer the sole possession of a few brilliant, inspired individuals, experts in the field can presumably breathe a little easier. Indeed, since most people in power are interested in remaining in power, they're likely to be more interested in acquiring persuasion skills than abolishing them.

preliminary conversation that precedes most meetings, there is almost always an opportunity to touch lightly on your relevant background and experience as a natural part of a sociable exchange. This initial disclosure of personal information gives you a chance to establish expertise early in the game, so that when the discussion turns to the business at hand, what you have to say will be accorded the respect it deserves.

The principle of scarcity: People want more of what they can have less of.

The application: Highlight unique benefits and exclusive information.

Study after study shows that items and opportunities are seen to be more valuable as they become less available. That's a tremendously useful piece of information for managers. They can harness the scarcity principle with the organizational equivalents of limited-time, limited-supply, and one-of-a-kind offers. Honestly informing a coworker of a closing window of opportunity—the chance to get the boss's ear before she leaves for an extended vacation, perhaps—can mobilize action dramatically.

Managers can learn from retailers how to frame their offers not in terms of what people stand to gain but in terms of what they stand to lose if they don't act on the information. The power of "loss language" was demonstrated in a 1988 study of California homeowners written up in the *Journal of Applied Psychology*. Half were told that if they fully insulated their homes, they would save a certain amount of money each day. The other half were told that if they failed to insulate, they would lose that amount each day. Significantly more people insulated their homes when exposed to the loss language. The same phenomenon occurs in business. According to a 1994 study in the journal *Organizational Behavior and Human Decision Processes,* potential losses figure far more heavily in managers' decision making than potential gains.

In framing their offers, executives should also remember that exclusive information is more persuasive than widely available data. A doctoral student of mine, Amram Knishinsky, wrote his 1982 dissertation on the purchase decisions of wholesale beef buyers. He observed that they more than doubled their orders when they were told that, because of certain weather conditions overseas, there was likely to be a scarcity of foreign beef in the near future. But their orders increased 600% when they were informed that no one else had that information yet.

The persuasive power of exclusivity can be harnessed by any manager who comes into possession of information that's not broadly available and that supports an idea or initiative he or she would like the organization to adopt. The next time that kind of information crosses your desk, round up your organization's key players. The information itself may seem dull, but exclusivity will give it a special sheen. Push it across your desk and say, "I just got this report today. It won't be distributed until next week, but I want to give you an early look at what it shows." Then watch your listeners lean forward.

Allow me to stress here a point that should be obvious. No offer of exclusive information, no exhortation to act now or miss this opportunity forever should be made unless it is genuine. Deceiving colleagues into compliance is not only ethically objectionable, it's foolhardy. If the deception is detected—and it certainly will be—it will snuff out any enthusiasm the offer originally kindled. It will also invite dishonesty toward the deceiver. Remember the rule of reciprocity.

Putting it all together

There's nothing abstruse or obscure about these six principles of persuasion. Indeed, they neatly codify our intuitive understanding of the ways people evaluate information and form decisions. As a result, the principles are easy for most people to grasp, even those with no formal education in psychology. But in the seminars and workshops I conduct, I have learned that two points bear repeated emphasis.

First, although the six principles and their applications can be discussed separately for the sake of clarity, they should be applied in combination to compound their impact. For instance, in discussing the importance of expertise, I suggested that managers use informal, social conversations to establish their credentials. But that conversation affords an opportunity to gain information as well as convey it. While you're showing your dinner companion that you have the skills and experience your business problem demands, you can also learn about your companion's background, likes, and dislikes—information that will help you locate genuine similarities and give sincere compliments. By letting your expertise surface and also establishing rapport, you double your persuasive power. And if you succeed in bringing your dinner partner on board, you may encourage other people to sign on as well, thanks to the persuasive power of social evidence.

The other point I wish to emphasize is that the rules of ethics apply to the science of social influence just as they do to any other technology. Not only is it ethically wrong to trick or trap others into assent, it's ill-advised in practical terms. Dishonest or high-pressure tactics work only in the short run, if at all. Their long-term effects are malignant, especially within an organization that can't function properly without a bedrock level of trust and cooperation.

That point is made vividly in the following account, which a department head for a large textile manufacturer related at a training workshop I conducted. She described a vice president in her company who wrung public commitments from department heads in a highly manipulative manner. Instead of giving his subordinates time to talk or think through his proposals carefully, he would approach them individually at the busiest moment of their workday and describe the benefits of his plan in exhaustive, patience-straining detail. Then he would move in for the kill. "It's very important for me to see you as being on my team on this," he would say. "Can I count on your support?" Intimidated, frazzled, eager to chase the man from their offices so they could get back to work, the department heads would invariably go along with his request. But because the commitments never felt voluntary, the department heads never followed through, and as a result the vice president's initiatives all blew up or petered out.

This story had a deep impact on the other participants in the workshop. Some gulped in shock as they recognized their own manipulative behavior. But what stopped everyone cold was the expression on the department head's face as she recounted the damaging collapse of her superior's proposals. She was smiling.

Nothing I could say would more effectively make the point that the deceptive or coercive use of the principles of social influence is ethically wrong and pragmatically wrongheaded. Yet the same principles, if applied appropriately, can steer decisions correctly. Legitimate expertise, genuine obligations, authentic similarities, real social proof, exclusive news, and freely made commitments can produce choices that are likely to benefit both parties. And any approach that works to everyone's mutual benefit is good business, don't you think? Of course, I don't want to press you into it, but, if you agree, I would love it if you could just jot me a memo to that effect.

ROBERT CIALDINI is the author of *Influence and Pre-Suasion: A Revolutionary Way to Influence and Persuade* (Simon & Schuster, 2016). He is Regents' Professor Emeritus of Psychology and Marketing at Arizona State University and president and CEO of INFLUENCE AT WORK, a global training and keynote company.

Reprinted from *Harvard Business Review*,
October 2001 (product #R0109D).

3

Three Things Managers Should Be Doing Every Day

By Linda A. Hill and Kent Lineback

Whe are we supposed to do all *that*?" That's the question we constantly get from new managers, only weeks or months into their positions, when we describe the three key activities they should be focusing on to be successful as leaders: building trust, building a team, and building a broader network. To their dismay, most of them have found they rarely end a day in their new positions having done what they planned to do. They spend most of their time solving unexpected problems and making sure their groups do their work on time, on budget, and up to standard. They feel desperately out of control because what's *urgent*—the daily work—always seems to highjack what's *important*—their ongoing work as managers and leaders.

So they push back because they think we've just made their to-do list even longer. And these key elements (we call them the "Three Imperatives of Leading and Managing") are not quick and easy wins—they are substantial and fundamental to one's ability to function effectively as a leader. Here's why:

- *Building trust.* Successful leadership is, at root, about influencing others, and trust is the foundation of all ability to influence others. You cannot influence anyone who does not trust you. Thus the manager must work to cultivate the trust of everyone they work with. They do this by demonstrating the two basic components of trust: competence and character. Competence doesn't mean being the resident expert in everything the group does; it does mean understanding the work well enough to make solid decisions about it and having the courage to ask questions where they may be less knowledge-able. Character means basing decisions and ac-tions on values that go beyond self-interest and truly caring about the work, about the custom-ers (internal or external) for whom they do the work, and about the people doing the work. If people believe in your competence and charac-ter, they will trust you to do the right thing.

- *Building a real team and managing through it.* An effective team is bound together by a common, compelling purpose, based on shared values. In a genuine team, the bonds among members are so strong that they truly believe they will all succeed or fail together and that no individual can win if the team loses. Be-sides purpose and values, strong teams also have rules of engagement: explicit and im-plicit understandings of how members work together. For example, what kinds of conflict are allowed, and what kinds are not? Smart leaders make sure all the elements that create a real team are in place—purpose, values, rules— and then manage *through* the team. So instead of saying, "Do it because I'm the boss," they say, "Do it for the team," which is a much more powerful approach. In a real team, members value their membership and strive mightily not to let their comrades down. The smart leader builds and uses these powerful ties to shape behavior.

- *Building a network.* Every team depends on the support and collaboration of outside people and groups. Effective group leaders proactively build and maintain a network of these outsiders, which includes not just those needed for today's work but also those the group will need to achieve future goals. This is without a doubt the imperative that most troubles new managers. They think "networking" is manipulative organizational politicking that requires them to pretend they like people just because they want something from them. They strive to be above that sort of thing. Alas, in the process, they unnecessarily limit their own and their group's ability to influence others for good ends. Building a network can be politicking, but it need not be if they do it honestly, openly, and with the genuine intent of creating relationships that benefit both sides.

It is here, after covering these imperatives, that we hear the question, "When are we supposed to build trust, build a team, and create a network? How do we do that on top of everything else we have to do?"

Our answer is that the "Three Imperatives" and all that each embodies are not discrete tasks to put on a to-do. Instead, strong, effective leaders manage and lead *through* the daily work. They do this in the way they define, assign, structure, talk about, review, and generally guide that work. They are masters at using the daily work and its inevitable crises to perform their work as managers and leaders.

How do they do this?

They build *trust* by taking the opportunity to demonstrate their ability as they do their daily work, by asking knowledgeable questions and offering insightful suggestions. They use daily decisions and choices to illustrate their own values, expressing their concern for those who work for them or those for whom the group does its work. They reveal themselves, but not in an egotistical way, showing what they know, what they believe, and what they value—and in doing this, they show themselves to be trustworthy.

They build a *team* by using problems and crises in the daily work to remind members of the team's purpose and what it values most. They explain their decisions in these terms. They immediately call out team members who violate a rule of engagement—treating each other disrespectfully, for example—or who place their interests above those of the team. And since the rules apply to all members, including the leader, they ask team members to hold the leader accountable if she ever forgets one of those rules.

They build a *network* by taking opportunities afforded by routine activities—a regular meeting of department heads, for example, or even a chance meeting in the elevator—to build and maintain relationships with colleagues outside their group. They consciously approach problems that involve another group leader in a way that both solves the problem and fosters a long-term relationship. They proactively share information with outsiders who would benefit from it. They encourage their group members to take the same approach when they deal with outsiders.

These are obviously only a few of the ways good managers use their daily work to fulfill the deeper imperatives of leadership, but you get the idea. In fact, if there's anything that might be called a "secret" for not getting overwhelmed by the challenges of becoming an effective manager, this is surely it. We've seen new managers light up when they finally grasp this principle: that the daily work isn't an impediment to doing what good leaders do. Instead, it's *the way*, the vehicle, to do most of what good managers do.

Once they learn this lesson, they look at their daily work differently. For every new task, for every unexpected problem, they take a moment to step back and ask, How can I use this to foster trust? To build and strengthen us as a team? To expand our network and make it stronger?

LINDA A. HILL is the Wallace Brett Donham Professor of Business Administration at Harvard Business School. She is the author of *Becoming a Manager* and a coauthor of *Being the Boss* and *Collective Genius: The Art and Practice of Leading Innovation* (Harvard Business Review Press, 2014). KENT LINEBACK spent many years as a manager and an executive in business and government. He is a coauthor of *Collective Genius: The Art and Practice of Leading Innovation* (Harvard Business Review Press, 2014).

Reprinted from hbr.org, originally published
September 24, 2015 (product #H02DCU).

4

Learning Charisma

By John Antonakis, Marika Fenley, and Sue Liechti

Jana stands at the podium, palms sweaty, looking out at hundreds of colleagues who are waiting to hear about her new initiative. Bill walks into a meeting after a failed product launch to greet an exhausted and demotivated team that desperately needs his direction. Robin gets ready to confront a brilliant but underperforming subordinate who needs to be put back on track.

We've all been in situations like these. What they require is charisma—the ability to communicate a clear, visionary, and inspirational message that captivates and motivates an audience. So how do you learn charisma? Many people believe that it's impossible.

They say that charismatic people are born that way—as naturally expressive and persuasive extroverts. After all, you can't teach someone to be Winston Churchill.

While we agree with the latter contention, we disagree with the former. Charisma is not all innate; it's a learnable skill or, rather, a set of skills that have been practiced since antiquity. Our research with managers in the laboratory and in the field indicates that anyone trained in what we call "charismatic leadership tactics" (CLTs) can become more influential, trustworthy, and "leader like" in the eyes of others. In this article we'll explain these tactics and how we help managers master them. Just as athletes rely on hard training and the right game plan to win a competition, leaders who want to become charismatic must study the CLTs, practice them religiously, and have a good deployment strategy.

What is charisma?

Charisma is rooted in values and feelings. It's influence born of the alchemy that Aristotle called the *logos*, the *ethos*, and the *pathos*; that is, to persuade others, you must use powerful and reasoned rhetoric, establish personal and moral credibility, and then rouse followers' emotions and passions. If a leader can do those three things well, he or she can then tap into the hopes and ideals of followers, give them a sense of purpose, and inspire them to achieve great things.

Several large-scale studies have shown that charisma can be an invaluable asset in any work context—small or large, public or private, Western or Asian. Politicians know that it's important. Yet many business managers don't use charisma, perhaps because they don't know how to or because they believe it's not as easy to master as transactional (carrot-and-stick) or instrumental (task-based) leadership. Let's be clear: Leaders need technical expertise to win the trust of followers, manage operations, and set strategy; they also benefit from the ability to punish and reward. But the most effective leaders layer charismatic leadership on top of transactional and instrumental leadership to achieve their goals.

In our research, we have identified a dozen key CLTs. Some of them you may recognize as long-standing techniques of oratory. Nine of them are verbal: metaphors, similes, and analogies; stories and anecdotes; contrasts; rhetorical questions; three-part lists; expressions of moral conviction; reflections of the group's sentiments; the setting of high goals; and conveying confidence that they can be achieved. Three tactics are nonverbal: animated voice, facial expressions, and gestures.

There are other CLTs that leaders can use—such as creating a sense of urgency, invoking history, using repetition, talking about sacrifice, and using humor—but the 12 described in this article are the ones that have the greatest effect and can work in almost any context. In studies and experiments, we have found that people who use them appropriately can unite followers around a vision in a way that others can't. In 8 of the past 10 U.S. presidential races, for instance, the candidate who deployed verbal CLTs more often won. And when we measured "good" presentation skills— such as speech structure, clear pronunciation, use of easy-to-understand language, tempo of speech, and speaker comfort—and compared their impact against that of the CLTs, we found that the CLTs played a much bigger role in determining who was perceived to be more leader like, competent, and trustworthy.

Still, these tactics don't seem to be widely known or taught in the business world. The managers who practice them typically learned them by trial and error, without thinking consciously about them. As one manager who attended our training remarked, "I use a lot of these tactics, some without even knowing it." Such learning should not be left to chance.

We teach managers the CLTs by outlining the concepts and then showing news and film clips that highlight examples from business, sports, and politics. Managers must then experiment with and practice the tactics—on video, in front of peers, and on their own. A group of midlevel European executives (with an average age of 35) that did so as part of our training almost doubled their use of CLTs in presentations. As a result, they saw observers' numerical ratings of their competence as leaders jump by about 60% on average. They were then able to take the tactics back to their jobs. We saw the same thing happen with another group of executives (with an average age of 42) in a large Swiss firm. Overall, we've found that about 65% of people who have been trained in the CLTs receive above-average ratings as leaders, in contrast with only 35% of those who have not been trained.

The aim is to use the CLTs not only in public speaking but also in everyday conversations—to be more charismatic all the time. The tactics work because they help you create an emotional connection with followers, even as they make you appear more powerful, competent, and worthy of respect. In Greek, the word "charisma" means special gift. Start to use the CLTs correctly, and that's what people will begin to think you have.

Let's now look at the tactics in detail.

Connect, compare, and contrast

Charismatic speakers help listeners understand, relate to, and remember a message. A powerful way to do this is by using *metaphors*, *similes*, and *analogies*. Martin Luther King Jr. was a master of the metaphor. In his "I Have a Dream" speech, for example, he likened the U.S. Constitution to "a promissory note" guaranteeing the unalienable rights of life, liberty, and the pursuit of happiness to all people but noted that America had instead given its black citizens "a bad check," one that had come back marked "insufficient funds." Everyone knows what it means to receive a bad check. The message is crystal clear and easy to retain.

Metaphors can be effective in any professional context, too. Joe, a manager we worked with, used one to predispose his team to get behind an urgent relocation. He introduced it by saying, "When I heard about this from the board, it was like hearing about a long-awaited pregnancy. The difference is that we have four months instead of nine months to prepare." The team instantly understood it was about to experience an uncomfortable but ultimately rewarding transition.

Stories and anecdotes also make messages more engaging and help listeners connect with the speaker. Even people who aren't born raconteurs can employ them in a compelling way. Take this example from a speech Bill Gates gave at Harvard, urging gradu-ates to consider their broader responsibilities: "My mother . . . never stopped pressing me to do more for others. A few days before my wedding, she hosted a bridal event, at which she read aloud a letter about marriage that she had written to Melinda. My mother was very ill with cancer at the time, but she saw one more opportunity to deliver her message, and at the close of the letter she [quoted]: 'From those to whom much is given, much is expected.'"

Lynn, another manager we studied, used the fol-lowing story to motivate her reports during a crisis: "This reminds me of the challenge my team and I faced when climbing the Eiger peak a few years ago. We got caught in bad weather, and we could have died up there. But working together, we managed to survive. And we made what at first seemed impossi-ble, possible. Today we are in an economic storm, but by pulling together, we can turn this situation around and succeed." The story made her team feel reassured and inspired.

Contrasts are a key CLT because they combine reason and passion; they clarify your position by pitting it against the opposite, often to dramatic effect. Think of John F. Kennedy's "Ask not what your country can do for you—ask what you can do for your country." In our experience, contrasts are one of the easiest tactics to learn and use, and yet they aren't used enough. Here are some examples from managers newly trained in the CLTs. Gilles, a senior VP, speaking to a direct report managing a stagnant team: "It seems to me that you're playing too much defense when you need to be playing more offense." (That's also a metaphor.) And Sally, introducing herself to her new team: "I asked to lead the medical division not because it has the best location but because I believe we can accomplish something great for our company and at the same time help save lives."

Engage and distill

Rhetorical questions might seem hackneyed, but charismatic leaders use them all the time to encourage engagement. Questions can have an obvious answer or pose a puzzle to be answered later. Think again of Martin Luther King Jr., who said, "There are those who are asking the devotees of civil rights, 'When will you be satisfied?'" and then went on to show that oppressed people can never be satisfied. Anita Roddick—founder of the Body Shop—once used three rhetorical questions to explain what led her to help start the social responsibility movement. The thinking, she said, "was really simple: How do you make business kinder? How do you embed it in the community? How do you make community a social purpose for business?"

This tactic works just as well in private conversations. Take Mika, a manager in our study, who effectively motivated an underperforming subordinate by asking, "So, where do you want to go from here? Will it be back to your office feeling sorry for yourself? Or do you want to show what you are capable of achieving?" Here's another question (also employing metaphor) used by Frank, an IT executive who needed to push back at the unrealistic goals being set for him: "How can you expect me to change an engine in a plane midflight?"

Three-part lists are another old trick of effective persuasion because they distill any message into key takeaways. Why three? Because most people can remember three things, three is sufficient to provide proof of a pattern, and three gives an impression of completeness. Three-part lists can be announced—as in "There are three things we need to do to get our bottom line back into the black"—or they can be under the radar, as in the sentence before this one.

Here's a list that Serge, a midlevel manager, used at a team meeting: "We have the best product on the market. We have the best team. Yet we did not make the sales target." And here's one that Karin, division head of a manufacturing company, employed in a speech to her staff: "We can turn this around with a three-point strategy: First, we need to look back and see what we did right. Next, we need to see where we went wrong. Then, we need to come up with a plan that will convince the board to give us the resources to get it right the next time."

Show integrity, authority, and passion

Expressions of moral conviction and *statements that reflect the sentiments of the group*—even when the sentiments are negative—establish your credibility by revealing the quality of your character to your listeners and making them identify and align themselves with you. On Victory Day at the end of the Second World War, Winston Churchill brilliantly captured the feelings of the British people and also conveyed a spirit of honor, courage, and compassion. He said: "This is your hour. This is not victory of a party or of any class. It's a victory of the great British nation as a whole. We were the first, in this ancient island, to draw the sword against tyranny. . . . There we stood, alone. The lights went out and the bombs came down. But every man, woman, and child in the country had no thought of quitting the struggle. . . . Now we have emerged from one deadly struggle—a terrible foe has been cast on the ground and awaits our judgment and our mercy."

Another nice example of moral conviction (plus a number of other CLTs) comes from Tina, a manager in an NGO pushing for a needed supply-chain change: "Who do you think will pay for the logistical mess we've created? It is not our donors who'll feel it but the children we're supposed to be feeding that will go to bed one more time with an empty belly and who may not make it through the night. Apart from wasting money, this is not right, especially because the fix is so simple." And here's Rami, a senior IT director trained in the CLTs, expertly reflecting the sentiments of his disheartened team: "I know what is going through your minds, because the same thing is going through mine. We all feel disappointed and demotivated. Some of you have told me you have had sleepless nights; others, that there are tensions in the team, even at home because of this. Personally, life to me has become dull and tasteless. I know how hard we have all worked and the bitterness we feel because success just slipped out of our reach. But it's not going to be like this for much longer. I have a plan."

Another CLT, which helps charismatic leaders demonstrate passion—and inspire it in their followers—is *setting high goals*. Gandhi set the almost impossible (and moral) goal of liberating India from British rule without using violence, as laid out in his famous "quit India" speech. An example from the business world that we often cite is the former CEO of Sharp, Katsuhiko Machida. In 1998, at a time when Sharp faced collapse, cathode-ray tubes dominated the TV market, and the idea of using LCD technology was commercially unviable, he energized his employees by stating the unthinkable: "By 2005, all TVs we sell in Japan will be LCD models."

But one must also *convey confidence that the goals can be achieved.* Gandhi noted: "I know the British Government will not be able to withhold freedom from us, when we have made enough self-sacrifice." In a later speech he expressed his conviction more forcefully: "Even if all the United Nations opposes me, even if the whole of India forsakes me, I will say, 'You are wrong. India will wrench with nonviolence her liberty from unwilling hands.' I will go ahead not for India's sake alone but for the sake of the world. Even if my eyes close before there is freedom, nonviolence will not end." Machida personally took his vision to Sharp's engineers to convince them that they could realize his risky goal. He made it the company's most important project, brought together cross-functional teams from LCD and TV development to work on it, and told them plainly that it was crucial to Sharp's survival. Or take Ray, an engineer we know, addressing his team after a setback: "The deadline the CEO gave us is daunting. Other teams would be right to tremble at the knees, but we are not just another team. I know you can rise to the challenge. I believe in each one of you, which means that I believe that we can get the prototype to manufacturing in three months. Let's commit to do what it takes to get the job done: We have the smarts. We have the experience. All we need is the will, and that's something only great teams have." Passion cannot emerge unless the leader truly believes that the vision and strategic goal can be reached.

The three nonverbal cues—*expressions of voice, body, and face*—are also key to charisma. They don't come naturally to everyone, however, and they are the most culturally sensitive tactics: What's perceived as too much passion in certain Asian contexts might be perceived as too muted in southern European ones. But they are nonetheless important to learn and practice because they are easier for your followers to process than the verbal CLTs, and they help you hold people's attention by punctuating your speech. (For more on these, see the sidebar "Charisma in Voice and Body.")

Putting it all into practice

Now that you've learned the CLTs, how do you start using them? Simple: preparation and practice. When you're mapping out a speech or a presentation, you should certainly plan to incorporate the tactics and rehearse them. We also encourage leaders to think about them before one-on-one conversations or team meetings in which they need to be persuasive. The idea is to arm yourself with a few key CLTs that feel comfortable to you and therefore will come out spontaneously—or at least look as if they did. The leaders we've trained worked on improving their charisma in groups and got feedback from one another. You could ask your spouse or a friendly colleague to do the same or videotape yourself and do a self-critique.

The goal isn't to employ all the tactics in every conversation but to use a balanced combination. With time and practice, they will start to come out on the fly. One manager we know, who met his wife after being trained in the CLTs, showed her his "before" videos and told us she couldn't believe it was him. The charismatic guy in the "after" videos—the one whose CLT use had more than doubled—was the person she had married. Another manager, who learned the tactics six years ago and has since become the chief operating officer of his company, says he now uses them every day—personally and professionally—such as in a recent talk to his team about a relocation, which went "much better than expected" as a result.

CHARISMA IN VOICE AND BODY

Three tactics for showing passion—and winning over listeners.

Animated voice

People who are passionate vary the volume with which they speak, whispering at appropriate points or rising to a crescendo to hammer home a point. Emotion—sadness, happiness, excitement, surprise—must come through in the voice. Pauses are also important because they convey control.

Facial expressions

These help reinforce your message. Listeners need to see as well as hear your passion—especially when you're telling a story or reflecting their sentiments. So be sure to make eye contact (one of the givens of charisma), and get comfortable smiling, frowning, and laughing at work.

Gestures

These are signals for your listeners. A fist can reinforce confidence, power, and certitude. Waving a hand, pointing, or pounding a desk can help draw attention.

If you think you can't improve because you're just not naturally charismatic, you're wrong. The managers with the lowest initial charisma ratings in our studies were able to significantly narrow the gap between themselves and their peers to whom the tactics came naturally. It's true that no amount of training or practice will turn you into Churchill or Martin Luther King Jr. But the CLTs can make you more charismatic in the eyes of your followers, and that will invariably make you a more effective leader.

JOHN ANTONAKIS is a professor of business and economics at the University of Lausanne in Switzerland and consults for companies on leadership development. MARIKA FENLEY has a PhD in management focusing on gender and leadership from the Faculty of Business and Economics at the University of Lausanne. SUE LIECHTI holds a master's degree in psychology from the University of Lausanne and is an organizational development consultant.

Reprinted from *Harvard Business Review*,
June 2012 (product #R1206K).

5

To Win People Over, Speak to Their Wants and Needs

By Nancy Duarte

P racticing empathy can be difficult, because you have to step outside your comfort zone to understand someone else's point of view. But it's essential to exercising influence.

It's how method actors move us to feel, think, or act differently—they deeply immerse themselves in their characters, trying on new ways of being and behaving. Sometimes their identity experiments are even part of the story line, as in *Being John Malkovich*, *Avatar*, and *Tootsie*.

During *Tootsie*, walking in the shoes of a woman had such a profound impact on Dustin Hoffman that, 30 years later, recalling his decision to make the film brought tears to his eyes in an interview with the American Film Institute.

Before agreeing to work on the movie, Hoffman did some makeup tests to see if he would be believable as a woman. When he discovered that he could pass, but he wouldn't be *beautiful*, he realized he had to do this project. As he explained to his wife: "I think I'm an interesting woman [as Dorothy Michaels]. And I know that if I met myself at a party, I wouldn't talk to that character because she doesn't fulfill physically the demands that we're brought up to think women have to have in order for us to ask them out . . . There's too many interesting women I have not had the experience to know in this life because I've been brainwashed." Empathy made Hoffman's performance—and the film's message—more convincing and powerful.

The same thing happens in business all the time. Whether you're trying to get your team on board with a new way of working, asking investors to fund you, persuading customers to buy your product, or imploring the public to donate to your cause, your success depends on your ability to grasp the wants and needs of the people around you. We've seen this over and over again at my firm as we've created presentations for clients and coached them on effective delivery. If people feel listened to, they become more receptive to your message. And by doing the listening, you become more informed about what they really need—not just what you think they need—which will fuel your relationships with stakeholders over the long run.

How do you build your capacity for empathy? Exercises can help, and they're used in many fields. Secret shoppers pose as retail customers and record their observations. Product developers brainstorm use cases and interview consumers to envision how they'll interact with a product. Negotiators do role-playing to imagine opposing points of view before they get to the table.

Once you've started to develop empathy as a skill, you can make it integral to the work you do. You might try visualizing stakeholders' various perspectives the way Airbnb CEO Brian Chesky and his team did. As described in a *Fast Company* post, they storyboarded the guest, host, and hiring processes—inspired by Disney's filmmaking. They created a list of the key moments in these three experiences and then developed the most important and most emotionally charged ones into fuller narratives. Cofounder Nathan Blecharczyk says they learned a lot: "What the storyboards made clear is that we were missing a big part of the picture. . . . There were a lot of important moments where we weren't doing anything." The storyboards ended up helping the company define its mobile strategy and even inspired new features, which allowed Airbnb to connect with traveling customers wherever the customers were.[1]

It's also essential to listen carefully to your stakeholders and check your understanding of what's being said. Arbitrators do this to get a handle on what both sides need in a dispute, before trying to carve out a solution. Executives who are new to a company often embark on listening tours with employees and customers to get their perspective on issues and opportunities.

That's what Lou Gerstner did in the 1990s, when the board at IBM brought him in to turn around the almost bankrupt company. Gerstner called his listening tour Operation Bear Hug. He gave managers three months to meet with customers and ask about issues they were grappling with and how IBM could help. Managers then had to recap the conversations in memos. Gerstner also called customers on his own every day. And he "bear-hugged" employees by touring IBM's various sites and hosting gatherings to share updates, test ideas, and tackle concerns. He held 90-minute unscripted Q&A sessions with the staff, during which he would talk to 20,000 workers directly.

Influence and Persuasion

"I listened, and I tried very hard not to draw con-clusions," Gerstner said.

It was an important step in the strategy-making process, one that enabled the executive team to build plans to make IBM relevant and competitive again. But it led to an even larger shift in IBM's culture that transformed the company from an inwardly focused bureaucracy to a market-driven innovator.

Empathize with the people you need to persuade to purchase your product or services or to work hard on your behalf. It gives you better ideas, and it makes you worth listening to. And if your stakeholders can empathize with you in return, you're on your way to building real, lasting relationships with them.

NANCY DUARTE is CEO of Duarte Design and the author of the *HBR Guide to Persuasive Presentations* (Harvard Business Review Press, 2012), as well as two books on the art of presenting, *Slide:ology: The Art and Science of Creating Great Presentations* (O'Reilly Media, 2008) and *Resonate: Present Visual Stories That Transform Audiences* (Wiley, 2010). She

88

is a coauthor with Patti Sanchez of *Illuminate: Ignite Change Through Speeches, Stories, Ceremonies, and Symbols* (Portfolio, 2016).

Note

1. S. Kessler, "How Snow White Helped Airbnb's Mobile Mission," *Fast Company*, November 8, 2012, http://www.fast cocreate.com/1681924/how-snow-white-helped-airbnbs -mobile-mission; N. Blecharczyk, "Visualizing the Customer Experience," Sequoia Capital, https://www.sequoia cap.com/article/visualizing-customer-experience/; A. Carr, "Inside Airbnb's Grand Hotel Plans," *Fast Company*, March 17, 2014, http://www.fastcompany.com/3027107/ punk-meet-rock-airbnb-brian-chesky-chip-conley.

Reprinted from hbr.org, originally published
May 12, 2015 (product #H0228V).

6

Storytelling That Moves People

An interview with Robert McKee by Bronwyn Fryer

ersuasion is the centerpiece of business activity. Customers must be convinced to buy your company's products or services, employees and colleagues to go along with a new strategic plan or reorganization, investors to buy (or not to sell) your stock, and partners to sign the next deal. But despite the critical importance of persuasion, most executives struggle to communicate, let alone inspire. Too often, they get lost in the accoutrements of companyspeak: PowerPoint slides, dry memos, and hyperbolic missives from the corporate communications department. Even the most carefully researched and considered efforts are routinely greeted with cynicism, lassitude, or outright dismissal.

Why is persuasion so difficult, and what can you do to set people on fire? In search of answers to those questions, HBR senior editor Bronwyn Fryer paid a visit to Robert McKee, the world's best known and most respected screenwriting lecturer, at his home in Los Angeles. An award-winning writer and director, McKee moved to California after studying for his PhD in cinema arts at the University of Michigan. He then taught at the University of Southern California's School of Cinema and Television before forming his own company, Two Arts, to take his lectures on the art of storytelling worldwide to an audience of writers, directors, producers, actors, and entertainment executives.

McKee's students have written, directed, and produced hundreds of hit films, including *Forrest Gump*, *Erin Brockovich*, *The Color Purple*, *Gandhi*, *Monty Python and the Holy Grail*, *Sleepless in Se-*

attle, Toy Story, and *Nixon.* They have won 18 Academy Awards, 109 Emmy Awards, 19 Writers Guild Awards, and 16 Directors Guild of America Awards. Emmy Award winner Brian Cox portrays McKee in the 2002 film *Adaptation,* which follows the life of a screenwriter trying to adapt the book *The Orchid Thief.* McKee also serves as a project consultant to film and television production companies such as Disney, Pixar, and Paramount as well as major corporations (including Microsoft) that regularly send their entire creative staffs to his lectures.

McKee believes that executives can engage listeners on a whole new level if they toss their PowerPoint slides and learn to tell good stories instead. In his best-selling book *Story: Substance, Structure, Style, and the Principles of Screenwriting,* published in 1997 by HarperCollins, McKee argues that stories "fulfill a profound human need to grasp the patterns of living—not merely as an intellectual exercise, but within a very personal, emotional experience."

What follows is an edited and abridged transcript of McKee's conversation with HBR.

Why should a CEO or a manager pay attention to a screenwriter?

A big part of a CEO's job is to motivate people to reach certain goals. To do that, he or she must engage their emotions, and the key to their hearts is story. There are two ways to persuade people. The first is by using conventional rhetoric, which is what most executives are trained in. It's an intellectual process, and in the business world it usually consists of a PowerPoint slide presentation in which you say, "Here is our company's biggest challenge, and here is what we need to do to prosper." And you build your case by giving statistics and facts and quotes from authorities. But there are two problems with rhetoric. First, the people you're talking to have their own set of authorities, statistics, and experiences. While you're trying to persuade them, they are arguing with you in their heads. Second, if you do succeed in persuading them, you've done so only on an intellectual basis. That's not good enough, because people are not inspired to act by reason alone.

The other way to persuade people—and ultimately a much more powerful way—is by uniting an idea with an emotion. The best way to do that is by telling a compelling story. In a story, you not only weave a lot of information into the telling but you also arouse your listener's emotions and energy. Persuading with a story is hard. Any intelligent person can sit down and make lists. It takes rationality but little creativity to design an argument using conventional rhetoric. But it demands vivid insight and storytelling skill to present an idea that packs enough emotional power to be memorable. If you can harness imagination and the principles of a well-told story, then you get people rising to their feet amid thunderous applause instead of yawning and ignoring you.

So, what is a story?

Essentially, a story expresses how and why life changes. It begins with a situation in which life is relatively in balance: You come to work day after day, week after week, and everything's fine. You expect it will go on that way. But then there's an event—in screenwriting, we call it the "inciting incident"—that throws life out of balance. You get a new job, or the boss dies of a heart attack, or a big customer threatens to leave. The story goes on to describe how, in an effort to restore balance, the protagonist's subjective expectations crash into an uncooperative objective reality. A good storyteller describes what it's like to deal with these opposing forces, calling on the protagonist to dig deeper, work with scarce resources, make difficult decisions, take action despite risks, and ultimately discover the truth. All great storytellers since the dawn of time—from the ancient Greeks through Shakespeare and up to the present day—have dealt with this fundamental conflict between subjective expectation and cruel reality.

How would an executive learn to tell stories?

Stories have been implanted in you thousands of times since your mother took you on her knee. You've read good books, seen movies, attended plays. What's more, human beings naturally *want* to work through stories. Cognitive psychologists describe how the human mind, in its attempt to understand and remember, assembles the bits and pieces of experience into a story, beginning with a personal desire, a life objective, and then portraying the struggle against the forces that block that desire. Stories are how we remember; we tend to forget lists and bullet points.

Businesspeople not only have to understand their companies' past, but then they must project the future. And how do you imagine the future? As a story. You create scenarios in your head of possible future events to try to anticipate the life of your company or your own personal life. So, if a businessperson understands that his or her own mind naturally wants to frame experience in a story, the key to moving an audience is not to resist this impulse but to embrace it by telling a good story.

What makes a good story?

You emphatically do not want to tell a beginning-to-end tale describing how results meet expectations. This is boring and banal. Instead, you want to display the struggle between expectation and reality in all its nastiness.

For example, let's imagine the story of a biotech startup we'll call Chemcorp, whose CEO has to persuade some Wall Street bankers to invest in the company. He could tell them that Chemcorp has discovered a chemical compound that prevents heart attacks and offer up a lot of slides showing them the size of the market, the business plan, the organizational chart, and so on. The bankers would nod politely and stifle yawns while thinking of all the other companies better positioned in Chemcorp's market.

Alternatively, the CEO could turn his pitch into a story, beginning with someone close to him— say, his father—who died of a heart attack. So nature itself is the first antagonist that the CEO-as-protagonist must overcome. The story might unfold like this: In his grief, he realizes that if there had been some chemical indication of heart disease, his father's death could have been prevented. His company discovers a protein that's present in the blood just before heart attacks and develops an easy-to-administer, low-cost test.

But now it faces a new antagonist: the FDA. The approval process is fraught with risks and dangers. The FDA turns down the first application, but new research reveals that the test performs even better than anyone had expected, so the agency approves a second application. Meanwhile, Chemcorp is running out of money, and a key partner drops out and goes off to start his own company. Now Chemcorp is in a fight-to-the-finish patent race.

This accumulation of antagonists creates great suspense. The protagonist has raised the idea in the bankers' heads that the story might not have a happy ending. By now, he has them on the edge of their seats, and he says, "We won the race, we got the patent, we're poised to go public and save a quarter-million lives a year." And the bankers just throw money at him.

Aren't you really talking about exaggeration and manipulation?

No. Although businesspeople are often suspicious of stories for the reasons you suggest, the fact is that statistics are used to tell lies and damn lies, while accounting reports are often BS in a ball gown—witness Enron and WorldCom.

When people ask me to help them turn their presentations into stories, I begin by asking questions. I kind of psychoanalyze their companies, and amazing dramas pour out. But most companies and executives sweep the dirty laundry, the difficulties, the antagonists, and the struggle under the carpet. They prefer to present a rosy—and boring—picture to the world. But as a storyteller, you want to position the problems in the foreground and then show how you've overcome them. When you tell the story of your struggles against real antagonists, your audience sees you as an exciting, dynamic person. And I know that the storytelling method works, because after I consulted with a dozen corporations whose principals told exciting stories to Wall Street, they all got their money.

What's wrong with painting a positive picture?

It doesn't ring true. You can send out a press release talking about increased sales and a bright future, but your audience knows it's never that easy. They know you're not spotless; they know your competitor doesn't wear a black hat. They know you've slanted your statement to make your company look good. Positive, hypothetical pictures and boilerplate press releases actually work against you because they foment distrust among the people you're trying to convince. I suspect that most CEOs do not believe their own spin doctors— and if they don't believe the hype, why should the public?

The great irony of existence is that what makes life worth living does not come from the rosy side.

We would all rather be lotus-eaters, but life will not allow it. The energy to live comes from the dark side. It comes from everything that makes us suffer. As we struggle against these negative powers, we're forced to live more deeply, more fully.

So acknowledging this dark side makes you more convincing?

Of course. Because you're more truthful. One of the principles of good storytelling is the understanding that we all live in dread. Fear is when you don't know what's going to happen. Dread is when you know what's going to happen and there's nothing you can do to stop it. Death is the great dread; we all live in an ever-shrinking shadow of time, and between now and then all kinds of bad things could happen.

Most of us repress this dread. We get rid of it by inflicting it on other people through sarcasm, cheating, abuse, indifference—cruelties great and small. We all commit those little evils that relieve the pressure and make us feel better. Then we rationalize our bad behavior and convince ourselves we're good people. Institutions do the same thing: They deny the existence of the negative while inflicting their dread on other institutions or their employees.

If you're a realist, you know that this is human nature; in fact, you realize that this behavior is the foundation of all nature. The imperative in nature is to follow the golden rule of survival: Do unto others what they do unto you. In nature, if you offer cooperation and get cooperation back, you get along. But if you offer cooperation and get antagonism back, then you give antagonism in return—in spades.

Ever since human beings sat around the fire in caves, we've told stories to help us deal with the dread of life and the struggle to survive. All great stories illuminate the dark side. I'm not talking about so-called "pure" evil, because there is no such thing. We are all evil and good, and these sides do continual battle. Kenneth Lay says wiping out people's jobs and life savings was unintentional. Hannibal Lecter is witty, charming, and brilliant, and he eats people's livers. Audiences appreciate the truthfulness of a storyteller who acknowledges the dark side of human beings and deals honestly with antagonistic events. The story engenders a positive but realistic energy in the people who hear it.

Does this mean you have to be a pessimist?

It's not a question of whether you're optimistic or pessimistic. It seems to me that the civilized human being is a skeptic—someone who believes nothing at face value. Skepticism is another principle of the storyteller. The skeptic understands the difference between text and subtext and always seeks what's really going on. The skeptic hunts for the truth beneath the surface of life, knowing that the real thoughts and feelings of institutions or individuals are unconscious and unexpressed. The skeptic is always looking behind the mask. Street kids, for example, with their tattoos, piercings, chains, and leather, wear amazing masks, but the skeptic knows the mask is only a persona. Inside anyone working that hard to look fierce is a marshmallow. Genuinely hard people make no effort.

So, a story that embraces darkness produces a positive energy in listeners?

Absolutely. We follow people in whom we believe. The best leaders I've dealt with—producers and directors—have come to terms with dark reality. Instead of communicating via spin doctors, they lead their actors and crews through the antagonism of a world in which the odds of getting the film made, distributed, and sold to millions of moviegoers are a thousand to one. They appreciate that the people who work for them love the work and live for the small triumphs that contribute to the final triumph.

CEOs, likewise, have to sit at the head of the table or in front of the microphone and navigate their companies through the storms of bad economies and tough competition. If you look your audience in the eye, lay out your really scary challenges, and say, "We'll be lucky as hell if we get through this, but here's what I think we should do," they will listen to you.

To get people behind you, you can tell a truthful story. The story of General Electric is wonderful and has nothing to do with Jack Welch's cult of celebrity. If you have a grand view of life, you can see it on all its complex levels and celebrate it in a story. A great CEO is someone who has come to terms with his or her own mortality and, as a result, has compassion for others. This compassion is expressed in stories.

Take the love of work, for example. Years ago, when I was in graduate school, I worked as an insurance fraud investigator. The claimant in one case was an immigrant who'd suffered a terrible head injury on a carmaker's assembly line. He'd been the fastest window assembler on the line and took great pride in his work. When I spoke to him, he was waiting to have a titanium plate inserted into his head.

The man had been grievously injured, but the company thought he was a fraud. In spite of that, he remained incredibly dedicated. All he wanted was to get back to work. He knew the value of work, no matter how repetitive. He took pride in it and even in the company that had falsely accused him. How wonderful it would have been for the CEO of that car company to tell the tale of how his managers recognized the falseness of their accusation and then rewarded the employee for his dedication. The company, in turn, would have been rewarded with redoubled effort from all the employees who heard that story.

How do storytellers discover and unearth the stories that want to be told?

The storyteller discovers a story by asking certain key questions. First, what does my protagonist want in order to restore balance in his or her life? Desire is the blood of a story. Desire is not a shopping list but a core need that, if satisfied, would stop the story in its tracks. Next, what is keeping my protagonist from achieving his or her desire? Forces within? Doubt? Fear? Confusion? Personal conflicts with friends, family, lovers? Social conflicts arising in the various institutions in society? Physical conflicts? The forces of Mother Nature? Lethal diseases in the air? Not enough time to get things done? The damned automobile that won't start? Antagonists come from people, society, time, space, and every object in it, or any combination of these forces at once. Then, how would my protagonist decide to act in order to achieve his or her desire in the face of these antagonistic forces? It's in the answer to that question that storytellers discover the truth of their characters, because the heart of a human being is revealed in the choices he or she makes under pressure. Finally, the storyteller leans back from the design of events he or she has created and asks, "Do I believe this? Is it neither an exaggeration nor a soft-soaping of the struggle? Is this an honest telling, though heaven may fall?"

Does being a good storyteller make you a good leader?

Not necessarily, but if you understand the principles of storytelling, you probably have a good understanding of yourself and of human nature, and that tilts the odds in your favor. I can teach the formal principles of stories, but not to a person who hasn't really lived. The art of storytelling takes intelligence, but it also demands a life experience that I've noted in gifted film directors: the pain of childhood. Childhood trauma forces you into a kind of mild schizophrenia that makes you see life simultaneously in two ways: First, it's direct, real-time experience, but at the same moment, your brain records it as material—material out of which you will create business ideas, science, or art. Like a double-edged knife, the creative mind cuts to the truth of self and the humanity of others.

Self-knowledge is the root of all great storytelling. A storyteller creates all characters from the self by asking the question, "If I were this character in these circumstances, what would I do?" The more you understand your own humanity, the more you can appreciate the humanity of others in all their good-versus-evil struggles. I would argue that the great leaders Jim Collins describes are people with enormous self-knowledge. They have self-insight and self-respect balanced by skepticism. Great storytellers—and, I suspect, great leaders—are skeptics who understand their own masks as well as the masks of life, and this understanding makes them humble. They see the humanity in others and deal with them in a compassionate yet realistic way. That duality makes for a wonderful leader.

ROBERT MCKEE is a celebrated screenwriting instructor formerly at the University of Southern California's School of Cinema and Television. His firm, Two Arts, brings his seminars on the art of storytelling worldwide to a broad audience of screenwriters, novelists, playwrights, poets, documentary makers, producers, and directors. BRONWYN FRYER is a collaborative writer and former senior editor with the *Harvard Business Review*.

Reprinted from *Harvard Business Review*,
June 2003 (product #R0306B).

7

The Surprising Persuasiveness of a Sticky Note

By Kevin Hogan

magine that you really need to convince someone to do something, such as follow through on a task. You might be surprised to learn that one of the best ways to get someone to comply with your request is through a tiny nuance that adds a personal touch: attaching a sticky note.

A brilliant set of experiments by Randy Garner at Sam Houston State University in Huntsville, Texas, found that a) adding a personal touch, and b) making someone feel like you're asking a favor of them (and not just anyone) can bring about impressive results when done in tandem.[1]

The goal of Garner's experiments was to see what was necessary to generate compliance in completing surveys—which are often quite lengthy and tedious—by fellow professors at the university, using only interoffice mail as the conduit of communication. The wild card factor in these experiments was the use of sticky notes. In one experiment, he sent surveys to three separate groups of 50 professors (150 professors total). Three groups received three different requests, as follows:

> *Group 1* received a survey with a sticky note attached asking for the return of the completed survey.

> *Group 2* received a survey with the same handwritten message on the cover letter instead of an attached sticky note.

> *Group 3* received a survey with a cover letter but no handwritten message.

What happened?

>*Group 3*: 36% of the professors returned the survey.

>*Group 2*: 48% of the professors returned the survey.

>*Group 1*: 76% of the professors returned the survey.

Generalizing this experiment in other contexts simply requires understanding *why* the sticky note worked so well. It represents many powerful behavioral triggers all in one little object:

1. It doesn't match the environment: The sticky note takes up space and looks a bit cluttered. The brain, therefore, wants it gone.

2. It gets attention first because of #1. It's difficult to ignore.

3. It's personalized. (That's the difference between Group 2 and Group 3 in the experiment.)

4. Ultimately, the sticky note represents *one person* communicating with *another important person*—almost as if it is a favor or special request, which makes the recipient feel important.

Garner couldn't help but explore the sticky note factor further. He decided to do a second experiment where he sent a group of professors a *blank* sticky note attached to one of the surveys. Here's what happened:

> *Group 1* received a survey with a personalized sticky note message.
>
> *Group 2* received a survey with a blank sticky note attached.

Group 3 received a survey with no sticky note.

What happened in the second study?

Group 3: 34% returned the survey with no sticky note (similar to the first experiment).

Group 2: 43% returned the survey with the blank sticky note

Group 1: 69% returned the survey with the personalized sticky note (similar to the first experiment).

The real magic, it seems, is not the sticky note itself but the sense of connection, meaning, and identity that the sticky note represents. The person sending the survey is *personally* asking *me* in a special way (not just writing it on the survey) to help him or her out.

But there's more to compliance than just the result. There's also the speed of compliance and the quality of the effort. Garner experimented to see how quickly people would return a follow-up survey if there was a sticky note attached and also measured how much information the person being surveyed returned if there was a sticky note attached versus the group that received no sticky note. Here's what he found:

> *Group 1* (with sticky note) returned their self-addressed stamped envelopes (SASEs) and surveys within an average of about 4 days.
>
> *Group 2* (no sticky note) returned their SASEs and surveys in an average of about 5 1/2 days.

But the most notable difference is that Group 1 also sent significantly more comments and answered other open-ended questions with more words than Group 2 did.

Further experiments revealed that if a task is easy to perform or comply with, a simple sticky note request needs no further personalization. But when the task is more involved, a more highly personalized sticky note was significantly more effective than a simple standard sticky note request. What makes it truly personal? Writing a brief message is effective, but adding the person's first name at the top and your initials at the bottom causes significantly greater compliance.

I've used this personalization theory with businesspeople around the world to great success. For example, a mortgage broker I worked with tested this approach in mailings, effectively doubling the number of phone calls from people pursuing a loan with the broker. And it's not just effective at the office or with clients. The people you live with are going to respond to the sticky note model as well. (Try sticking one on the bathroom mirror and see what happens.)

Recently, the personalized sticky note has been put into digital form for use in email, with mixed results. It's most effective in email when the two people have met or know each other. It had only a modest effect in sales letters designed to make an immediate sale, when the reader didn't know the author of the sales letter. Using the notes in sales letters designed for current clients and customers needs further testing.

The next time you need colleagues to comply with a request, or the next time you're giving a potential client a portfolio to review, try leaving a sticky note. A small personal touch will go a long way toward getting the results you want.

KEVIN HOGAN is the author of 21 books, including *The Science of Influence: How to Get Anyone to Say Yes* (Wiley, 2010) and *The Psychology of Persuasion: How to Persuade Others to Your Way of Thinking* (Pelican Publishing, 1996).

Note

1. R. Garner, "Post-it Note Persuasion: A Sticky Influence," and "What's In a Name? Persuasion Perhaps," *Journal of Consumer Psychology*, 2005.

Reprinted from hbr.org, originally published
May 26, 2015 (product #H023LE).

8

When to Sell with Facts and Figures, and When to Appeal to Emotions

By Michael D. Harris

When should salespeople sell with facts and figures, and when should they try to speak to the buyer's emotional subconscious instead? When do you talk to Mr. Intuitive and when to Mr. Rational?

I'd argue that too often, selling to Mr. Rational leads to analysis paralysis, especially for complex products or services. And yet many of us continue to market almost exclusively to Mr. Rational. The result is that we spend too much time chasing sales opportunities that eventually stall out. We need to improve our ability to sell to Mr. Intuitive.

We default to selling to Mr. Rational because when we think of ourselves, we identify with our conscious rational mind. We can't imagine that serious executives would make decisions based on emotion, because we view our emotional decisions as irrational and irresponsible.

But what if Mr. Intuitive has a logic of his own? In recent years, psychologists and behavioral economists have shown that our emotional decisions are neither irrational nor irresponsible. In fact, we now understand that our unconscious decisions do in fact follow a clear logic. They are based on a deeply empirical mental-processing system that is capable of effortlessly cycling through millions of bits of data without getting overwhelmed. Our conscious mind, on the other hand, has a strict bottleneck, because it can only process three or four new pieces of information at a time due to the limitations of our working memory.[1]

The Iowa Gambling Task study, for example, highlights how effective the emotional brain is at effortlessly figuring out the probability of success for maximum gain.[2] Subjects were given an imaginary budget and four stacks of cards. The objective of the game was to win as much money as possible, and to do so, subjects were instructed to draw cards from any of the four decks.

The subjects were not aware that the decks were carefully prepared. Drawing from two of the decks led to consistent wins, while the other two had high payouts but carried oversized punishments. The logical choice was to avoid the dangerous decks, and after about 50 cards, people did stop drawing from the risky decks. It wasn't until the 80th card, however, that people could explain why. Logic is slow.

But the researchers tracked the subjects' anxiety and found that people started to become nervous when reaching for the risky deck after drawing only 10 cards. Intuition is fast.

Harvard Business School professor Gerald Zaltman says that 95% of our purchase decisions take place unconsciously. But why, then, are we not able to look back through our decision history and find countless examples of emotional decisions? Because our conscious mind will always make up reasons to justify our unconscious decisions.

In a study of people who'd had the left and right hemisphere of their brains severed in order to prevent future epileptic seizures, scientists were able to deliver a message to the right side of the brain to "Go to the water fountain down the hall and get a drink."[3] After seeing the message, the subject would get up and start to leave the room, and that's when the scientist would deliver a message to the opposite, left side of the brain, asking, "Where are you going?" Now remember, the left side of the brain never saw the message about the fountain. But did the left brain admit it didn't know the answer? No. Instead it shamelessly fabricated a rational reason, something like, "It's cold in here. I'm going to get my jacket."

So if you can't reliably use your own decision-making history as a guide, when do you know you should be selling based on logic and when on emotion?

Here's the short rule of thumb: Sell to Mr. Rational for simple sales and to Mr. Intuitive for complex sales.

This conclusion is backed by a 2011 study based on subjects selecting the best used car from a selection of four cars. Each car was rated in four different categories (such as gas mileage). But one car clearly had the best attributes. In this "easy" situation with only four variables, the conscious deciders were 15% better at choosing the best car than the unconscious deciders. When the researchers made the decision more complex—ratcheting the number of variables up to 12—unconscious deciders were 42% better than conscious deciders at selecting the best car. Many other studies have shown how our conscious minds become overloaded by too much information.

If you want to influence how a customer feels about your product, provide an experience that creates the desired emotion. One of the best ways for a customer to experience your complex product is by sharing a vivid customer story. Research has shown that stories can activate the region of the brain that processes sights, sounds, tastes, and movement.[4] Contrast this approach with that of a salesperson delivering a data dump in the form of an 85-slide PowerPoint presentation.

Rather than thinking of the emotional mind as irrational, think of it this way: An emotion is simply the way the unconscious communicates its decision to the conscious mind.

MICHAEL D. HARRIS is the CEO of Insight Demand and the author of *Insight Selling: Surprising Research on What Sales Winners Do Differently* (Wiley, 2014).

Notes

1. N. Cowan, "The Magical Number 4 in Short-Term Memory: A Reconsideration of Mental Storage Capacity," *Behavioral Brain Science* 24, no. 1 (February 2001): 87–114.
2. A. Bechara et al., "Insensitivity to Future Consequences Following Damage to Human Prefrontal Cortex," *Cognition* 50, no. 1–3 (April–June 1995): 7–15.

3. M. S. Gazzaniga, "The Split Brain Revisited," *Scientific American*, July 1, 1998.
4. G. Everding, "Readers Build Vivid Mental Simulations of Narrative Situations, Brain Scans Suggest," Medical Xpress, January 26, 2009, https://medicalxpress .com/news/2009-01-readers-vivid-mental-simulations -narrative.html.

Reprinted from hbr.org, originally published
January 26, 2015 (product #H01U9Y).

Index

How to be human at work.

HBR's Emotional Intelligence Series features smart, essential reading on the human side of professional life from the pages of *Harvard Business Review*. Each book in the series offers uplifting stories, practical advice, and research from leading experts on how to tend to our emotional well-being at work.

Harvard Business Review Emotional Intelligence Series

Available in paperback or ebook format. The specially priced six-volume set includes:

- Mindfulness
- Resilience
- Influence and Persuasion

- Authentic Leadership
- Happiness
- Empathy

HBR.ORG

Buy for your team, clients, or event.
Visit hbr.org/bulksales for quantity discount rates.

Empathy

HBR EMOTIONAL INTELLIGENCE SERIES

HBR Emotional Intelligence Series

How to be human at work

The HBR Emotional Intelligence Series features smart, essential reading on the human side of professional life from the pages of *Harvard Business Review*.

Empathy

Happiness

Mindfulness

Resilience

Other books on emotional intelligence from *Harvard Business Review*:

HBR's 10 Must Reads on Emotional Intelligence

HBR Guide to Emotional Intelligence

Empathy

HBR EMOTIONAL INTELLIGENCE SERIES

Harvard Business Review Press

Boston, Massachusetts

HBR Press Quantity Sales Discounts

Harvard Business Review Press titles are available at significant quantity discounts when purchased in bulk for client gifts, sales promotions, and premiums. Special editions, including books with corporate logos, customized covers, and letters from the company or CEO printed in the front matter, as well as excerpts of existing books, can also be created in large quantities for special needs.

For details and discount information for both print and ebook formats, contact booksales@harvardbusiness.org, tel. 800-988-0886, or www.hbr .org/bulksales.

Copyright 2017 Harvard Business School Publishing Corporation
All rights reserved
Printed in the United States of America

23   22   21   20   19   18   17   16   15   14

No part of this publication may be reproduced, stored in or introduced into a retrieval system, or transmitted, in any form, or by any means (electronic, mechanical, photocopying, recording, or otherwise), without the prior permission of the publisher. Requests for permission should be directed to permissions@hbsp.harvard.edu, or mailed to Permissions, Harvard Business School Publishing, 60 Harvard Way, Boston, Massachusetts 02163.

The web addresses referenced in this book were live and correct at the time of the book's publication but may be subject to change.

Library of Congress Cataloging-in-Publication Data

Title: Empathy.
Other titles: HBR emotional intelligence series.
Description: Boston, Massachusetts : Harvard Business Review Press, [2017] | Series: HBR emotional intelligence series
Identifiers: LCCN 2016056297 | ISBN 9781633693258 (pbk.)
Subjects: LCSH: Empathy. | Management.
Classification: LCC BF575.E55 E45 2017 | DDC 152.4/1—dc23 LC record available at https://lccn.loc.gov/2016056297

ISBN: 978-1-63369-325-8
eISBN: 978-1-63369-326-5

The paper used in this publication meets the requirements of the American National Standard for Permanence of Paper for Publications and Documents in Libraries and Archives Z39.48-1992.

Contents

Contents

Contents

Empathy

1

What Is Empathy?

By Daniel Goleman

The word "attention" comes from the Latin *attendere*, meaning "to reach toward." This is a perfect definition of focus on others, which is the foundation of empathy and of an ability to build social relationships—the second and third pillars of emotional intelligence (the first is self-awareness).

Executives who can effectively focus on others are easy to recognize. They are the ones who find common ground, whose opinions carry the most weight, and with whom other people want to work. They emerge as natural leaders regardless of organizational or social rank.

The Empathy Triad

We talk about empathy most commonly as a single attribute. But a close look at where leaders are focusing when they exhibit it reveals three distinct kinds of empathy, each important for leadership effectiveness:

- *Cognitive empathy*: the ability to understand another person's perspective

- *Emotional empathy*: the ability to feel what someone else feels

- *Empathic concern*: the ability to sense what another person needs from you

Cognitive empathy enables leaders to explain themselves in meaningful ways—a skill essential to getting the best performance from their direct reports. Contrary to what you might expect, exercising cognitive empathy requires leaders to think about feelings rather than to feel them directly.

An inquisitive nature feeds cognitive empathy. As one successful executive with this trait puts it, "I've always just wanted to learn everything, to understand anybody that I was around—why they thought what they did, why they did what they did, what worked for them and what didn't work." But cognitive empathy is also an outgrowth of self-awareness. The executive circuits that allow us to think about our own thoughts and to monitor the feelings that flow from them let us apply the same reasoning to other people's minds when we choose to direct our attention that way.

Emotional empathy is important for effective mentoring, managing clients, and reading group dynamics. It springs from ancient parts of the brain beneath the cortex—the amygdala, the hypothalamus, the hippocampus, and the orbitofrontal cortex—that allow us to feel fast without thinking deeply. They tune us in by arousing in our bodies the emotional states of others: I literally feel your pain. My brain patterns match up with yours when I listen to you tell a gripping story. As Tania Singer, the director of the social neuroscience department at the Max Planck Institute for Human Cognitive and Brain Sciences, in Leipzig, Germany, says, "You need to understand your own feelings to understand the feelings of others." Accessing your capacity for emotional empathy depends on combining two kinds of attention: a deliberate focus on your own echoes of someone else's feelings and an open awareness of that person's face, voice, and other external signs of emotion. (See the sidebar "When Empathy Needs to Be Learned.")

WHEN EMPATHY NEEDS TO BE LEARNED

Emotional empathy can be developed. That's the conclusion suggested by research conducted with physicians by Helen Riess, the director of the Empathy and Relational Science Program at Boston's Massachusetts General Hospital. To help the physicians monitor

(Continued)

themselves, Riess set up a program in which they learned to focus using deep, diaphragmatic breathing and to cultivate a certain detachment—to watch an interaction from the ceiling, as it were, rather than being lost in their own thoughts and feelings. "Suspending your own involvement to observe what's going on gives you a mindful awareness of the interaction without being completely reactive," says Riess. "You can see if your own physiology is charged up or balanced. You can notice what's transpiring in the situation." If a doctor realizes that she's feeling irritated, for instance, that may be a signal that the patient is bothered too.

Those who are utterly at a loss may be able to prime emotional empathy essentially by faking it until they make it, Riess adds. If you act in a caring way—looking people in the eye and paying attention to their expressions, even when you don't particularly want to—you may start to feel more engaged.

Empathic concern, which is closely related to emotional empathy, enables you to sense not just how people feel but what they need from you. It's what you want in your doctor, your spouse—and your boss. Empathic concern has its roots in the circuitry that compels parents' attention to their children. Watch where people's eyes go when someone brings an adorable baby into a room, and you'll see this mammalian brain center leaping into action.

Research suggests that as people rise through the ranks, their ability to maintain personal connections suffers.

One neural theory holds that the response is triggered in the amygdala by the brain's radar for sensing danger and in the prefrontal cortex by the release of oxytocin, the chemical for caring. This implies that empathic concern is a double-edged feeling. We intuitively experience the distress of another as our own. But in deciding whether we will meet that person's needs, we deliberately weigh how much we value his or her well-being.

Getting this intuition-deliberation mix right has great implications. Those whose sympathetic feelings become too strong may themselves suffer. In the helping professions, this can lead to compassion fatigue; in executives, it can create distracting feelings of anxiety about people and circumstances that are beyond anyone's control. But those who protect themselves by deadening their feelings may lose touch with empathy. Empathic concern requires us to manage our personal distress without numbing ourselves to the pain of others. (See the sidebar "When Empathy Needs to Be Controlled.")

DANIEL GOLEMAN is a codirector of the Consortium for Research on Emotional Intelligence in Organizations at Rutgers University, coauthor of *Primal Leadership: Leading with Emotional Intelligence* (Harvard Business Review Press, 2013), and author of *The Brain and Emotional Intelligence: New Insights* and *Leadership: Selected Writings* (More Than Sound, 2011). His latest book is *A Force For Good: The Dalai Lama's Vision for Our World* (Bantam, 2015).

Excerpted from "The Focused Leader," adapted from *Harvard Business Review*, December 2013 (product #R1312B).

WHEN EMPATHY NEEDS TO BE CONTROLLED

Getting a grip on our impulse to empathize with other people's feelings can help us make better decisions when someone's emotional flood threatens to over-whelm us.

Ordinarily, when we see someone pricked with a pin, our brains emit a signal indicating that our own pain centers are echoing that distress. But physicians learn in medical school to block even such automatic responses. Their attentional anesthetic seems to be deployed by the temporal-parietal junction and re-gions of the prefrontal cortex, a circuit that boosts concentration by tuning out emotions. That's what is happening in your brain when you distance yourself from others in order to stay calm and help them. The same neural network kicks in when we see a problem in an emotionally overheated environment and need to focus on looking for a solution. If you're talking with someone who is upset, this system helps you understand the person's perspective intellectually by shifting from the heart-to-heart of emotional empathy to the head-to-heart of cognitive empathy.

What's more, some lab research suggests that the appropriate application of empathic concern is critical to making moral judgments. Brain scans have revealed that when volunteers listened to tales of people being subjected to physical pain, their own brain centers for experiencing such pain lit up instantly. But if the story was about psychological suffering, the higher brain centers involved in empathic concern and compassion took longer to activate. Some time is needed to grasp the psychological and moral dimensions of a situation. The more distracted we are, the less we can cultivate the subtler forms of empathy and compassion.

2

Why Compassion Is a Better Managerial Tactic Than Toughness

By Emma Seppala

S tanford University neurosurgeon James Doty
tells the story of performing surgery on a little
boy's brain tumor. In the middle of the procedure, the resident who is assisting him gets distracted
and accidentally pierces a vein. With blood shedding
everywhere, Doty is no longer able to see the delicate
brain area he is working on. The boy's life is at stake.
Doty is left with no other choice than to blindly reach
into the affected area in the hopes of locating and
clamping the vein. Fortunately, he is successful.

Most of us are not brain surgeons, but we certainly
are all confronted with situations in which an employee makes a grave mistake, potentially ruining a

critical project. The question is: How should we react when an employee is not performing well or makes a mistake?

Frustration is of course the natural response—and one we all can identify with. Especially if the mistake hurts an important project or reflects badly on us.

The traditional approach is to reprimand the employee in some way. The hope is that some form of punishment will be beneficial: It will teach the employee a lesson. Expressing our frustration also may relieve us of the stress and anger caused by the mistake. Finally, it may help the rest of the team stay on their toes to avoid making future errors.

Some managers, however, choose a different response when confronted by an underperforming employee: compassion and curiosity. Not that a part of them isn't frustrated or exasperated—maybe they still worry about how their employee's mistakes will reflect back on them—but they are somehow able to suspend judgment and may even be able to use the moment to do a bit of coaching.

What does research say is best? The more compassionate response will get you more powerful results.

First, compassion and curiosity increase employee loyalty and trust. Research has shown that feelings of warmth and positive relationships at work have a greater say over an employee's loyalty than the size of his or her paycheck.[1] In particular, a study by Jonathan Haidt of New York University shows that the more employees look up to their leaders and are moved by their compassion or kindness (a state he terms "elevation"), the more loyal they become to him or her.[2] So if you are more compassionate to your employee, not only will he or she be more loyal to you, but anyone else who has witnessed your behavior may also experience elevation and feel more devoted to you.

Conversely, responding with anger or frustration erodes loyalty. As Adam Grant, professor at the Wharton Business School and author of *Give and Take*, points out that, because of the law of reciprocity, if you embarrass or blame an employee too

17

harshly, your reaction may end up coming around to haunt you. "Next time you need to rely on that employee, you may have lost some of the loyalty that was there before," he told me.

We are especially sensitive to signs of trustworthiness in our leaders, and compassion increases our willingness to trust.[3] Simply put, our brains respond more positively to bosses who have shown us empathy, as neuroimaging research confirms.[4] Employee trust *in turn* improves performance.[5]

Doty, who is also director of Stanford University's Center for Compassion and Altruism Research and Education, recalls his first experience in the operating room. He was so nervous that he perspired profusely. Soon enough, a drop of sweat fell into the operation site and contaminated it. The operation was a simple one, and the patients' life was in no way at stake. As for the operation site, it could have been easily irrigated. However, the operating surgeon—one of the biggest names in surgery at the time—was so angry that he kicked Doty out of the OR. Doty recalls returning home and crying tears of devastation.

Tellingly, Doty explains in an interview how, if the surgeon had acted differently, he would have gained Doty's undying loyalty. "If the surgeon, instead of raging, had said something like: 'Listen young man, look what just happened—you contaminated the field. I know you're nervous. You can't be nervous if you want to be a surgeon. Why don't you go outside and take a few minutes to collect yourself. Readjust your cap in such a way that the sweat doesn't pour down your face. Then come back and I'll show you something.' Well, then he would have been my hero forever."

Not only does an angry response erode loyalty and trust, it also inhibits creativity by jacking up the employee's stress level. As Doty explains, "Creating an environment where there is fear, anxiety, and lack of trust makes people shut down. If people have fear and anxiety, we know from neuroscience that their threat response is engaged, and their cognitive control is impacted. As a consequence, their productivity and creativity diminish." For instance, brain-imaging studies show that when we feel safe, our brain's stress response is lower.[6]

Grant also agrees that "when you respond in a frustrated, furious manner, the employee becomes less likely to take risks in the future because he or she worries about the negative consequences of making mistakes. In other words, you kill the culture of experimentation that is critical to learning and innovation." Grant refers to research by Fiona Lee at the University of Michigan that shows that promoting a culture of safety—rather than of fear of negative consequences—helps encourage the spirit of experimentation that is so critical for creativity.[7]

There is, of course, a reason we feel anger. Research shows that feelings of anger can have beneficial results. For example, they can give us the energy to stand up against injustice.[8] Moreover, they make us appear more powerful.[9] However, when as a leader you express negative emotions like anger, your employees actually view you as less effective.[10] Conversely, being likable and projecting warmth—not toughness—gives leaders a distinct advantage, as Amy Cuddy of Harvard Business School has shown.[11]

So how can you respond with more compassion the next time an employee makes a serious mistake?

1. Take a moment. Doty explains that the first thing to do is to get a handle on your own emotions—anger, frustration, or whatever the case may be. "You have to take a step back and control your own emotional response, because if you act out of emotional engagement, you are not thoughtful about your approach to the problem. By stepping back and taking a period of time to reflect, you enter a mental state that allows for a more thoughtful, reasonable, and discerned response." Practicing meditation can help improve your self-awareness and emotional control.[12]

You don't want to operate from a place where you are just pretending not to be angry. Research shows that this kind of pretense actually ends up raising heart rates for both you and your employee.[13] Instead, take some time to cool off so you can see the situation with more detachment.

2. Put yourself in your employee's shoes. Taking a step back will help give you the ability to empathize with your employee. Why was Doty, in the near-tragic moment in the operating room, able to respond productively rather than with anger? As a consequence of recalling his own first experience in the OR, he could identify and empathize with the resident. This allowed him to curb his frustration, avoid degrading the already horrified resident, and maintain the presence of mind to save a little boy's life.

The ability to perspective-take is a valuable one. Studies have shown that it helps you see aspects of the situation you may not have noticed and leads to better results in interactions and negotiations.[14] And because positions of power tend to lower our natural inclination for empathy, it is particularly important that managers have the self-awareness to make sure they practice seeing situations from their employee's perspective.[15]

3. Forgive. Empathy, of course, helps you forgive. Forgiveness not only strengthens your relationship with your employee by promoting loyalty, it turns out that it is also good for you. Whereas carrying a grudge is bad for your heart (blood pressure and heart rate both go up), forgiveness lowers both your blood pressure *and* that of the person you're forgiving.[16] Other studies show that forgiveness makes you happier and more satisfied with life, significantly reducing stress and negative emotions.[17]

When trust, loyalty, and creativity are high and stress is low, employees are happier and more productive, and turnover is lower.[18] Positive interactions even make employees healthier and require fewer sick days.[19] Other studies have shown how compassionate management leads to improvements in customer service and client outcomes and satisfaction.[20]

Doty told me he's never thrown anyone out of his OR. "It's not that I let them off the hook, but by choosing a compassionate response when they know they have made a mistake, they are not destroyed, they have learned a lesson, and they want to improve for you because you've been kind to them."

EMMA SEPPALA, PH.D., is the Science Director of Stanford University's Center for Compassion and Altruism Research and Education and author of *The Happiness Track*. She is also founder of Fulfillment Daily. Follow her on Twitter @emmaseppala or her website www.emmaseppala.com.

Notes

1. "Britain's Workers Value Companionship and Recognition Over a Big Salary, a Recent Report Revealed," AAT press release, July 15, 2014, https://www.aat.org.uk/about-aat/press-releases/britains-workers-value-companionship-recognition-over-big-salary.
2. T. Qiu et al., "The Effect of Interactional Fairness on the Performance of Cross-Functional Product Develop-

ment Teams: A Multilevel Mediated Model," *The Journal of Product Innovation Management* 26, no. 2 (March 2009): 173–187.

3. K. T. Dirks et al., "Trust in Leadership: Meta-Analytic Findings and Implications for Research and Practice," *Journal of Applied Psychology* 87, no 4 (August 2002): 611–628.

4. R. Boyatzis et al., "Examination of the Neural Substrates Activated in Memories of Experiences with Resonant and Dissonant Leaders," *The Leadership Quarterly* 23, no. 2 (April 2012): 259–272.

5. T. Bartram et al., "The Relationship between Leadership and Follower In-Role Performance and Satisfaction with the Leader: The Mediating Effects of Empowerment and Trust in the Leader," *Leadership & Organization Development Journal* 28, no. 1, (2007): 4–19.

6. L. Norman et al., "Attachment-Security Priming Attenuates Amygdala Activation to Social and Linguistic Threat," *Social Cognitive and Affective Neuroscience*, Advance Access, November 5, 2014, http://scan.oxfordjournals.org/content/early/2014/11/05/scan.nsu127.

7. F. Lee et al., "The Mixed Effects of Inconsistency on Experimentation in Organizations," *Organization Science* 15, no. 3 (2004): 310–326.

8. D. Lindebaum and P. J. Jordan, "When It Can Feel Good to Feel Bad and Bad to Feel Good: Exploring Asymmetries in Workplace Emotional Outcomes," *Human Relations*, August 27, 2014, http://hum.sagepub.com/content/early/2014/07/09/0018726714535824.full.

9. L. Z. Tiedens, "Anger and Advancement Versus Sadness and Subjugation: The Effect of Negative Emotion Expressions on Social Status Conferral," *Journal of Personality and Social Psychology* 80, no. 1 (January 2001): 86–94.

10. K. M. Lewis, "When Leaders Display Emotion: How Followers Respond to Negative Emotional Expression of Male and Female Leaders," *Journal of Organizational Behavior* 21, no. 1 (March 2000): 221–234.

11. E. Seppala, "The Hard Data on Being a Nice Boss," *Harvard Business Review*, November 24, 2014, https://hbr.org/2014/11/the-hard-data-on-being-a-nice-boss; and A. J. C. Cuddy et al., "Connect, Then Lead," *Harvard Business Review* (July–August 2013).

12. "Know Thyself: How Mindfulness Can Improve Self-Knowledge," Association for Psychological Science, March 14, 2013, http://www.psychologicalscience.org/index.php/news/releases/know-thyself-how-mindfulness-can-improve-self-knowledge.html.

13. E. Butler et al., "The Social Consequences of Expressive Suppression," *Emotion* 3, no. 1 (2013): 48–67.

14. A. Galinsky, et al., "Why It Pays to Get Inside the Head of Your Opponent: The Differential Effects of Perspective Taking and Empathy in Negotiations," *Psychological Science* 19, no. 4 (April 2008): 378–384.

15. L. Solomon, "Becoming Powerful Makes You Less Empathetic," *Harvard Business Review*, April 21, 2015, https://hbr.org/2015/04/becoming-powerful-makes-you-less-empathetic.

16. P. A. Hannon et al., "The Soothing Effects of Forgiveness on Victims' and Perpetrators' Blood Pressure," *Personal Relationships* 19, no. 2 (June 2012): 279–289.

17. G. Bono et al., "Forgiveness, Feeling Connected to Others, and Well-Being: Two Longitudinal Studies," *Personality and Social Psychology Bulletin* 34, no. 2 (February 2008): 182–195; and K. A. Lawler, "The Unique Effects of Forgiveness on Health: An Exploration of Pathways," *Journal of Behavioral Medicine* 28, no. 2 (April 2005): 157–167.

18. American Psychological Association, "By the Numbers: A Psychologically Healthy Workplace Fact Sheet," *Good Company Newsletter*, November 20, 2013, http://www.apaexcellence.org/resources/goodcompany/newsletter/article/487.

19. E. D. Heaphy and J. E. Dutton; "Positive Social Interactions and the Human Body at Work: Linking Organizations and Physiology," *Academy of Management Review* 33, no. 1 (2008): 137–162; and S. Azagba and M. Sharaf, "Psychosocial Working Conditions and the Utilization of Health Care Services," *BMC Public Health* 11, no. 642 (2011).

20. S. G. Barsdale and D. E. Gibson, "Why Does Affect Matter in Organizations?" *Academy of Management Perspectives* 21, no. 1 (February 2007): 36–59; and S. G. Barsdale and O. A. O'Neill, "What's Love Got to Do with It? A Longitudinal Study of the Culture of Companionate Love and Employee and Client Outcomes in the Long-Term

Care Setting," *Administrative Science Quarterly* 59, no. 4 (December 2014): 551–598.

Adapted from content posted on hbr.org
on May 7, 2015 (product #H021MP).

3

What Great Listeners Actually Do

By Jack Zenger and Joseph Folkman

C hances are you think you're a good listener. People's appraisal of their listening ability is much like their assessment of their driving skills, in that the great bulk of adults think they're above average.

In our experience, most people think good listening comes down to doing three things:

- Not talking when others are speaking

- Letting others know you're listening through facial expressions and verbal sounds ("Mm-hmm")

- Being able to repeat what others have said, practically word for word

In fact, much management advice on listening suggests that people should do these very things—encouraging listeners to remain quiet, nod and "mm-hmm" encouragingly, and then repeat back to the talker something like, "So, let me make sure I understand. What you're saying is . . ." However, recent research that we've conducted suggests that these behaviors fall far short of describing good listening skills.

We analyzed data that describes the behavior of 3,492 participants in a development program designed to help managers become better coaches. As part of this program, participants' coaching skills were evaluated through 360-degree assessments. We identified the individuals who were perceived as being the most effective listeners (the top 5%). We then compared the best listeners with the average of all other people in the data set and identified the 20 characteristics that seemed to set them apart. With those results in hand we identified the factors that differed between great and average listeners and analyzed the data to determine which characteristics their colleagues identified as the behaviors that made them outstanding listeners.

We found some surprising characteristics, along with some qualities we expected to hear. We grouped them into four main findings:

- *Good listening is much more than being silent while the other person talks.* To the contrary, people perceive the best listeners to be those who periodically ask questions that promote discovery and insight. These questions gently challenge old assumptions but do so in a constructive way. Sitting there silently nodding does not provide sure evidence that a person is listening, but asking a good question tells the speaker the listener has not only heard what was said but that they comprehended it well enough to want additional information. Good listening was consistently seen as a two-way dialogue, rather than a one-way "speaker versus hearer" interaction. The best conversations were active.

- *Good listening includes interactions that build up a person's self-esteem.* The best listeners make the conversation a positive experience for the other party, which doesn't happen when the listener is passive (or critical, for that matter). Good listeners make the other person feel supported and convey confidence in the speaker. Good listening is characterized by the creation of a safe environment in which issues and differences can be discussed openly.

- *Good listening is seen as a cooperative conversation.* In the interactions we studied, feedback flowed smoothly in both directions with neither party becoming defensive about comments the other made. By contrast, poor listeners were seen as competitive—as listening only to identify errors in reasoning or logic, using their silence as a chance to prepare their next response. That might make you an excellent debater, but it doesn't make you a good listener. Good listeners may challenge assumptions and disagree, but the person being listened to feels the listener is trying to help rather than trying to win an argument.

- *Good listeners tend to make suggestions.* In the study, good listening invariably included some feedback that was provided in a way others would accept and that opened up alternative paths to consider. This finding somewhat surprised us, since it's not uncommon to hear complaints that "So-and-so didn't listen, he just jumped in and tried to solve the problem." Perhaps what the data is telling us is that making suggestions is not itself the problem; it may be more about the skill with which those suggestions are made. Another possibility is that we're more likely to accept suggestions from people we already think are good listeners. (Someone who is silent for the whole conversation and then jumps in with a suggestion may not be seen as credible. Someone who seems combative or critical and then tries to give advice may not be seen as trustworthy.)

While many of us may think of being a good listener like being a sponge that accurately absorbs what the other person is saying, what these findings show is that instead, good listeners are like trampolines: You can bounce ideas off of them, and rather than absorbing your ideas and energy, they amplify, energize, and clarify your thinking. They make you feel better not by merely passively absorbing, but by actively supporting. This lets you gain energy and height, just like a trampoline.

Of course, there are different levels of listening. Not every conversation requires the highest levels of listening, but many conversations would benefit from greater focus and listening skill. Consider which level of listening you'd like to aim for.

> *Level 1*: The listener creates a safe environment in which difficult, complex, or emotional issues can be discussed.

> *Level 2*: The listener clears away distractions like phones and laptops, focusing attention on the other person and making appropriate eye contact. (This behavior not only affects how you are perceived as the listener; it immediately influences the listener's *own* attitudes and inner feelings. Acting the part changes how you feel inside. This in turn makes you a better listener.)

> *Level 3*: The listener seeks to understand the substance of what the other person is saying.

They capture ideas, ask questions, and restate issues to confirm that their understanding is correct.

Level 4: The listener observes nonverbal cues, such as facial expressions, perspiration, respiration rates, gestures, posture, and numerous other subtle body language signals. It is estimated that 80% of what we communicate comes from these signals. It sounds strange to some, but you listen with your eyes as well as your ears.

Level 5: The listener increasingly understands the other person's emotions and feelings about the topic at hand and identifies and acknowledges them. The listener empathizes with and validates those feelings in a supportive, nonjudgmental way.

Level 6: The listener asks questions that clarify assumptions the other person holds and helps the other person see the issue in a new light. This could include the listener injecting some thoughts and ideas about the topic that could be useful to the other person. However, good listeners never highjack the conversation so that they or their issues become the subject of the discussion.

Each of the levels builds on the others; thus, if you've been criticized for offering solutions rather than listening, it may mean you need to attend to some of the other levels (such as clearing away distractions or empathizing) before your proffered suggestions can be appreciated.

We suspect that in being a good listener, most of us are more likely to stop short rather than go too far. Our hope is that this research will help by providing a new perspective on listening. We hope those who labor under an illusion of superiority about their listening skills will see where they really stand. We also hope the common perception that good listening is mainly about acting like an absorbent sponge will wane. Finally, we hope all will see that the highest and best form of listening comes in playing the same role for the other person that a trampoline would play for a child: It gives energy, acceleration, height, and amplification. These are the hallmarks of great listening.

JACK ZENGER is the CEO and JOSEPH FOLKMAN is President of Zenger Folkman, a leadership development consultancy. They are coauthors of the October 2011 HBR article "Making Yourself Indispensable" and the book *How to Be Exceptional: Drive Leadership Success by Magnifying Your Strengths* (McGraw-Hill, 2012).

Adapted from content posted on hbr.org
on July 14, 2016 (product #H030DC).

4

Empathy Is Key to a Great Meeting

By Annie McKee

Yes, we all hate meetings. Yes, they are usually a waste of time. And yes, they're here to stay. So it's your responsibility as a leader to make them better. This doesn't mean just making them shorter, more efficient, and more organized. People need to enjoy them and, dare I say it, have fun.

Happiness matters a lot at work. How could it not, when many of us spend most of our waking hours there. The alternatives—chronic frustration, discontent, and outright hatred of our jobs—are simply not acceptable. Negative feelings interfere with creativity and innovation, not to mention collaboration.[1] And let's face it: Meetings are, for the most part, still where lots of collaboration, creativity, and innovation happen.[2] If meetings aren't working, then chances are we're not able to do what we need to do.

So how do we fix meetings so they are more enjoyable and produce more positive feelings? Sure, invite the right people, create better agendas, and be better prepared. Those are baseline fixes. But if you really want to improve how people work together at meetings, you'll need to rely on—and maybe develop—a couple of key emotional intelligence competencies: empathy and emotional self-management.

Why empathy? Empathy is a competency that allows you to read people. Who is supporting whom? Who is pissed off, and who is coasting? Where is the resistance? This isn't as easy as it seems. Sometimes, the smartest resisters often look like supporters, but they're not supportive at all. They're smart, sneaky idea killers.

Carefully reading people will also help you understand the major and often hidden conflicts in the group. Hint: These conflicts probably have nothing to do with the topics discussed or decisions being made at the meeting. They are far more likely to be linked to very human dynamics like who is allowed to influence whom (headquarters vs. the field, expats vs. local nationals) and power dynamics between genders and among people of various races.

Empathy lets you see and manage these power dynamics. Many of us would like to think that these sorts of concerns—and office politics in general—are beneath us, unimportant, or just for those Machiavellian folks we all dislike. Realistically, though, power is hugely important in groups because it is the real currency in most organizations. And it plays out in meetings. Learning to read how the flow of power is moving and shifting can help you lead the meeting— and everything else.

Keep in mind that employing empathy will help you understand how people are responding to *you*. As a leader you may be the most powerful person at the meeting. Some people, the dependent types, will defer at every turn. That feels good, for a minute. Carry on that way, and you're likely to create a dependent group—or one that is polarized between those who will do anything you want and those who will not.

This is where emotional self-management comes in, for a couple of reasons. First, take a look at the dependent folks in your meetings. Again, it can feel really good to have people admire you and agree with your every word. In fact, this can be a huge relief in our conflict-ridden organizations. But again, if you don't manage your response, you will make group dynamics worse. You will also look like a fool. Others are reading the group, too, and they will rightly read that you like it when people go along with you. They will see that you are falling prey to your own ego or to those who want to please or manipulate you.

Second, strong emotions set the tone for the entire group. We take our cue from one another about how to feel about what's going on around us. Are we in danger? Is there cause for celebration? Should we be fed up and cynical or hopeful and committed? Here's why this matters in meetings: If you, as a leader, effectively project out your more positive emotions, such as hope and enthusiasm, others will "mirror" these feelings and the general tone of the group will be marked by optimism and a sense of "we're in this together, and we can do it."[3] And there is a strong neurological link between feelings and cognition. We think more clearly and more creatively when our feelings are largely positive and when we are appropriately challenged.[4]

The other side of the coin is obvious. Your negative emotions are also contagious, and they are almost always destructive if unchecked and unmanaged. Express anger, contempt, or disrespect, and you will definitely push people into fight mode—individually and collectively. Express disdain, and you'll alienate people far beyond the end of the meeting. And it doesn't matter who you feel this way about. All it takes is for people to see it, and they will catch it—and worry that next time your target will be them.

This is not to say that all positive emotions are good all the time or that you should never express negative emotions. The point is that the leader's emotions are highly infectious. Know this and manage your feelings accordingly to create the kind of environment where people can work together to make decisions and get things done.

It may go without saying, but you can't do any of this with your phone on. As Daniel Goleman shares in his book *Focus: The Hidden Driver of Excellence*, we are not nearly as good at multitasking as we think we are. Actually we stink at it. So turn it off and pay attention to the people you are with today.

In the end, it's your job to make sure people leave your meeting feeling pretty good about what's happened, their contributions, and you as the leader. Empathy allows you to read what's going on, and self-management helps you move the group to a mood that supports getting things done—and happiness.

ANNIE MCKEE is a senior fellow at the University of Pennsylvania, director of the PennCLO Executive Doctoral Program, and the founder of the Teleos Leadership Institute. She is the coauthor, with Daniel Goleman and Richard Boyatzis, of *Pri-*

mal Leadership (Harvard Business Review Press, 2013) as well as a coauthor of *Resonant Leadership* (Harvard Business Review Press, 2005) and *Becoming a Resonant Leader* (Harvard Business Review Press, 2008). Her new book, *How to Be Happy at Work*, is forthcoming from Harvard Business Review Press.

Notes

1. D. Goleman et al., *Primal Leadership: Unleashing the Power of Emotional Intelligence* (rev. ed.) (Boston: Harvard Business Review Press, 2013).
2. K. D'Costa, "Why Do We Need to Have So Many Meetings?" *Scientific American*, November 17, 2014, https://blogs.scientificamerican.com/anthropology-in-practice/why-do-we-need-to-have-so-many-meetings/.
3. V. Ramachandran, "The Neurons That Shaped Civilization," TED talk, November 2009, https://www.ted.com/talks/vs_ramachandran_the_neurons_that_shaped_civilization?language=en.
4. M. Csikzsentmihalyi, *Creativity: Flow and the Psychology of Discovery and Invention* (New York: Harper Perennial, 1997).

Adapted from content posted on hbr.org
on March 23, 2015 (product #H01YDY).

5

It's Harder to Empathize with People If You've Been in Their Shoes

By Rachel Ruttan, Mary-Hunter McDonnell, and Loran Nordgren

magine that you have just become a new parent. Overwhelmed and exhausted, your performance at work is suffering. You desperately want to work from home part time to devote more attention to your family. One of your supervisors has had children while climbing the corporate ladder, while the other hasn't. Which supervisor is more likely to embrace your request?

Most people would recommend approaching the supervisor who has children, drawing on the intuition that shared experience breeds empathy. After all, she has "been there" and thus would seem best placed to understand your situation.

Our recent research suggests that this instinct is very often wrong.[1]

In a series of recent experiments, we found that people who have endured challenges in the past (like divorce or being skipped over for a promotion) were less likely to show compassion for someone facing the same struggle, compared with people with no experience in that particular situation.

In the first experiment, we surveyed people participating in a "polar plunge": a jump into a very icy Lake Michigan in March. All participants read a story about a man named Pat who intended to complete the plunge but chickened out and withdrew from the event at the last minute. Critically, participants read about Pat either before they had completed the plunge themselves or one week after. We found that polar plungers who had successfully completed the plunge were less compassionate and more contemptuous of Pat than were those who had not yet completed the plunge.

In another study, we looked at compassion toward an individual struggling with unemployment. More than 200 people read a story about a man who—despite his best efforts—is unable to find a job. Struggling to make ends meet, the man ultimately stoops to selling drugs in order to earn money. We found that people who had overcome a period of unemployment in the past were less compassionate and more judgmental of the man than people who were currently unemployed or had never been involuntarily unemployed.

A third study examined compassion toward a bullied teenager. Participants were told either that the teen was successfully coping with the bullying or that he failed to cope by lashing out violently. Compared with participants who had no experience with bullying, participants who reported having been bullied in the past themselves were more compassionate toward the teen who was appropriately coping with the experience. But, as in our earlier studies, participants who were bullied in the past were the *least* compassionate toward the teen who failed to successfully cope with the bullying.

Taken together, these results suggest that people who have endured a difficult experience are particularly likely to penalize those who struggle to cope with a similar ordeal.

But why does this occur? We suggest that this phenomenon is rooted in two psychological truths.

First, people generally have difficulty accurately recalling just how difficult a past aversive experience was. Though we may remember that a past experience was painful, stressful, or emotionally trying, we tend to underestimate just how painful that experience felt in the moment. This phenomenon is called an "empathy gap."[2]

Second, people who have previously overcome an aversive experience know that they were able to successfully overcome it, which makes them feel especially confident about their understanding of just how difficult the situation is. The combined experience of "I can't recall how difficult it was" and "I know that I got through it myself" creates the perception that the event can be readily conquered, reducing empathy toward others struggling with the event.

This finding seems to run counter to our intuitions. When we asked participants to predict who would show the most compassion for the bullied teenager, for instance—a teacher who'd endured bullying himself or one who never had—an overwhelming 99 out of the 112 people chose the teacher who had been bullied. This means that many people may be instinctively seeking compassion from the very people who are least likely to provide it.

This clearly has implications for peer-to-peer office communication (choose the person you vent to carefully). And mentorship programs, which often pair people from similar backgrounds or experiences, may need to be reexamined. But there are also important lessons for leaders. When approached by employees in distress, leaders may believe that their own emotional reaction to the issue should guide their response. For example, an executive who broke the glass ceiling may focus on her own success when considering an employee's concerns about discrimination. Similarly, managers in overworked industries such as consulting and banking may respond to employees' concerns about burnout and fatigue with comments such as, "I had to work those hours, so why are you complaining?" (And in fact, there is some evidence that this mechanism is at play when older workers push back on reforms designed to help cut down on overwork.)[3]

Simply put, leaders need to get outside of their own heads—to place *less* emphasis, not more, on their own past challenges. To bridge the empathy gap, leaders may be best served by focusing on how upset the other person seems to be or by reminding themselves that many others struggle with the same challenge. Returning to the opening example, the supervisor approached by an exhausted new parent could instead think about the countless other new parents who struggle to find work-life balance, many of whom are ultimately pushed out of the workplace.

When we're trying to encourage someone to be more empathetic, we often say something like, "walk a mile in his shoes." As it turns out, that may be exactly the wrong thing to say to people who have worn those shoes themselves.

RACHEL RUTTAN is a doctoral student at the Kellogg School of Management. MARY-HUNTER MCDONNELL is an assistant professor of management at the Wharton School. LORAN NORDGREN is an associate professor of management and organizations at the Kellogg School of Management.

Notes

1. R. L. Ruttan et al., "Having 'Been There' Doesn't Mean I Care: When Prior Experience Reduces Compassion for Emotional Distress," *Journal of Personality and Social Psychology* 108, no. 4 (April 2015): 610–622.

2. L. F. Nordgren et al., "Visceral Drives in Retrospect: Explanations About the Inaccessible Past," *Psychological Science* 17, no. 7 (July 2006): 635–640.
3. K. C. Kellogg, *Challenging Operations: Medical Reform and Resistance in Surgery* (Chicago: University of Chicago Press, 2011).

Adapted from content posted on hbr.org on
October 20, 2015 (product #H02FKN).

6

Becoming Powerful Makes You Less Empathetic

By Lou Solomon

ast year, I worked with a senior executive—let's call him Steve—who had received feedback from his boss that he was wearing the power of his new title in an off-putting way. Steve's boss told him that he had developed a subtle way of being right in meetings that sucked all the oxygen out of the room. No one wanted to offer ideas once Steve had declared the right answer. Since his promotion, Steve had become less of a team player and more of a superior who knew better than others. In short, he had lost his empathy.

Why does this sort of shift in behavior happen to so many people when they're promoted to the ranks of management? Research shows that personal power actually interferes with our ability to empathize. Dacher Keltner, an author and social psychologist at the University of California, Berkeley, has conducted empirical studies showing that people who have power suffer deficits in empathy, the ability to read emotions, and the ability to adapt behaviors to other people. In fact, power can actually change how the brain functions, according to research from Sukhvinder Obhi, a neuroscientist at Wilfrid Laurier University in Ontario, Canada.[1]

The most common leadership failures don't involve fraud, the embezzlement of funds, or sex scandals. It's more common to see leaders fail in the area of every day self-management—and the use of power in a way that is motivated by ego and self-interest.

How does it happen? Slowly, and then suddenly. It happens with bad mini choices, made perhaps on an unconscious level. It might show up as the subtle act of throwing one's weight around. Demands for special treatment, isolated decision making, and getting one's way. Leaders who are pulled over by the police for speeding or driving drunk become indignant and rail, "Do you know who I am?" Suddenly the story hits social media, and we change our minds about the once-revered personality.

This points to a bigger story about power and fame. How do people start out in pursuit of a dream and wind up aggrandizing themselves instead? They reach a choke point, where they cross over from being generous with their power to using their power for their own benefit.

Take the case of former Charlotte, North Carolina, mayor Patrick Cannon. Cannon came from nothing. He overcame poverty and the violent loss of his father at the age of 5. He earned a degree from North Carolina A&T State University and entered public service at the age of 26, becoming the youngest council member in Charlotte history. He was known for being completely committed to serving the public and generous with the time he spent as a role model for young people.

But in 2014, Cannon, then 47, pleaded guilty to accepting $50,000 in bribes while in office.[2] As he entered the city's federal courthouse, he tripped and fell. The media was there to capture the fall, which was symbolic of the much bigger fall of an elected leader and small business owner who once embodied the very essence of personal achievement against staggering odds. Cannon now has the distinction of being the first mayor in the city's history to be sent to prison. Insiders say he was a good man but all too human, and he seemed vulnerable as he became isolated in his decision making. And while a local minister argued that Cannon's one lapse in judgment should not define the man and his career of exceptional public service, he is now judged only by his weakness: his dramatic move from humility and generosity to corruption. And that image of Cannon tripping on his way into court is now the image that people associate with him.

What can leaders do if they fear that they might be crossing the line from power to abuse of power? First, you must invite other people in. You must be willing to risk vulnerability and ask for feedback. A good executive coach can help you return to a state of empathy and value-driven decisions. However, be sure to ask for feedback from a wide variety of people. Dispense with the softball questions (How am I doing?) and ask the tough ones (How does my style and focus affect my employees?).

Preventive maintenance begins with self-awareness and a daring self-inventory. Here are some important questions to ask yourself:

1. Do you have a support network of friends, family, and colleagues who care about you without the title and can help you stay down-to-earth?

2. Do you have an executive coach, mentor, or confidant?

3. What feedback have you gotten about not walking the talk?

4. Do you demand privileges?

5. Are you keeping the small, inconvenient promises that fall outside of the spotlight?

6. Do you invite others into the spotlight?

7. Do you isolate yourself in the decision-making process? Do the decisions you're making reflect what you truly value?

8. Do you admit your mistakes?

9. Are you the same person at work, at home, and in the spotlight?

10. Do you tell yourself there are exceptions or different rules for people like you?

If a leader earns our trust, we hold them to non-negotiable standards. Nothing will blow up more dramatically than a failure to walk the talk or the selfish abuse of power. We all want our leaders to be highly competent, visionary, take-charge people. However, empathy, authenticity, and generosity are what distinguish competence and greatness. The most self-aware leaders recognize the signals of abuse of power and correct course before it's too late.

LOU SOLOMON is the CEO of Interact, a communications consultancy. She is the author of *Say Something Real* and an adjunct faculty member at the McColl School of Business at Queens University of Charlotte.

Notes

1. J. Hogeveen et al., "Power Changes How the Brain Responds to Others," *Journal of Experimental Psychology* 143, no. 2 (April 2014): 755–762.
2. M. Gordon et al., "Patrick Cannon Pleads Guilty to Corruption Charge," *The Charlotte Observer*, June 3, 2014, www.charlotteobserver.com/news/local/article9127154.html.

Adapted from content posted on hbr.org
on April 21, 2015 (product #H020S0).

7

A Process for Empathetic Product Design

By Jon Kolko

The discipline of product management is shifting from an external focus on the market, or an internal focus on technology, to an empathetic focus on people. While it's not too difficult to rally people around this general idea, it can be hard at first to understand how to translate it into tactics. So in this article, I'll walk through how we applied this approach to a particular product at a startup and how it led to large-scale adoption and, ultimately, the acquisition of the company.

I was previously VP of design at MyEdu, where we focused on helping students succeed in college, show their academic accomplishments, and gain employment. MyEdu started with a series of free academic planning tools, including a schedule planner. As we formalized a business model focused on college recruiting, we conducted behavioral, empathetic research with college students and recruiters. This type of qualitative research focuses on what people do, rather than what they say. We spent hours with students in their dorm rooms, watching them do their homework, watch TV, and register for classes. We watched them being college students, and our goal was not to identify workflow conflicts or utilitarian problems to solve; it was to build a set of intuitive feelings about what it means to be a college student. We conducted the same form of research with recruiters, watching them speak to candidates and work through their hiring process.

This form of research is misleadingly simple—you go and watch people. The challenge is in forging a disarming relationship with people in a very short period of time. Our goal is to form a master and apprentice relationship: We enter these research activities as a humble apprentice, expecting to learn from a master. It may sound a little funny, but college students are masters of being in academia, with all of the successes and failures this experience brings them.

As we complete our research, we transcribe the session in full. This time-consuming effort is critical, because it embeds the participants' collective voice in our heads. As we play, type, pause, and rewind our recordings, we begin to quite literally think from the perspective of the participant. I've found that I can repeat participant quotes and "channel" their voices years after a research session is over. We distribute the transcriptions into thousands of individual utterances, and then we post the utterances all over our war room.

The input of our behavioral research is a profile of the type of people we want to empathize with. The output of our research is a massive data set of verbatim utterances, exploded into individual, moveable parts.

Once we've generated a large quantity of data, our next step is to synthesize the contents into meaningful insights. This is an arduous, seemingly endless process—it will quite literally fill any amount of time you allot to it. We read individual notes, highlight salient points, and move the notes around. We build groups of notes in a bottom-up fashion, identifying similarities and anomalies. We invite the entire product team to participate: If they have 15 or 30 minutes, they are encouraged to pop in, read some notes, and shift them to places that make sense. Over time, the room begins to take shape. As groupings emerge, we give them action-oriented names. Rather than using pithy category labels like "Career Service" or "Employment," we write initial summary statements like "Students write résumés in order to find jobs."

When we've made substantial progress, we begin to provoke introspection on the categories by asking "why"-oriented questions. And the key to the whole process is that we answer these questions *even though we don't know the answer for sure.* We combine what we know about students with what we know about ourselves. We build on our own life experiences, and as we leverage our student-focused empathetic lens, we make inferential leaps. In this way, we drive innovation and simultaneously introduce risk. In this case, we asked the question, "Why do students develop résumés to find jobs?" and answered it, "Because they think employers want to see a résumé." This is what Roger Martin refers to as "abductive reasoning": a form of logical recombination to move past the expected and into the provocative world of innovation.[1]

Finally, when we've answered these "why" questions about each group, we create a series of insight statements, which are provocative statements of truth about human behavior. We'll build upon the why statement, abstracting our answer away from the students we spent time with and making a generalization about *all* students. We asked, "Why do students develop résumés to find jobs?" and we answered it, "Because they think employers want to see a résumé." Now we'll craft an insight statement: "Students think they have an idea of what employers want in a candidate, but they are often wrong." We've shifted from a passive statement to an active assertion. We've made a large inferential leap. And we've arrived at the scaffold for a new product, service, or idea.

We can create a similar provocative statement of truth about recruiters by learning from employers. Based on our research, we identified that recruiters spend very little time with each résumé but have very strong opinions about candidates. Our insight statement becomes "Recruiters make snap judgments, directly impacting a candidate's chances of success." (See table 1.)

The input of our synthesis process is the raw data from research, transcribed and distributed on a large wall. The output of our synthesis process is a series of insights: provocative statements of truth about human behavior.

TABLE 1

Student insight	Employer insight
Students think they have an idea of what employers want in a candidate, but they are often wrong.	**Recruiters make snap judgments, directly impacting a candidate's chances of success.**
"Your résumé is like your life: It is your golden ticket to the chocolate factory."—*Samantha, international business major*	"Don't apply to five of my jobs, because you aren't going to get any of them."—*Meg, recruiter*
• Emphasize bullets on a résumé rather than exhibit skills through artifacts (portfolio) • Think they should have a broad but shallow set of abilities rather than a depth of competency in one area • Typically apply for any and every job	• Form an opinion in seconds based on a single data point • Are looking for specific skills and evidence of competency in that skill • Create a mental narrative of what a candidate can do based on how the student presents herself

Now we can start to merge and compare insights in order to arrive at a value proposition. As we connect the two insights from students and employers and juxtapose them, we can narrow in on a "what-if" opportunity. What if we taught students new ways to think about finding a job? What if we showed students alternative paths to jobs? What if we helped students identify their skills and present them to employers in a credible way? (See table 2.)

If we subtly shift the language, we arrive at a capability value proposition: "MyEdu helps students identify their skills and present them to employers in a credible way."

This value proposition is a promise. We promise to students that if they use our products, we'll help them identify their skills and show those skills to employers. If we fail to deliver on that promise, students have a poor experience with our products—and leave. The same is true for any product or service company. If Comcast promises to deliver internet access to our

TABLE 2

Student insight	Employer Insight
Students think they have an idea of what employers want in a candidate, but they are often wrong.	**Recruiters make snap judgments, directly impacting a candidate's chances of success.**

What-if opportunity:
What if we helped students identify their skills and present them to employees in a credible way?

home but doesn't, we get frustrated. If they fail frequently enough, we dump them for a company with a similar or better value proposition.

Insights act as the input to this phase in the empathetic design process, and the output of this process is an emotionally charged value promise.

Armed with a value proposition, we have constraints around what we're building. In addition to providing an external statement of value, this statement also indicates how we can determine if the capabilities, features, and other details we brainstorm are appropriate to include in the offering. If we dream up a new feature and it doesn't help students identify their skills and present them to employers in a credible way, it's not appropriate for us to build. The value promise becomes the objective criteria in a subjective context, acting as a sieve through which we can pour our good ideas.

Now we tell stories—what we call "hero flows," or the main paths through our products that help people become happy or content. These stories paint a picture of how a person uses our product to receive the value promise. We write these, draw them as stick figures, and start to sketch the real product interfaces. And then, through a fairly standard product development process, we bring these stories to life with wireframes, visual comps, motion studies, and other traditional digital product assets.

Through this process, we developed the MyEdu Profile: a highly visual record that helps students highlight academic accomplishments and present them to employers in the context of recruiting.

During research, we heard from some college students that "LinkedIn makes me feel dumb." They don't have a lot of professional experiences, so asking them to highlight these accomplishments is a nonstarter. But as students use our academic planning tools, their behavior and activities translate to profile elements that highlight their academic accomplishments: We can deliver on our value proposition.

Our value proposition acts as the input to the core of product development. The output of this process is our products, which facilitate the iterative, incremental set of capabilities that shift behavior and help people achieve their wants, needs, and desires.

The LinkedIn example we highlighted illustrates what we call "empathetic research." We marinated in data and persevered through a rigorous process of sense making in order to arrive at insights. We leveraged these insights to provoke a value proposition, and then we built stories on top of the entire scaffold. And as a result of this process, we created a product with emotional resonance. The profile product attracted more than a million college students in about a year, and during a busy academic registration period, we saw growth of between 3,000 to 3,500 new student profiles a day. After we were acquired by education software company Blackboard and integrated this into the flagship learning management system, we saw growth of between 18,000 and 20,000 new student profiles a day.

The process described here is not hard, and it's not new—companies like Frog Design have been leveraging this approach for years, and I learned the fundamentals of empathetic design when I was an undergraduate at Carnegie Mellon. But for most companies, this process requires leaning on a different corporate ideology. It's a process informed by deep qualitative data rather than statistical market data. It celebrates people rather than technology. And it requires identifying and believing in behavioral insights, which are subjective and, in their ambiguity, full of risk.

JON KOLKO is the vice president of design at Blackboard, an education software company, the founder and director of Austin Center for Design, and the author of *Well-Designed: How to Use Empathy to Create Products People Love* (Harvard Business Review Press, 2014).

Note

1. R. Martin, *The Design of Business: Why Design Thinking Is the Next Competitive Advantage* (Boston: Harvard Business Review Press, 2009.)

Adapted from content posted on hbr.org
on April 23, 2015 (product #H0201E).

8

How Facebook Uses Empathy to Keep User Data Safe

By Melissa Luu-Van

Online security often focuses on technical details: software, hardware, vulnerabilities, and the like. But effective security is driven as much by people as it is by technology. After all, the point is to protect the consumers, employees, and partners who use our products.

The ways those people interact with technology and each other can completely change the effectiveness of your security strategy. So security products and tools must take into account the human context of the problems they're solving—and that requires empathy.

At Facebook, empathy helps us create solutions that work because they're designed around our users' experiences and well-being. Specifically, we see three ways to make security efforts more empathetic.

Consumer-driven goals that are actionable and specific. By researching the cultural and physical contexts in which people use the things you produce, you can define better, more precise goals for those products. Engaging with your users on a regular basis—through reporting tools built into your product, online surveys, or focus groups, for example—is a necessary step for understanding, rather than assuming you know, their challenges and needs.

For example, we recently asked several focus groups about their most important security concerns on Facebook. What are they worried about? What would help them feel safe? Overwhelmingly, people told us they wanted more control. Simply knowing that Facebook was working behind the scenes to protect their accounts wasn't enough. We learned that many Facebook users were unaware of all the security features we offer to add extra protection to their accounts. But once they learned about them, they were eager to use them. People also wanted to be able to control these features and to see how each tool protects their account. These findings told us two very important things about the security features. First, they needed to be easier to find. Second, they needed to be more visible and give people more control.

With that in mind, we created Security Checkup, a tool designed to make Facebook's security controls more visible and easier to use. During early testing and after our global launch, we asked people on Facebook about their experience using the new tool. They told us they found Security Checkup useful and helpful; the tool's completion rate quickly soared to over 90%. These results are validating—but not surprising, since we tailored Security Checkup to what we had learned about people's preferences and concerns.

Our primary goal has always been to protect the people who use Facebook, but through our research we've added the goal of helping people better protect themselves wherever they are on the web. The security lessons our users learn on Facebook could help them develop safer online habits—such as using unique passwords or checking app permissions—that can be used on other sites, too.

Collaborative, cross-functional teams. Security is often approached as an engineering-led effort in which cross-functional teams from research, design, or product are less important. However, we've found that disciplines besides engineering are just as critical to the thought process and product development, because diversity of thought is an important characteristic of empathy.

Cross-functional teams are particularly valuable for thinking through the various experiences people may have with a product. Car manufacturers have done this for years, adding seat belts and air bags to keep people safe even when a vehicle performs outside its intended purpose (that is, during a high-speed crash). The cars' designs were changed to make people's experiences safer by default. Similarly, Facebook's security tools are built with the belief that better product design leads to safer behavior. Many of our departments collaborate for this purpose, including research, security, user experience, marketing, product design, and communications.

Throughout various stages of the process, these teams convene to discuss potential engineering, design, or security challenges; identify solutions; and consider the impact any of these things might have on someone's overall experience using our products. We believe this collective expertise helps us avoid possible issues by addressing them early on in the development process. For example, during early iterations of Security Checkup we realized that simply drawing attention to our existing security features was interpreted by some people as a warning or alert that something was wrong. Because we had design and communication experts already working on the development team, we were able to create a security tool with a utilitarian tone to avoid making people feel unnecessarily concerned.

A focus on outcomes rather than inputs. Finally, and most important, empathy helps us keep people safe. If people don't have a safe experience, it doesn't matter how many security tools we make. That's why people's actual outcomes are always our highest priority. Empathy helps in a couple of ways.

First, having empathy for the people who use your products keeps you focused on helping them make small but useful tweaks (rather than major overhauls) to their online behavior. Because online security can be a daunting topic, many people shy away from being proactive about it. So encouraging people to start with small steps can go a long way. We've seen that even incremental progress helps people learn how to recognize risk and make safer choices. Simple behaviors like turning on extra security settings for online accounts can have a huge impact on someone's safety.

Second, using empathetic language in consumer communication makes security less intimidating and more accessible. This means using terms and concepts that are easily understood within local cultural and languages, even if they differ from the terms technical experts would use. Research shows that over time, fearful communications designed to scare people actually have a diminishing rate of return in helping consumers avoid online threats. On the other hand, building resiliency can help people better understand potential threats, recover from mistakes, and identify the most important preventative actions.

If you want to increase empathy on your team, one of the best ways to do it is to invite a diverse set of disciplines to be part of the product development process, both through hiring and through collaborating with other teams. Professionals with experience in psychology, behavioral sciences, or communications can bring invaluable perspectives for building an empathetic team. Then invest in research to understand the experience and security concerns of the people using your products; don't guess or assume you know what they are.

Empathy is not easy. It requires a commitment to deeply understanding the people you're protecting—but it also leads to significantly better security. And that's the whole point.

MELISSA LUU-VAN is a product manager at Facebook, where she leads a cross-functional team focused on helping people maintain access to their accounts and keep them secure.

Adapted from content posted on hbr.org
on April 28, 2016 (product #H02U0U).

9

The Limits of Empathy

By Adam Waytz

A few years ago, Ford Motor Company started asking its (mostly male) engineers to wear the Empathy Belly, a simulator that allows them to experience symptoms of pregnancy first-hand—the back pain, the bladder pressure, the 30 or so pounds of extra weight. They can even feel "movements" that mimic fetal kicking. The idea is to get them to understand the ergonomic challenges that pregnant women face when driving, such as limited reach, shifts in posture and center of gravity, and general bodily awkwardness.

It's unclear whether this has improved Ford's cars or increased customer satisfaction, but the engineers claim benefits from the experience. They're still using the belly; they're also simulating the foggy vision and stiff joints of elderly drivers with an "age suit." If nothing more, these exercises are certainly an attempt to "get the other person's point of view," which Henry Ford once famously said was the key to success.

Empathy is all the rage pretty much everywhere—not just at Ford and not just on engineering and product development teams. It's at the heart of design thinking and innovation more broadly defined. It's also touted as a critical leadership skill—one that helps you influence others in your organization, anticipate stakeholders' concerns, respond to social media followers, and even run better meetings.

But recent research (by me and many others) suggests that all this heat and light may be a bit too intense. Though empathy is essential to leading and managing others—without it, you'll make disastrous decisions and forfeit the benefits just described—

failing to recognize its limits can impair individual and organizational performance.

Here are some of the biggest problems you can run into and recommendations for getting around them.

Problem #1: It's exhausting

Like heavy-duty cognitive tasks, such as keeping multiple pieces of information in mind at once or avoiding distractions in a busy environment, empathy depletes our mental resources. So jobs that require constant empathy can lead to "compassion fatigue," an acute inability to empathize that's driven by stress, and burnout, a more gradual and chronic version of this phenomenon.

Health and human services professionals (doctors, nurses, social workers, corrections officers) are especially at risk, because empathy is central to their day-to-day jobs. In a study of hospice nurses, for example, the key predictors for compassion fatigue were psychological: anxiety, feelings of trauma, life demands, and what the researchers call excessive empathy, meaning the tendency to sacrifice one's own needs for others' (rather than simply "feeling" for people).[1] Variables such as long hours and heavy caseloads also had an impact, but less than expected. And in a survey of Korean nurses, self-reported compassion fatigue strongly predicted their intentions to leave their jobs in the near future.[2] Other studies of nurses show additional consequences of compassion fatigue, such as absenteeism and increased errors in administering medication.

People who work for charities and other nonprofits (think animal shelters) are similarly at risk. Voluntary turnover is exceedingly high, in part because of the empathically demanding nature of the work; low pay exacerbates the element of self-sacrifice. What's more, society's strict views of how nonprofits should operate mean they face a backlash when they act like businesses (for instance, investing in "overhead" to keep the organization running smoothly). They're expected to thrive through selfless outpourings of compassion from workers.

The demand for empathy is relentless in other sectors as well. Day after day, managers must motivate knowledge workers by understanding their experiences and perspectives and helping them find personal meaning in their work. Customer service professionals must continually quell the concerns of distressed callers. Empathy is exhausting in any setting or role in which it's a primary aspect of the job.

Problem #2: It's zero-sum

Empathy doesn't just drain energy and cognitive resources—it also depletes itself. The more empathy I devote to my spouse, the less I have left for my mother; the more I give to my mother, the less I can give my son. Both our desire to be empathic and the effort it requires are in limited supply, whether we're dealing with family and friends or customers and colleagues.

Consider this study: Researchers examined the trade-offs associated with empathic behaviors at work and at home by surveying 844 workers from various sectors, including hairstylists, firefighters, and telecom professionals.[3] People who reported workplace behaviors such as taking "time to listen to coworkers' problems and worries" and helping "others who have heavy workloads" felt less capable of connecting with their families. They felt emotionally drained and burdened by work-related demands.

Sometimes the zero-sum problem leads to another type of trade-off: Empathy toward insiders—say, people on our teams or in our organizations—can limit our capacity to empathize with people outside our immediate circles. We naturally put more time and effort into understanding the needs of our close friends and colleagues. We simply find it easier to do, because we care more about them to begin with. This uneven investment creates a gap that's widened by our limited supply of empathy: As we use up most of what's available on insiders, our bonds with them get stronger, while our desire to connect with outsiders wanes.

Preferential empathy can antagonize those who see us as protecting our own (think about how people reacted when the Pope praised the Catholic Church's handling of sexual abuse). It can also, a bit more surprisingly, lead to insiders' aggression toward outsiders. For example, in a study I conducted with University of Chicago professor Nicholas Epley, we looked at how two sets of participants—those sitting with a friend (to prime empathic connection) and those sitting with a stranger—would treat a group of terrorists, an outgroup with particularly negative associations. After describing the terrorists, we asked how much participants endorsed statements portraying them as subhuman, how acceptable waterboarding them would be, and how much voltage of electric shock they would be willing to administer to them. Merely sitting in a room with a friend significantly increased people's willingness to torture and dehumanize.

Although this study represents an extreme case, the same principle holds for organizations. Compassion for one's own employees and colleagues sometimes produces aggressive responses toward others. More often, insiders are simply uninterested in empathizing with outsiders—but even that can cause people to neglect opportunities for constructive collaboration across functions or organizations.

Problem #3: It can erode ethics

Finally, empathy can cause lapses in ethical judgment. We saw some of that in the study about terrorists. In many cases, though, the problem stems not from aggression toward outsiders but, rather, from extreme loyalty toward insiders. In making a focused effort to see and feel things the way people who are close to us do, we may take on their interests as our own. This can make us more willing to overlook transgressions or even behave badly ourselves.

Multiple studies in behavioral science and decision making show that people are more inclined to cheat when it serves another person.[4] In various settings, with the benefits ranging from financial to reputational, people use this ostensible altruism to rationalize their dishonesty. It only gets worse when they empathize with another's plight or feel the pain of someone who is treated unfairly: In those cases, they're even more likely to lie, cheat, or steal to benefit that person.

In the workplace, empathy toward fellow employees can inhibit whistle-blowing—and when that happens, it seems scandals often follow. Just ask the police, the military, Penn State University, Citigroup, JPMorgan, and WorldCom. The kinds of problems that have plagued those organizations—brutality, sexual abuse, fraud—tend to be exposed by outsiders who don't identify closely with the perpetrators.

In my research with Liane Young and James Dungan of Boston College, we studied the effects of loyalty on people using Amazon's Mechanical Turk, an online marketplace where users earn money for completing tasks. At the beginning of the study, we asked some participants to write an essay about loyalty and others to write about fairness. Later in the study, they were each exposed to poor work by someone else. Those who had received the loyalty nudge were less willing to blow the whistle on a fellow user for inferior performance. This finding complements research showing that bribery is more common in countries that prize collectivism.[5] The sense of group belonging and interdependence among members often leads people to tolerate the offense. It makes them feel less accountable for it, diffusing responsibility to the collective whole instead of assigning it to the individual.

In short, empathy for those within one's immediate circle can conflict with justice for all.

How to rein in excessive empathy

These three problems may seem intractable, but as a manager you can do a number of things to mitigate them in your organization.

Split up the work

You might start by asking each employee to zero in on a certain set of stakeholders, rather than empathize with anyone and everyone. Some people can focus primarily on customers, for instance, and others on coworkers—think of it as creating task forces to meet different stakeholders' needs. This makes the work of developing relationships and gathering perspectives less consuming for individuals. You'll also accomplish more in the aggregate, by distributing "caring" responsibilities across your team or company. Although empathy is finite for any one person, it's less bounded when managed across employees.

Make it less of a sacrifice

Our mindsets can either intensify or lessen our susceptibility to empathy overload. For example, we exacerbate the zero-sum problem when we assume that our own interests and others' are fundamentally opposed. (This often happens in deal making, when parties with different positions on an issue get stuck because they're obsessed with the gap between them.) An adversarial mindset not only prevents us from understanding and responding to the other party but also makes us feel as though we've "lost" when we don't get our way. We can avoid burnout by seeking integrative solutions that serve both sides' interests.

Take this example: A salary negotiation between a hiring manager and a promising candidate will become a tug-of-war contest if they have different numbers in mind and fixate on the money alone. But let's suppose that the candidate actually cares more about job security, and the manager is keenly interested in avoiding turnover. Building security into the contract would be a win-win: an empathic act by the manager that wouldn't drain his empathy reserves the way making a concession on salary would, because keeping new hires around is in line with his own desires.

There's only so much empathy to go around, but it's possible to achieve economies of sorts. By asking questions instead of letting assumptions go unchecked, you can bring such solutions to the surface.

Give people breaks

As a management and organizations professor, I cringe when students refer to my department's coursework—on leadership, teams, and negotiation—as "soft skills." Understanding and responding to the needs, interests, and desires of other human beings involves some of the *hardest* work of all. Despite claims that empathy comes naturally, it takes arduous mental effort to get into another person's mind—and then to respond with compassion rather than indifference.

We all know that people need periodic relief from technical and analytical work and from rote jobs like data entry. The same is true of empathy. Look for ways to give employees breaks. It's not sufficient to encourage self-directed projects that also benefit the company (and often result in more work), as Google did with its 20% time policy. Encourage individuals to take time to focus on their interests alone. Recent research finds that people who take lots of self-focused breaks subsequently report feeling more empathy for others.[6] That might seem counterintuitive, but when people feel restored, they're better able to perform the demanding tasks of figuring out and responding to what others need.

How do you give people respite from thinking and caring about others? Some companies are purchasing isolation chambers like Orrb Technologies' wellness and learning pods so that people can literally put themselves in a bubble to relax, meditate, or do whatever else helps them recharge. McLaren, for example, uses the pods to train F1 supercar drivers to focus. Other companies, such as electrical parts distributor Van Meter, are relying on much simpler interventions like shutting off employee email accounts when workers go on vacation to allow them to concentrate on themselves without interruption.

Despite its limitations, empathy is essential at work. So managers should make sure employees are investing it wisely.

When trying to empathize, it's generally better to talk with people about their experiences than to imagine how they might be feeling, as Nicholas Epley suggests in his book *Mindwise*. A recent study bears this out.[7] Participants were asked how capable they thought blind people were of working and living independently. But before answering the question, some were asked to complete difficult physical tasks while wearing a blindfold. Those who had done the blindness simulation judged blind people to be much less capable. That's because the exercise led them to ask "What would it be like if *I* were blind?" (the answer: very difficult!) rather than "What is it like for *a blind person* to be blind?" This finding speaks to why Ford's use of the Empathy Belly, while well-intentioned, may be misguided: After wearing it, engineers may overestimate or misidentify the difficulties faced by drivers who actually are pregnant.

Talking to people—asking them how they feel, what they want, and what they think—may seem simplistic, but it's more accurate. It's also less taxing to employees and their organizations, because it involves collecting real information instead of endlessly speculating. It's a smarter way to empathize.

ADAM WAYTZ is an associate professor of management and organizations at Northwestern University's Kellogg School of Management.

Notes

1. M. Abendroth and J. Flannery, "Predicting the Risk of Compassion Fatigue: A Study of Hospice Nurses," *Journal of Hospice and Palliative Nursing* 8, no. 6 (November–December 2006): 346–356.

2. K. Sung et al., "Relationships Between Compassion Fatigue, Burnout, and Turnover Intention in Korean Hospital Nurses," *Journal of Korean Academy of Nursing* 42, no. 7 (December 2012): 1087–1094.

3. J. Halbesleben et al., "Too Engaged? A Conservation of Resources View of the Relationships Between Work Engagement and Work Interference with Family," *Journal of Applied Psychology* 94, no. 6 (November 2009): 1452–1465.

4. F. Gino et al., "Self-Serving Altruism? The Lure of Unethical Actions That Benefit Others," *Journal of Economic Behavior & Organization* 93 (September 2013); and F. Gino and L. Pierce, "Dishonesty in the Name of Equity," *Psychological Science* 20, no. 9 (December 2009): 1153–1160.

5. N. Mazar and P. Aggarwal, "Greasing the Palm: Can Collectivism Promote Bribery?" *Psychological Science* 22, no. 7 (June 2011): 843–848.

6. G. Boyraz and J. B. Waits, "Reciprocal Associations Among Self-Focused Attention, Self-Acceptance, and Empathy: A Two-Wave Panel Study," *Personality and Individual Differences* 74 (2015): 84–89.

7. A. M. Silverman et al., "Stumbling in Their Shoes: Disability Simulations Reduce Judge Capabilities of Disabled People," *Social Psychological & Personality Science* 6, no. 4 (May 2015): 464–471.

Reprinted from *Harvard Business Review*,
January–February 2016 (product #R1601D).

10

What the Dalai Lama Taught Daniel Goleman About Emotional Intelligence

An interview with Daniel Goleman by Andrea Ovans

Two decades before Daniel Goleman first wrote about emotional intelligence in the pages of HBR, he met the Dalai Lama at Amherst College. The Dalai Lama mentioned to the young science journalist for the *New York Times* that he was interested in meeting with scientists. Thus began a long, rich friendship as Goleman became involved over the years in arranging a series of what he calls "extended dialogues" between the Buddhist spiritual leader and researchers in fields ranging from ecology to neuroscience. Over the next 30 years, as Goleman has pursued his own work as a psychologist and business thinker, he has come to see the Dalai Lama as a highly uncommon leader. And so he was understandably delighted when, on the occasion of his friend's 80th birthday, he was asked to write a book describing the Dalai Lama's compassionate approach to addressing the world's most intractable problems. Published in June 2015, *Force for Good: The Dalai Lama's Vision for Our World*, which draws both on Goleman's background in cognitive science and his long relationship with the Dalai Lama, is both an exploration of the science and the power of compassion and a call to action. Curious about the book and about how the Dalai Lama's views on compassion informed Goleman's thinking on emotional intelligence, I caught up with Goleman over the phone. What follows are edited excerpts from our conversation.

HBR: *Let's start with some definitions here. What is compassion, as you are describing it? It sounds a lot like empathy, one of the major components of emotional intelligence. Is there a difference?*

Goleman: Yes, an important difference. As I've written about recently in HBR, three kinds of empathy are important to emotional intelligence: *cognitive empathy*—the ability to understand another person's point of view, *emotional empathy*—the ability to feel what someone else feels, and *empathic concern*—the ability to sense what another person needs from you [see chapter 1, "What Is Empathy?"]. Cultivating all three kinds of empathy, which originate in different parts of the brain, is important for building social relationships.

But compassion takes empathy a step further. When you feel compassion, you feel distress when you witness someone else in distress—and because of that you want to help that person.

Why draw this distinction?

Simply put, compassion makes the difference between understanding and caring. It's the kind of love that a parent has for a child. Cultivating it more broadly means extending that to the other people in our lives and to people we encounter. I think that in the workplace, that attitude has a hugely positive effect, whether it's in how we relate to our peers, how we are as a leader, or how we relate to clients and customers. A positive disposition toward another person creates the kind of resonance that builds trust and loyalty and makes interactions harmonious. And the opposite of that—when you do nothing to show that you care—creates distrust and disharmony and causes huge dysfunction at home and in business.

When you put it that way, it's hard to disagree that if you treat people well things would go better than if you don't or that if you cared about them they would care a lot more about you. So why do you think that doesn't just happen naturally? Is it a cultural thing? Or a misplaced confusion about when competition is appropriate?

I think too often there's a muddle in people's thinking that if I'm nice to another person or if I have their interests at heart it means that I don't have my own interests at heart. The pathology of that is, "Well, I'll just care about me and not the other person." And that, of course, is the kind of attitude that leads to lots of problems in the business realm and in the personal realm. But compassion also includes yourself. If we protect ourselves and make sure we're okay—and also make sure the other person is okay—that creates a different framework for working with and cooperating with other people.

Could you give me an example of how that might work in the business world?

There's research that was done on star salespeople and on client managers that found that the lowest level of performance was a kind of "I'm going to get the best deal I can now, and I don't care how this affects the other person" attitude, which means that you might make the sale but that you lose the relationship. But at the top end, the stars were typified by the attitude, "I am working for the client as well as myself. I'm going to be completely straight with them, and I'm going to act as their advisor. If the deal I have is not the best deal they can get I'm going to let them know because that's going to strengthen the relationship, even though I might lose this specific sale." And I think that captures the difference between the "me first" and the "let's all do well" attitude that I'm getting at.

How would we cultivate compassion if we just weren't feeling it?

Neuroscientists have been studying compassion recently, and places like Stanford, Yale, UC Berkeley, and the University of Wisconsin, Madison, among others, have been testing methodologies for increasing compassion. Right now there's a kind of a trend toward incorporating mindfulness into the workplace, and it turns out there's data from the Max Planck Institute showing that enhancing mindfulness does have an effect in brain function but that the circuitry that's affected is not the circuitry for concern or compassion. In other words, there's no automatic boost in compassion from mindfulness alone.

Still, in the traditional methods of meditation that mindfulness in the workplace is based on, the two were always linked, so that you would practice mindfulness in a context in which you'd also cultivate compassion.

Stanford, for example, has developed a program that incorporates secularized versions of methods that have originally come from religious practices. It involves a meditation in which you cultivate an attitude of loving-kindness or of concern, or of compassion, toward people. First you do this for yourself, then for people you love, then for people you just know. And finally you do it for everyone. And this has the effect of priming the circuitry responsible for compassion within the brain so that you are more inclined to act that way when the opportunity arises.

You've remarked that the Dalai Lama is a very distinctive kind of leader. Is there something we could learn as leaders ourselves from his unique form of leadership?

Observing him over the years, and then doing this book for which I interviewed him extensively, and of course being immersed in leadership literature myself, three things struck me.

The first is that he's not beholden to any organization at all. He's not in any business. He's not a party leader. He's a citizen of the world at large. And this has freed him to tackle the largest problems we face. I think that to the extent that a leader is beholden to a particular organization or outcome, that creates a kind of myopia of what's possible and what matters. Focus narrows to the next quarter's results or the next election. He's way beyond that. He thinks in terms of generations and of what's best for humanity as a whole. Because his vision is so expansive, he can take on the largest challenges, rather than small, narrowly defined ones.

So I think there's a lesson here for all of us, which is to ask ourselves if there is something that limits our vision—that limits our capacity to care. And is there a way to enlarge it?

The second thing that struck me is that he gathers information from everywhere. He meets with heads of state, and he meets with beggars. He's getting information from people at every level of society worldwide. This casting a large net lets him understand situations in a very deep way, and he can analyze them in many different ways and come up with solutions that aren't confined by anyone. And I think that's another lesson everyday leaders can take from him.

The third thing would be the scope of his compassion, which I think is an ideal that we could strive for. It's pretty unlimited. He seems to care about everybody and the world at large.

You've said that the book is a call to action. What do you hope people will do after reading it?

The book is a call to action, but it is a very reasoned call to action. The Dalai Lama is a great believer in a deep analysis of problems and letting solutions come from that analysis. And then he is also passionate about people acting now. Not feeling passive, not feeling helpless, not feeling, "What's the point? I won't live to see the benefit," but rather having them start changes now even if the change won't come to fruition until future generations.

So my hope, and his, is to help people understand what they can do in the face of problems that
are so vast: creating a more inclusive economy;
making work meaningful; doing good and not just
well; cleaning up injustice and unfairness, corruption and collusion in society, whether in business,
politics, or religion; helping the environment heal;
the hope that one day conflict will be settled by dialogue rather than war.

These are very big issues. But everyone can do
something to move things in the right direction,
even if it's just reaching across the divide and becoming friendly with someone who belongs to
some other group. That actually has a very powerful end result: If you have two groups somewhere
in the world that have deep enmity toward each
other, and yet a few people in each group like each
other because they've had personal contact—they
have a friend in that other group. So something as
simple as reaching out across a divide is actually a

profound thing. In each of these areas, with whatever leverage we have, the point is to use it, not just to stand back.

DANIEL GOLEMAN is a codirector of the Consortium for Research on Emotional Intelligence in Organizations at Rutgers University, coauthor of *Primal Leadership: Leading with Emotional Intelligence* (Harvard Business Review Press, 2013), and author of *The Brain and Emotional Intelligence: New Insights* and *Leadership: Selected Writings* (More Than Sound, 2011). His latest book is *A Force For Good: The Dalai Lama's Vision for Our World* (Bantam, 2015). ANDREA OVANS is a former senior editor at *Harvard Business Review*.

Adapted from content published on hbr.org on May 4, 2015 (product #H021KQ).

Index

How to be human at work.

HBR's Emotional Intelligence Series features smart, essential reading on the human side of professional life from the pages of *Harvard Business Review*. Each book in the series offers uplifting stories, practical advice, and research from leading experts on how to tend to our emotional well-being at work.

Harvard Business Review Emotional Intelligence Series

Available in paperback or ebook format. The specially priced six-volume set includes:

- Mindfulness
- Resilience
- Influence and Persuasion

- Authentic Leadership
- Happiness
- Empathy

HBR.ORG

Buy for your team, clients, or event.
Visit hbr.org/bulksales for quantity discount rates.

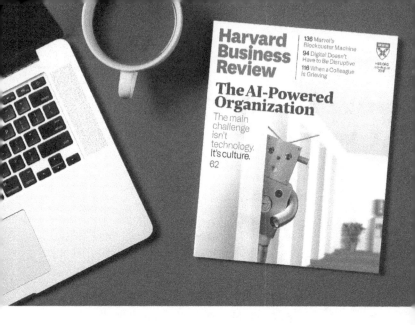

Engage with HBR content the way you want, on any device.

With HBR's new subscription plans, you can access world-renowned **case studies** from Harvard Business School and receive **four free eBooks**. Download and customize prebuilt **slide decks and graphics** from our **Visual Library**. With HBR's archive, top 50 best-selling articles, and five new articles every day, HBR is more than just a magazine.

Subscribe Today
hbr.org/success

The most important management ideas all in one place.

We hope you enjoyed this book from *Harvard Business Review*. For the best ideas HBR has to offer turn to HBR's 10 Must Reads Boxed Set. From books on leadership and strategy to managing yourself and others, this 6-book collection delivers articles on the most essential business topics to help you succeed.

HBR's 10 Must Reads Series

The definitive collection of ideas and best practices on our most sought-after topics from the best minds in business.

- Change Management
- Collaboration
- Communication
- Emotional Intelligence
- Innovation
- Leadership
- Making Smart Decisions

- Managing Across Cultures
- Managing People
- Managing Yourself
- Strategic Marketing
- Strategy
- Teams
- The Essentials

hbr.org/mustreads

Buy for your team, clients, or event.
Visit hbr.org/bulksales for quantity discount rates.

Harvard Business Review Press

Authentic
Leadership

HBR Emotional Intelligence Series

How to be human at work

The HBR Emotional Intelligence Series features smart, essential reading on the human side of professional life from the pages of *Harvard Business Review*.

Authentic Leadership

Empathy

Happiness

Influence and Persuasion

Mindfulness

Resilience

Other books on emotional intelligence from *Harvard Business Review*:

HBR's 10 Must Reads on Emotional Intelligence

HBR Guide to Emotional Intelligence

Authentic Leadership

HBR EMOTIONAL INTELLIGENCE SERIES

Harvard Business Review Press

Boston, Massachusetts

HBR Press Quantity Sales Discounts

Harvard Business Review Press titles are available at significant quantity discounts when purchased in bulk for client gifts, sales promotions, and premiums. Special editions, including books with corporate logos, customized covers, and letters from the company or CEO printed in the front matter, as well as excerpts of existing books, can also be created in large quantities for special needs.

For details and discount information for both print and ebook formats, contact booksales@harvardbusiness.org, tel. 800-988-0886, or www.hbr.org/bulksales.

Copyright 2018 Harvard Business School Publishing Corporation
All rights reserved
Printed in the United States of America

15

No part of this publication may be reproduced, stored in or introduced into a retrieval system, or transmitted, in any form, or by any means (electronic, mechanical, photocopying, recording, or otherwise), without the prior permission of the publisher. Requests for permission should be directed to permissions@hbsp.harvard.edu, or mailed to Permissions, Harvard Business School Publishing, 60 Harvard Way, Boston, Massachusetts 02163.

The web addresses referenced in this book were live and correct at the time of the book's publication but may be subject to change.

Library of Congress Cataloging-in-Publication Data

Title: Authentic leadership.
Other titles: HBR emotional intelligence series.
Description: Boston, Massachusetts : Harvard Business Review Press, [2017] | Series: HBR emotional intelligence series | Includes index.
Identifiers: LCCN 2017027307 | ISBN 9781633693913 (pbk. : alk. paper)
Subjects: LCSH: Leadership—Psychological aspects. | Self-consciousness (Awareness) | Authenticity (Philosophy) | Corporate culture.
Classification: LCC HD57.7 .A8496 2017 | DDC 658.4/092—dc23 LC record available at https://lccn.loc.gov/2017027307

The paper used in this publication meets the requirements of the American National Standard for Permanence of Paper for Publications and Documents in Libraries and Archives Z39.48-1992.

ISBN: 978-1-63369-391-3
eISBN: 978-1-63369-329-0

Contents

Contents

Authentic Leadership

HBR EMOTIONAL INTELLIGENCE SERIES

1

Discovering Your Authentic Leadership

By Bill George, Peter Sims, Andrew N. McLean, and Diana Mayer

During the past 50 years, leadership scholars have conducted more than 1,000 studies in an attempt to determine the definitive styles, characteristics, or personality traits of great leaders. None of these studies has produced a clear profile of the ideal leader. Thank goodness. If scholars had produced a cookie-cutter leadership style, individuals would be forever trying to imitate it. They would make themselves into personae, not people, and others would see through them immediately.

No one can be authentic by trying to imitate someone else. You can learn from others' experiences, but there is no way you can be successful when you are trying to be like them. People trust you when you are genuine and authentic, not a replica of someone else. Amgen CEO and president Kevin Sharer, who gained priceless experience working as Jack Welch's assistant in the 1980s, saw the downside of GE's cult of personality in those days. "Everyone wanted to be like Jack," he explains. "Leadership has many voices. You need to be who you are, not try to emulate somebody else."

Over the past five years, people have developed a deep distrust of leaders. It is increasingly evident that we need a new kind of business leader in the 21st century. In 2003, Bill George's book, *Authentic Leadership: Rediscovering the Secrets to Creating Lasting Value*, challenged a new generation to lead authentically. Authentic leaders demonstrate a passion for their purpose, practice their values consistently, and lead with their hearts as well as their heads. They establish long-term, meaningful relationships and have the self-discipline to get results. They know who they are.

Many readers of *Authentic Leadership*, including several CEOs, indicated that they had a tremendous desire to become authentic leaders and wanted to know how. As a result, our research team set out to answer the question, "How can people become and remain authentic leaders?" We interviewed 125 leaders to learn how they developed their leadership abilities. These interviews constitute the largest in-depth study of leadership development ever undertaken. Our interviewees discussed openly and honestly how they realized their potential and candidly shared their life stories, personal struggles, failures, and triumphs.

The people we talked with ranged in age from 23 to 93, with no fewer than 15 per decade. They were chosen based on their reputations for authenticity and effectiveness as leaders, as well as our personal knowledge of them. We also solicited recommendations from other leaders and academics. The resulting group includes women and men from a diverse array of racial, religious, and socioeconomic backgrounds and nationalities. Half of them are CEOs, and the other half comprises a range of profit and nonprofit leaders, midcareer leaders, and young leaders just starting on their journeys.

After interviewing these individuals, we believe we understand why more than 1,000 studies have not produced a profile of an ideal leader. Analyzing 3,000 pages of transcripts, our team was startled to see that these people did not identify any universal characteristics, traits, skills, or styles that led to their success. Rather, their leadership emerged from their life stories. Consciously and subconsciously, they were constantly testing themselves through real-world experiences and reframing their life stories to understand who they were at their core. In doing so, they discovered the purpose of their leadership and learned that being authentic made them more effective.

These findings are extremely encouraging: You do not have to be born with specific characteristics or traits of a leader. You do not have to wait for a tap on the shoulder. You do not have to be at the top of your organization. Instead, you can discover your potential right now. As one of our interviewees, Young & Rubicam chairman and CEO Ann Fudge, said, "All of us have the spark of leadership in us, whether it is in business, in government, or as a nonprofit volunteer. The challenge is to understand ourselves well enough to discover where we can use our leadership gifts to serve others."

Discovering your authentic leadership requires a commitment to developing yourself. Like musicians and athletes, you must devote yourself to a lifetime of realizing your potential. Most people Kroger CEO David Dillon has seen become good leaders were self-taught. Dillon said, "The advice I give to individuals in our company is not to expect the company to hand you a development plan. You need to take responsibility for developing yourself."

In the following pages, we draw upon lessons from our interviews to describe how people become authentic leaders. First and most important, they frame their life stories in ways that allow them to see themselves not as passive observers of their lives but rather as individuals who can develop self-awareness from their experiences. Authentic leaders act on that awareness by practicing their values and principles, sometimes at substantial risk to themselves. They are careful to balance their motivations so that they are driven by these inner values as much as by a desire for external rewards or recognition. Authentic leaders also keep a strong support team around them, ensuring that they live integrated, grounded lives.

Learning from your life story

The journey to authentic leadership begins with understanding the story of your life. Your life story provides the context for your experiences, and through it, you can find the inspiration to make an impact in the world. As the novelist John Barth once wrote, "The story of your life is not your life. It is your story." In other words, it is your personal narrative that matters, not the mere facts of your life. Your life narrative is like a permanent recording playing in your head. Over and over, you replay the events and personal interactions that are important to your life, attempting to make sense of them to find your place in the world.

While the life stories of authentic leaders cover the full spectrum of experiences—including the positive impact of parents, athletic coaches, teachers, and mentors—many leaders reported that their motivation came from a difficult experience in their lives. They described the transformative effects of the loss of a job; personal illness; the untimely death of a close friend or relative; and feelings of being excluded, discriminated against, and rejected by peers. Rather than seeing themselves as victims, though, authentic leaders used these formative experiences to give meaning to their lives. They reframed these events to rise above their challenges and to discover their passion to lead.

Let's focus now on one leader in particular, Novartis chairman and CEO Daniel Vasella, whose life story was one of the most difficult of all the people we interviewed. He emerged from extreme challenges in his youth to reach the pinnacle of the global pharmaceutical industry, a trajectory that illustrates the trials many leaders have to go through on their journeys to authentic leadership.

Vasella was born in 1953 to a modest family in Fribourg, Switzerland. His early years were filled with medical problems that stoked his passion to become a physician. His first recollections were of a hospital where he was admitted at age four when he suffered from food poisoning. Falling ill with asthma at age five, he was sent alone to the mountains of eastern Switzerland for two summers. He found the four-month separations from his parents especially difficult because his caretaker had an alcohol problem and was unresponsive to his needs.

At age eight, Vasella had tuberculosis, followed by meningitis, and was sent to a sanatorium for a year. Lonely and homesick, he suffered a great deal that year, as his parents rarely visited him. He still remembers the pain and fear when the nurses held him down during the lumbar punctures so that he would not move. One day, a new physician arrived and took time to explain each step of the procedure. Vasella asked the doctor if he could hold a nurse's hand rather than being held down. "The amazing thing is that this time the procedure didn't hurt," Vasella recalls. "Afterward, the doctor asked me, 'How was that?' I reached up and gave him a big hug. These human gestures of forgiveness, caring, and compassion made a deep impression on me and on the kind of person I wanted to become."

Throughout his early years, Vasella's life continued to be unsettled. When he was 10, his 18-year-old sister passed away after suffering from cancer for two years. Three years later, his father died in surgery. To support the family, his mother went to work in a distant town and came home only once every three weeks. Left to himself, he and his friends held beer parties and got into frequent fights. This lasted for three years until he met his first girlfriend, whose affection changed his life.

At 20, Vasella entered medical school, later graduating with honors. During medical school, he sought out psychotherapy so he could come to terms with his early experiences and not feel like a victim. Through analysis, he reframed his life story and realized that he wanted to help a wider range of people than he could as an individual practitioner. Upon completion of his residency, he applied to become chief physician at the University of Zurich; however, the search committee considered him too young for the position.

Disappointed but not surprised, Vasella decided to use his abilities to increase his impact on medicine. At that time, he had a growing fascination with finance and business. He talked with the head of the pharmaceutical division of Sandoz, who offered him the opportunity to join the company's US affiliate. In his five years in the United States, Vasella flourished in the stimulating environment, first as a sales representative and later as a product manager, and advanced rapidly through the Sandoz marketing organization.

When Sandoz merged with Ciba-Geigy in 1996, Vasella was named CEO of the combined companies, now called Novartis, despite his young age and limited experience. Once in the CEO's role, Vasella blossomed as a leader. He envisioned the opportunity to build a great global health care company that could help people through lifesaving new drugs, such as Gleevec, which has proved to be highly effective for patients with chronic myeloid leukemia. Drawing on the physician role models of his youth, he built an entirely new Novartis culture centered on compassion, competence, and competition. These moves established Novartis as a giant in the industry and Vasella as a compassionate leader.

Vasella's experience is just one of dozens provided by authentic leaders who traced their inspiration directly from their life stories. Asked what empowered them to lead, these leaders consistently replied that they found their strength through transformative experiences. Those experiences enabled them to understand the deeper purpose of their leadership.

Knowing your authentic self

When the 75 members of Stanford Graduate School of Business's Advisory Council were asked to recommend the most important capability for leaders to develop, their answer was nearly unanimous: self-awareness. Yet many leaders, especially those early in their careers, are trying so hard to establish themselves in the world that they leave little time for self-exploration. They strive to achieve success in tangible ways that are recognized in the external world—money, fame, power, status, or a rising stock price. Often their drive enables them to be professionally successful for a while, but they are unable to sustain that success. As they age, they may find something is missing in their lives and realize they are holding back from being the person they want to be. Knowing their authentic selves requires the courage and honesty to open up and examine their experiences. As they do so, leaders become more humane and willing to be vulnerable.

Of all the leaders we interviewed, David Pottruck, former CEO of Charles Schwab, had one of the most persistent journeys to self-awareness. An all-league football player in high school, Pottruck became MVP of his college team at the University of Pennsylvania. After completing his MBA at Wharton and a stint with Citigroup, he joined Charles Schwab as head of marketing, moving from New York to San Francisco. An extremely hard worker, Pottruck could not understand why his new colleagues resented the long hours he put in and his aggressiveness in pushing for results. "I thought my accomplishments would speak for themselves," he said. "It never occurred to me that my level of energy would intimidate and offend other people, because in my mind I was trying to help the company."

Pottruck was shocked when his boss told him, "Dave, your colleagues do not trust you." As he recalled, "That feedback was like a dagger to my heart. I was in denial, as I didn't see myself as others saw me. I became a lightning rod for friction, but I had no idea how self-serving I looked to other people. Still, somewhere in my inner core the feedback resonated as true." Pottruck realized that he could not succeed unless he identified and overcame his blind spots.

Denial can be the greatest hurdle that leaders face in becoming self-aware. They all have egos that need to be stroked, insecurities that need to be smoothed, fears that need to be allayed. Authentic leaders realize that they have to be willing to listen to feedback— especially the kind they don't want to hear. It was only after his second divorce that Pottruck finally was able to acknowledge that he still had large blind spots: "After my second marriage fell apart, I thought I had a wife-selection problem." Then he worked with a counselor who delivered some hard truths: "The good news is you do not have a wife-selection problem; the bad news is you have a husband-behavior problem." Pottruck then made a determined effort to change. As he described it, "I was like a guy who has had three heart attacks and finally realizes he has to quit smoking and lose some weight."

These days Pottruck is happily remarried and listens carefully when his wife offers constructive feedback. He acknowledges that he falls back on his old habits at times, particularly in high-stress situations, but now he has developed ways of coping with stress. "I have had enough success in life to have that foundation of self-respect, so I can take the criticism and not deny it. I have finally learned to tolerate my failures and disappointments and not beat myself up."

Practicing your values and principles

The values that form the basis for authentic leadership are derived from your beliefs and convictions, but you will not know what your true values are until they are tested under pressure. It is relatively easy to list your values and to live by them when things are going well. When your success, your career, or even your life hangs in the balance, you learn what is most important, what you are prepared to sacrifice, and what trade-offs you are willing to make.

Leadership principles are values translated into action. Having a solid base of values and testing them under fire enables you to develop the principles you will use in leading. For example, a value such as "concern for others" might be translated into a leadership principle such as "create a work environment where people are respected for their contributions, provided job security, and allowed to fulfill their potential."

Consider Jon Huntsman, the founder and chairman of Huntsman Corporation. His moral values were deeply challenged when he worked for the Nixon administration in 1972, shortly before Watergate. After a brief stint in the US Department of Health, Education, and Welfare (HEW), he took a job under H. R. Haldeman, President Nixon's powerful chief of staff. Huntsman said he found the experience of taking orders from Haldeman "very mixed. I wasn't geared to take orders, irrespective of whether they were ethically or morally right." He explained, "We had a few clashes, as plenty of things that Haldeman wanted to do were questionable. An amoral atmosphere permeated the White House."

One day, Haldeman directed Huntsman to help him entrap a California congressman who had been opposing a White House initiative. The congressman was part owner of a plant that reportedly employed undocumented workers. To gather information to embarrass the congressman, Haldeman told Huntsman to get the plant manager of a company Huntsman owned to place some undocumented workers at the congressman's plant in an undercover operation.

"There are times when we react too quickly and fail to realize immediately what is right and wrong," Huntsman recalled. "This was one of those times when I didn't think it through. I knew instinctively it was wrong, but it took a few minutes for the notion to percolate. After 15 minutes, my inner moral compass made itself noticed and enabled me to recognize this wasn't the right thing to do. Values that had accompanied me since childhood kicked in. Halfway through my conversation with our plant manager, I said to him, 'Let's not do this. I don't want to play this game. Forget that I called.'"

Huntsman told Haldeman that he would not use his employees in this way. "Here I was saying no to the second most powerful person in the country. He didn't appreciate responses like that, as he viewed

YOUR DEVELOPMENT AS AN AUTHENTIC LEADER

As you read this article, think about the basis for your leadership development and the path you need to follow to become an authentic leader. Then ask yourself these questions:

1. *Which people and experiences in your early life had the greatest impact on you?*

2. *What tools do you use to become self-aware?* What is your authentic self? What are the moments when you say to yourself, "This is the real me"?

3. *What are your most deeply held values?* Where did they come from? Have your values changed significantly since your childhood? How do your values inform your actions?

4. *What motivates you extrinsically?* What are your intrinsic motivations? How do you balance extrinsic and intrinsic motivation in your life?

(Continued)

YOUR DEVELOPMENT AS AN AUTHENTIC LEADER

5. *What kind of support team do you have?* How can your support team make you a more authentic leader? How should you diversify your team to broaden your perspective?

6. *Is your life integrated?* Are you able to be the same person in all aspects of your life—personal, work, family, and community? If not, what is holding you back?

7. *What does being authentic mean in your life?* Are you more effective as a leader when you behave authentically? Have you ever paid a price for your authenticity as a leader? Was it worth it?

8. *What steps can you take today, tomorrow, and over the next year to develop your authentic leadership?*

them as signs of disloyalty. I might as well have been saying farewell. So be it. I left within the next six months."

Balancing your extrinsic and intrinsic motivations

Because authentic leaders need to sustain high levels of motivation and keep their lives in balance, it is critically important for them to understand what drives them. There are two types of motivations—extrinsic and intrinsic. Although they are reluctant to admit it, many leaders are propelled to achieve by measuring their success against the outside world's parameters. They enjoy the recognition and status that come with promotions and financial rewards. Intrinsic motivations, on the other hand, are derived from their sense of the meaning of their life. They are closely linked to one's life story and the way one frames it. Examples include personal growth, helping other people develop, taking on social causes, and making a difference in the world. The key is to find a balance between your desires for external validation and the intrinsic motivations that provide fulfillment in your work.

Many interviewees advised aspiring leaders to be wary of getting caught up in social, peer, or parental expectations. Debra Dunn, who has worked in Silicon Valley for decades as a Hewlett-Packard executive, acknowledged the constant pressures from external sources: "The path of accumulating material possessions is clearly laid out. You know how to measure it. If you don't pursue that path, people wonder what is wrong with you. The only way to avoid getting caught up in materialism is to understand where you find happiness and fulfillment."

Moving away from the external validation of personal achievement is not always easy. Achievement-oriented leaders grow so accustomed to successive accomplishments throughout their early years that it takes courage to pursue their intrinsic motivations. But at some point, most leaders recognize that they need to address more difficult questions in order to pursue truly meaningful success. McKinsey's Alice Woodwark, who at 29 has already achieved notable success, reflected: "My version of achievement was pretty naive, born of things I learned early in life about praise and being valued. But if you're just chasing the rabbit around the course, you're not running toward anything meaningful."

Intrinsic motivations are congruent with your values and are more fulfilling than extrinsic motivations. John Thain, CEO of the New York Stock Exchange, said, "I am motivated by doing a really good job at whatever I am doing, but I prefer to multiply my impact on society through a group of people." Or as Ann Moore, chairman and CEO of Time, put it, "I came here 25 years ago solely because I loved magazines and the publishing world." Moore had a dozen job offers after business school but took the lowest-paying one with Time because of her passion for publishing.

Building your support team

Leaders cannot succeed on their own; even the most outwardly confident executives need support and advice. Without strong relationships to provide perspective, it is very easy to lose your way.

Authentic leaders build extraordinary support teams to help them stay on course. Those teams counsel them in times of uncertainty, help them in times of difficulty, and celebrate with them in times of success. After their hardest days, leaders find comfort in being with people on whom they can rely so they can be open and vulnerable. During the low points, they cherish the friends who appreciate them for who they are, not what they are. Authentic leaders find that their support teams provide affirmation, advice, perspective, and calls for course corrections when needed.

How do you go about building your support team? Most authentic leaders have a multifaceted support structure that includes their spouses or significant others, families, mentors, close friends, and colleagues. They build their networks over time, as the experiences, shared histories, and openness with people close to them create the trust and confidence they need in times of trial and uncertainty. Leaders must give as much to their supporters as they get from them so that mutually beneficial relationships can develop.

It starts with having at least one person in your life with whom you can be completely yourself, warts and all, and still be accepted unconditionally. Often that person is the only one who can tell you the honest truth. Most leaders have their closest relationships with their spouses, although some develop these bonds with another family member, a close friend, or a trusted mentor. When leaders can rely on unconditional support, they are more likely to accept themselves for who they really are.

Many relationships grow over time through an expression of shared values and a common purpose. Randy Komisar of venture capital firm Kleiner Perkins Caufield & Byers said his marriage to Hewlett-Packard's Debra Dunn is lasting because it is rooted in similar values. "Debra and I are very independent but extremely harmonious in terms of our personal aspirations, values, and principles. We have a strong resonance around questions like, 'What is your legacy in this world?' It is important to be in sync about what we do with our lives."

Many leaders have had a mentor who changed their lives. The best mentoring interactions spark mutual learning, exploration of similar values, and shared enjoyment. If people are only looking for a leg up from their mentors, instead of being interested in their mentors' lives as well, the relationships will not last for long. It is the two-way nature of the connection that sustains it.

Personal and professional support groups can take many forms. Piper Jaffray's Tad Piper is a member of an Alcoholics Anonymous group. He noted, "These are not CEOs. They are just a group of nice, hard-working people who are trying to stay sober, lead good lives, and work with each other about being open, honest, and vulnerable. We reinforce each other's behavior by talking about our chemical dependency in a disciplined way as we go through the 12 steps. I feel blessed to be surrounded by people who are thinking about those kinds of issues and actually doing something, not just talking about them."

Bill George's experiences echo Piper's: In 1974, he joined a men's group that formed after a weekend retreat. More than 30 years later, the group is still meeting every Wednesday morning. After an opening period of catching up on each other's lives and dealing with any particular difficulty someone may be facing, one of the group's eight members leads a discussion on a topic he has selected. These discussions are open, probing, and often profound. The key to their success is that people say what they really believe without fear of judgment, criticism, or reprisal. All the members consider the group to be one of the most important aspects of their lives, enabling them to clarify their beliefs, values, and understanding of vital issues, as well as serving as a source of honest feedback when they need it most.

Integrating your life by staying grounded

Integrating their lives is one of the greatest challenges leaders face. To lead a balanced life, you need to bring together all of its constituent elements—work, family, community, and friends—so that you can be the same person in each environment. Think of your life as a house, with a bedroom for your personal life, a study for your professional life, a family room for your family, and a living room to share with your friends. Can you knock down the walls between these rooms and be the same person in each of them?

As John Donahoe, president of eBay Marketplaces and former worldwide managing director of Bain, stressed, being authentic means maintaining a sense of self no matter where you are. He warned, "The world can shape you if you let it. To have a sense of yourself as you live, you must make conscious choices. Sometimes the choices are really hard, and you make a lot of mistakes."

Authentic leaders have a steady and confident presence. They do not show up as one person one day and another person the next. Integration takes discipline, particularly during stressful times when it is easy to become reactive and slip back into bad habits. Donahoe feels strongly that integrating his life has enabled him to become a more effective leader. "There is no nirvana," he said. "The struggle is constant, as the trade-offs don't get any easier as you get older." But for authentic leaders, personal and professional lives are not a zero-sum game. As Donahoe said, "I have no doubt today that my children have made me a far more effective leader in the workplace. Having a strong personal life has made the difference." Leading is high-stress work. There is no way to avoid stress when you are responsible for people, organizations, outcomes, and managing the constant uncertainties of the environment. The higher you go, the greater your freedom to control your destiny but also the higher the degree of stress. The question is not whether you can avoid stress but how you can control it to maintain your own sense of equilibrium.

Authentic leaders are constantly aware of the importance of staying grounded. Besides spending time with their families and close friends, authentic leaders get physical exercise, engage in spiritual practices, do community service, and return to the places where they grew up. All are essential to their effectiveness as leaders, enabling them to sustain their authenticity.

Empowering people to lead

Now that we have discussed the process of discovering your authentic leadership, let's look at how authentic leaders empower people in their organizations to achieve superior long-term results, which is the bottom line for all leaders.

Authentic leaders recognize that leadership is not about their success or about getting loyal subordinates to follow them. They know the key to a successful organization is having empowered leaders at all levels, including those who have no direct reports. They not only inspire those around them, they empower those individuals to step up and lead.

A reputation for building relationships and empowering people was instrumental in chairman and

CEO Anne Mulcahy's stunning turnaround of Xerox. When Mulcahy was asked to take the company's reins from her failed predecessor, Xerox had $18 billion in debt, and all credit lines were exhausted. With the share price in free fall, morale was at an all-time low. To make matters worse, the SEC was investigating the company's revenue recognition practices.

Mulcahy's appointment came as a surprise to everyone—including Mulcahy herself. A Xerox veteran, she had worked in field sales and on the corporate staff for 25 years, but not in finance, R&D, or manufacturing. How could Mulcahy cope with this crisis when she had had no financial experience? She brought to the CEO role the relationships she had built over 25 years, an impeccable understanding of the organization, and, above all, her credibility as an authentic leader. She bled for Xerox, and everyone knew it. Because of that, they were willing to go the extra mile for her.

After her appointment, Mulcahy met personally with the company's top 100 executives to ask them if they would stay with the company despite the challenges ahead. "I knew there were people who weren't supportive of me," she said. "So I confronted a couple of them and said, 'This is about the company.'"

The first two people Mulcahy talked with, both of whom ran big operating units, decided to leave, but the remaining 98 committed to stay. Throughout the crisis, people in Xerox were empowered by Mulcahy to step up and lead in order to restore the company to its former greatness. In the end, her leadership enabled Xerox to avoid bankruptcy as she paid back $10 billion in debt and restored revenue growth and profitability with a combination of cost savings and innovative new products. The stock price tripled as a result.

———————

Like Mulcahy, all leaders have to deliver bottom-line results. By creating a virtuous circle in which the results reinforce the effectiveness of their leadership, authentic leaders are able to sustain those results through good times and bad. Their success enables them to attract talented people and align employees' activities with shared goals, as they empower others on their team to lead by taking on greater challenges. Indeed, superior results over a sustained period of time is the ultimate mark of an authentic leader. It may be possible to drive short-term outcomes without being authentic, but authentic leadership is the only way we know to create sustainable long-term results.

For authentic leaders, there are special rewards. No individual achievement can equal the pleasure of leading a group of people to achieve a worthy goal. When you cross the finish line together, all the pain and suffering you may have experienced quickly vanishes. It is replaced by a deep inner satisfaction that you have empowered others and thus made the world a better place. That's the challenge and the fulfillment of authentic leadership.

BILL GEORGE is a professor of management practice at Harvard Business School and the former chair and CEO of Medtronic. PETER SIMS is a management writer and entrepreneur. He is the author of *Little Bets: How Breakthrough Ideas Emerge from Small Discoveries*. He is also the founder of the BLK SHP. ANDREW N. MCLEAN is a research associate at Harvard Business School. DIANA MAYER is a former Citigroup executive in New York. This article was adapted from *True North: Discover Your Authentic Leadership* by Bill George with Peter Sims.

Reprinted from *Harvard Business Review*,
February 2007 (product #R0702H).

2

The Authenticity Paradox

By Herminia Ibarra

Authenticity has become the gold standard for leadership. But a simplistic understanding of what it means can hinder your growth and limit your impact.

Consider Cynthia, a general manager in a health care organization. Her promotion into that role increased her direct reports tenfold and expanded the range of businesses she oversaw—and she felt a little shaky about making such a big leap. A strong believer in transparent, collaborative leadership, she bared her soul to her new employees: "I want to do this job," she said, "but it's scary, and I need your help." Her candor backfired; she lost credibility with people who wanted and needed a confident leader to take charge.

Or take George, a Malaysian executive in an auto parts company where people valued a clear chain of command and made decisions by consensus. When a Dutch multinational with a matrix structure acquired the company, George found himself working with peers who saw decision making as a freewheeling contest for the best-debated ideas. That style didn't come easily to him, and it contradicted everything he had learned about humility growing up in his country. In a 360-degree debrief, his boss told him that he needed to sell his ideas and accomplishments more aggressively. George felt he had to choose between being a failure and being a fake.

Because going against our natural inclinations can make us feel like impostors, we tend to latch on to authenticity as an excuse for sticking with what's comfortable. But few jobs allow us to do that for long. That's doubly true when we advance in our careers or when demands or expectations change, as Cynthia, George, and countless other executives have discovered.

In my research on leadership transitions, I have observed that career advances require all of us to move way beyond our comfort zones. At the same time, however, they trigger a strong countervailing impulse to protect our identities: When we are unsure of ourselves or our ability to perform well or measure up in a new setting, we often retreat to familiar behaviors and styles.

But my research also demonstrates that the moments that most challenge our sense of self are the ones that can teach us the most about leading effectively. By viewing ourselves as works in progress and evolving our professional identities through trial and error, we can develop a personal style that feels right to us and suits our organizations' changing needs.

That takes courage, because learning, by definition, starts with unnatural and often superficial behaviors that can make us feel calculating instead of genuine and spontaneous. But the only way to avoid being pigeonholed and ultimately become better leaders is to do the things that a rigidly authentic sense of self would keep us from doing.

Why leaders struggle with authenticity

The word "authentic" traditionally referred to any work of art that is an original, not a copy. When used to describe leadership, of course, it has other meanings—and they can be problematic. For example, the notion of adhering to one "true self" flies in the face of much research on how people evolve with experience, discovering facets of themselves they would never have unearthed through introspection alone. And being utterly transparent—disclosing every single thought and feeling—is both unrealistic and risky. (See figure 1, "What is authenticity?")

FIGURE 1

What is authenticity?

A too-rigid definition of authenticity can get in the way of effective leadership. Here are three examples and the problems they pose.

Being true to yourself.
Which self? We have many selves, depending on the different roles that we play in life. We evolve and even transform ourselves with experience in new roles. How can you be true to a future self that is still uncertain and unformed?

Maintaining strict coherence between what you feel and what you say or do.
You lose credibility and effectiveness as a leader if you disclose everything you think and feel, especially when you are unproven.

Making values-based choices.
When we move into bigger roles, values that were shaped by past experiences can lead us astray. For instance, "tight control over operating details" might produce authentic but wrong-headed behavior in the face of new challenges.

Leaders today struggle with authenticity for several reasons. First, we make more-frequent and more-radical changes in the kinds of work we do. As we strive to *improve* our game, a clear and firm sense of self is a compass that helps us navigate choices and progress toward our goals. But when we're looking to *change* our game, a too-rigid self-concept becomes an anchor that keeps us from sailing forth, as it did at first with Cynthia.

Second, in global business, many of us work with people who don't share our cultural norms and have different expectations for how we should behave. It can often seem as if we have to choose between what is expected—and therefore effective—and what feels authentic. George is a case in point.

Third, identities are always on display in today's world of ubiquitous connectivity and social media. How we present ourselves—not just as executives but as people, with quirks and broader interests—has become an important aspect of leadership. Having to carefully curate a persona that's out there for all to see can clash with our private sense of self.

In dozens of interviews with talented executives facing new expectations, I have found that they most often grapple with authenticity in the following situations.

Taking charge in an unfamiliar role

As everyone knows, the first 90 days are critical in a new leadership role. First impressions form quickly, and they matter. Depending on their personalities, leaders respond very differently to the increased visibility and performance pressure.

Psychologist Mark Snyder, of the University of Minnesota, identified two psychological profiles that inform how leaders develop their personal styles. "High self-monitors"—or chameleons, as I call them— are naturally able and willing to adapt to the demands of a situation without feeling fake. Chameleons care about managing their public image and often mask their vulnerability with bluster. They may not always get it right the first time, but they keep trying on different styles like new clothes until they find a good fit for themselves and their circumstances. Because of that flexibility, they often advance rapidly. But chameleons can run into problems when people perceive them as disingenuous or lacking a moral center—even though they're expressing their "true" chameleon nature.

By contrast, "true-to-selfers" (Snyder's "low self-monitors") tend to express what they really think and feel, even when it runs counter to situational demands. The danger with true-to-selfers like Cynthia and George is that they may stick too long with comfortable behavior that prevents them from meeting new requirements, instead of evolving their style as they gain insight and experience.

Cynthia (whom I interviewed after her story appeared in a *Wall Street Journal* article by Carol Hymowitz) hemmed herself in like this. She thought she was setting herself up for success by staying true to her highly personal, full-disclosure style of management. She asked her new team for support, openly acknowledging that she felt a bit at sea. As she scrambled to learn unfamiliar aspects of the business, she worked tirelessly to contribute to every decision and solve every problem. After a few months, she was on the verge of burnout. To make matters worse, sharing her vulnerability with her team members so early on had damaged her standing. Reflecting on her transition some years later, Cynthia told me: "Being authentic doesn't mean that you can be held up to the light and people can see right through you." But at the time, that was how she saw it—and instead of building trust, she made people question her ability to do the job.

Delegating and communicating appropriately are only part of the problem in a case like this. A deeper-seated issue is finding the right mix of distance and closeness in an unfamiliar situation. Stanford psychologist Deborah Gruenfeld describes this as managing the tension between authority and approachability. To be authoritative, you privilege your knowledge, experience, and expertise over the team's, maintaining a measure of distance. To be approachable, you emphasize your relationships with people, their input, and their perspective, and you lead with empathy and warmth. Getting the balance right presents an acute authenticity crisis for true-to-selfers, who typically have a strong preference for behaving one way or the other. Cynthia made herself too approachable and vulnerable, and it undermined and drained her. In her bigger role, she needed more distance from her employees to gain their confidence and get the job done.

Selling your ideas (and yourself)

Leadership growth usually involves a shift from having good ideas to pitching them to diverse stakeholders. Inexperienced leaders, especially true-to-selfers, often find the process of getting buy-in distasteful because it feels artificial and political; they believe that their work should stand on its own merits.

Here's an example: Anne, a senior manager at a transportation company, had doubled revenue and fundamentally redesigned core processes in her unit. Despite her obvious accomplishments, however, her boss didn't consider her an inspirational leader. Anne also knew she was not communicating effectively in her role as a board member of the parent company. The chairman, a broad-brush thinker, often became impatient with her detail orientation. His feedback to her was "step up, do the vision thing." But to Anne that seemed like valuing form over substance. "For me, it is manipulation," she told me in an interview. "I can do the storytelling too, but I refuse to play on people's emotions. If the string-pulling is too obvious, I can't make myself do it." Like many aspiring leaders, she resisted crafting emotional messages to influence and inspire others because that felt less authentic to her than relying on facts, figures, and spreadsheets. As a result, she worked at cross-purposes with the board chairman, pushing hard on the facts instead of pulling him in as a valued ally.

Many managers know deep down that their good ideas and strong potential will go unnoticed if they don't do a better job of selling themselves. Still, they can't bring themselves to do it. "I try to build a network based on professionalism and what I can deliver for the business, not who I know," one manager told me. "Maybe that's not smart from a career point of view. But I can't go against my beliefs . . . So I have been more limited in 'networking up.'"

Until we see career advancement as a way of extending our reach and increasing our impact in the organization—a collective win, not just a selfish pursuit—we have trouble feeling authentic when touting our strengths to influential people. True-to-selfers find it particularly hard to sell themselves to senior management when they most need to do so: when they are still unproven. Research shows, however, that this hesitancy disappears as people gain experience and become more certain of the value they bring.

Processing negative feedback

Many successful executives encounter serious negative feedback for the first time in their careers when they take on larger roles or responsibilities. Even when the criticisms aren't exactly new, they loom larger because the stakes are higher. But leaders often convince themselves that dysfunctional aspects of their "natural" style are the inevitable price of being effective.

Let's look at Jacob, a food company production manager whose direct reports gave him low marks in a 360 review on emotional intelligence, team building, and empowering others. One team member wrote that it was hard for Jacob to accept criticism.

Another remarked that after an angry outburst, he'd suddenly make a joke as if nothing had happened, not realizing the destabilizing effect of his mood changes on those around him. For someone who genuinely believed that he'd built trust among his people, all this was tough to swallow.

Once the initial shock had subsided, Jacob acknowledged that this was not the first time he'd received such criticism (some colleagues and subordinates had made similar comments a few years earlier). "I thought I'd changed my approach," he reflected, "but I haven't really changed so much since the last time." However, he quickly rationalized his behavior to his boss: "Sometimes you have to be tough in order to deliver results, and people don't like it," he said. "You have to accept that as part of the job description." Of course, he was missing the point. Because negative feedback given to leaders often centers on style rather than skills or expertise, it can feel like a threat to their identity—as if they're being

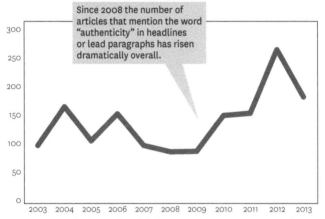

WHY COMPANIES ARE PUSHING AUTHENTICITY TRAINING

Since 2008 the number of articles that mention the word "authenticity" in headlines or lead paragraphs has risen dramatically overall.

Source: *New York Times, Financial Times, Washington Post, Economic Post, Forbes, Wall Street Journal,* and HBR

Managers can choose from countless books, articles, and executive workshops for advice on how to be more authentic at work. Two trends help explain the exploding popularity of the concept and the training industry it has fed.

(Continued)

WHY COMPANIES ARE PUSHING AUTHENTICITY TRAINING

First, trust in business leaders fell to an all-time low in 2012, according to the Edelman Trust Barometer. Even in 2013, when trust began to climb back up, only 18% of people reported that they trusted business leaders to tell the truth, and fewer than half trusted businesses to do the right thing.

Second, employee engagement is at a nadir. A 2013 Gallup poll found that only 13% of employees worldwide are engaged at work. Only one in eight workers—out of roughly 180 million employees studied—is psychologically committed to his or her job. In study after study, frustration, burnout, disillusionment, and misalignment with personal values are cited among the biggest reasons for career change.

At a time when public confidence and employee morale are so low, it's no surprise that companies are encouraging leaders to discover their "true" selves.

asked to give up their "secret sauce." That's how Jacob saw it. Yes, he could be explosive—but from his point of view, his "toughness" allowed him to deliver results year after year. In reality, though, he had succeeded up to this point *despite* his behavior. When his role expanded and he took on greater responsibility, his intense scrutiny of subordinates became an even bigger obstacle because it took up time he should have been devoting to more-strategic pursuits.

A great public example of this phenomenon is Margaret Thatcher. Those who worked with her knew she could be merciless if someone failed to prepare as thoroughly as she did. She was capable of humiliating a staff member in public, she was a notoriously bad listener, and she believed that compromise was cowardice. As she became known to the world as the "Iron Lady," Thatcher grew more and more convinced of the rightness of her ideas and the necessity of her coercive methods. She could beat anyone into submission with the power of her rhetoric and conviction, and she only got better at it. Eventually, though, it was her undoing—she was ousted by her own cabinet.

A playful frame of mind

Such a rigid self-concept can result from too much introspection. When we look only within for answers, we inadvertently reinforce old ways of seeing the world and outdated views of ourselves. Without the benefit of what I call outsight—the valuable external perspective we get from experimenting with new leadership behaviors—habitual patterns of thought and action fence us in. To begin thinking like leaders, we must first act: plunge ourselves into new projects and activities, interact with very different kinds of people, and experiment with new ways of getting things done. Especially in times of transition and uncertainty, thinking and introspection should follow experience—not vice versa. Action changes who we are and what we believe is worth doing.

Fortunately, there are ways of increasing outsight and evolving toward an "adaptively authentic" way of leading, but they require a playful frame of mind. Think of leadership development as trying on possible selves rather than working on yourself—which, let's face it, sounds like drudgery. When we adopt a playful attitude, we're more open to possibilities. It's OK to be inconsistent from one day to the next. That's not being a fake; it's how we experiment to figure out what's right for the new challenges and circumstances we face.

My research suggests three important ways to get started.

Learn from diverse role models

Most learning necessarily involves some form of imitation—and the understanding that nothing is "original." An important part of growing as a leader is viewing authenticity not as an intrinsic state but as the ability to take elements you have learned from others' styles and behaviors and make them your own.

But don't copy just one person's leadership style; tap many diverse role models. There is a big difference between imitating someone wholesale and borrowing selectively from various people to create your own collage, which you then modify and improve. As the playwright Wilson Mizner said, copying one author is plagiarism, but copying many is research.

I observed the importance of this approach in a study of investment bankers and consultants who were advancing from analytical and project work to roles advising clients and selling new business. Though most of them felt incompetent and insecure in their new positions, the chameleons among them consciously borrowed styles and tactics from successful senior leaders—learning through emulation how to use humor to break tension in meetings, for instance, and how to shape opinion without being overbearing. Essentially, the chameleons faked it until they found what worked for them. Noticing their efforts, their managers provided coaching and mentoring and shared tacit knowledge.

As a result, the chameleons arrived much faster at an authentic but more skillful style than the true-to-selfers in the study, who continued to focus solely on demonstrating technical mastery. Often the true-to-selfers concluded that their managers were "all talk and little content" and therefore not suitable role models. In the absence of a "perfect" model they had a harder time with imitation—it felt bogus. Unfortunately, their managers perceived their inability to adapt as a lack of effort or investment and thus didn't give them as much mentoring and coaching as they gave the chameleons.

Work on getting better

Setting goals for learning (not just for performance) helps us experiment with our identities without feeling like impostors, because we don't expect to get everything right from the start. We stop trying to protect our comfortable old selves from the threats that change can bring and start exploring what kinds of leaders we might become.

Of course, we all want to perform well in a new situation—get the right strategy in place, execute like crazy, deliver results the organization cares about. But focusing exclusively on those things makes us afraid to take risks in the service of learning. In a series of ingenious experiments, Stanford psychologist Carol Dweck has shown that concern about how we will appear to others inhibits learning on new or unfamiliar tasks. Performance goals motivate us to show others that we possess valued attributes, such as intelligence and social skill, and to prove to ourselves that we

THE CULTURAL FACTOR

Whatever the situation—taking charge in unfamiliar territory, selling your ideas and yourself, or processing negative feedback—finding authentic ways of being effective is even more difficult in a multicultural environment.

As my INSEAD colleague Erin Meyer finds in her research, styles of persuading others and the kinds of arguments that people find persuasive are far from universal; they are deeply rooted in a culture's philosophical, religious, and educational assumptions. That said, prescriptions for how leaders are supposed to look and sound are rarely as diverse as the leaders themselves. And despite corporate initiatives to build understanding of cultural differences and promote diversity, the fact is that leaders are still expected to express ideas assertively, to claim credit for them, and to use charisma to motivate and inspire people.

(Continued)

THE CULTURAL FACTOR

Authenticity is supposed to be an antidote to a single model of leadership. (After all, the message is to be yourself, not what someone else expects you to be.) But as the notion has gained currency, it has, ironically, come to mean something much more limiting and culturally specific. A closer look at how leaders are taught to discover and demonstrate authenticity—by telling a personal story about a hardship they have overcome, for example—reveals a model that is, in fact, very American, based on ideals such as self-disclosure, humility, and individualistic triumph over adversity.

This amounts to a catch-22 for managers from cultures with different norms for authority, communication, and collective endeavor because they must behave inauthentically in order to conform to the strictures of "authentic" leadership.

have them. By contrast, learning goals motivate us to develop valued attributes.

When we're in performance mode, leadership is about presenting ourselves in the most favorable light. In learning mode, we can reconcile our yearning for authenticity in how we work and lead with an equally powerful desire to grow. One leader I met was highly effective in small-group settings but struggled to convey openness to new ideas in larger meetings, where he often stuck to long-winded presentations for fear of getting derailed by others' comments. He set himself a "no PowerPoint" rule to develop a more relaxed, improvisational style. He surprised himself by how much he learned, not only about his own evolving preferences but also about the issues at hand.

Don't stick to "your story"

Most of us have personal narratives about defining moments that taught us important lessons. Consciously or not, we allow our stories, and the images of ourselves that they paint, to guide us in new situations. But the stories can become outdated as we grow, so sometimes it's necessary to alter them dramatically or even to throw them out and start from scratch.

That was true for Maria, a leader who saw herself as a "mother hen with her chicks all around." Her coach, former Ogilvy & Mather CEO Charlotte Beers, explains in *I'd Rather Be in Charge* that this self-image emerged from a time when Maria had to sacrifice her own goals and dreams to take care of her extended family. It eventually began to hold her back in her career: Though it had worked for her as a friendly and loyal team player and a peacekeeper, it wasn't helping her get the big leadership assignment she wanted. Together Maria and her coach looked for another defining moment to use as a touchstone— one that was more in keeping with Maria's desired future self, not who she had been in the past. They chose the time when Maria, as a young woman, had left her family to travel the world for 18 months. Acting from that bolder sense of self, she asked for—and got—a promotion that had previously been elusive.

Dan McAdams, a Northwestern psychology professor who has spent his career studying life stories, describes identity as "the internalized and evolving story that results from a person's selective appropriation of past, present, and future." This isn't just academic jargon. McAdams is saying that you have to believe your story—but also embrace how it changes over time, according to what you need it to do. Try out new stories about yourself, and keep editing them, much as you would your résumé.

Again, revising one's story is both an introspective and a social process. The narratives we choose should not only sum up our experiences and aspirations but also reflect the demands we face and resonate with the audience we're trying to win over.

Countless books and advisers tell you to start your leadership journey with a clear sense of who you are. But that can be a recipe for staying stuck in the past. Your leadership identity can and should change each time you move on to bigger and better things.

The only way we grow as leaders is by stretching the limits of who we are—doing new things that make us uncomfortable but that teach us through direct experience who we want to become. Such growth doesn't require a radical personality makeover. Small changes—in the way we carry ourselves, the way we communicate, the way we interact—often make a world of difference in how effectively we lead.

HERMINIA IBARRA is a professor of organizational behavior and the Cora Chaired Professor of Leadership and Learning at INSEAD. She is the author of *Act Like a Leader, Think Like a Leader* (Harvard Business Review Press, 2015) and *Working Identity: Unconventional Strategies for Reinventing*

Your Career (Harvard Business School Press, 2003). Follow her on Twitter @HerminiaIbarra and visit her website www .herminiaibarra.com.

Reprinted from *Harvard Business Review*, January–February 2015 (product #R1501C).

3

What Bosses Gain by Being Vulnerable

By Emma Seppala

One morning in Bangalore, South India, Archana Patchirajan, founder of a technology startup, called her entire staff in for a meeting. When everyone was seated, she announced that she had to let them go because the startup had run out of funds. She could no longer pay them. Shockingly, her staff of high-caliber engineers who had their pick of jobs in the booming Silicon Valley of India, refused to go. They said they would rather work for half their pay than leave her. They stayed and kept working so hard that, a few years later, Patchirajan's company—Hubbl, which provides internet advertising solutions—sold for $14 million.

Patchirajan continues to work on startups from the United States, and her staff, though thousands of miles away from her, continues to work for her.

What explains the connection and devotion that Patchirajan's staff had toward her?

Patchirajan's story is particularly extraordinary when you consider the alarming fact that according to a Gallup study, 70% of employees are "not engaged" or are "actively disengaged" at work.[1] As a consequence, they are "less emotionally connected" and also "less likely to be productive." What is it about Patchirajan that not only prevented this phenomenon in her staff but actually flipped it?

When I asked one of Patchirajan's longest-standing employees what drove him and the rest of the team to stay with her, these are some of the things he shared: "We all work as a family because she treats us as such." "She knows everyone in the office and has a personal relationship with each one of us." "She does not get upset when we make mistakes but gives us the time to learn how to analyze and fix the situation."

If you look at these comments, they suggest that Patchirajan's relationship with her employees runs deeper than that of the usual employer-employee relationship. Simply put, she is vulnerable and authentic with them. She shared her doubts honestly when the company was going downhill, she does not adhere to a strict hierarchy but treats her employees like family members, and she has a personal relationship with each one of them. Sound touchy-feely, daunting, or counterintuitive? Here's why it's not.

Brené Brown, an expert on social connection, conducted thousands of interviews to discover what lies at the root of social connections. A thorough analysis of the data revealed what it was: vulnerability. Vulnerability here does not mean being weak or submissive. To the contrary, it implies the courage to be oneself. It means replacing "professional distance and cool" with uncertainty, risk, and emotional exposure. Opportunities for vulnerability present themselves to us at work every day. Some examples Patchirajan gives of vulnerability include calling an employee or colleague whose child is not well, reaching out to someone who has just had a loss in their family, asking someone for help, taking responsibility for something that went wrong at work, or sitting by the bedside of a colleague or employee with a terminal illness.

More important, Brown describes vulnerability and authenticity as being at the root of human connection. And human connection is often dramatically absent from workplaces. Johann Berlin, CEO of Transformational Leadership for Excellence (TLEX), recounts an experience he had while teaching a workshop at a *Fortune* 100 company. The participants were all higher-level management. After an exercise in which pairs of participants shared an event from their life with each other, one of the top executive managers approached Berlin. Visibly moved by the experience, he said "I've worked with my colleague for more than 25 years and have never known about the difficult times in his life." In a short moment of authentic connection, this manager's understanding and connection with his colleague deepened in ways that hadn't happened in decades of working together.

Why is human connection missing at work? As leaders and employees, we are often taught to keep a distance and project a certain image—one of confidence, competence, and authority. We may disclose our vulnerability to a spouse or close friend behind closed doors at night, but we would never show it elsewhere during the day, let alone at work.

However, data suggests that we may want to revisit the idea of projecting an image. Research shows that people subconsciously register a lack of authenticity in others. Just by looking at someone, we download large amounts of information. "We are programmed to observe each other's states so we can more appropriately interact, empathize, or assert our boundaries—whatever the situation may require," says Paula Niedenthal, professor of psychology at the University of Wisconsin–Madison. We are wired to read each others' expressions in a very nuanced way. This process is called "resonance," and it is so automatic and rapid that it often happens below our awareness.

Like an acute sounding board, parts of our brain internally echo what others do and feel. Just by looking at someone, you experience them: You internally resonate with them. Ever seen someone trip and momentarily felt a twinge of pain for them? Observing them activates the "pain matrix" in your brain, research shows.[2] Ever been moved by the sight of a person helping someone? You vicariously experienced it and thereby felt elevation. Someone's smile activates the smile muscles in our face, while a frown activates our frown muscles, according to research by Ulf Dimberg at Uppsala University in Sweden.[3] We internally register what another person is feeling. As a consequence, if a smile is fake, we are more likely to feel uncomfortable than comfortable.

While we may try to appear perfect, strong, or intelligent to be respected by others, pretense often has the opposite effect intended. Paula Niedenthal's research shows that we resonate too deeply with one another to ignore inauthenticity.[4] Just think of how uncomfortable you feel around someone you perceive as "taking on airs" or "putting on a show." We tend to see right through them and feel less connected. Or think of how you respond when you know someone is upset, but they're trying to conceal it. "What's wrong?" you ask, only to be told, "Nothing!" Rarely does this answer satisfy—because we sense it's not true.

Our brains are wired to read cues so subtle that even when we don't consciously register the cues, our bodies respond. For example, when someone is angry but keeps their feelings bottled up, we may not realize that they are angry (they don't *look* angry) but still our blood pressure will increase, according to research by James Gross at Stanford University.[5]

Why do we feel more comfortable around someone who is authentic and vulnerable? Because we are particularly sensitive to signs of trustworthiness in our leaders.[6] Servant leadership, for example, which is characterized by authenticity and values-based leadership, yields more positive and constructive behavior in employees and greater feelings of hope and trust in both the leader and the organization.[7] In turn, trust in a leader improves employee performance.[8] You can even see this at the level of the brain. Employees who recall a boss who resonated with them show enhanced activation in parts of the brain related to positive emotion and social connection.[9] The reverse is true when they think of a boss who did not resonate.

One example of authenticity and vulnerability is forgiveness. Forgiveness doesn't mean tolerance of error but rather a patient encouragement of growth.

Forgiveness is what Archana Patchirajan's employee described as, "She does not get upset when we make mistakes but gives us the time to learn how to analyze and fix the situation." Forgiveness may be another soft-sounding term but, as University of Michigan researcher Kim Cameron points out in the book *Positive Organizational Behavior*, it has hard results: A culture of forgiveness in organizations can lead to increased employee productivity as well as less voluntary turnover.[10] Again, a culture that is forgiving breeds trust. As a consequence, an organization becomes more resilient in times of organizational stress or downsizing.

Why do we fear vulnerability or think it's inappropriate for the workplace? For one, we are afraid that if someone finds out who we really are or discovers a soft or vulnerable spot, they will take advantage of us. However, as I describe in my hbr.org article, "The Hard Data on Being a Nice Boss," kindness goes further than the old sink-or-swim paradigm.

Here's what may happen if you embrace an authentic and vulnerable stance: Your staff will see you as a human being; they may feel closer to you, they may be prompted to share advice, and—if you are attached to hierarchy—you may find that your team begins to feel more horizontal. While these types of changes might feel uncomfortable, you may see, as in Patchirajan's case, that the benefits are worth it.

There are additional benefits you may reap from a closer connection to employees, too. One study out of Stanford shows that CEOs are looking for more advice and counsel but that two thirds of them don't get it.[11] This isolation can skew perspectives and lead to potentially disadvantageous leadership choices. Who better to receive advice from than your own employees, who are intimately familiar with your product, your customers, and problems that might exist within the organization?

Rather than feeling like another peg in the system, your team members will feel respected and honored for their opinions and will consequently become more loyal. The research shows that the personal connection and happiness employees derive from their work fosters greater loyalty than the amount on their paycheck.[12]

EMMA SEPPALA, PH.D., is the science director of Stanford University's Center for Compassion and Altruism Research and Education and author of *The Happiness Track*. She is also founder of Fulfillment Daily. Follow her on Twitter @emmaseppala or her website www.emmaseppala.com.

Notes

1. "Report: State of the American Workplace," Gallup poll, September 22, 2014, http://www.gallup.com/services/176708/state-american-workplace.aspx.
2. C. Lamm et al., "What Are You Feeling? Using Functional Magnetic Resonance Imaging to Assess the Modulation of Sensory and Affective Responses During Empathy for Pain," *PLOS One* 2, no. 12 (2007): e1292.
3. U. Dimberg, M. Thunberg, K. Elmehed, "Unconscious Facial Reactions to Emotional Facial Expressions," *Psychological Science* 11, no. 1 (2000): 86–89.

4. S. Korb et al., "The Perception and Mimicry of Facial Movements Predict Judgments of Smile Authenticity," *PLOS One* 9, no. 6 (2014): e99194.

5. J. Gross and R. Levenson, "Emotional Suppression: Physiology, Self-Report, and Expressive Behavior," *Journal of Personality and Social Psychology* 64, no. 6 (1993): 970–986.

6. K. Dirks and D. Ferrin, "Trust in Leadership: Meta-Analytic Findings and Implications for Research and Practice," *Journal of Applied Psychology* 87, no. 4 (2002): 611–628.

7. E. Joseph and B. Winston, "A Correlation of Servant Leadership, Leader Trust, and Organizational Trust," *Leadership & Organization Development Journal* 26, no. 1 (2005): 6–22; T. Searle and J. Barbuto, "Servant Leadership, Hope, and Organizational Virtuousness: A Framework Exploring Positive Micro and Macro Behaviors and Performance Impact," *Journal of Leadership & Organizational Studies* 18, no. 1 (2011): 107–117.

8. T. Bartram and G. Casimir, "The Relationship Between Leadership and Follower In-Role Performance and Satisfaction with the Leader: The Mediating Effects of Empowerment and Trust in the Leader," *Leadership & Organization Development Journal* 28, no. 1 (2007): 4–19.

9. R. Boyatzis et al., "Examination of the Neural Substrates Activated in Memories of Experiences with Resonant and Dissonant Leaders," *The Leadership Quarterly* 23, no. 2 (2012): 259–272.

10. K. Cameron, "Forgiveness in Organizations," *Positive Organizational Behavior*, ed. D. L. Nelson and C. L. Cooper (London: Sage Publications, 2007), 129–142.

11. Stanford GSB staff, "David Larcker: 'Lonely at the Top' Resonates for Most CEOs," *Insights* by Stanford Graduate School of Business, July 31, 2013, https://www.gsb.stanford.edu/insights/david-larcker-lonely-top-resonates-most-ceos.

12. The Association of Accounting Technicians, "Britain's Workers Value Companionship and Recognition Over a Big Salary, a Recent Report Revealed," July 15, 2014, https://www.aat.org.uk/about-aat/press-releases/britains-workers-value-companionship-recognition-over-big-salary.

Adapted from content posted on hbr.org,
December 11, 2014 (product #H01R7U).

4

Practice Tough Empathy

By Rob Goffee and Gareth Jones

There's altogether too much hype nowadays about the idea that leaders *must* show concern for their teams. There's nothing worse than seeing a manager return from the latest interpersonal-skills training program with "concern" for others. Real leaders don't need a training program to convince their employees that they care. Real leaders empathize fiercely with the people they lead. They also care intensely about the work their employees do.

Consider Alain Levy, the former CEO of Polygram. Although he often comes across as a rather aloof intellectual, Levy is well able to close the distance between himself and his followers. On one occasion, he helped some junior record executives in Australia choose singles off albums. Picking singles is a critical task in the music business: The selection of a song can make or break the album. Levy sat down with the young people and took on the work with passion. "You bloody idiots," he added his voice to the melee, "you don't know what the hell you're talking about; we always have a dance track first!" Within 24 hours, the story spread throughout the company; it was the best PR Levy ever got. "Levy really knows how to pick singles," people said. In fact, he knew how to identify with the work, and he knew how to enter his followers' world—one where strong, colorful language is the norm—to show them that he cared.

Clearly, as the above example illustrates, we do not believe that the empathy of inspirational leaders is the soft kind described in so much of the management literature. On the contrary, we feel that real leaders manage through a unique approach we call tough empathy. Tough empathy means giving people what they need, not what they want. Organizations like the Marine Corps and consulting firms specialize in tough empathy. Recruits are pushed to be the best that they can be; "grow or go" is the motto. Chris Satterwaite, the CEO of Bell Pottinger Communications and a former chief executive of several ad agencies, understands what tough empathy is all about. He adeptly handles the challenges of managing creative people while making tough decisions. "If I have to, I can be ruthless," he says. "But while they're with me, I promise my people that they'll learn."

At its best, tough empathy balances respect for the individual and for the task at hand. Attending to both, however, isn't easy, especially when the business is in survival mode. At such times, caring leaders have to give selflessly to the people around them and know when to pull back. Consider a situation at Unilever at a time when it was developing Persil Power, a detergent that eventually had to be removed from the market because it destroyed clothes that were

laundered in it. Even though the product was showing early signs of trouble, CEO Niall FitzGerald stood
by his troops. "That was the popular place to be, but
I should not have been there," he says now. "I should
have stood back, cool and detached, looked at the
whole field, watched out for the customer." But caring
with detachment is not easy, especially since, when
done right, tough empathy is harder on you than on
your employees. "Some theories of leadership make
caring look effortless. It isn't," says Paulanne Man-
cuso, president and CEO of Calvin Klein Cosmetics. "You have to do things you don't want to do, and
that's hard." It's tough to be tough.

Tough empathy also has the benefit of impelling
leaders to take risks. When Greg Dyke took over at
the BBC, his commercial competitors were able to
spend substantially more on programs than the BBC
could. Dyke quickly realized that in order to thrive
in a digital world, the BBC needed to increase its ex-

penditures. He explained this openly and directly to the staff. Once he had secured their buy-in, he began thoroughly restructuring the organization. Although many employees were let go, he was able to maintain people's commitment. Dyke attributed his success to his tough empathy with employees: "Once you have the people with you, you can make the difficult decisions that need to be made."

One final point about tough empathy: Those more apt to use it are people who really care about something. And when people care deeply about something—anything—they're more likely to show their true selves. They will not only communicate authenticity, which is the precondition for leadership, but they will show that they are doing more than just playing a role. People do not commit to executives who merely live up to the obligations of their jobs. They want more. They want someone who cares passionately about the people and the work—just as they do.

ROB GOFFEE is Emeritus Professor of Organisational Behaviour at London Business School, where he teaches in the world-renowned Senior Executive Programme. GARETH JONES is a Fellow of the Centre for Management Development at London Business School and a visiting professor at Spain's IE Business School in Madrid. Goffee and Jones consult to the boards of several global companies and are coauthors of *Why Should Anyone Be Led by You?*, *Clever*, and *Why Should Anyone Work Here?*, all published by Harvard Business Review Press.

Excerpted from "Why Should Anyone Be
Led By You?" in *Harvard Business Review*,
September–October 2000 (product #R00506).

5

Cracking the Code That Stalls People of Color

By Sylvia Ann Hewlett

I t's a topic that corporations once routinely ignored, then dismissed, and are only now beginning to discuss: the dearth of professionals of color in senior positions. Professionals of color hold only 11% of executive posts in corporate America.[1] Among *Fortune* 500 CEOs, only six are black, eight are Asian, and eight are Hispanic.[2]

Performance and hard work, along with sponsors, get top talent recognized and promoted, but leadership potential isn't enough to lever men and women into the executive suite. Top jobs are given to those who also look and act the part, who manifest "executive presence" (EP). According to research by the Center for Talent Innovation (CTI), EP constitutes 26% of what senior leaders say it takes to get the next promotion.[3] Yet because senior leaders are overwhelmingly Caucasian, professionals of color (African American, Asian, and Hispanic individuals) find themselves at an immediate disadvantage in trying to look, sound, and act like a leader. And the feedback that might help them do so is markedly absent at all levels of management.

Executive presence rests on three pillars: gravitas (the core characteristic, according to 67% of the 268 senior executives surveyed), an amalgam of behaviors that convey confidence, inspire trust, and bolster credibility; communication skills (according to 28%); and appearance, the filter through which communication skills and gravitas become more apparent. While they are aware of the importance of EP, men and women of color are nonetheless hard-pressed to interpret and embody aspects of a code written by and for white men.

Research from CTI finds that professionals of color, like their Caucasian counterparts, prioritize gravitas over communication and communication over appearance. Yet, "cracking the code" of executive presence presents unique challenges for professionals of color because standards of appropriate behavior, speech, and attire demand they suppress or sacrifice aspects of their cultural identity in order to conform. They overwhelmingly feel that EP at their firm is based on white male standards—African Americans, especially, were 97% more likely than their Caucasian counterparts to agree with this assessment—and that conforming to these standards requires altering their authenticity, a new version of "bleached-out professionalism" that contributes to feelings of resentment and disengagement. (See figures 2 and 3.) People of color already feel they have to work harder than their

FIGURE 2

Executive presence at my company is defined as conforming to traditionally white male standards

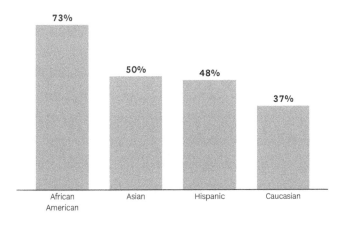

Source: Center for Talent Innovation

Caucasian counterparts just to be perceived as being on a par with them; more than half (56%) of minority professionals also feel they are held to a stricter code of EP standards.

FIGURE 3

I feel the need to compromise my authenticity to conform to executive presence standards at my company

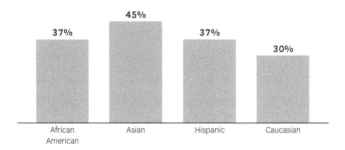

Source: Center for Talent Innovation

Executive presence further eludes professionals of color because they're not likely to get feedback on their "presentation of self." Qualitative findings affirm that their superiors, most of whom are white, hesitate to call attention to gravitas shortfalls or communication blunders for fear of coming across as racially insensitive or discriminatory. While sponsors might close this gap by specifically addressing EP issues with their high potentials, CTI's 2012 research shows that professionals of color are much less likely to have a sponsor than Caucasians (8% versus 13%).[4] When they do get feedback, they're unclear about how to act on it, particularly if they were born outside the United States. (See figure 4.) This is a serious problem for corporations that need local expertise to expand their influence in global markets.

In short, because feedback is either absent, overly vague, or contradictory, executive presence remains an inscrutable set of rules for professionals of color— rules they're judged by but cannot interpret and embody except at considerable cost to their authenticity. Consequently, in a workplace where unconscious bias continues to permeate the corridors of power and leadership is mostly white and male, professionals of color are measurably disadvantaged in their efforts to be perceived as leaders.

FIGURE 4

Unclear on how to correct issues raised by feedback

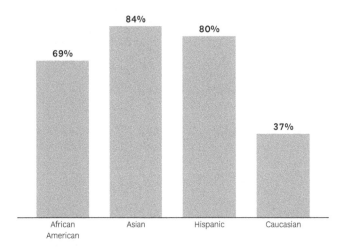

Source: Center for Talent Innovation

As America becomes more diverse at home and its companies are increasingly engaged in the global marketplace, winning in today's fiercely competitive economy requires a diverse workforce that "matches the market." Such individuals are better attuned to the unmet needs of consumers or clients like themselves. Research from CTI shows, however, that their insights need a key ingredient to reach full-scale implementation: a cadre of equally diverse leaders.[5] Yet the power of difference is missing at the top, just when it matters most.

SYLVIA ANN HEWLETT is the founder and CEO of the Center for Talent Innovation and the founder of Hewlett Consulting Partners LLC.

Notes

1. U.S. Equal Employment Opportunity Commission, *Job Patterns For Minorities And Women In Private Industry* (2009 EEO-1 National Aggregate Report), 2009.
2. DiversityInc. staff, "Where's the Diversity in *Fortune* 500 CEOs?" October 8, 2012, https://www.diversityinc.com/diversity-facts/wheres-the-diversity-in-fortune-500-ceos/.
3. S. Hewlett et al., "Cracking the Code: Executive Presence and Multicultural Professionals," Center for Talent Innovation, 2013.

4. S. Hewlett et al., "Vaulting the Color Bar: How Sponsorship Levers Multicultural Professionals into Leadership," Center for Talent Innovation, 2012.

5. S. Hewlett et al., "Innovation, Diversity, and Market Growth," Center for Talent Innovation, 2013.

Adapted from content posted on hbr.org,
January 22, 2014 (product #H00MV0).

6

For a Corporate Apology to Work, the CEO Should Look Sad

By Sarah Green Carmichael

S traight up, we made some mistakes," Whole Foods co-CEOs John Mackey and Walter Robb said in a video apology in response to an over-charging scandal.

"We weren't prepared for the crisis, and we dropped the ball," wrote Airbnb CEO Brian Chesky on the Airbnb blog in 2011, after a guest trashed a host's home.

"This should never have happened. It is simply unacceptable," said Mary Barra, CEO of GM, in one of several public apologies in the wake of safety scandals at the automaker.

The corporate apology, once a relative rarity, has become a normal part of business discourse. Stuff happens, and then we say we're sorry for it. But just because corporate apologies have become commonplace doesn't mean they're all created equal.

Two new studies shed light on what makes some apologies effective and what makes others backfire.

First, Leanne ten Brinke of the UC Berkeley Haas School of Business and Gabrielle S. Adams of the London Business School examine how expressions of emotion affect corporate apologies. Publishing in the journal *Organizational Behavior and Human Decision Processes*, they present the findings of two studies.[1]

In the first study, they looked at how investors reacted to real apologies from executives. They examined 29 online videos of apologies made between 2007 and 2011. Using an established system for distinguishing facial expressions (the Facial Action Coding System, or FACS), their researchers watched each video second by second, without sound, and tracked the expressions that flitted across the executives' faces. Were they frowning? Smiling? Looking sad? Then Brinke and Adams looked at what happened to the company's stock price after the apology. They found that for those leaders who had apologized with a smile, the stock price dropped—perhaps because the leader seemed insincere delivering his apology, or even seemed to be enjoying the suffering his company had caused. The more the person smiled, the worse his company performed.

For the leaders who appeared genuinely contrite, at first it seemed like there was no impact on stock price: The company neither performed worse nor performed better. "Normative emotions simply allow the company to move forward," they write.

But then the researchers took a closer look at CEO apologies, specifically—16 out of the 29 cases. They found that when an apology was delivered by a CEO who looked sad, the company's stock price actually rose post-apology. They determined that "a good apology can build investor confidence," especially in the long term.

To investigate this further, Brinke and Adams conducted an experiment in which they hired an actor to portray an airline CEO apologizing for a computer malfunction that canceled 140 flights, stranding thousands of passengers—a scenario based on a real Alaska Airlines snafu. They made sure his fictional apology contained all the verbal elements of a good apology: the components previous research has identified as being central to repairing relationships, including an explicit "I'm sorry," an offer of repair, an explanation, taking responsibility, and a promise of forbearance. They then recruited subjects to watch this fictional CEO apologize—either happily, sadly, or neutrally. When the CEO appeared sad, participants rated him as more sincere and were more likely to want to reconcile with him. When the CEO delivered his apology with a smile on his face—or, interestingly, a neutral expression—the study participants were less likely to trust him, and the apology even seemed to exacerbate their negative feelings.

Even seasoned leaders are likely to find delivering an apology to be an uncomfortable experience, and when we feel uncomfortable, a normal reaction is to grimace, laugh awkwardly, or even try to break the tension with a joke. Leaders (especially Americans) may also feel they can't show too much sadness or anguish but instead must present a positive front at all times. The research by Brinke and Adams reminds us how these understandable impulses can backfire.

Another paper that appeared in the *Journal of Corporate Finance* adds an interesting wrinkle to this subject.[2] Researchers Don Chance, James Cicon, and Stephen P. Ferris examined 150 press releases from 1993 to 2009 to examine how companies fared when they blamed themselves for poor performance as opposed to blaming external factors. They found that while companies are twice as likely to blame external factors when things go wrong, passing the buck results in continued financial decline. Conversely, companies that take responsibility for their missed earnings stabilize and eventually see an uptick in financial performance. (Interestingly, both groups were about equally likely to fire their CEOs.)

Why? After eliminating numerous factors, the researchers conclude that being honest and specific about the source of the problem—both characteristics of self-blaming statements—not only cheers up investors, it likely helps the company turn around the issue more quickly. Conversely, the companies that blamed external factors were often vague (blaming "economic forces" for instance) and seen as less honest (since many of their wounds had actually been self-inflicted).

The message is loud and clear: When you mess up, admit it. And look appropriately sad about it.

SARAH GREEN CARMICHAEL is a senior editor at *Harvard Business Review*. Follow her on Twitter @skgreen.

Notes

1. L. ten Brinke and G. Adams, "Saving Face? When Emotion Displays During Public Apologies Mitigate Damage to Organizational Performance," *Organizational Behavior and Human Decision Processes* 130 (2015): 1–12.
2. D. Chance, J. Cicon, and S. Ferris, "Poor Performance and the Value of Corporate Honesty," *Journal of Corporate Finance* 33 (2015): 1–18.

Adapted from "Research: For a Corporate Apology to Work, the CEO Should Look Sad," hbr.org, August 24, 2015 (product #H02AMD).

7

Are Leaders Getting Too Emotional?

An interview with Gautam Mukunda
and Gianpiero Petriglieri by Adi Ignatius
and Sarah Green Carmichael

There's a lot of crying and shouting both in politics and at the office. Gautam Mukunda of Harvard Business School and Gianpiero Petriglieri of INSEAD help us try to make sense of it all.

Sarah Green Carmichael: *It seems today, with leaders being in public more, there is an emphasis on our leaders always being authentic—that's the buzzword. And tears and shouting do seem to exude authenticity. Gianpiero, what do you make of that? Are our leaders crying and shouting to prove to us that they are real in some way?*

Gianpiero Petriglieri: I don't think people care about leaders being authentic. I think people care about leaders being consistent. Emotions are a great way to convey that you mean what you're saying.

I think we also need to make a distinction between people in positions of power, where emotional expression is always problematic because you expect a certain contained demeanor—although norms are changing, as Gautam has said—and leaders, where emotions are the whole thing. Emotions constitute the connection between people whom we follow and ourselves. So just because you happen to be in a position of visible power, that doesn't mean people regard you as a leader.

In fact, demonstrating emotion is a way of claiming, "Hey, I'm here. I think you should pay attention to this. And I am credibly voicing a concern that we should all care about." Emotions are a way in which people in power try to lead.

Adi Ignatius: *Gianpiero, let me follow up on that because you said that people don't care about their leaders being authentic, and that's basically challenging an entire industry—a sub-industry in the management business that says leaders do need to be authentic. Talk about that a little bit, particularly in the context of emotions. You almost sounded Machiavellian in what you were saying, that a leader can be whatever—they can be emotional—but the point is to be consistent and therefore effective. Can you talk more about that?*

GP: Now when you talk about authenticity, you're talking about two different things. One is spontaneity, which is to say, "I voice my feelings of the moment." Now that might—or much more likely might not—be appropriate for you as a leader.

Then, another part of authenticity means, "I voice credibly, consistently, and authentically the feelings that other people are also feeling. I am showing that we are, in a way, sharing the same concern. I am, in many ways, concerned and I care about the same things that you care about."

This is what you see leaders doing all the time. Sometimes in a Machiavellian way. But sometimes in a very genuine way. In fact, one of the very reasons why we end up following someone is because they seem to be genuinely concerned about things we care about. In politics you see it a lot. You see in political campaigns one candidate saying, "I am one of you guys. I am like you. I have your same background. I care about the same things. But this other guy, he or she is really out for themselves." And the other person is saying the same thing: "No, no, no. *I'm* actually talking about what we all care about. And this other person is out for themselves."

Whoever manages to define themselves as one of us and define the opponent as personally interested wins. So what I'm saying is we don't particularly care that our leader is expressing something that's authentic to them. What we really care about is that our leader is expressing emotions that are meaningful to us.

This is why emotional expression is a double-edged sword. Because sometimes people interpret an emotion as essentially an act of selfishness—that the emotion is really an expression of you being more preoccupied with yourself than with me.

But sometimes people interpret an emotion as an act of generosity: This really shows that you were feeling what I am also feeling. Remember Bill Clinton? In '92 there was a moment during his first campaign where he said in a rally, "I feel your pain." And that remained a legendary moment in his first election. Because he was doing what leaders always try to do, not always manipulatively or in a way that's Machiavellian, but often very genuinely to convey that the leader shares not just the same *understanding* of our situation but the same *experience* of our situation. This is what most of us have always wanted in the people that

we then trust to lead, not just that they intellectually understand our circumstances, but that they
feel what it's like to be in our circumstances—that
they feel our pain, they feel our concerns, they aspire to our same aspirations, they desire our same
desires.

That's ultimately what we care about when we
say we want leaders to be authentic. We want them
to have a lived understanding of our predicament.
We don't just want them to express what happens
to be true to them at that particular moment.

AI: *Gautam, do you agree with that? Because that
seems to be a statement that empathy and emotional
intelligence are really the key to leadership. I'm sim-
plifying, but does that all make sense to you?*

Gautam Mukunda: I think empathy and emotional intelligence are extraordinarily powerful
keys to leadership. You do often hear people

saying—if you look at the Trump phenomenon here in the United States, for example—that they want leaders to tell them what they really think, as opposed to just telling them what the leader *thinks* they want to hear in order to gain power.

But of course it's worth noting that the same people who say this then support those who tell them what they want to hear, not in fact what they really think. So there is some level of doublethink, where, "Donald Trump says what I think, so that must be what he really thinks."

It's that ability to tell people what they want to hear in a way that they believe that you're being sincere that strikes me as being a pretty effective tool in getting power. And certainly, what I got from Gianpiero's comment is the extent to which we want our leaders to be not just self-interested but interested in the welfare of the group, of the people they lead, as much as themselves. And that, essentially, many of these contests for power involve people struggling to define their opponents as only being self-interested.

I think that's true across almost any organization. A leader who is self-interested is one whose followers will be much less likely to lead. But to me, then, you get this question: What are emotions?

Even a very skilled actor, for example, finds it difficult to fake tears on cue. That's something that even professional actors can struggle with. So when President Obama cries over children who are murdered in a school, there is a sense that he's revealing some deeply held emotion.

It is also striking, of course, that so much of the conservative response to that statement was to suggest that he had onions or something under the podium that were allowing him to fake it, both because I think the people saying this realize how powerful it was to see a president break down in tears and because it reveals something about themselves—that they felt that the murder of many innocent children was somehow something that wouldn't move a person to tears.

GP: You see, I don't think people just want to hear leaders tell them what they think. I think people want to see leaders show them what they themselves feel. They want to see their leaders express the feeling that they also sense to be true.

Of course, not everyone shares the same feelings. The example Gautam brings up—President Obama crying—it's an extremely powerful message. And it humanizes a leader. For people who share the same dismay, the same discomfort, that humanization actually enhances his leadership. And for people who oppose his understanding of the situation, for people who don't share his sentiments, that humanization diminishes his leadership. This is where emotional expression is always a double-edged sword. Because the people who share the sentiments you are expressing will actually feel closer to you and, therefore, feel that you are more of a leader. And the people who don't share those sentiments will suddenly feel more distant from you, and they will suspect that you are being manipulative, Machiavellian, and whatnot.

In that moment, you have a man who occupies one of the most powerful positions of leadership in the world facing, on his watch, a tragedy. A tragedy that, despite all his power, he cannot reverse. He is therefore expressing frustration at the limitation of that power—a frustration that's not just his own but is also expressed on behalf of a large group of people who probably feel that it is a tragedy that could easily have been prevented with political will, with political action. And it isn't prevented simply because there is not enough political will to implement the changes that you would need for gun control.

SGC: *In that moment, President Obama crying—would that moment have been different if he were a female president? Is there something different about when you see a man break down that way and a female leader of that stature break down that way?*

GM: I mean, surely, without a doubt. The criticism that someone is too emotional is one of the classic gendered tropes that are used to go after female leaders. It's worth noting that when Hillary Clinton cried a little bit in 2008 in New Hampshire it was highlighted as one of the high points of her campaign. This was one of the moments that turned it around and put her back into the race against Obama in 2008.

But it's illustrative that one of the criticisms of Hillary is that she's robotic. Right? So that was a breakthrough of that facade.

I think for most women leaders it's a much riskier proposition to cry than for a male leader to do so. It just plays into gendered stereotypes that opponents of that leader can use to weaken them very rapidly.

SGC: *We should also probably mention here that there may be racial stereotypes. There may be other emotions, like maybe anger, that Obama might get in trouble for expressing that Hillary would not.*

GM: Without a doubt. On those few occasions when Barack Obama has revealed how he thinks about the way he presents himself—and it's clear that he is someone who thinks deeply about this kind of thing and is very self-reflective on these issues—he has said that, above all else, the thing that he most strives to avoid is being perceived as the angry black man. That's the phrase that he used. And that this is a profound force that is shaping how he wants to be seen.

He essentially feels that visible expressions of anger are, because of racial dynamics in the United States, almost entirely off limits to him as a leader. And in fact, if you note, before he was reelected, anger was in fact entirely off limits to him as a leader. I can't think of any time that he expressed anger in those first four years. What we've started to see after he was reelected, and particularly in the past year, is that he essentially has more freedom to express these emotions. And he is taking advantage of it quite powerfully on some occasions.

AI: *So given what you said, would you advise female executives to hold their emotions in check? That it may not be fair, but society will still hold it against them if they cry in public in front of their teams?*

GM: First, I would advise any leader, male or female, to work pretty hard to do that. The power of these moments is at least in part precisely because they are rare.

John Boehner's tendency to break down in tears became a punch line in Washington. I don't think it was an asset to his leadership. When Barack Obama did it, it was striking because we had never seen a president do something like that, that I can recall.

So male or female, I would say, if you are extraordinarily emotional at all times, that is likely to be a handicap for you as a leader at least to some extent. I would tell female executives that it is deeply unfair, but they are being judged more harshly.

And they surely know that better than I ever could; I've never spoken with a woman leader who wasn't well aware of that fact and who hadn't thought through the fact that they were being judged by standards that their male counterparts were not.

But it is too easy to use gendered attacks—to argue that someone is overly emotional and not thinking things through—against a female leader, or any female leader in a contentious situation where there are people trying to undercut her, to not be extremely cautious of that concern.

SGC: *Gianpiero, do you have anything to add either about the anger issue or the weeping issue?*

GP: I generally think outrage is a lot easier to fake than sadness. And perhaps a lot easier to mistrust, frankly. See, I think we risk spending too much tension under the stereotypes about what you should or shouldn't do.

I would tend to agree that, especially for a senior or a visible leader in politics or business, it's a good rule of thumb to have a relatively contained demeanor. I also think that anyone who wants to really be a leader—not just call themselves one—

has to have some kind of relationship with their emotional life. They ought to be able to ask themselves not just, "Do I express emotions or not?" but to be a little bit more sophisticated with themselves and with others to ask, "How do I express emotions?"

If you are attentive to the undercurrent of organizational lives, emotions are constantly being expressed. When I work with senior management teams, my first question is never, "Do you openly express emotions or not?" My first question is, "How do you tend to express emotions?"

So, for example, one classic way to scream your divergence with a group's opinion is simply not to show up. Or to show up late to a meeting and say nothing when everyone else is very animated. That's a very overt, very visible expression of disappointment or even aggression. Now, whether that's discussed, whether that's decoded, whether that's verbalized is a different thing. Just because we aren't verbalizing our emotions or melting into tears doesn't mean we aren't expressing strong emotions or that we aren't expressing emotions appropriately. Too detached of an emotional response can very often be extremely inappropriate and extremely ineffective.

So I think, as a leader, the more important questions are: Do you know what you're feeling? And do you know whose feelings those are? Do you know why you're feeling that way? Are you interpreting those feelings just as an expression of your emotional state of the moment? Or are you able to think more deeply about what those feelings are telling you about what's happening around you—what's happening to the people that you're responsible for? And can you make sense of and then articulate them in a way that is useful, in a way that actually advances the task?

GAUTAM MUKUNDA is an assistant professor in the Organizational Behavior Unit of Harvard Business School. He received his Ph.D. from MIT in political science. His first book is *Indispensable: When Leaders Really Matter* (Harvard Business Review Press, 2012). GIANPIERO PETRIGLIERI is an associate professor of organizational behavior at INSEAD, where he directs the Management Acceleration Programme, the school's flagship executive program for emerging leaders. A medical doctor and psychiatrist by training, he researches and practices leadership development. Follow him on Twitter @gpetriglieri. ADI IGNATIUS is the editor in chief of *Harvard Business Review*. SARAH GREEN CARMICHAEL is a senior editor at *Harvard Business Review*. Follow her on Twitter @skgreen.

Adapted from "Are Leaders Getting Too Emotional?"
on *HBR IdeaCast* (podcast), March 17, 2016.

Index

Index

How to be human at work.

HBR's Emotional Intelligence Series features smart, essential reading on the human side of professional life from the pages of *Harvard Business Review*. Each book in the series offers uplifting stories, practical advice, and research from leading experts on how to tend to our emotional well-being at work.

Harvard Business Review Emotional Intelligence Series

Available in paperback or ebook format. The specially priced six-volume set includes:

- Mindfulness
- Resilience
- Influence and Persuasion
- Authentic Leadership
- Happiness
- Empathy

HBR.ORG

Buy for your team, clients, or event.
Visit hbr.org/bulksales for quantity discount rates.

Happiness

HBR EMOTIONAL INTELLIGENCE SERIES

1

Happiness Isn't the Absence of Negative Feelings

By Jennifer Moss

Happiness feels intolerably elusive for many of us. Like fog, you can see it from afar, dense and full of shape. But upon approach, its particles loosen, and suddenly it becomes out of reach, even though it's all around you.

We put so much emphasis on the pursuit of happiness, but if you stop and think about it, to pursue is to chase something without a guarantee of ever catching it.

Up until about six years ago, I was fervently and ineffectively chasing happiness. My husband, Jim, and I were living in San Jose, California, with our two-year-old son and a second baby on the way. On

3

paper, our life appeared rosy. Still, I couldn't seem to find the joy. I always felt so guilty about my sadness. My problems were embarrassingly "first world."

Then in September 2009, my world tilted. Jim fell severely ill. He was diagnosed with Swine Flu (H1N1) and West Nile virus, then Guillain-Barré Syndrome, due to his compromised immune system.

Jim never worried about death. I did.

When we were told Jim's illness was letting up, that he'd won this round, we were relieved. When we were told Jim might not walk for some time—likely a year, maybe longer—we were alarmed. We knew this prognosis meant the end of Jim's career as a pro lacrosse player. What we didn't know was how we'd pay the medical bills or how much energy Jim would have for parenting.

With 10 weeks to go until the baby arrived, I had very little time to think and reflect. Jim, on the other hand, *only* had time. He was used to moving at high speeds, both in life and on the field, so minutes passed like hours in the hospital. He was kept busy with physical and occupational therapy, but he was also in need of psychological support.

He put out a note to people in his social networks, asking them for reading suggestions that would help him to mentally heal. Suggestions flowed in. Books and audio tapes were delivered bedside with notes about how they'd "helped so much" after whatever difficulty this person had also experienced but overcame.

Jim would spend his days reading motivational books from Tony Robbins and Oprah or watching TED talks, like Jill Bolte Taylor's "My Stroke of Insight," about the impacts of brain trauma. He would analyze spiritual books by Deepak Chopra and the Dalai Lama. Or review scientific research papers about happiness and gratitude written by researchers Martin Seligman, Shawn Achor, Sonja Lyubomirsky, and many others.

There was a repeated theme throughout all the literature—gratitude. It would weave in and out of the science, the true stories, and the drivers for success. Jim responded by starting a gratitude journal of his own. He got very thankful—thankful for the people who changed his sheets, thankful for the family that would bring him hot meals at dinner. Thankful for the nurse who would encourage him and thankful for the extra attention his rehab team would give him on their own time. (The team once told Jim that they were only putting in extra time because they knew how grateful he was for their efforts.)

He asked that I participate in his approach, and because I wanted to help him to heal so badly and I was seeing how hard it was for him, I tried hard to be in a positive place when I came into his world inside that hospital room. I wasn't always at my best. I sometimes resented that I couldn't break down—but after a while I started to see how rapidly he was getting better. And although our paths weren't congruent, we were making it work. I was "coming around."

It was shaky and scary, but when Jim walked out of the hospital on crutches (he stubbornly refused the wheelchair) only six weeks after he was rushed by ambulance to the ER, we decided there was something more to his healing than just dumb luck.

One of those early books that influenced Jim was Seligman's *Flourish*. A psychologist and former president of the American Psychology Association, Seligman was responsible for defining the term "PERMA," the root of many positive psychology research projects around the world. The acronym stands for the five elements essential to lasting contentment:

- *Positive emotion*: Peace, gratitude, satisfaction, pleasure, inspiration, hope, curiosity, and love fall into this category.

- *Engagement*: Losing ourselves in a task or project provides us with a sense of "disappeared time" because we are so highly engaged.

7

- *Relationships*: People who have meaningful, positive relationships with others are happier than those who do not.

- *Meaning*: Meaning comes from serving a cause bigger than ourselves. Whether it's a religion or a cause that helps humanity in some way, we all need meaning in our lives.

- *Accomplishment/achievement*: To feel significant life satisfaction, we must strive to better ourselves.

We slowly brought these five tenets back into our lives. Jim returned to Wilfrid Laurier University in Ontario to research neuroscience, and we promptly started up Plasticity Labs to help teach others what we'd learned about the pursuit of happiness. As our lives came to include more empathy, gratitude, and meaning, I stopped feeling sad.

So when I see skepticism directed at the positive psychology movement, I take it personally. Do these critics have a problem with gratitude? Relationships? Meaning? Hope?

Perhaps part of the problem is that we oversimplify happiness in our pop culture and media, which makes it easy to discard as unproven. As Vanessa Buote, a postdoctoral fellow in social psychology, put it to me in an email:

One of the misconceptions about happiness is that happiness is being cheerful, joyous, and content all the time; always having a smile on your face. It's not—being happy and leading rich lives is about taking the good with the bad, and learning how to reframe the bad. In fact, in the recent [article in the Journal of Experimental Psychology*], "Emodiversity and the Emotional Ecosystem," by Harvard [researcher Jordi] Quoidbach, found that experiencing a wide range of* *emotions—both positive and negative—was linked to positive mental and physical well-being.*

Not only do we tend to misunderstand what happiness is, we also tend to chase it the wrong way. Shawn Achor, the researcher and corporate trainer who wrote the HBR article "Positive Intelligence," told me that most people think about happiness the wrong way: "The biggest misconception of the happiness industry is that happiness is an end, not a means. We think that if we get what we want, then we'll be happy. But it turns out that our brains actually work in the opposite direction."

Buote agrees: "We sometimes tend to see 'being happy' as the end goal, but we forget that what's really important is the journey; finding out what makes us the happiest and regularly engaging in those activities to help us lead a more fulfilling life."

In other words, we're not happy when we're chasing happiness. We're happiest when we're not thinking about it, when we're enjoying the present moment because we're lost in a meaningful project, working toward a higher goal, or helping someone who needs us.

Healthy positivity doesn't mean cloaking your authentic feelings. Happiness is not the absence of suffering; it's the ability to rebound from it. And happiness is not the same as joy or ecstasy; happiness includes contentment, well-being, and the emotional flexibility to experience a full range of emotions. At our company, some of us have dealt with anxiety and depression. Some have experienced PTSD. Some of us have witnessed severe mental illness in our families, and some of us have not. We openly share. Or we don't—either way is fine. We support tears in the office, if the situation calls for it (in both sorrow and in laughter).

Some people—perhaps looking for a fresh angle—have even argued that happiness is harmful (see, for example, the last two articles in this book). But the point of practicing exercises that help increase mental and emotional fitness is not to learn to paste a smile on your face or wish away your problems. It's to learn how to handle stressors with more resilience through training, just as you would train to run a marathon.

During my time with Jim in the hospital, I watched him change. It happened in subtle ways at first, but then all at once I realized that practicing gratitude and the happiness that comes with it had given me a gift: It gave me back Jim. If happiness is harmful—then I say, bring it on.

JENNIFER MOSS is a cofounder and chief communications officer of Plasticity Labs.

Adapted from content posted on hbr.org on August 20, 2015 (product #H02AEB).

2

Being Happy at Work Matters

By Annie McKee

People used to believe that you didn't have to be happy at work to succeed. And you didn't need to like the people you worked with, or even share their values. "Work is *not* personal," the thinking went. This is bunk.

My research with dozens of companies and hundreds of people—along with the research conducted by neuroscientists like Richard Davidson and V.S. Ramachandran and scholars such as Shawn Achor—increasingly points to a simple fact: Happy people are better workers. Those who are engaged with their jobs and colleagues work harder—and smarter.

And yet, an alarmingly high number of people aren't engaged. According to a sobering 2013 Gallup report, only 30% of the U.S. workforce *is* engaged. This echoes what I've seen in my work. Not very many people are truly "emotionally and intellectually committed" to their organizations.[1] Far too many couldn't care less about what's happening around them. For them, Wednesday is "hump day" and they're just working to get to Friday. And then there's the other end of the bell curve—the nearly one out of five employees who is actively *disengaged*, according to the same Gallup report. These people are sabotaging projects, backstabbing colleagues, and generally wreaking havoc in their workplaces.

The Gallup report also notes that employee engagement has remained largely constant over the years despite economic ups and downs. Scary: We're not engaged with work, and we haven't been for a long time.

Disengaged, unhappy people aren't any fun to work with and don't add much value; they impact our or-

ganizations (and our economy) in profoundly negative ways. It's even worse when leaders are disengaged because they infect others with their attitude.
Their emotions and mindsets impact others' moods
and performance tremendously. After all, how we feel
is linked to what and how we think. In other words,
thought influences emotion, and emotion influences
thinking.[2]

It's time to finally blow up the myth that feelings don't matter at work. Science is on our side:
There are clear neurological links between feelings,
thoughts, and actions.[3] When we are in the grip of
strong negative emotions, it's like having blinders on.
We focus mostly—sometimes only—on the source of
the pain. We don't process information as well, think
creatively, or make good decisions. Frustration, anger, and stress cause an important part of us to shut
down—the part that's thinking and engaged.[4] Disengagement is a natural neurological and psychological
response to pervasive negative emotions.

But it's not just negative emotions we need to watch out for. Extremely strong positive emotions can have the same effect.[5] Some studies show that too much happiness can make you less creative and prone to engaging in riskier behaviors (think about how we act like fools when we fall in love). On the work front: I've seen groups of people worked up into a frenzy at sales conferences and corporate pep rallies. Little learning or innovation comes out of these meetings. Throw in a lot of alcohol, and you've got a whole host of problems.

If we can agree that our emotional states at work matter, what can we do to increase engagement and improve performance?

Over the past few years, my team at the Teleos Leadership Institute and I have studied dozens of organizations and interviewed thousands of people. The early findings about the links between people's feelings and engagement are fascinating. There are clear similarities in what people say they want and need, no matter where they are from, whom they work for, or what field they're in. We often assume that there are huge differences across industries and around the world, but the research challenges that assumption.

To be fully engaged and happy, virtually everyone tells, we need three things:

1. *A meaningful vision of the future.* When people talked with our research team about what was working and what wasn't in their organizations and what helped or hindered them the most, they talked about *vision.* People want to be able to see the future and know how they fit in. And, as we know from our work with organizational behavior expert Richard Boyatzis on intentional change, people learn and change when they have a personal vision that is linked to an organizational vision.[6] Sadly, far too many leaders don't paint a very compelling

vision of the future, they don't try to link it to people's personal visions, and they don't communicate well. And they lose people as a result.

2. *A sense of purpose.* People want to feel as if their work matters, that their contributions help achieve something really important. And except for those at the tippy top, shareholder value isn't a meaningful goal that excites and engages them. They want to know that they— and their organizations—are doing something big that matters to other people.

3. *Great relationships.* We know that people join an organization and leave a boss.[7] A dissonant relationship with one's boss is downright painful. So too are bad relationships with colleagues. Leaders, managers, and employees have all told us that close, trusting, and supportive relationships are hugely important to their state of mind—and their willingness contribute to a team.

Added up, brain science and organizational research are in fact debunking the old myths: Emotions matter a lot at work. Happiness is important. To be fully engaged, people need vision, meaning, purpose, and resonant relationships.

It's on us as individuals to find ways to live our values at work and build great relationships. And it's on leaders to create an environment where people can thrive. It's simple and it's practical: If you want an engaged workforce, pay attention to how you create a vision, link people's work to your company's larger purpose, and reward individuals who resonate with others.

ANNIE MCKEE is a senior fellow at the University of Pennsylvania, director of the PennCLO executive doctoral program, and the founder of the Teleos Leadership Institute. She is a co-author with Daniel Goleman and Richard Boyatzis of *Primal Leadership, Resonant Leadership*, and *Becoming a Resonant Leader.* The ideas in this article are expanded in McKee's latest book, *How to Be Happy at Work*, forthcoming from Harvard Business Review Press.

Notes

1. A. K. Goel et al., "Measuring the Level of Employee Engagement: A Study from the Indian Automobile Sector." *International Journal of Indian Culture and Business Management* 6, no. 1 (2013): 5–21.
2. J. Lite, "*MIND* Reviews: *The Emotional Life of Your Brain*," *Scientific American MIND*, July 1, 2012, http:// www.scientificamerican.com/article/mind-reviews-the -emotional-life-of/.
3. D. Goleman, *Destructive Emotions: A Scientific Dialogue with the Dalai Lama.* (New York: Bantam, 2004).
4. D. Goleman et al., *Primal Leadership: Unleashing the Power of Emotional Intelligence.* (Boston: Harvard Business Review Press, 2013).
5. J. Gruber, "Four Ways Happiness Can Hurt You," *Greater Good*, May 3, 2012, http://greatergood.berkeley.edu/ article/item/four_ways_happiness_can_hurt_you.
6. R. E. Boyatzis and C. Soler, "Vision, Leadership, and Emotional Intelligence Transforming Family Business," *Journal of Family Business Management* 2, no. 1 (2012) 23–30; and A. McKee et al., *Becoming a Resonant Leader: Develop Your Emotional Intelligence, Renew Your Relationships, Sustain Your Effectiveness.* (Boston: Harvard Business Review Press, 2008). http://www.amazon.com/ Becoming-Resonant-Leader-Relationships-Effectiveness/ dp/1422117340.

7. "How Managers Trump Companies," *Gallup Business Journal*, August 12, 1999, http://businessjournal.gallup .com/content/523/how-managers-trump-companies.aspx.

Adapted from content posted on hbr.org on
November 14, 2014 (product #H012CE).

3

The Science Behind the Smile

An interview with Daniel Gilbert by Gardiner Morse

arvard psychology professor Daniel Gilbert is widely known for his 2006 best seller, *Stumbling on Happiness*. His work reveals, among other things, the systematic mistakes we all make in imagining how happy (or miserable) we'll be. In this edited interview with HBR's Gardiner Morse, Gilbert surveys the field of happiness research and explores its frontiers.

HBR: *Happiness research has become a hot topic in the past 20 years. Why?*

Gilbert: It's only recently that we realized we could marry one of our oldest questions—"What is the nature of human happiness?"—to our newest way of getting answers: science. Until just a few decades ago, the problem of happiness was mainly in the hands of philosophers and poets.

Psychologists have always been interested in emotion, but in the past two decades the study of emotion has exploded, and one of the emotions that psychologists have studied most intensively is happiness. Recently economists and neuroscientists joined the party. All these disciplines have distinct but intersecting interests: Psychologists want to understand what people feel, economists want to know what people value, and neuroscientists want to know how people's brains respond to rewards. Having three separate disciplines all interested in a single topic has put that topic on the scientific map. Papers on happiness are published in *Science*, people who study happiness win Nobel prizes, and governments all over the world are rushing to figure out how to measure and increase the happiness of their citizens.

How is it possible to measure something as subjective as happiness?

Measuring subjective experiences is a lot easier than you think. It's what your eye doctor does when she fits you for glasses. She puts a lens in front of your eye and asks you to report your experience, and then she puts another lens up, and then another. She uses your reports as data, submits the data to scientific analysis, and designs a lens that will give you perfect vision—all on the basis of your reports of your subjective experience. People's real-time reports are very good approximations of their experiences, and they make it possible for us to see the world through their eyes. People may not be able to tell us how happy they were yesterday or how happy they will be tomorrow, but they *can* tell us how they're feeling at the moment we ask them. "How are you?" may be the world's most frequently asked question, and nobody's stumped by it.

There are many ways to measure happiness. We can ask people "How happy are you right now?" and have them rate it on a scale. We can use magnetic resonance imaging to measure cerebral blood flow, or electromyography to measure the activity of the "smile muscles" in the face. But in most circumstances those measures are highly correlated, and you'd have to be the federal government to prefer the complicated, expensive measures over the simple, inexpensive one.

But isn't the scale itself subjective? Your five might be my six.

Imagine that a drugstore sold a bunch of cheap thermometers that weren't very well calibrated. People with normal temperatures might get readings other than 98.6, and two people with the same temperature might get different readings. These inaccuracies could cause people to seek medical treatment they didn't need or to miss getting treatment they did need. So buggy thermometers are sometimes a problem—but not always. For example, if I brought 100 people to my lab, exposed half of them to a flu virus, and then used those buggy thermometers to take their temperatures a week later, the average temperature of the people who'd been exposed would almost surely be higher than the average temperature of the others. Some thermometers would underestimate, some would overestimate, but as long as I measured enough people, the inaccuracies would cancel themselves out. Even with poorly calibrated instruments, we can compare large groups of people.

A rating scale is like a buggy thermometer. Its inaccuracies make it inappropriate for some kinds of measurement (for example, saying exactly how happy John was at 10:42 am on July 3, 2010), but it's perfectly appropriate for the kinds of measurements most psychological scientists make.

What did all these happiness researchers discover?

Much of the research confirms things we've always suspected. For example, in general people who are in good romantic relationships are happier than those who aren't. Healthy people are happier than sick people. People who participate in their churches are happier than those who don't. Rich people are happier than poor people. And so on.

That said, there have been some surprises. For example, while all these things do make people happier, it's astonishing how little any one of them matters. Yes, a new house or a new spouse will make you happier, but not much and not for long. As it turns out, people are not very good at predicting what will make them happy or how long that happiness will last. They expect positive events to make them much happier than those events actually do, and they expect negative events to make them unhappier than they actually do. In both field and lab studies, we've found that winning or losing an election, gaining or losing a romantic partner, getting or not getting a promotion, passing or failing an exam all have less impact on happiness than people think they will. A recent study showed that very few experiences affect us for more than three months. When good things happen, we celebrate for a while and then sober up. When bad things happen, we weep and whine for a while and then pick ourselves up and get on with it.

Why do events have such a fleeting effect on happiness?

One reason is that people are good at synthesizing happiness—at finding silver linings. As a result, they usually end up happier than they expect after almost any kind of trauma or tragedy. Pick up any newspaper, and you'll find plenty of examples. Remember Jim Wright, who resigned in disgrace as

Speaker of the House of Representatives because of a shady book deal? A few years later he told the *New York Times* that he was "so much better off, physically, financially, emotionally, mentally and in almost every other way." Then there's Moreese Bickham, who spent 37 years in the Louisiana State Penitentiary; after his release he said, "I don't have one minute's regret. It was a glorious experience." These guys appear to be living in the best of all possible worlds. Speaking of which, Pete Best, the original drummer for the Beatles, was replaced by Ringo Starr in 1962, just before the Beatles got big. Now he's a session drummer. What did he have to say about missing out on the chance to belong to the most famous band of the 20th century? "I'm happier than I would have been with the Beatles."

One of the most reliable findings of the happiness studies is that we do not have to go running to a therapist every time our shoelaces break. We have a remarkable ability to make the best of things. Most people are more resilient than they realize.

Aren't they deluding themselves? Isn't real happiness better than synthetic happiness?

Let's be careful with terms. Nylon is real; it's just not natural. Synthetic happiness is perfectly real; it's just man-made. Synthetic happiness is what we produce when we don't get what we want, and natural happiness is what we experience when we do. They have different origins, but they are not necessarily different in terms of how they feel. One is not obviously better than the other.

Of course, most folks don't see it that way. Most folks think that synthetic happiness isn't as "good" as the other kind—that people who produce it are just fooling themselves and aren't really happy. I know of no evidence demonstrating that that's the case. If you go blind or lose a fortune, you'll find that there's a whole new life on the other side of those events. And you'll find many things about that new life that are quite good. In fact, you'll undoubtedly find a few things that are even better than what you had before. You're not lying to yourself; you're not delusional. You're discovering things you didn't know—*couldn't* know—until you were in that new life. You are looking for things that make your new life better, you are finding them, and they are making you happy. What is most striking to me as a scientist is that most of us don't realize how good we're going to be at finding these things. We'd never say, "Oh, of course, if I lost my money or my wife left me, I'd find a way to be just as happy as I am now." We'd never say it—but it's true.

Is being happy always desirable? Look at all the unhappy creative geniuses—Beethoven, van Gogh, Hemingway. Doesn't a certain amount of unhappiness spur good performance?

Nonsense! Everyone can think of a historical example of someone who was both miserable and creative, but that doesn't mean misery generally promotes creativity. There's certainly someone out there who smoked two packs of cigarettes a day and lived to be 90, but that doesn't mean cigarettes are good for you. The difference between using anecdotes to prove a point and using science to prove a point is that in science you can't just cherry-pick the story that suits you best. You have to examine *all* the stories, or at least take a fair sample of them, and see if there are more miserable creatives or happy creatives, more miserable noncreatives or happy noncreatives. If misery promoted creativity, you'd see a higher percentage of creatives among the miserable than among the delighted. And you don't. By and large, happy people are more creative and more productive. Has there ever been a human being whose misery was the source of his creativity? Of course. But that person is the exception, not the rule.

Many managers would say that contented people aren't the most productive employees, so you want to keep people a little uncomfortable, maybe a little anxious, about their jobs.

Managers who collect data instead of relying on intuition don't say that. I know of no data showing that anxious, fearful employees are more creative or productive. Remember, contentment doesn't mean sitting and staring at the wall. That's what people do when they're bored, and people *hate* being bored. We know that people are happiest when they're appropriately challenged—when they're trying to achieve goals that are difficult but not out of reach. Challenge and threat are not the same thing. People blossom when challenged and wither when threatened. Sure, you can get results from threats: Tell someone, "If you don't get this to me by Friday, you're fired," and you'll probably have it by Friday. But you'll also have an employee who will thereafter do his best to undermine you, who will feel no loyalty to the organization, and who will never do more than he must. It would be much more effective to tell your employee, "I don't think most people could get this done by Friday. But I have full faith and confidence that you can. And it's hugely important to the entire team." Psychologists have studied reward and punishment for a century, and the bottom line is perfectly clear: Reward works better.

So challenge makes people happy. What else do we know now about the sources of happiness?

If I had to summarize all the scientific literature on the causes of human happiness in one word, that word would be "social." We are by far the most social species on Earth. Even ants have nothing on us. If I wanted to predict your happiness, and I could know only one thing about you, I wouldn't want to know your gender, religion, health, or income. I'd want to know about your social network—about your friends and family and the strength of your bonds with them.

Beyond having rich networks, what makes us happy day to day?

The psychologist Ed Diener has a finding I really like. He essentially shows that the *frequency* of your positive experiences is a much better predictor of your happiness than is the *intensity* of your positive experiences. When we think about what would make us happy, we tend to think of intense events—going on a date with a movie star, winning a Pulitzer, buying a yacht. But Diener and his colleagues have shown that how good your experiences are doesn't matter nearly as much as how many good experiences you have. Somebody who has a dozen mildly nice things happen each day is likely to be happier than somebody who has a single truly amazing thing happen. So wear comfortable shoes, give your wife a big kiss, sneak a french fry. It sounds like small stuff, and it is. But the small stuff matters.

I think this helps explain why it's so hard for us to forecast our affective states. We imagine that one or two big things will have a profound effect. But it looks like happiness is the sum of hundreds of small things. Achieving happiness requires the same approach as losing weight. People trying to lose weight want a magic pill that will give them instant results. Ain't no such thing. We know exactly how people lose weight: They eat less and exercise more. They don't have to eat *much* less or exercise *much* more— they just have to do those things consistently. Over time it adds up. Happiness is like that. The things you can do to increase your happiness are obvious and small and take just a little time. But you have to do them every day and wait for the results.

What are those little things we can do to increase our happiness?

They won't surprise you any more than "eat less and exercise more" does. The main things are to commit to some simple behaviors—meditating, exercising, getting enough sleep—and to practice altruism. One of the most selfish things you can do is help others. Volunteer at a homeless shelter. You may or may not help the homeless, but you will almost surely help yourself. And nurture your social connections. Twice a week, write down three things you're grateful for, and tell someone why. I know these sound like homilies from your grandmother. Well, your grandmother was smart. The secret of happiness is like the secret of weight loss: It's not a secret!

If there's no secret, what's left to study?

There's no shortage of questions. For decades psychologists and economists have been asking,

"Who's happy? The rich? The poor? The young? The old?" The best we could do was divide people into groups, survey them once or maybe twice, and try to determine if the people in one group were, on average, happier than those in the others. The tools we used were pretty blunt instruments. But now millions of people are carrying little computers in their pockets—smartphones—and this allows us to collect data in real time from huge numbers of people about what they are doing and feeling from moment to moment. That's never been possible before.

One of my collaborators, Matt Killingsworth, has built an experience-sampling application called Track Your Happiness. He follows more than 15,000 people by iPhone, querying them several times a day about their activities and emotional states. Are they at home? On a bus? Watching television? Praying? How are they feeling? What are they thinking about? With this technology, Matt's beginning to answer a much better question than the one we've been asking for decades. Instead of asking *who* is happy, he can ask *when* they are happy. He doesn't get the answer by asking, "When are you happy?"—because frankly, people don't know. He gets it by tracking people over days, months, and years and measuring what they are doing and how happy they are while they are doing it. I think this kind of technology is about to revolutionize our understanding of daily emotions and human well-being. (See the sidebar "The Future of Happiness Research.")

What are the new frontiers of happiness research?

We need to get more specific about what we are measuring. Many scientists say they are studying happiness, but when you look at what they're measuring, you find they are actually studying depression or life satisfaction. These things are related to happiness, of course, but they are not the same as happiness. Research shows that people with children are typically less happy on a moment-to-moment basis than people without children. But people who have kids may feel fulfilled in a way that people without kids do not. It doesn't make sense to say that people with kids are happier, or that people without kids are happier; each group is happier in some ways and less happy in others. We need to stop painting our portrait of happiness with such a fat brush.

Will all this research ultimately make us happier?

We are learning and will continue to learn how to maximize our happiness. So yes, there is no doubt that the research has helped and will continue to help us increase our happiness. But that still leaves the big question: What kind of happiness *should* we want? For example, do we want the average happiness of our moments to be as large as possible, or do we want the sum of our happy moments to be as large as possible? Those are different things.

Do we want lives free of pain and heartache, or is there value in those experiences? Science will soon be able to tell us how to live the lives we want, but it will never tell us what kinds of lives we should want to live. That will be for us to decide.

THE FUTURE OF HAPPINESS RESEARCH

by Matthew Killingsworth

You'd think it would be easy to figure out what makes us happy. Until recently, though, researchers have had to rely mainly on people's reports about their average emotional states over long periods of time and on easily surveyed predictors of happiness, such as demographic variables. As a result, we know that married or wealthy people are, on average, happier than unmarried or less-well-off people. But what is it about being married or having money that makes people happy?

Focusing on average emotional states also smoothes out short-term fluctuations in happiness and consequently diminishes our ability to understand the causes of those fluctuations. For example, how do the moment-by-moment details of a person's day affect that person's happiness?

We can now begin to answer questions like these, thanks to the smartphone. For an ongoing research project called Track Your Happiness, I have recruited more than 15,000 people in 83 countries to report their emotional states in real time, using devices they carry with them every day. I created an iPhone web app that queries users at random intervals, asking them about their mood (respondents slide a button along a scale that ranges from "very bad" to "very good"), what they are doing (they can select from 22 options, including commuting, working, exercising,

(Continued)

and eating), and factors such as their level of productivity, the nature of their environment, the amount and quality of their sleep, and their social interactions. Since 2009 we have collected more than half a million data points—making this, to my knowledge, the first-ever large-scale study of happiness in daily life.

One major finding is that people's minds wander nearly half the time, and this appears to lower their mood. Wandering to unpleasant or even neutral topics is associated with sharply lower happiness; straying to positive topics has no effect either way. The amount of mind-wandering varies greatly depending on the activity, from roughly 60% of the time while commuting to 30% when talking to someone or playing a game to 10% during sex. But no matter what people are doing, they are much less happy when their minds are wandering than when their minds are focused.

All of this strongly suggests that to optimize our emotional well-being, we should pay at least as much attention to where our minds are as to what our bodies are doing. Yet for most of us, the focus of our thoughts isn't part of our daily planning. When you wake up on a Saturday morning and ask, "What am I going to do today?" the answer is usually about where you'll take your body—to the beach, to the kids' soccer practice, for a run. You ought to also ask, "What am I going to do with my mind today?"

A related stream of research examines the relationship between mind-wandering and productivity. Many managers, particularly those whose employees do creative knowledge work, may sense that a certain amount of daydreaming is a good thing, providing a mental break and perhaps leading people to reflect on related work matters. Unfortunately, the data so far suggest that, in addition to reducing happiness, mind-wandering on the job reduces productivity. And employees' minds stray much more than managers

(Continued)

probably imagine—about 50% of the workday—and almost always veer toward personal concerns. Managers may want to look for ways to help employees stay focused, for the employees' *and* the company's sakes.

The data are also beginning to paint a picture of variations in happiness within an individual and from one individual to the next. The most striking finding here is that happiness differs more from moment to moment than it does from person to person. This suggests that it's not the stable conditions of our lives, such as where we live or whether we're married, that are the principal drivers of happiness; it could be the small, everyday things that count the most.

It also suggests that happiness on the job may depend more on our moment-to-moment experiences—our routine interactions with coworkers, the projects we're involved in, our daily contributions—than on the

A focused mind is a happy mind

Participants were queried about mood and mind-wandering during 22 activities. The balls represent their activities and thoughts. The farther to the right a ball is, the happier people were, on average. The larger the ball, the more frequently they engaged in the activity or thought.

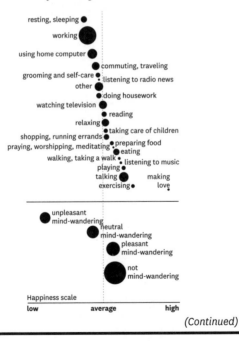

(Continued)

stable conditions thought to promote happiness, such as a high salary or a prestigious title. A priority of my current and future research is to deploy this tracking technology in the workplace and, I hope, at last reveal what actually makes employees happy.

Matthew Killingsworth is a doctoral student in psychology at Harvard University. He is the creator of www.trackyour happiness.com.

DANIEL GILBERT is the Edgar Pierce Professor of Psychology at Harvard University. He has won numerous awards for his research and teaching, including the American Psychological Association's Distinguished Scientific Award for an Early Career Contribution to Psychology. He is the author of *Stumbling on Happiness* and host and co-writer of the PBS television series *This Emotional Life*. GARDINER MORSE is a senior editor at *Harvard Business Review*.

Reprinted from *Harvard Business Review*,
January–February 2012 (product #R1201E).

4

The Power of Small Wins

By Teresa M. Amabile and Steven J. Kramer

What is the best way to drive innovative work inside organizations? Important clues hide in the stories of world-renowned creators. It turns out that ordinary scientists, marketers, programmers, and other unsung knowledge workers, whose jobs require creative productivity every day, have more in common with famous innovators than most managers realize. The workday events that ignite their emotions, fuel their motivation, and trigger their perceptions are fundamentally the same.

The Double Helix, James Watson's 1968 memoir about discovering the structure of DNA, describes the roller coaster of emotions he and Francis Crick experienced through the progress and setbacks of the work that eventually earned them the Nobel Prize. After the excitement of their first attempt to build a DNA model, Watson and Crick noticed some serious flaws. According to Watson, "Our first minutes with the models . . . were not joyous." Later that evening, "a shape began to emerge which brought back our spirits." But when they showed their "breakthrough" to colleagues, they found that their model would not work. Dark days of doubt and ebbing motivation followed. When the duo finally had their bona fide breakthrough, and their colleagues found no fault with it, Watson wrote, "My morale skyrocketed, for I suspected that we now had the answer to the riddle." Watson and Crick were so driven by this success that they practically lived in the lab, trying to complete the work.

Throughout these episodes, Watson and Crick's progress—or lack thereof—ruled their reactions. In our recent research on creative work inside businesses, we stumbled upon a remarkably similar phenomenon. Through exhaustive analysis of diaries kept by knowledge workers, we discovered the "progress principle": Of all the things that can boost emotions, motivation, and perceptions during a workday, the single most important is making progress in meaningful work. And the more frequently people experience that sense of progress, the more likely they are to be creatively productive in the long run. Whether they are trying to solve a major scientific mystery or simply produce a high-quality product or service, everyday progress—even a small win—can make all the difference in how they feel and perform.

The power of progress is fundamental to human nature, but few managers understand it or know how to leverage progress to boost motivation. In fact, work motivation has been a subject of long-standing debate. In a survey asking about the keys to motivating workers, we found that some managers ranked recognition for good work as most important, while others put more stock in tangible incentives. Some focused on the value of interpersonal support, while still others thought clear goals were the answer. Interestingly, very few of our surveyed managers ranked progress first. (See the sidebar "A Surprise for Managers.")

If you are a manager, the progress principle holds clear implications for where to focus your efforts. It suggests that you have more influence than you may realize over employees' well-being, motivation, and creative output. Knowing what serves to catalyze and nourish progress—and what does the opposite— turns out to be the key to effectively managing people and their work.

In this article, we share what we have learned about the power of progress and how managers can leverage it. We spell out how a focus on progress translates into concrete managerial actions and provide a checklist to help make such behaviors habitual. But to clarify why those actions are so potent, we first

A SURPRISE FOR MANAGERS

In a 1968 issue of HBR, Frederick Herzberg published a now-classic article titled "One More Time: How Do you Motivate Employees?" Our findings are consistent with his message: People are most satisfied with their jobs (and therefore most motivated) when those jobs give them the opportunity to experience achievement. The diary research we describe in this article— in which we microscopically examined the events of thousands of workdays, in real time—uncovered the mechanism underlying the sense of achievement: making consistent, meaningful progress.

But managers seem not to have taken Herzberg's lesson to heart. To assess contemporary awareness of the importance of daily work progress, we recently administered a survey to 669 managers of varying levels from dozens of companies around the world. We asked about the managerial tools that can affect employees'

(Continued)

motivation and emotions. The respondents ranked five tools—support for making progress in the work, recognition for good work, incentives, interpersonal support, and clear goals—in order of importance.

Of the managers who took our survey, 95% would probably be surprised to learn that supporting progress is the primary way to elevate motivation—because that's the percentage who failed to rank progress number one. In fact, only 35 managers ranked progress as the number one motivator—a mere 5%. The vast majority of respondents ranked support for making progress dead last as a motivator and third as an influence on emotion. They ranked "recognition for good work (either public or private)" as the most important factor in motivating workers and making them happy. In our diary study, recognition certainly did boost inner work life. But it wasn't nearly as prominent as progress. Besides, without work achievements, there is little to recognize.

describe our research and what the knowledge workers' diaries revealed about their "inner work lives."

Inner work life and performance

For nearly 15 years, we have been studying the psychological experiences and the performance of people doing complex work inside organizations. Early on, we realized that a central driver of creative, productive performance was the quality of a person's inner work life: the mix of emotions, motivations, and perceptions over the course of a workday. How happy workers feel; how motivated they are by an intrinsic interest in the work; how positively they view their organization, their management, their team, their work, and themselves—all these combine either to push them to higher levels of achievement or to drag them down.

To understand such interior dynamics better, we asked members of project teams to respond individually to an end-of-day email survey during the course of the project—just over four months, on average. (For more on this research, see our article "Inner Work Life: Understanding the Subtext of Business Performance," HBR May 2007.) The projects—inventing kitchen gadgets, managing product lines of cleaning tools, and solving complex IT problems for a hotel empire, for example—all involved creativity. The daily survey inquired about participants' emotions and moods, motivation levels, and perceptions of the work environment that day, as well as what work they did and what events stood out in their minds.

Twenty-six project teams from seven companies participated, comprising 238 individuals. This yielded nearly 12,000 diary entries. Naturally, every individual in our population experienced ups and downs. Our goal was to discover the states of inner work life and the workday events that correlated with the highest levels of creative output.

In a dramatic rebuttal to the commonplace claim that high pressure and fear spur achievement, we found that, at least in the realm of knowledge work, people are more creative and productive when their inner work lives are positive—when they feel happy, are intrinsically motivated by the work itself, and have positive perceptions of their colleagues and the organization. Moreover, in those positive states, people are more committed to the work and more collegial toward those around them. Inner work life, we saw, can fluctuate from one day to the next— sometimes wildly—and performance along with it. A person's inner work life on a given day fuels his or her performance for the day and can even affect performance the *next* day.

Once this "inner work-life effect" became clear, our inquiry turned to whether and how managerial action could set it in motion. What events could evoke positive or negative emotions, motivations, and perceptions? The answers were tucked within our research participants' diary entries. There are predictable triggers that inflate or deflate inner work life, and, even accounting for variation among individuals, they are pretty much the same for everyone.

The power of progress

Our hunt for inner work-life triggers led us to the progress principle. When we compared our research participants' best and worst days (based on their overall mood, specific emotions, and motivation levels), we found that the most common event triggering a "best day" was any progress in the work by the individual or the team. The most common event triggering a "worst day" was a setback.

Consider, for example, how progress relates to one component of inner work life: overall mood ratings. Steps forward occurred on 76% of people's best-mood days. By contrast, setbacks occurred on only 13% of those days. (See the figure "What happens on good days and bad days?")

Two other types of inner work-life triggers also occur frequently on best days: *catalysts*, actions that directly support work, including help from a person or group, and *nourishers*, events such as shows of respect and words of encouragement. Each has an opposite: *inhibitors*, actions that fail to support or actively hinder work, and *toxins*, discouraging or undermining events. Whereas catalysts and inhibitors are directed at the project, nourishers and toxins are directed at the person. Like setbacks, inhibitors and toxins are rare on days of great inner work life.

Events on worst-mood days are nearly the mirror image of those on best-mood days. Here, setbacks predominated, occurring on 67% of those days; progress occurred on only 25% of them. Inhibitors and toxins also marked many worst-mood days, and catalysts and nourishers were rare.

This is the progress principle made visible: If a person is motivated and happy at the end of a workday, it's a good bet that he or she made some progress.

If the person drags out of the office disengaged and joyless, a setback is most likely to blame.

When we analyzed all 12,000 daily surveys filled out by our participants, we discovered that progress and setbacks influence all three aspects of inner work life. On days when they made progress, our participants reported more positive *emotions*. They not only were in a more upbeat mood in general but also expressed more joy, warmth, and pride. When they suffered setbacks, they experienced more frustration, fear, and sadness.

Motivations were also affected: On progress days, people were more intrinsically motivated—by interest in and enjoyment of the work itself. On setback days, they were not only less intrinsically motivated but also less extrinsically motivated by recognition. Apparently, setbacks can lead a person to feel generally apathetic and disinclined to do the work at all.

Perceptions differed in many ways, too. On progress days, people perceived significantly more positive

What happens on good days and bad days?

Progress—even a small step forward—occurs on many of the days people report being in a good mood. Events on bad days—setbacks and other hindrances—are nearly the mirror image of those on good days.

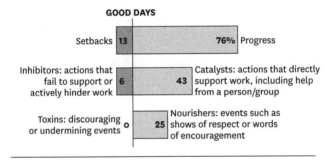

GOOD DAYS

Setbacks	13	**76%** Progress
Inhibitors: actions that fail to support or actively hinder work	6	43 Catalysts: actions that directly support work, including help from a person/group
Toxins: discouraging or undermining events	0	25 Nourishers: events such as shows of respect or words of encouragement

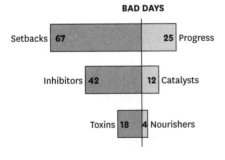

BAD DAYS

Setbacks	67	25 Progress
Inhibitors	42	12 Catalysts
Toxins	18	4 Nourishers

challenge in their work. They saw their teams as more mutually supportive and reported more positive interactions between the teams and their supervisors. On a number of dimensions, perceptions suffered when people encountered setbacks. They found less positive challenge in the work, felt that they had less freedom in carrying it out, and reported that they had insufficient resources. On setback days, participants perceived both their teams and their supervisors as less supportive.

To be sure, our analyses establish correlations but do not prove causality. Were these changes in inner work life the result of progress and setbacks, or was the effect the other way around? The numbers alone cannot answer that. However, we do know, from reading thousands of diary entries, that more-positive perceptions, a sense of accomplishment, satisfaction, happiness, and even elation often followed progress. Here's a typical post-progress entry, from a programmer: "I smashed that bug that's been frustrating me for almost a calendar week. That may not be an event to you, but I live a very drab life, so I'm all hyped."

Likewise, we saw that deteriorating perceptions, frustration, sadness, and even disgust often followed setbacks. As another participant, a product marketer, wrote, "We spent a lot of time updating the cost reduction project list, and after tallying all the numbers, we are still coming up short of our goal. It is discouraging to not be able to hit it after all the time spent and hard work."

Almost certainly, the causality goes both ways, and managers can use this feedback loop between progress and inner work life to support both.

Minor milestones

When we think about progress, we often imagine how good it feels to achieve a long-term goal or experience a major breakthrough. These big wins are great—but they are relatively rare. The good news is that even small wins can boost inner work life tremendously. Many of the progress events our research participants reported represented only minor steps forward. Yet they often evoked outsize positive reactions. Consider this diary entry from a programmer in a high-tech company, which was accompanied by very positive self-ratings of her emotions, motivations, and perceptions that day: "I figured out why something was not working correctly. I felt relieved and happy because this was a minor milestone for me."

Even ordinary, incremental progress can increase people's engagement in the work and their happiness during the workday. Across all the types of events our participants reported, a notable proportion (28%) that had a minor impact on the project had a major impact on people's feelings about it. Because inner work life has such a potent effect on creativity and productivity, and because small but consistent steps forward shared by many people can accumulate into excellent execution, progress events that often go unnoticed are critical to the overall performance of organizations.

Unfortunately, there is a flip side. Small losses or setbacks can have an extremely negative effect on inner work life. In fact, our study and research by others show that negative events can have a more powerful impact than positive ones. Consequently, it is especially important for managers to minimize daily hassles. (See again the figure "What happens on good days and bad days?")

Progress in meaningful work

We've shown how gratifying it is for workers when they are able to chip away at a goal, but recall what we said earlier: The key to motivating performance is supporting progress in *meaningful* work. Making headway boosts your inner work life, but only if the work matters to you.

Think of the most boring job you've ever had. Many people nominate their first job as a teenager—washing pots and pans in a restaurant kitchen, for example, or checking coats at a museum. In jobs like those, the power of progress seems elusive. No matter how hard you work, there are always more pots to wash and coats to check; only punching the time clock at the end of the day or getting the paycheck at the end of the week yields a sense of accomplishment.

In jobs with much more challenge and room for creativity, like the ones our research participants had, simply "making progress"—getting tasks done—doesn't guarantee a good inner work life, either. You may have experienced this rude fact in your own job, on days (or in projects) when you felt demotivated, devalued, and frustrated, even though you worked hard and got things done. The likely cause is your perception of the completed tasks as peripheral or irrelevant. For the progress principle to operate, the work must be meaningful to the person doing it.

In 1983, Steve Jobs was trying to entice John Sculley to leave a wildly successful career at PepsiCo to become Apple's new CEO. Jobs reportedly asked him, "Do you want to spend the rest of your life selling sugared water or do you want a chance to change the world?" In making his pitch, Jobs leveraged a potent psychological force: the deep-seated human desire to do meaningful work.

Fortunately, to feel meaningful, work doesn't have to involve putting the first personal computers in the hands of ordinary people, or alleviating poverty, or helping to cure cancer. Work with less profound importance to society can matter if it contributes value to something or someone important to the worker. Meaning can be as simple as making a useful and high-quality product for a customer or providing

a genuine service for a community. It can be supporting a colleague or boosting an organization's profits
by reducing inefficiencies in a production process.
Whether the goals are lofty or modest, as long as they
are meaningful to the worker and it is clear how his
or her efforts contribute to them, progress toward
them can galvanize inner work life.

In principle, managers shouldn't have to go to
extraordinary lengths to infuse jobs with meaning.
Most jobs in modern organizations are potentially
meaningful for the people doing them. However,
managers can make sure that employees know just
how their work is contributing. And, most important, they can avoid actions that negate its value. (See
the sidebar "How Work Gets Stripped of Its Meaning.") All the participants in our research were doing
work that should have been meaningful; no one was
washing pots or checking coats. Shockingly often,
however, we saw potentially important, challenging
work losing its power to inspire.

HOW WORK GETS STRIPPED OF ITS MEANING

Diary entries from 238 knowledge workers who were members of creative project teams revealed four primary ways in which managers unwittingly drain work of its meaning.

Managers may dismiss the importance of employees' work or ideas. Consider the case of Richard, a senior lab technician at a chemical company, who found meaning in helping his new-product development team solve complex technical problems. However, in team meetings over the course of a three-week period, Richard perceived that his team leader was ignoring his suggestions and those of his teammates. As a result, he felt that his contributions were not meaningful, and his spirits flagged. When at last he believed that he was again making a substantive contribution to the success of the project, his mood

(Continued)

improved dramatically: "I felt much better at today's team meeting. I felt that my opinions and information were important to the project and that we have made some progress."

They may destroy employees' sense of owner-ship of their work. Frequent and abrupt reassign-ments often have this effect. This happened repeat-edly to the members of a product development team in a giant consumer products company, as de-scribed by team member Bruce: "As I've been hand-ing over some projects, I do realize that I don't like to give them up. Especially when you have been with them from the start and are nearly to the end. You lose ownership. This happens to us way too often."

Managers may send the message that the work employees are doing will never see the light of day. They can signal this—unintentionally—by shifting their priorities or changing their minds about how something should be done. We saw the latter in an internet technology company after user-interface developer Burt had spent weeks designing seamless transitions for non-English-speaking users. Not surprisingly, Burt's mood was seriously marred on the day he reported this incident: "Other options for the international [interfaces] were [given] to the team during a team meeting, which could render the work I am doing useless."

They may neglect to inform employees about unexpected changes in a customer's priorities. Often, this arises from poor customer management or inadequate communication within the company. For example, Stuart, a data transformation expert at an IT company, reported deep frustration and low

(Continued)

motivation on the day he learned that weeks of the team's hard work might have been for naught: "Found out that there is a strong possibility that the project may not be going forward, due to a shift in the client's agenda. Therefore, there is a strong possibility that all the time and effort put into the project was a waste of our time."

Supporting progress: catalysts and nourishers

What can managers do to ensure that people are motivated, committed, and happy? How can they support workers' daily progress? They can use catalysts and nourishers, the other kinds of frequent "best day" events we discovered.

Catalysts are actions that support work. They include setting clear goals, allowing autonomy, providing sufficient resources and time, helping with the work, openly learning from problems and successes, and allowing a free exchange of ideas. Their opposites, inhibitors, include failing to provide support and actively interfering with the work. Because of their impact on progress, catalysts and inhibitors ultimately affect inner work life. But they also have a more immediate impact: When people realize that they have clear and meaningful goals, sufficient resources, helpful colleagues, and so on, they get an instant boost to their emotions, their motivation to do a great job, and their perceptions of the work and the organization.

Nourishers are acts of interpersonal support, such as respect and recognition, encouragement, emotional comfort, and opportunities for affiliation. Toxins, their opposites, include disrespect, discouragement, disregard for emotions, and interpersonal conflict. For good and for ill, nourishers and toxins affect inner work life directly and immediately.

Catalysts and nourishers—and their opposites—can alter the meaningfulness of work by shifting people's perceptions of their jobs and even themselves. For instance, when a manager makes sure that people have the resources they need, it signals to them that what they are doing is important and valuable. When managers recognize people for the work they do, it signals that they are important to the organization. In this way, catalysts and nourishers can lend greater meaning to the work—and amplify the operation of the progress principle.

The managerial actions that constitute catalysts and nourishers are not particularly mysterious; they may sound like Management 101, if not just common sense and common decency. But our diary study reminded us how often they are ignored or forgotten. Even some of the more attentive managers in the companies we studied did not consistently provide catalysts and nourishers. For example, a supply chain specialist named Michael was, in many ways and on most days, an excellent subteam manager. But he was occasionally so overwhelmed that he became toxic toward his people. When a supplier failed to complete a "hot" order on time and Michael's team had to resort to air shipping to meet the customer's deadline, he realized that the profit margin on the sale would be blown. In irritation, he lashed out at his subordinates, demeaning the solid work they had done and disregarding their own frustration with the supplier. In his diary, he admitted as much: "As of Friday, we have spent \$28,000 in air freight to send 1,500 \$30 spray jet mops to our number two customer. Another 2,800 remain on this order, and there is a good probability that they too will gain wings. I have turned from the kindly supply chain manager into the black-masked executioner. All similarity to civility is gone, our backs are against the wall, flight is not possible, therefore fight is probable."

Even when managers don't have their backs against the wall, developing long-term strategy and launching new initiatives can often seem more important—and perhaps sexier—than making sure subordinates have what they need to make steady progress and feel supported as human beings. But as we saw repeatedly in our research, even the best strategy will fail if managers ignore the people working in the trenches to execute it.

A model manager—and a tool for emulating him

We could explain the many (and largely unsurprising) moves that can catalyze progress and nourish spirits, but it may be more useful to give an example of a manager who consistently used those moves—and then to provide a simple tool that can help any manager do so.

Our model manager is Graham, whom we observed leading a small team of chemical engineers within a multinational European firm we'll call Kruger-Bern. The mission of the team's NewPoly project was clear and meaningful enough: Develop a safe, biodegradable polymer to replace petrochemicals in cosmetics and, eventually, in a wide range of consumer products. As in many large firms however, the project was nested in a confusing and sometimes threatening corporate setting of shifting top-management priorities, conflicting signals, and wavering commitments. Resources were uncomfortably tight, and uncertainty loomed over the project's future—and every team member's career. Even worse, an incident early in the project, in which an important customer reacted angrily to a sample, left the team reeling. Yet Graham was able to sustain team members' inner work lives by repeatedly and visibly removing obstacles, materially supporting progress, and emotionally supporting the team.

Graham's management approach excelled in four ways. First, he established a positive climate, one event at a time, which set behavioral norms for the entire team. When the customer complaint stopped the project in its tracks, for example, he engaged immediately with the team to analyze the problem, without recriminations, and develop a plan for repairing the relationship. In doing so, he modeled how to respond to crises in the work: not by panicking or pointing fingers but by identifying problems and their causes and developing a coordinated action plan. This is both a practical approach and a great way to give subordinates a sense of forward movement even in the face of the missteps and failures inherent in any complex project.

Second, Graham stayed attuned to his team's everyday activities and progress. In fact, the nonjudgmental climate he had established made this happen naturally. Team members updated him frequently—

without being asked—on their setbacks, progress, and plans. At one point, one of his hardest-working colleagues, Brady, had to abort a trial of a new material because he couldn't get the parameters right on the equipment. It was bad news, because the New-Poly team had access to the equipment only one day a week, but Brady immediately informed Graham. In his diary entry that evening, Brady noted, "He didn't like the lost week but seemed to understand." That understanding assured Graham's place in the stream of information that would allow him to give his people just what they needed to make progress.

Third, Graham targeted his support according to recent events in the team and the project. Each day, he could anticipate what type of intervention—a catalyst or the removal of an inhibitor; a nourisher or some antidote to a toxin—would have the most impact on team members' inner work lives and progress. And if he could not make that judgment, he asked. Most days it was not hard to figure out, as on the day he received some uplifting news about his bosses' commitment to the project. He knew the team was jittery about a rumored corporate reorganization and could use the encouragement. Even though the clarification came during a well-earned vacation day, he immediately got on the phone to relay the good news to the team.

Finally, Graham established himself as a resource for team members rather than a micromanager; he was sure to check in while never seeming to check *up* on them. Superficially, checking in and checking up seem quite similar, but micromanagers make four kinds of mistakes. First, they fail to allow autonomy in carrying out the work. Unlike Graham, who gave the NewPoly team a clear strategic goal but respected members' ideas about how to meet it, micromanagers dictate every move. Second, they frequently ask subordinates about their work without providing any real help. By contrast, when one of Graham's team members reported problems, Graham helped analyze them—remaining open to alternative interpretations—and often ended up helping to get things back on track. Third, micromanagers are quick to affix personal blame when problems arise, leading subordinates to hide problems rather than honestly discuss how to surmount them, as Graham did with Brady. And fourth, micromanagers tend to hoard information to use as a secret weapon. Few realize how damaging this is to inner work life. When subordinates perceive that a manager is withholding potentially useful information, they feel infantilized, their motivation wanes, and their work is handicapped. Graham was quick to communicate upper management's views of the project, customers' opinions and needs, and possible sources of assistance or resistance within and outside the organization.

In all those ways, Graham sustained his team's positive emotions, intrinsic motivation, and favorable perceptions. His actions serve as a powerful example of how managers at any level can approach each day determined to foster progress.

We know that many managers, however well-intentioned, will find it hard to establish the habits that seemed to come so naturally to Graham. Awareness, of course, is the first step. However, turning an awareness of the importance of inner work life into routine action takes discipline. With that in mind, we developed a checklist for managers to consult on a daily basis (see the sidebar "The Daily Progress Checklist"). The aim of the checklist is managing for meaningful progress, one day at a time.

The progress loop

Inner work life drives performance; in turn, good performance, which depends on consistent progress, enhances inner work life. We call this the "progress loop"—it reveals the potential for self-reinforcing benefits.

So, the most important implication of the progress principle is this: By supporting people and their daily progress in meaningful work, managers improve not only the inner work lives of their employees but also the organization's long-term performance, which enhances inner work life even more. Of course, there is a dark side—the possibility of negative feedback loops. If managers fail to support progress and the people trying to make it, inner work life suffers and so does performance; and degraded performance further undermines inner work life.

A second implication of the progress principle is that managers needn't fret about trying to read the psyches of their workers or manipulate complicated incentive schemes to ensure that employees are motivated and happy. As long as managers show basic respect and consideration, they can focus on supporting the work itself.

To become an effective manager, you must learn to set this positive feedback loop in motion. That may require a significant shift. Business schools, business books, and managers themselves usually focus on managing organizations or people. But if you focus on managing progress, the management of people—and even of entire organizations—becomes much more feasible. You won't have to figure out how to x-ray the inner work lives of subordinates; if you facilitate their steady progress in meaningful work, make that progress salient to them, and treat them well, they will experience the emotions, motivations, and perceptions necessary for great performance. Their superior work will contribute to organizational success. And here's the beauty of it: They will love their jobs.

TERESA M. AMABILE is the Edsel Bryant Ford Professor of Business Administration at Harvard Business School and the author of *Creativity in Context* (Westview Press, 1996). STEVEN J. KRAMER is an independent researcher, writer, and consultant. He is a coauthor of "Creativity Under the Gun" (HBR August 2002) and "Inner Work Life" (HBR May 2007). Amabile and Kramer are the coauthors of *The Progress*

Principle: Using Small Wins to Ignite Joy, Engagement, and Creativity at Work (Harvard Business Review Press, 2011).

Reprinted from *Harvard Business Review*,
May 2011 (product # R1105C).

THE DAILY PROGRESS CHECKLIST

Near the end of each workday, use this checklist to review the day and plan your managerial actions for the next day. After a few days, you will be able to identify issues by scanning the boldface words.

First, focus on progress and setbacks and think about specific events (catalysts, nourishers, inhibitors, and toxins) that contributed to them. Next, consider any clear inner-work-life clues and what further information they provide about progress and other events. Finally, prioritize for action.

The action plan for the next day is the most important part of your daily review: What is the one thing you can do to best facilitate progress?

(Continued)

Progress

Which 1 or 2 events today indicated either a small win or a possible breakthrough? (Describe briefly.)

_____

_____

Catalysts

- ☐ Did the team have clear short- and long-term **goals** for meaningful work?

- ☐ Did team members have sufficient **autonomy** to solve problems and take ownership of the project?

- ☐ Did they have all the **resources** they needed to move forward efficiently?

- ☐ Did they have sufficient **time** to focus on meaningful work?

- ☐ Did I discuss **lessons** from today's successes and problems with my team?

- ☐ Did I give or get them **help** when they needed or requested it? Did I encourage team members to help one another?

- ☐ Did I help **ideas** flow freely within the group?

Nourishers

- ☐ Did I show **respect** to team members by recognizing their contributions to progress, attending to their ideas, and treating them as trusted professionals?

- ☐ Did I **encourage** team members who faced difficult challenges?

- ☐ Did I **support** team members who had a personal or professional problem?

- ☐ Is there a sense of personal and professional **affiliation** and camaraderie within the team?

(Continued)

Setbacks

Which 1 or 2 events today indicated either a small setback or a possible crisis? (Describe briefly.)

_____

_____

Inhibitors

- ☐ Was there any confusion regarding long- or short-term **goals** for meaningful work?

- ☐ Were team members overly **constrained** in their ability to solve problems and feel ownership of the project?

- ☐ Did they lack any of the **resources** they needed to move forward effectively?

- ☐ Did they lack sufficient **time** to focus on meaningful work?

- ☐ Did I or others fail to provide needed or requested **help**?

- ☐ Did I "punish" failure or neglect to find **lessons** and/or opportunities in problems and successes?

- ☐ Did I or others cut off the presentation or debate of **ideas** prematurely?

Toxins

- ☐ Did I **disrespect** any team members by failing to recognize their contributions to progress, not attending to their ideas, or not treating them as trusted professionals?

- ☐ Did I **discourage** a member of the team in any way?

- ☐ Did I **neglect** a team member who had a personal or professional problem?

- ☐ Is there tension or **antagonism** among members of the team or between team members and me?

(Continued)

Inner work life

- Did I see any indications of the quality of my sub-ordinates' inner work lives today? _____

  _____

  _____

- Perceptions of the work, team, management, firm _____

  _____

- Emotions_____

  _____

  _____

- Motivation _____

  _____

- What specific events might have affected inner work life today? _____

  _____

Action plan

- What can I do tomorrow to strengthen the catalysts and nourishers identified and provide the ones that are lacking? _____

  _____

  _____

  _____

  _____

- What can I do tomorrow to start eliminating the inhibitors and toxins identified? _____

  _____

  _____

  _____

  _____

5

Creating Sustainable Performance

By Gretchen Spreitzer and Christine Porath

When the economy's in terrible shape, when any of us is lucky to have a job—let alone one that's financially and intellectually rewarding—worrying about whether or not your employees are happy might seem a little over the top. But in our research into what makes for a consistently high-performing workforce, we've found good reason to care: Happy employees produce more than unhappy ones over the long term. They routinely show up at work, they're less likely to quit, they go above and beyond the call of duty, and they attract people who are just as committed to the job. Moreover, they're not sprinters; they're more like marathon runners, in it for the long haul.

So what does it mean to be happy in your job? It's not about *contentment*, which connotes a degree of complacency. When we and our research partners at the Ross School of Business's Center for Positive Organizational Scholarship started looking into the factors involved in sustainable individual and organizational performance, we found a better word: *thriving*. We think of a thriving workforce as one in which employees are not just satisfied and productive but also engaged in creating the future—the company's and their own. Thriving employees have a bit of an edge: They are highly energized—but they know how to avoid burnout.

Across industries and job types, we found that people who fit our description of thriving demonstrated 16% better overall performance (as reported by their managers) and 125% less burnout (self-reported) than their peers. They were 32% more committed to the organization and 46% more satisfied with their jobs. They also missed much less work and reported significantly fewer doctor visits, which meant health care savings and less lost time for the company.

We've identified two components of thriving. The first is *vitality*: the sense of being alive, passionate, and excited. Employees who experience vitality spark energy in themselves and others. Companies generate vitality by giving people the sense that what they do on a daily basis makes a difference.

The second component is *learning*: the growth that comes from gaining new knowledge and skills. Learning can bestow a technical advantage and status as an expert. Learning can also set in motion a virtuous cycle: People who are developing their abilities are likely to believe in their potential for further growth.

The two qualities work in concert; one without the other is unlikely to be sustainable and may even damage performance. Learning, for instance, creates momentum for a time, but without passion it can lead to burnout. What will I do with what I've learned? Why should I stick with this job? Vitality alone—even when you love the kudos you get for delivering results—can be deadening: When the work doesn't give you opportunities to learn, it's just the same thing over and over again.

The combination of vitality and learning leads to employees who deliver results and find ways to grow. Their work is rewarding not just because they successfully perform what's expected of them today but also because they have a sense of where they and the company are headed. In short, they are thriving, and the energy they create is contagious. (See the sidebar "About the Research.")

How organizations can help employees thrive

Some employees thrive no matter the context. They naturally build vitality and learning into their jobs, and they inspire the people around them. A smart

ABOUT THE RESEARCH

Over the past seven years, we have been researching the nature of thriving in the workplace and the factors that enhance or inhibit it.

Across several studies with our colleagues Cristina Gibson and Flannery Garnett, we surveyed or interviewed more than 1,200 white- and blue-collar employees in an array of industries, including higher education, health care, financial services, maritime, energy, and manufacturing. We also studied metrics reflecting energy, learning, and growth, based on information supplied by employees and bosses, along with retention rates, health, overall job performance, and organizational citizenship behaviors.

We developed a definition of thriving that breaks the concept into two factors: *vitality*—the sense that

(Continued)

you're energized and alive; and *learning*—the gaining of knowledge and skills.

When you put the two together, the statistics are striking. For example, people who were high energy and high learning were 21% more effective as leaders than those who were only high energy. The outcomes on one measure in particular—health—were even more extreme. Those who were high energy and low learning were 54% worse when it came to health than those who were high in both.

hiring manager will look for those people. But most employees are influenced by their environment. Even those predisposed to flourish can fold under pressure.

The good news is that—without heroic measures or major financial investments—leaders and managers can jump-start a culture that encourages employees to thrive. That is, managers can overcome organizational inertia to promote thriving and the productivity that follows it—in many cases with a relatively modest shift in attention.

Ideally, you'd be blessed with a workforce full of people who naturally thrive. But there's a lot you can do to release and sustain enthusiasm. Our research has uncovered four mechanisms that create the conditions for thriving employees: providing decision-making discretion, sharing information, minimizing incivility, and offering performance feedback. The mechanisms overlap somewhat. For instance, if you let people make decisions but give them incomplete information, or leave them exposed to hostile reactions, they'll suffer rather than thrive. One mechanism by itself will get you part of the way, but all four are necessary to create a culture of thriving. Let's look at each in turn.

Providing decision-making discretion

Employees at every level are energized by the ability to make decisions that affect their work. Empowering them in this way gives them a greater sense of control, more say in how things get done, and more opportunities for learning.

The airline industry might seem like an unlikely place to find decision-making discretion (let alone a thriving workforce), but consider one company we studied, Alaska Airlines, which created a culture of empowerment that has contributed to a major turnaround over the past decade. In the early 2000s the airline's numbers were flagging, so senior management launched the 2010 Plan, which explicitly invited employee input into decisions that would improve service while maintaining a reputation for timely departures. Employees were asked to set aside their current perceptions of "good" service and consider new ways to contribute, coming up with ideas that could take service from good to truly great. Agents embraced the program, which gave them, for instance, the discretion to find solutions for customers who had missed flights or were left behind for any other reason. Ron Calvin, the director of the eastern region, told us of a call he had recently received on his cell phone from a customer he hadn't seen or spoken to since working at the Seattle airport, five years earlier. The customer had a three-month-old grandchild who had just gone into cardiac arrest. The grandparents were trying to get back to Seattle from Honolulu. Everything was booked. Ron made a few calls and got them on a flight right away. That day the grandfather sent Ron a text saying, simply, "We made it."

Efforts like this to meet individual needs without holding up flights have led to a number one rating for on-time performance and a full trophy case. The airline has also expanded considerably into new markets, including Hawaii, the Midwest, and the East Coast.

Southwest is a better-known story, largely because of the company's reputation for having a fun and caring culture. Flight attendants are often eager to sing, joke around, and in general entertain customers. They also radiate energy and a passion for learning. One decided to offer the preflight safety instructions in rap format. He was motivated to put his special talents to work, and the passengers loved it, reporting that it was the first time they had actually paid attention to the instructions.

At Facebook, decision-making discretion is fundamental to the culture. One employee posted a note on the site expressing his surprise, and pleasure, at the company's motto, "Move fast and break things," which encourages employees to make decisions and act. On just his second day of work, he found a fix to a complicated bug. He expected some sort of hierarchical review, but his boss, the vice president of product, just smiled and said, "Ship it." He marveled that so early on he had delivered a solution that would instantly reach millions of people.

The challenge for managers is to avoid cutting back on empowerment when people make mistakes. Those situations create the best conditions for learning—not only for the parties concerned but also for others, who can learn vicariously.

Sharing information

Doing your job in an information vacuum is tedious and uninspiring; there's no reason to look for innovative solutions if you can't see the larger impact. People can contribute more effectively when they understand how their work fits with the organization's mission and strategy.

Alaska Airlines has chosen to invest management time in helping employees gain a broad view of the company's strategy. The 2010 Plan was launched with traditional communications but also with a months-long road show and training classes designed to help employees share ideas. The CEO, the president, and the COO still go on the road quarterly to gather information about the idiosyncrasies of various markets; they then disseminate what they've learned. The benefits show up in yearly measures of employee pride in the company—now knocking it out of the park at 90%.

At Zingerman's (an Ann Arbor, Michigan, community of food-related businesses that has worked closely with Wayne Baker, a colleague of ours at the Center for Positive Organizational Scholarship), information is as transparent as possible. The organization had never consciously withheld its numbers—financial information was tacked up for employees to see—but when cofounders Ari Weinzweig and Paul Saginaw studied open book management in the mid-

1990s, they came to believe that employees would show more interest if they got involved in the "game."

Implementation of a more formal and meaningful open book policy was not easy. People could look at the numbers, but they had little reason to pay attention and didn't get much insight into how the data related to their daily work. For the first five or six years, the company struggled to build the concept into its systems and routines and to wrap people's minds around what Baker calls "the rigor of the huddle": weekly gatherings around a whiteboard at which teams track results, "keep score," and forecast the next week's numbers. Although people understood the rules of open book management, at first they didn't see the point of adding yet another meeting to their busy schedules. It wasn't until senior leaders made huddling non-negotiable that employees grasped the true purpose of the whiteboards, which displayed not just financial figures but also service and food quality measures, check averages, internal satisfaction figures, and "fun," which could mean anything from weekly contests to customer satisfaction ratings to employees' ideas for innovation.

Some Zingerman's businesses began instituting "mini games": short-term incentives to find a problem or capitalize on an opportunity. For instance, the staff at Zingerman's Roadhouse restaurant used the greeter game to track how long it took for customers to be greeted. "Ungreeted" customers expressed less satisfaction, and employees found themselves frequently comping purchases to make up for service lapses. The greeter game challenged the host team to greet every customer within five minutes of being seated, with a modest financial reward for 50 straight days of success. It inspired hosts to quickly uncover and fill holes in the service process. Service scores improved considerably over the course of a month. Other Zingerman's businesses started similar games, with incentives for faster delivery, fewer knife injuries in the bakery (which would lower insurance costs), and neater kitchens.

The games have naturally created some internal tensions by delivering the bad news along with the good, which can be demoralizing. But overall they have greatly increased frontline employees' sense of ownership, contributing to better performance. From 2000 to 2010 Zingerman's revenue grew by almost 300%, to more than $35 million. The company's leaders credit open book management as a key factor in that success.

Simple anecdotes lend credence to their claim. For instance, a couple of years ago we saw Ari Weinzweig give a talk at the Roadhouse. A guest asked him whether it was realistic to expect the average waiter or busboy to understand company strategy and finance. In response, Ari turned to a busboy, who had been oblivious to the conversation: Would the teenager mind sharing Zingerman's vision and indicating how well the restaurant was meeting its weekly goals?

Without batting an eye, the busboy stated the vision in his own words and then described how well the restaurant was doing that week on "meals sent back to the kitchen."

While Zingerman's is a fairly small business, much larger ones—such as Whole Foods and the transportation company YRC Worldwide—have also adopted open book management. Systems that make information widely available build trust and give employees the knowledge they need to make good decisions and take initiative with confidence.

Minimizing incivility

The costs of incivility are great. In our research with Christine Pearson, a professor at Arizona State University's Thunderbird School of Global Management, we discovered that half of employees who had experienced uncivil behavior at work intentionally decreased their efforts. More than a third deliberately decreased the quality of their work. Two-thirds spent a lot of time avoiding the offender, and about the same number said their performance had declined.

Most people have experienced rude behavior at work. Here are a few quotes from our research:

> "My boss asked me to prepare an analysis. This was my first project, and I was not given any instructions or examples. He told me the assignment was crap."

> "My boss said, 'If I wanted to know what you thought, I'd ask you.'"

> "My boss saw me remove a paper clip from some documents and drop it in my wastebasket. In front of my 12 subordinates he rebuked me for being wasteful and required me to retrieve it."

"On speakerphone, in front of peers, my boss told me that I'd done 'kindergarten work.'"

We have heard hundreds of stories, and they're sadly familiar to most working people. But we don't hear so much about the costs.

Incivility prevents people from thriving. Those who have been the targets of bad behavior are often, in turn, uncivil themselves: They sabotage their peers. They "forget" to copy colleagues on memos. They spread gossip to deflect attention. Faced with incivility, employees are likely to narrow their focus to avoid risks—and lose opportunities to learn in the process.

A management consultancy we studied, Caiman Consulting, was founded as an alternative to the larger firms. Headquartered in Redmond, Washington, in offices that are not particularly sleek, the firm is recognized for its civil culture. Background checks in its hiring process include a candidate's record of civility.

"People leave a trail," says Caiman's director, Greg Long. "You can save yourself from a corrosive culture by being careful and conscientious up front." The managing director, Raazi Imam, told us, "I have no tolerance for anyone to berate or disrespect someone." When it does happen, he pulls the offender aside to make his policy clear. Long attributes the firm's 95% retention rate to its culture.

Caiman passes up highly qualified candidates who don't match that culture. It also keeps a list of consultants who might be good hires when an appropriate spot opens up. The HR director, Meg Clara, puts strong interpersonal skills and emotional intelligence among her prime criteria for candidates.

At Caiman, as at all companies, managers establish the tone when it comes to civility. A single bad player can set the culture awry. One young manager told us about her boss, an executive who had a habit of yelling from his office "You made a mistake!" for a sin as minor as a typo. His voice would resonate across the floor, making everyone cringe and the recipient feel acutely embarrassed. Afterward, colleagues would gather in a common area for coffee and commiseration. An insider told us that those conversations focused not on how to get ahead at the company or learn to cope by developing a thick skin but on how to get even and get out.

In our research, we were surprised by how few companies consider civility—or incivility—when evaluating candidates. Corporate culture is inherently contagious; employees assimilate to their environment. In other words, if you hire for civility, you're more likely to breed it into your culture. (See the sidebar "Individual Strategies for Thriving.")

Offering performance feedback

Feedback creates opportunities for learning and the energy that's so critical for a culture of thriving. By resolving feelings of uncertainty, feedback keeps

INDIVIDUAL STRATEGIES FOR THRIVING

Although organizations benefit from enabling employees to thrive, leaders have so much on their plates that attention to this important task can slip. However, anyone can adopt strategies to enhance learning and vitality without significant organizational support. And because thriving can be contagious, you may find your ideas quickly spreading.

Take a break

Research by Jim Loehr and Tony Schwartz has shown that breaks and other renewal tactics, no matter how small, can create positive energy.

In our teaching, we let students design regular breaks and activities into the class to ensure that they stay energized. In one term, students decided to halt every class for two minutes at the midpoint to get up and do something active. Each week a different

(Continued)

foursome designed the quick activity—watching a funny YouTube video, doing the cha-cha slide, or playing a game. The point is that the students figure out what is energizing for them and share it with the class.

Even if your organization doesn't offer formal mechanisms for renewal, it's nearly always possible to schedule a short walk, a bike ride, or a quick lunch in the park. Some people write it into their schedules so that meetings can't impinge.

Craft your own work to be more meaningful

You can't ignore the requirements of your job, but you can watch for opportunities to make it more meaningful. Consider Tina, the staff administrator of a policy think tank within a large organization. When her boss took a six-month sabbatical, Tina needed to find a short-term replacement project. After some scouting, she uncovered a budding initiative to develop staff members' ability to speak up with their ideas about the organization. The effort needed an innovative spirit to kick it off. The pay was lower, but the nature of the work energized Tina. When her boss returned, she renegotiated the terms of her think tank job to consume only 80% of her time, leaving the rest for the staff development project.

Look for opportunities to innovate and learn

Breaking out of the status quo can trigger the learning that is so essential to thriving. When Roger became the head of a prestigious high school in the Midwest, he was brimming with innovative ideas. He quickly ascertained, however, that quite a few staff members were not open to new ways of doing things.

(Continued)

He made sure to listen to their concerns and tried to bring them along, but he invested more of his effort in the growth and learning of those who shared his passion for breakthrough ideas. Mentoring and encouraging them, Roger began to achieve small wins, and his initiatives gained some momentum. A few of the resisters ended up leaving the school, and others came around when they saw signs of positive change. By focusing on those bright spots rather than the points of resistance, Roger was able to launch an effort that is propelling the school toward a radically different future.

Invest in relationships that energize you

All of us have colleagues who may be brilliant but are difficult and corrosive to work with. Individuals who thrive look for opportunities to work closely with colleagues who generate energy and to minimize interaction with those who deplete it. In fact, when we built the research team to study thriving, we chose colleagues we enjoyed, who energized us, with whom we looked forward to spending time, and from whom we knew we could learn. We seek to build good relationships by starting every meeting with good news or expressions of gratitude.

Recognize that thriving can spill over outside the office

There's evidence that high levels of engagement at work will not lessen your ability to thrive in your personal life but instead can enhance it. When one of us (Gretchen) was dealing with her husband's difficult medical diagnosis, she found that her work,

(Continued)

even though it was demanding, gave her the energy to thrive professionally and in her family life. Thriving is not a zero-sum game. People who feel energized at work often bring that energy to their lives beyond work. And people inspired by outside activities—volunteering, training for a race, taking a class—can bring their drive back to the office.

people's work-related activities focused on personal and organizational goals. The quicker and more direct the feedback, the more useful it is.

The Zingerman's huddle, described earlier, is a tool for sharing near-real-time information about individual as well as business performance. Leaders outline daily ups and downs on the whiteboard, and employees are expected to "own" the numbers and come up with ideas for getting back on track when necessary. The huddles also include "code reds" and "code greens," which document customer complaints and compliments so that all employees can learn and grow on the basis of immediate and tangible feedback.

Quicken Loans, a mortgage finance company that measures and rewards employee performance like no other organization, offers continually updated performance feedback using two types of dashboards: a ticker and kanban reports. (*Kanban*, a Japanese word meaning "signal," is used frequently in operations.)

The ticker has several panels that display group and individual metrics along with data feeds that show how likely an employee is to meet his or her daily goals. People are hardwired to respond to scores and goals, so the metrics help keep them energized through the day; essentially, they're competing against their own numbers.

The kanban dashboard allows managers to track people's performance so that they know when an employee or a team needs some coaching or other type of assistance. A version of the kanban chart is also displayed on monitors, with a rotating list of the top 15 salespeople for each metric. Employees are constantly in competition to make the boards, which are almost like a video game's ranking of high scorers.

Employees could feel overwhelmed or even oppressed by the constant nature of the feedback. Instead, the company's strong norms for civility and respect and for giving employees a say in how they accomplish their work create a context in which the feedback is energizing and promotes growth.

The global law firm O'Melveny & Myers lauds the use of 360-degree evaluations in helping workers thrive. The feedback is open-ended and summarized rather than shared verbatim, which has encouraged a 97% response rate. Carla Christofferson, the managing partner of the Los Angeles offices, learned from her evaluation that people saw her behavior as not matching the firm's stated commitment to work-life balance—which was causing stress among employees. She started to spend more time away from the office and to limit weekend work to things she could do at home. She became a role model for balance, which went a long way toward eliminating the worry of employees who wanted a life outside of work.

The four mechanisms that help employees thrive don't require enormous efforts or investments. What they do require is leaders who are open to empowering employees and who set the tone. As we've noted, each mechanism provides a different angle that's necessary for thriving. You can't choose one or two from the menu; the mechanisms reinforce one another. For example, can people be comfortable making decisions if they don't have honest information about current numbers? Can they make effective decisions if they're worried about being ridiculed?

Creating the conditions for thriving requires your concerted attention. Helping people grow and remain energized at work is valiant on its own merits—but it can also boost your company's performance in a sustainable way.

GRETCHEN SPREITZER is the Keith E. and Valerie J. Alessi Professor of Business Administration at the University of Michigan's Ross School of Business where she is a core faculty member in the Center for Positive Organizations. CHRISTINE PORATH is an associate professor of management at Georgetown University, the author of *Mastering Civility: A Manifesto for the Workplace* (Grand Central Publishing, 2016), and a coauthor of *The Cost of Bad Behavior* (Portfolio, 2009).

Reprinted from *Harvard Business Review*, January–February 2012 (product #R1201F).

6

The Research We've Ignored About Happiness at Work

By André Spicer and Carl Cederström

Recently, we found ourselves in motivational seminars at our respective places of employment. Both events preached the gospel of happiness. In one, a speaker explained that happiness could make you healthier, kinder, more productive, and even more likely to get promoted.

The other seminar involved mandatory dancing of the wilder kind. It was supposed to fill our bodies with joy. It also prompted one of us to sneak out and take refuge in the nearest bathroom.

Ever since a group of scientists switched the lights on and off at the Hawthorne factory in the mid-1920s, scholars and executives alike have been obsessed with increasing their employees' productivity. In particular, happiness as a way to boost productivity seems to have gained traction in corporate circles as of late.[1] Firms spend money on happiness coaches, team-building exercises, gameplays, funsultants, and chief happiness officers (yes, you'll find one of those at Google). These activities and titles may appear jovial or even bizarre, but companies are taking them extremely seriously. Should they?

When you look closely at the research—which we did after the dancing incident—it's not clear that encouraging happiness at work is always a good idea. Sure, there is evidence to suggest that happy employees are less likely to leave, more likely to satisfy customers, are safer, and more likely to engage in citizenship behavior.[2] However, we also discovered alternate findings, which indicates that some of the taken-for-granted wisdoms about what happiness can achieve in the workplace are mere myths.

To start, we don't really know what happiness is or how to measure it. Measuring happiness is about as easy as taking the temperature of the soul or determining the exact color of love. As historian Darrin M. McMahon shows in his illuminating book *Happiness: A History*, ever since the sixth century BC, when Croesus is said to have quipped "No one who lives is happy," this slippery concept has served as a proxy for all sorts of other concepts, from pleasure and joy to plenitude and contentment. Being happy in the moment, Samuel Johnson said, could be achieved only when drunk.[3] For Jean-Jacques Rousseau, happiness was to lie in a boat, drifting aimlessly, feeling like a God (not exactly the picture of productivity). There are other definitions of happiness, too, but they are neither less nor more plausible than those of Johnson or Rousseau.

And just because we have more-advanced technology today doesn't mean we're any closer to pinning down a definition, as Will Davies reminds us in his book *The Happiness Industry.* He concludes that even as we have developed more-advanced techniques for measuring emotions and predicting behaviors, we have also adopted increasingly simplified notions of what it means to be human, let alone what it means to pursue happiness. A brain scan that lights up may *seem* like it's telling us something concrete about an elusive emotion, for example, when it actually isn't.

Happiness doesn't necessarily lead to increased productivity. A stream of research shows some contradictory results about the relationship between happiness—which is often defined as "job satisfaction"—and productivity.[4] One study on British supermarkets even suggests there might be a negative correlation between job satisfaction and corporate productivity: The more miserable the employees were, the better the profits.[5] Sure, other studies have pointed in the opposite direction, saying that there is a link between feeling content with work and being productive. But even these studies, when considered as a whole, demonstrate a relatively weak correlation.

Happiness can also be exhausting. The pursuit of happiness may not be wholly effective, but it doesn't really hurt, right? Wrong. Ever since the eighteenth century, people have been pointing out that the demand to be happy brings with it a heavy burden, a responsibility that can never be perfectly fulfilled. Focusing on happiness can actually make us feel less happy.

A psychological experiment recently demonstrated this.[6] The researchers asked their subjects to watch a film that would usually make them happy: a figure skater winning a medal. But before watching the film, half of the group was asked to read a statement aloud about the importance of happiness in life. The other half did not read the statement. The researchers were surprised to find that those who had read the statement were actually *less* happy after watching the film. Essentially, when happiness becomes a duty, it can make people feel worse if they fail to accomplish it.

This is particularly problematic at the present era, in which happiness is preached as a moral obligation.[7] As the French philosopher Pascal Bruckner put it, "Unhappiness is not only unhappiness; it is, worse yet, a failure to be happy."[8]

Happiness won't necessarily get you through the workday. If you've worked in a frontline customer service job, like a call center or a fast food restaurant, you know that being upbeat is not optional—it's compulsory. And as tiring as that may be, it makes some sense when you're in front of customers.

But today, many non-customer-facing employees are also asked to be upbeat. This could have some unforeseen consequences. One study found that people who were in a good mood were worse at picking out acts of deception than those who were in a bad mood.[9] Another piece of research found that people who were angry during a negotiation achieved better outcomes than people who were happy.[10] This suggests that being happy may not be good for all aspects of our work or for jobs that rely heavily on certain abilities. In fact, in some cases, happiness can actually make our performance worse.

Happiness could damage your relationship with your boss. If we believe that work is where we will find happiness, we might, in some cases, start to mistake our boss for a surrogate spouse or parent. In her study of a media company, researcher Susanne Ekmann found that those who expected work to make them happy would often become emotionally needy.[11] They wanted their managers to provide them with a steady stream of recognition and emotional reassurance. And when they *didn't* receive the expected emotional response (which was often), these employees felt neglected and started overreacting. Even minor setbacks were interpreted as being rejected by their bosses. So in many ways, expecting a boss to bring happiness makes us emotionally vulnerable.

Happiness could also hurt your relationships with friends and family. In her book *Cold Intimacies*, sociology professor Eva Illouz points out a strange side effect of people trying to live more emotionally at work: They started to treat their private lives like work tasks. The people she spoke with saw their personal lives as something that needed to be carefully administered using a range of tools and techniques they had learned from corporate life. As a result, their home lives became increasingly cold and calculating. It's no wonder then that many of the people she spoke with preferred to spend time at work rather than at home.

Happiness could make losing your job that much more devastating. When we expect the workplace to provide happiness and meaning in our lives, we become dangerously dependent on it. When studying professionals, sociology professor Richard Sennett noticed that people who saw their employer as an important source of personal meaning were those who became most devastated if they were fired.[12] When these people lost their jobs, they weren't just losing an income—they were losing the promise of happiness. This suggests that, when we see our work as a great source of happiness, we make ourselves emotionally vulnerable during periods of change. In an era of constant corporate restructuring, this can be dangerous.

Happiness could also make you selfish. Being happy makes you a better person, right? Not so, according to an interesting piece of research.[13] Participants were given lottery tickets and then given a choice about how many tickets they wanted to give to others and how many they wished to keep for themselves. Those who were in a good mood ended up keeping more tickets for themselves. This implies that, at least in some settings, being happy doesn't necessarily mean we will be generous. In fact, the opposite could be true.

Finally, happiness could also make you lonely. In one experiment, psychologists asked a number of people to keep a detailed diary for two weeks. What they found at the end of the study was that those who greatly valued happiness felt lonelier than those who valued happiness less.[14] It seems that focusing too much on the pursuit of happiness can make us feel disconnected from other people.

So why, contrary to all of this evidence, do we continue to hold on to the belief that happiness can improve a workplace? The answer, according to one study, comes down to aesthetics and ideology. Happiness is a convenient idea that looks good on paper (the aesthetic part). But it's also an idea that helps us shy away from more serious issues at work, such as conflicts and workplace politics (the ideological part).[15]

When we assume that happy workers are better workers, we may sweep more uncomfortable questions under the rug, especially since happiness is often seen as a choice. It becomes a convenient way of dealing with negative attitudes, party poopers, miserable bastards, and other unwanted characters in corporate life. Invoking happiness, in all its ambiguity, is an excellent way of getting away with controversial decisions, such as choosing to let people go. As Barbara Ehrenreich points out in her book *Bright-Sided*, positive messages about happiness have proved particularly popular in times of crisis and mass layoffs.

Given all these potential problems, we think there is a strong case for rethinking our expectation that work should always make us happy. It can be exhausting, make us overreact, drain our personal life of meaning, increase our vulnerability, and make us more gullible, selfish, and lonely. Most striking is that consciously pursuing happiness can actually drain the sense of joy we usually get from the really good things we experience.

In reality, work—like all other aspects of life—is likely to make us feel a wide range of emotions. If your job feels depressing and meaningless, it might be because it *is* depressing and meaningless. Pretending otherwise can just make it worse. Happiness, of course, is a great thing to experience, but it can't be willed into existence. Maybe the less we seek to actively pursue happiness through our jobs, the more likely we will be to actually experience a sense of joy in our work—a joy that is spontaneous and pleasurable rather than constructed and oppressive. But most important, we will be better equipped to cope with work in a sober manner. To see it for what it is and not what we—whether as executives, employees, or dancing motivational seminar leaders—pretend that it is.

ANDRÉ SPICER is a professor of organizational behavior at
Cass Business School in London. CARL CEDERSTRÖM is an
associate professor of organization theory at Stockholm University. They are the coauthors of *The Wellness Syndrome*
(Polity 2015).

Notes

1. C. D. Fisher, "Happiness at Work." *International Journal of Management Reviews* 12, no. 4 (December 2010):
   384–412.
2. Ibid.
3. D. M. McMahon, *Happiness: A History.* (New York: Atlan-
   tic Monthly Press, 2006.)
4. Fisher, "Happiness at Work."
5. McMahon, *Happiness: A History.*
6. I. B. Mauss et al., "Can Seeking Happiness Make People
   Happy? Paradoxical Effects of Valuing Happiness." *Emotion* 11, no. 4 (August 2011): 807–815.
7. P. Bruckner, *Perpetual Euphoria: On the Duty to Be
   Happy*, tr. Steven Rendall. (Princeton, New Jersey: Princeton University Press, 2011.)
8. Ibid, 5.
9. J. P. Forgas and R. East, "On Being Happy and Gullible:
   Mood Effects on Skepticism and the Detection of Deception." *Journal of Experimental Social Psychology* 44
   (2008): 1362–1367.

10. G. A. van Kleef et al., "The Interpersonal Effects of Anger and Happiness in Negotiations." *Journal of Personality and Social Psychology* 86, no. 1 (2004): 57–76.

11. S. Ekman, "Fantasies About Work as Limitless Potential—How Managers and Employees Seduce Each Other through Dynamics of Mutual Recognition." *Human Relations* 66, no. 9 (December 2012): 1159–1181.

12. R. Sennett, *The Corrosion of Character: The Personal Consequences of Work in New Capitalism.* (New York: W.W. Norton, 2000.)

13. H. B. Tan and J. Forgas, "When Happiness Makes Us Selfish, But Sadness Makes Us Fair: Affective Influences on Interpersonal Strategies in the Dictator Game." *Journal of Experimental Social Psychology* 46, no. 3 (May 2010): 571–576.

14. I. B. Mauss, "The Pursuit of Happiness Can Be Lonely." *Emotion* 12, no. 5 (2012): 908–912.

15. G. E. Ledford, "Happiness and Productivity Revisited." *Journal of Organizational Behavior* 20, no. 1 (January 1999): 25–30.

Adapted from content posted on hbr.org on
July 21, 2015 (product #H027TW).

7

The Happiness Backlash

By Alison Beard

Nothing depresses me more than reading about happiness. Why? Because there's entirely too much advice out there about how to achieve it. As Frédéric Lenoir points out in *Happiness: A Philosopher's Guide* (recently translated from its original French), great thinkers have been discussing this topic for more than 2,000 years. But opinions on it still differ. Just scan the 14,700 titles listed in the "happiness" subgenre of self-help books on Amazon, or watch the 55 TED talks tagged in the same category. What makes us happy? Health, money, social connection, purpose, "flow," generosity, gratitude, inner peace, positive thinking . . . research shows that any (or all?) of the above answers are correct. Social scientists tell us that even the simplest of tricks—counting our blessings, meditating for 10 minutes a day, forcing smiles—can push us into a happier state of mind.

And yet for me and many others, happiness remains elusive. Of course, I sometimes feel joyful and content—reading a bedtime story to my kids, interviewing someone I greatly admire, finishing a tough piece of writing. But despite having good health, supportive family and friends, and a stimulating and flexible job, I'm often awash in negative emotions: worry, frustration, anger, disappointment, guilt, envy, regret. My default state is dissatisfied.

The huge and growing body of happiness literature promises to lift me out of these feelings. But the effect is more like kicking me when I'm down. I know I should be happy. I know I have every reason to be and that I'm better off than most. I know that happier people are more successful. I know that just a few mental exercises might help me. Still, when I'm in a bad mood, it's hard to break out of it. And—I'll admit—a small part of me regards my nonbliss not as unproductive negativity but as highly productive realism. I can't imagine being happy all the time; indeed, I'm highly suspicious of anyone who claims to be.

I agreed to write this essay because over the past several years I've sensed a swell of support for this point of view. Barbara Ehrenreich's 2009 book *Bright-Sided*, about the "relentless promotion" and undermining effects of positive thinking, was followed last year by *Rethinking Positive Thinking*, by the NYU psychology professor Gabriele Oettingen, and *The Upside of Your Dark Side*, by two experts in positive psychology, Todd Kashdan and Robert Biswas-Diener. This year brought a terrific *Psychology Today* article by Matthew Hutson titled "Beyond Happiness: The Upside of Feeling Down"; *The Upside of Stress*, by Stanford's Kelly McGonigal; *Beyond Happiness*, by the British historian and commentator Anthony Seldon; and *The Happiness Industry:*

How the Government and Big Business Sold Us Well-Being, by another Brit, the Goldsmiths lecturer in politics William Davies.

Are we finally seeing a backlash against happiness? Sort of. Most of these recent releases rail against our modern obsession with *feeling* happy and *thinking* positively. Oettingen explains the importance of damping sunny fantasies with sober analysis of the obstacles in one's way. Kashdan and Biswas-Diener's book and Hutson's article detail the benefits we derive from all the negative emotions I cited earlier; taken together, those feelings spur us to better our circumstances and ourselves. (The Harvard psychologist Susan David, a coauthor of the HBR article "Emotional Agility," also writes thoughtfully on this topic.)

McGonigal shows how viewing one unhappy condition—stress—in a kinder light can turn it into something that improves rather than hurts our health. Those who accept feeling stressed as the body's natural response to a challenge are more resilient and live longer than those who try to fight it.

Seldon describes his own progression from pleasure seeking to more-meaningful endeavors that
bring him (and should bring us) joy. Sadly, he trivial-
izes his advice by alphabetizing it: Accepting oneself;
Belonging to a group; having good Character, Discipline, Empathy, Focus, Generosity, and Health; using
Inquiry; embarking on an inner Journey; accepting
Karma; and embracing both Liturgy and Meditation. (One wonders what he'll use for X and Z in the
next book.)

Davies comes at the issue from a different angle.
He's fed up with organizational attempts to tap into
what is essentially a "grey mushy process inside our
brains." In his view, there's something sinister about
the way advertisers, HR managers, governments, and
pharmaceutical companies are measuring, manipu-
lating, and ultimately making money from our insa-
tiable desire to be happier.

But none of these authors is arguing against individuals' aspiring to have a generally happy life. We
call that the pursuit of "happiness," but what we really

mean is "long-term fulfillment." Martin Seligman, the father of positive psychology, calls it "flourishing" and said years ago that positive emotion (that is, feeling happy) is only one element of it, along with engagement, relationships, meaning, and achievement. In the parlance Arianna Huffington uses in her recent book, it's "thriving," and Lenoir, whose history of happiness philosophy is probably the most enlightening and entertaining of the bunch, describes it as simply "love of life." Who can argue against any of those things?

Where most of the happiness gurus go wrong is insisting that daily if not constant happiness is a means to long-term fulfillment. For some glass-half-full optimists, that may be true. They can "stumble on happiness" the way the field's most prominent researcher, Dan Gilbert, suggests; or gain "the happiness advantage" that the professor-turned-consultant Shawn Achor talks about; or "broadcast happiness," as Michelle Gielan, Achor's wife and partner at the firm GoodThink, recommends in her new book. As I said, it apparently takes just a few simple tricks.

But for the rest of us, that much cheer feels forced, so it's unlikely to help us mold meaningful relationships or craft the perfect career. It certainly can't be drawn out of us by employers or other external forces. We pursue fulfillment in different ways, without reading self-help books. And I suspect that in the long run we'll be OK—perhaps even happy.

ALISON BEARD is a senior editor at *Harvard Business Review*.

Reprinted from *Harvard Business Review*,
July–August 2015.

Index

How to be human at work.

HBR's Emotional Intelligence Series features smart, essential reading on the human side of professional life from the pages of *Harvard Business Review*. Each book in the series offers uplifting stories, practical advice, and research from leading experts on how to tend to our emotional well-being at work.

Harvard Business Review Emotional Intelligence Series

Available in paperback or ebook format. The specially priced six-volume set includes:

- Mindfulness
- Resilience
- Influence and Persuasion
- Authentic Leadership
- Happiness
- Empathy

HBR.ORG

Buy for your team, clients, or event.
Visit hbr.org/bulksales for quantity discount rates.

Happiness

HBR EMOTIONAL INTELLIGENCE SERIES

HBR Emotional Intelligence Series

How to be human at work

The HBR Emotional Intelligence Series features smart, essential reading on the human side of professional life from the pages of *Harvard Business Review*.

Empathy

Happiness

Mindfulness

Resilience

Other books on emotional intelligence from *Harvard Business Review*:

HBR's 10 Must Reads on Emotional Intelligence

HBR Guide to Emotional Intelligence

Happiness

HBR EMOTIONAL INTELLIGENCE SERIES

Harvard Business Review Press

Boston, Massachusetts

HBR Press Quantity Sales Discounts

Harvard Business Review Press titles are available at significant quantity discounts when purchased in bulk for client gifts, sales promotions, and premiums. Special editions, including books with corporate logos, customized covers, and letters from the company or CEO printed in the front matter, as well as excerpts of existing books, can also be created in large quantities for special needs.

For details and discount information for both print and ebook formats, contact booksales@harvardbusiness.org, tel. 800-988-0886, or www.hbr.org/bulksales.

Copyright 2017 Harvard Business School Publishing Corporation
All rights reserved
Printed in the United States of America

20 19 18 17 16 15 14 13

No part of this publication may be reproduced, stored in or introduced into a retrieval system, or transmitted, in any form, or by any means (electronic, mechanical, photocopying, recording, or otherwise), without the prior permission of the publisher. Requests for permission should be directed to permissions@hbsp.harvard.edu, or mailed to Permissions, Harvard Business School Publishing, 60 Harvard Way, Boston, Massachusetts 02163.

The web addresses referenced in this book were live and correct at the time of the book's publication but may be subject to change.

Library of Congress Cataloging-in-Publication Data

Title: Happiness.
Other titles: HBR emotional intelligence series.
Description: Boston, Massachusetts : Harvard Business Review Press, [2017]
    Series: HBR emotional intelligence series
Identifiers: LCCN 2016056298 | ISBN 9781633693210 (pbk. : alk. paper)
Subjects: LCSH: Happiness. | Work—Psychological aspects.
Classification: LCC BF575.H27 H362 2017 | DDC 152.4/2—dc23 LC record available at https://lccn.loc.gov/2016056298

ISBN: 978-1-63369-321-0
eISBN: 978-1-63369-322-7

The paper used in this publication meets the requirements of the American National Standard for Permanence of Paper for Publications and Documents in Libraries and Archives Z39.48-1992.

Contents

Contents

Purpose, Meaning, and Passion

HBR EMOTIONAL INTELLIGENCE SERIES

HBR Emotional Intelligence Series

The HBR Emotional Intelligence Series features smart, essential reading on the human side of professional life from the pages of *Harvard Business Review*.

Authentic Leadership

Dealing with Difficult People

Empathy

Happiness

Influence and Persuasion

Leadership Presence

Mindfulness

Purpose, Meaning, and Passion

Resilience

Other books on emotional intelligence from *Harvard Business Review*:

HBR's 10 Must Reads on Emotional Intelligence

HBR Guide to Emotional Intelligence

HBR Everyday Emotional Intelligence

Purpose, Meaning, and Passion

HBR EMOTIONAL INTELLIGENCE SERIES

Harvard Business Review Press

Boston, Massachusetts

HBR Press Quantity Sales Discounts

Harvard Business Review Press titles are available at significant quantity discounts when purchased in bulk for client gifts, sales promotions, and premiums. Special editions, including books with corporate logos, customized covers, and letters from the company or CEO printed in the front matter, as well as excerpts of existing books, can also be created in large quantities for special needs.

For details and discount information for both print and ebook formats, contact booksales@harvardbusiness.org, tel 800-988-0886, or www.hbr .org/bulksales.

Copyright 2018 Harvard Business School Publishing Corporation
All rights reserved
Printed in the United States of America

10 9 8

No part of this publication may be reproduced, stored in or introduced into a retrieval system, or transmitted, in any form, or by any means (electronic, mechanical, photocopying, recording, or otherwise), without the prior permission of the publisher. Requests for permission should be directed to permissions@hbsp.harvard.edu, or mailed to Permissions, Harvard Business School Publishing, 60 Harvard Way, Boston, Massachusetts 02163.

The web addresses referenced in this book were live and correct at the time of the book's publication but may be subject to change.

Library of Congress Cataloging-in-Publication Data

Title: Purpose, meaning, and passion.
Other titles: HBR emotional intelligence series.
Description: Boston, Massachusetts : Harvard Business Review Press, [2018] | Series: HBR emotional intelligence series
Identifiers: LCCN 2017053590 | ISBN 9781633696273 (pbk. : alk. paper)
Subjects: LCSH: Work--Psychological aspects. | Job satisfaction. | Meaning (Psychology) | Employee motivation. | Enthusiasm.
Classification: LCC BF481 .P87 2018 | DDC 158.7--dc23 LC record available at https://lccn.loc.gov/2017053590

The paper used in this publication meets the requirements of the American National Standard for Permanence of Paper for Publications and Documents in Libraries and Archives Z39.48-1992.

Contents

Contents

Contents

Purpose, Meaning, and Passion

HBR EMOTIONAL INTELLIGENCE SERIES

1

Finding Meaning at Work, Even When Your Job Is Dull

By Morten Hansen and Dacher Keltner

D o you experience meaning at work—or just emptiness?

In the United States, people spend an average of 35 to 40 hours working every week. That's some 80,000 hours during a career—more time than you will spend with your kids probably. Beyond the paycheck, what does work give you? Few questions could be more important. It is sad to walk through life experiencing work as empty, dreadful, a chore—something that saps energy out of your body and soul. Yet many employees feel this way, as evidenced by one large-scale study showing that only 31% of employees were engaged.[1]

Work can, however, provide an array of meaningful experiences, even though many employees do not enjoy them in their current job. So what are the sources of meaningful experiences at work?

We have compiled a list based on our reading of literature in organization behavior and psychology. Many theories speak to meaning at work, including need-based, motivational, status, power, and community theories. The phrase "meaning at work" refers to a person's experience of something meaningful—something of value—that work provides. That is not the same as "meaningful work," which refers to the task itself. Work is a social arena that offers other kinds of meaningful experiences as well.

Before we run through the list, it is important to note:

- Different people look for different types of meaning.

- Different workplaces provide different meanings.

Purpose

Contributions beyond yourself

The people at nonprofit Kiva channel microloans to poor people who can use the money to get a small business going and improve their lives. Their work clearly has a greater purpose—that of helping people in need. This taps into a longing to have a meaningful life defined as making contributions beyond oneself.

The problem is, however, that most work doesn't have such a higher purpose, either because the job is basically mundane or because—let's face it—the company doesn't really have a social mission. Critics of workplace culture like economics researcher Umair Haque argue that work that involves selling yet more burgers, sugar water, high-fashion clothing, and the like has no broader purpose whatsoever. In this view, Coke's "Open happiness" tagline is just a slogan devoid of meaning. However, as researchers Teresa Amabile and Steve Kramer argue, much work can be

5

infused with some level of purpose. (See chapter 9 of this book for more on gradual steps toward meaningful work.) Companies that make real efforts in social responsibilities do this. For example, Danone, the $25 billion large and highly successful consumer goods company that sells yogurt, has defined their business as providing healthy foods (which led them to sell off their biscuit business). The litmus test here is whether employees experience that their work makes positive contributions to others. If they do, then they experience meaning at work.

Self-realization

Learning

Many MBA graduates flock to McKinsey, BCG, and other consultancies so that they can rapidly acquire valuable skills. General Electric is renowned for developing general managers, and people who want to become marketers crave to learn that trade at Procter & Gamble. Work offers opportunities to learn, expand one's horizon, and improve self-awareness. This kind of personal growth is meaningful.

Accomplishment

Work is also a place to accomplish things and be recognized, which leads to greater satisfaction, confidence, and self-worth. In the documentary *Jiro Dreams of Sushi* we see Japan's greatest sushi chef devote his life to making perfect sushi. Some critics like Lucy Kellaway at the *Financial Times* say there isn't a real social mission here. But the main character's quest for perfection—to make better sushi all the time—gives his life a deep sense of meaning. And for Jiro, the work itself—making the sushi—gives him a deep intrinsic satisfaction.

Prestige

Status

At cocktail parties, a frequent question is "Where do you work?" The ability to rattle off "Oh, I am a doctor at Harvard Medical School" oozes status. For some, that moment is worth all the grueling night shifts. A high-status organization confers respect, recognition, and a sense of worth to employees, and that provides meaning at work for some.

Power

As Paul Lawrence and Nitin Nohria write about in their book *Driven*, for those drawn to power, work provides an arena for acquiring and exercising power. You may not be one of those, but if you are, you experience work as meaningful because you have and can use power.

Social rewards

Belonging to a community

Companies like Southwest Airlines go out of their way to create a company atmosphere where people feel they belong. In a society where people increasingly are "bowling alone," people crave a place where they can forge friendships and experience a sense of community. (In his book of the same name, Robert Putnam describes the American decline in bowling leagues as a metaphor for a larger cultural shift away from formal social structures.[2]) The workplace can complement or even be a substitute for other communities (family, the neighborhood, clubs and so on). Workplaces that provide a sense of community give people meaning.

Agency

Employees also experience meaning at work when what they do actually matters for the organization, when their ideas are listened to and when they see that their contributions have an impact on how the place performs. A sense of real involvement gives people meaning.

Autonomy

As Dan Pink shows in his book *Drive*, autonomy—the absence of others who tell you what to do and the freedom to do your own work in your own time—is a great intrinsic motivator. Some people are drawn to certain kinds of work that provides a great deal of autonomy. For example, entrepreneurs frequently go into business by themselves so that they can be their own boss. This kind of freedom gives work meaning.

———————————

There are no doubt other sources as well, but the ones listed here seem to be especially important. Which of them are important to you? And which do you receive from your current workplace? Having more sources of meaning is not necessarily better; experiencing one deeply may just be enough. But it's an issue if you don't experience any at all.

MORTEN HANSEN is a professor at the University of California, Berkeley, and at INSEAD, France, and is the author of *Collaboration: How Leaders Avoid the Traps, Build Common Ground, and Reap Big Results* (Harvard Business Review Press, 2009). DACHER KELTNER is a professor of psychology at UC Berkeley and the author of *Born to Be Good: The Science of a Meaningful Life* (W. W. Norton, 2009).

Notes

1. "Employee Engagement Research Report," Blessing White, January 2013; http://blessingwhite.com/research-report/ 2013/01/01/employee-engagement-research-report -update-jan-2013.

2. R. D. Putnam, *Bowling Alone: The Collapse and Revival of American Community* (New York: Touchstone Books, 2001).

Adapted from content posted on hbr.org, originally published December 20, 2012 (product #H009WH).

2

What to Do When Your Heart Isn't in Your Work Anymore

By Andy Molinsky

n an ideal world, our work lives would be completely fulfilling, full of meaning, and intrinsically
motivating. But what if they're not? What if you're
stuck in a job or a career that you once loved, but
your heart isn't in it anymore?

More people fit this profile than you'd think. According to a 2017 Gallup survey, only one-third of
U.S. employees feel engaged at work; that is, only one
in three workers brings a consistently high level of
initiative, commitment, passion, and productivity to
their job.[1] That leaves the majority of employees less
than satisfied with their work.

And truth be told, there could be any number of reasons for this sense of malaise. You might feel stuck doing the same thing over and over again. You might question the ultimate meaning of the work you're doing. You might feel micromanaged or that company leaders don't know or care about your learning and growth. Or maybe your own growth and development since starting your career has caused you to change your passions and priorities in life.

I see and hear examples of career malaise all the time—in my work teaching and training people in companies, in discussions following my corporate talks, and in conversations with my family and friends. Though the tendency among some of us in this situation is to simply grin and bear it, current scientific research suggests ways to reimagine—or reenvision—an uninspired professional existence.

Assess what you want out of your work— at this point in your life

Not everyone wants a high-powered career. In fact, according to research by Yale associate professor of organizational psychology Amy Wrzesniewski, people tend to fall into one of three categories: Some see their work as a career, others see it as just a job, and still others see it as a calling.[2] It's this third category of people, perhaps unsurprisingly, who exhibit higher performance and a greater sense of satisfaction with their jobs. The key for you is to determine what you care about *now*—what drives you, what you're passionate about, what truly motivates you—and build from there. It's quite possible that what drove your career in your twenties is no longer appealing. Don't force your 40-, 50-, or 60-year-old self into your 20-year-old sense of ambition. Even if you don't find your true calling, you will at least increase the odds of finding a meaningful work experience.

See if parts of your job are "craftable"

There has been considerable research on the idea of job crafting, in which you tweak certain aspects of your job to gain a greater sense of meaning and satisfaction. Research by Wrzesniewski and two other organizational behavior scholars, Justin Berg and Jane Dutton, has shown that people can be quite imaginative and effective at reimagining the design of their job in personally meaningful ways.

For example, if you enjoy analysis but not sales, can you adjust your responsibilities in that direction? If you love interacting with others but feel lonely, can you find ways to partner more on projects? One participant from Berg, Dutton, and Wrzesniewski's research redesigned her marketing job to include

more event planning, even though it wasn't originally part of her job. The reason was quite simple:
She liked it and was good at it, and by doing so, she
could add value to the company and to her own work
experience.[3]

Or consider this activity: Imagine that you're a job
architect, and do a "before" and "after" sketch of your
job responsibilities, with the "before" representing
the uninspiring status quo and the "after" representing future possibilities.[4] What novel tweaks can you
make to redesign your job, even slightly? Sometimes
even the smallest adjustments can lead to qualita-
tively meaningful changes in your work experience.

Ignite your passion outside of work

It might be a latent hobby you've told yourself you
don't have the time for, a personal project that isn't
related to your job or career, or a "side hustle" where

you can experiment with innovative or entrepreneurial ideas on a smaller scale. Having an outlet for your passion outside of work can counterbalance the monotony of the nine-to-five daily grind. These inspirational endeavors can even have unintended positive spillover effects at work, giving you energy and inspiration to craft your job or reengage with parts of it you actually like.[5]

If all else fails, make a change

Think about changing your career like you'd think about changing your house. When you originally bought your house, you had certain requirements. But since then, your priorities may have changed, or maybe you have simply outgrown it. Do you move, renovate, or stay put? You can think the exact same way about your job and career. Have your priorities and needs changed? Can you tweak or "renovate" your job? Or do you need to move on?

Of course, if you choose to change your career, you'll want to think it through and prepare yourself before jumping in with both feet. Network with people in professions you might be interested in, get your finances in order, and test out the new career (perhaps on the weekend or at night) before making the change. It can feel daunting to change everything so suddenly, but it's important to consider the option if you're truly feeling a deep sense of malaise at work.

The most important thing, though, if you're finding your interest waning at work, is not to lose hope. You *can* find ways to ignite your passion again—or at least make slight changes so you won't feel so hopeless. You'll likely be surprised at how resilient and resourceful you are as you walk down the path of career renovation.

ANDY MOLINSKY is a professor of organizational behavior at the Brandeis International Business School. He's the author of *Global Dexterity: How to Adapt Your Behavior Across Cultures Without Losing Yourself in the Process* (Harvard Business Review Press, 2013) and *Reach: A New Strategy to Help You*

Step Outside Your Comfort Zone, Rise to the Challenge, and Build Confidence (Avery, 2017).

Notes

1. E. O'Boyle and A. Mann, "American Workplace Changing at a Dizzying Pace," Gallup News, February 15, 2017.
2. K. Brooks, "Job, Career, Calling: Key to Happiness and Meaning at Work?" *Psychology Today*, June 29, 2012, https://www.psychologytoday.com/blog/career-transitions/201206/job-career-calling-key-happiness-and-meaning-work.
3. J. M. Berg, J. E. Dutton, and A. Wrzesniewski, "What Is Job Crafting and Why Does It Matter?" working paper, Center for Positive Organizational Scholarship, Ross School of Business, University of Michigan, 2007.
4. L. Lee, "Should Employees Design Their Own Jobs?" *Insights by Stanford Business*, January 22, 2016.
5. "The Positive Effect of Creative Hobbies on Performance at Work," *PsyBlog* (blog), April 28, 2014, http://www.spring.org.uk/2014/04/the-positive-effect-of-creative-hobbies-on-performance-at-work.php.

Reprinted from hbr.org, originally published
July 10, 2017 (product #H03RL0).

3

You Don't Find Your Purpose— You Build It

By John Coleman

ow do I find my purpose?"

Ever since Daniel Gulati, Oliver Segovia, and I published our book *Passion and Purpose* six years ago, I've received hundreds of questions—from younger and older people alike—about purpose. We're all looking for purpose. Most of us feel that we've never found it, we've lost it, or in some way we're falling short.

But in the midst of all this angst, I think we're also suffering from what I see as fundamental misconceptions about purpose, neatly encapsulated by the question I receive most frequently: *How do I find my purpose?* Challenging these misconceptions can help us all develop a more well-rounded vision of purpose.

Misconception #1:
Purpose is only a thing you find

On social media, I often see an inspiring quotation attributed to Mark Twain: "The two most important days in your life are the day you are born and the day you find out why." It neatly articulates what I'll call the "Hollywood version" of purpose. Like Neo in *The Matrix* or Rey in *Star Wars*, we're all just moving through life waiting until fate delivers a higher calling to us.

Make no mistake: That can happen, at least in some form. I recently saw Scott Harrison, founder and CEO of respected nonprofit Charity: Water, speak, and in many ways his story was about how he found a higher purpose after a period of wandering. But I think it's more rare than most people think. For the average 20-year-old in college or 40-year-old in an unfulfilling job, searching for the silver bullet to give life meaning is more likely to end in frustration than fulfillment.

In achieving professional purpose, most of us have to focus as much on *making* our work meaningful as in *taking* meaning from it. Put differently, purpose is a thing you build, not a thing you find. Almost any work can possess remarkable purpose. School bus drivers bear enormous responsibility—caring for and keeping safe dozens of children—and are an essential part of assuring our children receive the education they need and deserve. Nurses play an essential role not simply in treating people's medical conditions but also in guiding them through some of life's most difficult times. Cashiers can be a friendly, uplifting interaction in someone's day—often desperately needed—or a forgettable or regrettable one. But in each of these instances, purpose is often primarily derived from focusing on what's so meaningful and purposeful about the job and on doing it in such a way that that meaning is enhanced and takes center stage. Sure, some jobs more naturally lend themselves to a sense of meaning, but many require at least some deliberate effort to invest them with the purpose we seek.

Misconception #2:
Purpose is a single thing

The second misconception I often hear is that purpose can be articulated as a single thing. Some people genuinely do seem to have an overwhelming purpose in their lives. Mother Teresa lived her life to serve the poor. Samuel Johnson poured every part of himself into his writing. Marie Curie devoted her energy to her work.

And yet even these luminaries had other sources of purpose in their lives. Mother Teresa served the poor as part of what she believed was a higher calling. Curie, the Nobel prize–winning scientist, was also a devoted wife and mother (she wrote a biography of her husband, Pierre, and one of her daughters—Irene—won her own Nobel prize). And Johnson, beyond his writing, was known to be a great humanitarian in his community, often caring personally for the poor.

Most of us will have multiple sources of purpose in our lives. I find purpose in my children, my marriage, my faith, my writing, my work, and my community. For almost everyone, there's no one thing we can find. It's not *purpose* but *purposes* we are looking for: the multiple sources of meaning that help us find value in our work and lives. Professional commitments are only one component of this meaning, and often our work isn't central to our purpose but a conduit to helping others, including our families and communities. Acknowledging that there are multiple sources of purpose takes the pressure off of finding one single thing to give our lives meaning.

Misconception #3:
Purpose is stable over time

It's common now for people to have multiple careers in their lifetimes. I know one individual, for example, who recently left a successful private equity career to found a startup. I know two more who recently left business careers to run for elective office. And whether or not we switch professional commitments, most of us will experience personal phases in which our sources of meaning change—childhood, young adulthood, parenthood, and empty-nesting, to name a few.

This evolution in our sources of purpose isn't flaky or demonstrative of a lack of commitment but rather natural and good. Just as we all find meaning in multiple places, the sources of that meaning can and do change over time. My focus and sense of purpose at 20 was dramatically different in many ways than it is now, and the same could be said of almost anyone you meet.

How do you find your purpose? That's the wrong question to ask. We should be looking to endow everything we do with purpose, to allow for the multiple sources of meaning that will naturally develop in our lives, and to be comfortable with those sources changing over time. Unpacking what we mean by "purpose" can allow us to better understand its presence and role in our lives.

JOHN COLEMAN is a coauthor of the book *Passion and Purpose: Stories from the Best and Brightest Young Business Leaders* (Harvard Business Review Press, 2013).

Reprinted from hbr.org, originally published October 20, 2012 (product #H03YZX).

4

How to Find Meaning in a Job That Isn't Your True Calling

By Emily Esfahani Smith

W hy do so few people find fulfillment in their work?

A few years ago I posed this question to Amy Wrzesniewski, a Yale School of Management professor who studies these issues, and she offered an explanation that made a lot of sense. Students, she told me, "think their calling is under a rock, and if they turn over enough rocks, they will find it."

Surveys confirm that meaning is the top thing millennials say they want from a job. And yet her research shows that less than 50% of people see their work as a calling. So many of her students are left feeling anxious and frustrated and completely unsatisfied by the good jobs and careers they do secure.[1]

What they—and many of us, I think—fail to realize is that work can be meaningful even if you don't think of it as a calling. The four most common occupations in America are retail salesperson, cashier, food preparer or server, and office clerk—jobs that aren't typically associated with meaning.[2] But all have something in common with roles that are considered meaningful, such as clergy, teachers, and doctors: They exist to help others. And as Adam Grant, an organizational psychologist and professor at the University of Pennsylvania's Wharton School, has shown, people who see their work as a form of giving consistently rank their jobs as more meaningful.[3]

That means you can find meaning in nearly any role in nearly any organization. After all, most companies create products or services to fill a need in the world, and all employees contribute in their own way. The key is to become more conscious about the service you're providing—as a whole and personally.

How? One way is to connect with the end user or beneficiary. In one study, Grant and his colleagues found that fundraisers in a university call center who'd been introduced to a student whose education was being paid for by the money raised spent 142% more time on the phone with potential donors and raised 171% more cash than peers who hadn't met those scholarship recipients. Whether your customers are external or internal, an increased focus on them, and how you help them live their lives or do their jobs, can help you find more meaning in yours.

Another strategy is to constantly remind yourself of your organization's overarching goal. There's a great story about a janitor that John F. Kennedy ran into at NASA in 1962. When the president asked him what he was doing, the man said, "I'm helping put a man on the moon." Life is Good is an apparel company best known for colorful T-shirts with stick-figure designs, but its mission is to spread optimism and hope throughout the world, and that's something that even the company's warehouse employees understand. If you work for an accounting firm, you're helping people or companies with the unpleasant task of doing their taxes. If you're a fast-food cook, you're providing a family with a cheap and delicious meal. Each of these jobs serves a purpose in the world.

Even if you can't get excited about your company's mission or customers, you can still adopt a service mindset by thinking about how your work helps those you love. Consider a study of women working in a coupon-processing factory in Mexico. Researchers led by Jochen Menges, a professor of leadership and organizational behavior at WHU–Otto Beisheim School of Management, found that those who described the work as dull were generally less productive than those who said it was rewarding. But the effects went away for those in the former group who saw the work (however tedious) as a way to support their families. With that attitude, they were just as productive and energized as the coupon processors who didn't mind the task. Many people understand the purpose of their jobs in a similar manner. The work they do helps them pay their mortgage, go on vacation—or even support a hobby that gives meaning to their lives, like volunteer tutoring, gardening, or woodworking.

Not everyone finds their one true calling. But that doesn't mean we're doomed to work meaningless jobs. If we reframe our tasks as opportunities to help others, any occupation can feel more significant.

EMILY ESFAHANI SMITH is the author of *The Power of Meaning: Crafting a Life That Matters* (Crown, 2017) and an editor at Stanford University's Hoover Institution, where she manages the Ben Franklin Circles project, a collaboration with the 92nd Street Y and Citizen University to build meaning in local communities.

Notes

1. E. Esfahani Smith and J. L. Aaker, "Millennial Searchers," *New York Times*, November 30, 2013; and A. Wrzesniewski et al., "Jobs, Careers, and Callings: People's

Relations to Their Work," *Journal of Research in Personality* 31 (1997).

2. Bureau of Labor Statistics, U.S. Department of Labor, "Retail Salespersons and Cashiers Were Occupations with Highest Employment in May 2015," *The Economics Daily*, November 2017.

3. A. Grant, "In the Company of Givers and Takers," *Harvard Business Review*, April 2013.

Reprinted from hbr.org, originally published
August 3, 2012 (product #H03T83).

5

You're Never Done Finding Purpose at Work

By Dan Pontefract

D o you dread going into the office on Monday morning? Maybe a new boss has entered the equation, creating a rift between how you once felt and how you feel now. Perhaps your company has recently been acquired, and the culture has changed. Maybe you simply have outgrown your role and are bored to tears in your cubicle.

I have found that whether or not we enjoy our work often boils down to how our job fits with our sense of purpose. Where we work, the role we hold, our broader sense of purpose—all three are subject to change. Thus, if we want to stay in the "sweet spot" among these three, we must not fear career transitions or even change itself; indeed, we must seek them out.

Having a sense of purpose in our life is critical to well-being. In fact, in a longitudinal study, researchers found that people who demonstrate a sense of purpose in their lives have a 15% lower risk of early death.[1] Having a sense of purpose in our roles at work is equally important. And yet it's not enough to find that sense of purpose once—you have to continually find it as circumstances (and you) change.

"I am cautious and alert and mindful that the battle is not won yet" is how Céline Schillinger, an executive at vaccine maker Sanofi Pasteur, describes staying on this learning journey. "I will not fall into complacency. No matter what, I will continue to hone myself." In 2001 Schillinger landed a position in France at the company. To date, she has occupied positions in human resources, product development, and stakeholder engagement. She moved to Boston in 2015 to focus on quality innovation. "I would define myself as a person under construction," she told me. "I'm always trying to enrich my experience by adding bits and pieces wherever I go. I experiment in my roles and push for uncomfortableness to eventually gain new knowledge out of each situation."

Schillinger's story shows that you don't have to quit your company to stay engaged. However, sometimes a more radical change is needed. Consider the story of Mana Ionescu. She worked hard to climb the ladder at the U.S.-based company she worked for, and she was in line for the director role. But Ionescu was frustrated by the transactional nature of her work. Creativity was minimal. Inspiration was nominal. "There must be more to my working life than just sitting here making money and not actually making an impact," she thought. She decided to leave her organization and founded Lightspan Digital, a digital marketing company based in Chicago that specializes in social media, email, and content marketing. Ionescu recognized that she had to take charge of both her personal life and her working life—and ever since, she has been living *and* working with a sense of purpose. It's up to each of us to know when to make that leap.

Try this exercise. At the end of the workday, jot down approximately how much time you spent in each of the following three mindsets:

- *Job mindset.* When someone has a job mindset, they resort to a "paycheck mentality," performing their duties in return for compensation and not much else.

- *Career mindset.* This mindset occurs when an individual is focused on increasing or advancing their salary, title, power, team size, or sphere of control.

- *Purpose mindset.* Feeling passionate, innovative, and committed are hallmarks of this mindset, as is having an outward-looking focus on serving the broader organization or key stakeholders. Here, your professional purpose feels aligned with your personal purpose.

Keep a log for a couple of weeks, and see whether you fall into one of these mindsets more than the others. If the job and career mindsets total more than 50% of your time, that may be a warning sign that you need to restate or redefine your personal purpose.

No one lives in the purpose mindset all the time, but spending too much time in the career or job mindsets is destructive: You are certain to be dissatisfied with your job, and these mindsets can end up harming your reputation, chances of promotion, and long-term prospects. While everyone should be trying to develop and grow, focusing too much on your career or your paycheck can lead to bad behaviors such as bullying and selfishness or simply trying to exert too much control over others. Before that happens, seek a new role, and perhaps a new organization, that rebalances your equation.

If you have never created a personal declaration of purpose, now is the time. A declaration of purpose is a simple statement about how you will decide to live each and every day. Make it succinct, specific, jargon free, and expressive. Your statement ought to be personal, and it should integrate your strengths, interests, and core ambitions. Here's mine: "We're not here to see through each other; we're here to see each other through." (For more on a personal declaration of purpose, see chapter 6 of this book.)

Take into account all three types of purpose: personal, job, and organization. But don't shortchange your personal purpose, which is a common error, according to A. R. Elangovan, a professor of organizational behavior at the University of Victoria in Canada. As he told me, "Especially in contrast to organizational and role purpose, where multiple stakeholders shape the outcomes, my advice is to invest as much effort [as possible] into figuring out our personal purpose."

Life is short. You deserve to work in a role, and for an organization, where your personal purpose shines. But you cannot leave it up to the organization, your boss, or your team. It really does come down to you defining and enacting your purpose.

DAN PONTEFRACT is the author of *The Purpose Effect: Building Meaning in Yourself, Your Role, and Your Organization* (2016) and *Flat Army: Creating a Connected and Engaged Organization* (Wiley, 2013). He is chief envisioner at wireless and internet services company TELUS.

Note

1. P. L. Hill and N. A. Turiano, "Purpose in Life as a Predictor of Mortality Across Adulthood," *Psychological Science* 25, no. 7 (2014).

Reprinted from hbr.org, originally published May 20, 2016 (product #H02WJI).

6

From Purpose to Impact

By Nick Craig and Scott A. Snook

The two most important days in
your life are the day you are born
and the day you find out why.

—Mark Twain

O ver the past five years, there's been an explosion of interest in purpose-driven leadership. Academics argue persuasively that an executive's most important role is to be a steward of the organization's purpose. Business experts make the case that purpose is a key to exceptional performance, while psychologists describe it as the pathway to greater well-being.

Doctors have even found that people with purpose in their lives are less prone to disease. Purpose is increasingly being touted as the key to navigating the complex, volatile, ambiguous world we face today, where strategy is ever changing and few decisions are obviously right or wrong.

Despite this growing understanding, however, a big challenge remains. In our work training thousands of managers at organizations from GE to the Girl Scouts, and teaching an equal number of executives and students at Harvard Business School, we've found that fewer than 20% of leaders have a strong sense of their own individual purpose. Even fewer can distill their purpose into a concrete statement. They may be able to clearly articulate their organization's mission: Think of Google's "To organize the world's information and make it universally accessible and useful," or Charles Schwab's "A relentless ally for the individual investor." But when asked to describe their own purpose, they typically fall back on something generic and nebulous: "Help others excel." "Ensure success." "Empower my people." Just as problematic, hardly any of them have a clear plan for translating purpose into action. As a result, they limit their aspirations and often fail to achieve their most ambitious professional and personal goals.

Our purpose is to change that—to help executives find and define their leadership purpose and put it to use. Building on the seminal work of our colleague Bill George, our programs initially covered a wide range of topics related to authentic leadership, but in recent years purpose has emerged as the cornerstone of our teaching and coaching. Executives tell us it is the key to accelerating their growth and deepening their impact, in both their professional and personal lives. Indeed, we believe that the process of articulating your purpose and finding the courage to live it— what we call *purpose to impact*—is the single most important developmental task you can undertake as a leader.

Consider Dolf van den Brink, the president and CEO of Heineken USA. Working with us, he identified a decidedly unique purpose statement—"To be the wuxia master who saves the kingdom"—which reflects his love of Chinese kung fu movies, the inspiration he takes from the wise, skillful warriors in them, and the realization that he, too, revels in high-risk situations that compel him to take action. With that impetus, he was able to create a plan for reviving a challenged legacy business during extremely difficult economic conditions. We've also watched a retail operations chief call on his newly clarified purpose—"Compelled to make things better, whomever, wherever, however"—to make the "hard, cage-rattling changes" needed to beat back a global competitor. And we've seen a factory director in Egypt use his purpose—"Create families that excel"—to persuade employees that they should honor the 2012 protest movement not by joining the marches but by maintaining their loyalties to one another and keeping their shared operation running.

We've seen similar results outside the corporate world. Kathi Snook (Scott's wife) is a retired army colonel who'd been struggling to reengage in work after several years as a stay-at-home mom. But after nailing her purpose statement—"To be the gentle, behind-the-scenes, kick-in-the-ass reason for success," something she'd done throughout her military career and with her kids—she decided to run for a hotly contested school committee seat, and won.

And we've implemented this thinking across organizations. Unilever is a company that is committed to purpose-driven leadership, and Jonathan Donner, the head of global learning there, has been a key partner in refining our approach. Working with his company and several other organizations, we've helped more than 1,000 leaders through the purpose-to-impact process and have begun to track and review their progress over the past two to three years. Many have seen dramatic results, ranging from two-step promotions to sustained improvement in business results. Most important, the vast majority tell us they've developed a new ability to thrive in even the most challenging times.

In this article, we share our step-by-step framework to start you down the same path. We'll explain how to identify your purpose and then develop an impact plan to achieve concrete results.

What is purpose?

Most of us go to our graves with our music still inside us, unplayed.

—Oliver Wendell Holmes

Your leadership purpose is who you are and what makes you distinctive. Whether you're an entrepreneur at a startup or the CEO of a *Fortune* 500 company, a call center rep or a software developer, your purpose is your brand, what you're driven to achieve, the magic that makes you tick. It's not *what* you do, it's *how* you do your job and *why*—the strengths and passions you bring to the table no matter where you're seated. Although you may express your purpose in different ways in different contexts, it's what everyone close to you recognizes as uniquely you and would miss most if you were gone.

When Kathi Snook shared her purpose statement with her family and friends, the response was instantaneous and overwhelming: "Yes! That's you—all business, all the time!" In every role and every context—as captain of the army gymnastics team, as a math teacher at West Point, informally with her family and friends—she had always led from behind, a gentle but forceful catalyst for others' success. Through this new lens, she was able to see herself—and her future—more clearly. When Dolf van den Brink revealed his newly articulated purpose to his wife, she easily recognized the "wuxia master" who had led his employees through the turmoil of serious fighting and unrest in the Congo and was now ready to attack the challenges at Heineken USA head-on.

At its core, your leadership purpose springs from your identity, the essence of who you are. Purpose is not a list of the education, experience, and skills you've gathered in your life. We'll use ourselves as examples. The fact that Scott is a retired army colonel with an MBA and a PhD is not his purpose. His purpose is "to help others live more 'meaning-full' lives." Purpose is also not a professional title, limited to your current job or organization. Nick's purpose is not "To lead the Authentic Leadership Institute." That's his job. His purpose is "To wake you up and have you find that you are home." He has been doing just that since he was a teenager, and if you sit next to him on the shuttle from Boston to New York, he'll wake you up (figuratively), too. He simply can't help himself.

Purpose is definitely not some jargon-filled catch-all ("Empower my team to achieve exceptional business results while delighting our customers"). It should be specific and personal, resonating with you and you alone. It doesn't have to be aspirational or cause based ("Save the whales" or "Feed the hungry"). And it's not what you think it should be—it's who you can't help being. In fact, it might not necessarily be all that flattering ("Be the thorn in people's side that keeps them moving!").

How do you find it?

To be nobody but yourself in a world
which is doing its best, night and day,
to make you everybody else, means to
fight the hardest battle which any human
being can fight; and never stop fighting.

—E.E. Cummings

Finding your leadership purpose is not easy. If it were, we'd all know exactly why we're here and be living that purpose every minute of every day. As E.E. Cummings suggests, we are constantly bombarded by powerful messages (from parents, bosses, management gurus, advertisers, celebrities) about what we should be (smarter, stronger, richer) and about how to lead (empower others, lead from behind, be authentic, distribute power). To figure out who you are in such a world, let alone "be nobody but yourself," is indeed hard work. However, our experience shows that when you have a clear sense of who you are, everything else follows naturally.

Some people will come to the purpose-to-impact journey with a natural bent toward introspection and reflection. Others will find the experience uncomfortable and anxiety provoking. A few will just roll their eyes. We've worked with leaders of all stripes and can attest that even the most skeptical discover personal and professional value in the experience. At one multinational corporation, we worked with a senior lawyer who characterized himself as "the least likely person to ever find this stuff useful." Yet he became such a supporter that he required all his people to do the program. "I have never read a self-help book, and I don't plan to," he told his staff. "But if you want to become an exceptional leader, you have to know your leadership purpose." The key to engaging both the dreamers and the skeptics is to build a process that has room to express individuality but also offers step-by-step practical guidance.

The first task is to mine your life story for common threads and major themes. The point is to identify your core, lifelong strengths, values, and passions—those pursuits that energize you and bring you joy. We use a variety of prompts but have found three to be most effective:

- What did you especially love doing when you were a child, before the world told you what you should or shouldn't like or do? Describe a moment and how it made you feel.

- Tell us about two of your most challenging life experiences. How have they shaped you?

- What do you enjoy doing in your life now that helps you sing your song?

We strongly recommend grappling with these questions in a small group of a few peers, because we've found that it's almost impossible for people to identify their leadership purpose by themselves. You can't get a clear picture of yourself without trusted colleagues or friends to act as mirrors.

After this reflective work, take a shot at crafting a clear, concise, and declarative statement of purpose: "My leadership purpose is _____." The words in your purpose statement must be yours. They must capture your essence. And they must call you to action.

To give you an idea of how the process works, consider the experiences of a few executives. When we asked one manager about her childhood passions, she told us about growing up in rural Scotland and delighting in "discovery" missions. One day, she and a friend set out determined to find frogs and spent the whole day going from pond to pond, turning over every stone. Just before dark, she discovered a single frog and was triumphant. The purpose statement she later crafted—"Always find the frogs!"—is perfect for her current role as the senior VP of R&D for her company.

Another executive used two "crucible" life experiences to craft her purpose. The first was personal: Years before, as a divorced young mother of two, she found herself homeless and begging on the street, but she used her wits to get back on her feet. The second was professional: During the economic crisis of 2008, she had to oversee her company's retrenchment from Asia and was tasked with closing the flagship operation in the region. Despite the near hopeless job environment, she was able to help every one of her employees find another job before letting them go. After discussing these stories with her group, she shifted her purpose statement from "Continually and consistently develop and facilitate the growth and development of myself and others leading to great performance" to "With tenacity, create brilliance."

Dolf came to his "wuxia master" statement after exploring not only his film preferences but also his extraordinary crucible experience in the Congo, when militants were threatening the brewery he managed and he had to order it barricaded to protect his employees and prevent looting. The Egyptian factory director focused on family as his purpose because his stories revealed that familial love and support had been the key to facing every challenge in his life, while the retail operations chief used "Compelled to improve" after realizing that his greatest achievements had always come when he pushed himself and others out of their comfort zones.

As you review your stories, you will see a unifying thread, just as these executives did. Pull it, and you'll uncover your purpose. (The exhibit "Purpose Statements" offers a sampling of purpose statements.)

Purpose statements

FROM BAD . . .	TO GOOD . . .
Lead new markets department to achieve exceptional business results	Eliminate chaos
Be a driver in the infrastructure business that allows each person to achieve their needed outcomes while also mastering the new drivers of our business as I balance my family and work demands	Bring water and power to the two billion people who do not have it
Continually and consistently develop and facilitate the growth and development of myself and others, leading to great performance	With tenacity, create brilliance

How do you put your purpose into action?

*This is the true joy in life, the being
used for a purpose recognized by
yourself as a mighty one.*

—George Bernard Shaw

Clarifying your purpose as a leader is critical, but writing the statement is not enough. You must also envision the impact you'll have on your world as a result of living your purpose. Your actions—not your words—are what really matter. Of course, it's virtually impossible for any of us to fully live into our purpose 100% of the time. But with work and careful planning, we can do it more often, more consciously, wholeheartedly, and effectively.

Purpose-to-impact plans differ from traditional development plans in several important ways: They start with a statement of leadership purpose rather than of a business or career goal. They take a holistic view of professional and personal life rather than ignore the fact that you have a family or outside interests and commitments. They incorporate meaningful, purpose-infused language to create a document that speaks to you, not just to any person in your job or role. They force you to envision long-term opportunities for living your purpose (three to five years out) and then help you to work backward from there (two years out, one year, six months, three months, 30 days) to set specific goals for achieving them.

When executives approach development in this purpose-driven way, their aspirations—for instance, Kathi's decision to get involved in the school board, or the Egyptian factory director's ambition to run manufacturing and logistics across the Middle East— are stoked. Leaders also become more energized in their current roles. Dolf's impact plan inspired him to tackle his role at Heineken USA with four mottos

Purpose-to-impact planning versus traditional development planning

PURPOSE-TO-IMPACT PLANNING	TRADITIONAL DEVELOPMENT PLANNING
Uses meaningful, purpose-infused language	Uses standard business language
Is focused on strengths to realize career aspirations	Is focused on weaknesses to address performance
Elicits a statement of leadership purpose that explains how you will lead	States a business- or career-driven goal
Sets incremental goals related to living your leadership purpose	Measures success using metrics tied to the firm's mission and goals
Focuses on the future, working backward	Focuses on the present, working forward
Is unique to you; addresses who you are as a leader	Is generic; addresses the job or role
Takes a holistic view of work and family	Ignores goals and responsibilities outside the office

for his team: "Be brave," "Decide and do," "Hunt as a pack," and "Take it personally." When Unilever executive Jostein Solheim created a development plan around his purpose—"To be part of a global movement that makes changing the world seem fun and achievable"—he realized he wanted to stay on as CEO of the Ben & Jerry's business rather than moving up the corporate ladder.

Let's now look at a hypothetical purpose-to-impact plan (representing a composite of several people with whom we've worked) for an in-depth view of the process. "Richard" arrived at his purpose only after being prodded into talking about his lifelong passion for sailing; suddenly, he'd found a set of experiences and language that could redefine how he saw his job in procurement.

Richard's development plan leads with the *purpose statement* he crafted: "To harness all the elements to win the race." This is followed by *an explanation* of why that's his purpose: Research shows that understanding what motivates us dramatically increases our ability to achieve big goals.

Next, Richard addresses his *three- to five-year goals* using the language of his purpose statement. We find that this is a good time frame to target first; several years is long enough that even the most disillusioned managers could imagine they'd actually be living into their purpose by then. But it's not so distant that it creates complacency. A goal might be to land a top job—in Richard's case, a global procurement role—but the focus should be on how you will do it, what kind of leader you'll be.

Then he considers *two-year goals*. This is a time frame in which the grand future and current reality begin to merge. What new responsibilities will you take on? What do you have to do to set yourself up for the longer term? Remember to address your personal life, too, because you should be more fully living into your purpose everywhere. Richard's goals explicitly reference his family, or "shore team."

A PURPOSE-TO-IMPACT PLAN

This sample plan shows how "Richard" uses his unique leadership purpose to envision big-picture aspirations and then work backward to set more-specific goals.

1. Create purpose statement

To harness all the elements to win the race

2. Write explanation

I love to sail. In my teens and twenties, I raced high-performance three-man skiffs and almost made it to the Olympics. Now sailing is my hobby and passion—a challenge that requires discipline, balance, and coordination. You never know what the wind will do next, and in the end, you win the race only by relying on your team's combined capabilities, intuition, and flow. It's all about how you read the elements.

(Continued)

A PURPOSE-TO-IMPACT PLAN

3. Set three- to five-year goals

Be known for training the best crews and winning the big races: Take on a global procurement role, and use the opportunity to push my organization ahead of competitors

How will I do it?

- Make everyone feel they're part of the same team
- Navigate unpredictable conditions by seeing wind shears before everyone else
- Keep calm when we lose individual races; learn and prepare for the next ones

Celebrate my shore team: Make sure the family has one thing we do that binds us

---

4. Set two-year goals

Win the gold: Implement a new procurement model, redefining our relationship with suppliers and generating 10% cost savings for the company

Tackle next-level racing challenge: Move into a European role with broader responsibilities

How will I do it?

- Anticipate and then face the tough challenges
- Insist on innovative yet rigorous and pragmatic solutions
- Assemble and train the winning crew

Develop my shore team: Teach the boys to sail

(Continued)

A PURPOSE-TO-IMPACT PLAN

5. Set one-year goals

Target the gold: Begin to develop new procurement process

Win the short race: Deliver Sympix project ahead of expectations

Build a seaworthy boat: Keep TFLS process within cost and cash forecast

How will I do it?

- Accelerate team reconfiguration
- Get buy-in from management for new procurement approach

Invest in my shore team: Take a two-week vacation, no email

6. Map out critical next steps

Assemble the crew: Finalize key hires

Chart the course: Lay the groundwork for Sympix and TFLS projects

How will I do it?

Six months:

- Finalize succession plans
- Set out Sympix timeline

Three months:

- Land a world-class replacement for Jim
- Schedule "action windows" to focus with no email

30 days:

- Bring Alex in Shanghai on board
- Agree on TFLS metrics
- Conduct one-day Sympix off-site

(Continued)

A PURPOSE-TO-IMPACT PLAN

Reconnect with my shore team: Be more present with Jill and the boys

7. Examine key relationships

Sarah, HR manager

Jill, manager of my shore team

The fifth step—setting *one-year goals*—is often the most challenging. Many people ask, "What if most of what I am doing today isn't aligned in any way with my leadership purpose? How do I get from here to there?" We've found two ways to address this problem. First, think about whether you can rewrite the narrative on parts of your work, or change the way you do some tasks, so that they become an expression of your purpose. For example, the phrase "seaworthy boat" helps Richard see the meaning in managing a basic procurement process. Second, consider whether you can add an activity that is 100% aligned with your purpose. We've found that most people can manage to devote 5% to 10% of their time to something that energizes them and helps others see their strengths. Take Richard's decision to contribute to the global strategic procurement effort: It's not part of his "day job," but it gets him involved in a more purpose-driven project.

Now we get to the nitty-gritty. What are the *critical next steps* that you must take in the coming six months, three months, and 30 days to accomplish the one-year goals you've set out? The importance of small wins is well documented in almost every management discipline from change initiatives to innovation. In detailing your next steps, don't write down all the requirements of your job. List the activities or results that are most critical given your newly clarified leadership purpose and ambitions. You'll probably notice that a number of your tasks seem much less urgent than they did before, while others you had pushed to the side take priority.

Finally, we look at the *key relationships* needed to turn your plan into reality. Identify two or three people who can help you live more fully into your leadership purpose. For Richard, it is Sarah, the HR manager who will help him assemble his crew, and his wife, Jill, the manager of his "shore team."

Executives tell us that their individual purpose-to-impact plans help them stay true to their short- and long-term goals, inspiring courage, commitment, and focus. When they're frustrated or flagging, they pull out the plans to remind themselves what they want to accomplish and how they'll succeed. After creating his plan, the retail operations chief facing global competition said he's no longer "shying away from things that are too hard." Dolf van den Brink said: "I'm much clearer on where I really can contribute and where not. I have full clarity on the kind of roles

I aspire to and can make explicit choices along the way." What creates the greatest leaders and companies? Each of them operates from a slightly different set of assumptions about the world, their industry, what can or can't be done. That individual perspective allows them to create great value and have significant impact. They all operate with a unique leadership purpose. To be a truly effective leader, you must do the same. Clarify your purpose, and put it to work.

NICK CRAIG is the president of the Authentic Leadership Institute. SCOTT A. SNOOK is currently an associate professor of organizational behavior at Harvard Business School. He served in the U.S. Army Corps of Engineers for over 22 years.

Reprinted from *Harvard Business Review*,
May 2014 (product #R1405H).

7

Five Questions to Help Your Employees Find Their Inner Purpose

By Kristi Hedges

How can leaders help employees find meaning at work?

Organizations spend considerable resources on corporate values and mission statements, but even the most inspiring of these—from Volvo's commitment to safety to Facebook's desire to connect people—tend to fade into the background during the daily bustle of the workday.

What workers really need to feel engaged in and satisfied by their jobs is an inner sense of purpose. As Deloitte found in a 2016 study, people feel loyal to companies that support their own career and life ambitions—in other words, what's meaningful to them.[1]

And, although that research focused on millennials, in the decade I've spent coaching seasoned executives, I've found that it's a common attitude across generations. No matter one's level, industry, or career, we all need to find a personal sense of meaning in what we do.

Leaders can foster this inner sense of purpose—what matters right now, in each individual's life and career—with simple conversation. One technique is action identification theory, which posits that there are many levels of description for any action.[2] For example, right now I'm writing this article. At a low level, I'm typing words on a keyboard. At a high level, I'm creating better leaders. When leaders walk employees up this ladder, they can help them find meaning in even the most mundane tasks.

Regular check-ins that use five areas of inquiry are another way to help employees explore and call out their inner purpose. Leaders can ask:

What are you good at doing? Which work activities require less effort for you? What do you take on because you believe you're the best person to do it? What have you gotten noticed for throughout your career? The idea here is to help people identify their strengths and open possibilities from there.

What do you enjoy? In a typical workweek, what do you look forward to doing? What do you see on your calendar that energizes you? If you could design your job with no restrictions, how would you spend your time? These questions help people find or rediscover what they love about work.

What feels most useful? Which work outcomes make you most proud? Which of your tasks are most critical to the team or organization? What are the highest priorities for your life and how does your work fit in? This line of inquiry highlights the inherent value of certain work.

What creates a sense of forward momentum? What are you learning that you'll use in the future? What do you envision for yourself next? How is your work today getting you closer to what you want for yourself? The goal here is to show how today's work helps the individual advance toward future goals.

How do you relate to others? Which working partnerships are best for you? What would an office of your favorite people look like? How does your work enhance your family and social connections? These questions encourage people to think about and foster relationships that make work more meaningful.

It's not easy to guide others toward purpose, but these strategies can help.

KRISTI HEDGES is a senior leadership coach who specializes in executive communications and the author of *The Inspiration Code: How the Best Leaders Energize People Every Day* (AMACOM, 2017) and *The Power of Presence: Unlock Your Potential to Influence and Engage Others* (AMACOM, 2011). She is the president of the Hedges Company and a faculty member at Georgetown University's Institute for Transformational Leadership.

Notes

1. Deloitte, "2016 Deloitte Millennial Survey: Winning Over the Next Generation of Leaders," 2016, https://www2 .deloitte.com/content/dam/Deloitte/global/Documents/ About-Deloitte/gx-millenial-survey-2016-exec-summary .pdf.
2. R. R. Vallacher and D. M. Wegner, *A Theory of Action Identification* (Hillsdale, NJ: Lawrence Erlbaum Associates, 1985).

Reprinted from hbr.org, originally published
August 17, 2017 (product #H03U96).

8

How to Make Work More Meaningful for Your Team

By Lewis Garrad and Tomas Chamorro-Premuzic

There is a well-known story about a janitor at NASA who, when asked by John F. Kennedy what his job was, responded, "I'm helping to put a man on the moon." This anecdote is often used to show how even the most mundane job can be seen as meaningful with the right mindset and under good leadership.

Today, more and more employees demand much more than a good salary from their jobs. Money may lure people into particular positions, but purpose, meaning, and the prospect of interesting and valuable work determines both their tenure and how hard they will work while they are on the job. Finding meaning at work has become so important that there are even public rankings for the most meaningful jobs.[1] Although there are many factors that determining how appealing a position tends to be, those that contribute to improving other people's lives (such as those in health care and social work) are ranked at the top. Interestingly, meta-analytic studies indicate that there is only a marginal association between pay and job satisfaction.[2] By that reasoning, a lawyer who earns $150,000 a year is no more engaged than a freelance designer who earns $35,000 a year.

Research consistently shows that people who experience meaningful work report better health, more well-being, and a clearer sense of teamwork and engagement. They bounce back faster from setbacks and are more likely to view mistakes as learning opportunities rather than failures. In other words, people at work who experience their job as meaningful are more likely to thrive and grow. This is why businesses with a stronger and clearer sense of purpose tend to perform better financially. Unsurprisingly, the most successful companies in the world are also the best places in the world to work.[3]

Over the past few decades, a great deal of research has shown that leaders play a significant role in helping employees understand why their roles matter. Furthermore, the leadership characteristics that enable these cultures of meaning and purpose to engage employees are a reflection of a leader's personality—which has been proven to have a strong impact on team and organizational performance.[4]

In particular, research suggests that there are four key personality characteristics that determine leaders' ability to make other people's jobs more meaningful, namely:

> *They are curious and inquisitive.* Studies show that people tend to experience work as meaningful when they feel like they are contributing to creating something new—especially when

they feel able to explore, connect and have an impact.[5] Curious leaders help people find meaning at work by exploring, asking questions, and engaging people in ideas about the future. In a way, curious leaders help employees find something meaningful by providing a wider range of possibilities for how work gets done, as opposed to being very prescriptive and micromanaging people. Curious leaders also detest monotony and are more likely to get bored, so they will always be looking for people to come up with new ideas to make their own experience of work more interesting.

They are challenging and relentless. One of the greatest problems organizations must solve is the inertia and stagnation that follow, or even anticipate, success. Research shows that optimistic people who expect to do well don't try as hard as people who expect to struggle or

fail.[6] Leaders who remain ambitious in the face
of both failure and success, and who push their
people to remain dissatisfied with their accomplishments, instill a deeper sense of purpose
in their teams and organizations. As a result
employees feel a sense of progress, reinvention,
and growth, which in turn results in a more
meaningful and positive work experience.

They hire for values and culture fit. Research
shows that people only find something valuable
if it aligns with their core needs and motives.
This is why the fit between an individual's
personal values and the culture of the organization they work in is such an important driver
of their performance. In fact, you are better off
not hiring the "best" people but instead looking
for those who are a good fit for your organization. Values function like an inner compass or
lens through which we assign meaning to the

world. Leaders who pay attention to what *each* individual values are more likely to hire people who will find it easier to connect with their colleagues and the wider organization, all of which help to drive a sense of meaning.[7]

They are able to trust people. Most individuals hate being micromanaged. Overpowering and controlling bosses are a serious source of disempowerment for employees. They drain the value from the work they do and make employees feel worthless. In stark contrast, leaders who know how to trust people are more likely to give them room to experiment and grow. In particular, they help their employees mold their roles—something researchers call "job crafting." Employees who customize their job tend to feel a much greater sense of importance and value because they feel that their manager actually trusts them.

Note that all of the above four qualities ought to exist in concert. A boss who is relentless but not trusting might seek to "keep people on their toes" by being erratic or unpredictable—a sure way to hurt performance and morale. A boss who is challenging but not curious may come across as a bully, while a boss who's trusting but not challenging will seem like a pushover. In short, there is a clear difference between making work meaningful and making it fun or easy, just like there is a big difference between an engaged and a happy employee. Whereas engagement results in enthusiasm, drive, and motivation—all of which increase performance and are therefore valuable to the organization—happiness can lead to complacency. To be a good leader, focus on helping employees find meaning in their achievements, rather than just enjoy their time at the office.

LEWIS GARRAD is a senior consultant and advisor at Mercer | Sirota. TOMAS CHAMORRO-PREMUZIC is the CEO of Hogan

Assessments, a professor of business psychology at University College London and at Columbia University, and an associate at Harvard's Entrepreneurial Finance Lab. His latest book is *The Talent Delusion: Why Data, Not Intuition, Is the Key to Unlocking Human Potential* (2017).

Notes

1. "The Most and Least Meaningful Jobs," Payscale, http://www.payscale.com/data-packages/most-and-least-meaningful-jobs/least-meaningful-jobs.
2. T. A. Judge et al., "The Relationship Between Pay and Job Satisfaction: A Meta-Analysis of the Literature," *Journal of Vocational Behavior* 77, no. 2 (2010).
3. M. F. Steger, "Measuring Meaningful Work: The Work and Meaning Inventory (WAMI)," *Journal of Career Assessment* 20, no. 3 (2012); G. Spreitzer et al., "A Socially Embedded Model of Thriving at Work," *Organization Science* 16, no. 5 (2005); and C. M. Gartenberg et al., "Corporate Purpose and Financial Performance," Columbia Business School Research Paper no. 16–69, June 30, 2016.
4. M. Carton, "'I'm Not Mopping the Floors, I'm Putting a Man on the Moon': How NASA Leaders Enhanced the Meaningfulness of Work by Changing the Meaning of Work," *Administrative Science Quarterly*, 2017; and C. A. O'Reilly et al., "The Promise and Problems of

Organizational Culture," *Group and Organization Management* 39, no. 6 (2014).

5. A. Wrzesniewski and J. E. Dutton, "Crafting a Job: Revisioning Employees as Active Crafters of Their Work," *Academy of Management Review* 26, no. 2 (2001).

6. H. B. Kappes and G. Oettingen, "Positive Fantasies About Idealized Futures Sap Energy," *Journal of Experimental Social Psychology* 47, no. 4 (2011).

7. T. Schnell et al., "Predicting Meaning in Work: Theory, Data, Implications," *Journal of Positive Psychology* 8, no. 6 (2013); A. L. Kristof-Brown et al., "Consequences of Individuals' Fit at Work: A Meta-Analysis of Person-Job, Person-Organization, Person-Group, and Person-Supervisor Fit," *Personnel Psychology* 58 (2005); and A. Bhaduri, *Don't Hire the Best: An Essential Guide to Building the Right Team* (Hogan Press, 2013).

Reprinted from hbr.org, originally published
August 9, 2017 (product #H03U4D).

9

The Power of Small Wins

By Teresa M. Amabile and Steven J. Kramer

What is the best way to drive innovative work inside organizations? Important clues hide in the stories of world-renowned creators. It turns out that ordinary scientists, marketers, programmers, and other unsung knowledge workers, whose jobs require creative productivity every day, have more in common with famous innovators than most managers realize. The workday events that ignite their emotions, fuel their motivation, and trigger their perceptions are fundamentally the same.

The Double Helix, James Watson's 1968 memoir about discovering the structure of DNA, describes the roller coaster of emotions he and Francis Crick experienced through the progress and setbacks of the work that eventually earned them the Nobel Prize. After the excitement of their first attempt to build a DNA model, Watson and Crick noticed some serious flaws. According to Watson, "Our first minutes with the models . . . were not joyous." Later that evening, "a shape began to emerge which brought back our spirits." But when they showed their "breakthrough" to colleagues, they found that their model would not work. Dark days of doubt and ebbing motivation followed. When the duo finally had their bona fide breakthrough, and their colleagues found no fault with it, Watson wrote, "My morale skyrocketed, for I suspected that we now had the answer to the riddle." Watson and Crick were so driven by this success that they practically lived in the lab, trying to complete the work.

Throughout these episodes, Watson and Crick's progress—or lack thereof—ruled their reactions. In our recent research on creative work inside businesses, we stumbled upon a remarkably similar phenomenon. Through exhaustive analysis of diaries kept by knowledge workers, we discovered the "progress principle": Of all the things that can boost emotions, motivation, and perceptions during a workday, the single most important is making progress in meaningful work. And the more frequently people experience that sense of progress, the more likely they are to be creatively productive in the long run. Whether they are trying to solve a major scientific mystery or simply produce a high-quality product or service, everyday progress—even a small win—can make all the difference in how they feel and perform.

The power of progress is fundamental to human nature, but few managers understand it or know how to leverage progress to boost motivation. In fact, work motivation has been a subject of long-standing debate. In a survey asking about the keys to motivating workers, we found that some managers ranked recognition for good work as most important, while others put more stock in tangible incentives. Some focused on the value of interpersonal support, while still others thought clear goals were the answer. Interestingly, very few of our surveyed managers ranked progress first. (See the sidebar "A Surprise for Managers.")

If you are a manager, the progress principle holds clear implications for where to focus your efforts. It suggests that you have more influence than you may realize over employees' well-being, motivation, and creative output. Knowing what serves to catalyze and nourish progress—and what does the opposite— turns out to be the key to effectively managing people and their work.

In this article, we share what we have learned about the power of progress and how managers can leverage it. We spell out how a focus on progress translates into concrete managerial actions and pro- vide a checklist to help make such behaviors habitual. But to clarify why those actions are so potent, we first

A SURPRISE FOR MANAGERS

In a 1968 issue of HBR, Frederick Herzberg published a now-classic article titled "One More Time: How Do You Motivate Employees?" Our findings are consistent with his message: People are most satisfied with their jobs (and therefore most motivated) when those jobs give them the opportunity to experience achievement. The diary research we describe in this article—in which we microscopically examined the events of thousands of workdays, in real time—uncovered the mechanism underlying the sense of achievement: making consistent, meaningful progress.

But managers seem not to have taken Herzberg's lesson to heart. To assess contemporary awareness of the importance of daily work progress, we recently administered a survey to 669 managers of varying levels from dozens of companies around the world. We asked about the managerial tools that can affect employees'

(Continued)

A SURPRISE FOR MANAGERS

motivation and emotions. The respondents ranked five tools—support for making progress in the work, recognition for good work, incentives, interpersonal support, and clear goals—in order of importance.

Of the managers who took our survey, 95% would probably be surprised to learn that supporting progress is the primary way to elevate motivation—because that's the percentage who failed to rank progress number one. In fact, only 35 managers ranked progress as the number one motivator—a mere 5%. The vast majority of respondents ranked support for making progress dead last as a motivator and third as an influence on emotion. They ranked "recognition for good work (either public or private)" as the most important factor in motivating workers and making them happy. In our diary study, recognition certainly did boost inner work life. But it wasn't nearly as prominent as progress. Besides, without work achievements, there is little to recognize.

describe our research and what the knowledge workers' diaries revealed about their "inner work lives."

Inner work life and performance

For nearly 15 years, we have been studying the psychological experiences and the performance of people doing complex work inside organizations. Early on, we realized that a central driver of creative, productive performance was the quality of a person's inner work life: the mix of emotions, motivations, and perceptions over the course of a workday. How happy workers feel; how motivated they are by an intrinsic interest in the work; how positively they view their organization, their management, their team, their work, and themselves—all these combine either to push them to higher levels of achievement or to drag them down.

To understand such interior dynamics better, we asked members of project teams to respond individually to an end-of-day email survey during the course of the project—just over four months, on average. (For more on this research, see our article "Inner Work Life: Understanding the Subtext of Business Performance," HBR, May 2007.) The projects—inventing kitchen gadgets, managing product lines of cleaning tools, and solving complex IT problems for a hotel empire, for example—all involved creativity. The daily survey inquired about participants' emotions and moods, motivation levels, and perceptions of the work environment that day, as well as what work they did and what events stood out in their minds.

Twenty-six project teams from seven companies participated, comprising 238 individuals. This yielded nearly 12,000 diary entries. Naturally, every individual in our population experienced ups and downs. Our goal was to discover the states of inner work life and the workday events that correlated with the highest levels of creative output.

In a dramatic rebuttal to the commonplace claim that high pressure and fear spur achievement, we found that, at least in the realm of knowledge work, people are more creative and productive when their inner work lives are positive—when they feel happy, are intrinsically motivated by the work itself, and have positive perceptions of their colleagues and the organization. Moreover, in those positive states, people are more committed to the work and more collegial toward those around them. Inner work life, we saw, can fluctuate from one day to the next—sometimes wildly—and performance along with it. A person's inner work life on a given day fuels his or her performance for the day and can even affect performance the *next* day.

Once this "inner work-life effect" became clear, our inquiry turned to whether and how managerial action could set it in motion. What events could evoke positive or negative emotions, motivations, and perceptions? The answers were tucked within our research participants' diary entries. There are predictable triggers that inflate or deflate inner work life, and, even accounting for variation among individuals, they are pretty much the same for everyone.

The power of progress

Our hunt for inner work-life triggers led us to the progress principle. When we compared our research participants' best and worst days (based on their overall mood, specific emotions, and motivation levels), we found that the most common event triggering a "best day" was any progress in the work by the individual or the team. The most common event triggering a "worst day" was a setback.

Consider, for example, how progress relates to one component of inner work life: overall mood ratings. Steps forward occurred on 76% of people's best-mood days. By contrast, setbacks occurred on only 13% of those days. (See the figure "What happens on good days and bad days?")

Two other types of inner work-life triggers also occur frequently on best days: *catalysts*, actions that directly support work, including help from a person or group, and *nourishers*, events such as shows of respect and words of encouragement. Each has an opposite: *inhibitors*, actions that fail to support or actively hinder work, and *toxins*, discouraging or undermining events. Whereas catalysts and inhibitors are directed at the project, nourishers and toxins are directed at the person. Like setbacks, inhibitors and toxins are rare on days of great inner work life.

Events on worst-mood days are nearly the mirror image of those on best-mood days. Here, setbacks predominated, occurring on 67% of those days; progress occurred on only 25% of them. Inhibitors and toxins also marked many worst-mood days, and catalysts and nourishers were rare.

This is the progress principle made visible: If a person is motivated and happy at the end of a workday, it's a good bet that he or she made some progress.

If the person drags out of the office disengaged and joyless, a setback is most likely to blame.

When we analyzed all 12,000 daily surveys filled out by our participants, we discovered that progress and setbacks influence all three aspects of inner work life. On days when they made progress, our participants reported more positive *emotions*. They not only were in a more upbeat mood in general but also expressed more joy, warmth, and pride. When they suffered setbacks, they experienced more frustration, fear, and sadness.

Motivations were also affected: On progress days, people were more intrinsically motivated—by interest in and enjoyment of the work itself. On setback days, they were not only less intrinsically motivated but also less extrinsically motivated by recognition. Apparently, setbacks can lead a person to feel generally apathetic and disinclined to do the work at all.

Perceptions differed in many ways, too. On progress days, people perceived significantly more positive

What happens on good days and bad days?

Progress—even a small step forward—occurs on many of the days people report being in a good mood. Events on bad days—setbacks and other hindrances—are nearly the mirror image of those on good days.

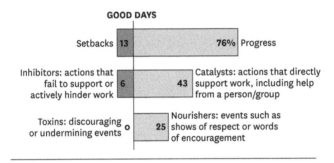

GOOD DAYS

Setbacks **13** — **76%** Progress

Inhibitors: actions that fail to support or actively hinder work **6** — **43** Catalysts: actions that directly support work, including help from a person/group

Toxins: discouraging or undermining events **0** — **25** Nourishers: events such as shows of respect or words of encouragement

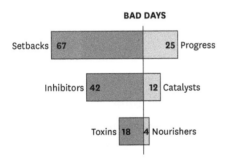

BAD DAYS

Setbacks **67** — **25** Progress

Inhibitors **42** — **12** Catalysts

Toxins **18** — **4** Nourishers

challenge in their work. They saw their teams as more mutually supportive and reported more positive interactions between the teams and their supervisors. On a number of dimensions, perceptions suffered when people encountered setbacks. They found less positive challenge in the work, felt that they had less freedom in carrying it out, and reported that they had insufficient resources. On setback days, participants perceived both their teams and their supervisors as less supportive.

To be sure, our analyses establish correlations but do not prove causality. Were these changes in inner work life the result of progress and setbacks, or was the effect the other way around? The numbers alone cannot answer that. However, we do know, from reading thousands of diary entries, that more-positive perceptions, a sense of accomplishment, satisfaction, happiness, and even elation often followed progress. Here's a typical post-progress entry, from a programmer: "I smashed that bug that's been frustrating me for almost a calendar week. That may not be an event to you, but I live a very drab life, so I'm all hyped."

Likewise, we saw that deteriorating perceptions, frustration, sadness, and even disgust often followed setbacks. As another participant, a product marketer, wrote, "We spent a lot of time updating the cost reduction project list, and after tallying all the numbers, we are still coming up short of our goal. It is discouraging to not be able to hit it after all the time spent and hard work."

Almost certainly, the causality goes both ways, and managers can use this feedback loop between progress and inner work life to support both.

Minor milestones

When we think about progress, we often imagine how good it feels to achieve a long-term goal or experience a major breakthrough. These big wins are great—but they are relatively rare. The good news is that even small wins can boost inner work life tremendously. Many of the progress events our research participants reported represented only minor steps forward. Yet they often evoked outsize positive reactions. Consider this diary entry from a programmer in a high-tech company, which was accompanied by very positive self-ratings of her emotions, motivations, and perceptions that day: "I figured out why something was not working correctly. I felt relieved and happy because this was a minor milestone for me."

Even ordinary, incremental progress can increase people's engagement in the work and their happiness during the workday. Across all the types of events our participants reported, a notable proportion (28%) that had a minor impact on the project had a major impact on people's feelings about it. Because inner work life has such a potent effect on creativity and productivity, and because small but consistent steps forward shared by many people can accumulate into excellent execution, progress events that often go unnoticed are critical to the overall performance of organizations.

Unfortunately, there is a flip side. Small losses or setbacks can have an extremely negative effect on inner work life. In fact, our study and research by others show that negative events can have a more powerful impact than positive ones. Consequently, it is especially important for managers to minimize daily hassles. (See again the figure "What happens on good days and bad days?")

Progress in meaningful work

We've shown how gratifying it is for workers when they are able to chip away at a goal, but recall what we said earlier: The key to motivating performance is supporting progress in *meaningful* work. Making headway boosts your inner work life, but only if the work matters to you.

Think of the most boring job you've ever had. Many people nominate their first job as a teenager—washing pots and pans in a restaurant kitchen, for example, or checking coats at a museum. In jobs like those, the power of progress seems elusive. No matter how hard you work, there are always more pots to wash and coats to check; only punching the time clock at the end of the day or getting the paycheck at the end of the week yields a sense of accomplishment.

In jobs with much more challenge and room for creativity, like the ones our research participants had, simply "making progress"—getting tasks done—doesn't guarantee a good inner work life, either. You may have experienced this rude fact in your own job, on days (or in projects) when you felt demotivated, devalued, and frustrated, even though you worked hard and got things done. The likely cause is your perception of the completed tasks as peripheral or irrelevant. For the progress principle to operate, the work must be meaningful to the person doing it.

In 1983, Steve Jobs was trying to entice John Sculley to leave a wildly successful career at PepsiCo to become Apple's new CEO. Jobs reportedly asked him, "Do you want to spend the rest of your life selling sugared water or do you want a chance to change the world?" In making his pitch, Jobs leveraged a potent psychological force: the deep-seated human desire to do meaningful work.

Fortunately, to feel meaningful, work doesn't have to involve putting the first personal computers in the hands of ordinary people, or alleviating poverty, or helping to cure cancer. Work with less profound importance to society can matter if it contributes value to something or someone important to the worker. Meaning can be as simple as making a useful and high-quality product for a customer or providing a genuine service for a community. It can be supporting a colleague or boosting an organization's profits by reducing inefficiencies in a production process. Whether the goals are lofty or modest, as long as they are meaningful to the worker and it is clear how his or her efforts contribute to them, progress toward them can galvanize inner work life.

In principle, managers shouldn't have to go to extraordinary lengths to infuse jobs with meaning. Most jobs in modern organizations are potentially meaningful for the people doing them. However, managers can make sure that employees know just how their work is contributing. And, most important, they can avoid actions that negate its value. (See the sidebar "How Work Gets Stripped of Its Meaning.") All the participants in our research were doing work that should have been meaningful; no one was washing pots or checking coats. Shockingly often, however, we saw potentially important, challenging work losing its power to inspire.

HOW WORK GETS STRIPPED OF ITS MEANING

Diary entries from 238 knowledge workers who were members of creative project teams revealed four primary ways in which managers unwittingly drain work of its meaning.

Managers may dismiss the importance of employees' work or ideas. Consider the case of Richard, a senior lab technician at a chemical company, who found meaning in helping his new-product development team solve complex technical problems. However, in team meetings over the course of a three-week period, Richard perceived that his team leader was ignoring his suggestions and those of his teammates. As a result, he felt that his contributions were not meaningful, and his spirits flagged. When at last he believed that he was again making a substantive contribution to the success of the project, his mood

(Continued)

HOW WORK GETS STRIPPED OF ITS MEANING

improved dramatically: "I felt much better at today's team meeting. I felt that my opinions and information were important to the project and that we have made some progress."

They may destroy employees' sense of ownership of their work. Frequent and abrupt reassignments often have this effect. This happened repeatedly to the members of a product development team in a giant consumer products company, as described by team member Bruce: "As I've been handing over some projects, I do realize that I don't like to give them up. Especially when you have been with them from the start and are nearly to the end. You lose ownership. This happens to us way too often."

Managers may send the message that the work employees are doing will never see the light of day. They can signal this—unintentionally—by shifting

█████████████████████████████████████

their priorities or changing their minds about how something should be done. We saw the latter in an internet technology company after user-interface developer Burt had spent weeks designing seamless transitions for non-English-speaking users. Not surprisingly, Burt's mood was seriously marred on the day he reported this incident: "Other options for the international [interfaces] were [given] to the team during a team meeting, which could render the work I am doing useless."

They may neglect to inform employees about unexpected changes in a customer's priorities. Often, this arises from poor customer management or inadequate communication within the company. For example, Stuart, a data transformation expert at an IT company, reported deep frustration and low

(Continued)

HOW WORK GETS STRIPPED OF ITS MEANING

motivation on the day he learned that weeks of the team's hard work might have been for naught: "Found out that there is a strong possibility that the project may not be going forward, due to a shift in the client's agenda. Therefore, there is a strong possibility that all the time and effort put into the project was a waste of our time."

Supporting progress:
catalysts and nourishers

What can managers do to ensure that people are motivated, committed, and happy? How can they support workers' daily progress? They can use catalysts and nourishers, the other kinds of frequent "best day" events we discovered.

Catalysts are actions that support work. They include setting clear goals, allowing autonomy, providing sufficient resources and time, helping with the work, openly learning from problems and successes, and allowing a free exchange of ideas. Their opposites, inhibitors, include failing to provide support and actively interfering with the work. Because of their impact on progress, catalysts and inhibitors ultimately affect inner work life. But they also have a more immediate impact: When people realize that they have clear and meaningful goals, sufficient resources, helpful colleagues, and so on, they get an instant boost to their emotions, their motivation to do a great job, and their perceptions of the work and the organization.

Nourishers are acts of interpersonal support, such as respect and recognition, encouragement, emotional comfort, and opportunities for affiliation. Toxins, their opposites, include disrespect, discouragement, disregard for emotions, and interpersonal conflict. For good and for ill, nourishers and toxins affect inner work life directly and immediately.

Catalysts and nourishers—and their opposites—can alter the meaningfulness of work by shifting people's perceptions of their jobs and even themselves. For instance, when a manager makes sure that people have the resources they need, it signals to them that what they are doing is important and valuable. When managers recognize people for the work they do, it signals that they are important to the organization. In this way, catalysts and nourishers can lend greater meaning to the work—and amplify the operation of the progress principle.

The managerial actions that constitute catalysts and nourishers are not particularly mysterious; they may sound like Management 101, if not just common sense and common decency. But our diary study reminded us how often they are ignored or forgotten. Even some of the more attentive managers in the companies we studied did not consistently provide catalysts and nourishers. For example, a supply chain specialist named Michael was, in many ways and on most days, an excellent subteam manager. But he was occasionally so overwhelmed that he became toxic toward his people. When a supplier failed to complete a "hot" order on time and Michael's team had to resort to air shipping to meet the customer's deadline, he realized that the profit margin on the sale would be blown. In irritation, he lashed out at his subordinates, demeaning the solid work they had done and disregarding their own frustration with the supplier. In his diary, he admitted as much: "As of Friday, we have spent $28,000 in air freight to send 1,500 $30 spray jet mops to our number two customer. Another 2,800 remain on this order, and there is a good probability that they too will gain wings. I have turned from the kindly supply chain manager into the black-masked executioner. All similarity to civility is gone, our backs are against the wall, flight is not possible, therefore fight is probable."

Even when managers don't have their backs against the wall, developing long-term strategy and launching new initiatives can often seem more important—and perhaps sexier—than making sure subordinates have what they need to make steady progress and feel supported as human beings. But as we saw repeatedly in our research, even the best strategy will fail if managers ignore the people working in the trenches to execute it.

A model manager—and a tool for emulating him

We could explain the many (and largely unsurprising) moves that can catalyze progress and nourish spirits, but it may be more useful to give an example of a manager who consistently used those moves—and then to provide a simple tool that can help any manager do so.

Our model manager is Graham, whom we observed leading a small team of chemical engineers within a multinational European firm we'll call Kruger-Bern. The mission of the team's NewPoly project was clear and meaningful enough: Develop a safe, biodegradable polymer to replace petrochemicals in cosmetics and, eventually, in a wide range of consumer products. As in many large firms however, the project was nested in a confusing and sometimes threatening corporate setting of shifting top-management priorities, conflicting signals, and wavering commitments. Resources were uncomfortably tight, and uncertainty loomed over the project's future—and every team member's career. Even worse, an incident early in the project, in which an important customer reacted angrily to a sample, left the team reeling. Yet Graham was able to sustain team members' inner work lives by repeatedly and visibly removing obstacles, materially supporting progress, and emotionally supporting the team.

Graham's management approach excelled in four ways. First, he established a positive climate, one event at a time, which set behavioral norms for the entire team. When the customer complaint stopped the project in its tracks, for example, he engaged immediately with the team to analyze the problem, without recriminations, and develop a plan for repairing the relationship. In doing so, he modeled how to respond to crises in the work: not by panicking or pointing fingers but by identifying problems and their causes and developing a coordinated action plan. This is both a practical approach and a great way to give subordinates a sense of forward movement even in the face of the missteps and failures inherent in any complex project.

Second, Graham stayed attuned to his team's everyday activities and progress. In fact, the nonjudgmental climate he had established made this happen naturally. Team members updated him frequently—

without being asked—on their setbacks, progress, and plans. At one point, one of his hardest-working colleagues, Brady, had to abort a trial of a new material because he couldn't get the parameters right on the equipment. It was bad news, because the New-Poly team had access to the equipment only one day a week, but Brady immediately informed Graham. In his diary entry that evening, Brady noted, "He didn't like the lost week but seemed to understand." That understanding assured Graham's place in the stream of information that would allow him to give his people just what they needed to make progress.

Third, Graham targeted his support according to recent events in the team and the project. Each day, he could anticipate what type of intervention—a catalyst or the removal of an inhibitor; a nourisher or some antidote to a toxin—would have the most impact on team members' inner work lives and progress. And if he could not make that judgment, he asked. Most days it was not hard to figure out, as on the day he received some uplifting news about his bosses' commitment to the project. He knew the team was jittery about a rumored corporate reorganization and could use the encouragement. Even though the clarification came during a well-earned vacation day, he immediately got on the phone to relay the good news to the team.

Finally, Graham established himself as a resource for team members rather than a micromanager; he was sure to check in while never seeming to check *up* on them. Superficially, checking in and checking up seem quite similar, but micromanagers make four kinds of mistakes. First, they fail to allow autonomy in carrying out the work. Unlike Graham, who gave the NewPoly team a clear strategic goal but respected members' ideas about how to meet it, micromanagers dictate every move. Second, they frequently ask subordinates about their work without providing any real help. By contrast, when one of Graham's team

members reported problems, Graham helped analyze them—remaining open to alternative interpretations—and often ended up helping to get things
back on track. Third, micromanagers are quick to
affix personal blame when problems arise, leading
subordinates to hide problems rather than honestly
discuss how to surmount them, as Graham did with
Brady. And fourth, micromanagers tend to hoard information to use as a secret weapon. Few realize how
damaging this is to inner work life. When subordinates perceive that a manager is withholding potentially useful information, they feel infantilized, their
motivation wanes, and their work is handicapped.
Graham was quick to communicate upper management's views of the project, customers' opinions and
needs, and possible sources of assistance or resistance within and outside the organization.

In all those ways, Graham sustained his team's
positive emotions, intrinsic motivation, and favorable

perceptions. His actions serve as a powerful example of how managers at any level can approach each day determined to foster progress.

We know that many managers, however well-intentioned, will find it hard to establish the habits that seemed to come so naturally to Graham. Awareness, of course, is the first step. However, turning an awareness of the importance of inner work life into routine action takes discipline. With that in mind, we developed a checklist for managers to consult on a daily basis (see the sidebar "The Daily Progress Checklist"). The aim of the checklist is managing for meaningful progress, one day at a time.

The progress loop

Inner work life drives performance; in turn, good performance, which depends on consistent progress, enhances inner work life. We call this the "progress loop"—it reveals the potential for self-reinforcing benefits.

So, the most important implication of the progress principle is this: By supporting people and their daily progress in meaningful work, managers improve not only the inner work lives of their employees but also the organization's long-term performance, which enhances inner work life even more. Of course, there is a dark side—the possibility of negative feedback loops. If managers fail to support progress and the people trying to make it, inner work life suffers and so does performance; and degraded performance further undermines inner work life.

A second implication of the progress principle is that managers needn't fret about trying to read the psyches of their workers or manipulate complicated incentive schemes to ensure that employees are motivated and happy. As long as managers show basic respect and consideration, they can focus on supporting the work itself.

To become an effective manager, you must learn to set this positive feedback loop in motion. That may require a significant shift. Business schools, business books, and managers themselves usually focus on managing organizations or people. But if you focus on managing progress, the management of people—and even of entire organizations—becomes much more feasible. You won't have to figure out how to x-ray the inner work lives of subordinates; if you facilitate their steady progress in meaningful work, make that progress salient to them, and treat them well, they will experience the emotions, motivations, and perceptions necessary for great performance. Their superior work will contribute to organizational success. And here's the beauty of it: They will love their jobs.

TERESA M. AMABILE is the Edsel Bryant Ford Professor of Business Administration at Harvard Business School and the author of *Creativity in Context* (Westview Press, 1996). STEVEN J. KRAMER is an independent researcher, writer, and consultant. He is a coauthor of "Creativity Under the Gun" (HBR, August 2002) and "Inner Work Life" (HBR, May 2007). Amabile and Kramer are the coauthors of *The Progress*

Principle: Using Small Wins to Ignite Joy, Engagement, and Creativity at Work (Harvard Business Review Press, 2011).

Reprinted from *Harvard Business Review*,
May 2011 (product #R1105C).

THE DAILY PROGRESS CHECKLIST

Near the end of each workday, use this checklist to review the day and plan your managerial actions for the next day. After a few days, you will be able to identify issues by scanning the boldface words.

First, focus on progress and setbacks and think about specific events (catalysts, nourishers, inhibitors, and toxins) that contributed to them. Next, consider any clear inner-work-life clues and what further information they provide about progress and other events. Finally, prioritize for action.

The action plan for the next day is the most important part of your daily review: What is the one thing you can do to best facilitate progress?

(Continued)

THE DAILY PROGRESS CHECKLIST

Progress

Which 1 or 2 events today indicated either a small win or a possible breakthrough? (Describe briefly.)

_____

_____

Catalysts

- ☐ Did the team have clear short- and long-term **goals** for meaningful work?

- ☐ Did team members have sufficient **autonomy** to solve problems and take ownership of the project?

- ☐ Did they have all the **resources** they needed to move forward efficiently?

- ☐ Did they have sufficient **time** to focus on meaningful work?

- ☐ Did I discuss **lessons** from today's successes and problems with my team?

▮▮▮▮▮▮▮▮▮▮▮▮▮▮▮▮▮▮▮▮▮▮▮▮▮▮▮▮

- ☐ Did I give or get them **help** when they needed or requested it? Did I encourage team members to help one another?
- ☐ Did I help **ideas** flow freely within the group?

Nourishers

- ☐ Did I show **respect** to team members by recognizing their contributions to progress, attending to their ideas, and treating them as trusted professionals?
- ☐ Did I **encourage** team members who faced difficult challenges?
- ☐ Did I **support** team members who had a personal or professional problem?
- ☐ Is there a sense of personal and professional **affiliation** and camaraderie within the team?

(Continued)

THE DAILY PROGRESS CHECKLIST

Setbacks

Which 1 or 2 events today indicated either a small setback or a possible crisis? (Describe briefly.)

_____

_____

Inhibitors

- ☐ Was there any confusion regarding long- or short-term **goals** for meaningful work?

- ☐ Were team members overly **constrained** in their ability to solve problems and feel ownership of the project?

- ☐ Did they lack any of the **resources** they needed to move forward effectively?

- ☐ Did they lack sufficient **time** to focus on meaningful work?

- ☐ Did I or others fail to provide needed or requested **help**?

□ Did I "punish" failure or neglect to find **lessons** and/or opportunities in problems and successes?

□ Did I or others cut off the presentation or debate of **ideas** prematurely?

Toxins

□ Did I **disrespect** any team members by failing to recognize their contributions to progress, not attending to their ideas, or not treating them as trusted professionals?

□ Did I **discourage** a member of the team in any way?

□ Did I **neglect** a team member who had a personal or professional problem?

□ Is there tension or **antagonism** among members of the team or between team members and me?

(Continued)

THE DAILY PROGRESS CHECKLIST

Inner work life

- Did I see any indications of the quality of my subordinates' inner work lives today? _____

  _____

  _____

- Perceptions of the work, team, management, firm _____

  _____

- Emotions _____

  _____

  _____

- Motivation _____

  _____

- What specific events might have affected inner work life today? _____

  _____

Action plan

- What can I do tomorrow to strengthen the catalysts and nourishers identified and provide the ones that are lacking? _____

  _____

  _____

  _____

  _____

  _____

- What can I do tomorrow to start eliminating the inhibitors and toxins identified? _____

  _____

  _____

  _____

  _____

  _____

  _____

10

The Founder of TOMS on Reimagining the Company's Mission

By Blake Mycoskie

n the fall of 2012 I did something I never thought I'd do: I took a sabbatical from TOMS. It was not your typical travel-the-world sabbatical. My wife, Heather, and I moved to Austin, Texas, where I'd grown up, and I used the physical and psychological separation from the company to do some soul-searching.

In the six years since I'd founded TOMS, it had grown from a startup based in my Venice, California, apartment to a global company with more than $300 million in revenue. I still owned 100% of it, and we were still delivering on our promise to give a pair of shoes to someone in need for every pair sold, but

I felt disillusioned. My days were monotonous, and I had lost my connection to many of the executives who were running daily operations. What had once been my reason for being now felt like a job.

During my months away, I did a lot of thinking about my personal "why." I knew why I had started the company and why people joined me in the early days. And I still believed in our mission and the impact we were making. But I was no longer sure why I wanted—or even if I did want—to continue driving the business forward.

Eventually I came to a surprising conclusion: I felt lost because TOMS had become more focused on process than on purpose. We were concentrating so hard on the "what" and "how" of scaling up that we'd forgotten our overarching mission, which is to use business to improve lives. That is our greatest competitive advantage: It allows us to build an emotional bond with customers and motivate employees, because they know they are shopping and working for a movement bigger than themselves.

After my time away from the business, I returned with renewed energy. My mission was clear: Make TOMS a movement again.

The company's genesis

I got the idea for TOMS on something like a sabbatical. After founding and selling several companies (a door-to-door laundry business, an outdoor advertising company, an online driver's education service) and making a brief detour into reality TV (I competed on *The Amazing Race* with my sister and created an all-reality cable channel), I decided to take some time off in 2006 to learn to play polo in Argentina. I know that sounds like a strange mix of pursuits, but I've always been happiest chasing my latest interest.

While in Buenos Aires, I met a woman who worked for a nonprofit, delivering shoes to children in poor rural areas. She invited me to accompany her, and the experience was truly life changing. In every town we were greeted with cheers and tears. I met a pair of brothers, ages 10 and 12, who had been sharing a single pair of adult-size shoes. Because the local schools required footwear, they had to take turns going to class. Their mother wept when I handed her shoes that actually fit her boys' feet. I couldn't believe that such a simple act could have such an enormous impact on people's lives.

I decided to do something more. Rather than go home and ask my friends to donate their hand-me-downs or make financial contributions, I would start a for-profit company based on the buy-one, give-one idea. I named it Shoes for Tomorrow, later shortened to Tomorrow's Shoes, and finally to TOMS so that the name would fit on the little tag on our shoes. (To this day, some people are puzzled when they meet me, because they're expecting a guy named Tom.)

My polo instructor, Alejo, and I persuaded a local shoemaker to help us make a more fashionable version of the *alpargata*, a canvas shoe worn by Argentines for a century. To borrow a term from Eric Ries's *The Lean Startup*, our first shoes were a "minimum viable product." They had glue stains on them, were in Argentine rather than U.S. sizes, and didn't always fit the same from pair to pair. But they were just good enough to test the concept among my friends in Los Angeles. My goal was to sell 250 pairs so that I could give away 250 pairs in Argentina.

Back home, I hosted a dinner party for some women friends to get their advice. They loved the shoes and were even more excited when I shared my vision of helping children in need. They suggested a number of local boutiques that might serve as retail outlets, so I went to one of them, American Rag, and asked to speak with the shoe buyer. I knew my shoes couldn't compete on quality or price alone, so I told the buyer why I wanted to sell them and give them away. The store became our first retail account.

On a Saturday morning soon after that, I woke up to find my BlackBerry vibrating. At the time, the TOMS website was set to email my phone every time we made a sale. Usually it was just family and friends placing orders, and the occasional buzzing was a nice surprise. But on this day the phone kept buzzing . . . and buzzing . . . and buzzing. At brunch I started flipping through the *Los Angeles Times* and saw that what I'd expected would be a short piece by its fashion writer on TOMS had landed on the front page of the Calendar section. By the end of the day we had sold 2,200 pairs of shoes. This was incredible—but it was also the company's first supply-chain management challenge. We had fewer than 200 pairs in my apartment.

Over the next six months I worked with a team of interns to turn my "shoe project" into a real company. We received a flood of additional press from *Vogue*, *People*, *Time*, *Elle*. Soon celebrities such as Tobey Maguire, Keira Knightley, and Scarlett Johansson were being photographed wearing TOMS. Nordstrom insisted on carrying our shoes. By the end of the summer we had sold 10,000 pairs. The "why" of TOMS was clearly resonating.

Disillusionment

By 2011 TOMS had an annual growth rate (for five years running) of 300%, and we'd recently given away our 10 millionth pair of shoes. The one-for-one model—initially dismissed by traditional businesspeople as nice but not financially sustainable—was clearly a success, and we'd decided to extend it to eyewear, giving away pairs of glasses or medical treatments to restore sight for pairs sold. We had set ourselves apart in other ways, too: A third of our revenue was coming from direct-to-consumer sales via our website, and we spent virtually nothing on traditional advertising, relying instead on our 5 million social media followers to create word-of-mouth buzz.

In September 2012 Heather and I got married. I'd brought in an experienced team of executives to manage the day-to-day operations, and for the first time since founding the business, I felt I could take a break from it. I was relieved but also deeply unsettled. The excitement and camaraderie of our startup was beginning to be replaced by a more hierarchical culture. The leadership team was bogged down in personality conflicts and bickering, with key members insisting that we implement processes and systems similar to those used at their previous companies. As an organization, we were so focused on protecting what we'd already built that no one was thinking about new possibilities. I noticed that longtime employees were starting to leave for more-entrepreneurial organizations, and I realized that, secretly, I wanted to follow them.

I'd started and sold companies before—but TOMS was different. It was more than a company to me: It was my life. So this period of uncertainty felt like having problems in a marriage. You thought you'd found your business soul mate, but you're not in love anymore. What do you do? For me, the sabbatical was like going into couples counseling. I wasn't walking away; I was putting in the work to see if TOMS and I could reconcile. If it had been a pure business problem, I would have organized a strategic offsite. But this was both corporate and personal. I needed to figure out the future course of the company and my role in it. And I tend to do my best thinking alone.

When I left for Austin, I was careful not to make a big deal of it—I told people the break was an extended honeymoon with Heather. But once there, I dedicated a lot of time to private contemplation. I also started talking to anyone I thought might offer good advice and inspire me. I spoke regularly with my executive coach, entrepreneur friends, and business and nonprofit leaders I admire. I traveled to conferences around the country to learn from experts in social enterprise and international development.

It was during this time that I read Simon Sinek's fantastic book *Start with Why*, which looks at leaders who inspire action, such as Martin Luther King Jr., and companies, such as Apple, that create products so compelling that fans will line up to buy them. Sinek argues that one can build and sustain these movements only when leading with the "why." People follow you, buy from you, when they believe what you believe.

The more I thought about this idea, the more I realized that TOMS had veered away from its "why." In the early days we always led with our story: We weren't selling shoes; we were selling the promise that each purchase would directly and tangibly benefit a child who needed shoes. But our desire to sustain the company's hypergrowth had pushed us away from that mission and into competing on the "what" and "how," just as every other shoe company does. In an effort to meet aggressive sales goals, we had begun promoting deals and discounts on our website—something we'd never done before. Our marketing increasingly felt product focused rather than purpose focused. And as the leader of TOMS, I was ultimately accountable for those mistakes. That was a tough pill to swallow.

Another breakthrough came during a Dallas Cowboys game. I was introduced to a man named Joe Ford, who told me that his son, Scott, was also using business to improve lives, but through the coffee trade in Rwanda. Joe explained the importance of water in the coffee supply chain. When beans are processed with clean as opposed to dirty water, they are transformed from a commodity to a specialty and can be sold at dramatically higher prices. Scott's company, Westrock Coffee, was helping Rwandan growers build community-owned washing stations to increase the value of their product and to prevent the spread of waterborne disease. It was also buying direct from growers, helping to break up unfair industry price controls, and offering low-interest loans as an alternative to those from predatory lenders. Best of all, Westrock was a profitable business that sold fantastic coffee.

After meeting Scott, I realized that a TOMS coffee venture could have a real impact—and maybe lift me out of the funk I was in. Like most entrepreneurs, I get a high from starting things and doing the unexpected. No one doubted our shoe business anymore, but few people would imagine that we could also sell coffee. And the expansion could pave the way for a new TOMS retail experience, something I had long wanted to try. We could create cafés and use them as community gathering places to share ideas, get inspired, and connect guests with the "why" of TOMS. The vision—and the challenge—pumped new life into me.

I told our senior executives about my idea. Like TOMS Shoes, TOMS Roasting would have a one-for-one model: For every bag of coffee we sold, we would provide a week's worth of water to a person in need. When they gave me the green light, I quickly assembled a small team of TOMS employees to get the project (code-named "Burlap") off the ground. I was still living in Austin, but the more I discussed my plans with Heather (an early TOMS employee who knew the business—and me—better than most people), the more she realized it was time for my sabbatical to end. We'd just bought a house, and we had a great group of friends, but in early 2013 she said to me, "Blake, we need to move back to L.A." If I was going to fully recommit to TOMS, it couldn't happen from afar.

The reentry

Coming back was great, but I quickly made some of the classic mistakes that founders do upon rejoining their companies. First, when I outlined my vision for using the coffee business to reinspire the "why" of TOMS, I did so without a fully thought-out plan. That made some of my coworkers anxious. Second, I asked the company's CMO to step down so that I could take over brand marketing and communications, which I considered to be key pieces of our new direction—not only for integrating the new business but also for reigniting the passion of our customers. But I quickly realized that I'm better in the founder's role—setting the vision and traveling the country to communicate it, not running marketing or any other department.

Despite these hiccups, by the end of 2013 we had launched the coffee business nationally in Whole Foods stores, opened up three of our own cafés, and started exploring international expansion. To date we have provided more than 175,000 weeks of clean drinking water to people in need around the world. The new product generated a ton of PR and got our customers excited about TOMS again. But most important, I believe, it gave our employees permission to think bigger, to challenge the status quo, and to reconnect with the mission of the business.

It also got me thinking bigger. I realized that my ultimate aim was to create the most influential, inspirational company in the world, which would be possible only with more help. I decided to meet with private equity firms that had a track record of helping entrepreneurial companies into the next stage of growth, and after a thorough search, I sold 50% of TOMS to Bain Capital in mid-2014. We clearly defined my role and responsibilities and agreed to hire a world-class CEO.

The man we found, Jim Alling, embodies the core values of TOMS. Although he scratched his head a bit over the "coffee decision" (he spent much of his career in senior roles at Starbucks), he understood what the move represented. Creating TOMS Roasting wasn't an attempt to compete with big chains but, rather, a bold move to reengage with the community and help more people. Over the past year Jim has brought great stability and strategic thinking to the business. We now also sell handbags to fund safe births for mothers and babies in need and backpacks to support anti-bullying programs.

As TOMS approaches its 10th anniversary, I feel more energized and committed than ever. As far as we've come, I still see tremendous opportunities to grow our movement. The "why" of TOMS—using business to improve lives—is bigger than myself, the shoes we sell, or any future products we might launch. It took going on a sabbatical to realize the power of what we've created—and the best way for me to move it forward. Now that I have a clear purpose and amazing partners supporting me, I'm ready for the company's next 10 years and the many adventures ahead.

BLAKE MYCOSKIE is the founder and chief shoe giver of TOMS.

Reprinted from *Harvard Business Review*,
January–February 2016 (product #R1601A).

Index

How to be human at work.

HBR's Emotional Intelligence Series features smart, essential reading on the human side of professional life from the pages of *Harvard Business Review*. Each book in the series offers uplifting stories, practical advice, and research from leading experts on how to tend to our emotional well-being at work.

Harvard Business Review Emotional Intelligence Series

Available in paperback or ebook format. The specially priced six-volume set includes:

- Mindfulness
- Resilience
- Influence and Persuasion
- Authentic Leadership
- Happiness
- Empathy

HBR.ORG

Buy for your team, clients, or event.
Visit hbr.org/bulksales for quantity discount rates.

Leadership Presence

HBR EMOTIONAL INTELLIGENCE SERIES

HBR Emotional Intelligence Series

The HBR Emotional Intelligence Series features smart, essential reading on the human side of professional life from the pages of *Harvard Business Review*.

Authentic Leadership

Dealing with Difficult People

Empathy

Happiness

Influence and Persuasion

Leadership Presence

Mindfulness

Purpose, Meaning, and Passion

Resilience

Other books on emotional intelligence from *Harvard Business Review*:

HBR's 10 Must Reads on Emotional Intelligence

HBR Guide to Emotional Intelligence

HBR Everyday Emotional Intelligence

Leadership Presence

HBR EMOTIONAL INTELLIGENCE SERIES

Harvard Business Review Press

Boston, Massachusetts

HBR Press Quantity Sales Discounts

Harvard Business Review Press titles are available at significant quantity discounts when purchased in bulk for client gifts, sales promotions, and premiums. Special editions, including books with corporate logos, customized covers, and letters from the company or CEO printed in the front matter, as well as excerpts of existing books, can also be created in large quantities for special needs.

For details and discount information for both print and ebook formats, contact booksales@harvardbusiness.org, tel. 800-988-0886, or www.hbr.org/bulksales.

Copyright 2018 Harvard Business School Publishing Corporation
All rights reserved
Printed in the United States of America

10 9 8

No part of this publication may be reproduced, stored in or introduced into a retrieval system, or transmitted, in any form, or by any means (electronic, mechanical, photocopying, recording, or otherwise), without the prior permission of the publisher. Requests for permission should be directed to permissions@hbsp.harvard.edu, or mailed to Permissions, Harvard Business School Publishing, 60 Harvard Way, Boston, Massachusetts 02163.

The web addresses referenced in this book were live and correct at the time of the book's publication but may be subject to change.

Library of Congress Cataloging-in-Publication Data

Title: Leadership presence.
Other titles: HBR emotional intelligence series.
Description: Boston, Massachusetts : Harvard Business Review Press, [2018] | Series: HBR emotional intelligence series
Identifiers: LCCN 2017054135 | ISBN 9781633696242 (pbk. : alk. paper)
Subjects: LCSH: Leadership. | Executive ability. | Emotional intelligence.
Classification: LCC HD57.7 .L4347 2018 | DDC 658.4/092--dc23 LC record available at https://lccn.loc.gov/2017054135

The paper used in this publication meets the requirements of the American National Standard for Permanence of Paper for Publications and Documents in Libraries and Archives Z39.48-1992.

Contents

Contents

Leadership
Presence

HBR EMOTIONAL INTELLIGENCE SERIES

1

Deconstructing Executive Presence

By John Beeson

f you ask a group of managers who aspire to the C-suite what it takes to get there, they'll invariably mention executive presence, but they aren't always so clear about what it means. Not too long ago, I conducted a series of off-the-record interviews with senior executives responsible for executive placement in their organizations. I asked them about the "make or break" factors they consider in making C-suite promotion decisions. Executive presence was one of the handful of decision criteria they cited, but even these experienced executives struggled to define what it is and why one person has it and another doesn't. In an increasingly diverse world where senior executives are no longer all six-feet-two-inch males who look like they were sent from central casting, what does it take to create a commanding executive presence? The right clothes? A firm handshake? Those matter, but they don't tell the whole story.

Although executive presence is highly intuitive and difficult to pin down, it ultimately boils down to your ability to project mature self-confidence, a sense that you can take control of difficult, unpredictable situations; make tough decisions in a timely way and hold your own with other talented and strong-willed members of the executive team. If that's the nub of the issue, what style, what behaviors combine to signal that level of self-confidence to others? For some answers, consider three talented managers—two of whom didn't make it to the executive level and one who did.

Every manager would love to have a Frank Simmons on his or her management team. Experienced, results oriented, collaborative, and committed to the company, Frank showed up on succession lists for a number of years, but was never promoted. Although a top performer in his area, Frank always looked a little rumpled and his posture was a bit hunched. When he made presentations to the executive team, he was invariably well prepared, but his lack of comfort was evident in his body language. Normally highly articulate, his presentations were long-winded and rambling. In the Q&A portion of his presentations, he tended to be overly deferential to members of the executive team, and he was hesitant to insert himself into the conversation when the executives got into a debate. As one senior executive said privately, "Frank's an incredible asset to the company, but I just can't envision putting him in front of a customer."

Alicia Wallace was a highly trained marketing manager who had succeeded in every assignment she'd had. However, when it came time to select high-potential people for promotion to more senior levels, she always missed the cut. As much as the senior marketing executives liked and respected her, they were never quite comfortable moving her to the next level. The reason: her apparent disorganization. People would talk about "Alicia being Alicia" when she arrived late to yet another meeting, rushed, harried, and with her files askew. Was this trivial and petty? Perhaps, but on a visceral level, it caused senior people to question her ability to manage a larger staff and maintain the necessary focus on implementing key priorities.

If you entered a room filled with 20 managers, Lydia Taylor, a member of the legal department, wouldn't stand out, but that would change once the dialogue started. Although soft spoken and not terribly aggressive, she was highly respected by her peers as well as the executives with whom she worked. Lydia possessed outstanding listening skills and had an unerring sense of when to enter the conversation to make her point. Unrushed, straightforward, and unflappable, she maintained her calm, even demeanor when others got emotional, and she used her dry sense of humor to defuse difficult situations. When challenged by others, she stood her ground in a firm, nonconfrontational way. Although highly supportive of her internal customers, she was prepared to put her foot down if anyone advocated a position that might put the company at risk. As a result, Lydia was identified as a top candidate and groomed to succeed the company's general counsel.

The age-old question is whether executive presence can be developed? The answer is yes, if you have a baseline of self-confidence and a willingness to deal with the unpredictable situations that go with the territory at the executive level. Start by addressing the basics. Find a couple of trusted people who will give you unvarnished feedback about your dress and grooming and the level of self-confidence you project. As noted, dress and grooming aren't the whole deal, but major problems can create an impediment. One highly talented female manager was privately described by her peers as dressing like a "school marm," while others said a hard-charging manager came off like a "used car salesman." The connotations aren't flattering, nor are they insignificant. People tend not to trust a used car salesman, and school marms aren't typically thought of as creative and risk taking, two qualities central to leading innovation and change at the executive level.

Look for opportunities to hone your presentation skills. Not only is public speaking an important executive requirement, but your ability to "stand and deliver" to an executive group or large audience is frequently viewed as an indicator of your ability to handle pressure. Rehearse a major presentation until you can come off as relaxed and in command, and pay special attention to the Q&A portion since your poise when questioned and ability to think on your feet help you project a sense of self-confidence.

Most important, find your voice as an executive: that is, identify your assets and leverage them to the hilt. Some people are naturally gregarious and can fill a room with their personality. Others, like Lydia Taylor, rely on their listening ability, sense of timing, and ability to maintain their composure when others get emotional. In an increasingly diverse world, executive presence will look very different from one executive to another. However, the constant is building the confidence of others that you can step up as a leader when times get tough.

JOHN BEESON is principal of Beeson Consulting, a management consulting firm specializing in succession planning, executive assessment and coaching, and organization design. He is also the author of *The Unwritten Rules: The Six Skills You Need to Get Promoted to the Executive Level* (Jossey-Bass). Follow him on Twitter @johnrbeeson.

Reprinted from hbr.org, originally published August 22, 2012 (product #H0099M).

2

How New Managers Can Send the Right Leadership Signals

By Amy Jen Su

One of the most exciting and sometimes anxiety-producing transitions in a career comes when you move from being an individual contributor to becoming a manager. At this juncture, *what you think, what you say, and how you show up*—in effect, your leadership presence—can have a direct impact on those you are now leading and managing for the first time. So, as a new manager, how do you build an authentic and connected leadership presence that has a positive impact on your team and colleagues?

Set a leadership values-based goal. An authentic and connected presence begins from the inside out. How you define the role and what you value will telegraph out to those you work with. As a new manager, spend time to consider the kind of leader you are and hope to be. Set an aspirational goal to serve as a guiding compass. As one new manager shared recently, "my professional leadership goal is to be a genuine and emotionally intelligent manager who inspires others to excellence."

As Ram Charan, Stephen Drotter, and James Noel describe in their book, *The Leadership Pipeline*, "Though this might seem like an easy, natural leadership passage, it's often one where people trip . . . [T]hey make the job transition from individual contribution to manager without making a behavioral or values-based transition . . . They must believe that making time for others, planning, [and] coaching . . . are necessary tasks and their responsibility. More than that, they must view this other-directed work as mission-critical to their success."

Increase your emotional intelligence and situational awareness. As the job now shifts to getting more work done through others, recognize that what motivates or influences you may not be how others are motivated or influenced. In advance of important interactions or meetings, ask yourself:

- Who is the other person or audience?

- What might their perspective on this topic be?

- How are they best motivated or influenced?

- What does the situation at hand call for?

- What are the optimal outcomes and tone?

These questions remind us that leadership presence is not about finding a one-size-fits-all solution. Leadership presence is therefore an "and/both" versus an "either/or." On the one hand, having an effective leadership presence includes being authentic, genuine, and clear on your guiding compass, core values, and convictions. And, on the other hand, it includes being adaptive and agile, demonstrating an ability to connect with different kinds of people through many different communication platforms and technologies.

Be clear and direct, always with respect. As your new role will likely increase your interactions with people of many different styles, having an effective leadership presence includes continually building and practicing the skills of being clear and direct while finding ways of making connections and showing respect. Leadership presence is dynamic and fluid, and encourages a two-way dialogue where we can give authentic voice to our views while staying open to the views and perspectives of others as we work toward a common goal, best outcome, or solution. Here are a few examples of things that can help you cultivate your own voice and listen to the voices of others:

- *Know what you think:* If you are naturally
  strong at listening and hearing other's opinions,
  flex your muscles in getting to your own convictions and thoughts more quickly. Before important meetings or interactions, jot down a few
  bullet points to yourself: *What are the three to
  five things I believe about this topic or issue?*

- *Ask, listen, and acknowledge:* Conversely, if
  you are naturally strong at having your own
  opinions, settle into a greater patience, so that
  you can make space to hear others. Show you
  are really listening by asking great questions,
  clarifying what you've heard, or acknowledging
  how you're processing the information. In some
  cases, you might share: *"With this new information, I am experiencing this quite differently. My view has changed."* In other cases, you
  might end up saying: *"In digesting what you
  have shared, I am finding I just can't get myself*

comfortable with that direction. Ultimately, this is coming down to a difference of opinion."

- *Share the "why":* As a new manager, it's also critical to share the "why" behind your vision, priorities, expectations, feedback, or requests. Don't dilute your message. Instead, make it more powerful by sharing more about the context. Help connect work deliverables or professional development to what's happening at the organizational level. For example, in giving developmental feedback to someone, you could include additional context such as: *"Because the organization is growing so fast, there is opportunity for each member of the team to stretch and step up in the following ways. I'd love to see you take on . . ."* Or, you can strengthen the message by painting the picture of the aspiration: *"I'd love to see us become best in class at this, and here's what will be required."*

Bring a stable and grounded presence in the face of change, stress, or difficult news. The reality is that most of us can exude an effective presence, especially when business is going well or when we are having a good day. As a new manager, however, it's equally important to ask yourself: *What do people experience when I'm stressed out, tired, under deadline, or when someone is bringing me bad news?*

Recognize that what may feel like a passing or fleeting moment of anger, impatience, or hurried insincerity may end up negatively impacting your team and its overall morale and engagement. As author Daniel Goleman writes in his book *Primal Leadership*: "Quite simply, in any human group, the leader has maximal power to sway everyone's emotions . . . [H]ow well leaders manage their moods affects everyone else's moods, which becomes not just a private matter, but a factor in how well a business will do."

Maintaining a stable and grounded presence increases the likelihood that your team will feel comfortable bringing you important information, even if it's bad news, so that you can help to remove obstacles, reset priorities, or get the team back on track. Professor Amy Edmondson's research finds that teams can optimize their learning and performance when there is an environment or culture—most often set by the manager—that promotes both psychological safety and accountability.

To help maintain and sustain a more stable and grounded presence, be sure that you are setting the right priorities for yourself, and that you have strategies for managing the workload of being a leader as you take on this larger role and responsibility as a new manager.

Becoming a new manager is an important leadership passage in your career. Step back and think about your leadership presence and if you are *thinking, saying, and showing up* as you most hope to and intend. Set a values-based leadership goal, increase your emotional intelligence and situational awareness, be direct with respect, and find strategies to maintain and sustain a stable and grounded presence. It's easy in our humbleness to underestimate the impact we have on other's lives as managers.

As professor Clayton Christensen writes in his classic HBR article, "How Will You Measure Your Life?":

In my mind's eye I saw one of my managers leave for work one morning with a relatively strong level of self-esteem. Then, I pictured her driving home to her family 10 hours later, feeling unappreciated, frustrated, underutilized, and demeaned. I imagined how profoundly her lowered self-esteem affected the way she interacted with her children. The vision in my mind then fast-forwarded to another day, when she drove home with greater self-esteem—feeling that she had learned a lot, had been recognized for achieving valuable things, and had played a significant role in the success of some important initiatives. I then imagined how positively that affected her as a spouse and a parent. My conclusion: Management is the most noble of professions if it's practiced well. No other occupation offers as many ways to help others learn and grow, take responsibility, be recognized for achievement, and contribute to the success of a team.

AMY JEN SU is a cofounder and managing partner of Paravis Partners, an executive coaching and leadership development firm. She is the author of the forthcoming book, *The Leader You Want to Be: Five Essential Principles for Bringing Out Your Best Self—Every Day,* and coauthor, with Muriel Maignan Wilkins, of *Own the Room: Discover Your Signature Voice to Master Your Leadership Presence.* Follow Amy on Twitter @amyjensu.

Reprinted from hbr.org, originally published
August 8, 2017 (product #H03S6X).

3

To Sound Like a Leader, Think About What You Say, and How and When You Say It

By Rebecca Shambaugh

Nancy started her day feeling prepared to brief her executive team on a high-stakes project she had been working on for the past two months. She had rehearsed her slide deck repeatedly, to the point where she had every level of content practically memorized. She arrived at the meeting early and waited patiently, yet anxiously, for her part of the agenda. The meeting began, and within a few minutes Jack, one of the cochairs, asked her to brief the executives on her project and recommendations.

Nancy enthusiastically launched into her presentation, hitting every talking point that she had meticulously rehearsed. With a solid command of the material, she felt at the top of her game and was relieved that she'd spent so much time practicing and preparing for this meeting. But just as she was about to move into her recommendations, Jack interrupted and said, "Nancy, I appreciate your hard work on this project, but it is not relevant to our agenda, and it doesn't have merit for the business objectives we're covering today." Mortified, Nancy retreated to her chair and sat in silence for the rest of the meeting. She couldn't wait to bolt from the room the moment the meeting ended to reflect on how this moment—which she expected would be a positive turning point in her career—had turned into a disaster.

What just happened here? While Nancy was prepared to participate in the meeting, she had failed to think strategically. This common problem trips up many capable managers, executives, and leaders when determining their role in communications, meetings, and other forums. Learning how to develop and convey a more strategic executive voice—in part by understanding context—can help leaders avoid finding themselves, as Nancy did, in a potentially career-damaging situation.

Whether you are an associate manager or a senior executive, what you say, how you say it, when you say it, to whom you say it, and whether you say it in the proper context are critical components for tapping into your full strategic leadership potential. If you want to establish credibility and influence people, particularly when interacting with other executives or senior leadership, it's important to be concise and let individuals know clearly what role you want them to play in the conversation. It's also important to demystify the content of any message you deliver by avoiding jargon and being a person of few—but effective—words.

All of these factors relate to developing a strategic executive voice. Your executive voice is less about your performance; it relates more to your strategic instincts, understanding of context, and awareness of the signals you send in your daily interactions and communications. Like its sister attribute, executive presence, executive voice can seem somewhat intangible and thus difficult to define. But the fact is, we all have a preferred way to communicate with others, and doing this with strategic intent and a solid grasp of context can mean the difference between success and failure in your communication and leadership style.

One of the most important aspects of having an executive voice relates to being a strategic leader. I frequently hear from top executives that they would like to promote one of their high-potential leaders but feel the person is not strategic enough to advance. When I hear managers say this, I try to gently push back and suggest that maybe the problem isn't the candidate's lack of strategic leadership potential; perhaps they are failing to tap into their abilities as a strategic leader.

Whether you have someone on your team who you think lacks strategic readiness or you're worried that *you* might be a leader with untapped strategic potential due to an undeveloped executive voice, read on. Below are some coaching strategies that I use frequently with both male and female executives to help them add a more strategic executive voice to their leadership tool kit.

Understand the context. How often do you find yourself throwing out an unformed idea in a meeting, not speaking up when people are looking for your ideas, or saying something that doesn't quite fit the agenda and suddenly getting that "deer in the headlights" feeling? If these situations sound familiar, what is it that went wrong? In short, these types of tactical errors come down to failing to understand the context of the call, meeting, or discussion that you are in.

For example, if you are the primary authority on a topic, then it's likely that the context would require you to lead the meeting and make any final decisions. But if you are one of several executives who might have input, then sharing your view and connecting the dots with others (rather than stealing the spotlight with your great ideas) would be your role. If you are in learning mode and are not asked to present at a meeting, then your role when it comes to communication would be to observe and listen. Knowing or finding out in advance what your expected role is in a group forum or event can guide you in determining the kind of voice you need for that particular venue and can help ensure that you understand the context before you speak up.

Be a visionary. Sometimes we fail to tap into an executive voice because we focus too much on our own function or role. Strategic leaders are more visionary than that, taking an enterprise view that focuses less on themselves and more on the wider organization. Another part of being visionary is developing the ability to articulate aspirations for the future and a rationale for transformation.

This type of executive vision helps guide decisions around individual and corporate action. You should work toward connecting the dots with your recommendations to show how your decisions affect others around the table, including your staff and the organization as a whole.

Cultivate strategic relationships. One of the best ways to build your strategic thinking is by leveraging relationships more intentionally, with specific business goals in mind. This calls for having senior leaders and executives who bring a strategic perspective of the organization's goals, changes, and top priorities that we may normally not have access to. When you cultivate and invest in broad strategic relationships, it helps you avoid getting caught up in day-to-day minutiae.

It's easy to lose sight of the significance of cultivating new and diverse relationships when you already have a full plate, but part of being able to access a strong executive voice is expanding your knowledge beyond your specific position, department, or area of expertise. To develop your executive voice, take time to reach out to at least one person each week outside of your immediate team or functional area. Try to learn:

- How they fit into the business as a whole

- Their goals and challenges

- Ways you might support them as a strategic business partner

Bring solutions, not just problems. While coaching a wide range of executives, I've seen firsthand that most feel frustrated when people point out challenges but don't offer any resolutions. Leading strategically with a strong executive voice involves problem solving, not just finger-pointing at difficult issues.

You can show up more strategically by doing your homework and taking the lead in analyzing situations. Brainstorm fresh ideas that go beyond the obvious. Even if you don't have the perfect answer, you can demonstrate your ability to come up with clever solutions.

Stay calm in the pressure cooker. People with an effective executive voice aren't easily rattled. Can you provide levelheaded leadership even when—in fact, particularly when—everyone around you is losing their composure? When you can stick with facts instead of getting swept into an emotional tailspin no matter how stressed you feel, you'll be able to lead with a more powerful executive voice.

It can be uncomfortable to recognize and admit personal challenges regarding your executive voice, and at first you may get pushback when making suggestions to improve the executive voice of those on your team. But once you overcome this initial resistance, whether in yourself or others, you'll find it's worth the up-front effort to investigate how to contribute most effectively to important meetings and other communications. By making the necessary adjustments to your approach to participation, you can avoid flying blind and start showing up more strategically in every setting.

REBECCA SHAMBAUGH is an internationally recognized leadership expert, author, and keynote speaker. She's president of SHAMBAUGH, a global leadership development organization, and founder of Women in Leadership and Learning (WILL).

Reprinted from hbr.org, originally published
October 31, 2017 (product #H03ZDX).

4

Connect, Then Lead

By Amy J. C. Cuddy, Matthew Kohut,
and John Neffinger

s it better to be loved or feared?

Niccolò Machiavelli pondered that timeless conundrum 500 years ago and hedged his bets. "It
may be answered that one should wish to be both,"
he acknowledged, "but because it is difficult to unite
them in one person, it is much safer to be feared than
loved."

Now behavioral science is weighing in with research showing that Machiavelli had it partly right.
When we judge others—especially our leaders—we
look first at two characteristics: how lovable they
are (their warmth, communion, or trustworthiness)
and how fearsome they are (their strength, agency,

or competence). Although there is some disagreement about the proper labels for the traits, researchers agree that they are the two primary dimensions of social judgment.

Why are these traits so important? Because they answer two critical questions: "What are this person's intentions toward me?" and "Is he or she capable of acting on those intentions?" Together, these assessments underlie our emotional and behavioral reactions to other people, groups, and even brands and companies.[1] Research by one of us, Amy Cuddy, and colleagues Susan Fiske of Princeton and Peter Glick of Lawrence University, shows that people judged to be competent but lacking in warmth often elicit envy in others, an emotion involving both respect and resentment that cuts both ways. When we respect someone, we want to cooperate or affiliate ourselves with him or her, but resentment can make that person vulnerable to harsh reprisal (think of disgraced Tyco CEO Dennis Kozlowski, whose extravagance made him an unsympathetic public figure). On the other hand, people judged as warm but incompetent tend to elicit pity, which also involves a mix of emotions: Compassion moves us to help those we pity, but our lack of respect leads us ultimately to neglect them (think of workers who become marginalized as they near retirement or of an employee with outmoded skills in a rapidly evolving industry).

To be sure, we notice plenty of other traits in people, but they're nowhere near as influential as warmth and strength. Indeed, insights from the field of psychology show that these two dimensions account for more than 90% of the variance in our positive or negative impressions we form of the people around us.

So which is better, being lovable or being strong? Most leaders today tend to emphasize their strength, competence, and credentials in the workplace, but that is exactly the wrong approach. Leaders who project strength before establishing trust run the risk of eliciting fear, and along with it, a host of dysfunctional behaviors. Fear can undermine cognitive potential, creativity, and problem solving, and cause employees to get stuck and even disengage. It's a "hot" emotion, with long-lasting effects. It burns into our memory in a way that cooler emotions don't. Research by Jack Zenger and Joseph Folkman drives this point home: In a study of 51,836 leaders, only 27 of them were rated in the bottom quartile in terms of likability and in the top quartile in terms of overall leadership effectiveness—in other words, the chances that a manager who is strongly disliked will be considered a good leader are only about one in 2,000.

A growing body of research suggests that the way to influence—and to lead—is to begin with warmth. Warmth is the conduit of influence: It facilitates trust and the communication and absorption of ideas. Even a few small nonverbal signals—a nod, a smile, an open gesture—can show people that you're pleased to be in their company and attentive to their concerns. Prioritizing warmth helps you connect immediately with those around you, demonstrating that

you hear them, understand them, and can be trusted
by them.

When strength comes first

Most of us work hard to demonstrate our competence. We want to see ourselves as strong—and want
others to see us the same way. We focus on warding
off challenges to our strength and providing abundant evidence of competence. We feel compelled to
demonstrate that we're up to the job, by striving to
present the most innovative ideas in meetings, being
the first to tackle a challenge, and working the longest hours. We're sure of our own intentions and thus
don't feel the need to prove that we're trustworthy,
despite the fact that evidence of trustworthiness is
the first thing we look for in others.

Organizational psychologists Andrea Abele of the
University of Erlangen-Nuremberg and Bogdan Woj-
ciszke of the University of Gdańsk have documented

this phenomenon across a variety of settings. In one experiment, when asked to choose between training programs focusing on competence-related skills (such as time management) and warmth-related ones (providing social support, for instance), most participants opted for competence-based training for themselves but soft-skills training for others. In another experiment, in which participants were asked to describe an event that shaped their self-image, most told stories about themselves that emphasized their own competence and self-determination ("I passed my pilot's license test on the first try"), whereas when they described a similar event for someone else, they focused on that person's warmth and generosity ("My friend tutored his neighbor's child in math and refused to accept any payment").

But putting competence first undermines leadership: Without a foundation of trust, people in the organization may comply outwardly with a leader's wishes, but they're much less likely to conform privately—to adopt the values, culture, and mission of the organization in a sincere, lasting way. Workplaces lacking in trust often have a culture of "every employee for himself," in which people feel that they must be vigilant about protecting their interests. Employees can become reluctant to help others because they're unsure of whether their efforts will be reciprocated or recognized. The result: Shared organizational resources fall victim to the tragedy of the commons.

When warmth comes first

Although most of us strive to demonstrate our strength, warmth contributes significantly more to others' evaluations of us, and it's judged before competence. Princeton social psychologist Alex Todorov and colleagues study the cognitive and neural mechanisms that drive our "spontaneous trait inferences"—

the snap judgments we make when briefly looking at faces. Their research shows that when making those judgments, people consistently pick up on warmth faster than on competence. This preference for warmth holds true in other areas as well. In a study led by Oscar Ybarra of the University of Michigan, participants playing a word game identified warmth-related words (such as "friendly") significantly faster than competence-related ones (such as "skillful").

Behavioral economists, for their part, have shown that judgments of trustworthiness generally lead to significantly higher economic gains. For example, Mascha van 't Wout of Brown University and Alan Sanfey of the University of Arizona asked subjects to determine how an endowment should be allocated. Players invested more money, with no guarantee of return, in partners whom they perceived to be more trustworthy on the basis of a glance at their faces.[2]

In management settings, trust increases information sharing, openness, fluidity, and cooperation. If coworkers can be trusted to do the right thing and live up to their commitments, planning, coordination, and execution are much easier. Trust also facilitates the exchange and acceptance of ideas—it allows people to hear others' messages—and boosts the quantity and quality of the ideas that are produced within an organization. Most important, trust provides the opportunity to change people's attitudes and beliefs, not just their outward behavior. That's the sweet spot when it comes to influence and the ability to get people to fully accept your message.

The happy warrior

The best way to gain influence is to combine warmth and strength—as difficult as Machiavelli says that may be to do. The traits can actually be mutually reinforcing: Feeling a sense of personal strength

HOW WILL PEOPLE REACT TO YOUR STYLE?

Research by Amy Cuddy, Susan Fiske, and Peter Glick suggests that the way others perceive your levels of warmth and competence determines the emotions you'll elicit and your ability to influence a situation. For example, if you're highly competent but show only moderate warmth, you'll get people to go along with you, but you won't earn their true engagement and support. And if you show no warmth, beware of those who may try to derail your efforts—and maybe your career.

helps us to be more open, less threatened, and less threatening in stressful situations. When we feel confident and calm, we project authenticity and warmth.

Understanding a little bit about our chemical makeup can shed some light on how this works. The

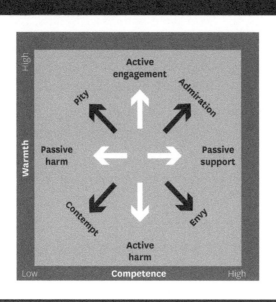

neuropeptides oxytocin and arginine vasopressin, for instance, have been linked to our ability to form human attachments, to feel and express warmth, and to behave altruistically. Recent research also suggests that, across the animal kingdom, feelings of strength and power have close ties to two hormones: testosterone (associated with assertiveness, reduced fear, and willingness to compete and take risks) and cortisol (associated with stress and stress reactivity).

One study, by Jennifer Lerner, Gary Sherman, Amy Cuddy, and colleagues, brought hundreds of people participating in Harvard executive-education programs into the lab and compared their levels of cortisol with the average levels of the general population. The leaders reported less stress and anxiety than did the general population, and their physiology backed that up: Their cortisol levels were significantly lower. Moreover, the higher their rank and the more subordinates they managed, the lower their cortisol levels. Why? Most likely because the leaders had a heightened sense of control—a psychological factor known to have a powerful stress-buffering effect. According to research by Pranjal Mehta of the University of Oregon and Robert Josephs of the University of Texas, the most effective leaders, regardless of gender, have a unique physiological profile, with relatively high testosterone and relatively low cortisol.

Such leaders face troubles without being troubled. Their behavior is not relaxed, but they are relaxed emotionally. They're often viewed as "happy warriors," and the effect of their demeanor on those around them is compelling. Happy warriors reassure us that whatever challenges we may face, things will work out in the end. Ann Richards, the former governor of Texas, played the happy warrior by pairing her assertiveness and authority with a big smile and a quick wit that made it clear she did not let the rough-and-tumble world of politics get her down.

During crises, these are the people who are able to keep that influence conduit open and may even expand it. Most people hate uncertainty, but they tolerate it much better when they can look to a leader who they believe has their back and is calm, clearheaded, and courageous. These are the people we trust. These are the people we listen to.

There are physical exercises that can help to summon self-confidence—and even alter your body's chemistry to be more like that of a happy warrior. Dana Carney, Amy Cuddy, and Andy Yap suggest that people adopt "power poses" associated with dominance and strength across the animal kingdom. These postures are open, expansive, and space-occupying (imagine Wonder Woman and Superman standing tall with their hands on their hips and feet spread apart). By adopting these postures for just two minutes before social encounters, their research shows, participants significantly increased their testosterone and decreased their cortisol levels.

Bear in mind that the signals we send can be ambiguous—we can see someone's reaction to our presence, but we may not be sure exactly what the person is reacting to. We may feel a leader's warmth but remain unsure whether it is directed at us; we sense her strength but need reassurance that it is squarely aimed at the shared challenge we face. And, as we noted earlier, judgments are often made quickly, on the basis of nonverbal cues. Especially when facing a high-pressure situation, it is useful for leaders to go through a brief warm-up routine beforehand to get in the right state of mind, practicing and adopting an attitude that will help them project positive nonverbal signals. We refer to this approach as "inside out," in contrast to the "outside-in" strategy of trying to consciously execute specific nonverbal behaviors in the moment. Think of the difference between method acting and classical acting: In method acting, the actor experiences the emotions of the character and naturally produces an authentic performance, whereas in classical acting, actors learn to exercise precise control of their nonverbal signals. Generally speaking, an inside-out approach is more effective.

There are many tactics for projecting warmth and competence, and these can be dialed up or down as needed. Two of us, John Neffinger and Matt Kohut, work with leaders from many walks of life in mastering both nonverbal and verbal cues. Let's look now at some best practices.

WHY WARMTH TRUMPS STRENGTH

The primacy of warmth manifests in many interrelated ways that powerfully underscore the importance of connecting with people before trying to lead them.

The Need to Affiliate

People have a need to be included, to feel a sense of belonging. In fact, some psychologists would argue that the drive to affiliate ranks among our primary needs as humans. Experiments by neuroscientist Naomi Eisenberger and colleagues suggest that the need is so strong that when we are ostracized—even by virtual strangers—we experience pain that is akin to strong physical pain.

"Us" Versus "Them"

In recent decades, few areas have received as much attention from social psychology researchers as group dynamics, and for good reason: The preference for the groups to which one belongs is so strong that even under extreme conditions—such as knowing that membership in a group was randomly assigned and that the groups themselves are arbitrary—people consistently prefer fellow group members to nonmembers. As a leader, you must make sure you're a part of the key groups in your organization. In fact, you want to be the aspirational member of the group, the chosen representative of the group. As soon as you become one of "them"—the management, the leadership—you begin to lose people.

(Continued)

WHY WARMTH TRUMPS STRENGTH

The Desire to Be Understood

People deeply desire to be heard and seen. Sadly, as important as perspective taking is to good leadership, being in a position of power decreases people's understanding of others' points of view. When we have power over others, our ability to see them as individuals diminishes. So leaders need to consciously and consistently make the effort to imagine walking in the shoes of the people they are leading.

How to project warmth

Efforts to appear warm and trustworthy by consciously controlling your nonverbal signals can backfire: All too often, you'll come off as wooden and inauthentic instead. Here are ways to avoid that trap.

Find the right level

When people want to project warmth, they sometimes amp up the enthusiasm in their voice, increasing their volume and dynamic range to convey
delight. That can be effective in the right setting,
but if those around you have done nothing in particular to earn your adulation, they'll assume either
that you're faking it or that you fawn over everyone
indiscriminately.

A better way to create vocal warmth is to speak
with lower pitch and volume, as you would if you
were comforting a friend. Aim for a tone that suggests that you're leveling with people—that you're
sharing the straight scoop, with no pretense or emotional adornment. In doing so, you signal that you
trust those you're talking with to handle things the
right way. You might even occasionally share a personal story—one that feels private but not inappropriate—in a confiding tone of voice to demonstrate

that you're being forthcoming and open. Suppose, for instance, that you want to establish a bond with new employees you're meeting for the first time. You might offer something personal right off the bat, such as recalling how you felt at a similar point in your career. That's often enough to set a congenial tone.

Validate feelings

Before people decide what they think of your message, they decide what they think of *you*. If you show your employees that you hold roughly the same worldview they do, you demonstrate not only empathy but, in their eyes, common sense—the ultimate qualification for being listened to. So if you want colleagues to listen and agree with you, first agree with them.

Imagine, for instance, that your company is undergoing a major reorganization and your group is feeling deep anxiety over what the change could mean—for quality, innovation, job security. Acknowledge people's fear and concerns when you speak to them, whether in formal meetings or during watercooler chats. Look them in the eye and say, "I know everybody's feeling a lot of uncertainty right now, and it's unsettling." People will respect you for addressing the elephant in the room, and will be more open to hearing what you have to say.

ARE YOU PROJECTING WARMTH?

How you present yourself in workplace settings matters a great deal to how you're perceived by others. Even if you're not feeling particularly warm, practicing these approaches and using them in formal and informal situations can help clear your path to influence.

(Continued)

ARE YOU PROJECTING WARMTH?

Warm

- When standing, balance your weight primarily on one hip to avoid appearing rigid or tense.
- Tilt your head slightly and keep your hands open and welcoming.

Cold

- Avoid standing with your chin pointed down.
- Don't pivot your body away from the person you're engaging with.
- Avoid closed-hand positions and cutting motions.

(Continued)

ARE YOU PROJECTING WARMTH?

Warm

- Lean inward in a nonaggressive manner to signal interest and engagement.
- Place your hands comfortably on your knees or rest them on the table.
- Aim for body language that feels professional but relaxed.

Cold

- Try not to angle your body away from the person you're engaging.
- Crossing your arms indicates coldness and a lack of receptivity.
- Avoid sitting "at attention" or in an aggressive posture.

Illustration: Colin Hayes

Smile—and mean it

When we smile sincerely, the warmth becomes self-reinforcing: Feeling happy makes us smile, and smiling makes us happy. This facial feedback is also contagious. We tend to mirror one another's nonverbal expressions and emotions, so when we see someone beaming and emanating genuine warmth, we can't resist smiling ourselves.

Warmth is not easy to fake, of course, and a polite smile fools no one. To project warmth, you have to genuinely feel it. A natural smile, for instance, involves not only the muscles around the mouth but also those around the eyes—the crow's feet.

So how do you produce a natural smile? Find some reason to feel happy wherever you may be, even if you have to resort to laughing at your predicament. Introverts in social settings can single out one person to focus on. This can help you channel the sense of comfort you feel with close friends or family.

For example, KNP Communications worked with a manager who was having trouble connecting with her employees. Having come up through the ranks as a highly analytic engineer, she projected competence and determination, but not much warmth. We noticed, however, that when she talked about where she grew up and what she learned about life from the tight-knit community in her neighborhood, her demeanor relaxed and she smiled broadly. By including a brief anecdote about her upbringing when she kicked off a meeting or made a presentation, she was able to show her colleagues a warm and relatable side of herself.

One thing to avoid: smiling with your eyebrows raised at anyone over the age of five. This suggests that you are overly eager to please and be liked. It also signals anxiety, which, like warmth, is contagious. It will cost you much more in strength than you will gain in warmth.

How to project strength

Strength or competence can be established by virtue of the position you hold, your reputation, and your actual performance. But your presence, or demeanor, always counts, too. The way you carry yourself doesn't establish your skill level, of course, but it is taken as strong evidence of your attitude—how serious you are and how determined to tackle a challenge—and that is an important component of overall strength. The trick is to cultivate a demeanor of strength without seeming menacing.

Feel in command

Warmth may be harder to fake, but confidence is harder to talk yourself into. Feeling like an impostor—that you don't belong in the position you're in and are going to be "found out"—is very common. But self-doubt completely undermines your ability to project confidence, enthusiasm, and passion, the qualities that make up presence. In fact, if you see yourself as an impostor, others will, too. Feeling in command and confident is about connecting with yourself. And when we are connected with ourselves, it is much easier to connect with others.

Holding your body in certain ways, as we discussed previously, can help. Although we refer to these postures as power poses, they don't increase your dominance over others. They're about personal power—your agency and ability to self-regulate. Recent research led by Dacher Keltner of the University of California, Berkeley, shows that feeling powerful in this way allows you to shed the fears and inhibitions that can prevent you from bringing your fullest, most authentic and enthusiastic self to a high-stakes professional situation, such as a pitch to investors or a speech to an influential audience.

Stand up straight

It is hard to overstate the importance of good posture in projecting authority and an intention to be taken seriously. As Maya Angelou wrote, "Stand up straight and realize who you are, that you tower over your circumstances." Good posture does not mean the exaggerated chest-out pose known in the military as standing at attention, or raising one's chin up high. It just means reaching your full height, using your muscles to straighten the S-curve in your spine rather than slouching. It sounds trivial, but maximizing the physical space your body takes up makes a substantial difference in how your audience reacts to you, regardless of your height.

Get ahold of yourself

When you move, move deliberately and precisely to a specific spot rather than casting your limbs about loose-jointedly. And when you are finished moving, be still. Twitching, fidgeting, or other visual static sends the signal that you're not in control. Stillness demonstrates calm. Combine that with good posture, and you'll achieve what's known as poise, which telegraphs equilibrium and stability, important aspects of credible leadership presence.

Standing tall is an especially good way to project strength because it doesn't interfere with warmth in the way that other signals of strength—cutting gestures, a furrowed brow, an elevated chin—often do. People who instruct their children to stand up straight and smile are on to something: This simple combination is perhaps the best way to project strength and warmth simultaneously. If you want to effectively lead others, you have to get the warmth-competence dynamic right. Projecting both traits at once is difficult, but the two can be mutually reinforcing—and the rewards substantial. Earning the trust and appreciation of those around you feels good. Feeling in command of a situation does, too. Doing both lets you influence people more effectively.

The strategies we suggest may seem awkward at first, but they will soon create a positive feedback loop. Being calm and confident creates space to be warm, open, and appreciative, to choose to act in ways that reflect and express your values and priorities. Once you establish your warmth, your strength is received as a welcome reassurance. Your leadership becomes not a threat but a gift.

AMY J. C. CUDDY is a former associate professor of business administration at Harvard Business School. MATTHEW KOHUT and JOHN NEFFINGER are the authors of *Compelling People: The Hidden Qualities That Make Us Influential* (Hudson Street Press, 2013) and principals at KNP Communications.

Notes

1. A. J. C. Cuddy, P. Glick, and A. Beninger, "The Dynamics of Warmth and Competence Judgments, and Their

Outcomes in Organizations," *Research in Organizational Behavior* 31 (2011): 73–98.

2. M. van 't Wout and A. G. Sanfey, "Friend or Foe: The Effect of Implicit Trustworthiness Judgments in Social Decision-Making," *Cognition* 108, no. 3 (2008): 796–803.

Reprinted from *Harvard Business Review*,
July–August 2013 (product #R1307C).

5

The Power of Talk: Who Gets Heard and Why

By Deborah Tannen

The head of a large division of a multinational corporation was running a meeting devoted to performance assessment. Each senior manager stood up, reviewed the individuals in his group, and evaluated them for promotion. Although there were women in every group, not one of them made the cut. One after another, each manager declared, in effect, that every woman in his group didn't have the self-confidence needed to be promoted. The division head began to doubt his ears. How could it be that all the talented women in the division suffered from a lack of self-confidence?

In all likelihood, they didn't. Consider the many women who have left large corporations to start their own businesses, obviously exhibiting enough confidence to succeed on their own. Judgments about confidence can be inferred only from the way people present themselves, and much of that presentation is in the form of talk.

The CEO of a major corporation told me that he often has to make decisions in five minutes about matters on which others may have worked five months. He said he uses this rule: If the person making the proposal seems confident, the CEO approves it. If not, he says no. This might seem like a reasonable approach. But my field of research, socio-linguistics, suggests otherwise. The CEO obviously thinks he knows what a confident person sounds like. But his judgment, which may be dead right for some people, may be dead wrong for others.

Communication isn't as simple as saying what you mean. How you say what you mean is crucial, and differs from one person to the next, because using language is learned social behavior: How we talk and listen are deeply influenced by cultural experience. Although we might think that our ways of saying what we mean are natural, we can run into trouble if we interpret and evaluate others as if they necessarily felt the same way we'd feel if we spoke the way they did.

Since 1974, I have been researching the influence of linguistic style on conversations and human relationships. In the past four years, I have extended that research to the workplace, where I have observed how ways of speaking learned in childhood affect judgments of competence and confidence, as well as who gets heard, who gets credit, and what gets done.

The division head who was dumbfounded to hear that all the talented women in his organization lacked confidence was probably right to be skeptical. The senior managers were judging the women in their groups by their own linguistic norms, but

Leadership Presence

women—like people who have grown up in a different culture—have often learned different styles of speaking than men, which can make them seem less competent and self-assured than they are.

What is linguistic style?

Everything that is said must be said in a certain way—in a certain tone of voice, at a certain rate of speed, and with a certain degree of loudness. Whereas often we consciously consider what to say before speaking, we rarely think about how to say it, unless the situation is obviously loaded—for example, a job interview or a tricky performance review. Linguistic style refers to a person's characteristic speaking pattern. It includes such features as directness or indirectness, pacing and pausing, word choice, and the use of such elements as jokes, figures of speech, stories, questions, and apologies. In other words, linguistic style

76

is a set of culturally learned signals by which we not only communicate what we mean but also interpret others' meaning and evaluate one another as people.

Consider turn taking, one element of linguistic style. Conversation is an enterprise in which people take turns: One person speaks, then the other responds. However, this apparently simple exchange requires a subtle negotiation of signals so that you know when the other person is finished and it's your turn to begin. Cultural factors such as country or region of origin and ethnic background influence how long a pause seems natural. When Bob, who is from Detroit, has a conversation with his colleague Joe, from New York City, it's hard for him to get a word in edgewise because he expects a slightly longer pause between turns than Joe does. A pause of that length never comes because, before it has a chance to, Joe senses an uncomfortable silence, which he fills with more talk of his own. Both men fail to realize that differences in conversational style are getting in their way. Bob thinks that Joe is pushy and uninterested in what he has to say, and Joe thinks that Bob doesn't have much to contribute. Similarly, when Sally relocated from Texas to Washington, D.C., she kept searching for the right time to break in during staff meetings—and never found it. Although in Texas she was considered outgoing and confident, in Washington she was perceived as shy and retiring. Her boss even suggested she take an assertiveness training course. Thus, slight differences in conversational style—in these cases, a few seconds of pause—can have a surprising impact on who gets heard and on the judgments, including psychological ones, that are made about people and their abilities.

Every utterance functions on two levels. We're all familiar with the first one: Language communicates ideas. The second level is mostly invisible to us, but it plays a powerful role in communication. As a form of social behavior, language also negotiates relationships. Through ways of speaking, we signal—and create—the relative status of speakers and their level of rapport. If you say, "Sit down!" you are signaling that you have higher status than the person you are addressing, that you are so close to each other that you can drop all pleasantries, or that you are angry. If you say, "I would be honored if you would sit down," you are signaling great respect—or great sarcasm, depending on your tone of voice, the situation, and what you both know about how close you really are. If you say, "You must be so tired. Why don't you sit down," you are communicating either closeness and concern or condescension. Each of these ways of saying "the same thing"—telling someone to sit down—can have a vastly different meaning.

In every community known to linguists, the patterns that constitute linguistic style are relatively different for men and women. What's "natural" for most men speaking a given language is, in some cases, different from what's "natural" for most women. That is because we learn ways of speaking as children growing up, especially from peers, and children tend to play with other children of the same sex. The research of sociologists, anthropologists, and psychologists observing American children at play has shown that, although both girls and boys find ways of creating rapport and negotiating status, girls tend to learn conversational rituals that focus on the rapport dimension of relationships whereas boys tend to learn rituals that focus on the status dimension.

Girls tend to play with a single best friend or in small groups, and they spend a lot of time talking. They use language to negotiate how close they are; for example, the girl you tell your secrets to becomes your best friend. Girls learn to downplay ways in which one is better than the others and to emphasize ways in which they are all the same. From childhood, most girls learn that sounding too sure of themselves will make them unpopular with their peers—although nobody really takes such modesty literally. A group of girls will ostracize a girl who calls attention to her own superiority and criticize her by saying, "She thinks she's something"; and a girl who tells others what to do is called "bossy." Thus, girls learn to talk in ways that balance their own needs with those of others—to save face for one another in the broadest sense of the term.

Boys tend to play very differently. They usually play in larger groups in which more boys can be included, but not everyone is treated as an equal. Boys with high status in their group are expected to emphasize rather than downplay their status, and usually one or several boys will be seen as the leader or leaders. Boys generally don't accuse one another of being bossy, because the leader is expected to tell lower-status boys what to do. Boys learn to use language to negotiate their status in the group by displaying their abilities and knowledge, and by challenging others and resisting challenges. Giving orders is one way of getting and keeping the high-status role. Another is taking center stage by telling stories or jokes.

This is not to say that all boys and girls grow up this way or feel comfortable in these groups or are equally successful at negotiating within these norms. But, for the most part, these childhood play groups are where boys and girls learn their conversational styles. In this sense, they grow up in different worlds. The result is that women and men tend to have different habitual ways of saying what they mean, and conversations between them can be like cross-cultural communication: You can't assume that the other person means what you would mean if you said the same thing in the same way.

My research in companies across the United States shows that the lessons learned in childhood carry over into the workplace. Consider the following example: A focus group was organized at a major multinational company to evaluate a recently implemented flextime policy. The participants sat in a circle and discussed the new system. The group concluded that it was excellent, but they also agreed on ways to improve it. The meeting went well and was deemed a success by all, according to my own observations and everyone's comments to me. But the next day, I was in for a surprise.

I had left the meeting with the impression that Phil had been responsible for most of the suggestions adopted by the group. But as I typed up my notes, I noticed that Cheryl had made almost all those suggestions. I had thought that the key ideas came from Phil because he had picked up Cheryl's points and supported them, speaking at greater length in doing so than she had in raising them.

It would be easy to regard Phil as having stolen Cheryl's ideas—and her thunder. But that would be inaccurate. Phil never claimed Cheryl's ideas as his own. Cheryl herself told me later that she left the meeting confident she had contributed significantly, and that she appreciated Phil's support. She volunteered, with a laugh, "It was not one of those times when a woman says something and it's ignored, then a man says it and it's picked up." In other words, Cheryl and Phil worked well as a team, the group fulfilled its charge, and the company got what it needed. So what was the problem?

I went back and asked all the participants who they thought had been the most influential group member, the one most responsible for the ideas that had been adopted. The pattern of answers was revealing. The two other women in the group named Cheryl. Two of the three men named Phil. Of the men, only Phil named Cheryl. In other words, in this instance, the women evaluated the contribution of another woman more accurately than the men did.

Meetings like this take place daily in companies around the country. Unless managers are unusually good at listening closely to how people say what they mean, the talents of someone like Cheryl may well be undervalued and underutilized.

One up, one down

Individual speakers vary in how sensitive they are to the social dynamics of language—in other words, to the subtle nuances of what others say to them. Men tend to be sensitive to the power dynamics of interaction, speaking in ways that position themselves as one up and resisting being put in a one-down position by others. Women tend to react more strongly to the rapport dynamic, speaking in ways that save face for others and buffering statements that could be seen as putting others in a one-down position. These linguistic patterns are pervasive; you can hear them in hundreds of exchanges in the workplace every day. And, as in the case of Cheryl and Phil, they affect who gets heard and who gets credit.

Getting credit

Even so small a linguistic strategy as the choice of pronoun can affect who gets credit. In my research in the workplace, I heard men say "I" in situations where I heard women say "we." For example, one publishing company executive said, "I'm hiring a new manager. I'm going to put him in charge of my marketing division," as if he owned the corporation. In stark contrast, I recorded women saying "we" when referring to work they alone had done. One woman explained that it would sound too self-promoting to claim credit in an obvious way by saying, "I did this." Yet she expected—sometimes vainly—that others would know it was her work and would give her the credit she did not claim for herself.

Managers might leap to the conclusion that women who do not take credit for what they've done should be taught to do so. But that solution is problematic because we associate ways of speaking with moral qualities: The way we speak is who we are and who we want to be.

Veronica, a senior researcher in a high-tech company, had an observant boss. He noticed that many of the ideas coming out of the group were hers but that often someone else trumpeted them around the office and got credit for them. He advised her to "own" her ideas and make sure she got the credit. But Veronica found she simply didn't enjoy her work if she had to approach it as what seemed to her an unattractive and unappealing "grabbing game." It was her dislike of such behavior that had led her to avoid it in the first place.

Whatever the motivation, women are less likely than men to have learned to blow their own horn. And they are more likely than men to believe that if they do so, they won't be liked.

Many have argued that the growing trend of assigning work to teams may be especially congenial to women, but it may also create complications for performance evaluation. When ideas are generated and work is accomplished in the privacy of the team, the outcome of the team's effort may become associated with the person most vocal about reporting results. There are many women and men—but probably relatively more women—who are reluctant to put themselves forward in this way and who consequently risk not getting credit for their contributions.

Confidence and boasting

The CEO who based his decisions on the confidence level of speakers was articulating a value that is widely shared in U.S. businesses: One way to judge confidence is by an individual's behavior, especially verbal behavior. Here again, many women are at a disadvantage.

Studies show that women are more likely to downplay their certainty and men are more likely to minimize their doubts. Psychologist Laurie Heatherington and her colleagues devised an ingenious experiment, which they reported in the journal *Sex Roles*.[1] They asked hundreds of incoming college students to predict what grades they would get in their first year.

Some subjects were asked to make their predictions privately by writing them down and placing them in an envelope; others were asked to make their predictions publicly, in the presence of a researcher. The results showed that more women than men predicted lower grades for themselves if they made their predictions publicly. If they made their predictions privately, the predictions were the same as those of the men—and the same as their actual grades. This study provides evidence that what comes across as lack of confidence—predicting lower grades for oneself—may reflect not one's actual level of confidence but the desire not to seem boastful.

These habits with regard to appearing humble or confident result from the socialization of boys and girls by their peers in childhood play. As adults, both women and men find these behaviors reinforced by the positive responses they get from friends and relatives who share the same norms. But the norms of behavior in the U.S. business world are based on the style of interaction that is more common among men—at least, among American men.

Asking questions

Although asking the right questions is one of the hallmarks of a good manager, how and when questions are asked can send unintended signals about competence and power. In a group, if only one person asks questions, he or she risks being seen as the only ignorant one. Furthermore, we judge others not only by how they speak but also by how they are spoken to. The person who asks questions may end up being lectured to and looking like a novice under a schoolmaster's tutelage. The way boys are socialized makes them more likely to be aware of the underlying power dynamic by which a question asker can be seen in a one-down position.

One practicing physician learned the hard way that any exchange of information can become the basis for judgments—or misjudgments—about competence. During her training, she received a negative evaluation that she thought was unfair, so she asked her supervising physician for an explanation. He said that she knew less than her peers. Amazed at his answer, she asked how he had reached that conclusion. He said, "You ask more questions."

Along with cultural influences and individual personality, gender seems to play a role in whether and when people ask questions. For example, of all the observations I've made in lectures and books, the one that sparks the most enthusiastic flash of recognition is that men are less likely than women to stop and ask for directions when they are lost. I explain that men often resist asking for directions because they are aware that it puts them in a one-down position and because they value the independence that comes with finding their way by themselves. Asking for directions while driving is only one instance—along with many others that researchers have examined—

in which men seem less likely than women to ask questions. I believe this is because they are more attuned than women to the potential face-losing aspect of asking questions. And men who believe that asking questions might reflect negatively on them may, in turn, be likely to form a negative opinion of others who ask questions in situations where they would not.

Conversational rituals

Conversation is fundamentally ritual in the sense that we speak in ways our culture has conventionalized and expect certain types of responses. Take greetings, for example. I have heard visitors to the United States complain that Americans are hypocritical because they ask how you are but aren't interested in the answer. To Americans, "How are you?" is obviously a ritualized way to start a conversation rather than a literal request for information. In other parts of the world, including the Philippines, people ask each other, "Where are you going?" when they meet. The question seems intrusive to Americans, who do not realize that it, too, is a ritual query to which the only expected reply is a vague "Over there."

It's easy and entertaining to observe different rituals in foreign countries. But we don't expect differences, and are far less likely to recognize the ritualized nature of our conversations, when we are with our compatriots at work. Our differing rituals can be even more problematic when we think we're all speaking the same language.

Apologies

Consider the simple phrase *I'm sorry.*

Catherine: How did that big presentation go?

Bob: Oh, not very well. I got a lot of flak from the VP for finance, and I didn't have the numbers at my fingertips.

Catherine: Oh, I'm sorry. I know how hard you worked on that.

In this case, *I'm sorry* probably means "I'm sorry that happened," not "I apologize," unless it was Catherine's responsibility to supply Bob with the numbers for the presentation. Women tend to say *I'm sorry* more frequently than men—and often they intend it in this way—as a ritualized means of expressing concern. It's one of many learned elements of conversational style that girls often use to establish rapport. Ritual apologies—like other conversational rituals—work well when both parties share the same assumptions about their use. But people who utter frequent ritual apologies may end up appearing weaker, less confident, and literally more blameworthy than people who don't.

Apologies tend to be regarded differently by men, who are more likely to focus on the status implications of exchanges. Many men avoid apologies because they see them as putting the speaker in a one-down position. I observed with some amazement an encounter among several lawyers engaged in a negotiation over a speakerphone. At one point, the lawyer in whose office I was sitting accidentally elbowed the telephone and cut off the call. When his secretary got the parties back on again, I expected him to say what I would have said: "Sorry about that. I knocked the phone with my elbow." Instead, he said, "Hey, what happened? One minute you were there; the next minute you were gone!" This lawyer seemed to have an automatic impulse not to admit fault if he didn't have to. For me, it was one of those pivotal moments when you realize that the world you live in is not the one everyone lives in and that the way you assume is the way to talk is really only one of many.

Those who caution managers not to undermine their authority by apologizing are approaching interaction from the perspective of the power dynamic. In many cases, this strategy is effective. On the other hand, when I asked people what frustrated them in their jobs, one frequently voiced complaint was working with or for someone who refuses to apologize or admit fault. In other words, accepting responsibility for errors and admitting mistakes may be an equally effective or superior strategy in some settings.

Feedback

Styles of giving feedback contain a ritual element that often is the cause for misunderstanding. Consider the following exchange: A manager had to tell her marketing director to rewrite a report. She began this potentially awkward task by citing the report's strengths and then moved to the main point: the weaknesses that needed to be remedied. The marketing director seemed to understand and accept his supervisor's comments, but his revision contained only minor changes and failed to address the major weaknesses. When the manager told him of her dissatisfaction, he accused her of misleading him: "You told me it was fine."

The impasse resulted from different linguistic styles. To the manager, it was natural to buffer the criticism by beginning with praise. Telling her subordinate that his report is inadequate and has to be rewritten puts him in a one-down position. Praising him for the parts that are good is a ritualized way of saving face for him. But the marketing director did not share his supervisor's assumption about how feedback should be given. Instead, he assumed that what she mentioned first was the main point and that what she brought up later was an afterthought.

Those who expect feedback to come in the way the manager presented it would appreciate her tact and would regard a more blunt approach as unnecessarily callous. But those who share the marketing director's assumptions would regard the blunt approach as honest and no-nonsense, and the manager's as obfuscating. Because each one's assumptions seemed self-evident, each blamed the other: The manager thought the marketing director was not listening, and he thought she had not communicated clearly or had changed her mind. This is significant because it illustrates that incidents labeled vaguely as "poor communication" may be the result of differing linguistic styles.

Compliments

Exchanging compliments is a common ritual, especially among women. A mismatch in expectations about this ritual left Susan, a manager in the human resources field, in a one-down position. She and her colleague Bill had both given presentations at a national conference. On the airplane home, Susan told Bill, "That was a great talk!" "Thank you," he said. Then she asked, "What did you think of mine?" He responded with a lengthy and detailed critique, as she listened uncomfortably. An unpleasant feeling of having been put down came over her. Somehow she had been positioned as the novice in need of his expert advice. Even worse, she had only herself to blame, since she had, after all, asked Bill what he thought of her talk.

But had Susan asked for the response she received? When she asked Bill what he thought about her talk, she expected to hear not a critique but a compliment. In fact, her question had been an attempt to repair a ritual gone awry. Susan's initial compliment to Bill was the kind of automatic recognition she felt was more or less required after a colleague gives a presentation, and she expected Bill to respond with a matching compliment. She was just talking automatically, but he either sincerely misunderstood the ritual or simply took the opportunity to bask in the one-up position of critic. Whatever his motivation, it was Susan's attempt to spark an exchange of compliments that gave him an opening.

Although this exchange could have occurred between two men, it does not seem coincidental that it happened between a man and a woman. Linguist

Janet Holmes discovered that women pay more compliments than men.[2] And, as I have observed, fewer men are likely to ask, "What did you think of my talk?" precisely because the question might invite an unwanted critique.

In the social structure of the peer groups in which they grow up, boys are indeed looking for opportunities to put others down and take the one-up position for themselves. In contrast, one of the rituals girls learn is taking the one-down position but assuming that the other person will recognize the ritual nature of the self-denigration and pull them back up.

The exchange between Susan and Bill also suggests how women's and men's characteristic styles may put women at a disadvantage in the workplace. If one person is trying to minimize status differences, maintain an appearance that everyone is equal, and save face for the other, while another person is trying to maintain the one-up position and avoid being positioned as one down, the person seeking the one-up position is likely to get it. At the same time, the person who has not been expending any effort to avoid the one-down position is likely to end up in it. Because women are more likely to take (or accept) the role of advice seeker, men are more inclined to interpret a ritual question from a woman as a request for advice.

Ritual opposition

Apologizing, mitigating criticism with praise, and exchanging compliments are rituals common among women that men often take literally. A ritual common among men that women often take literally is ritual opposition.

A woman in communications told me she watched with distaste and distress as her office mate argued heatedly with another colleague about whose division should suffer budget cuts. She was even more surprised, however, that a short time later they were as friendly as ever. "How can you pretend that fight never happened?" she asked. "Who's pretending it never happened?" he responded, as puzzled by her question as she had been by his behavior. "It happened," he said, "and it's over." What she took as literal fighting to him was a routine part of daily negotiation: a ritual fight.

Many Americans expect the discussion of ideas to be a ritual fight—that is, an exploration through verbal opposition. They present their own ideas in the most certain and absolute form they can, and wait to see if they are challenged. Being forced to defend an idea provides an opportunity to test it. In the same spirit, they may play devil's advocate in challenging their colleagues' ideas—trying to poke holes and find weaknesses—as a way of helping them explore and test their ideas.

This style can work well if everyone shares it, but those unaccustomed to it are likely to miss its ritual nature. They may give up an idea that is challenged, taking the objections as an indication that the idea was a poor one. Worse, they may take the opposition as a personal attack and may find it impossible to do their best in a contentious environment. People unaccustomed to this style may hedge when stating their ideas in order to fend off potential attacks. Ironically, this posture makes their arguments appear weak and is more likely to invite attack from pugnacious colleagues than to fend it off.

Ritual opposition can even play a role in who gets hired. Some consulting firms that recruit graduates from the top business schools use a confrontational interviewing technique. They challenge the candidate to "crack a case" in real time. A partner at one firm told me, "Women tend to do less well in this kind of interaction, and it certainly affects who gets hired. But, in fact, many women who don't 'test well' turn out to be good consultants. They're often smarter than some of the men who looked like analytic powerhouses under pressure."

The level of verbal opposition varies from one company's culture to the next, but I saw instances of it in all the organizations I studied. Anyone who is uncomfortable with this linguistic style—and that includes some men as well as many women—risks appearing insecure about his or her ideas.

Negotiating authority

In organizations, formal authority comes from the position one holds. But actual authority has to be negotiated day to day. The effectiveness of individual managers depends in part on their skill in negotiating authority and on whether others reinforce or undercut their efforts. The way linguistic style reflects status plays a subtle role in placing individuals within a hierarchy.

Managing up and down

In all the companies I researched, I heard from women who knew they were doing a superior job and knew that their coworkers (and sometimes their immediate bosses) knew it as well, but believed that the higher-ups did not. They frequently told me that something outside themselves was holding them back and found it frustrating because they thought that all that should be necessary for success was to do a great job, that superior performance should be recognized and rewarded. In contrast, men often told me that if women weren't promoted, it was because they simply weren't up to snuff. Looking around, however, I saw evidence that men more often than women behaved in ways likely to get them recognized by those with the power to determine their advancement.

In all the companies I visited, I observed what happened at lunchtime. I saw young men who regularly ate lunch with their boss, and senior men who ate with the big boss. I noticed far fewer women who sought out the highest-level person they could eat with. But one is more likely to get recognition for work done if one talks about it to those higher up, and it is easier to do so if the lines of communication are already open. Furthermore, given the opportunity for a conversation with superiors, men and women are likely to have different ways of talking about their accomplishments because of the different ways in which they were socialized as children. Boys are rewarded by their peers if they talk up their achievements, whereas girls are rewarded if they play theirs down. Linguistic styles common among men may tend to give them some advantages when it comes to managing up.

All speakers are aware of the status of the person they are talking to and adjust accordingly. Everyone speaks differently when talking to a boss than when talking to a subordinate. But, surprisingly, the ways in which they adjust their talk may be different and thus may project different images of themselves.

Communications researchers Karen Tracy and Eric Eisenberg studied how relative status affects the way people give criticism. They devised a business letter that contained some errors and asked 13 male and 11 female college students to role-play delivering criticism under two scenarios. In the first, the speaker was a boss talking to a subordinate; in the second, the speaker was a subordinate talking to his or her boss. The researchers measured how hard the speakers tried to avoid hurting the feelings of the person they were criticizing.

One might expect people to be more careful about how they deliver criticism when they are in a subordinate position. Tracy and Eisenberg found that hypothesis to be true for the men in their study but not for the women. As they reported in *Research on Language and Social Interaction*, the women showed more concern about the other person's feelings when they were playing the role of superior.[3] In other words, the women were more careful to save face for the other person when they were managing down than when they were managing up. This pattern recalls the way girls are socialized: Those who are in some way superior are expected to downplay rather than flaunt their superiority.

In my own recordings of workplace communication, I observed women talking in similar ways. For example, when a manager had to correct a mistake made by her secretary, she did so by acknowledging that there were mitigating circumstances. She said, laughing, "You know, it's hard to do things around here, isn't it, with all these people coming in!" The manager was saving face for her subordinate, just like the female students role-playing in the Tracy and Eisenberg study.

Is this an effective way to communicate? One must ask, effective for what? The manager in question established a positive environment in her group, and the work was done effectively. On the other hand, numerous women in many different fields told me that their bosses say they don't project the proper authority.

Indirectness

Another linguistic signal that varies with power and status is indirectness—the tendency to say what we mean without spelling it out in so many words. Despite the widespread belief in the United States that it's always best to say exactly what we mean, indirectness is a fundamental and pervasive element in human communication. It also is one of the elements that vary most from one culture to another, and it can cause enormous misunderstanding when speakers have different habits and expectations about how it is used. It's often said that American women are more indirect than American men, but in fact everyone tends to be indirect in some situations and in different ways. Allowing for cultural, ethnic, regional, and individual differences, women are especially likely to be indirect when it comes to telling others what to do, which is not surprising, considering girls' readiness to brand other girls as bossy. On the other hand, men are especially likely to be indirect when it comes to admitting fault or weakness, which also is not surprising, considering boys' readiness to push around boys who assume the one-down position.

At first glance, it would seem that only the powerful can get away with bald commands such as, "Have that report on my desk by noon." But power in an organization also can lead to requests so indirect that they don't sound like requests at all. A boss who says, "Do we have the sales data by product line for each region?" would be surprised and frustrated if a subordinate responded, "We probably do" rather than "I'll get it for you." Examples such as these notwithstanding, many researchers have claimed that those in subordinate positions are more likely to speak indirectly, and that is surely accurate in some situations. For example, linguist Charlotte Linde examined the black-box conversations that took place between pilots and copilots before airplane crashes.[4] In one particularly tragic instance, an Air Florida plane crashed into the Potomac River immediately after attempting takeoff from National Airport in Washington, D.C., killing all but 5 of the 74 people on board. The pilot, it turned out, had little experience flying in icy weather. The copilot had a bit more, and it became heartbreakingly clear on analysis that he had tried to warn the pilot but had done so indirectly. Alerted by Linde's observation, I examined the transcript of the conversations and found evidence of her hypothesis. The copilot repeatedly called attention to the bad weather and to ice buildup on other planes:

Copilot: Look how the ice is just hanging on his, ah, back, back there, see that? See all those icicles on the back there and everything?

Pilot: Yeah.

[The copilot also expressed concern about the long waiting time since deicing.]

Copilot: Boy, this is a, this is a losing battle here on trying to deice those things; it [gives] you a false feeling of security, that's all that does.
[Just before they took off, the copilot expressed another concern—about abnormal instrument readings—but again he didn't press the matter when it wasn't picked up by the pilot.]

Copilot: That don't seem right, does it? [3-second pause]. Ah, that's not right. Well—

Pilot: Yes it is, there's 80.

Copilot: Naw, I don't think that's right. [7-second pause] Ah, maybe it is.

Shortly thereafter, the plane took off, with tragic results. In other instances, as well as this one, Linde observed that copilots, who are second in command, are more likely to express themselves indirectly or otherwise mitigate, or soften, their communication when they are suggesting courses of action to the pilot. In an effort to avert similar disasters, some airlines now offer training for copilots to express themselves in more assertive ways.

This solution seems self-evidently appropriate to most Americans. But when I assigned Linde's article in a graduate seminar I taught, a Japanese student pointed out that it would be just as effective to train pilots to pick up on hints. This approach reflects assumptions about communication that typify Japanese culture, which places great value on the ability of people to understand one another without putting everything into words. Either directness or indirectness can be a successful means of communication as long as the linguistic style is understood by the participants.

In the world of work, however, there is more at stake than whether the communication is understood.

People in powerful positions are likely to reward styles similar to their own, because we all tend to take as self-evident the logic of our own styles. Accordingly, there is evidence that in the U.S. workplace, where instructions from a superior are expected to be voiced in a relatively direct manner, those who tend to be indirect when telling subordinates what to do may be perceived as lacking in confidence.

Consider the case of the manager at a national magazine who was responsible for giving assignments to reporters. She tended to phrase her assignments as questions. For example, she asked, "How would you like to do the X project with Y?" or said, "I was thinking of putting you on the X project. Is that okay?" This worked extremely well with her staff; they liked working for her, and the work got done in an efficient and orderly manner. But when she had her midyear evaluation with her own boss, he criticized her for not assuming the proper demeanor with her staff.

In any work environment, the higher-ranking person has the power to enforce his or her view of appropriate demeanor, created in part by linguistic style. In most U.S. contexts, that view is likely to assume that the person in authority has the right to be relatively direct rather than to mitigate orders. There also are cases, however, in which the higher-ranking person assumes a more indirect style. The owner of a retail operation told her subordinate, a store manager, to do something. He said he would do it, but a week later he still hadn't. They were able to trace the difficulty to the following conversation: She had said, "The bookkeeper needs help with the billing. How would you feel about helping her out?" He had said, "Fine." This conversation had seemed to be clear and flawless at the time, but it turned out that they had interpreted this simple exchange in very different ways. She thought he meant, "Fine, I'll help the bookkeeper out." He thought he meant, "Fine, I'll think about how I would feel about helping the bookkeeper out." He did think about it and came to the conclusion that he had more important things to do and couldn't spare the time.

To the owner, "How would you feel about helping the bookkeeper out?" was an obviously appropriate way to give the order "Help the bookkeeper out with the billing." Those who expect orders to be given as bald imperatives may find such locutions annoying or even misleading. But those for whom this style is natural do not think they are being indirect. They believe they are being clear in a polite or respectful way.

What is atypical in this example is that the person with the more indirect style was the boss, so the store manager was motivated to adapt to her style. She still gives orders the same way, but the store manager now understands how she means what she says. It's more common in U.S. business contexts for the highest-ranking people to take a more direct style, with the result that many women in authority risk being judged by their superiors as lacking the appropriate demeanor—and, consequently, lacking confidence.

What to do?

I am often asked, What is the best way to give criticism? or What is the best way to give orders?—in other words, What is the best way to communicate? The answer is that there is no one best way. The results of a given way of speaking will vary depending on the situation, the culture of the company, the relative rank of speakers, their linguistic styles, and how those styles interact with one another. Because of all those influences, any way of speaking could be perfect for communicating with one person in one situation and disastrous with someone else in another. The critical skill for managers is to become aware of the workings and power of linguistic style, to make sure that people with something valuable to contribute get heard.

It may seem, for example, that running a meeting in an unstructured way gives equal opportunity to all. But awareness of the differences in conversational style makes it easy to see the potential for unequal access. Those who are comfortable speaking up in groups, who need little or no silence before raising their hands, or who speak out easily without waiting to be recognized are far more likely to get heard at meetings. Those who refrain from talking until it's clear that the previous speaker is finished, who wait to be recognized, and who are inclined to link their comments to those of others will do fine at a meeting where everyone else is following the same rules but will have a hard time getting heard in a meeting with people whose styles are more like the first pattern. Given the socialization typical of boys and girls, men are more likely to have learned the first style and women the second, making meetings more congenial for men than for women. It's common to observe women who participate actively in one-on-one discussions or in all-female groups but who are seldom heard in meetings with a large proportion of men. On the other hand, there are women who share the style more common among men, and they run a different risk—of being seen as too aggressive.

A manager aware of those dynamics might devise any number of ways of ensuring that everyone's ideas are heard and credited. Although no single solution will fit all contexts, managers who understand the dynamics of linguistic style can develop more adaptive and flexible approaches to running or participating in meetings, mentoring or advancing the careers of others, evaluating performance, and so on. Talk is the lifeblood of managerial work, and understanding that different people have different ways of saying what they mean will make it possible to take advantage of the talents of people with a broad range of linguistic styles. As the workplace becomes more culturally diverse and business becomes more global, managers will need to become even better at reading interactions and more flexible in adjusting their own styles to the people with whom they interact.

DEBORAH TANNEN is University Professor and a professor of linguistics at Georgetown University in Washington, D.C. She is the author of 15 books, including *You Just Don't Understand: Women and Men in Conversation* (William Morrow, 1990), which introduced to the general public the idea of female and male styles of communication. The material in this article is drawn from *Talking from 9 to 5* (Avon Books, 1995).

Notes

1. L. Heatherington et al., "Two Investigations of 'Female Modesty' in Achievement Situations," *Sex Roles* 29, no. 11 (1993): 739–754.
2. J. Holmes, "Compliments and Compliment Responses in New Zealand English," *Anthropological Linguistics* 28, no. 4 (1986): 485–508.
3. K. Tracy and E. Eisenberg, "Giving Criticism: A Multiple Goals Case Study," *Research and Social Interaction* 24, no. 1 (1990/1991): 37–70.

4. C. Linde, "The Quantitative Study of Communicative
   Success: Politeness and Accidents in Aviation Discourse,"
   Language in Society 17, no. 3 (1988): 375–399.

Reprinted from *Harvard Business Review*,
September–October 1995 (product #95510).

6

Too Much Charisma Can Make Leaders Look Less Effective

By Jasmine Vergauwe, Bart Wille, Joeri Hofmans, Robert B. Kaiser, and Filip de Fruyt

onventional wisdom suggests that the most charismatic leaders are also the best leaders. Charismatic leaders have, for instance, the ability to inspire others toward higher levels of performance and to instill deep levels of commitment, trust, and satisfaction. As a result, they are generally perceived by their subordinates to be more effective, compared with less charismatic leaders.[1]

But our research shows that while having at least a moderate level of charisma is important, having too much may hinder a leader's effectiveness. We conducted three studies, involving 800 business leaders globally and around 7,500 of their superiors, peers, and subordinates. Leaders occupied different managerial levels, ranging from supervisors to general managers. Our paper is forthcoming in the *Journal of Personality and Social Psychology*.

First, it's important to understand what charisma is. Traditional models of charismatic leadership state that charisma is not a personality trait, but simply exists in the eye of the beholder. In other words, charisma is *attributed to* someone, as opposed to being grounded in one's personality.[2]

However, the observation that people tend to agree in their perceptions of others' charisma levels suggests that it is not only a matter of attribution, and that this agreement might result from a personality-based foundation underlying these perceptions.[3] So the first goal of our research was to establish a measure of *charismatic personality*.

We gave leaders the Hogan Development Survey (HDS), a personality inventory specifically designed for work applications, and looked at how they scored on four personality tendencies: bold, colorful, mischievous, and imaginative. More-charismatic leaders score high on these traits, which is reflected in their high self-confidence, dramatic flair, readiness to test the limits, and expansive visionary thinking.

Next, we conducted a study to confirm this cluster of traits as a valid measure of charismatic personality. Using a sample of 204 business leaders, we showed that charismatic personality related to subordinates' perceptions of charismatic leadership. So leaders with a highly charismatic personality, as measured with HDS charisma, were also perceived to be highly charismatic by their subordinates. Using an archival data set from 1998 on a sample of 156 people, we further showed that HDS charisma levels could be predicted by people's charismatic behaviors (for example, being energetic, assertive, and generating enthusiasm).[4]

Our second goal was to investigate the relationship between charismatic personality and leader effectiveness. In a second study, 306 leaders (65% of them men) provided HDS self-ratings of their charismatic personality, while their coworkers provided ratings of their overall effectiveness using a 10-point rating scale, where 5 is *adequate* and 10 is *outstanding*. Taken together, 4,345 of their coworkers participated in this study: 666 superiors; 1,659 peers; and 2,020 subordinates. An average of 14 people rated each leader in terms of overall effectiveness.

Consistent with our expectations, we found that as charisma increased, so did perceived effectiveness—but only up to a certain point. As charisma scores continued to increase beyond the 60th percentile, which is just above the average score relative to the general population of working adults, perceived effectiveness started to decline. This trend was consistent across the three observer groups (subordinates, peers, and supervisors).

We also asked the leaders to evaluate their own effectiveness. As shown later, the more charismatic the leaders were, the higher they rated their own effectiveness. This discrepancy between self-perceptions and observer ratings is in line with other research demonstrating that leaders with high self-esteem typically overrate their performance on a variety of criteria.[5]

In a third study, we tested whether the effects of charismatic personality on effectiveness could be explained by looking at specific leader behaviors. To test this, we asked 287 business leaders (81% men) to rate their charismatic personality, and an average of 11 coworkers—including supervisors, peers, and subordinates—to rate each leader in terms of overall effectiveness. Additionally, coworkers now also rated leaders on two pairs of opposing leader-behavior dimensions: the extent to which they were *forceful* and *enabling* (tapping into the interpersonal behavior dimensions, or *how* they led), and the extent to which they were *strategic* and *operational* (representing the organizational dimensions, or *what* they led).

Although we did not find significant relationships between charisma and the interpersonal behavior dimensions, we found that highly charismatic leaders were perceived to engage in more strategic behavior and less operational behavior. But how can this explain lower effectiveness ratings for the most charismatic?

One explanation is that the costs associated with the desired trait (charisma) eventually come to outweigh its benefits. For highly charismatic leaders, we expected that the costs associated with a lack of operational behavior would come to outweigh the benefits delivered by strategic behavior when a certain level of charisma is exceeded. And that's exactly what we found: Highly charismatic leaders may be strategically ambitious, but this comes at the expense of getting day-to-day work activities executed in a proper manner, which can hurt perceived effectiveness. They failed, for example, in managing the day-to-day operations needed to implement their big strategic vision and in taking a methodical approach to getting things done in the near term. Further analysis showed that for leaders with lower levels of charisma, the opposite was true: They were found to be less effective because they lacked strategic behavior. For example, they did not spend enough time on long-term planning, and failed in taking a big-picture perspective, questioning the status quo, and encouraging innovation.

In terms of practical implications, our findings suggest that leaders should be aware of the potential drawbacks of being highly charismatic. Although it's difficult to draw a precise line between "just enough" and "too much" charisma, these are a few traits to look out for that can influence one's effectiveness. Self-confidence, for instance, may turn into overconfidence and narcissism in highly charismatic leaders, while risk tolerance and persuasiveness may start to translate into manipulative behavior. Further, the enthusiastic and entertaining nature of charisma may turn into attention-seeking behaviors that distract the organization from its mission, and extreme creativity may make highly charismatic leaders think and act in fanciful, eccentric ways.

For those whose charisma may be above optimal, coaching and development programs aimed at managing potential operational weaknesses, enhancing self-awareness, and improving self-regulation can be useful. Highly charismatic leaders would also benefit from receiving feedback from their coworkers on their effectiveness. That way, any gap between their perception and the perceptions of others will become clear. In contrast, coaching programs for leaders low on charisma might focus more on boosting their strategic behavior.

In sum, we found support for the idea that a leader can be too charismatic. Our findings suggest that highly charismatic leaders are perceived to be less effective, not for interpersonal reasons like self-centeredness but for business-related reasons that specifically relate to a lack of operational leader behavior.

We do want to point out that we didn't include situational factors in our study, which could influence the strength and shape of the relationship between leader charisma and effectiveness. Under certain conditions, such as in low-stress situations, this relationship may be strictly linear ("the more charisma the better"). However, we believe that high-stress and high-pressure situations are rather typical for a "normal" leadership context, enhancing the likelihood of finding a too-much-of-a-good-thing effect.[6] Additional studies will be important to further investigate the specific conditions under which charisma is desirable or not.

JASMINE VERGAUWE is a PhD candidate at the Department of Developmental, Personality, and Social Psychology, Ghent University. Her research interests include general and maladaptive personality traits, personality assessment, and leadership, with particular emphasis on traits as predictors of managerial performance and derailment. BART WILLE is assistant professor at the Department of Training and Education Sciences, University of Antwerp. His research focuses on professional development, strategic human resource development, career management and unfolding, and person-environment fit. JOERI HOFMANS is associate professor at the Research Group of Work and Organizational Psychology, Vrije Universiteit Brussel. His research interests include personality, emotions, and motivation at work, with particular emphasis on temporal dynamics. ROBERT B. KAISER is the president of Kaiser Leadership Solutions, based in Greensboro, N.C. His latest book, with coauthor Robert E. Kaplan, is *Fear Your Strengths: What You Are Best At Could Be Your Biggest Problem* (Berrett-Koehler, 2013). Find him online at kaiserleadership.com. FILIP DE FRUYT is senior full professor at the Department of Developmental, Personality, and Social Psychology, Ghent University. His research spans adaptive and maladaptive traits, their structure and development, cross-cultural manifestations of personality, and applied personality psychology.

Notes

1. B. Shamir, R. J. House, and M. B. Arthur, "The Motivational Effects of Charismatic Leadership: A Self-Concept Based Theory," *Organization Science* 4, no. 4 (1993); T. Dvir et al., "Impact of Transformational Leadership on Follower Development and Performance: A Field Experiment," *Academy of Management Journal* 45, no. 4 (2002): 735–744; and J. A. Conger, R. N. Kanungo., and S. T. Menon, "Charismatic Leadership and Follower Effects," *Journal of Organizational Behavior* 21 (2000): 747–767.

2. Conger et al., "Charismatic Leadership and Follower Effects."

3. J. J. Sosik, "Self-Other Agreement on Charismatic Leadership," *Group and Organization Management* 26, no. 4 (2001).

4. L. R. Goldberg, "The Eugene-Springfield Community Sample." *ORI Technical Report* 48, no. 1 (2008).

5. T. A. Judge, J. A. LePine, and B. L. Rich, "Loving Yourself Abundantly: Relationship of Narcissistic Personality to Self- and Other Perceptions of Workplace Deviance, Leadership and Task and Contextual Performance," *Journal of Applied Psychology* 91, no. 4 (2006): 762–776.

6. J. R. Pierce and H. Aguinis, "The Too-Much-of-a-Good-Thing Effect in Management." *Journal of Management* 39, no. 2 (2013).

Reprinted from hbr.org, originally published
September 26, 2017 (product #H03WYV).

Index

How to be human at work.

HBR's Emotional Intelligence Series features smart, essential reading on the human side of professional life from the pages of *Harvard Business Review*. Each book in the series offers uplifting stories, practical advice, and research from leading experts on how to tend to our emotional well-being at work.

Harvard Business Review Emotional Intelligence Series

Available in paperback or ebook format. The specially priced six-volume set includes:

- Mindfulness
- Resilience
- Influence and Persuasion
- Authentic Leadership
- Happiness
- Empathy

HBR.ORG

Buy for your team, clients, or event.
Visit hbr.org/bulksales for quantity discount rates.

Harvard Business Review Press

Dealing with
Difficult People

HBR EMOTIONAL INTELLIGENCE SERIES

HBR Emotional Intelligence Series

The HBR Emotional Intelligence Series features smart, essential reading on the human side of professional life from the pages of *Harvard Business Review*.

Authentic Leadership

Dealing with Difficult People

Empathy

Happiness

Influence and Persuasion

Leadership Presence

Mindfulness

Purpose, Meaning, and Passion

Resilience

Other books on emotional intelligence from *Harvard Business Review*:

HBR's 10 Must Reads on Emotional Intelligence

HBR Guide to Emotional Intelligence

HBR Everyday Emotional Intelligence

Dealing with Difficult People

HBR EMOTIONAL INTELLIGENCE SERIES

Harvard Business Review Press

Boston, Massachusetts

HBR Press Quantity Sales Discounts

Harvard Business Review Press titles are available at significant quantity discounts when purchased in bulk for client gifts, sales promotions, and premiums. Special editions, including books with corporate logos, customized covers, and letters from the company or CEO printed in the front matter, as well as excerpts of existing books, can also be created in large quantities for special needs.

For details and discount information for both print and ebook formats, contact booksales@harvardbusiness.org, tel. 800-988-0886, or www.hbr.org/bulksales.

Copyright 2018 Harvard Business School Publishing Corporation
All rights reserved
Printed in the United States of America

20 19 18 17 16 15 14 13 12 11

No part of this publication may be reproduced, stored in or introduced into a retrieval system, or transmitted, in any form, or by any means (electronic, mechanical, photocopying, recording, or otherwise), without the prior permission of the publisher. Requests for permission should be directed to permissions@hbsp.harvard.edu, or mailed to Permissions, Harvard Business School Publishing, 60 Harvard Way, Boston, Massachusetts 02163.

The web addresses referenced in this book were live and correct at the time of the book's publication but may be subject to change.

Library of Congress Cataloging-in-Publication Data

Title: Dealing with difficult people.
Other titles: HBR emotional intelligence series.
Description: Boston, Massachusetts : Harvard Business Review Press, [2018] | Series: HBR emotional intelligence series
Identifiers: LCCN 2017051988 | ISBN 9781633696082 (pbk. : alk. paper)
Subjects: LCSH: Conflict management. | Problem employees. | Emotional intelligence. | Problem solving. | Work—Psychological aspects.
Classification: LCC HD42 .D43 2018 | DDC 658.3/045—dc23 LC record available at https://lccn.loc.gov/2017051988

The paper used in this publication meets the requirements of the American National Standard for Permanence of Paper for Publications and Documents in Libraries and Archives Z39.48-1992.

Contents

Contents

Dealing with Difficult People

HBR EMOTIONAL INTELLIGENCE SERIES

1

To Resolve a Conflict, First Decide: Is It Hot or Cold?

By Mark Gerzon

As a leader, you're going to face conflict. It comes with the territory. But before you try to deal with a conflict, you first need to stop and ask yourself the following question:

Is it *hot* or *cold*?

To help you answer this vital question, consider these two definitions:

> *Hot conflict* is when one or more parties are highly emotional and doing one or more of the following: speaking loudly or shouting; being physically aggressive, wild, or

threatening; using language that is incendiary; appearing out of control and potentially explosive.

Cold conflict is when one or more parties seem to be suppressing emotions or are appearing "unemotional" and are doing one or more of the following: muttering under their breath or pursing their lips; being physically with-drawn or controlled; turning away or otherwise deflecting contact; remaining silent or speaking in a tone that is passively aggressive; appearing shut down or somehow frozen.

Neither of these types of conflict is constructive. Conflicts that are warm—that is, already open for discussion but not inflamed with intense hostility—are far more likely to be productive. So if you're dealing with cold conflict, you need skills to "warm it up." If you're dealing with hot conflict, you need skills to "cool it down."

Conflict resolution, like cooking, works best at the optimal temperature. If too hot, your conflict may explode, burning your deal or causing your relationship to flame out in anger or overt hostility. Too cold, and your deal may be frozen, not moving forward at all, or the relationship may become icy with unexpressed emotions and withheld concerns. As a leader, you want to bring conflict into a temperature zone where it can become useful and productive.

In the 20 years that I've been dealing with conflict professionally, I've operated in both hot and cold settings. In my work with companies, educational institutions, and faith-based organizations in the United States, I have generally found cold conflict. However, in my work with politicians both in the United States and in conflict zones around the world as a United Nations mediator, I have often dealt with hot conflict. And I've learned firsthand that understanding this hot/cold distinction is a crucial first step before you start trying to act like a mediator in any organization.

Once you've made a definitive hot/cold diagnosis, you'll need to understand what some of the dynamics behind each situation might be.

If the conflict is hot. You don't want to bring participants in a hot conflict together in the same room without setting ground rules that are strong enough to contain the potentially explosive energy. For example, if you are dealing with a conflict between two board members who have already attacked each other verbally, you would set clear ground rules—*and obtain agreement to them*—at the outset of your board meeting before anyone has a chance to speak.

Try this approach: Have everyone sit in a circle, and then ask each person to speak in turn with strict limits (three minutes each, for example). Pick a question for everyone to answer that requires each person to speak about themselves and their own feelings. For example, when I worked with members of the US House of Representatives, the question that opened the retreats I designed was, "How does the way the

House deals with its differences affect you and your family personally?" The result of this sort of question-and-answer session would be an opening round of conversation that avoided personal attacks, allowed everyone to speak, and ideally deepened trust before people entered more-difficult territory.

If the conflict is cold. In a cold conflict situation, you can usually go ahead and bring the participants or stakeholders in the conflict together and engage them in constructive communication. That dialogue, if properly facilitated, should "warm up" the conflict enough so that it can begin to thaw out and start the process of transformation. But you will still need to be vigilant and prepared. Conflict is often cold pre-cisely because so much feeling is being repressed. So you'll need to know how to warm things up without the temperature unexpectedly skyrocketing.

To do this, use debate and dialogue. If a group is avoiding tackling a tough issue, frame the differences as a debate. Then form two (or, if necessary, more) teams, and hold an actual debate. This will accentuate the differences and inspire the group to recognize the conflict that is under the surface.

For both hot and cold conflict. Whether the conflict is hot or cold, the goal is not compromise but rather bridging the divide and innovating new options or solutions. Bridging means creating stronger ties and deeper trust between the former antagonists. Innovating—which is distinct from compromising—means that some new resolution or possibility has emerged.

Conflict resolution isn't something you learn overnight. It takes time, practice, and reflection. If you find yourself in the middle of a conflict and you haven't yet developed the skills to address it, consider bringing in a third party or a professional mediator to help. With that said, if you're reading this in the middle of an intense, immediate conflict that requires urgent action, keep the following advice in mind:

- Make time your ally. Don't rush to act. Unless you're in danger, take stock of your options. Otherwise you might say or do something you regret.

- Determine your goal, and focus on it. Don't get distracted; stick to what matters.

- Avoid name-calling and finger-pointing. Focus on the problem, not the people.

- Beware of self-righteousness. Keep an open mind; you may find that you can learn something of value.

- Listen to everything, but respond selectively. You don't have to address every point—just the ones that make a difference.

- Take stock before you take sides. Don't speak—or take any other action—until you've really heard the other person out. Don't leap to conclusions before you have a firm grasp of the situation at hand.

- Consider calling in a third party. Someone who is not involved in the conflict may be able to provide vital perspective for both parties.

- Allow your adversary to know you. Letting down your guard and letting the other person in may help them understand your point of view.

- Check the temperature gauge. If the conflict is still too hot, don't try to resolve it right away. Agree to come back when things have cooled.

- Observe the golden rule. Do unto others as you would have them do unto you. Be polite. Be compassionate. It may inspire your adversary to do the same.

Keep in mind that showing your ability to navigate conflict is one of the primary ways that you reveal your character as a leader. The best time to learn is when conflict is neither too hot nor too cold. By learning to control the temperature, you make it much more likely that you'll be well positioned to deal creatively with the next conflict that's inevitably coming your way.

MARK GERZON is the author of *Leading Through Conflict: How Successful Leaders Transform Differences into Opportunities* (Harvard Business School Press, 2006) and the president of the Mediators Foundation.

Reprinted from hbr.org, originally published
June 26, 2014 (product #H00VQZ).

2

Taking the Stress Out of Stressful Conversations

By Holly Weeks

We live by talking. That's just the kind of animal we are. We chatter and tattle and gossip and jest. But sometimes—more often than we'd like—we have stressful conversations, those sensitive exchanges that can hurt or haunt us in ways no other kind of talking does. Stressful conversations are unavoidable in life, and in business they can run the gamut from firing a subordinate to, curiously enough, receiving praise. But whatever the context, stressful conversations differ from other conversations because of the emotional loads they carry. These conversations call up embarrassment, confusion, anxiety, anger, pain, or fear—if not in us, then in our counterparts. Indeed, stressful conversations cause such anxiety that most people simply avoid them. This strategy is not necessarily wrong. One of the first rules of engagement, after all, is to pick your battles. Yet sometimes it can be extremely costly to dodge issues, appease difficult people, and smooth over antagonisms because the fact is that avoidance usually makes a problem or relationship worse.

Since stressful conversations are so common—and so painful—why don't we work harder to improve them? The reason is precisely because our feelings are so enmeshed. When we are not emotionally entangled in an issue, we know that conflict is normal, that it can be resolved—or at least managed. But when feelings get stirred up, most of us are thrown off balance. Like a quarterback who chokes in a tight play, we lose all hope of ever making it to the goal line.

For the past 20 years, I have been teaching classes and conducting workshops at some of the top corporations and universities in the United States on how to communicate during stressful conversations. With classrooms as my laboratory, I have learned that most people feel incapable of talking through sensitive issues. It's as though all our skills go out the window and we can't think usefully about what's happening or what we could do to get good results.

Stressful conversations, though, need not be this way. I have seen that managers can improve difficult conversations unilaterally if they approach them with greater self-awareness, rehearse them in advance, and apply just three proven communication techniques. Don't misunderstand me: There will never be a cookie-cutter approach to stressful conversations. There are too many variables and too much tension, and the interactions between people in difficult situations are always unique. Yet nearly every stressful conversation can be seen as an amalgam of a limited number of basic conversations, each with its own distinct set of problems. In the following pages, we'll explore how you can anticipate and handle those problems. But first, let's look at the three basic stress-ful conversations that we bump up against most often in the workplace.

"I have bad news for you"

Delivering unpleasant news is usually difficult for both parties. The speaker is often tense, and the listener is apprehensive about where the conversation is headed. Consider David, the director of a nonprofit institution. He was in the uncomfortable position of needing to talk with an ambitious researcher, Jeremy, who had a much higher opinion of his job performance than others in the organization did. The complication for David was that, in the past, Jeremy had received artificially high evaluations. There were several reasons for this. One had to do with the organization's culture: The nonprofit was not a confrontational kind of place. Additionally, Jeremy had tremendous confidence in both his own abilities and the quality of his academic background. Together with his defensive response to even the mildest criticism, this confidence led others—including David—to let slide discussions of weaknesses that were interfering with Jeremy's ability to deliver high-quality work. Jeremy had a cutting sense of humor, for instance, which had offended people inside and outside his unit. No one had ever said anything to him directly, but as time passed, more and more people were reluctant to work with him. Given that Jeremy had received almost no concrete criticism over the years, his biting style was now entrenched and the staff was restive.

In conversations like this, the main challenge is to get off to the right start. If the exchange starts off reasonably well, the rest of it has a good chance of going well. But if the opening goes badly, it threatens to bleed forward into the rest of the conversation. In an effort to be gentle, many people start these conversations on a light note. And that was just what David did, opening with, "How about those Red Sox?"

Naturally Jeremy got the wrong idea about where David was heading; he remained his usual cocky, superior self. Sensing this, David felt he had to take off the velvet gloves. The conversation quickly became brutally honest, and David did almost all the talking. When the monologue was over, Jeremy stared icily at the floor. He got up in stiff silence and left. David was relieved. From his point of view, the interaction had been painful but swift. There was not too much blood on the floor, he observed wryly. But two days later, Jeremy handed in his resignation, taking a lot of institutional memory—and talent—with him.

"What's going on here?"

Often we have stressful conversations thrust upon us. Indeed, some of the worst conversations—especially for people who are conflict averse—are the altogether unexpected ones that break out like crackling summer storms. Suddenly the conversation becomes intensely charged emotionally, and electricity flies in all directions. What's worse, nothing makes sense. We seem to have been drawn into a black cloud of twisted logic and altered sensibilities.

Consider the case of Elizabeth and Rafael. They were team leaders working together on a project for a major consulting firm. It seemed that everything that could have gone wrong on the project had, and the work was badly bogged down. The two consultants were meeting to revise their schedule, given the delays, and to divide up the discouraging tasks for the week ahead. As they talked, Elizabeth wrote and erased on the white board. When she had finished, she looked at Rafael and said matter-of-factly, "Is that it, then?"

Rafael clenched his teeth in frustration. "If you say so," he sniped.

Elizabeth recoiled. She instantly replayed the exchange in her mind but couldn't figure out what had provoked Rafael. His reaction seemed completely disconnected from her comment. The most common reaction of someone in Elizabeth's place is to guiltily defend herself by denying Rafael's unspoken accusation. But Elizabeth was uneasy with confrontation so she tried appeasement. "Rafael," she stammered, "I'm sorry. Is something wrong?"

"Who put you in charge?" he retorted. "Who told you to assign work to me?"

Clearly, Rafael and Elizabeth have just happened into a difficult conversation. Some transgression has occurred, but Elizabeth doesn't know exactly what it is. She feels blindsided—her attempt to expedite the task at hand has clearly been misconstrued. Rafael feels he's been put in a position of inferiority by what he sees as Elizabeth's controlling behavior. Inexplicably, there seem to be more than two people taking part in this conversation, and the invisible parties are creating lots of static. What childhood experience, we may wonder, is causing Elizabeth to assume that Rafael's tension is automatically her fault? And who is influencing Rafael's perception that Elizabeth is taking over? Could it be his father? His wife? It's impossible to tell. At the same time, it's hard for us to escape the feeling that Rafael is overreacting when he challenges Elizabeth about her alleged need to take control.

Elizabeth felt Rafael's resentment like a wave, and she apologized again. "Sorry. How do you want the work divided?" Deferring to Rafael in this way smoothed the strained atmosphere for the time being. But it set a precedent for unequal status that neither Elizabeth nor the company believed was correct. Worse, though Rafael and Elizabeth remained on the same team after their painful exchange, Elizabeth chafed under the status change and three months later transferred out of the project.

"You are attacking me!"

Now let's turn our attention to aggressively stressful conversations, those in which people use all kinds of psychological and rhetorical mechanisms to throw their counterparts off balance, to undermine their positions, even to expose and belittle them. These "thwarting tactics" take many forms—profanity, manipulation, shouting—and not everyone is triggered or stumped by the same ones. The red zone is not the thwarting tactic alone but the pairing of the thwarting tactic with individual vulnerability.

Consider Nick and Karen, two senior managers working at the same level in an IT firm. Karen was leading a presentation to a client, and the information was weak and disorganized. She and the team had not been able to answer even basic questions. The client had been patient, then quiet, then clearly exasperated. When the presentation really started to fall apart, the client put the team on the spot with questions that made them look increasingly inadequate.

On this particular day, Nick was not part of the presenting team; he was simply observing. He was as surprised as the client at Karen's poor performance. After the client left, he asked Karen what happened. She lashed out at him defensively: "You're not my boss, so don't start patronizing me. You always undercut me no matter what I do." Karen continued to shout at Nick, her antagonism palpable. Each time he spoke, she interrupted him with accusations and threats: "I can't wait to see how you like it when people leave you flailing in the wind." Nick tried to remain reasonable, but Karen didn't wind down. "Karen," he said, "pull yourself together. You are twisting every word I say."

Here, Nick's problem is not that Karen is using a panoply of thwarting tactics but that all her tactics—

accusation, distortion, and digression—are aggressive. This raises the stakes considerably. Most of us are vulnerable to aggressive tactics because we don't know whether, or how far, the aggression will escalate. Nick wanted to avoid Karen's aggression, but his insistence on rationality in the face of emotionalism was not working. His cool approach was trumped by Karen's aggressive one. As a result, Nick found himself trapped in the snare of Karen's choosing. In particular, her threats that she would pay him back with the client rattled him. He couldn't tell whether she was just huffing or meant it. He finally turned to the managing director, who grew frustrated and later angry at Nick and Karen for their inability to resolve their problems. In the end, their lack of skill in handling their difficult conversations cost them dearly. Both were passed over for promotion after the company pinned the loss of the client directly on their persistent failure to communicate.

Preparing for a stressful conversation

So how can we prepare for these three basic stressful conversations before they occur? A good start is to become aware of your own weaknesses to people and situations. David, Elizabeth, and Nick were unable to control their counterparts, but their stressful conversations would have gone much better if they had been more usefully aware of their vulnerabilities. It is important for those who are vulnerable to hostility, for example, to know how they react to it. Do they withdraw or escalate? Do they clam up or retaliate? While one reaction is not better than the other, knowing how you react in a stressful situation will teach you a lot about your vulnerabilities, and it can help you master stressful situations.

Recall Nick's problem. If he had been more self-aware, he would have known that he acts stubbornly

27

rational in the face of aggressive outbursts such as Karen's. Nick's choice of a disengaged demeanor gave Karen control over the conversation, but he didn't have to allow Karen—or anyone else—to exploit his vulnerability. In moments of calm self-scrutiny, when he's not entangled in a live stressful conversation, Nick can take time to reflect on his inability to tolerate irrational aggressive outbursts. This self-awareness would free him to prepare himself—not for Karen's unexpected accusations but for his own predictable vulnerability to any sudden assault like hers.

Though it might sound like it, building awareness is not about endless self-analysis. Much of it simply involves making our tacit knowledge about ourselves more explicit. We all know from past experience, for instance, what kinds of conversations and people we handle badly. When you find yourself in a difficult conversation, ask yourself whether this is one of those situations and whether it involves one of those people. For instance, do you bare your teeth when faced with an overbearing competitor? Do you shut down when you feel excluded? Once you know what your danger zones are, you can anticipate your vulnerability and improve your response.

Explicit self-awareness will often help save you from engaging in a conversation in a way that panders to your feelings rather than one that serves your needs. Think back to David, the boss of the nonprofit institution, and Jeremy, his cocky subordinate. Given Jeremy's history, David's conversational game plan—easing in, then when that didn't work, the painful-but-quick bombshell—was doomed. A better approach would have been for David to split the conversation into two parts. In a first meeting, he could have raised the central issues of Jeremy's biting humor and disappointing performance. A second meeting could have been set up for the discussion itself. Handling the situation incrementally would have allowed time for both David and Jeremy to prepare for a two-way conversation instead of one of them delivering a monologue. After all, this wasn't an emergency; David didn't have to exhaust this topic immediately. Indeed, if David had been more self-aware, he might have recognized that the approach he chose was dictated less by Jeremy's character than by his own distaste for conflict.

An excellent way to anticipate specific problems that you may encounter in a stressful conversation is to rehearse with a neutral friend. Pick someone who doesn't have the same communication problems as you. Ideally, the friend should be a good listener, honest but nonjudgmental. Start with content. Just tell your friend what you want to say to your counterpart without worrying about tone or phrasing. Be vicious, be timid, be sarcastically witty, jump around in your argument, but get it out. Now go over it again and think about what you would say if the situation weren't emotionally loaded. Your friend can help you because he or she is not in a flush of emotion over the situation. Write down what you come up with together because if you don't, you'll forget it later.

Now fine-tune the phrasing. When you imagine talking to the counterpart, your phrasing tends to be highly charged—and you can think of only one way to say anything. But when your friend says, "Tell me how you want to say this," an interesting thing happens: Your phrasing is often much better, much more temperate, usable. Remember, you can say what you want to say, you just can't say it *like that*. Also, work on your body language with your friend. You'll both soon be laughing because of the expressions that sneak out unawares—eyebrows skittering up and down, legs wrapped around each other like licorice twists, nervous snickers that will certainly be misinterpreted. (For more on preparing for stressful conversations, see the sidebar "The DNA of Conversation Management.")

THE DNA OF CONVERSATION MANAGEMENT

The techniques I have identified for handling stressful conversations all have tucked within them three deceptively simple ingredients that are needed to make stressful conversations succeed. These are clarity, neutrality, and temperance. They are the building blocks of all good communication. Mastering them will multiply your chances of responding well to even the most strained conversation. Let's take a look at each of the components in turn.

Clarity means letting words do the work for us. Avoid euphemisms or talking in circles, and tell people clearly what you mean: "Emily, from your family's point of view, the Somerset Valley Nursing Home would be the best placement for your father. His benefits don't cover it." Unfortunately, delivering clear content when the news is bad is particularly hard to do. Under strained circumstances, we all tend to shy away from clarity because we equate it with brutality. Instead, we say things like, "Well, Dan, we're still not sure yet what's going to happen with this job, but in the future we'll keep our eyes open." This is a roundabout—and terribly misleading—way to inform someone that he didn't get the promotion he was seeking. And in reality, there's nothing inherently brutal about honesty. It is not the content but the delivery of the news that makes it brutal or humane. Ask a surgeon. Ask a priest; ask a cop. If a message is given skillfully—even though the news is bad—the content may still be tolerable. When a senior executive, for example, directly tells a subordinate that "the promotion has gone to someone else," the news is likely to be highly unpleasant, and the appropriate reaction is sadness, anger, and anxiety.

(Continued)

33

THE DNA OF CONVERSATION MANAGEMENT

But if the content is clear, the listener can better begin to process the information. Indeed, bringing clarity to the content eases the burden for the recipient rather than increases it.

Tone is the nonverbal part of delivery in stressful conversations. It is intonation, facial expressions, and conscious and unconscious body language. Although it's hard to have a neutral tone when overcome by strong feelings, neutrality is the desired norm in crisis communications, including stressful conversations. Consider the classic neutrality of NASA. Regardless of how dire the message, NASA communicates its content in uninflected tones: "Houston, we have a problem." It takes practice to acquire such neutrality. But a neutral tone is the best place to start when a conversation turns stressful.

Temperate phrasing is the final element in this triumvirate of skills. English is a huge language, and there are lots of different ways to say what you need to say. Some of these phrases are temperate, while others will baldly provoke the recipient to dismiss your words—and your content. In the United States, for example, some of the most intemperate phrasing revolves around threats of litigation: "If you don't get a check to me by April 23, I'll be forced to call my lawyer." Phrases like this turn up the heat in all conversations, particularly in strained ones. But remember, we're not in stressful conversations to score points or to create enemies. The goal is to advance the conversation, to hear and be heard accurately, and to have a functional exchange between two people. So the next time you want to snap at someone— "Stop interrupting me!"—try this: "Can you hold on a minute? I want to finish before I lose my train of thought." Temperate phrasing will help you take the strain out of a stressful conversation.

Managing the conversation

While it is important to build awareness and to practice before a stressful conversation, those steps are not enough. Let's look at what you can do as the conversation unfolds. Consider Elizabeth, the team leader whose colleague claimed she was usurping control. She couldn't think well on her feet in confrontational situations, and she knew it, so she needed a few hippocket phrases—phrases she could recall on the spot so that she wouldn't have to be silent or invent something on the spur of the moment. Though such a solution sounds simple, most of us don't have a tool kit of conversational tactics ready at hand. Rectifying this gap is an essential part of learning how to handle stressful conversations better. We need to learn communications skills, in the same way that we learn CPR: well in advance, knowing that when we need to use them, the situation will be critical and tense.

Here are three proven conversational approaches. The particular wording may not suit your style, and that's fine. The important thing is to understand how the techniques work, and then choose phrasing that is comfortable for you.

Honor thy partner

When David gave negative feedback to Jeremy, it would have been refreshing if he had begun with an admission of regret and some responsibility for his contribution to their shared problem. "Jeremy," he might have said, "the quality of your work has been undercut—in part by the reluctance of your colleagues to risk the edge of your humor by talking problems through with you. I share responsibility for this because I have been reluctant to speak openly about these difficulties with you, whom I like and respect and with whom I have worked a long time." Acknowledging responsibility as a technique—

37

particularly as an opening—can be effective because it immediately focuses attention, but without provocation, on the difficult things the speaker needs to say and the listener needs to hear.

Is this always a good technique in a difficult conversation? No, because there is never any one good technique. But in this case, it effectively sets the tone for David's discussion with Jeremy. It honors the problems, it honors Jeremy, it honors their relationship, and it honors David's responsibility. Any technique that communicates honor in a stressful conversation—particularly a conversation that will take the counterpart by surprise—is to be highly valued. Indeed, the ability to act with dignity can make or break a stressful conversation. More important, while Jeremy has left the company, he can still do harm by spreading gossip and using his insider's knowledge against the organization. The more intolerable the conversation with David has been, the more Jeremy is likely to want to make the organization pay.

Disarm by restating your intentions

Part of the difficulty in Rafael and Elizabeth's "What's going on here?" conversation is that Rafael's misinterpretation of Elizabeth's words and actions seems to be influenced by instant replays of other stressful conversations that he has had in the past. Elizabeth doesn't want to psychoanalyze Rafael; indeed, exploring Rafael's internal landscape would exacerbate this painful situation. So what can Elizabeth do to defuse the situation unilaterally?

Elizabeth needs a technique that doesn't require her to understand the underlying reasons for Rafael's strong reaction but that helps her handle the situation effectively. "I can see how you took what I said the way you did, Rafael. That wasn't what I meant. Let's go over this list again." I call this the clarification technique, and it's a highly disarming one. Using it, Elizabeth can unilaterally change the confrontation into a point of agreement. Instead of arguing with Rafael about his perceptions, she grants him his perceptions—after all, they're his. Instead of arguing about her intentions, she keeps the responsibility for aligning her words with her intentions. And she goes back into the conversation right where they left off. (For a fuller discussion of the disconnect between what we mean and what we say, see the sidebar "The Gap Between Communication and Intent.")

THE GAP BETWEEN COMMUNICATION AND INTENT

One of the most common occurrences in stressful conversations is that we all start relying far too much on our intentions. As the mercury in the emotional thermometer rises, we presume that other people automatically understand what we mean. We assume, for instance, that people know we mean well. Indeed, research shows that in stressful conversations, most speakers assume that the listener believes that they have good intentions, regardless of what they say.

Intentions can never be that powerful in communications—and certainly not in stressful conversations.

To see what I mean, just think of the last time someone told you not to take something the wrong way. This may well have been uttered quite sincerely by the speaker; nevertheless, most people automatically react by stiffening inwardly, anticipating something at least mildly offensive or antagonistic. And that is exactly the reaction that phrase is always going to get. Because the simplest rule about stressful conversations is that people don't register intention *despite* words; we register intention *through* words. In stressful conversations in particular, the emphasis is on what is actually said, not on what we intend or feel. This doesn't mean that participants in stressful conversations don't have feelings or intentions that are valid and valuable. They do. But when we talk

(Continued)

41

THE GAP BETWEEN COMMUNICATION AND INTENT

about people in stressful communication, we're talking about communication between people—and not about intentions.

Of course, in difficult conversations we may all wish that we didn't have to be so explicit. We may want the other person to realize what we mean even if we don't spell it out. But that leads to the wrong division of labor: with the listener interpreting rather than the speaker communicating. In all conversations, but especially in stressful ones, we are all responsible for getting across to one another precisely what we want to say. In the end, it's far more dignified for an executive to come right out and tell an employee, "Corey, I've arranged for you to speak with HR, because you won't be with us after the end of July." Forcing someone to guess your intentions only prolongs the agony of the inevitable.

This technique will work for Elizabeth regardless of Rafael's motive. If Rafael innocently misunderstood what she was saying, she isn't fighting him. She accepts his take on what she said and did and corrects it. If his motive is hostile, Elizabeth doesn't concur just to appease him. She accepts and retries. No one loses face. No one scores points off the other. No one gets drawn off on a tangent.

Fight tactics, not people

Rafael may have baffled Elizabeth, but Karen was acting with outright malice toward Nick when she flew off the handle after a disastrous meeting with the client. Nick certainly can't prevent her from using the thwarting tactics with which she has been so successful in the past. But he can separate Karen's character from her behavior. For instance, it's much more useful for him to think of Karen's reactions as thwarting tactics rather than as personal characteristics. If he thinks of Karen as a distorting, hostile, threatening person, where does that lead? What can anyone ever do about another person's character? But if Nick sees Karen's behavior as a series of tactics that she is using with him because they have worked for her in the past, he can think about using countering techniques to neutralize them.

The best way to neutralize a tactic is to name it. It's much harder to use a tactic once it is openly identified. If Nick, for instance, had said, "Karen, we've worked together pretty well for a long time. I don't know how to talk about what went wrong in the meeting when your take on what happened, and what's going on now, is so different from mine," he would have changed the game completely. He neither would have attacked Karen nor remained the pawn of her tactics. But he would have made Karen's tactics in the conversation the dominant problem.

Openly identifying a tactic, particularly an aggressive one, is disarming for another reason. Often we think of an aggressive counterpart as persistently, even endlessly, contentious, but that isn't true. People have definite levels of aggression that they're comfortable with—and they are reluctant to raise the bar. When Nick doesn't acknowledge Karen's tactics, she can use them unwittingly, or allegedly so. But if Nick speaks of them, it would require more aggression on Karen's part to continue using the same tactics. If she is at or near her aggression threshold, she won't continue because that would make her uncomfortable. Nick may not be able to stop Karen, but she may stop herself.

People think stressful conversations are inevitable. And they are. But that doesn't mean they have to have bad resolutions. Consider a client of mine, Jacqueline, the only woman on the board of an engineering company. Another board member repeatedly ribbed her about being a feminist and, on this occasion, he was telling a sexist joke.

This wasn't the first time that something like this had happened, and Jacqueline felt the usual internal cacophony of reactions. But because she was aware that this was a stressful situation for her, Jacqueline was prepared. First, she let the joke hang in the air for a minute and then went back to the issue they had been discussing. When Richard didn't let it go but escalated with a new poke—"Come on, Jackie, it was a *joke*"—Jacqueline stood her ground. "Richard," she said, "this kind of humor is frivolous to you, but it is wrong, and moreover, it makes me, the only woman on this board, feel pushed aside." Jacqueline didn't need to say more. If Richard had continued to escalate, he would have lost face. In fact, he backed down: "Well, I wouldn't want my wife to hear about my bad behavior a second time," he snickered. Jacqueline was silent. She had made her point; there was no need to take it further.

Stressful conversations are never easy, but we can all fare better if, like Jacqueline, we prepare for them by developing greater awareness of our vulnerabilities and better techniques for handling ourselves.

The advice and tools described in this article can be helpful in unilaterally reducing the strain in stressful conversations. All you have to do is try them. If one technique doesn't work, try another. Find phrasing that feels natural. But keep practicing—you'll find what works best for you.

HOLLY WEEKS publishes, teaches, and consults on communications issues. She is an adjunct lecturer in public policy at the Harvard Kennedy School and the author of *Failure to Communicate: How Conversations Go Wrong and What You Can Do to Right Them* (Harvard Business Review Press, 2008).

Adapted from an article in *Harvard Business Review*,
July–August 2001 (product #R0107H).

3

The Secret to Dealing with Difficult People: It's About You

By Tony Schwartz

D o you have someone at work who consistently triggers you? Doesn't listen? Takes credit for work you've done? Wastes your time with trivial issues? Acts like a know-it-all? Can only talk about himself? Constantly criticizes?

Our core emotional need is to feel valued and valuable. When we don't, it's deeply unsettling, a challenge to our sense of equilibrium, security, and well-being. At the most primal level, it can feel like a threat to our very survival.

This is especially true when the person you're struggling with is your boss. The problem is that being in charge of other people rarely brings out the best in us.

"Power tends to corrupt, and absolute power corrupts absolutely," Lord Acton said way back in 1887. "There is no worse heresy than the office that sanctifies the holder of it."

The easy default when we feel devalued is to play the role of victim, and it's a seductive pull. Blaming others for how we're feeling is a form of self-protection. Whatever is going wrong isn't our fault. By off-loading responsibility, we feel better in the short term.

The problem with being a victim is that you cede the power to influence your circumstances. The painful truth when it comes to the people who trigger you is this: You're not going to change them. The only person you have the possibility of changing is yourself.

Each of us has a default lens through which we see the world. We call it reality, but in fact it's a selective filter. We have the power to view the world through other lenses. There are three worth trying on when you find yourself defaulting to negative emotions.

The lens of realistic optimism. Using this lens requires asking yourself two simple questions when you feel you're being treated badly or unfairly. The first one is, "What are the facts in this situation?" The second is, "What's the story I'm telling myself about those facts?"

Making this distinction allows you to stand outside your experience rather than simply reacting to it. It also opens the possibility that whatever story you're currently telling yourself isn't necessarily the only way to look at your situation.

Realistic optimism, a term coined by the psychologist Sandra Schneider, means telling yourself the most hopeful and empowering story about a given circumstance without subverting the facts. It's about moving beyond your default reaction to feel under attack and exploring whether there is an alternative way of viewing the situation that would ultimately serve you better. Another way of discovering an alternative is to ask yourself, "How would I act here at my best?"

The reverse lens. This lens requires viewing the world through the lens of the person who triggered you. It doesn't mean sacrificing your own point of view but rather widening your perspective.

It's nearly certain that the person you perceive as difficult views the situation differently than you do. With the reverse lens, you ask yourself, "What is this person feeling, and in what ways does that make sense?" Or put more starkly: "Where's my responsibility in all this?"

Counterintuitively, one of the most powerful ways to reclaim your value, when it feels threatened, is to find a way to appreciate the perspective of the person you feel devalued by. It's called empathy.

Just as you do, others tend to behave better when they feel seen and valued—especially since insecurity is what usually prompts them to act badly in the first place.

The long lens. Sometimes your worst fears about another person turn out to be true. He is someone who bullies you unreasonably, and seeing it from his perspective doesn't help. She does invariably take credit for your work.

When your current circumstances are incontrovertibly bad, the long lens provides a way of looking beyond the present to imagine a better future. Begin with this question: "Regardless of how I feel about what's happening right now, how can I grow and learn from this experience?" How many times has something that felt terrible to you in the moment turned out to be trivial several months later or actually led you to an important opportunity or in a positive new direction?

My last boss fired me. It felt awful at the time, but it also pushed me way out of my comfort zone, which is where it turned out I needed to go.

Looking back, the story I tell myself is that for all his deficiencies, I learned a lot from that boss, and it all serves me well today. I can understand, from his point of view, why he found me difficult as an employee, without feeling devalued. Most important, getting fired prompted me to make a decision— founding the company I now run—that has brought me more happiness than any other work I've ever done.

TONY SCHWARTZ is the president and CEO of The Energy Project and the author of *Be Excellent at Anything* (Free-Press, 2011). Become a fan of The Energy Project on Facebook and connect with Tony on Twitter at @TonySchwartz and @Energy_Project.

Reprinted from hbr.org, originally published October 12, 2011.

4

How to Deal with a Mean Colleague

By Amy Gallo

When a colleague is mean to you, it can be hard to know how to respond. Some people are tempted to let aggressive behavior slide in the hopes that the person will stop. Others find themselves fighting back. When you're being treated poorly by a coworker, how can you change the dynamic? And if the behavior persists or worsens, how do you know when you're dealing with a true bully?

What the experts say

"When it comes to bad behavior at work, there's a broad spectrum," with outright bullies on one end and people who are simply rude on the other, says Michele Woodward, an executive coach and host of HBR's webinar "Bullies, Jerks, and Other Annoyances: Identify and Defuse the Difficult People at Work." You may not know which end of the spectrum you're dealing with until you actually address the behavior. If it's a bully, it can be difficult—if not impossible—to get the person to change, says Gary Namie, founder of the Workplace Bullying Institute and author of *The Bully at Work*. But in most cases, you can—and should—take action. "Know that you have a solution, you're not powerless," says Woodward. Here are some tactics to consider when dealing with an aggressive colleague.

Understand why

The first step is to understand what's causing the behavior. Research from Nathanael Fast, an assistant professor at the University of Southern California's

Marshall School of Business, proves a commonly held idea: People act out when their ego is threatened. "We often see powerful people behave aggressively toward less powerful people when their competence is questioned," he says. Namie agrees: "People who are skilled and well-liked are the most frequent targets precisely because they pose a threat." So it may help to stroke the aggressor's ego. "In our study, we saw that if the subordinate offered gratitude to the boss, it wiped out the effect," Fast explains. Even a small gesture, such as ending an email with "Thanks so much for your help" or complimenting the person on something you genuinely admire, can help.[1]

Look at what you're doing

These situations also require introspection. "It's very easy to say, 'Oh, that person is a jerk,'" Woodward says. But perhaps you work in a highly competitive culture or one that doesn't prioritize politeness. Consider whether you might be misinterpreting the behavior or overreacting to it or whether you've unknowingly contributed to the problem. Have you in any way caused the person to feel threatened or to see you as disloyal? Self-evaluation can be tough, so get a second opinion from someone you trust, who will tell you the truth, not just what you want to hear. Don't put too much of the blame on yourself, however. "It's important to balance not being threatening with not being a doormat, which just invites more aggression," Fast says. "Targets regularly assume it's their fault," when it's not, Namie agrees.

Stand up for yourself

Don't be afraid to call out the bad behavior when it happens. "I believe very strongly in making immediate corrections," says Woodward. "If someone calls you 'Honey' in a meeting, say right then: 'I don't like being called that. Please use my name,'" she says. If you're uncomfortable with an immediate, public response, Woodward advises saying something as soon as you're able. After the meeting, you could say, "I didn't like being called 'Honey.' It demeans me." Show that there is no reward for treating you that way. "The message should be: Don't mess with me; it won't be worth your effort," Namie says.

Enlist help

"Everybody should have alliances at work—peers and people above and below, who can be your advocates and champions," says Woodward. Talk to those supporters and see what they can do to help, whether it's simply confirming your perspective or speaking on your behalf. Of course, you may need to escalate the situation to someone more senior or to HR. But before that, "you owe it to the relationship to try to solve it informally," says Woodward.

Demonstrate the cost to the business

If you do need to take formal action, start with your boss (assuming he isn't the aggressor). But you may need to take the issue higher up the hierarchy. When you have someone's ear, Namie recommends focusing the conversation on how the person's behavior is hurting the business. "Talk about how it's affecting morale and performance," says Fast. Personal pleas rarely work and too often degenerate into he said-she said type arguments. "Don't tell a story of emotional wounds," Namie advises. "Make an argument that the person is costing the organization money."

Know the limitations

When none of the above works you have to consider: Is this uncivil, mean behavior, or am I being bullied? If you are in an abusive situation (not just a tough one), Namie and Woodward agree that chances of change are low. "The only time I've seen a bully change is when they are publicly fired. Sanctions don't work," says Woodward. Instead, you need to take action to protect yourself. Of course, in an ideal world, senior leaders would immediately fire people who are toxic to a workplace. But both Namie and Woodward agree that it rarely happens. "Even though the statistics are clear on the impact [of bullying] on morale, retention, and performance, it's very hard for organizations to take action," Woodward says. If you're in an abusive situation at work, the most tenable solution may be to leave—if that's a possibility. The Workplace Bullying Institute has done online surveys that show more people stay in a bullying situation because of pride (40% of respondents) than because of economics (38%). If you're worried about letting the bully win, Namie says, you're better off worrying about your own well-being.[2]

Principles to remember

Do:

- Know that most people act aggressively at work because they feel threatened.

- Ask yourself whether you're being overly sensitive or misinterpreting the situation.

- Call out the inappropriate behavior in the moment.

Don't:

- Take the blame. Many bullies pick targets that are highly skilled and well-liked.

- Escalate the situation until you've tried to solve it informally and with the help of your allies.

- Suffer unnecessarily. If the situation persists and you can leave, do it.

Case study #1: Don't stay and suffer

Eleven years ago Heather Reynolds took a new position at a veterinary clinic owned by another veterinarian named Adam with the intention of buying into the practice (names and details in these case studies have been changed). At first, Adam seemed thrilled about Heather coming to work with him. "He was positive, supportive, and encouraging. He was over the moon about me joining," she says. After several months, she bought half of the firm and became Adam's business partner.

Things continued to go well until a year later when, after what seemed like a minor disagreement, Adam stopped speaking to Heather for six weeks. When she confronted him, he told her he was considering dropping her as a partner. Heather was shocked. She had taken out a loan to buy into the firm and felt stuck.

Eventually they got back on track, but Heather soon learned that this was a pattern of behavior. Any time there was conflict, Adam reacted the same way. "If I disagreed, he would ice me out. If I confronted him, he'd ice me out longer," she says. She eventually figured out that stroking his ego was more effective. "You could flatter him, tell him how great he was, how he did well in a case, and he'd be back on your side. I learned to do this sort of dance in order to survive."

But Adam's harsh behavior took its toll on Heather. Last year, things got so bad that he didn't speak to her for three months. Heather sought the advice of a professional coach, who helped her see that Adam was a narcissist and a bully who was threatened by her skills. Late last year, she told him she was looking for someone to buy out her part of the business and he offered to do it. "It was the best thing I could've done," she says. "I wished I'd left when he first showed me who he truly was."

Case study #2: Call out the bad behavior

Christine Johnson was excited about her new role as deputy editor at a San Francisco–based media company. The position had just been created, so she would be managing a team of existing staff, and everyone welcomed her except for one person, Terry. "What I didn't know and I learned later was that he wanted the role and was angry that he didn't get it," she says.

During her first weeks on the job, Terry was aggressive. "I was constantly fending off little attacks from him," she remembers. He kept asking her how she wanted to supervise their work, what processes she wanted to put in place, how he should interact with her about his projects. Looking back, Heather realizes these were all questions designed to make her look unprepared and incompetent. "And I was too green to say I didn't know yet," she says.

Terry started sending Christine 50 emails with return receipt before 9:00 a.m. When she hadn't responded by 11:00 a.m., he would start emailing her to ask if she'd seen his emails. "He was constantly badgering me. I actually considered quitting. I didn't feel like I had any allies and wasn't sure this was the job I wanted," she says. After five weeks of this abuse, Christine stood up to Terry in a staff meeting. "He kept asking me questions over and over, and I just lost my cool," she says. She snapped at Terry and said, "I'm sick of you asking me so many unnecessary questions. Can you please stop?" Terry backed down.

Christine was embarrassed by her behavior, but later, when she was in her office, people began stopping by to thank her for standing up to Terry. "Once I had a small amount of reinforcement from my peers, I knew I could take him on," she says. And once he saw that she wasn't willing to take his abuse, he stood down. "It got better and we were cordial, but it was an awful start," she says.

AMY GALLO is a contributing editor at *Harvard Business Review* and the author of the *HBR Guide to Dealing with Conflict* (Harvard Business Review Press, 2017). She writes and speaks about workplace dynamics. See her website amyegallo .com and follow her on Twitter @amyegallo.

Notes

1. N. J. Fast and S. Chen, "When the Boss Feels Inadequate: Power, Incompetence, and Aggression," *Psychological Science* 20, no. 11 (November 2009): 1406–1413; and "A Simple 'Thanks' Can Tame the Barking Boss," *Psychological Science*, October 30, 2013, http://www.psychological science.org/index.php/news/minds-business/a-simple -thanks-can-tame-the-barking-boss.html.
2. G. Namie, "2014 WBI U.S. Workplace Bullying Survey," Workplace Bullying Institute, February 2014, http://www .workplacebullying.org/wbiresearch/wbi-2014-us-survey/.

Adapted from content posted on hbr.org,
October 16, 2014 (product #H011T2).

5

How to Deal with a Passive-Aggressive Colleague

By Amy Gallo

Your colleague says one thing in a meeting but then does another. He passes you in the hallway without saying hello and talks over you in meetings. But when you ask to speak with him about his behavior, he insists that everything's fine and the problem is all in your head. But it's not: He's being passive-aggressive. Working with someone like this can be so frustrating. Do you address the behavior directly? Or try to ignore it? How can you get to the core issue when your colleague pretends that nothing's going on?

What the experts say

It's not uncommon for colleagues to occasionally make passive-aggressive remarks to one another over particularly sensitive issues or when they feel they can't be direct. "We're all guilty of doing it once in a while," says Amy Su, coauthor of *Own the Room: Discover Your Signature Voice to Master Your Leadership Presence*. But persistent passive-aggressive behavior is a different ballgame. "These are people who will often do anything to get what they need, including lie," says Annie McKee, founder of the Teleos Leadership Institute and coauthor of *Primal Leadership: Unleashing the Power of Emotional Intelligence*. In these cases, you have to take special precautions that help you, and hopefully your counterpart, both get your jobs done. Here are some tips.

Don't get caught up

When your coworker pretends nothing is going on or accuses you of overreacting, it's hard not to get angry and defensive. But "this is not one of those situations to fight fire with fire," McKee says. Do your best to remain calm. "The person may want you to get mad so they can then blame you, which is a release of their own anxiety," Su explains. "Responding in an emotional way will likely leave you looking—and feeling—like the fool. This is your opportunity to be the bigger person."

Consider what's motivating the behavior

People who routinely act in a passive-aggressive way aren't necessarily complete jerks. It could be that they don't know how to communicate or are afraid of conflict. McKee says that passive-aggressive behavior is often a way for people to "get their emotional point across without having true, healthy conflict." There's also a self-centeredness to it. "They make the flawed assumption that others should know what they're feeling and that their needs and preferences are more important than [those of] others'," says Su. Understand this, but don't try to diagnose all your colleague's problems. "You just have to see it for what it is," Su adds: "an unproductive expression of emotions that they can't share constructively."

Own your part

Chances are that you're not blameless in the situation. Ask yourself if something you're doing is contributing to the dynamic or causing the person to be passive-aggressive. "Own your half," says Su. Also, consider whether you've dished out the same behavior; know the signs.[1] "It can happen to even the best of us, whether we're procrastinating or wanting to avoid something. We might leak emotions in a way that's hurtful to others," says Su.

Focus on the content, not the delivery

It might be the last thing you want to do, but try to see the situation from your colleague's perspective. What is the underlying opinion or perspective she's attempting to convey with her snarky comment? "Analyze the position the person is trying to share with you," says McKee. Does she think that the way you're running the project isn't working? Or does she disagree about your team goals? "Not everyone knows how to publicly discuss or express what they think," says Su. If you can focus on the underlying business concern or question rather than the way she's expressing herself, you can move on to addressing the actual problem.

Acknowledge the underlying issue

Once you're calm and able to engage in a productive conversation, go back to the person. Say something like, "You made a good point in that exchange we had the other day. Here's what I heard you saying." This will help them talk about the substance of their concerns." By joining *with* them, you'll have a better chance of turning the energy around," McKee explains. Do this in a matter-of-fact way, without discussing how the sentiment was expressed. "Don't listen or give any credence to the toxic part," advises Su. "Sometimes it's that they just want their opinion heard."

Watch your language

Whatever you say, don't accuse the person of being passive-aggressive. "That can hurt your cause," says McKee. Su agrees: "It's such a loaded word. It would put someone who's already on the defensive into a more angry position. Don't label or judge them." Instead, McKee suggests recounting how some of your previous interactions have played out and explaining the impact it's having on you and possibly others. If feasible, show that the behavior is working against something your counterpart cares about, like achieving the team's goals.

Find safety in numbers

You don't have to deal with this situation alone. "It's OK to reality check with others and have allies in place to say you're not crazy," says Su. But be sure to frame your discussions as an attempt to constructively improve the relationship, so it doesn't come across as gossiping or bad-mouthing your colleague. Su suggests you ask for honest opinions, something like "I was wondering how Emily's comment landed with you. How did you interpret that?"

Set guidelines for everyone

You might also enlist the help of others in coming up with a long-term solution. "As a team, you can build healthy norms," McKee says. Together you can agree to be more up-front about frustrations and model the honest and direct interactions you want to happen. You can also keep one another accountable. If your problematic colleague tends to ignore agreements, you might take notes in meetings about who's supposed to do what by when, so there are clear action items. The worst offenders are likely to give in to the positive peer pressure and public accountability.

Get help in extreme situations

When a colleague persistently tries to undermine you or prevent you from doing your job and outside observers confirm your take on the situation, you might have to go further. "If you share the same manager, you may be able to ask for help," says McKee. You might tell your boss, "A lot of us have noticed a particular behavior, and I want to talk about how it's impacting my ability to do my work." But "step into those waters carefully," she warns. "Your manager may be hoodwinked by the person and may not see the same behaviors or be conflict averse himself and not want to see it."

Protect yourself

"If there's an interdependence in your work, make sure you're meeting your commitments and dead-lines," Su says. "Copy others on important emails. Don't let that person speak for you or represent you in meetings. After a meeting, document agreements and next steps." McKee also suggests keeping records. "Track specific behaviors so that you have examples if needed," she says. "It's hard to argue with the facts." She also recommends you try to avoid working with the person and "keep contact to a minimum. If you have to work together, do it in a group setting" where your colleague is likely to be on better behavior. You might not be able to break the person of his passive-aggressive habits, but you can control your reaction to it.

Principles to remember

Do:

- Understand why people typically act this way: Their needs probably aren't being met.

- Focus on the message your colleague is trying to convey, even if their delivery is misguided.

- Take a step back and ask yourself if you're contributing to the issue in some way.

Don't:

- Lose your cool. Address the underlying business issue in a calm, matter-of-fact way.

- Accuse the person of acting passive-aggressively—that will only make them madder.

- Assume you can change your colleague's behavior.

Case study #1: Make your coworker publicly accountable

One of Mitch Davis's coworkers in the student guidance office of the public high school where he worked was making things difficult for him (names and details in both these case studies have been changed). "She would agree to a plan in a meeting but then sabotage it by not following through," he explains. His colleague, Sarah, defended herself by saying things like "That's not how I remember it" or "I didn't think we had finalized the plan." He tried to talk about these "misunderstandings" with her, but she always shrugged him off. "She'd say she was busy or didn't have time to talk," he explained.

When Mitch told Jim, his and Sarah's boss, that a certain project hadn't gotten done because of this strange dynamic, Jim said that he had noticed the pattern too. Together, they devised a plan to make Sarah more accountable. "He and I agreed that he would publicly ask for a volunteer to take notes on each meeting, [documenting] who would be responsible for accomplishing each task and by when," Mitch recalls. He was the first volunteer.

And the approach worked. After Mitch sent around the task list, Sarah couldn't make excuses. She was accountable to everyone who attended the meetings. And Mitch didn't mind the additional work: "The extra effort I put in was less than the time I was spending fuming about my coworker and running around to pick up the pieces of the things she didn't complete. It actually helped everyone in our department be more productive and was something we should have done a long time ago."

Case study #2: Get help sooner rather than later

Emily Sullivan, a digital marketing consultant at a small agency, had recently been promoted and managed an eight-person team. One of her direct reports, Will, had only been at the agency for three months before Emily's promotion, and he clearly wasn't thrilled to suddenly have her as a new boss. But "he was a top performer and extremely competent," Emily recalls, and since they'd worked "fairly harmoniously together as colleagues," she was happy to have him in the group.

Unfortunately, Will became very difficult to manage. He didn't communicate with Emily unless absolutely necessary, he didn't actively engage in training sessions that she offered, and he "poked holes" in her initiatives. "He took every opportunity to make it clear that he didn't value my input," she explains.

Surprised and dismayed by his attitude, Emily decided to address it as she would with any other team member: directly and clearly. She started by asking him in their one-on-one meetings whether something was wrong. He said there wasn't, but the behavior persisted, so she tried taking him out for coffee and asking whether she had unknowingly offended him or if he wanted to be managed in a different way. He acknowledged that there was a "personality clash," but he ended the conversation there and continued to treat her dismissively at the office. She heard from other staff members that he had even called her "lazy and useless."

"The last thing I wanted was to pass the issue further up the chain and potentially harm Will's career," she says. After all, he was a valuable team member, and she wanted to protect him. But she came to see that she should have gone to her manager from the start. When she eventually did, her boss pointed out that her failure to effectively manage a key team member amounted to poor performance on her part.

Within a year both Emily and Will voluntarily left the agency, but neither was happy with the circumstances. She says that if she could do it over again she would've talked to her manager sooner, kept better records on Will's "toxic attitude," and, when there weren't drastic improvements, fired him "without hesitation."

AMY GALLO is a contributing editor at *Harvard Business Review* and the author of the *HBR Guide to Dealing with Conflict* (Harvard Business Review Press, 2017). She writes and speaks about workplace dynamics. See her website amyegallo .com and follow her on Twitter @amyegallo.

Note

1. See, for example, Muriel Maignan Wilkins, "Signs You're Being Passive-Aggressive," hbr.org, June 20, 2014, https:// hbr.org/2014/06/signs-youre-being-passive-aggressive/.

Adapted from content posted on hbr.org,
January 11, 2016 (product #H02LQP).

6

How to Work with Someone Who's Always Stressed Out

By Rebecca Knight

We all know people who seem to be constantly stressed out—who claim to be buried in work, overloaded with projects, and without a minute to spare. Colleagues like that can be difficult to work with, but you probably don't have a choice. How do you deal with coworkers who can't handle stress? Should you address the issue directly? Or try other tactics to help them calm down and focus? And how can you protect yourself from their toxic emotions?

What the experts say

Stress is part of everyday life. "We all go through periods when we are dealing with a lot of stress," says Caroline Webb, author of *How to Have a Good Day*. "Those periods might last 10 minutes, 10 days, or 10 months." But for certain people, "stress is a habitual pattern." These folks always "feel overwhelmed, constantly stretched, and always out of their depth." Working closely with a person like this can be a real challenge. "But you mustn't make them the villain," says Holly Weeks, author of *Failure to Communicate*. "Don't think, *What can I do to change this person?* Think about how to neutralize the situation and what you can do for yourself." Whether you regard your colleague with annoyance or sympathy, here are some tips on how to collaborate more effectively.

Don't judge

First things first: Check that you're not being too judgmental. "There's an enormous range in people's tolerance level for stress, and stress that may feel toxic to you may be stimulating to someone else," Weeks explains. "So unless you're a psychologist, judging someone's way of handling stress as inappropriate is fraught." Try to think of your colleague's disposition "as not a character flaw but a characteristic." Webb notes that your coworker may just be responding to the "always-on nature of work" nowadays. "There was a time when we could go home and forget about work until the next day," but the modern era's "pressure to stay connected" weighs on some more than others.

Acknowledge the stress

It's important to make the stressed-out person feel "seen and heard," Webb says. "Say something like,

'I notice you were working late last night, and it wasn't the first time. How are things going?'" Then, after your colleague recites the usual catalog of pressures, "say, 'That must be hard.' It doesn't matter if you believe it or not. That's how this person is feeling. Acknowledging it gives you both a chance to move beyond." At the same time, Weeks says, you mustn't "enable" or agitate your colleague by making comments like, "I don't know how you can you stand it! This company is working you to death!" That's not helpful. Instead, she says, say something more neutral, like "You have a lot of balls in the air."

Offer praise

One of the best ways to "get a stressed person out of fight-or-flight mode [is to] pay a compliment," Webb says. "This person is feeling out of control, incompetent, and disrespected. A compliment is your easy way to help them get back to their better self." Praising someone's performance in the workplace gives the person an alternative "self-image of being a competent, positive professional," Weeks adds. Cite something specific. For instance, you could say, "The way you handled that presentation last week was admirable. You were so calm and collected and the clients were impressed." Appreciation can be a powerful intervention. "When you tell people how you see them, they step into that role."

Offer your assistance

Another strategy is to offer your support. "Say, 'Is there anything that I, or anyone on my team, can do to help to you?'" Webb suggests. "Chances are that you can't do anything, but your offer will give the other person a chance to think about solutions and feel that he's not out on his own." Be clear, however, that this isn't a blanket invitation to be used anytime, anywhere, Weeks says. "Give caveats about what you're able to do." The message should be, "I'm a limited resource, but I want to help you if you are in a pickle."

Break down your requests

When dealing with stressed-out colleagues, think about ways to "reduce their cognitive load," Webb says. "Don't add to their sense of being overwhelmed." You might, for instance, shorten your emails to the person, split your larger requests into several smaller steps, or encourage the idea of dividing work into manageable chunks. "Be smart about how you break down your ask," she adds. But don't go too far. You'll have to reconcile your colleague's deficiencies with your own desire and need to complete tasks. After all, "your job is to get done what you need to get done."

Ask for a read

If your coworker's anxieties seem to be having an impact on their ability to focus—and you're genuinely worried about their health—ask them to provide more detail, Weeks recommends. "Say, 'On a scale of 1 to 10, how worried should I be about your level of stress?' Signal that you can't read how bad it is for them." The answers may surprise you. "They may tell you, 'Oh, this is a 5,' in which case you don't need to call an ambulance. Or they may reveal that their wife has cancer and they're going through something very hard." To a large degree, the roots of the tension "are none of your business."

Get some distance

Stress can be contagious, so "have the self-awareness to know the effect it's having on you," Webb says. "When someone is toxic and draining your energy, you sometimes have to figure out how you can get distance from that person or limit your interactions with them." Of course, this isn't always easy—particularly if you work in the same department and are assigned to the same projects. In that case, Weeks says, look at the bright side of the situation. "When it comes to office characters, the laconic, laid-back, doesn't-carry-their-weight type is the person who's going to leave you in a jam," she explains. "While you may not prefer the stress case's temperament, it's less of a problem."

Principles to remember

Do:

- Offer support by asking if there's anything you can do to help. This will help your stressed-out colleague feel less alone.

- Improve your colleague's self-image by offering praise.

- Think about ways to reduce the person's cognitive load by, for instance, breaking work up into more-manageable chunks.

Don't:

- Judge. Your colleague may express stress differently than you, but that's not necessarily a character flaw.

- Enable the person. Simply acknowledge the stress, then try to help your colleague move beyond it.

- Get sucked in. Instead, figure out ways to get distance from your colleague.

Case study #1: Offer your help and perspective

Karoli Hindriks, founder and CEO of Jobbatical, the international job placement firm, previously worked at a company where she supervised a highly anxious marketing executive. The colleague—we'll call her

Jenny—"was so overwhelmed and stressed out by her work that her overall performance was really beginning to suffer," Karoli recalls. "Everyone could see how hard she was working. But I also saw the dark circles under her eyes, her jumpy mood, and her irritability."

Karoli knew that it wasn't her place to judge; Jenny just seemed to be wired that way. Instead, she offered support and talked about the work that Jenny had to do in terms of small steps rather than a single large, daunting task. "I asked her to imagine a messy room that she needed to clean up. I told her to think of stepping into that room and seeing the clothes scattered all over the floor, the mountain of candy wrappers under the bed, and the layer of dust covering every surface."

"I told her she had two options: She could give up, fall apart, and surrender to the mess, or she could pick up the first pair of socks you see and feel good about being one step closer to cleaning up that mess.

Step by step, inch by inch, item by item, she would create order."

Karoli says that message got through to Jenny. "I started to see her sharing more of her small victories and how happy that was making her," she says. "Her performance improved drastically, and her team members felt comfortable communicating with her again."

Case study #2: Be empathetic and praise your stressed-out colleague's strengths

Earlier in her career, Jan Bruce worked as a publisher and editor at a consumer health and wellness magazine. "It was a high-stress environment in a pressure-cooker industry," she recalls. "There were a lot of big personalities strutting around the office. The culture was toxic, and people were inclined to be disparaging."

One of her closest colleagues—we'll call her Abby—became consumed by the strain of her job. "She had been very successful in the organization and had gotten many promotions, so she was under extreme pressure," Jan explains. At a certain point, she started working so hard that "she was unable to focus. The stress was making her sick."

Jan remembers approaching Abby with a "spirit of empathy" and concern. "I said, 'I know that you're under a lot of pressure. How are you coping?' which made Abby want to talk to me and confide in me."

Through subsequent conversations, Jan saw that Abby was determined to achieve and be successful, but she also needed to give herself a break and let some of the stress go. "She had an attitude of, 'I will overcome this. If I just work longer and harder, everything will be okay.'"

Jan responded by complimenting Abby's skills and abilities. "I said, 'You are doing all of this great work, and you've been put in charge of a whole new division, plus you have four small children at home. No matter what you're feeling today, you are enormously smart and competent. You have to remember that. If you ever forget, I'm here to remind you.'"

Abby appreciated the support, and the two ultimately developed a strong working relationship.

Today Jan is the cofounder and CEO of MeQuilibrium, a software platform that helps companies and workers better manage their productivity, health, and well-being.

REBECCA KNIGHT is a freelance journalist in Boston and a lecturer at Wesleyan University. Her work has been published in the *New York Times*, *USA Today*, and the *Financial Times*.

Reprinted from hbr.org, originally published
August 7, 2017 (product #H03TO8).

7

How to Manage Someone Who Thinks Everything Is Urgent

By Liz Kislik

We've all been in situations where we couldn't wait for a slow-moving or overly cautious employee to take action. But at the other extreme, some employees have such a deep need to get things resolved that they move too quickly, or too intensely, and make a mess. They may make a bad deal just to say they've made it or issue a directive without thinking through the ramifications just to say they've handled a problem decisively.

The problem is that these employees may have been praised in the past for this very behavior, even when it results in mistakes that they can then heroically "save." And when urgency is a part of the organizational culture, it may feel like a requirement to move fast, whether you're a leader or a frontline employee. At a basic level, because urgency generates so much activity, it can be hard to recognize it as an organizational problem. But it's a significant one. Executives report that thousands of dollars are lost every business day when decisions are rote or arbitrary because of pro forma, nonstrategic decision making.

And yet, despite the damage that unaddressed urgency can do, urgent employees are usually some of the most committed and are often very productive. Here are steps you can take to mitigate the negative impact of their urgency, to help them focus their intensity on the right targets, and to ensure they make better long-term decisions before taking action.

Help them recognize their impact on others. Show your urgent employees how collaboration pays off for everyone—including them. One assistant VP I worked with was correct about what needed to be accomplished, but he was driven to get it over with and put it behind him and often operated unilaterally to get things done. Because he was only urgent about his own goals and tasks, he was perceived as a bad partner and not a team player. I encouraged his manager to affirm the importance of collaboration and to ask him to prepare the equivalent of "impact statements" as a way to force interaction and cooperation with other parties. His manager also learned to stop praising him for every accomplishment and to praise him instead for the process: joint planning, coordination, and interdepartmental success.

Encourage them to identify all the consequences of their actions. It's typical for urgent employees to see only the upside of acting quickly, not the negative effects of acting *too* quickly. A VP at a nonprofit client had a history of making decisions hastily and without sufficient data. These decisions led to some unfortunate employee layoffs, even though she had been asked to consult with others and weigh such decisions carefully. After we had her rehearse termination conversations with the employees she had just hired, we dramatized the impact the firings would have on them as individuals and on their families. The exposure to the pain she was causing finally got her attention.

Pair them with long-term thinkers. Effective interventions let urgent employees actually experience the success that comes from a more deliberate, thoughtful approach. A senior sales specialist brought in many deals because he was both diligent and intense. But he was so eager to get the deals that as soon as a prospect indicated even a tentative yes, he would offer anything they seemed to want to close their initial order rather than strengthening his own presentation to get better value. After he brought in several new accounts that were significantly smaller than potential or that had too many strings attached, his management paired him with a more cerebral colleague who excelled in research and planning. The combination of high energy and careful planning increased the number and size of deals.

Coach them to separate urgency from what actually needs to be done. Addressing underlying concerns often mitigates the apparent need for urgency. During a period of organizational growth, a previously solid team leader made people nuts because he seemed to not take others' input, needed to manage everything himself, and didn't share enough information or decision making with his team. His team's growth and development was suppressed, and he was almost always overwhelmed and holding up progress. We discussed various aspects of project management so that he could see he had all the elements under control, and then I asked, "What's the actual pressure?" After some discussion, it became clear that the pressure wasn't from the work itself so much as from feeling alone with the awesome responsibility of handling it all. We used mindfulness techniques to help him cope with the feeling and various other techniques for engaging his team so that they understood the ramifications, how to anticipate, how to shoulder more responsibility, and how to warn him if anything was going off course.

Employees who are driven by excessive urgency often act like they're scratching an itch rather than making intentional efforts to accomplish and grow as much as they can, either for themselves or their organizations. Once they realize that additional re-flection and deliberation can generate significantly better results, they can learn to corral their urgency in service of being a better leader and achieving bet-ter performance.

LIZ KISLIK has helped organizations from the *Fortune* 500 to national nonprofits and family-run businesses—such as American Express, the American Red Cross, Staples, and Highlights for Children—solve their biggest challenges in organizational performance, talent management, and leadership development while strengthening their top and bottom lines in the process. She has served as adjunct faculty at Hofstra University and New York University, and speaks frequently on the topics of collaboration, managing teams, developing leaders, and improving customer loyalty.

Reprinted from hbr.org, originally published
August 2, 2017 (product #H03TJ0).

8

Do You Hate Your Boss?

By Manfred F. R. Kets de Vries

Stacey really loved her job at a top tech company—that is, until her boss left for another firm. The new manager, Peter, seemed to dislike pretty much everyone on the team he had inherited, regardless of individual or collective performance. He was aloof, prone to micromanaging, and apt to write off any project that wasn't his brainchild. Within a year he had replaced a number of Stacey's colleagues.

At first Stacey (whose name, like others in this article, has been changed to protect her confidentiality) tried to win her new boss's trust and respect by asking for his feedback and guidance. But Peter was unresponsive. Despite her best efforts, Stacey couldn't make the relationship click. When, several months in, she finally decided to approach HR about the problem, she got nothing more than sympathy. The firm was not willing to sanction Peter, because his unit's performance had not materially deteriorated and no one else had lodged a complaint.

Unable to escape or change the dynamic with Peter, Stacey felt stressed, depressed, and increasingly unable to do good work. She worried that the only way out was to leave the company she loved.

Stacey's situation is not uncommon. According to the most recent Gallup State of the Global Workplace study, half of all employees in the United States have quit jobs at some point in their career in order to get away from their bosses. The figures are similar or even higher for workers in Europe, Asia, the Middle East, and Africa.[1]

The same survey, consistent with previous ones, also shows a clear correlation between an employee's engagement (that is, motivation and effort to achieve organizational goals) and his or her relationship with the boss. While 77% of employees who said they were engaged at work described interactions with their managers in positive terms (for example, "my supervisor focuses on my strengths"), only 23% of those who were "not engaged" and a mere 4% of those who were "actively disengaged" did the same. This is worrying, because research has shown that an engaged workforce is a key driver of organizational success. And yet according to Gallup, only 13% of employees worldwide fall into that category.

What are the "bad" bosses doing? Frequently cited grievances include micromanaging, bullying, avoiding conflict, ducking decisions, stealing credit, shifting blame, hoarding information, failing to listen, setting a poor example, slacking, and not developing staff. Such dysfunctional behavior would make anyone unhappy and unproductive. However, whatever sins your boss commits, managing your relationship with them is a critical part of your job. Doing it well is a key indicator of how effective you are.

In my work as a researcher, management coach, and psychoanalyst, I have spent many decades working with senior and high-potential executives to help them resolve dysfunctional dynamics with their managers. This article explores the options available to anyone in the same predicament. Much of it will feel like common sense. But I have found that people often forget that it's in their power to improve bad situations, so having the options systematically laid out can be very helpful.

Practice empathy

The first step is to consider the external pressures your manager is under. Remember, most bad bosses are not inherently bad people; they're good people with weaknesses that can be exacerbated by the pressure to lead and deliver results. So it's important to consider not just how they act but why they're acting that way.

Research has shown time and again that practicing empathy can be a game changer in difficult boss-subordinate relationships and not just as a top-down phenomenon. Experts such as Stephen Covey and Daniel Goleman emphasize the importance of using this key aspect of emotional intelligence to manage up. Neuroscience also suggests that it's an effective strategy, since mirror neurons in the human brain naturally prompt people to reciprocate behaviors. Bottom line: If you work on empathizing with your boss, chances are they will start empathizing with you, and that will benefit everyone.

It may seem difficult to feel for a manager who isn't giving you what you need or whom you actively dislike. But as Goleman showed years ago, empathy can be learned. And recent research from other scholars, including experts at the Menninger Clinic, suggests that if you practice empathy consciously, your perceptions of others' feelings will be more accurate.[2]

I recall the case of George, a sales manager in a big U.S. firm, who had been going out of his way to please his boss, Abby—to no avail. George was extremely frustrated by Abby's lack of attention and support until a colleague told him to imagine being in the boss's shoes. George knew that Abby's own manager was a real taskmaster, famous for setting impossible stretch goals. Once George took that into account, he realized that Abby was not deliberately ignoring him; she simply didn't have time to be supportive, as she was working on several important new business initiatives at once.

Although it may be a conscious exercise, a display of empathy is still best delivered in an informal setting. You don't make an appointment; instead you look for the right moment when the other person will be receptive to your efforts. In George's case it came on a shared business trip to some high-profile accounts in Singapore. Over dinner the first day, he carefully offered Abby an opportunity to open up about the pressures she felt by asking how the new business projects in mainland China were coming along.

Abby turned out to be only too ready to share her stresses and frustrations, and the exchange marked a turning point in what eventually became a very satisfactory working relationship between the two. George worried less about the attention he was (or wasn't) getting, and Abby seemed readier to listen to his problems.

Consider your role

The second step is to look at yourself. In my experience, people who struggle to work well with their bosses are nearly always part of the problem themselves: Their behavior is in some way preventing them from being recognized and valued. This probably isn't what you want to hear, but by acknowledging that you might be doing something wrong, figuring out what it is, and adjusting accordingly, you might be able to salvage the relationship.

Start with some introspection. Consider, as objectively as you can, any criticisms your boss has offered. In what areas do you need to improve? What aspects of your behavior or output might irk him or her?

Also ask yourself what might make your personalities clash. I often find after a fairly short discussion with clients that their managers are "transferential figures," representing authority figures from the past with whom the clients have unresolved issues. Transference of this kind has a powerful influence on behavior and should always be explicitly considered in figuring out dysfunctions in any boss-subordinate relationship.

One client, for example, told me that her boss reminded her of a primary school teacher who had bullied her and whom she had never been able to please. The two resembled each other physically and shared a similar peremptory manner of communicating.

When we surface transference, we can usually take steps to correct for it. After our sessions, my client reported that she found it easier to step back and separate her past resentments from her present reactions and view her boss's comments in a positive light.

Next, observe and seek advice from colleagues who work successfully with your boss. Try to understand the boss's preferences, quirks, and hot buttons, and get some pointers on how you might do things differently. When you approach colleagues, though, make sure to frame any questions carefully. For instance, instead of asking a coworker why the boss always interrupts you when you speak, ask the person, "How do *you* know whether to speak up or not? How can you tell when the boss does or doesn't want input? How do you express disagreement?"

Also take advantage of group training programs to get advice from peers. I remember the case of Tom, who, during a leadership development workshop was asked (like everyone else in his small group) to present an issue that was troubling him. He confessed that he needed to improve his relationship with his boss; whatever he did, it never seemed good enough. His peers were frank in their responses. They said that he often sounded muddled in meetings when trying to explain his business unit goals and that he seemed to be doing a poor job of empowering his direct reports. In the view of his colleagues, this was why the boss was dissatisfied with Tom's performance.

They suggested he spend more time rehearsing and framing his presentations and, in particular, work on proposing less-generic goals and identifying measures of success. They also recommended that he have his subordinates copresent with him and make reports on their own. Tom asked a few clarifying questions and left the workshop eager to apply the advice he'd received. At the next year's planning session, his boss congratulated him on the quality of his group's presentation and followed up with an email praising the teamwork his unit was starting to display.

If feedback from your colleagues doesn't provide any insights into how your behavior might be hurting you, the next step is to try talking to your boss about the problem. Again, approach the conversation delicately, framing your questions in a positive way: "How can I better help you achieve your goals?" rather than "What am I doing wrong?" Position yourself as seeking advice or even mentoring. Request a one-on-one meeting to do this, and give your boss an idea of what you'd like to discuss: performance issues and the development of your management skills.

If you're lucky, he or she will appreciate your willingness to engage and will point out areas to improve, building the foundation for a closer relationship. If your boss stonewalls or rebuffs you, however, that's a clue that the problem isn't you, and you need to figure out what—if anything—you can do to alter things.

Offer a chance to change

If you conclude you're not the one derailing the relationship with your boss, only then should you openly suggest that the two of you don't seem to interact well and that you'd like to remedy the situation.

There are a number of ways into this conversation. If you have the opportunity, you can tack it on as an extension of a frank discussion you're already having. Jeanne, a French executive I once taught, told me about a visit she'd made with her British boss, Richard, to meet a customer. The client gave them both an extremely rough ride, which prompted an exchange between the two of them about what had gone wrong. This gave Jeanne an opening to express some of her frustrations with her boss's behavior, and the two were able to work out how they could improve their own relationship.

If a moment like this does not present itself, you have to initiate the conversation yourself. Most conflict management experts recommend doing that in a private setting where you can't easily be interrupted and where it will be difficult for either of you to leave. To have a constructive talk, it's important that people feel they are in a safe place. Invite your boss out to lunch, perhaps, at a restaurant where you are unlikely to meet colleagues. Explain that you have some private concerns you want to discuss away from the office. If a specific business problem, such as the failure to meet a crucial deadline, came about because of the friction between you, you can say you wish to talk about this event and its implications for other projects—the kind of postmortem that Jeanne and Richard had. Let your boss know to expect a difficult conversation—one that can't be sidestepped. If you just say you want to discuss interpersonal issues, the boss may find some crisis that takes priority.

When you begin a dialogue, you may even discover that your boss is not consciously aware of the degree of your discontent. With Jeanne, for example, one problem was that Richard never asked her for an opinion, listening only to colleagues (also largely British and male) who volunteered their ideas. When they talked about it, Richard explained that he didn't want to put her on the spot in meetings but he had no intention of silencing her.

Organize a mutiny

If you can't improve things by changing your behavior or opening lines of communication with your boss, and if your colleagues feel the same way you do, you should consider alerting HR and the boss's bosses to the problem.

In taking this route, however, you need to make a substantial business case for why your boss is a liability, someone whose poor management will ultimately cause the team's, unit's, or organization's performance to suffer. You must also be prepared to make a credible threat of litigation against the corporation. You'll need documented evidence of the boss's negative impact and inappropriate behavior, such as witness statements and examples of correspondence that clearly breach company rules or HR guidelines. The more people willing to go on record with similar complaints and evidence, the harder it will be for senior managers to ignore or deny the problem.

In the absence of compelling data indicating a pattern of bad behavior, HR representatives are unlikely to be allies; very often they will take the boss's side. Maria, another executive I counseled who had had issues with her boss, initially went to HR for help. But her boss was extremely skilled at self-promotion and persuaded HR that in fact Maria was the problem.

The head of HR not only declined to pursue the matter but even suggested that it was up to Maria to adapt to her boss.

Stories like that are all too common, and many subordinates who have not prepared a strong case against the boss have ended up losing their jobs rather than forcing a change of behavior or practice. Mutiny and whistle-blowing can also damage your future job prospects. Lodging a formal complaint, therefore, should definitely be a last resort.

Play for time or move on

If you are unable to change your relationship with your boss by taking the steps described here, and if there isn't potential for group action, then your options become more limited.

In these situations, most employees simply go through the motions at work and minimize contact with the boss. There is always the possibility, or hope, that he or she will move on. But remember that in playing for time, you also need to set a time limit, so that hanging in doesn't become a way of life. If it does, you will feel disengaged, disenchanted, and even embittered. And that may spill over to other realms, contributing to depression and a range of additional psychosomatic reactions.

The better solution is to look for another job while you're still employed, exiting on your own terms. Beef up your résumé, contact headhunters, line up references, and start interviewing. Having a bad boss isn't your fault, but staying with one will be.

That's ultimately what Stacey concluded. After some soul-searching, she started to hunt for another job. It didn't take her long to find an interesting position in another organization working under a boss with whom she had great rapport. Some months later a former colleague told Stacey that Peter had left the company soon after her. Although his departure was announced as his own choice, the inside scoop was that top management had forced him out because he was losing too many valuable people.

MANFRED F. R. KETS DE VRIES is an executive coach, psychoanalyst, and management scholar. He is the Distinguished Clinical Professor of Leadership Development and Organizational Change at INSEAD in France, Singapore, and Abu Dhabi. His most recent book is *Riding the Leadership Rollercoaster: An Observer's Guide* (Springer, 2017).

Notes

1. "State of the Global Workplace Report 2013," Gallup, http://www.gallup.com/services/178517/state-global-workplace.aspx.
2. J. G. Allen, E. Bleiberg, and T. Haslam-Hopwood, "Understanding Mentalizing: Mentalizing as a Compass for Treatment," Menninger Clinic website, 2003, http://www.menningerclinic.com/education/clinical-resources/mentalizing.

Reprinted from *Harvard Business Review*,
December 2016 (product #R1612H).

Index

The most important management ideas all in one place.

We hope you enjoyed this book from *Harvard Business Review*. For the best ideas HBR has to offer turn to HBR's 10 Must Reads Boxed Set. From books on leadership and strategy to managing yourself and others, this 6-book collection delivers articles on the most essential business topics to help you succeed.

HBR's 10 Must Reads Series

The definitive collection of ideas and best practices on our most sought-after topics from the best minds in business.

- Change Management
- Collaboration
- Communication
- Emotional Intelligence
- Innovation
- Leadership
- Making Smart Decisions

- Managing Across Cultures
- Managing People
- Managing Yourself
- Strategic Marketing
- Strategy
- Teams
- The Essentials

hbr.org/mustreads

Buy for your team, clients, or event.
Visit hbr.org/bulksales for quantity discount rates.

Focus

HBR EMOTIONAL INTELLIGENCE SERIES

HBR Emotional Intelligence Series

How to be human at work

The HBR Emotional Intelligence Series features smart, essential reading on the human side of professional life from the pages of *Harvard Business Review*.

Authentic Leadership	Leadership Presence
Confidence	Mindful Listening
Dealing with Difficult People	Mindfulness
Empathy	Purpose, Meaning, and Passion
Focus	Resilience
Happiness	Self-Awareness
Influence and Persuasion	

Other books on emotional intelligence from *Harvard Business Review*:

HBR Everyday Emotional Intelligence

HBR Guide to Emotional Intelligence

HBR's 10 Must Reads on Emotional Intelligence

Focus

HBR EMOTIONAL INTELLIGENCE SERIES

Harvard Business Review Press

Boston, Massachusetts

HBR Press Quantity Sales Discounts

Harvard Business Review Press titles are available at significant quantity discounts when purchased in bulk for client gifts, sales promotions, and premiums. Special editions, including books with corporate logos, customized covers, and letters from the company or CEO printed in the front matter, as well as excerpts of existing books, can also be created in large quantities for special needs.

For details and discount information for both print and ebook formats, contact booksales@harvardbusiness.org, tel 800-988-0886, or www.hbr.org/bulksales.

Copyright 2019 Harvard Business School Publishing Corporation
All rights reserved
Printed in the United States of America

20 19 18 17 16 15 14 13 12 11

No part of this publication may be reproduced, stored in or introduced into a retrieval system, or transmitted, in any form, or by any means (electronic, mechanical, photocopying, recording, or otherwise), without the prior permission of the publisher. Requests for permission should be directed to permissions@hbsp.harvard.edu, or mailed to Permissions, Harvard Business School Publishing, 60 Harvard Way, Boston, Massachusetts 02163.

The web addresses referenced in this book were live and correct at the time of the book's publication but may be subject to change.

Library of Congress Cataloging-in-Publication Data

Title: Focus.
Other titles: HBR emotional intelligence series.
Description: Boston, Massachusetts : Harvard Business Review Press, [2018]
    Series: HBR emotional intelligence series
Identifiers: LCCN 2018022310 | ISBN 9781633696587 (pbk. : alk. paper)
Subjects: LCSH: Attention. | Interest (Psychology) | Executives—Psychology. |
    Leadership. | Emotional intelligence.
Classification: LCC BF323.I52 F63 2018 | DDC 658.4/094--dc23
LC record available at https://lccn.loc.gov/2018022310

ISBN: 978-1-63369-658-7
eISBN: 978-1-63369-659-4

The paper used in this publication meets the requirements of the American National Standard for Permanence of Paper for Publications and Documents in Libraries and Archives Z39.48-1992.

Contents

Contents

Focus

1

The Focused Leader

By Daniel Goleman

A primary task of leadership is to direct attention. To do so, leaders must learn to focus their own attention. When we speak about being focused, we commonly mean thinking about one thing while filtering out distractions. But a wealth of recent research in neuroscience shows that we focus in many ways, for different purposes, drawing on different neural pathways—some of which work in concert, while others tend to stand in opposition.

Grouping these modes of attention into three broad buckets—focusing on *yourself*, focusing on *others*, and focusing on *the wider world*—sheds new light on the practice of many essential leadership skills. Focusing inward and focusing constructively on others helps leaders cultivate the primary elements of emotional intelligence. A fuller understanding of how they focus on the wider world can improve their ability to devise strategy, innovate, and manage organizations.

Every leader needs to cultivate this triad of awareness, in abundance and in the proper balance, because a failure to focus inward leaves you rudderless, a failure to focus on others renders you clueless, and a failure to focus outward may leave you blindsided.

Focusing on yourself

Emotional intelligence begins with self-awareness—getting in touch with your inner voice. Leaders who heed their inner voices can draw on more resources to make better decisions and connect with their authentic selves. But what does that entail? A look at how people focus inward can make this abstract concept more concrete.

Self-awareness

Hearing your inner voice is a matter of paying careful attention to internal physiological signals. These subtle cues are monitored by the insula, which is tucked behind the frontal lobes of the brain. Attention given to any part of the body amps up the insula's sensitivity to that part. Tune in to your heartbeat, and the insula activates more neurons in that circuitry. How well people can sense their heartbeats has, in fact, become a standard way to measure their self-awareness.

Gut feelings are messages from the insula and the amygdala, which neuroscientist Antonio Damasio, of the University of Southern California, calls "somatic markers." Those messages are sensations that something "feels" right or wrong. Somatic markers simplify decision making by guiding our attention toward better options. They're hardly foolproof (how often was that feeling that you left the stove on correct?), so the more comprehensively we read them, the better we use our intuition. (See the sidebar "Are You Skimming This Sidebar?")

Consider, for example, the implications of an analysis of interviews conducted by a group of British researchers with 118 professional traders and 10 senior managers at four City of London investment banks. The most-successful traders (whose annual income averaged £500,000) were neither the ones who relied entirely on analytics nor the ones who just went with their guts. They focused on a full range of emotions, which they used to judge the value of their intuition. When they suffered losses, they acknowledged their anxiety, became more cautious, and took fewer risks. The least-successful traders (whose income averaged only £100,000) tended to ignore their anxiety and keep going with their gut. Because they failed to heed a wider array of internal signals, they were misled.

Zeroing in on sensory impressions of ourselves in the moment is one major element of self-awareness. But another is critical to leadership: combining our experiences across time into a coherent view of our authentic selves.

To be authentic is to be the same person to others as you are to yourself. In part that entails paying attention to what others think of you, particularly people whose opinions you esteem and who will be candid in their feedback. A variety of focus that is useful here is *open awareness,* in which we broadly notice what's going on around us without getting caught up in or swept away by any particular thing. In this mode we don't judge, censor, or tune out; we simply perceive.

Leaders who are more accustomed to giving input than to receiving it may find this tricky. Someone who has trouble sustaining open awareness typically gets snagged by irritating details, such as fellow travelers in the airport security line who take forever getting

ARE YOU SKIMMING THIS SIDEBAR?

Do you have trouble remembering what someone has just told you in conversation? Did you drive to work this morning on autopilot? Do you focus more on your smartphone than on the person you're having lunch with?

Attention is a mental muscle; like any other muscle, it can be strengthened through the right kind of exercise. The fundamental rep for building deliberate attention is simple: When your mind wanders, notice that it has wandered, bring it back to your desired point of focus, and keep it there as long as you can. That basic exercise is at the root of virtually every kind of meditation. Meditation builds concentration and calmness and facilitates recovery from the agitation of stress.

So does a video game called Tenacity, developed by a design group and neuroscientists. The game offers a leisurely journey through any of half a dozen scenes, from a barren desert to a fantasy staircase spiraling heavenward. At the beginner's level you tap an iPad screen with one finger every time you exhale; the challenge is to tap two fingers with every fifth breath. As you move to higher levels, you're presented with more distractions—a helicopter flies into view, a plane does a flip, a flock of birds suddenly scuds by.

When players are attuned to the rhythm of their breathing, they experience the strengthening of selective attention as a feeling of calm focus, as in meditation. Stanford University is exploring that connection at its Calming Technology Lab, which is developing relaxing devices, such as a belt that detects your breathing rate. Should a chock-full inbox, for instance, trigger what has been called "email apnea," an iPhone app can guide you through exercises to calm your breathing and your mind.

their carry-ons into the scanner. Someone who can keep her attention in open mode will notice the travelers but not worry about them, and will take in more of her surroundings. (See the sidebar "Expand Your Awareness.")

Of course, being open to input doesn't guarantee that someone will provide it. Sadly, life affords us few chances to learn how others really see us and even fewer for executives as they rise through the ranks. That may be why one of the most popular and over-enrolled courses at Harvard Business School is Bill George's Authentic Leadership Development, in which George has created what he calls True North groups to heighten this aspect of self-awareness.

These groups (which anyone can form) are based on the precept that self-knowledge begins with self-revelation. Accordingly, they are open and intimate, "a safe place," George explains, "where members can discuss personal issues they do not feel they can raise elsewhere—often not even with their closest family members." What good does that do? "We don't know who we are until we hear ourselves speaking the story of our lives to those we trust," George says. It's a structured way to match our view of our true selves with the views our most trusted colleagues have—an external check on our authenticity.

Self-control

"Cognitive control" is the scientific term for putting one's attention where one wants it and keeping it there in the face of temptation to wander. This focus is one aspect of the brain's executive function, which is located in the prefrontal cortex. A colloquial term for it is "willpower."

Cognitive control enables executives to pursue a goal despite distractions and setbacks. The same neural circuitry that allows such a single-minded pursuit of goals also manages unruly emotions. Good cognitive control can be seen in people who stay calm

EXPAND YOUR AWARENESS

Just as a camera lens can be set narrowly on a single point or more widely to take in a panoramic view, you can focus tightly or expansively.

One measure of open awareness presents people with a stream of letters and numbers, such as S, K, O, E, 4, R, T, 2, H, P. In scanning the stream, many people will notice the first number, 4, but after that their attention blinks. Those firmly in open awareness mode will register the second number as well.

Strengthening the ability to maintain open awareness requires leaders to do something that verges on the unnatural: cultivate at least sometimes a willingness to not be in control, not offer up their own views, not judge others. That's less a matter of deliberate action than of attitude adjustment.

One path to making that adjustment is through the classic power of positive thinking, because pessimism narrows our focus, whereas positive emotions widen our attention and our receptiveness to the new and unexpected. A simple way to shift into positive mode is to ask yourself, "If everything worked out perfectly in my life, what would I be doing in 10 years?" Why is that effective? Because when you're in an upbeat mood, the University of Wisconsin neuroscientist Richard Davidson has found, your brain's left prefrontal area lights up. That area harbors the circuitry that reminds us how great we'll feel when we reach some long-sought goal.

"Talking about positive goals and dreams activates brain centers that open you up to new possibilities," says Richard Boyatzis, a psychologist at Case Western Reserve. "But if you change the conversation to what you should do to fix yourself, it closes you down . . . You need the negative to survive but the positive to thrive."

in a crisis, tame their own agitation, and recover from a debacle or defeat.

Decades' worth of research demonstrates the singular importance of willpower to leadership success. Particularly compelling is a longitudinal study tracking the fates of all 1,037 children born during a single year in the 1970s in the New Zealand city of Dunedin. For several years during childhood the children were given a battery of tests of willpower, including the psychologist Walter Mischel's legendary "marshmallow test"—a choice between eating one marshmallow right away and getting two by waiting 15 minutes. In Mischel's experiments, roughly a third of children grab the marshmallow on the spot, another third hold out for a while longer, and a third manage to make it through the entire quarter hour.

Years later, when the children in the Dunedin study were in their thirties and all but 4% of them had been tracked down again, the researchers found that those who'd had the cognitive control to resist the marshmallow longest were significantly healthier, more successful financially, and more law-abiding than the ones who'd been unable to hold out at all. In fact, statistical analysis showed that a child's level of self-control was a more powerful predictor of financial success than IQ, social class, or family circumstance.

How we focus holds the key to exercising willpower, Mischel says. Three subvarieties of cognitive control are at play when you pit self-restraint against self-gratification: the ability to voluntarily disengage your focus from an object of desire; the ability to resist distraction so that you don't gravitate back to that object; and the ability to concentrate on the future goal and imagine how good you will feel when you achieve it. As adults the children of Dunedin may have been held hostage to their younger selves, but they need not have been, because the power to focus can be developed. (See the sidebar "Learning Self-Restraint.")

LEARNING SELF-RESTRAINT

Quick, now. Here's a test of cognitive control. In what direction is the middle arrow in each row pointing?

→ → → ← ←
→ ← ← ← ←
→ → ← → →

The test, called the Eriksen Flanker Task, gauges your susceptibility to distraction. When it's taken under laboratory conditions, differences of a thousandth of a second can be detected in the speed with which subjects perceive which direction the middle arrows are pointing. The stronger their cognitive control, the less susceptible they are to distraction.

Interventions to strengthen cognitive control can be as unsophisticated as a game of Simon Says or Red Light, Green Light—any exercise in which you are asked to stop on cue. Research suggests that the better a child gets at playing Musical Chairs, the stronger his or her prefrontal wiring for cognitive control will become.

Operating on a similarly simple principle is a social and emotional learning (SEL) method that's used to strengthen cognitive control in schoolchildren across the United States. When confronted by an upsetting problem, the children are told to think of a traffic signal. The red light means stop, calm down, and think before you act. The yellow light means slow down and think of several possible solutions. The green light means try out a plan and see how it works. Thinking in these terms allows the children to shift away from amygdala-driven impulses to prefrontal-driven deliberate behavior.

It's never too late for adults to strengthen these circuits as well. Daily sessions of mindfulness practice work in a way similar to Musical Chairs and SEL.

(Continued)

LEARNING SELF-RESTRAINT

In these sessions you focus your attention on your breathing and practice tracking your thoughts and feelings without getting swept away by them. Whenever you notice that your mind has wandered, you simply return it to your breath. It sounds easy—but try it for 10 minutes, and you'll find there's a learning curve.

Focusing on others

The word "attention" comes from the Latin *attendere*, meaning "to reach toward." This is a perfect definition of focus on others, which is the foundation of empathy and of an ability to build social relationships—the second and third pillars of emotional intelligence.

Executives who can effectively focus on others are easy to recognize. They are the ones who find common ground, whose opinions carry the most weight, and with whom other people want to work. They emerge as natural leaders regardless of organizational or social rank.

The empathy triad

We talk about empathy most commonly as a single attribute. But a close look at where leaders are focusing when they exhibit empathy reveals three distinct kinds, each important for leadership effectiveness:

- *Cognitive empathy:* the ability to understand another person's perspective

- *Emotional empathy:* the ability to feel what someone else feels

- *Empathic concern:* the ability to sense what another person needs from you

Cognitive empathy enables leaders to explain themselves in meaningful ways—a skill essential to getting the best performance from their direct reports.

Contrary to what you might expect, exercising cognitive empathy requires leaders to think about feelings rather than to feel them directly.

An inquisitive nature feeds cognitive empathy. As one successful executive with this trait puts it, "I've always just wanted to learn everything, to understand anybody that I was around—why they thought what they did, why they did what they did, what worked for them, and what didn't work." But cognitive empathy is also an outgrowth of self-awareness. The executive circuits that allow us to think about our own thoughts and to monitor the feelings that flow from them let us apply the same reasoning to other people's minds when we choose to direct our attention that way.

Emotional empathy is important for effective mentoring, managing clients, and reading group dynamics. It springs from ancient parts of the brain beneath the cortex—the amygdala, the hypothalamus, the hippocampus, and the orbitofrontal cortex—that allow us to feel fast without thinking deeply. They tune us in by arousing in our bodies the emotional states of others: I literally feel your pain. My brain patterns match up with yours when I listen to you tell a gripping story. As Tania Singer, the director of the social neuroscience department at the Max Planck Institute for Human Cognitive and Brain Sciences in Leipzig, Germany, says, "You need to understand your own feelings to understand the feelings of others." Accessing your capacity for emotional empathy depends on combining two kinds of attention: a deliberate focus on your own echoes of someone else's feelings and an open awareness of that person's face, voice, and other external signs of emotion. (See the sidebar "When Empathy Needs to Be Learned.")

Empathic concern, which is closely related to emotional empathy, enables you to sense not just how people feel but what they need from you. It's what you want in your doctor, your spouse—and your boss. Empathic concern has its roots in the circuitry that

WHEN EMPATHY NEEDS TO BE LEARNED

Emotional empathy can be developed. That's the conclusion suggested by research conducted with physicians by Helen Riess, the director of the Empathy and Relational Science Program at Boston's Massachusetts General Hospital. To help the physicians monitor themselves, she set up a program in which they learned to focus using deep, diaphragmatic breathing and to cultivate a certain detachment—to watch an interaction from the ceiling, as it were, rather than being lost in their own thoughts and feelings. "Suspending your own involvement to observe what's going on gives you a mindful awareness of the interaction without being completely reactive," says Riess. "You can see if your own physiology is charged up or balanced. You can notice what's transpiring in the situation." If a doctor realizes that she's feeling irritated, for instance, that may be a signal that the patient is bothered too.

Those who are utterly at a loss may be able to prime emotional empathy essentially by faking it until they make it, Riess adds. If you act in a caring way—looking people in the eye and paying attention to their expressions, even when you don't particularly want to—you may start to feel more engaged.

compels parents' attention to their children. Watch where people's eyes go when someone brings an adorable baby into a room, and you'll see this mammalian brain center leaping into action.

One neural theory holds that the response is triggered in the amygdala by the brain's radar for sensing danger and in the prefrontal cortex by the release of oxytocin, the chemical for caring. This implies that empathic concern is a double-edged feeling. We intuitively experience the distress of another as our own. But in deciding whether we will meet that person's needs, we deliberately weigh how much we value his or her well-being.

Getting this intuition-deliberation mix right has great implications. Those whose sympathetic feelings become too strong may themselves suffer. In the helping professions, this can lead to compassion fatigue; in executives, it can create distracting feelings of anxiety about people and circumstances that are beyond anyone's control. But those who protect themselves by deadening their feelings may lose touch with empathy. Empathic concern requires us to manage our personal distress without numbing ourselves to the pain of others. (See the sidebar "When Empathy Needs to Be Controlled.")

What's more, some lab research suggests that the appropriate application of empathic concern is critical to making moral judgments. Brain scans have revealed that when volunteers listened to tales of people subjected to physical pain, their own brain centers for experiencing such pain lit up instantly. But if the story was about psychological suffering, the higher brain centers involved in empathic concern and compassion took longer to activate. Some time is needed to grasp the psychological and moral dimensions of a situation. The more distracted we are, the less we can cultivate the subtler forms of empathy and compassion.

WHEN EMPATHY NEEDS TO BE CONTROLLED

Getting a grip on our impulse to empathize with other people's feelings can help us make better decisions when someone's emotional flood threatens to overwhelm us.

Ordinarily, when we see someone pricked with a pin, our brains emit a signal indicating that our own pain centers are echoing that distress. But physicians learn in medical school to block even such automatic responses. Their attentional anesthetic seems to be deployed by the temporal-parietal junction and regions of the prefrontal cortex, a circuit that boosts

---

Building relationships

People who lack social sensitivity are easy to spot—at least for other people. They are the clueless among us. The CFO who is technically competent but bul-

concentration by tuning out emotions. That's what is happening in your brain when you distance yourself from others in order to stay calm and help them. The same neural network kicks in when we see a problem in an emotionally overheated environment and need to focus on looking for a solution. If you're talking with someone who is upset, this system helps you understand the person's perspective intellectually by shifting from the heart-to-heart of emotional empathy to the head-to-heart of cognitive empathy.

lies some people, freezes out others, and plays favorites—but when you point out what he has just done, shifts the blame, gets angry, or thinks that you're the problem—is not trying to be a jerk; he's utterly unaware of his shortcomings.

Social sensitivity appears to be related to cognitive empathy. Cognitively empathic executives do better at overseas assignments, for instance, presumably because they quickly pick up implicit norms and learn the unique mental models of a new culture. Attention to social context lets us act with skill no matter what the situation, instinctively follow the universal algorithm for etiquette, and behave in ways that put others at ease. (In another age this might have been called good manners.)

Circuitry that converges on the anterior hippocampus reads social context and leads us intuitively to act differently with, say, our college buddies than with our families or our colleagues. In concert with the deliberative prefrontal cortex, it squelches the impulse to do something inappropriate. Accordingly, one brain test for sensitivity to context assesses the function of the hippocampus. The University of Wisconsin neuroscientist Richard Davidson hypothesizes that people who are most alert to social situations exhibit stronger activity and more connections between the hippocampus and the prefrontal cortex than those who just can't seem to get it right.

The same circuits may be at play when we map social networks in a group—a skill that lets us navigate the relationships in those networks well. People who excel at organizational influence can not only sense the flow of personal connections but also name the people whose opinions hold most sway—and so focus on persuading those who will persuade others.

Alarmingly, research suggests that as people rise through the ranks and gain power, their ability to perceive and maintain personal connections tends to suffer a sort of psychic attrition. In studying encounters between people of varying status, Dacher Keltner, a psychologist at Berkeley, has found that higher-ranking individuals consistently focus their gaze less on lower-ranking people and are more likely to interrupt or to monopolize the conversation.

In fact, mapping attention to power in an organization gives a clear indication of hierarchy: The longer it takes Person A to respond to Person B, the more relative power Person A has. Map response times across an entire organization, and you'll get a remarkably accurate chart of social standing. The boss leaves emails unanswered for hours; those lower down respond within minutes. This is so predictable that an algorithm for it—called automated social hierarchy detection—has been developed at Columbia University. Intelligence agencies reportedly are applying the algorithm to suspected terrorist gangs to piece together chains of influence and identify central figures.

But the real point is this: Where we see ourselves on the social ladder sets the default for how much attention we pay. This should be a warning to top executives, who need to respond to fast-moving competitive situations by tapping the full range of ideas and talents within an organization. Without a deliberate shift in attention, their natural inclination may be to ignore smart ideas from the lower ranks.

Focusing on the wider world

Leaders with a strong outward focus are not only good listeners but also good questioners. They are visionaries who can sense the far-flung consequences of local decisions and imagine how the choices they make today will play out in the future. They are open to the surprising ways in which seemingly unrelated data can inform their central interests. Melinda and Bill Gates offered up a cogent example when Melinda remarked on *60 Minutes* that her husband was the kind of person who would read an entire book about fertilizer. Charlie Rose asked, "Why fertilizer?" The connection was obvious to Bill, who is constantly looking for technological advances that can save lives on a massive scale. "A few billion people would have to die if we hadn't come up with fertilizer," he replied.

Focusing on strategy

Any business school course on strategy will give you the two main elements: exploitation of your current advantage and exploration for new ones. Brain scans that were performed on 63 seasoned business decision makers as they pursued or switched between exploitative and exploratory strategies revealed the specific circuits involved. Not surprisingly, exploitation requires concentration on the job at hand, whereas exploration demands open awareness to recognize new possibilities. But exploitation is accompanied by activity in the brain's circuitry for anticipation and reward. In other words, it feels good to coast along in a familiar routine. When we switch to exploration, we have to make a deliberate cognitive effort to disengage from that routine in order to roam widely and pursue fresh paths.

What keeps us from making that effort? Sleep deprivation, drinking, stress, and mental overload all interfere with the executive circuitry used to make the cognitive switch. To sustain the outward focus that leads to innovation, we need some uninterrupted time in which to reflect and refresh our focus.

The wellsprings of innovation

In an era when almost everyone has access to the same information, new value arises from putting ideas together in novel ways and asking smart questions that open up untapped potential. Moments before we have a creative insight, the brain shows a third-of-a-second spike in gamma waves, indicating the synchrony of far-flung brain cells. The more neurons firing in sync, the bigger the spike. Its timing suggests that what's happening is the formation of a new neural network—presumably creating a fresh association.

But it would be making too much of this to see gamma waves as a secret to creativity. A classic model of creativity suggests how the various modes of attention play key roles. First we prepare our minds by gathering a wide variety of pertinent information, and then we alternate between concentrating intently on the problem and letting our minds wander freely. Those activities translate roughly into vigilance, when while immersing ourselves in all kinds of input, we remain alert for anything relevant to the problem at hand; selective attention to the specific creative challenge; and open awareness, in which we allow our minds to associate freely and the solution to emerge spontaneously. (That's why so many fresh ideas come to people in the shower or out for a walk or a run.)

The dubious gift of systems awareness

If people are given a quick view of a photo of lots of dots and asked to guess how many there are, the strong systems thinkers in the group tend to make the best estimates. This skill shows up in those who are good at designing software, assembly lines, matrix organizations, or interventions to save failing ecosystems—it's a very powerful gift indeed. After all, we live within extremely complex systems. But, suggests the Cambridge University psychologist Simon Baron-Cohen (a cousin of actor Sacha's), in a small but significant number of people, a strong systems awareness is coupled with an empathy deficit—a blind spot for what other people are thinking and feeling and for reading social situations. For that reason, although people with a superior systems understanding are organizational assets, they are not necessarily effective leaders.

An executive at one bank explained to me that it has created a separate career ladder for systems analysts so that they can progress in status and salary on the basis of their systems smarts alone. That way, the bank can consult them as needed while recruiting leaders from a different pool—one containing people with emotional intelligence.

Putting it all together

For those who don't want to end up similarly compartmentalized, the message is clear. A focused leader is not the person concentrating on the three most important priorities of the year, or the most brilliant systems thinker, or the one most in tune with the corporate culture. Focused leaders can command the full range of their own attention: They are in touch with their inner feelings, they can control their impulses, they are aware of how others see them, they understand what others need from them, and they can weed out distractions and also allow their minds to roam widely, free of preconceptions.

This is challenging. But if great leadership were a paint-by-numbers exercise, great leaders would be more common. Practically every form of focus can be strengthened. What it takes is not talent so much as diligence—a willingness to exercise the attention circuits of the brain just as we exercise our analytic skills and other systems of the body.

The link between attention and excellence remains hidden most of the time. Yet attention is the basis of the most essential of leadership skills—emotional, organizational, and strategic intelligence. And never has it been under greater assault. The constant onslaught of incoming data leads to sloppy shortcuts—triaging our email by reading only the subject lines, skipping many of our voicemails, skimming memos and reports. Not only do our habits of attention make us less effective, but the sheer volume of all those messages leaves us too little time to reflect on what they really mean. This was foreseen decades ago by the Nobel Prize–winning economist Herbert Simon. Information "consumes the attention of its recipients," he wrote in 1971. "Hence a wealth of information creates a poverty of attention."

My goal here is to place attention center stage so that you can direct it where you need it when you need it. Learn to master your attention, and you will be in command of where you, and your organization, focus.

DANIEL GOLEMAN is codirector of the Consortium for Research on Emotional Intelligence in Organizations at Rutgers University and coauthor of *Primal Leadership: Unleashing the Power of Emotional Intelligence* (Harvard Business Review Press, 2013). His latest book is *Altered Traits: Science Reveals How Meditation Changes Your Mind, Brain, and Body.*

Reprinted from *Harvard Business Review*,
December 2013 (product #R1312B).

2

Break the Cycle of Stress and Distraction by Using Your Emotional Intelligence

By Kandi Wiens

Being able to focus helps us succeed.[1] Whether it's focusing inward and attuning ourselves to our intuitions and values or outward and navigating the world around us, honing our attention is a valuable asset.

All too often though, our focus and attention get hijacked, leaving us feeling frazzled, forgetful, and unable to concentrate. In my coaching work with executives, these are the kinds of statements I most often hear when they've lost their focus (I may have uttered a few of them myself):

- "I feel completely overwhelmed."

- "My workload is insane, and there's never enough time to get things done when I'm in meetings and dealing with urgent issues all day long."

- "I'm mentally exhausted from the pressure and constant distractions in my office. I just can't seem to focus."

Constant distractions and a lack of time certainly interrupt our focus, but stress also plays a major role.[2]

Chronic stress floods our nervous system with cortisol and adrenaline that short-circuits important cognitive functions.[3] Researchers have studied the negative effects of stress on focus, memory, and other cognitive functions for decades. The findings are consistent: Short-term stress raises cortisol levels (the so-called stress hormone) for short periods and can jump-start our adrenaline and motivate us to perform more efficiently in response to impending deadlines.[4] Long-term stress, however, can lead to prolonged increases in cortisol and can be toxic to the brain. Scientists also suspect that high levels of cortisol over a long period of time are a key contributor to Alzheimer's and other forms of dementia.[5]

When we can't focus at work because of distractions, it may lead us to feel stressed about not being productive, which then causes us to focus less, further feeding the cycle. Unfortunately, most of us don't notice our focus declining until we become completely overwhelmed. When mental and emotional exhaustion sets in, it further drains our ability to focus, concentrate, and recall information.

Fortunately, there are things we can do to break the cycle. I've found in my research that one of the reasons why some people get burned out and others don't is because they use their emotional intelligence (EI) to manage their stress.[6] You can use these same competencies, in particular self-awareness and self-management, to improve your focus. Here's how.

Start by using your self-awareness to help you notice several things:

- *Why you feel stressed or anxious.* Before you can deal with stress, you need to know what's causing it. As simple as it may sound, it can be helpful to make a list of the sources of your stress. Write down each thing in your life and at work that's causing you anxiety. You might categorize items into things you have the ability to change and things you don't. For the stressors in the latter category, you will need to figure out how to change your attitude toward them.[7]

- *How you lose your ability to focus.* According to clinical psychologist Michael Lipson, you can learn to sharpen your focus by understanding how exactly your concentration strays in the first place.[8] By paying attention to the patterns that lead to your lack of focus, you can begin to develop your ability to dismiss distractions and stay with your original point of attention.

- *How you feel when you can't focus.* Does it make you anxious when you can't recall information when you need it—perhaps during a job interview, a high-stakes presentation, or an important client meeting? Do you feel tense and dazed when you're racking your brain trying to find just the right words for an important email? These can be clues that you're more stressed than you may realize—and that your inability to concentrate is causing even more stress.

- *When you lose your ability to focus.* If, for example, you find yourself worrying yourself sick over something while you're driving 65 mph on the highway with a car full of kids, you're putting yourself and others in real danger. This can be a wake-up call to bring your attention back to what you're doing and make a decision to think about your concerns later.

Once you've increased your awareness of what's causing you stress and how and when you lose your focus, you can use the following strategies, which depend on your self-management abilities, to make better choices that keep you focused.

- *Do a digital detox.*[9] In its 2017 Stress in America survey, The American Psychological Association (APA) found that "constant checkers"—people who check their emails, texts, and social media on a constant basis—experience more stress than those who don't.[10] More than 42% of respondents attribute their stress to political and cultural discussions on social media, compared with 33% of non-constant checkers. While it may feel impossible to take a cold turkey break from technology, the APA says that periodically unplugging or limiting your digital access can be great for your mental health.

- *Rest your brain.* Most of us have experienced sleepless nights caused by ruminating over past events or fears and anxieties about the future. When you add a few of these nights together, sleep deprivation can set in, making it more difficult to focus and more challenging to receive and recall information.[11] Our interpretation of events and our judgment may be affected, too.[12] Lack of sleep can negatively affect our decisions because it impairs our ability to accurately assess a situation, plan accordingly, and behave appropriately. Committing to the recommended seven to eight hours of sleep each night may seem impossible when you're stressed and overworked, but the payoff is worth it.[13]

- *Practice mindfulness.* The research on mindfulness is clear and compelling. Having a mindfulness practice decreases our tendency to jump to conclusions and have knee-jerk reactions we may regret later (and potentially cause more stress).[14] Neuroscientist Richard Davidson says that "Mindfulness boosts the classic attention network in the brain's frontoparietal system that works together to allocate attention."[15] In other words, mindfulness is key to emotional resilience, which is a key contributor in our ability to quickly recover from stress. Don't worry, you don't have to be a serious yogi to practice mindfulness.[16]

- *Shift your focus to others.* When we fixate on our own worries and fears, it can take our attention away from those we care about. Studies (mine included) show that shifting our focus to others produces physiological effects that calm us and strengthen our resilience.[17] If you pay more attention to other people's feelings and needs and show concern for them, you can not only take your mind off of your stress but also reap the benefits of knowing that you're doing something meaningful for someone you care about.[18]

Too many people feel like they need to work harder when they struggle to focus. But this strategy is likely to backfire.[19] Instead, pay attention to the causes of your stress and inability to focus, and then take actions that promote improvements in the specific brain functions that drive concentration and awareness.

KANDI WIENS is a faculty member at the University of Pennsylvania Graduate School of Education in the PennCLO executive doctoral program and the Penn Master's in Medical Education program. She is also an executive coach, national speaker, and organizational change consultant.

Notes

1. Daniel Goleman, *Focus: The Hidden Driver of Excellence* (New York: Harper, 2013).
2. William Treseder, "The Two Things Killing Your Ability to Focus," hbr.org, August 3, 2016, https://hbr.org/2016/08/the-two-things-killing-your-ability-to-focus.
3. Madhumita Murgia, "How Stress Affects Your Brain," TED-Ed video, 4:15, https://ed.ted.com/lessons/how-stress-affects-your-brain-madhumita-murgia.
4. Francesca Gino, "Are You Too Stressed to Be Productive? Or Not Stressed Enough?" hbr.org, April 14, 2016, https://

hbr.org/2016/04/are-you-too-stressed-to-be-productive
-or-not-stressed-enough.

5. Elaine Karen Hebda-Bauer and Huda Akil, "How Over-expression of a Stress Gene Modifies Alzheimer's Disease Pathology," grant from the Alzheimer's Association, 2007–2010, https://www.alz.org/research/alzheimers_grants/for_researchers/overview-2007.asp?grants=2007 hebda-bauer.

6. Kandi Weins, "Leading Through Burnout: The Influence of Emotional Intelligence on the Ability of Executive Level Physician Leaders to Cope with Occupational Stress and Burnout," dissertation, University of Pennsylvania, 2016, https://repository.upenn.edu/dissertations/AAI10158565/.

7. David Brendel, "Stress Isn't a Threat, It's a Signal to Change," hbr.org, May 5, 2014, https://hbr.org/2014/05/stress-isnt-a-threat-its-a-signal-to-change.

8. Michael Lipson, "To Improve Your Focus, Notice How You Lose It," hbr.org, November 4, 2015, https://hbr.org/2015/11/to-improve-your-focus-notice-how-you-lose-it. (This article is reproduced in chapter 3 of this book.)

9. Charlotte Lieberman, "Device-Free Time Is as Important as Work-Life Balance," hbr.org, April 13, 2017, https://hbr.org/2017/04/device-free-time-is-as-important-as-work-life-balance.

10. American Psychological Association, "APA's Survey Finds Constantly Checking Electronic Devices Linked to Significant Stress for Most Americans," press release, Febru-

ary 23, 2017, http://www.apa.org/news/press/releases/
2017/02/checking-devices.aspx.

11. Nick van Dam and Els van der Helm, "There's a Proven
    Link Between Effective Leadership and Getting
    Enough Sleep," hbr.org, February 16, 2016, https://hbr
    .org/2016/02/theres-a-proven-link-between-effective
    -leadership-and-getting-enough-sleep.

12. Cristiano Guarana and Christopher M. Barnes, "Research:
    Sleep Deprivation Can Make It Harder to Stay Calm at
    Work," hbr.org, August 21, 2017, https://hbr.org/2017/08/
    research-sleep-deprivation-can-make-it-harder-to-stay
    -calm-at-work.

13. Larry Rosen, "Relax, Turn Off Your Phone, and Go to
    Sleep," hbr.org, August 31, 2015, https://hbr.org/2017/08/
    research-sleep-deprivation-can-make-it-harder-to-stay
    -calm-at-work.

14. Rasmus Hougaard, Jacqueline Carter, and Gitte Dybkjaer,
    "Spending 10 Minutes a Day on Mindfulness Subtly
    Changes the Way You React to Everything," hbr.org,
    January 18, 2017, https://hbr.org/2017/01/spending-10
    -minutes-a-day-on-mindfulness-subtly-changes-the-way
    -you-react-to-everything

15. Richard J. Davidson and Jon Kabat-Zinn, "Alterations in
    Brain and Immune Function Produced by Mindfulness
    Meditation: Three Caveats: Response," *Psychosomatic
    Medicine* 66, no. 1 (January–February 2004): 149–152.

16. Positive Psychology Program, "22 Mindfulness Exercises,
    Techniques, and Activities for Adults," January 18, 2017,

https://positivepsychologyprogram.com/mindfulness
-exercises-techniques-activities/.

17. Annie McKee and Kandi Wiens, "Prevent Burnout by
    Making Compassion a Habit," hbr.org, May 11, 2017,
    https://hbr.org/2017/05/prevent-burnout-by-making
    -compassion-a-habit.

18. Cassie Mogilner, "You'll Feel Less Rushed If You Give
    Time Away," hbr.org, September 2012, https://hbr
    .org/2012/09/youll-feel-less-rushed-if-you-give-time
    -away.

19. Sarah Green Carmichael, "The Research Is Clear: Long
    Hours Backfire for People and for Companies," hbr.org,
    August 19, 2015, https://hbr.org/2015/08/the-research-is
    -clear-long-hours-backfire-for-people-and-for-companies.

Reprinted from hbr.org, originally published
December 12, 2017 (product #H04351).

3

To Improve Your Focus, Notice How You Lose It

By Michael Lipson

We've all been there: You try to focus on a task, and soon you're looking out the window, wondering about dinner, analyzing your golf game, fantasizing about your lover. How did your mind end up in Cancún when you were supposed to be thinking about first-quarter strategy?

The normal act of concentration or attention is a mess, but it's a mess with a specific structure. To learn to sharpen your focus, you can start by understanding this "structure of distraction"—how, exactly, your concentration strays in the first place.

Over the past 20 years working as a clinical psychologist, I have led workshops and meditation groups that have taught people from all walks of life to see the structure of their own distraction. In my work with clinicians in end-of-life care, understanding this structure has helped them distinguish between the needs of dying patients and their own emotional responses. This same skill has helped families to drop resentments and choose togetherness. It has helped business leaders clarify their strategic goals and develop the courage both to initiate and to end internal and external relationships. It has even helped golf players keep their mind on their swing and their eye on the ball.

What follows is my reformulation of wisdom that has been around since people first noticed they had minds—and simultaneously noticed that the mind could be distracted from its intentional focus. It didn't start with the cell phone, as scholar and innovator Cathy Davidson points out.[1] In Greek mythology, Hercules distracts Atlas and tricks him into losing his focus and his freedom. Homer has Circe distract Odysseus from his journey—probably not the first or last sexual distraction. Plato's Socrates explains in his last dialogue that the mind is normally in shreds, and the purpose of philosophy is to "gather" and concentrate the mind in spite of its centrifugal forces. Shakespeare points to a distracted mind, for example, in Claudius's monologue in *Hamlet*.

Like Plato, most writers not only complain about distraction but point implicitly or explicitly to ways to address its downsides. In the meditative traditions, everyone from Gautama Buddha to mindfulness expert Andy Puddicombe of Headspace has said that the prime way to deal with distraction is first to be okay with it, which means noticing it.[2] You notice the distraction, and bring your mind back.

The approach I use summarizes and condenses the wisdom from these disparate traditions. You begin by simply noticing that there are four phases of attention and distraction that happen every time you try to focus:

1. *First, you choose a focus.* It might be anything, from any sphere of life. At work, it's supposed to be some aspect of work—let's say, whom to include in an important meeting.

2. *Sooner or later, your attention wanders.* This isn't what you plan to do. It just happens. (If it *were* a plan, it would be another focus, not a wandering.)

3. *Sooner or later, you wake up to the fact that your mind has wandered.* You notice the distraction. You realize how far you are from the thing you first wanted to focus on. Again, you can't exactly plan or choose this.

4. *Having woken up, you may choose to return to the original theme.* For example, whom to invite to that meeting. Then again, you may choose to give up and do something else. It's up to you; it's a choice.

If you do return to the original theme at step 4, the whole thing tends to begin again. Sooner or later, your mind wanders.

Reviewing these four steps, you'll notice that steps 1 and 4 are conscious choices. Steps 2 and 3 are unconscious—they just happen. The unconscious force at work in the second step, when your mind "just wanders," seems to be hostile to the project of focusing; the force operating in the third step, when you notice your distraction, is not exactly friendly to your focus, but it is friendly to your freedom. It wakes you up to the fact of having wandered from your theme, then leaves it up to you to return to that original focus or not.

Just by noticing these stages over and over as they play out in real time, you'll find that the pattern changes. At first you may simply note that these four stages occur. With repeated attention to the process, you will tend to stay with the original focus longer before distraction sets in. You will wander less far away from the theme, and for a shorter length of time, before waking up. And having woken up from a distraction, you will choose more often to return to the original theme rather than give up and stretch your legs.

Here's how to get started. Pick a theme, any theme: something you want to focus on that would potentially help your business. It could be a personnel decision, it could be a strategic decision, it could be a management issue. That's step 1, your focus. Think about it as clearly and creatively as you can. Soon, your attention will wander. But the very act of noticing the distraction, and the *structure* of distraction, will gradually strengthen your ability to stay focused and head off distraction in the first place.

MICHAEL LIPSON is a clinical psychologist and a former associate clinical professor at Columbia University's medical school. He is the author of *Stairway of Surprise: Six Steps to a Creative Life*.

Notes

1. Cathy N. Davidson, "The History of Distraction, 4000 BCE to the Present," blog post, November 13, 2011, http://www.cathydavidson.com/blog/the-history-of-distraction-4000-bce-to-the-present/.
2. Andy Puddicombe, "Headspace," website, 2018, https://www.headspace.com.

Reprinted from hbr.org, originally published
November 4, 2015 (product #H02GHT).

4

What to Do When You're Feeling Distracted at Work

By Amy Gallo

Sometimes there's so much going on in your life, and in the world, that you can't focus. What can you do when every time you sit down at your desk, you feel distracted? How can you get back to feeling focused and productive?

What the experts say

Feeling distracted and unproductive is something most people struggle with, says Susan David, founder of the Harvard/McLean Institute of Coaching and author of *Emotional Agility*.[1] This is especially true because most of us are constantly bombarded by news alerts, text messages, and other interruptions. And even on days when you might feel industrious, you have to contend with what's going on with your coworkers. "We very subtly pick up on others' behaviors and emotions," David says.[2] "When this happens, we can start to lose our way." Rich Fernandez, CEO of the nonprofit Search Inside Yourself Leadership Institute, a global mindfulness and emotional intelligence training organization, notes that we're actually wired this way. "One thing we all have in common is a fundamental neuroanatomy that orients us toward stress that isn't always productive," he explains. To overcome this and regain your focus, take the following eight steps.

Understand the dangers of multitasking

Start by understanding the impact that distractions, like a constantly pinging phone or quick Twitter break, have on your brain. Fernandez explains that we have a network of brain structures related to focus.[3] There's the *default mode network*, which is responsible for analyzing the past, forecasting or planning for the future, and reflecting on oneself and others. "We're in this mode at least half of the time," he says. But when you need to focus your mind, you tap into the *direct attention network*, which allows you to put aside ruminations and stay on task. Distractions, in whatever form they take, pull you back into default mode, and the cognitive cost of regaining your focus is high.[4] "Some research shows it can take ten to eighteen minutes to get the same level of attention back," Fernandez says.[5] This is why it's critical to reduce interruptions.

Allow for your emotional response, but stay in charge

Feeling overwhelmed can bring up a lot of emotions— frustration, anger, anxiety—that take a further toll on your productivity. So you have to break the cycle,

David says. To regain a sense of agency, so you don't feel "at the mercy of the events going on in the world or in your office," she suggests labeling your feelings and then asking yourself questions about them.[6] You might say, "OK, I'm feeling angry, but who's in charge—the anger or me, the person having the emotion?" Fernandez agrees with this approach: "You want to acknowledge that these feelings are there—they're legitimate and significant—but not get swept away by them."

Gather your attention

When you do find yourself distracted, Fernandez says, "Pause, take stock, be aware that you're being triggered. Then switch the spotlight of your attention." This might feel easier said than done, but remind yourself that most of the things we worry about "aren't immediate existential threats." To reconnect with the logical part of your brain, focus it on "some-

thing more immediate or visceral, like your breath."
You might say to yourself, "I've become consumed
by this Twitter thread. I'm going to pay attention to
my breathing" to pivot away from what's causing the
anxiety.[7] Fernandez says this isn't the same as trying
to ignore the distraction: "You don't have to stifle it or
suppress it. Make note of it, acknowledge it, and put
it in a mental parking lot to think about later, when
you can discuss it with someone else, or when you're
not at work and have lots to do."

Rely on your values

Once you've gathered your attention, you can choose
where to focus it. David says that concentrating on
your values gives you a sense of control. "When you're
overwhelmed, it feels like a lot of power and choices
are being taken away from you," she says. "But you
still get to choose who you want to be. If one of your
core values is to be collaborative, focus on that. How

can you help people feel like part of the team?" And consider how your lack of focus is affecting your sense of self. "If fairness is important to you, how is your distraction contributing to your ability to be fair? If you're on Facebook for three hours a day, how fair is that to your team or your family?"

Put up boundaries

Once you have more awareness about what distracts you, set rules for yourself. If you realize that checking news in the morning means that you're upset and un-focused when you get to the office, tell yourself that you won't catch up on world events until lunchtime.[8] Or you can decide that you're going to get a certain amount of work done before you go on Facebook. If you don't have the self-control for this, there are apps you can install in your browsers or on your phone to control how much time you spend on particular sites. You also have to practice. "There's a lot of research that suggests the difference between elite focus and non-elite focus is deliberate focus," Fernandez says.[9] He points to athletes who train by telling themselves, for example, "I'm not going to leave the free-throw line until I make 10 free throws." So spend time training your brain to stay on task.

Choose whom you interact with wisely

Social contagion is real. "We've all had that experience when you go into an elevator and everyone is looking at their cell phones, so you start looking at yours," David says. She points to recent research that shows that if someone next to you on an airplane buys candy—even if you don't know the person— you're 30% more likely to make a similar purchase.[10] The same goes for productivity.[11] If you have colleagues who are constantly distracted themselves or who tend to pull you away from work, try to spend less time with them. You don't have to be rude; you can say something simple like, "Can we continue this conversation later? I want to get this report done and then I can take a break."

Support and be supported by your colleagues

Instead of avoiding your distracted colleagues, you could try to encourage each other to stay focused. Make a pact with your coworkers. Set up a time where you will work without interrupting each other or without getting on social media or workplace messaging app Slack. The team I work with at HBR designated Thursday afternoons as uninterrupted work time after listening to a podcast about this.[12] You can take this collegial support one step further and actively support each other. "Your peers are in the trenches with you and they can relate because they're in the same culture and organization," Fernandez says. Go out to coffee with a coworker and "ask for advice, counsel, and coaching." They may have tactics that have worked for them that you haven't thought of. Make a commitment to each other that you're going to change your behavior and check in regularly on your progress. When you tell someone else that you want to reform your ways, you're more likely to follow through.[13]

Take care of your body

If you're tired and worn out, you're going to be more vulnerable to feeling overwhelmed, David says. It's important to get enough sleep and exercise. Also, she suggests making "tiny tweaks in your environment" that improve your well-being.[14] Take breaks, eat a healthy lunch, put your phone on silent. "If you normally spend your lunch hour on Facebook, leave your phone behind and go outside for a walk instead," she says.

Principles to remember

Do:

- Use breathing to break the immediate cycle of anxiety and frustration with being distracted.

- Think about how you want to act as a colleague and a leader, and let that self-image guide your behavior.

- Set boundaries around when you'll go on social media or check email.

Don't:

- Fool yourself into thinking distractions aren't harmful to your focus—they have high cognitive costs.

- Spend time with people who are distracted. You're likely to end up feeling the same way.

- Neglect self-care. Instead, take breaks, eat healthily, and get enough sleep.

Case study #1: Schedule time to focus

Over the past year, Emily Lin, a vice president at a financial services company, had a lot on her plate. She was building her private coaching practice and had received a promotion at work. Because of the expanded scope of her responsibilities, she was dealing with a whole host of new distractions. "I got so many more emails, instant messages, and phone calls. And people were coming by my office much more frequently," she says.

Emily was having trouble getting her work done. "I would see all these instant messages or email alerts popping up, and even if it just took a few seconds to read them or send a quick response, it would take me away from what I was doing," she says. And it was affecting her mood. "Certain messages would stress me out. I was becoming very short-tempered with my coworkers."

She had previously learned to set boundaries for herself around social media by scheduling in time for distractions. "I gave myself pockets of time when I could go on Facebook. It might be a 10-minute break between meetings or while I was waiting for the elevator to go to lunch. Once I baked those breaks in, I found it a lot easier to control the impulse to check social media while I was working," she explains.

She did something similar to address the work interruptions: she allowed herself time to read and respond to messages, but only after getting her most important work completed. "At the beginning of each week, I ask myself, 'What are the most critical things I have to complete?' And each day, I ask, 'Today, what is the one thing I absolutely have to do?'" She says that helped her determine how much time she needed to focus, and then she would block that time out in two-hour chunks. "For a two-hour window, I turn off email, put 'do not disturb' on instant messenger, and send my phone directly to voicemail." She would even put on headphones as a way to signal to would-be visitors that she was busy.

Two hours seems to be the right amount of time, she says. It gives her enough time to get deeply involved in a task, and it's a "tolerable amount of time to be unreachable," she says. "After that, people start to call back or email again." Plus, it gives her a sense of urgency. "I have the adrenaline to get things done."

Emily says this approach has worked: "It's had a noticeable effect on my productivity." And she feels less stressed. "Because I'm not constantly looking at my email throughout the day, my blood pressure isn't always escalated. I'm a lot more patient now when I am interrupted."

She points out that getting more sleep has also helped her resist distractions. A few years ago she was only sleeping three or four hours a night, but she has drastically revamped her sleep schedule and is now getting from six and a half to seven hours a night. "I went from feeling overwhelmed and unable to focus to being able to think clearly," she says. "When I'm well rested, I have more perspective. I know I don't have to respond to an email right away." She's even become "a huge sleep evangelist" with her coaching clients.

Case study #2: Set boundaries

Sarah Taylor (not her real name), an HR manager at an international humanitarian organization, struggled to stay focused at work for several months before and after the 2016 U.S. presidential election. She says she couldn't stay away from the news. "I was spending several hours a day—throughout the workday, not just in the evenings—compulsively checking for updates on various sites, like the *New York Times*, the *Washington Post*, and CNN." Because of these distractions, she would get behind and found herself working late into the evening and on weekends to try to keep up.

"I was miserable because I wasn't getting sufficient rest—not to mention I was being continually exposed to bad news every day." While she knew this wasn't good for her, she struggled to set limits on her own.

She saw a reference to StayFocusd, a browser extension that sets time limits for selected websites. She checked online reviews and saw that it had helped others like her, so she decided to try it out. "At that point, I was desperate to find ways to fix my bad habit, which I was clearly unable to do through my own willpower," she says.

She put a 10-minute daily limit on the three news sites she mentioned earlier. Once that limit has passed, a window pops up that says, "Shouldn't you be working?" She says it definitely helps—though she does find ways around it. "My sneaky mind starts looking at sites that I haven't yet blocked, such as the BBC."

She's set other rules for herself as well. When she works from home, she keeps all of her personal devices out of the room where she's working. She still stays up-to-date on current events, she says, "but at least I'm no longer risking being seriously behind on my core work duties."

AMY GALLO is a contributing editor at *Harvard Business Review* and the author of the *HBR Guide to Dealing with Conflict*. She writes and speaks about workplace dynamics. Follow her on Twitter @amyegallo.

Notes

1. Susan David, *Emotional Agility: Get Unstuck, Embrace Change, and Thrive in Work and Life* (New York: Avery, 2016).
2. Shawn Achor and Michelle Gielan, "Make Yourself Immune to Secondhand Stress," hbr.org, September 2, 2015, https://hbr.org/2015/09/make-yourself-immune -to-secondhand-stress.

3. Matthew McKinnon, "Neuroscience of Mindfulness: Default Mode Network, Meditation, and Mindfulness," mindfulnessmd.com, June 17, 2017, https://www.mindful nessmd.com/2014/07/08/neuroscience-of-mindfulness -default-mode-network-meditation-mindfulness/.

4. Bob Sullivan and Hugh Thompson, "Brain, Interrupted," *New York Times*, May 3, 2013.

5. American Psychological Association, "Multitasking: Switching Costs," March 20, 2006, http://www.apa.org/ research/action/multitask.aspx.

6. Susan David, "3 Ways to Better Understand Your Emotions," hbr.org, November 10, 2016, https://hbr.org/ 2016/11/3-ways-to-better-understand-your-emotions.

7. Leah Weiss, "A Simple Way to Stay Grounded in Stressful Moments," hbr.org, November 18, 2016, https://hbr .org/2016/11/a-simple-way-to-stay-grounded-in-stressful -moments.

8. Shawn Achor and Michelle Gielan, "Consuming Negative News Can Make You Less Effective at Work," hbr.org, September 14, 2015, https://hbr.org/2015/09/consuming -negative-news-can-make-you-less-effective-at-work.

9. K. Anders Ericcson, Michael J. Prietula, and Edward T. Cokely, "The Making of an Expert," *Harvard Business Review*, July–August 2007, 114.

10. Eilene Zimmerman, "Pedro M. Gardete: Fellow Airline Passengers Influence What You Buy," *Insights by Stanford Business*, Stanford Graduate School of Business, February 6, 2015, https://www.gsb.stanford.edu/insights/pedro

-m-gardete-fellow-airline-passengers-influence-what
-you-buy.

11. Jason Corsello and Dylan Minor, "Want to Be More
    Productive? Sit Next to Someone Who Is," hbr.org, Febru-
    ary 14, 2017, https://hbr.org/2017/02/want-to-be-more
    -productive-sit-next-to-someone-who-is.

12. Jason Fried, "Restoring Sanity to the Office," interview
    by Sarah Green-Carmichael, *Harvard Business Review*,
    Audio, 31:32, December 29, 2016, https://hbr.org/
    ideacast/2016/12/restoring-sanity-to-the-office.

13. Rebecca Knight, "Make Your Work Resolutions Stick,"
    hbr.org, December 29, 2014, https://hbr.org/2014/12/
    make-your-work-resolutions-stick.

14. Amy Jen Su, "6 Ways to Weave Self-Care into Your Work-
    day," hbr.org, June 19, 2017, https://hbr.org/2017/06/6
    -ways-to-weave-self-care-into-your-workday.

Reprinted from hbr.org, originally published
December 20, 2017 (product #H0433F).

5

How to Make Yourself Work When You Just Don't Want To

By Heidi Grant

There's that project you've left on the back burner—the one with the deadline that's growing uncomfortably near. And there's the client whose phone call you really should return—the one who does nothing but complain and eat up your valuable time. Wait, weren't you going to try to go to the gym more often this year?

Can you imagine how much less guilt, stress, and frustration you would feel if you could somehow just make yourself do the things you don't want to do when you are actually supposed to do them? Not to mention how much happier and more effective you would be?

The good news (and it's very good news) is that you can get better about not putting things off if you use the right strategy. Figuring out which strategy to use depends on why you are procrastinating in the first place. Here are some of the most likely reasons.

Reason #1: You are putting something off because you are afraid you'll screw it up

Solution: Adopt a "prevention focus"

There are two ways to look at any task. You can do something because you see it as a way to end up better off than you are now—as an achievement or accomplishment. As in, "If I complete this project successfully I will impress my boss," or "If I work out regularly, I will look amazing." Psychologists call this a **promotion focus,** and research shows that when you have one, you are motivated by the thought of making gains, and you work best when you feel eager and optimistic. Sounds good, doesn't it? Well, if you are afraid you will screw up on the task in question, this is *not* the focus type for you. Anxiety and doubt undermine promotion motivation, leaving you less likely to take any action at all.

What you need is a way of looking at what you need to do that *isn't* undermined by doubt but rather, ideally, thrives on it. When you have a **prevention focus**, instead of thinking about how you can end up better off, you see the task as a way to hang on to what you already have—to avoid loss. For the prevention focused, successfully completing a project is a way to keep your boss from being angry or thinking less of you. Working out regularly is a way to not "let yourself go." Decades of research, which I describe in my book *Focus*, shows that prevention motivation is actually enhanced by anxiety about what might go wrong. When you are focused on avoiding loss, it becomes clear that the only way to get out of danger is to take immediate action. The more worried you are, the faster you are out of the gate.

I know this doesn't sound like a barrel of laughs, particularly if you are usually more the promotion-minded type, but there is probably no better way to get over your anxiety about screwing up than to give some serious thought to all the dire consequences of doing nothing at all. So go on, scare the pants off yourself. It feels awful, but it works.

Reason #2: You are putting something off because you don't feel like doing it

Solution: Make like Spock and ignore your feelings. They're getting in your way

In his excellent book *The Antidote: Happiness for People Who Can't Stand Positive Thinking*, Oliver

Burkeman points out that often when we say things like "I just can't get out of bed early in the morning," or "I just can't get myself to exercise," what we really mean is that we can't get ourselves to *feel* like doing these things. After all, no one is tying you to your bed every morning. Intimidating bouncers aren't blocking the entrance to your gym. Physically, nothing is stopping you: You just don't feel like it. But as Burkeman asks, "Who says you need to wait until you 'feel like' doing something in order to start doing it?"

Think about that for a minute, because it's really important. Somewhere along the way, we've all bought into the idea—without consciously realizing it—that to be motivated and effective we need to *feel* like we want to take action. We need to be eager to do so. I really don't know why we believe this, because it is 100% nonsense. Yes, on some level you need to be committed to what you are doing—you need to want to see the project finished, or get healthier, or get an earlier start to your day. But you don't need to *feel like doing it.*

In fact, as Burkeman points out, many of the most prolific artists, writers, and innovators have become successful in part because of their reliance on work routines that forced them to put in a certain number of hours a day, no matter how uninspired (or, in many instances, hung over) they might have felt. Burkeman reminds us of renowned artist Chuck Close's observation that "Inspiration is for amateurs. The rest of us just show up and get to work."

So if you're sitting there, putting something off because you don't feel like doing it, remember that you don't actually *need* to feel like it. There is nothing stopping you.

Reason #3: You are putting something off because it's hard, boring, or otherwise unpleasant

Solution: Use if-then planning

Too often, we try to solve this particular problem with sheer will: *Next time, I will* make *myself start working on this sooner.* Of course, if we actually had the willpower to do that, we would never put it off in the first place. Studies show that people routinely over-estimate their capacity for self-control and rely on it too often to keep them out of hot water.

Do yourself a favor and embrace the fact that your willpower is limited. Your will may not always be up to the challenge of getting you to do things you find difficult, tedious, or otherwise awful. Instead, use **if-then planning** to get the job done.

Making an if-then plan is more than just deciding what specific steps you need to take to complete a project: It's also deciding where and when you will take those steps. For example:

> *If it is 2 p.m., **then** I will stop what I'm doing and start work on the report Bob asked for. If my boss doesn't mention my request for a raise at our meeting, **then** I will bring it up again before the meeting ends.*

By deciding in advance *exactly* what you're going to do—and when and where you're going to do it— there's no deliberating when the time comes. There's no *Do I really have to do this now?* Or *Can this wait till later?* Or *Maybe I should do something else instead.* It's when we deliberate that willpower becomes necessary to make the tough choice. If-then plans dramatically reduce the demands placed on your willpower by ensuring that you've made the right decision way ahead of the critical moment. In fact, if-then planning has been shown in more than 200 studies to increase rates of goal attainment and productivity by 200% to 300% on average.

I realize that the three strategies I'm offering you—thinking about the consequences of failure, ignoring your feelings, and engaging in detailed planning—don't sound as fun as advice like "Follow your passion!" or "Stay positive!" But they have the decided advantage of actually being *effective*—which, as it happens, is exactly what you'll be if you use them.

HEIDI GRANT is a senior scientist at the NeuroLeadership Institute and the associate director for the Motivation Science Center at Columbia University. She is the author of *Nine Things Successful People Do Differently*, *No One Understands You and What to Do About It*, and *Reinforcements: How to Get People to Help You.* Follow her on Twitter @heidgrantphd.

Reprinted from hbr.org, originally published February 14, 2014 (product #H00OF8).

6

Productivity Tips for People Who Hate Productivity Tips

By Monique Valcour

T raditional approaches to staying focused don't work for me." "I know what I should do to be more productive, but I just don't do it." I hear sentences like these repeatedly from coaching clients. Many have read articles and books—and have even been trained in productivity methods—but still find staying focused to be an uphill battle. Why do people who know a lot about what helps people focus still struggle to focus? Through my work, I've identified several reasons, as well as strategies that may help you gain control.

Assuming that others' preferred productivity strategies should work for you can yield frustration and a sense of defeat. A friend or an author may advocate their own approach so enthusiastically that it seems foolproof if properly implemented. But if you experience the approach as inauthentic or constraining, it may not be right for you. Trying to make it work can send you into a rut where you repeat unhelpful behaviors while beating yourself up over your lack of focus.

For example, a subset of my coaching clients has an aversion to structuring their time usage with widely recommended tools like spreadsheets, planners, calendars, if-then rules, and timers. These are often the same clients who are closely attuned to the quality of their work experience, who find joy in flow and seek to create more of it, and for whom the introduction of industrial productivity levers feels stifling. If this describes you, you'll benefit by paying attention to what's happening within yourself as you work and using what you observe to inform your strategies.

If you feel defeated, two things will help you move forward and feel more in control. The first is to accept where you are and have compassion for yourself. When you admit to yourself, "I'm stuck. This feels awful," and let that admission sit in your awareness without fighting it or using it to berate yourself, it loses its power to derail you. Treat yourself with compassion by recognizing your strengths, recalling challenges you've overcome in the past, and affirming your capacity to solve problems.

Then move forward by experimenting and reflecting. I encourage my clients to check in with how their work process feels at different points throughout the day and make adjustments to improve the quality of their work experience. Being flexible helps. If one approach isn't working, try another rather than continuing to hammer away fruitlessly. Frustrated sitting at your desk? Take your work outside or to a coffee shop for a couple of hours. Computer screen making your eyes go buggy? Switch to working on paper or using voice recognition. Perhaps you're determined to complete something before lunch. But if frustration is building, stepping away, taking a walk, and getting something to eat may be exactly what you need to facilitate smooth and rapid completion of the task after lunch.

Leveraging the connection between mind and body is key to knowing when to make a change. For instance, I've learned that I need to get out of my chair to stretch several times a day. Tightness in my shoulders or numbness in my buttocks triggers the urge to move. If I feel myself hunching or my jaw getting tight, I'll walk to the window or go outside and breathe for few minutes. I also build in exercise nearly every day, typically toward the end of the workday or before something that doesn't require close attention as I find that it diffuses rather than sharpens my focus. Your body can provide you with important cues to optimally manage your focus.

Some people like to keep track of what they plan to accomplish by when. On the other hand, focusing on the process of work rather than the output is a powerfully facilitative perspective shift for many. For instance, my client Nora learned that if she framed her main goal for the day as "finish project," she felt increasingly stressed as time went by if the project wasn't moving along as quickly as she'd hoped—and she was ultimately demoralized at the end of the day if the project remained incomplete. She found she's much better served by an intention to "work on project" or "make progress on project," particularly when she identifies discrete tasks and little milestones that can serve as indicators of progress.

Staying focused doesn't have to be a struggle. While it may not be easy, managing your focus can and should be self-affirming and fulfilling. Making progress on work that is meaningful is among the most energizing and satisfying experiences anyone can have.

Therefore, it makes sense to engineer your workflow for ease and progress. University of Minnesota professor Theresa Glomb recommends organizing your work for a "downhill start."[1] Like parking your car on a slope facing downhill, what can you do to set conditions such that you need only lift your foot from the brake to get moving? Clear off your desk before you start a new task? Write down your two top priorities for the next day before leaving in the evening? Perhaps you're a big-picture person who gets bogged down in details. To move your big idea toward realization, you must pinch a manageable task out of your vision and perform it. Ask yourself, "What's one tiny step I could take?" For example, if I get an idea for an article I'd like to write, I know that the inspiration will dissipate if I don't convert it to action. I can do a rough outline in a few minutes (tangible progress). If I have time, I'll develop it into a more extensive outline (more progress). Outlining is much faster and easier than writing a whole draft, yet it's a concrete step forward that feels good and facilitates the next phase of writing. Waiting for inspiration to create something big from scratch doesn't work; in fact, it slams the brakes on productivity. What does work is finding ways to take small steps and enjoying the resulting sense of progress.

If someone else's productivity strategy feels artificial to you, it probably won't motivate you. For instance, some people can increase their productivity by setting a series of deadlines for themselves. For others, a deadline only promotes focus when it's real, interpersonally relevant, and has serious consequences attached, not when it's made up by themselves or someone else for seemingly arbitrary reasons. A real deadline for me is, for example, knowing there will be an audience waiting to hear me speak at a particular time. With that kind of deadline, I'll be ready and I will deliver an excellent talk. By contrast, me stating to myself or someone else that I plan to have my slides done two weeks in advance won't help me focus.

Productivity strategies also lose their potential to motivate when they don't feel meaningful. Try reframing something you have to do in terms of your core values for stronger and more sustained focus. Let's say I need to schedule interviews with employees at a client firm. Managing the emails and the scheduling process feels tedious if I consider these tasks mindless administrative details. But when I think of them as opening conversations that hold the key to helping people grow and thrive, they become engaging.

Many people fall prey to distractions, both internal and external, in their quest to focus. A useful tool to fend off distraction is an inquiry into the costs of giving in to it. Surrendering to distraction, while temporarily soothing, will later generate feelings of regret and even incompetence. On the other hand, making progress boosts the wonderfully self-affirming sense of mastery. In the face of temptation to give in to distraction, ask yourself the following question: "What are you saying no to right now?" When you take stock of the fact that tumbling down an internet rabbit hole means letting go of the reins and giving up time for the things you really want to do, you may well find the strength to focus.

Finally, accept that focus is dynamic, a work in progress. There's no single tool that will help you develop laser-like focus that never wanders. The best response to a few hours given over to distraction is not self-recrimination but self-compassion paired with curiosity. Regardless of whether your focus has been ideal or not, take a few moments at the end of each day to note what you accomplished and to set yourself up for a smooth downhill start on the next day's targets for progress.

MONIQUE VALCOUR is an executive coach, keynote speaker, and management professor. You can follow her on Twitter @moniquevalcour.

Note

1. Theresa Glomb, "Let's Make Work Better," filmed July 21, 2015 in Minneapolis, Minnesota, TedX Talks video, 18:35, https://www.youtube.com/watch?v=oCYeEt94EMc.

Reprinted from hbr.org, originally published December 6, 2017 (product #H03XEH).

7

5 Ways to Focus Your Energy During a Work Crunch

By Amy Jen Su

Work invariably ebbs and flows, cycling between steady states, where we feel more in control of the pace and workload, and peak periods, where the work crunch hits us hard. Unexpected setbacks, project sprints, or even vacations and holidays can create mayhem and tension. Maintaining focus and managing energy levels become critical as tasks pile onto an already full load. When you're in your next work crunch, there are a few things you can do to focus and manage your energy more productively.

Accept the situation

When an acute period hits, it's easy to resist the fact that it's happening. We wish for things to be like they were last month, or we long for the pace we had during vacation. By not being present to the here and now, we drain our energy by ruminating on the situation. In fact, physicists define resistance as "the degree to which a substance or device opposes the passage of an electrical current, causing energy dissipation." In the case of a work crunch, the more you oppose what's happening, the more energy you'll lose. Acceptance does not mean giving in.[1] On the contrary, it means acknowledging the reality of the situation with awareness so that you can take clear action.

Observe and label your underlying emotions

Acceptance is particularly difficult given the underlying emotions that an acute work crunch can bring. Negative thoughts such as *I'm not going to do a good job, I don't know if I'll be able to get it all done*, or *I feel like I'm dropping the ball at both home and work* often predominate. David Rock, director of the Neuro-Leadership Institute, suggests in his book *Your Brain at Work* that rather than suppressing or denying an emotion, an effective cognitive technique is labeling, whereby you take a situation and put a label on your emotions.[2] "The most successful executives have developed an ability to be in a state of high limbic system arousal and still remain calm," Rock says. "Partly, this is their ability to label emotion states."

The next time you are in a tough work crunch or you're experiencing a setback at work, take Rock's advice to step back, observe your thinking and emotional state, and assign a word to what's happening, such as "pressure," "guilt," or "worry." By using just one or two words, Rock's research shows, you can reduce the arousal of the limbic brain's fight-or-flight system and instead activate the prefrontal cortex, which is responsible for our executive functioning skills.

Preserve your sense of choice and agency

Accepting the situation and labeling our emotions can help reduce the anxiety that comes with a work crunch. This is critical, because, as research out of the University of Pittsburgh shows, anxiety directly impacts our cognitive functioning, especially areas that are responsible for making sound decisions.[3] Don't fall into a victim mentality, in which you believe that there are no choices or that you don't have control.

Instead, bring greater vigilance to assessing your priorities, making tough trade-offs, and incorporating self-care where you can. For example, ask yourself:

- What are the one or two things that are mission critical today?

- What is something I can do to recharge my batteries (get to bed early one night this week, listen to my favorite music while working, or catch a nap on a plane)?

- Who or what will I have to say no to during this time?

Communicate with your colleagues and loved ones

People can be a real energy drain—or gain—during work crunches and setbacks. Pause and consider how you can renegotiate deadlines, set tighter boundaries, or ask for more support during this time. Here are some suggestions.

- *Renegotiate deadlines.* Loop back with colleagues to ensure that you understand when someone really needs something and is going to review it. In other cases, if you anticipate not being able to meet a deadline, be sure to inform your colleagues of the new timing, or renegotiate it. Keep your integrity by doing what you say you're going to do and by being up front when you need to shift gears.

- *Set tighter boundaries.* Our boundaries and guardrails need to change during work crunches or acute periods. Let others in your life, both professionally and personally, know when you'll be available or not, so they will be aware of your more-limited schedule.

- *Ask for help and support.* Many of us pride ourselves on not bothering others and being self-reliant. These are great qualities, but there are times when we need to ask for help. In such times, ask your loved ones for more help on the home front. Share the weight of the account-ability for projects with your colleagues by del-egating or teaming up, instead of trying to do it all on your own.

Practice self-compassion

Probably the toughest thing of all during a work crunch or setback is how easy it is to beat yourself up—especially when you aren't hitting your own high standards for work or time at home. Annie McKee, author of the book *How to Be Happy at Work* and coauthor of several books on emotional intelligence, says this about self-compassion: "If you really want to deal with stress, you've got to stop trying to be a hero and start caring for and about yourself."[4]

To be truly self-compassionate, especially during an acute period of work stress, accept the situation by acknowledging it with awareness and compassion, observe and label your emotions (don't suppress or deny them), preserve your sense of choice and agency, communicate with your colleagues and loved ones, and ask for help when you need it. By taking these actions, you'll move through your next crunch with greater ease and peace.

AMY JEN SU is a cofounder and managing partner of Paravis Partners, an executive coaching and leadership development firm. She is the author of the forthcoming book, *The Leader You Want to Be: Five Essential Principles for Bringing Out Your Best Self—Every Day,* and coauthor, with Muriel Maignan Wilkins, of *Own the Room: Discover Your Signature Voice to Master Your Leadership Presence.* Follow Amy on Twitter @amyjensu.

Notes

1. Steve Taylor, "How Acceptance Can Transform Your Life," *Psychology Today* blog, August 19, 2015, https://www

.psychologytoday.com/us/blog/out-the-darkness/201508/
how-acceptance-can-transform-your-life.

2. David Rock, *Your Brain at Work: Strategies for Overcoming Distraction, Regaining Focus, and Working Smarter All Day* (New York: HarperBusiness, 2009).

3. Christopher Bergland, "How Does Anxiety Short Circuit the Decision-Making Process?" *Psychology Today* blog, March 17, 2016, https://www.psychologytoday.com/us/blog/the-athletes-way/201603/how-does-anxiety-short-circuit-the-decision-making-process.

4. Annie McKee and Kandi Wiens, "Prevent Burnout by Making Compassion a Habit," hbr.org, May 11, 2017, https://hbr.org/2017/05/prevent-burnout-by-making-compassion-a-habit.

Reprinted from hbr.org, originally published
September 22, 2017 (product #H03WMD).

8

Your Team's Time Management Problem Might Be a Focus Problem

By Maura Thomas

M y team has a time management problem," leaders often tell me. Executives might say, for example, that their teams aren't moving the needle on important projects, yet staffers seem busy and stressed. "Time management" becomes a catchall solution to this problem, and they want to hire me to offer tips and techniques on things like prioritizing and using their calendars better.

What we soon uncover, however, is that the root of the team's problems is not managing time, but managing *attention*. And these attention management issues are due not to a skills gap on the part of the employees but to a wider cultural problem unintentionally reinforced, or at least tolerated, by senior leadership.[1]

Distraction is one of the biggest hurdles to high-quality knowledge work, costing almost $1 trillion annually.[2] The first step to addressing this problem is to treat it as a company culture issue that deserves the attention of senior executives.

In my experience, many leaders inadvertently allow or even actively promote the following four situations that impede their team's ability to focus and produce their best work.

They create an environment that undermines focus

The products of knowledge work are creativity, ideas, decisions, information, and communication. All of these require extended periods of sustained focus. However, many offices have a culture in which all communication, regardless of the subject or source, carries the same level of presumed urgency and is expected to produce an immediate response.

Sometimes this happens out of a customer service requirement: Leadership mandates that customers or clients should receive timely responses to all communication. But if "timely" isn't specific and realistic, the assumption grows that faster is better—and immediate is best. Since workers never know whether incoming messages are from customers or from someone else, they must monitor messages constantly. Therefore every *other* task is tackled intermittently, in increments of 30 to 120 seconds, around the handling of messages.

Saying, "Just acknowledge the message, and let them know you'll get back to them soon" does not alleviate the problem, since workers still have to monitor their messages to know that this response is required. The problem is exacerbated when employees are issued a second computer monitor, which they use to have their email open on one screen while keeping whatever work they are trying to get done up on the other screen. This is a recipe for constant distraction, seemingly endorsed by the leaders who provide the hardware.

To solve this problem, divert customer- or client-facing issues to dedicated customer service personnel, whose role is more geared toward reactive tasks. Free up high-impact employees to have more uninterrupted time to focus on their responsibilities. If you can't designate employees for specific customer response roles, then create a realistic response window, such as four hours or one business day, perhaps with an auto-responder instructing clients to call when a timely response is required. Will your customers really leave you if you don't respond to their emails immediately? When considering customer response times, think of it this way: If your customer were sitting across from one of your employees, you wouldn't want the employee checking email. So even when the customer isn't present, the work your company provides to them deserves the same amount of respect and undivided attention, correct? If so, then your team has to have time away from incoming communication. And an added benefit is that, as studies show, that work will get done faster and better.[3]

They don't offer clear instruction on which communication channel is appropriate in which situation

Email was not designed for urgent or time-sensitive communication. Instant messaging can be a better vehicle, but it is used for trivial issues, critical issues, and everything in between. When every communication tool is used in every circumstance, there's no way to vet incoming communication except to check everything as it arrives. This ensures constant distraction.

Consider using an auto-responder or a line in your email signature that tells customers how to reach you if the matter is urgent. Also ensure that internal communication doesn't carry an expectation of immediate response. Staff, especially millennials, increasingly tend to avoid the phone and in-person communication, yet sensitive information and urgent information are better suited to these channels. Offer guidelines that are flexible yet specific regarding how to make effective use of all company communication channels.

They assign the same workers to receive and solve customer issues

Even if you designate specific staff to be the front line to customers, you will have a problem if those staff members have to both *receive* the problems and *solve* them. After all, they won't be able to bring their full attention to solving the problem if they can't take a break from receiving more problems.

Try organizing your support staff's daily schedule so that each person has time away from phone and email to thoughtfully address problems and get other meaningful work done. Another option would be to appoint a "triage" person, who only handles intake and assigns problems to others for solutions. Either choice gives support staff opportunities to devote their full attention to solving problems. This will likely result in happier customers. When staff members have a chance to reflect on issues, they are better primed to recognize systemic problems and opportunities for product and policy improvements. Train your staff to understand that good customer service means not only responding to customers in a timely manner but also solving their problems in a thorough, attentive, and satisfactory way.

They don't realize that monitoring internal systems is still work, even if there is rarely an emergency

I have this experience in almost every training session I deliver: I introduce the idea that downtime and vacation are critical for knowledge workers' success, and then the head of IT or another system-monitoring department speaks up and says that they can never be out of touch in case of a system failure. This is followed by a member of leadership jumping in to say, "But it's okay, because those kinds of emergencies rarely happen."

It's *not* okay, because monitoring work for emergencies is still *work*. If you have a staffer who is expected to be available 24/7/365 in case of an "emergency," then that person essentially gets *no* time off, because they still have to monitor their work communication "just in case." Even if there is no emergency, there's still other work happening that this staffer will see. Even if they choose not to respond, their mind will be engaged in work all the time, and there will never be a time when they can truly unplug.

To address this, every role in your organization needs to have a trusted backup. When an employee has no backup, there is risk to the business whether that employee stays or leaves. If they leave and take all of that business knowledge with them, it could take your company years to recover. If they stay, they are likely to experience high stress (which is not good for their output) or burnout (causing you to need to replace them anyway, temporarily or permanently).[4]

If you are a leader and think your employees might be struggling with "time management," examine these issues first. Your first step may be to address your culture problem around attention management. While many employees do struggle with time and attention management, the solutions won't stick unless leaders address the underlying culture issues.

MAURA THOMAS is an international speaker and trainer on individual and corporate productivity, attention management, and work-life balance. She is a TEDx speaker, was named one of *Inc.* Magazine's Top Leadership Speakers for 2018, and is the author of *Personal Productivity Secrets* and *Work Without Walls.* Follow her on Twitter @mnthomas.

Reprinted from hbr.org, originally published February 27, 2017 (product #H03H6V).

Notes

1. Maura Thomas, "Time Management Training Doesn't Work," hbr.org, April 22, 2015, https://hbr.org/2015/04/time-management-training-doesnt-work.
2. Larry Rosen and Alexandra Samuel, "Conquering Digital Distraction," *Harvard Business Review*, June 2015, 110.
3. Peter Bregman, "How (and Why) to Stop Multitasking," hbr.org, May 20, 2010, https://hbr.org/2010/05/how-and-why-to-stop-multitaski.html.
4. Diane Coutu, "The Science of Thinking Smarter," *Harvard Business Review*, May 2008, 51.

9

How to Practice Mindfulness Throughout Your Work Day

By Rasmus Hougaard and Jacqueline Carter

You probably know the feeling all too well: You arrive at the office with a clear plan for the day, and then, in what feels like just a moment, you find yourself on your way back home. Nine or ten hours have passed but you've accomplished only a few of your priorities. And, most likely, you can't even remember exactly what you did all day. If this sounds familiar, don't worry: You're not alone. Research shows that people spend nearly 47% of their waking hours thinking about something other than what they're doing.[1] In other words, many of us operate on autopilot.

Add to this that we have entered what many people are calling the "attention economy." In the attention economy, the ability to maintain focus and concentration is every bit as important as technical or management skills. And because leaders must be able to absorb and synthesize a growing flood of information in order to make good decisions, they're hit particularly hard by this emerging trend.

The good news is you can train your brain to focus better by incorporating mindfulness exercises throughout your day. Based on our experience with thousands of leaders in more than 250 organizations, here are some guidelines for becoming a more focused and mindful leader.

First, start off your day right. Researchers have found that we release the most stress hormones within minutes after waking.[2] Why? Because thinking of the day ahead triggers our fight-or-flight instinct and releases cortisol into our blood. Instead, try this: When you wake up, spend two minutes in your bed simply noticing your breath. As thoughts about the day pop into your mind, let them go and return to your breath.

Next, when you get to the office, take 10 minutes at your desk or in your car to boost your brain with the following short mindfulness practice before you dive into activity. Close your eyes, relax, and sit upright. Place your full focus on your breath. Simply maintain an ongoing flow of attention on the experience of your breathing: Inhale, exhale; inhale, exhale. To help your focus stay on your breathing, count silently at each exhalation. Any time you find your mind distracted, simply release the distraction by returning your focus to your breath. Most important, allow yourself to enjoy these minutes. Throughout the rest of the day, other people and competing urgencies will fight for your attention. But for these 10 minutes, your attention is all your own.

Once you finish this practice and get ready to start working, mindfulness can help increase your effectiveness. Two skills define a mindful mind: *focus* and *awareness*. Focus is the ability to concentrate on what you're doing in the moment, while awareness is the ability to recognize and release unnecessary distractions as they arise. Understand that mindfulness is not just a sedentary practice; it is about developing a sharp, clear mind. And mindfulness in action is a great alternative to the illusory practice of multitasking. Mindful working means applying focus and awareness to everything you do from the moment you enter the office. Focus on the task at hand, and recognize and release internal and external distractions as they arise. In this way, mindfulness helps increase effectiveness, decrease mistakes, and even enhance creativity.

To better understand the power of focus and awareness, consider an affliction that touches nearly all of us: email addiction. Emails have a way of seducing our attention and redirecting it to lower-priority tasks because completing small, quickly accomplished tasks releases dopamine, a pleasurable hormone, in our brains. This release makes us addicted to email and compromises our concentration. Instead, apply mindfulness when opening your inbox. *Focus* on what is important and maintain *awareness* of what is merely noise. To get a better start to your day, avoid checking your email first thing in the morning. Doing so will help you sidestep an onslaught of distractions and short-term problems during a time of day that holds the potential for exceptional focus and creativity.

As the day moves on and the inevitable back-to-back meetings start, mindfulness can help you lead shorter, more effective meetings. To avoid entering a meeting with a wandering mind, take two minutes to practice mindfulness, which you can do en route. Even better, let the first two minutes of the meeting be silent, allowing everybody to arrive both physically and mentally. Then, if possible, end the meeting five minutes before the hour to allow all participants a mindful transition to their next appointment.

As the day progresses and your brain starts to tire, mindfulness can help you stay sharp and avoid poor decisions. After lunch, set a timer on your phone to ring every hour. When the timer rings, cease your current activity and do one minute of mindfulness practice. These mindful performance breaks will help keep you from resorting to autopilot and lapsing into action addiction.

Finally, as the day comes to an end and you start your commute home, apply mindfulness. For at least 10 minutes of the commute, turn off your phone, shut off the radio, and simply be. Let go of any thoughts that arise. Attend to your breath. Doing so will allow you to let go of the stresses of the day so you can return home and be fully present with your family.

Mindfulness is not about living life in slow motion. It's about enhancing focus and awareness both in work and in life. It's about stripping away distractions and staying on track with both individual and organizational, goals. Take control of your own mindfulness: Test these tips for 14 days, and see what they do for you.

RASMUS HOUGAARD is the founder and managing director of Potential Project, a global leadership and organizational development. JACQUELINE CARTER is a partner and the North American director of Potential Project. They are the coauthors of *One Second Ahead: Enhancing Performance at Work with Mindfulness* and *The Mind of the Leader: How to Lead Yourself, Your People, and Your Organization for Extraordinary Results* (Harvard Business Review Press, 2018).

Notes

1. S. Bradt, "Wandering Mind Not a Happy Mind," *Harvard Gazette*, November 11, 2010.
2. J. C. Pruessner et al., "Free Cortisol Levels After Awakening: A Reliable Biological Marker for the Assessment of Adrenocortical Activity," *Life Sciences* 61, no. 26 (November 1997): 2539–2549.

Adapted from content posted on hbr.org on
March 4, 2016 (#H02OTU).

10

Your Brain Can Only Take So Much Focus

By Srini Pillay

The ability to focus is an important driver of excellence. Focused techniques such as to-do lists, timetables, and calendar reminders all help people stay on task. Few would argue with that, and even if they did, there is evidence to support the idea that resisting distraction and staying present have benefits. Practicing mindfulness for 10 minutes a day, for example, can enhance leadership effectiveness by helping you become more able to regulate your emotions and make sense of past experiences.[1] Yet as helpful as focus can be, there's also a downside to focus as it is commonly viewed.

The problem is that excessive focus exhausts the focus circuits in your brain. It can drain your energy and make you lose control.[2] This energy drain can also make you more impulsive and less helpful.[3] As a result, decisions are poorly thought out, and you become less collaborative.

So what do we do then? Focus or unfocus?

Recent research shows that both focus *and* unfocus are vital. The brain operates optimally when it toggles between focus and unfocus, allowing us to develop resilience, enhance creativity, and make better decisions.[4]

When you unfocus, you engage a brain circuit called the "default mode network" (DMN). We used to think of this circuit as the "do mostly nothing" circuit because it only came on when you stopped focusing with effort. Yet when "at rest," this circuit uses 20% of the body's energy (compared with the comparatively small 5% that any effort would require).[5]

The DMN needs this energy because it is doing anything *but* resting. Under the brain's conscious radar, it activates old memories; goes back and forth between the past, present, and future; and recombines different ideas.[6] Using this new and previously inaccessible data, you develop enhanced self-awareness and a sense of personal relevance.[7] And you can imagine creative solutions or predict what might happen in the future, thereby leading to better decision-making too.[8] The DMN also helps you tune in to other people's thinking, thereby improving team understanding and cohesion.[9]

There are many simple and effective ways to activate this circuit in the course of a day. Here are some examples.

Using positive constructive daydreaming (PCD)

Positive constructive daydreaming (PCD) is a type of mind wandering that is different from slipping into a daydream or guiltily rehashing worries.[10] When you build PCD into your day deliberately, it can boost your creativity, strengthen your leadership ability, and also reenergize the brain. To activate PCD, you choose a low-key activity such as knitting, gardening, or casual reading, then wander into the recesses of your mind.[11] But unlike slipping into a daydream or guilty-dysphoric daydreaming, you might first imagine something playful and wishful—like running through the woods, or lying on a yacht. Then you swivel your attention from the external world to the internal space of your mind with this image in mind while still doing the low-key activity.

Studied for decades by psychologist Jerome Singer, PCD activates the DMN and metaphorically changes the silverware that your brain uses to find information.[12] While focused attention is like a fork that picks up obvious conscious thoughts that you have, PCD commissions a different set of silverware: a spoon for scooping up the delicious mélange of flavors of your identity (the scent of your grandmother, the feeling of satisfaction with the first bite of apple pie on a crisp fall day), chopsticks for connecting ideas across your brain (to enhance innovation), and a marrow spoon for getting into the nooks and crannies of your brain to pick up long-lost memories that are a vital part of your identity.[13] In this state, your sense of self is enhanced—which, according to organizational consultant Warren Bennis, is the essence of leadership.[14] I call this the psychological center of gravity, a grounding mechanism (part of your mental "six-pack") that helps you enhance your agility and manage change more effectively.[15]

Taking a nap

In addition to building in time for PCD, leaders can also consider authorized napping. Not all naps are the same. When your brain is in a slump, your clarity and creativity are compromised. After a 10-minute nap, studies show, you become much clearer and more alert.[16] But if it's a creative task you have in front of you, you will likely need a full 90 minutes of sleep for more complete brain refreshing.[17] Your brain requires this longer time to make more associations and dredge up ideas that reside in the nooks and crannies of your memory network.

Pretending to be someone else

When you're stuck in a creative process, unfocus can come to the rescue if you embody and live out an entirely different personality. In 2016, educational psychologists Denis Dumas and Kevin Dunbar found that people who try to solve creative problems are more successful if they behave like an eccentric poet than a rigid librarian.[18] Given a test in which they had to come up with as many uses as possible for any object (such as a brick), those who behaved like eccentric poets had superior creative performance. This finding holds even if the same person takes on a different identity.

When you're in a creative deadlock, try embodying a different identity. It will likely get you out of your own head and allow you to think from another person's perspective. (I call this "psychological halloweenism.")[19]

For years, focus has been the venerated ability amongst all abilities. Since we spend 46.9% of our days with our minds wandering away from a task at hand, we crave the ability to keep it fixed and on task.[20] Yet, if we built PCD, 10- and 90-minute naps, and psychological halloweenism into our days, we would likely preserve focus for when we needed it, and use it much more efficiently too. More important, unfocus would allow us to update information in the brain, giving us access to deeper parts of ourselves and enhancing our agility, creativity, and decision-making.

SRINI PILLAY, MD, is an executive coach and CEO of Neuro-Business Group. He is also a technology innovator and entrepreneur in the health and leadership development sectors and the author of *Tinker, Dabble, Doodle, Try: Unlock the Power of the Unfocused Mind*. He is also a part-time assistant professor at Harvard Medical School and teaches in the executive education programs at Harvard Business School and Duke Corporate Education.

Notes

1. Louise Wasylkiw et al., "The Impact of Mindfulness on Leadership in a Health Care Setting: A Pilot Study," *Journal of Health Organization and Management* 29, no. 7 (2015): 893–911; Megan Reitz and Michael Chaskalson, "Mindfulness Works, But Only If You Work at It," hbr.org, November 4, 2016, https://hbr.org/2016/11/mindfulness-works-but-only-if-you-work-at-it; Rasmus Hougaard, Jacqueline Carter, and Gitte Dybkjaer, "Spending 10 Minutes a Day on Mindfulness Subtly Changes the Way You React to Everything," hbr.org, January 18, 2017, https://hbr.org/2017/01/spending-10-minutes-a-day-on-mindfulness-subtly-changes-the-way-you-react-to-everything; Christina Congleton, Britta K. Hölzel, and Sara W. Lazar, "Mindfulness Can Literally Change Your Brain," hbr.org, January 8, 2015, https://hbr.org/2015/01/mindfulness-can-literally-change-your-brain.

2. Todd F. Heatherton and Dylan D. Wagner, "Cognitive Neuroscience of Self-Regulation Failure," *Trends in Cognitive Sciences* 15, no. 3 (March 2011): 132–139.

3. Roy F. Baumeister, "Ego Depletion and Self-Regulation Failure: A Resource Model of Self-Control," *Alcoholism: Clinical and Experimental Research* 27, no. 2 (February 2003): 281–284; C. Nathan Dewall et al., "Depletion Makes the Heart Grow Less Helpful: Helping as a Function of Self-Regulatory and Genetic Relatedness," *Personality and Social Psychology Bulletin* 34, no. 12 (December 2008): 1653–1662.

4. Jinyi Long et al., "Distinct Interactions Between Fronto-Parietal and Default Mode Networks in Impaired Consciousness," *Scientific Reports* 6 (2016): 1–11.

5. Marcus E. Raichle and Deborah A. Gusnard, "Appraising the Brain's Energy Budget," *Proceedings of the National Academy of Sciences (PNAS)* 99, no. 16 (August 2002): 10237–10239.

6. Carlo Sestieri et al., "Episodic Memory Retrieval, Parietal Cortex, and the Default Mode Network: Functional and Topical Analyses," *The Journal of Neuroscience* 31, no. 12 (March 2011): 4407–4420; Ylva Østby et al., "Mental Time Travel and Default-Mode Network Functional Connectivity in the Developing Brain," *PNAS* 109, no. 42 (October 2012): 16800–16804; Roger E. Beaty et al., "Creativity and the Default Network: A Functional Connectivity Analysis of the Creative Brain at Rest," *Neuropsychologia* 64 (November 2014): 92–98.

7. Christopher G. Davey, Jesus Pujol, and Ben J. Harrison, "Mapping the Self in the Brain's Default Mode Network," *Neuroimage* 132 (May 2016): 390–397.

8. Beaty et al., "Creativity and the Default Network," 92–98; Fabiana M. Carvalho et al., "Time-Perception Network and Default Mode Network Are Associated with Temporal Prediction in a Periodic Motion Task," *Frontiers in Human Neuroscience* 10 (June 2016): 268.

9. Christopher J. Hyatt et al., "Specific Default Mode Subnetworks Support Mentalizing as Revealed Through Opposing Network Recruitment by Social and Semantic FMRI Tasks," *Human Brain Mapping* 36, no. 8 (August 2015): 3047–3063.

10. Rebecca L. McMillan, Scott Barry Kaufman, and Jerome L. Singer, "Ode to Positive Constructive Daydreaming," *Frontiers in Psychology* 4 (September 2013): 626.

11. Benjamin Baird et al., "Inspired by Distraction: Mind Wandering Facilitates Creative Incubation," *Psychological Science* 23, no. 10 (October 2013): 1117–1122.

12. Jerome L. Singer, "Researching Imaginative Play and Adult Consciousness: Implications for Daily and Literary Creativity," *Psychology of Aesthetics, Creativity, and the Arts* 3, no. 4 (2009): 190–199.

13. Jeroen J. A. van Boxtel, Naotsugu Tsuchiya, and Christof Koch, "Consciousness and Attention: On Sufficiency and Necessity," *Frontiers in Psychology* (December 2010): 217; Christopher G. Davey, Jesus Pujol, and Ben J. Harrison, "Mapping the Self in the Brain's Default Mode Network,"

Neuroimage 132 (May 2016): 390–397; Roger E. Beaty et al., "Creativity and the Default Network," 92–98; Carlo Sestieri et al., "Episodic Memory Retrieval, Parietal Cortex, and the Default Mode Network: Functional and Topical Analyses," *The Journal of Neuroscience* 31, no. 12 (March 2011): 4407–4420.

14. Adi Ignatius, "Becoming a Leader, Becoming Yourself," *Harvard Business Review*, May 2015, 10.
15. Srini Pillay, *Tinker, Dabble, Doodle, Try: Unlock the Power of the Unfocused Mind* (New York: Ballantine Books, 2017).
16. Nicole Lovato and Leon Lack, "The Effects of Napping on Cognitive Functioning," *Progress in Brain Research* 185 (2010): 155–166.
17. Denise J. Kai et al., "REM, Not Incubation, Improves Creativity by Priming Associative Networks," *PNAS* 106, no. 25 (June 2009): 10130–10134.
18. Denise Dumas and Kevin N. Dunbar, "The Creative Stereotype Effect," *PLOS One* 11, no. 2 (February 2016): e0142567.
19. Srini Pillay, *Tinker, Dabble, Doodle, Try*.
20. Matthew A. Killingsworth and Daniel T. Gilbert, "A Wandering Mind Is an Unhappy Mind," *Science* 330, no. 6006 (November 2010): 932.

Reprinted from hbr.org, originally published
May 12, 2017 (product #H03NKH).

Index

How to be human at work.

HBR's Emotional Intelligence Series features smart, essential reading on the human side of professional life from the pages of *Harvard Business Review*. Each book in the series offers uplifting stories, practical advice, and research from leading experts on how to tend to our emotional well-being at work.

Harvard Business Review Emotional Intelligence Series

Available in paperback or ebook format. The specially priced six-volume set includes:

- Mindfulness
- Resilience
- Influence and Persuasion

- Authentic Leadership
- Happiness
- Empathy

HBR.ORG

Buy for your team, clients, or event.
Visit hbr.org/bulksales for quantity discount rates.

Mindful
Listening

HBR EMOTIONAL INTELLIGENCE SERIES

HBR Emotional Intelligence Series

How to be human at work

The HBR Emotional Intelligence Series features smart, essential reading on the human side of professional life from the pages of *Harvard Business Review*.

Authentic Leadership	*Leadership Presence*
Confidence	*Mindful Listening*
Dealing with Difficult People	*Mindfulness*
Empathy	*Power and Impact*
Focus	*Purpose, Meaning, and Passion*
Happiness	*Resilience*
Influence and Persuasion	*Self-Awareness*

Other books on emotional intelligence from *Harvard Business Review*:

HBR Everyday Emotional Intelligence

HBR Guide to Emotional Intelligence

HBR's 10 Must Reads on Emotional Intelligence

Mindful Listening

HBR EMOTIONAL INTELLIGENCE SERIES

Harvard Business Review Press

Boston, Massachusetts

HBR Press Quantity Sales Discounts

Harvard Business Review Press titles are available at significant quantity discounts when purchased in bulk for client gifts, sales promotions, and premiums. Special editions, including books with corporate logos, customized covers, and letters from the company or CEO printed in the front matter, as well as excerpts of existing books, can also be created in large quantities for special needs.

For details and discount information for both print and ebook formats, contact booksales@harvardbusiness.org, tel. 800-988-0886, or www.hbr.org/bulksales.

Copyright 2019 Harvard Business School Publishing Corporation
All rights reserved
Printed in the United States of America

10 9 8 7 6

No part of this publication may be reproduced, stored in or introduced into a retrieval system, or transmitted, in any form, or by any means (electronic, mechanical, photocopying, recording, or otherwise), without the prior permission of the publisher. Requests for permission should be directed to permissions@hbsp.harvard.edu, or mailed to Permissions, Harvard Business School Publishing, 60 Harvard Way, Boston, Massachusetts 02163.

The web addresses referenced in this book were live and correct at the time of the book's publication but may be subject to change.

Library of Congress Cataloging-in-Publication Data

Title: Mindful listening.
Other titles: HBR emotional intelligence series.
Description: Boston, Massachusetts : Harvard Business Review Press, [2019] | Series: HBR emotional intelligence series | Includes index.
Identifiers: LCCN 2018044757 | ISBN 9781633696679 (pbk.)
Subjects: LSCH: Listening. | Mindful (Psychology) | Listening comprehension. | Emotional intelligence. | Communication in management. | Leadership. | Industrial management.
Classification: LCC BF323.L5 M56 2019 | DDC 153.6/8—dc 23
LC record available at https://lccn.loc.gov/2018044757

ISBN: 978-1-63369-667-9
eISBN: 978-1-63369-668-6

The paper used in this publication meets the requirements of the American National Standard for Permanence of Paper for Publications and Documents in Libraries and Archives Z39.48-1992.

Contents

Contents

Contents

Mindful
Listening

HBR EMOTIONAL INTELLIGENCE SERIES

1

What Great Listeners Actually Do

By Jack Zenger and Joseph Folkman

Chances are you think you're a good listener. People's appraisal of their listening ability is much like their assessment of their driving skills, in that the great bulk of adults think they're above average.

In our experience, most people think good listening comes down to doing three things:

- Not talking when others are speaking

- Letting others know you're listening through facial expressions and verbal sounds ("mm-hmm")

- Being able to repeat what others have said, practically word-for-word

In fact, much management advice on listening suggests doing these very things: encouraging listeners to remain quiet, nod and "mm-hmm" encouragingly, and then repeat back to the talker something like, "So, let me make sure I understand. What you're saying is . . ." However, recent research that we conducted suggests that these behaviors fall far short of describing good listening skills.

We analyzed data describing the behavior of 3,492 participants in a development program designed to help managers become better coaches. As part of this program, managers' coaching skills were assessed by others in 360-degree assessments. We identified those who were perceived as being the most effective listeners (the top 5%). We then compared the best listeners to the average of all other people in the data set and identified the 20 items that showed the largest significant difference. With those results in hand we identified the differences between great and average listeners and analyzed the data to determine what characteristics their colleagues identified as the behaviors that made them outstanding listeners.

We found some surprising conclusions, along with some qualities we expected to hear. We grouped them into four main findings:

- *Good listening is much more than being silent while the other person talks.* To the contrary, people perceive the best listeners to be those who periodically ask questions that promote discovery and insight. These questions gently challenge old assumptions but do so in a constructive way. Sitting there silently nodding does not provide sure evidence that a person is listening, but asking a good question tells the speaker the listener has not only heard what was said but that they comprehended it well enough to want additional information. Good listening was consistently seen as a two-way dialogue, rather than a one-way "speaker versus hearer" interaction. The best conversations were active.

- *Good listening includes interactions that build a person's self-esteem.* The best listeners made the conversation a positive experience for the other party; that doesn't happen when the listener is passive (or, for that matter, critical). Good listeners made the other person feel supported and conveyed confidence in them. Good listening was characterized by the creation of a safe environment in which issues and differences could be discussed openly.

- *Good listening is seen as a cooperative conversation.* In these interactions, feedback flowed smoothly in both directions with neither party becoming defensive about comments the other made. By contrast, poor listeners were seen as competitive—as listening only to identify errors in reasoning or logic, using their silence as a chance to prepare their next response. That might make you an excellent debater, but it doesn't make you a good listener. Good listeners may challenge assumptions and disagree, but the person being listened to feels the listener is trying to help, not trying to win an argument.

- *Good listeners tend to make suggestions.* Good listening invariably included some feedback provided in a way others would accept and that opened up alternative paths to consider. This finding surprised us somewhat, since it's not uncommon to hear complaints that "So-and-so didn't listen, he just jumped in and tried to solve the problem." Perhaps what the data is telling us is that making suggestions is not itself the problem; it may be the skill with which those suggestions are made. Another possibility is that we're more likely to accept suggestions from people we already think are good listeners. (Someone who is silent for the whole conversation and then jumps in with a suggestion may not be seen as credible. Someone who seems combative or critical and then tries to give advice may not be seen as trustworthy.)

While many of us have thought of being a good listener as being like a sponge that accurately absorbs what the other person is saying, what these findings show instead is that good listeners are like trampolines: They are someone you can bounce ideas off of and, rather than absorbing your ideas and energy, they amplify, energize, and clarify your thinking. They make you feel better not by merely passively absorbing but by actively supporting. This lets you gain energy and height, just like someone jumping on a trampoline.

Of course, there are different levels of listening. Not every conversation requires the highest levels, but many conversations would benefit from greater focus and listening skill. Consider which level of listening you'd like to aim for:

Level 1: The listener creates a safe environment in which difficult, complex, or emotional issues can be discussed.

Level 2: The listener clears away distractions like phones and laptops, focusing attention on the other person and making appropriate eye contact. (This behavior not only affects how you are perceived as the listener; it immediately influences the listener's *own* attitudes and inner feelings. Acting the part changes how you feel inside. This in turn makes you a better listener.)

Level 3: The listener seeks to understand the substance of what the other person is saying. They capture ideas, ask questions, and restate issues to confirm that their understanding is correct.

Level 4: The listener observes nonverbal cues, such as facial expressions, perspiration, respiration rates, gestures, posture, and numerous other subtle body language signals. It is estimated that 80% of what we communicate comes from these signals. It sounds strange to some, but you listen with your eyes as well as your ears.

Level 5: The listener increasingly understands the other person's emotions and feelings about the topic at hand and identifies and acknowledges them. The listener empathizes with and validates those feelings in a supportive, non-judgmental way.

Level 6: The listener asks questions that clarify assumptions the other person holds and helps the other person see the issue in a new light. This could include the listener injecting some thoughts and ideas about the topic that could be useful to the other person. However, good listeners never highjack the conversation so that they or their issues become the subject of the discussion.

Each of these levels builds on the others. Thus, if you've been criticized (for example) for offering solutions rather than listening, it may mean you need to attend to some of the other levels (such as clearing away distractions or empathizing) before your proffered suggestions can be appreciated.

We suspect that in being a good listener, most of us are more likely to stop short rather than go too far. Our hope is that this research will help by providing a new perspective on listening. We hope those who labor under an illusion of superiority about their listening skills will see where they really stand. We also hope the common perception that good listening is mainly about acting like an absorbent sponge will wane. Finally, we hope all will see that the highest and best form of listening comes in playing the same role for the other person that a trampoline plays for a child: It gives energy, acceleration, height, and amplification. These are the hallmarks of great listening.

JACK ZENGER is the CEO of Zenger Folkman, a leadership development consultancy. Follow him on Twitter @jhzenger. JOSEPH FOLKMAN is the president of Zenger Folkman. Follow him on Twitter @joefolkman. Zenger and Folkman are coauthors of the October 2011 HBR article "Making Yourself Indispensable" and the book *Speed: How Leaders Accelerate Successful Execution*.

Adapted from content posted on hbr.org,
July 14, 2016 (product #H030DC).

2

What Gets in the Way of Listening

By Amy Jen Su and Muriel Maignan Wilkins

As your role grows in scale and influence, so too must your ability to listen. But listening is one of the toughest skills to master—and it requires uncovering deeper barriers within oneself.

Take, for example, our client, Janet, a successful principal in a management-consulting firm. She recently received 360-degree feedback from colleagues that she needed to improve her listening skills. This confused her: She had always thought of herself as an active listener. When we asked her colleagues why, they described how she wouldn't exactly answer questions in meetings—and how she often had different takeaways from the rest of the team. Janet wanted to explore what was happening. It seemed simple enough, and yet why was she having trouble? The key, ironically, was for her to focus on herself. Here's what she—and you—should do.

Ignore your inner critic

Janet realized that she wasn't tracking to the dialogue because she was nervous about her own performance. Her mind was attuned to a different voice— that of her own inner critic—monitoring how she was doing in the meeting. This was especially true during presentations. Janet's performance anxiety overshadowed her ability to hear the concerns underlying each question and kept her from noticing the audience's cues to move along. *Shift your focus from "getting a good grade" to the presentation's greater purpose. What excites you about the topic or audience?*

Expand how you see your role

To fully listen, you must first believe doing so is a critical part of your job. To quote from Boris Groysberg and Michael Slind's *Harvard Business Review* article "Leadership Is a Conversation," "Leaders who take organizational conversation seriously know when to stop talking and start listening." As Janet continued to explore why she wasn't listening, she realized she'd boxed herself in. As a management consultant, she described her role as "providing efficient solutions to clients." We discussed how she might update her view from problem solver to trusted adviser: one that not only provided counsel but also listened deeply to clients' issues and concerns. *Consider if you've boxed yourself in by role definition. Do you believe your only job is to provide direction?*

Put aside your fear and anticipation

Listening demands being fully present and ready to respond to what might get thrown your way. But our listening shuts down when we're anticipating what might happen next. Janet found that while another person was talking, her mind was already thinking about what she might say next or anticipating what might be said. This was especially true during difficult conversations, when she anticipated confrontation. She'd rush through what she wanted to say without listening as a way to avoid her fears of conflict. But listening is an especially important skill in navigating difficult conversations, where multiple interests and agendas must be aligned. Our full attention is demanded to understand what the hot-button issues are or what the potential misunderstandings might be. *Notice if your listening shuts down when you're emotionally uncomfortable. Are you aware of your triggers?*

What Gets in the Way of Listening

Be open to having your mind changed

Janet also realized that she was working hard to appear confident and to make sure she was offering her point of view in meetings. In trying to be more assertive, she came off as having prematurely made up her mind. One of Janet's partners shared this tip: "I do have a viewpoint going in, but I don't assume or try to show I'm the smartest person in the room. In fact, I go in with the assumption that my colleagues are smart too and therefore might have good reason for having a different position. I'm willing to hear them out for the sake of getting to the best answer, not just my answer." Listening, then, is actually a sign of incredible self-confidence. *Are you trying too hard to convey confidence and missing others' perspectives in the process?*

While tactically there are many ways to strengthen your listening skills, you must focus on the deeper, internal issues at stake to really improve. Listening is a skill that enables you to align people, decisions, and agendas. You cannot have leadership presence without hearing what others have to say.

AMY JEN SU is a cofounder and managing partner of Paravis Partners, a boutique executive coaching and leadership development firm. Follow her on Twitter @amyjensu. MURIEL MAIGNAN WILKINS is a cofounder and managing partner of Paravis Partners. They are the coauthors of *Own the Room: Discover Your Signature Voice to Master Your Leadership Presence* (Harvard Business Review Press, 2013).

Adapted from content posted on hbr.org,
April 14, 2014 (product #H00RDP).

3

Listening to People

By Ralph G. Nichols and Leonard A. Stevens

Editor's note: In their classic 1957 article, Ralph G. Nichols and Leonard A. Stevens explain why listening is a key component in business communication and why so many people struggle with it. In this excerpt, they describe how emotions can affect what we hear—and provide two ways to train yourself to get more out of your conversations.

I n different degrees and in many different ways, listening ability is affected by our emotions.[1] Figuratively we reach up and mentally turn off what we do not want to hear. Or, on the other hand, when someone says what we especially want to hear, we open our ears wide, accepting everything—truths, half-truths, or fiction. We might say, then, that our emotions act as aural filters. At times they in effect cause deafness, and at other times they make listening altogether too easy. If we hear something that opposes our most deeply rooted prejudices, notions, convictions, mores, or complexes, our brains may become overstimulated, and not in a direction that leads to good listening. We mentally plan a rebuttal to what we hear, formulate a question designed to embarrass the talker, or perhaps simply turn to thoughts that support our own feelings on the subject at hand. For example:

The firm's accountant goes to the general manager and says: "I have just heard from the Bureau of Internal Revenue, and . . . " The general manager suddenly breathes harder as he thinks, "That blasted bureau! Can't they leave me alone? Every year the government milks my profits to a point where . . ." Red in the face, he whirls and stares out the window. The label "Bureau of Internal Revenue" cuts loose emotions that stop the general manager's listening.

In the meantime, the accountant may go on to say that here is a chance to save $3,000 this year if the general manager will take a few simple steps. The fuming general manager may hear this—if the

accountant presses hard enough—but the chances
are he will fail to comprehend it.

When emotions make listening too easy, it usually results from hearing something that supports the deeply rooted inner feelings that we hold. When we hear such support, our mental barriers are dropped and everything is welcomed. We ask few questions about what we hear; our critical faculties are put out of commission by our emotions. Thinking drops to a minimum because we are hearing thoughts that we have harbored for years in support of our inner feelings. It is good to hear someone else think those thoughts, so we lazily enjoy the whole experience.

What can we do about these emotional filters? The solution is not easy in practice, although it can be summed up in this simple admonition: *Hear the man out.* Following are two pointers that often help in training people to do this:

1. *Withhold evaluation.* This is one of the most important principles of learning, especially learning through the ear. It requires self-control, sometimes more than many of us can muster, but with persistent practice it can be turned into a valuable habit. While listening, the main object is to comprehend each point made by the talker. Judgments and decisions should be reserved until after the talker has finished. At that time, and only then, review his main ideas and assess them.

2. *Hunt for negative evidence.* When we listen, it is human to go on a militant search for evidence that proves us right in what we believe. Seldom do we make a search for evidence to prove ourselves wrong. The latter type of effort is not easy, for behind its application must lie a generous spirit and real breadth of outlook. However, an important part of listening comprehension is found in the search for negative

evidence in what we hear. If we make up our minds to seek out the ideas that might prove us wrong, as well as those that might prove us right, we are less in danger of missing what people have to say.

RALPH G. NICHOLS was nationally known for his many articles and lectures on communication problems. He served as the president of the National Society for the Study of Communication. LEONARD A. STEVENS is a freelance writer and a consultant on oral presentation to a number of leading companies and also is affiliated with Management Development Associates of New York. Nichols and Stevens coauthored the book *Are You Listening?*

Note

1. See Wendell Johnson, "The Fateful Process of Mr. A Talking to Mr. B," *Harvard Business Review*, January–February 1953, 49.

Reprinted from *Harvard Business Review*,
September 1957 (product #57507).

4

Three Ways Leaders Can Listen with More Empathy

By Christine M. Riordan

Study after study has shown that listening is critical to leadership effectiveness. So why are so few leaders good at it?

Too often, leaders seek to take command, direct conversations, talk too much, or worry about what they will say next in defense or rebuttal. Additionally, leaders can react quickly, get distracted during a conversation, or fail to make the time to listen to others. Finally, leaders can be ineffective at listening if they are competitive, if they multitask such as by reading emails or text messages, or if they let their egos get in the way of listening to what others have to say.

Instead, leaders need to start by really caring about what other people have to say about an issue. Research also shows that active listening, combined with empathy or trying to understand others' perspectives and points of view, is the most effective form of listening.[1] Henry Ford once said, "If there is any great secret of success in life, it lies in the ability to get the other person's point of view and to see things from that person's angle as well as from one's own."

Research has linked several notable behavior sets with empathic listening.[2] The first behavior set involves recognizing all verbal and nonverbal cues, including tone, facial expressions, and other body language. In short, leaders receive information through all senses, not just hearing. Sensitive leaders pay attention to what others are *not* saying and probe a bit deeper. They also understand how others are feeling and acknowledge those feelings. Sample phrases include, "Thank you for sharing how you feel about this situation, it is important to understand where everyone is coming from on the issue," "Would you share a bit more on your thoughts on this situation," and "You seem excited (happy, upset) about this situation, and I would like to hear more about your perspective."

The second set of empathic listening behaviors is processing, which includes the behaviors we most commonly associate with listening. It involves understanding the meaning of the messages and keeping track of the points of the conversation. Leaders who are effective at processing assure others that they are remembering what others say, summarize points of agreement and disagreement, and capture global themes and key messages from the conversation. Sample phrases include, "Here are a couple of key points that I heard from this meeting," "Here are our points of agreement and disagreement," "Here are a few more pieces of information we should gather," and "Here are some suggested next steps—what do you think?"

The third set of behaviors, responding, involves assuring others that listening has occurred and encouraging communication to continue. Leaders who are effective responders give appropriate replies through verbal acknowledgments, deep and clarifying questioning, or paraphrasing. Important nonverbal behaviors include facial expressions, eye contact, and body language. Other effective responses might include head nods, full engagement in the conversation, and the use of acknowledging phrases such as "That is a great point."

Overall, it is important for leaders to recognize the multidimensionality of empathetic listening and engage in all forms of behaviors. Among its benefits are that empathic listening builds trust and respect, enables people to reveal their emotions (including tensions), facilitates openness of information sharing, and creates an environment that encourages collaborative problem-solving.

Beyond exhibiting the behaviors associated with empathetic listening, follow-up is an important step to ensure that others understand that true listening has occurred. This assurance may come in the form of incorporating feedback and making changes, following through on promises made in meetings, summarizing the meeting through notes, or—if the leader is not incorporating the feedback—explaining why they made other decisions. In short, the leader can find many ways to demonstrate that they have heard the messages.

The ability and willingness to listen with empathy is often what sets a leader apart. Hearing words is not adequate; the leader truly needs to work at understanding the position and perspective of the others involved in the conversation. In an interview, Paul Bennett, chief creative officer at IDEO, advises leaders to listen more and ask the right questions. Bennett shared that, "For most of my twenties, I assumed that the world was more interested in me than I was in it, so I spent most of my time talking, usually in a quite uninformed way, about whatever I thought, rushing to be clever, thinking about what I was going to say to someone rather than listening to what they were saying to me."[3]

Slowing down, engaging with others rather than endlessly debating, taking the time to hear and learn from others, and asking brilliant questions are ultimately the keys to success.

CHRISTINE M. RIORDAN is the provost and professor of management at the University of Kentucky. Her research focuses on labor force diversity issues, leadership effectiveness, and career success.

Notes

1. Christopher C. Gearhart and Graham D. Bodie, "Active-Empathic Listening as a General Social Skill: Evidence from Bivariate and Canonical Correlations," *Communication Reports* 24, no. 2 (2011): 86–98.

2. Tanya Drollinger, Lucette B. Comer, and Patricia T. Warrington, "Development and Validation of the Active Empathic Listening Scale," *Psychology & Marketing* 23, no. 2 (2005): 160–180.

3. Grace Nasri, "8 Successful Entrepreneurs Give Their Younger Selves Lessons They Wish They Had Known Then," *Fast Company*, May 9, 2013, https://www.fast company.com/3009482/8-successful-entrepreneurs-give -their-younger-selves-lessons-they-wish-theyd-known-th.

Adapted from content posted on hbr.org, January 16, 2014 (product #H00MQE).

5

If You Aspire to Be a Great Leader, Be Present

By Rasmus Hougaard and Jacqueline Carter

Some years ago, we worked with a director of a multinational pharma company who'd been receiving poor grades for engagement and leadership effectiveness. Although he tried to change, nothing seemed to work. As his frustration grew, he started tracking the time he spent with each of his direct reports—and every time he received bad feedback, he pulled out his data and exclaimed, "But look how much time I spend with everyone!"

Things improved when he began a daily 10-minute mindfulness practice. After a couple of months, people found him more engaging, nicer to work with, and more inspiring. He was surprised and elated by the results. The real surprise? When he pulled out his time-tracking spreadsheet, he saw that he was spending, on average, 21% *less* time with his people.

The difference? He was actually *there*.

He came to understand that, even though he was in the same room with someone, he wasn't always fully present. He let himself become pre-occupied with other activities or let his mind drift to other things. And, most of all, he'd listen to his inner voice when someone was talking. Because of his lack of presence, people felt unheard and frustrated.

Our inner voices are the commentaries we lend to our experiences. They often say things like, "I wish he would stop talking." Or, "I know what she's going to say next." Or, "I've heard this all before." Or, "I wonder if Joe has responded to my text."

To truly engage other human beings and create meaningful connections, we need to silence our inner voices and be fully present—and being more mindful can help.

As part of the research for our book, *The Mind of the Leader*, we surveyed more than 1,000 leaders who indicated that a more mindful presence is the optimal strategy to engage their people, create better connections, and improve performance.

Other research bears this out. In a survey of 2,000 employees, Bain & Company found that among 33 leadership traits—including creating compelling objectives, expressing ideas clearly, and being receptive to input—the ability to be mindfully present (also called *centeredness*) is the most essential of all.[1]

Research also suggests that there's a direct correlation between leaders' mindfulness and the well-being and performance of their people.[2] In other words, the more a leader is present with their people, the better they will perform.

Based on our work, here are some tips and strategies that may help in your quest to be more present in your daily life.

Be here now

Like all CEOs, Dominic Barton, who was global managing director of McKinsey & Company, knows about having a daily schedule of back-to-back meetings. All of these meetings are important, all include complex information, and most require far-reaching decisions. Under these conditions, being present moment to moment, meeting after meeting, is a challenge. But in Barton's experience, presence is not a choice. It's a necessity.

"When I'm with people during the day, I'm doing my best to be focused, I'm present with them," he told us. "Part of this is because I get energy from being with people. But the other part is because if you're not focused, if you're not present, it's discouraging to the other people. They lose motivation. If you're not present, I think you may as well not have the meeting. It can sometimes be difficult to do, but it's always important."

The person in front of you does not know what you were dealing with a moment ago, nor should they. It's your responsibility to show up and be fully present to effectively use the limited time you have with each person you meet.

Barton believes being mindfully present requires discipline and skill. It takes discipline to stay on task and not let yourself be affected by nagging challenges or distracted by mental chatter. And it requires skill to have the mental ability to stay laser focused and present. When he's present throughout his day, he finds it deeply gratifying. Being present becomes the cornerstone to getting the most out of every moment with each person.

Plan for presence

In his decade as CEO of Campbell Soup Company, Doug Conant developed rituals for physically and psychologically connecting with people at all levels in the company, which he called touchpoints.

Every morning, Conant allocated a good chunk of his time to walking around the plant, greeting people, and getting to know them. He would memorize their names and the names of their family members. He would take a genuine interest in their lives. He also handwrote letters of gratitude to recognize extraordinary efforts. And when people in the company were having tough times, he wrote them personal messages of encouragement. During his tenure, he sent more than 30,000 such letters.

To Conant, these behaviors were not just strategies to enhance productivity; they were heartfelt efforts to support his people.

Do less, be more

Gabrielle Thompson, senior vice president at Cisco, has found that when an employee comes to her with a challenge, sometimes it needs a simple solution. But often, the problem just needs to be heard. "Many situations simply need an ear, not action. Oftentimes, problems don't need solutions—they need presence and time," she says. As leaders, having the ability to be fully present and listen with an open mind is often the most powerful way to solve issues.

As a leader, your role can be simply to create the safe space for people to air their frustrations and process their problems. Through mindful presence, you become the container in which they have space to process the issue, without you stepping in to solve, fix, manipulate, or control the situation. Presence in itself can help resolve the issue. This kind of presence not only solves the problem but also creates greater connection and engagement.

Embodied presence

Loren Shuster, chief people officer at the LEGO Group, explained that when he has very important meetings or presentations, he takes five minutes to ground himself in his body. He visualizes coming fully alive in each cell of his body. As he explained to us, "When you're not grounded, when you're not connected to your body and surrounding environment, you don't have a strong sense of direction or purpose. You're just floating. The smallest thing can distract you. This grounding technique helps me clear my mind, recharge my energy, strengthen my instincts, and calm my emotions."

After this five-minute practice, he walks differently, he talks differently. With more gravitas. With more weight. With more vigor. And as a result, he's able to be more fully present mentally *and* physically with those around him. It grounds him in the room like a rock.

When we have embodied presence, our posture shifts. Rather than slouching, crossing our arms, and literally closing in on ourselves, we assume a more balanced, uplifted, open, and inclusive posture. This includes sitting up straight, with our arms open.

This shift in posture can influence how we think, behave, and communicate. In the same way that we can catalyze qualities like confidence through assuming a bold posture, we can induce qualities like awareness, focus, inclusion, and compassion through an uplifted, dignified posture.

The act of sitting up and opening up has a positive effect on the chemistry of our brains. It cultivates our capacity for higher-functioning thought processes. It gives us access to wisdom that comes from heightened awareness, compassion that comes from increased openness, and confidence that comes from the strength of vertical alignment.

RASMUS HOUGAARD is the founder and managing director of Potential Project, a global leadership and organizational development firm that serves Microsoft, Accenture, Cisco, and hundreds of other organizations. JACQUELINE CARTER is a partner and the North American director of Potential Project. Hougaard and Carter are coauthors of *The Mind of the Leader: How to Lead Yourself, Your People, and Your Organization for Extraordinary Results* and *One Second Ahead: Enhance Your Performance at Work with Mindfulness*.

Notes

1. Mark Horwitch and Meredith Whipple Callahan, "How Leaders Inspire: Cracking the Code," Bain & Company, June 9, 2016, https://www.bain.com/insights/how-leaders-inspire-cracking-the-code.
2. Jochen Matthias REB, J. Narayanan and S. Chaturvedi, "Leading Mindfully: Two Studies of the Influence of Supervisor Trait Mindfulness on Employee Well-Being and Performance," *Mindfulness* 5, no. 1 (2014): 36–45.

Adapted from content posted on hbr.org,
December 13, 2017 (product #H042IC).

6

Become a Better Listener

An interview with Mark Goulston
by Sarah Green Carmichael

Mark Goulston is a psychiatrist and the author of many books, including *Just Listen: Discover the Secret to Getting Through to Absolutely Anyone*. In this interview, he discusses how you can improve your listening skills by helping your counterpart "feel felt" and encouraging them to open up to you at deeper and deeper levels.

Sarah Green Carmichael: *When you talk about listening and helping people become better listeners, are you working from one definition? Or do you have many definitions?*

Mark Goulston: There are four levels of talking: talking over, at, to, or with. They parallel the four kinds of listening, and there's a one-to-one correlation.

What goes along with talking over someone is what I call *removed listening*. Removed listening is when you're really not there. Now, if you're someone who can multitask, you can be kind of foolish, and while someone's trying to get your attention—perhaps a spouse or something like that—you can put down your iPad and you'll parrot back exactly what they said, because you're a great multitasker. And if you then smile, taking delight in how you were able to spout that back to them, you're going to spend the night in the den. So removed listening is insulting, and it goes along with when someone's talking over you.

Now, when someone's talking *at* you, that is the second level, which is *reactive listening*. That's when no matter what the other person says, you get defensive. You take an issue with it. You're taking it personally. Doing that is actually fairly upsetting to the conversation.

When someone's talking *to* you, that goes along with *responsible listening*. You're being responsible to the conversation.

But the gold standard—and for me it's the gold standard because I think we need to connect better in the world—is what I call *receptive listening*, which goes along with talking *with* someone. The difference between responsible listening and receptive listening is that if you can imagine a young child is freezing and they knock on the door and come in, responsible listening is to say, "Oh, you were out in the rain. You must have been out there for a long time. You're drenched." That's responsible listening, while that little child is shivering.

In receptive listening, you don't even need the words. You can say, "My god. You look chilled to the bone. Let's get you into some dry clothes. Let's get you near the heater, and let's get you out of those things."

So can you feel the difference between responsible and receptive listening? One of the things that I talk about in *Just Listen* is the difference between feeling figured out, feeling understood, and feeling felt. And again—you're already catching my bias—I go to the feeling felt issue.

There's an anecdote that I often speak about from *Just Listen*, where I was meeting with a CEO. I was trying to get an appointment. It wasn't easy. He was a big footballer type of guy, must've been 270 pounds, with trophies behind him. As I'm seated with him, I can see that the last thing he wants to do is have a conversation with me.

Now, I can be a little bit bold. So I'm seated there, and I'm not keeping his attention. So imagine this (and this is what you can do when you don't work for a company, because your company would fire you): I said to him, "How much time do you have for me?" And he looked at me. He said, "What?" I said, "Yeah. Look on your schedule. How much time do you have for me?" I knew he was going to throw me out then.

He said, "20 minutes." I knew I had about 30 seconds to turn this around.

But I got his attention. I said, "Look, we're into minute three, and what I wanted to talk to you about is worth your undivided attention, I believe. You can't give me your undivided attention because you've got a lot of things on your mind and there are several things that I think you need to take care of.

"So here's the deal. Let's stop now. You take the next 16 minutes, take care of whatever's on your mind, and we'll reschedule this. Or you can just tell your assistant that I was just too rude and bold, and you never have to see me again. But take the next 16 minutes, which maybe you don't have the rest of the day, and take care of whatever's on your mind. We'll redo this another time. It's less important."

At that point, he looked at me and he teared up. And I said to myself, Mark, you promised yourself you wouldn't make these people cry in the business world. I mean, you're a psychiatrist. Can't you just leave that behind?

Yeah, that escalated very quickly.

It did. It did. And he looked at me and said, "You know, you've known me for three minutes. There are people 20 yards from where we are that don't know what you know, because I'm very private. My wife's having a biopsy and it doesn't look good.

"My wife's stronger than me. And she told me, 'You go to work.' So I'm here at work, but I'm really not here."

Then I immediately switched from brazen to compassion. I said, "Wow. I'm sorry to hear that.

Go be with her. You're not here. Go be with her or make a call. Go do that."

And it was interesting. He was like a big Newfoundland dog coming in from the rain. He shook his shoulders and went, "pfff." He centered himself and said, "You know, I'm not as strong as my wife, but I'm pretty strong. I served a couple tours in Vietnam. You've got my undivided attention, and you've got your full 20 minutes."

What's the point of this story? He felt *felt*. There he was, feeling alone in this and didn't want to burden his wife. And he was this big CEO. It shouldn't surprise you that not only did I get his undivided attention, we've been friends ever since.

Well, and that raises a really interesting point, which is that we can all be doing everything we can to listen at all these different levels that you've mentioned, but it doesn't really count unless the other person feels like we've heard them. So walk me through how we can do a better job at making other people feel heard or feel felt.

In my training of people to be better listeners—and I work with major consulting companies about how to turn a conversation into getting hired—when I've finished the presentation, what I've said is, your main goal when you first meet a prospect, a potential client, is to get a second meeting that they initiate. It's not to sell them anything in the first meeting.

As you're asking them questions, there will be a point at which they say, "What do you think?" What I suggest—and this is not for all cases, you have to pick and choose—but I suggest that you never answer the first question they ask you after you've had some conversation. Instead, what you focus on are four things: hyperbole, inflection, adverbs, and adjectives.

Hyperbole is when people use words like "outlandish," "horrendous," or "wonderful." Inflection is when they raise their voice. Notice adverbs and adjectives, because an adverb is a way of embellishing a verb: "We need to do this quickly." And an adjective is a way of embellishing a noun: "This is an amazing opportunity." You need to notice. Be a first-class *noticer*.

When you notice hyperbole, inflection, adverbs, and adjectives, you're being given an invitation to a deeper conversation. You have the chance to take the conversation to a level that your competitors don't.

So when they've said something and they ask you, "What do you think?" you say, "I can tell you what I think, but say more about having to do this thing quickly," or "Say more about the amazing opportunity." What you'll notice, if you're face-to-face with them, is that they will start to use hand gestures, and their hands will go up from their hips to midabdomen.

Then, there's something else I talk about in *Just Listen* called *conversation deepeners*. "Say more about such and such" is one of them. But then after they finish whatever they're saying, another conversation deepener is to say, "Really?" Then what you'll see is they're going to raise their hands even more. "Oh, yeah. This is really amazing. If we could do this, this would change everything."

In your mind's eye what you're trying to do is to get them to open up at deeper and deeper levels, because then they'll be invested in the conversation more than just at a transactional level. You're helping them get everything off their chest, from the positive to the negative. And even then, if they ask "So what do you think"—because now they're really intrigued—I say, "I can tell you what I think, but I'd like to take our conversation to the ICU."

Now, I can get away with saying that because I'm a medical doctor, but they're going to say, "What?" Tell them, "ICU stands for important, critical, and urgent. Important is a year, two years from now. Critical is three to six months. And urgent is this week. I can guess at which of the things we talked about are important, critical, and urgent. But rather than my guessing, why don't you tell me?"

What you're trying to do is get them to just dump everything into the conversation at deeper levels. They may be a little bit off balance, because you've just invited them to dump it all out, but now you're giving them the opportunity to focus it and prioritize it. And what you really want to focus them on is what's urgent.

Can you get a sense of just how this is uncovering all kinds of things in the conversation? If I'm dealing with training a consultant, at that point they're going to say, "Well, what do you think? I've told you what's important, critical, and urgent."

Even then what I say is, "You know, I can give you an answer right now. But it would be a B, B+ answer. You've just shared with me things that are important, critical, and urgent, and it would be my best answer, based on what I know now. I'd like to take a day or two days to check on something so I could give you an even better answer. What it comes down to is, how urgent is this that you've talked to me about, and how interested would you be in my getting my best answer for it. What do you think?"

What you want them to do is say, "It's urgent, and I'd like that best answer soon." And then you let them initiate it, as opposed to the unfortunate thing that many of us do, where, out of our own nervousness, we need to prove how smart we are. Sometimes in a conversation, we're there impressing them with all this brightness, and then at the end they pause, and they start to disengage. On the heels of us impressing them with all our brightness, we're scurrying, saying, "So what do we do next? Do you have any other questions?" By then, the cow has left the barn.

So can you picture this? It's almost like a surgical approach to a conversation.

It's interesting because I feel like we started out talking about listening. And I had this assumption that it was all about reining in your own feelings and any distractions so you could be fully present. But actually it seems like a lot of what we've ended up talking about is getting other people to talk, like getting other people to share the information with you that maybe is in their head but that they just weren't disclosing before.

Absolutely true. The key is helping them talk about what's most important, critical, and urgent to them. I think we're in a world in which people want to buy, but nobody wants to be sold. People don't want to be persuaded. And people don't even like to do the persuading.

MARK GOULSTON, MD, FAPA, is a business psychiatrist, executive advisor, keynote speaker, and the CEO and founder of the Goulston Group. He is the author of *Talking to "Crazy": How to Deal with the Irrational and Impossible People in Your*

Life and *Just Listen: Discover the Secret to Getting Through to Absolutely Anyone,* and a coauthor of *Real Influence: Persuade Without Pushing and Gain Without Giving In.* He can be reached at markgoulston.com. Follow him on Twitter @markgoulston. **SARAH GREEN CARMICHAEL** was an executive editor at *Harvard Business Review.* Follow her on Twitter at @skgreen.

Adapted from "Become a Better Listener" on
HBR IdeaCast (podcast), August 13, 2015.

7

To Change Someone's Mind, Stop Talking and Listen

By Nilofer Merchant

Samar Minallah Khan, the feminist Pakistani anthropologist and filmmaker, was enraged. Local tribal leaders were trading little girls as compensation for their male family members' crimes.

These leaders, responsible for settling legal disputes in their villages, act as local judges. A long-standing practice was to address major crimes by "compensating" a harmed family with a daughter of the family doing the harm. The guilty father or uncle was then considered "free" and the village was told this issue was "resolved." Samar thought this tradition, called *swara*, was horrendous: It forever changed a young girl's life, through no fault of her own. But although Samar was angry, she realized she'd never get to the outcome she wanted if she led with that anger.

So she tried something else. First, she listened more than she talked. She listened to the religious (male) leaders explain the use of swara and its benefits, and she asked how that tradition would have been interpreted by the Prophet Mohammad. She listened to the fathers and uncles who allowed their crimes to be expiated this way. And by listening, Samar learned so much that it enabled her to bridge a seemingly unbridgeable chasm of difference.

Samar had first assumed that the fathers whose crimes were being forgiven this way were happy to let their daughters suffer for their crimes, but when she listened to them, she heard that they were not. They wanted another way. She heard from local leaders that they placed an extremely high value on tradition. She heard from religious Muslim legal scholars that swara was a form of "vicarious liability," which is not allowed in Islam. And finally, she heard that in earlier times, disputes were also resolved by sending a girl to an enemy's family, but she didn't stay there permanently; instead, she would be given gifts and then sent back to her parents' home. All of this, she taped.

She convened local communities to watch these videos and talk with one another about the tradition and its implications. One by one, local tribal leaders changed what they considered true justice. They decided that swara could be replaced by monetary compensation. Samar created change not by selling *her* idea, but creating a way for everyone to arrive at a new idea, together.

What Samar did was to ask people to share their perspective, without trying to convince them of hers. It sounds like something for a movie script, not necessarily practical advice for business leaders. But maybe it should be.

I found myself thinking, somewhat wistfully, of Samar the other day during a terrible, but not unusual, meeting. A leader had asked 30 of his best and brightest to gather so that he could hear their input on what he perceived as a marketing gap. But the very design of the meeting meant he would be hearing very little: The agenda called for three hours of presentations and about 15 minutes total of Q&A (if none of the presentations ran over, that is).

I left feeling that he didn't really want to listen, that what he wanted was to convince the 30 people present of his perspective so that we could become his mouthpiece and fix his "marketing gap" for him. And because of the format of the meeting, I left unconvinced that I wanted to do that.

Even though it doesn't work very well, this approach is, of course, common—in any setting where one party is trying to convince another party to change, whether that's in an organization, during a political debate, or at a contentious family dinner. *Identify what key ideas could convince them. Find persuasive facts. Enthusiastically share. Beat their facts back with your facts.*

That isn't the way to create lasting change. The best way to sway others is not to tell them *your* answer, but to arrive at an answer together. Listening is the key pathway to go from *your* idea to *our* idea. To reshape the idea as needed. And ultimately to create the kind of shared ownership that is needed for any idea to become a new reality.

The next time you head into a meeting where a major decision will be made or an important issue discussed, try the following exercise I've used to prepare for the workshops I run on innovation and leadership:

Find an index card or sheet of paper (even a paper napkin will do). On one side, write key ideas that could be useful for you to share. I say "could" because you will reevaluate any of it once you learn more. On the other side, brainstorm questions you want to ask and things you hope to learn.

For example, at last year's Drucker Forum conference in Vienna, I was part of an executive round table with John Hagel, Julia Kirby, and Hal Gregersen to talk about "the power to innovate." Before our session kicked off, I jotted down a handful of questions on the back of an index card:

- Why are these executives attending our session? What is their motivation?

- What is the core "power to innovate" problem at their firms? What does that *specifically* look like?

- Do they think they have enough ideas, too many ideas, or ideas of poor quality?

- Is innovation, to them, a problem of idea selection, market connection or execution, or something else?

- Can "innovation" be discussed in general terms—without a specific context—and have it be useful?

- Who or what set of ideas are they listening to now about innovation? What is missing, or why is that idea set not working?

I didn't end up asking all of these questions, but writing them down meant that I was *primed* to be curious and to listen for motivations, needs, and emotions. Developing a list of questions can help you be ready to really listen to what is actually going on.

Most of us don't do that. Most of us listen to the degree that we can understand points of agreement or disagreement, or to prepare what to say in response, rather than to learn. But when we do that, we're not so much hearing other people as we are waiting for our turn to speak.

To listen is to pay attention to. Listening means stepping outside one's own interests, to actually want to know more, and to care what others' interests are. To not just hear words but to pay attention to the underlying needs and frames of reference.

Which gets to why we aren't already great listeners. We're afraid that if we're listening, we're not advocating for our own ideas and why those ideas matter. We're afraid we're giving up on our convictions.

But we can all have more faith in ourselves. And each other.

NILOFER MERCHANT has personally launched 100 products amounting to $18 billion in revenue and has served on both public and private boards. Today, she lectures at Stanford, gives talks around the world, and has been ranked one of the most influential management thinkers in the world by Thinkers50. Her latest book is *The Power of Onlyness: Make Your Wild Ideas Mighty Enough to Dent the World.*

Adapted from content posted on hbr.org,
February 6, 2018 (product #H044YR).

8

Defusing an Emotionally Charged Conversation with a Colleague

By Ron Friedman

Work with anyone long enough and you're bound to encounter a difference of opinion. Most of the time, these disagreements are resolved amicably. But if you're like most people, every now and then you find yourself immersed in a conversation so emotionally charged it seems to have nothing to do with the issues you're supposedly discussing.

What do you do when a conversation is spiraling out of control? When you've tried all the patient listening you can muster, and the other person still won't budge? How do you get the conversation back on track?

Anthony Suchman has invested a good portion of his career in searching for an answer. A charming physician with a profound intellect, Suchman has been studying the dynamics of human relationships for more than three decades and has published his results in some of the world's leading medical journals.[1]

According to Suchman, every workplace conversation operates on two levels: a task channel and a relationship channel. Occasionally the two get fused, which is when disagreements intensify and collaborations break down.

Here's what he means: Suppose you and I are working together on a project. Along the way, we have a difference of opinion about our next steps. Perhaps I think we should use PowerPoint to deliver an important presentation, and you see Power-Point as a poor communication tool. When I express a point of view that's different from yours, you may take our disagreement at face value by saying, "Hmm, I guess Ron sees it differently." But if we're new to working together, or if we've had a few run-ins in the past, you're likely to read beyond my suggestion and use it to draw inferences about our relationship. For instance, you may misinterpret my suggestion as a lack of trust, a sign of disrespect, or even proof of competition.

It's at this point, Suchman argues, that our task-focused disagreement becomes contaminated with concerns about our relationship. And when that happens, things escalate. Fast.

Neurologically, what Suchman is describing is the activation of a fear response. When we perceive danger, our hypothalamus sends a signal that releases adrenaline and cortisol into the bloodstream. That triggers a fight-or-flight response that sends our bodies into overdrive, short-circuiting our ability to concentrate or think creatively. We experience tunnel vision.

In the evolutionary past, having an automatic reaction to fear was quite useful. It helped protect us from oncoming predators and kept us alive long enough to reproduce. But in today's workplace, an involuntary fear response can interfere with our ability to work collaboratively with others. It's one reason why the greater the emotional charge, the harder it is to get either side to listen.

To defuse an emotionally volatile situation like this, Suchman believes the first step is to disentangle the task and relational channels. "When people disagree, it's often because one party misinterprets the feedback they've received as a personal attack," he says. "So it becomes: 'If you like my idea, you like me,' and 'If you don't like my idea, you don't like me.' That puts a huge encumbrance on the task channel and makes it really hard to speak openly."

Our mental capacity is limited, Suchman points out, which means we can attend to either the task channel or the relationship channel. It's when we get the two channels crossed that our ability to collaborate constructively suffers. One approach to reducing tensions during disagreements involves deliberately attending to the relational channel and reaffirming your commitment to the relationship. This way there's no confusion about what the argument is really about. By momentarily focusing on the relationship, you disentangle the personal from the business.

Suchman recommends using a specific series of relationship-building statements to make the conversation more productive, which are represented in the acronym PEARLS:

Partnership

- "I really want to work on this with you."

- "I bet we can figure this out together."

Empathy

- "I can feel your enthusiasm as you talk."

- "I can hear your concern."

Acknowledgment

- "You clearly put a lot of work into this."

- "You invested in this, and it shows."

Respect

- "I've always appreciated your creativity."

- "There's no doubt you know a lot about this."

Legitimation

- "This would be hard for anyone."

- "Who wouldn't be worried about something like this?"

Support

- "I'd like to help you with this."

- "I want to see you succeed."

Using relationship-building statements can feel unnatural at first, especially when you're not accustomed to complimenting others. I know they did for me when I first started using them in workplace conversations. The key, I've discovered, is to employ them sparingly at first and to only say the ones that genuinely reflect how you feel.

Almost immediately, you'll notice that inserting a well-timed PEARLS statement can dramatically alter the tenor of a conversation. Because no matter how far up we climb on an organizational ladder, we are still stuck using an emotionally driven brain. When fear enters the equation, it's impossible to get people to do their best work, which is why restoring confidence in the relationship can be a powerful tool.

The value of relationship-building statements extends far beyond the workplace. They're as effective with spouses, children, and friends as they are with colleagues. The reason is simple: Anytime you attend to people's psychological need for connection, you have the potential to improve the quality of an exchange. The more heated the argument, the more vital the statements become.

RON FRIEDMAN, PhD, is an award-winning psychologist and the founder of ignite80, a company that teaches leaders practical, evidence-based strategies for working smarter and creating thriving organizations. He is the author of *The Best Place to Work: The Art and Science of Creating an Extraordinary Workplace* and frequently delivers keynote speeches and workshops on the science of workplace excellence.

Note

1. Anthony L. Suchman, "A New Theoretical Foundation for Relationship-Centered Care," *Journal of General Internal Medicine* 21, no. 1 (2006): S40–S44.

Adapted from content posted on hbr.org,
January 12, 2016 (product #H02LNI).

9

The Power of Listening in Helping People Change

By Guy Itzchakov and Avraham N. (Avi) Kluger

Giving performance feedback is one of the most common ways managers help their subordinates learn and improve. Yet research has revealed that feedback can actually hurt performance: More than 20 years ago, one of us (Avraham) analyzed 607 experiments on feedback effectiveness and found that feedback caused performance to decline in 38% of cases.[1] This happened with both positive and negative feedback, mostly when the feedback threatened how people saw themselves.

One reason that giving feedback (even when it's positive) often backfires is that it signals that the boss is in charge and the boss is judgmental. This can make employees stressed and defensive, which makes it harder for them to see another person's perspective. For example, employees can handle negative feedback by downplaying the importance of the person providing the feedback or the feedback itself. People may even reshape their social networks to avoid the feedback source in order to restore their self-esteem.[2] In other words, they defend themselves by bolstering their attitudes against the person giving feedback.

We wanted to explore whether a more subtle intervention, namely asking questions and listening, could prevent these consequences. Whereas feedback is about telling employees that they need to change, listening to employees and asking them questions might make them *want* to change. In a recent paper, we consistently demonstrated that experiencing high-quality (attentive, empathic, and nonjudgmental) listening can positively shape speakers' emotions and attitudes.[3]

WHAT MAKES LISTENING POWERFUL?

Listening as an avenue for self-change was advocated by the psychologist Carl Rogers in a classic 1952 HBR article, "Barriers and Gateways to Communication." Rogers theorized that when speakers feel that listeners are being empathic, attentive, and nonjudgmental, they relax and share their inner feelings and thoughts without worrying about what listeners will think of them. This safe state enables speakers to delve deeper into their consciousness and discover new insights about themselves—even those that may challenge previously held beliefs and perceptions.

For example, consider an employee who believes that she always respects her colleagues' and customers' feelings. If someone tells her this isn't true, it will likely lead her to protect her view of herself by doubling down on her belief and discounting the other

(Continued)

WHAT MAKES LISTENING POWERFUL?

person's judgment. By contrast, if someone asks her to describe her interactions with other people at work and listens attentively while encouraging her to occasionally elaborate, she is likely to feel more secure with the listener and open up in ways she might not otherwise. She might remember incidents where she was disrespectful to customers or got angry at her colleagues and be more open to discussing them and ways to change.

For example, in one laboratory experiment, we assigned 112 undergraduate students to serve as either a speaker or a listener and paired them up, sitting face-to-face. We asked speakers to talk for 10 minutes about their attitudes toward a proposal for universal basic income or a possible requirement that all university students must also volunteer. We instructed the listeners to "listen as you listen when you are at your best." But we randomly distracted half of the listeners by sending them text messages (such as "What event irritated you the most recently?") and instructed them to answer briefly (so the speakers saw that they were distracted). Afterward, we asked the speakers questions about whether they were worried about what their partner thought of them, whether they acquired any insight while talking, and whether they were confident in their beliefs.

We found that speakers paired with good listeners (versus those paired with distracted listeners) felt less anxious and more self-aware and reported higher clarity about their attitudes on the topics. Speakers paired with undistracted listeners also reported wanting to *share* their attitude with other people more compared with speakers paired with distracted listeners.

Another benefit of high-quality listening is that it helps speakers see both sides of an argument (what we call "attitude complexity"). In another paper we found that speakers who conversed with a good listener reported attitudes that were more complex and less extreme—in other words, not one-sided.[4]

In a lab experiment we instructed 114 undergraduates at a business school to talk for 12 minutes about their fitness to become a manager in the future. We randomly assigned these speakers to one of three listening groups (good, moderate, and poor). Speakers in the good listening condition talked to a trained listener, who was either a certified management coach or a trained social work student. We asked these trained listeners to use all their listening skills, such as asking questions and reflecting. Speakers in the moderate listening condition talked to another undergraduate at the business school who was instructed to listen as he or she usually does. Speakers in the poor listening condition talked with a student from the theatre department who was instructed to act distracted (such as by looking aside and playing with their smartphone).

After the conversation, we asked the speakers to indicate separately the extent to which they thought they were suitable for becoming managers. Based on these answers, we calculated their attitude complexity (whether they saw both strengths and weaknesses that would affect their ability to be a manager) and extremity (whether they saw only one side). We found that speakers who talked to a good listener saw both strengths and weaknesses more than those in the other conditions. Speakers who talked to a distracted listener mostly described their strengths and barely acknowledged their weaknesses. Interestingly, the speakers in the poor listening condition were those that, on average, reported feeling the most suitable for becoming a manager.

We tested the relevance of these lab findings in three field studies conducted among city hall employees, high-tech workers, and teachers (180 workers, in total).[5] In these studies, we asked employees to talk about their colleagues, their supervisor, or about a meaningful experience at work, before and after participating in a listening intervention known as a listening circle. In the listening circle, employees are invited to talk openly and honestly about an issue, like a meaningful experience they had at work. They're trained to listen without interrupting, and only one person talks at a time.

We replicated all of our lab findings. Namely, employees who participated in the listening circles reported lower social anxiety, higher attitude complexity, and lower attitude extremity regarding various work-related topics (such as attitude toward a manager) by comparison with employees who participated in one of the control conditions that did not involve trained listeners.

In concert, our findings suggest that listening seems to make an employee more relaxed, more self-aware of his or her strengths and weaknesses, and more willing to reflect in a nondefensive manner. This can make employees more likely to cooperate (versus compete) with other colleagues—as they become more interested in sharing their attitudes but not necessarily in trying to persuade others to adopt them—and more open to considering other points of view.

Going back to giving feedback, of course we do not claim that listening must replace feedback. Rather, it seems that listening to employees talk about their own experiences first can make giving feedback more productive by helping them feel psychologically safe and less defensive.[6]

Listening has its enemies

Our findings support existing evidence that managers who listen well are perceived as people leaders, generate more trust, instill higher job satisfaction, and increase their team's creativity.[7] Yet if listening is so beneficial for employees and for organizations, why is it not more prevalent in the workplace? Why are most employees not listened to in the way they want? Research shows that a few barriers often stand in the way.

1. *Loss of power.* Research from our team has shown that some managers may feel that if they listen to their employees they are going to be looked upon as weak.[8] But at the same time, it's been shown that being a good listener means gaining prestige. So it seems managers must make a trade-off between attaining status based on intimidation and getting status based on admiration.

2. *Listening consumes time and effort.* In many instances, managers listen to employees under time pressure or while they're distracted by

other thoughts or work. So listening is an investment decision: Managers must put in the time to listen in order to see the future benefits.

3. *Fear of change.* High-quality listening can be risky because it entails entering a speaker's perspective without trying to make judgments. This process could potentially change the listener's attitudes and perceptions. We observed several times that when we trained managers to truly listen, they gained crucial insights about their employees; they were stunned to learn how little they knew about the lives of people they'd worked with for many years.

For example, several managers reported that when they tried listening to employees whom they'd confronted about poor attendance, they learned that these employees were struggling with supporting a family member (a wife dying of cancer, a sibling with a mental disability). This realization threatened managers' attitudes and views about themselves—an experience called cognitive dissonance that can be difficult.

Tips for becoming a better listener

Listening resembles a muscle. It requires training, persistence, effort, and, most important, the intention to become a good listener. It requires clearing your mind from internal and external noise—and if that's not possible, postponing the conversation for when you can truly listen without being distracted. Here are some best practices.

Give 100% of your attention, or do not listen. Put aside your smartphone, tablet, or laptop, and look at the speaker, even if they do not look back at you. In an ordinary conversation, a speaker looks at you occasionally to see that you're still listening. Constant eye contact lets the speaker feel that you are listening.

Do not interrupt. Resist the urge to interrupt before the speaker indicates that they are done for the moment. In our workshop, we give managers the following instruction: "Go to someone at your work who makes listening very hard on you. Let them know that you are learning and practicing listening and that today, you will only listen for ___ minutes (where the blank could be 3, 5, or even 10 minutes), and delay responding until the predetermined listening time is up or even until the following day."

Managers are often amazed at their discoveries. One shared, "In six minutes, we completed a transaction that otherwise would have taken more than an hour." Another told us, "The other person shared things with me that I had prevented her from saying for 18 years."

Do not judge or evaluate. Listen without jumping to conclusions and interpreting what you hear. You may notice your judgmental thoughts, but push them aside. If you notice that you've lost track of the conversation due to your judgments, apologize and explain to the speaker that your mind was distracted, and ask them to repeat. Don't pretend to listen.

Don't impose your solutions. The role of the listener is to help the speaker draw up a solution on their own. Therefore, when listening to a fellow colleague or subordinate, refrain from suggesting solutions. If you believe you have a good solution and feel an urge to share it, frame it as a question, such as "I wonder what will happen if you choose to do X?"

Ask more (good) questions. Listeners shape conversations by asking questions that benefit the speaker.[9] Good listening requires being thoughtful about what the speaker needs help with most and crafting a question that would lead the speaker to search for an answer. Ask questions to help someone delve deeper into their thoughts and experiences.

Before you ask a question, ask yourself, "Is this question intended to benefit the speaker or satisfy my curiosity?" Of course, there is room for both, but a good listener prioritizes the needs of the other. One of the best questions you can ask is "Is there anything else?" This often exposes novel information and unexpected opportunities.

Reflect. When you finish a conversation, reflect on your listening, and think about missed opportunities—moments in which you ignored potential leads or remained silent when you could have asked questions. When you feel that you were an excellent listener, consider what you gained and how you can apply this type of listening in more challenging circumstances.

GUY ITZCHAKOV is a lecturer on the faculty of Business Administration at Ono Academic College. He received his PhD from the Hebrew University of Jerusalem in 2017. His research draws on Carl Rogers's theory and focuses on how attentive and nonjudgmental listening facilitates a change in the speakers' emotions and cognitions. It has appeared in *Personality and Social Psychology Bulletin*, the *European Journal of Work and Organizational Psychology*, and the *Journal of Experimental Social Psychology*. AVRAHAM N. (AVI) KLUGER is a professor of organizational behavior at the School of Business at Hebrew University of Jerusalem. He has studied the destructive effects of performance feedback for more than 20 years. In his ongoing meta-analyses of listening, he has found that good listeners are good performers and are perceived as good leaders. For more on his research, visit his website avikluger.wixsite.com/avi-kluger.

Notes

1. Avraham N. Kluger and Angelo DeNisi, "The Effects of Feedback Interventions on Performance: A Historical Review, a Meta-Analysis, and a Preliminary Feedback Intervention Theory," *Psychological Bulletin* 119, no. 2 (1996): 254–284.
2. Paul Green Jr., Francesca Gino, Bradley Staats, "Shopping for Confirmation: How Disconfirming Feedback Shapes

Social Networks," working paper 18-028, Harvard Business School, 2017, https://www.hbs.edu/faculty/Publication%20Files/18-028_5efa4295-edc1-4fac-bef5-0111064c9e08.pdf.

3. Guy Itzchakov et al., "The Listener Sets the Tone: High-Quality Listening Increases Attitude Clarity and Behavior-Intention Consequences," *Personality and Social Psychology Bulletin* 44, no. 5 (2018): 762–778.

4. Guy Itzchakov, Avraham N. Kluger, Dotan R. Castro, "I Am Aware of My Inconsistencies but Can Tolerate Them: The Effect of High-Quality Listening on Speakers' Attitude Ambivalence," *Personality and Social Psychology Bulletin* 43, no. 1 (2016): 105–120.

5. Liora Lipetz, Avraham N. Kluger, and Graham D. Bodie, "Listening Is Listening Is Listening: Employees' Perception of Listening as a Holistic Phenomenon," *International Journal of Listening* (2018): 1–26.

6. Marie-Hélène Budworth, Gary P. Latham, Laxmikant Manroop, "Looking Forward to Performance Improvement: A Field Test of the Feedforward Interview for Performance Management," *Human Resource Management* 54, no. 1 (2015): 45–54.

7. Avraham N. Kluger and Keren Zaidel, "Are Listeners Perceived as Leaders?" *International Journal of Listening* 27, no. 2 (2013): 73–84; Mary Stine, Teresa Thompson, and Louis Cusella, "The Impact of Organizational Structure and Supervisory Listening Indicators on Subordinate Support, Trust, Intrinsic Motivation, and Performance,"

International Journal of Listening 9, 1995, no. 1 (2012): 84–105; V. Tellis-Nayak, "A Person-Centered Workplace: The Foundation for Person-Centered Caregiving in Long-Term Care," *Journal of the American Medical Directors Association* 8, no. 2 (2007): 46–54; and Dotan R. Castro et al., "Mere-Listening Effect on Creativity and the Mediating Role of Psychological Safety," *Psychology of Aesthetics, Creativity and the Arts,* May 17, 2018.

8. Anat Hurwitz and Avraham N. Kluger, "The Power of Listeners: How Listeners Transform Status and Co-Create Power," *Academy of Management Proceedings* 2017, no. 1 (2017).

9. Niels Van Quaquebeke and Will Felps, "Respectful Inquiry: A Motivational Account of Leading Through Asking Questions and Listening," *Academy of Management Review* 43, no. 1 (2016).

Adapted from content posted on hbr.org,
May 17, 2018 (product #H04C0H).

10

When You're the Person Your Colleagues Always Vent To

By Sandra L. Robinson and Kira Schabram

D ivani (not her real name) is a senior analyst at a large telecommunications firm. She proudly describes herself as her department's "resident cheer-upper." As she says, "I have always been the person that people turn to for support . . . I listen really well, and I like to listen, I like to help." But the year before I spoke with her, Divani's organization was going through a major change initiative: "I already had so much on my plate, and so many colleagues were leaning on me, turning to me to process, commiserate, ask for advice. It was hard to get through my own deadlines and also be there for my coworkers. I was drowning in stress and nearing burnout." She told us about feeling down on Sunday nights, feeling increasingly angry and cynical, and having trouble sleeping because she couldn't "shut my mind off." She took up smoking after having given it up for four years and let her exercise routine falter.

Divani is what the late organizational behavior professor Peter Frost and one of us (Sandra) termed a "toxic handler," someone who voluntarily shoulders the sadness, frustration, bitterness, and anger that are endemic to organizational life just as are joy and success. Toxic handlers can be found at all levels of an organization, but particularly in roles that span disparate groups. And they are by no means confined to management roles. Their work is difficult and critical even if it often goes uncelebrated; it keeps organizations positive and productive even as the individuals within it necessarily clash and tussle. By carrying others' confidences, suggesting solutions to interpersonal issues, working behind the scenes to prevent pain, and reframing difficult messages in constructive ways, toxic handlers absorb the negativity in day-to-day professional life and allow employees to focus on constructive work.

This isn't easy, and as Sandra's and Frost's research of over 70 toxic handlers (or those who managed them) revealed, individuals in these roles frequently experience untenably high levels of stress and strain that affect their physical health and career paths and often mean they have a diminished capacity to help others in the long run—a side effect that is most troubling for handlers.

But if handlers can recognize that they're playing a role that is both highly valuable *and* burdensome, they can see their own emotional competence in a new light and recognize the signs of serious strain while there's still something they can do about it.

How do you know if *you're* a toxic handler? Here are some questions to ask yourself:

- Are you working in an organization that is characterized by lots of change, dysfunction, or politics?

- Are you working in a role that spans different groups or different levels?

- Do you spend a lot of time listening to and offering advice to colleagues at work?

- Do people come to you to unload their worries, emotions, secrets, or workplace problems?

- Do you have a hard time saying no to colleagues, especially when they need you?

- Do you spend time behind the scenes, managing politics and influencing decisions so that others are protected?

- Do you tend to mediate communication between a toxic individual and others?

- Are you a person who feels compelled to stand up for the people at work who need your help?

- Do you think of yourself as a counselor, mediator, or peacemaker?

If you answered yes to four or more of these questions, then you may be a toxic handler. Before you panic at that label, recognize that there are both positives and negatives to fulfilling this role. On the positive side, being a toxic handler means you have valuable emotional strengths: You're probably a good listener, you're empathetic, and you're good at suggesting solutions instead of piling on problems. The people around you value the support you provide. It's important too to understand that this role is strategically critical to organizations: You likely defuse tough situations and reduce dysfunction.

Now for the bad news. Chances are that you're taking on more work than is covered in your formal job description (and in fact, as an unsung hero, you may not be getting any kind of formal credit from the organization for these efforts and how much of yourself you bring to them). Listening, mediating, and working behind the scenes to protect others takes important time away from your other responsibilities. More important, being a toxic handler also takes tremendous emotional energy to listen, comfort, and counsel others. Because you are not a trained therapist, you may also be inadvertently taking on others' pain and slowly paying a price for it. Sandra's research shows that toxic handlers tend to take on others' emotions but have no way to offload them. As a person who is constantly helping others, you may be unlikely to seek support for yourself. And finally, this role may be part of your identity, something that brings you fulfillment—so it is difficult to step away from.

Consider Sheung-Li (not his real name). His manager was a star with a great track record, but he created a lot of turmoil. The manager wouldn't take the time to get to know anyone on Sheung-Li's team personally and totally disregarded more-junior members. He was also obsessed with lofty performance goals that seemed to come out of nowhere. "My main role became protecting everyone on my team, reassuring them, keeping them focused on our objectives and away from the tensions this guy continually created," Sheung-Li described. "I spent an inordinate amount of time massaging the message, trying to persuade my boss to reconsider his decisions so as to avoid the obvious fallout they would bring, and playing mediator when our team was not delivering. I felt like I was treading water all the time. And I'm not even sure I was protecting my team from the pain he was causing. I was losing sleep over what was happening to my team, I lost weight, and I was starting to get sick with one bug after another. I don't know if that was the cause, but I know this was a really tough time in my life. It was hard to concentrate on anything else."

So if Sheung-Li's and Divani's stories sound familiar, how can you continue to help your colleagues (and your organization) while also protecting yourself? How can you keep playing your valuable role in a sustainable way?

Start by assessing whether the role is indeed taking a toll. Some toxic handlers are naturally able to take on more than others; you need to know what's right for you at any given time. Look for evidence of strain and burnout: physical symptoms like insomnia, jaw pain and TMJ, heart palpitations, and more sickness than usual. Do you have a shorter fuse than normal or an inability to concentrate? Sometimes these symptoms can sneak up on you, so it may help to check in with others to see if they've noticed a change. If you're not experiencing stress as a result, there's nothing you need to change other than being aware and keeping an eye out. Being a toxic handler only needs to be fixed if it's actually hurting you. If it is, here's how.

Reduce symptoms of stress. Turn to tried-and-true methods for stress relief: meditation, exercise, enough sleep, and healthful eating. Because toxic handlers have trouble doing things just for themselves, keep in mind that you're helping your colleagues by taking care of yourself. Set your colleagues as the intention for your meditation or yoga practice.

Pick your battles. It's hard to ask yourself where you'll have the most impact if you're emotionally drawn to every problem, but it's an exercise that will allow you to be more helpful where you can actually make a difference. Who is likely to be fine without your help? In which situations have you not even made a dent, despite your best efforts? Step away from those interactions.

Learn to say no. It's hard to say no to things you want to do, but it's important. Here's how to do it while still being supportive:

- Convey empathy: Make it clear that you feel for your colleague in their pain—you're not denying that they are having a legitimate emotional response to a situation.

- Tell them you're currently not in a position to be most helpful to them right now, and, to the extent you are comfortable, explain the reasons why.

- Consider alternative sources of support: Refer them to another support person in the organization or someone having a similar experience (so they can provide mutual support to one another). Suggest an article, book, or other resource on the topic, be it something on managing conflict or handling office politics. Or, if you know from experience that the person is good at coming up with creative solutions on their own, you can simply offer them encouragement to do so.

Let go of the guilt. If you feel guilty that you're not stepping in to help someone, here are some things to consider.

- Recognize that conflicts are often better solved by the parties directly involved. If you're stepping in repeatedly, you're not helping people acquire the skills and tools they need to succeed.

- Question whether you are truly the only one that can help in a particular situation. Enlist trusted others in the organization to help you think this through—you may identify a way to share the load.

- Remember that there is only so much of you to go around: Saying yes to one more person means you are agreeing to do less for those people and projects you have already committed to.

Form a community. Find other toxic handlers to turn to for support. These could be others in similar roles in your organization or other team members whom you see dealing with the fallout from the same toxic leader. You can also identify a pal to vent to or create a more formal group that comes together regularly to share their experiences. This is a particularly good option if your whole team or organization is going through turmoil and you know there are others experiencing the same challenges. Keep these outlets from turning into repetitive venting sessions by focusing the conversation on creative problem solving and advice.

Take breaks. These can be as small or as dramatic as you need. Divani started working with her door closed, which she had never done before. "I felt terrible about it, as if I were abandoning my coworkers who needed me. But if I lost my job I wasn't going to be much good to anybody," she explained. Consider giving yourself a mental health day off from work or planning a significant vacation. In more dramatic situations, you could also consider a temporary re-assignment of your role. Because jobs that require you to mediate between multiple teams or groups tend to come under particular fire, if you are able to step away from that role for a time you're more likely to get the respite you need.

These breaks don't need to be forever, though. "Things have since calmed down at work," Divani has reported, "and I find I have gravitated back to being the person people lean on for emotional support. But at this point, it is totally doable."

Make a change. If nothing you are doing has resulted in a shift, your best option may be to leave. Sheung-Li explained: "After two years of this [toxic situation], and at the encouragement of my wife, I saw a thera-pist. It then became clear to me this work reality was not going to change, this toxic manager was not go-ing anywhere, the stress was eating me alive, and I am the one who needed to change. I did a bunch of things, but I think the key thing I did was make a lateral move in the company to escape this role and to protect my long-term well-being. It was the best decision I ever made."

Consider therapy. It may sound dramatic, but Sheung-Li's bid to talk to a therapist is a highly useful one. A trained psychologist can help you identify burnout, manage your symptoms of stress, help you learn to say no, and work through any guilt. Not only can they help you protect yourself from the emotional vagaries of being a toxic handler, they can also assist you in your role. Clinical psychologists are themselves trained to listen to their clients empathetically without taking on their emotions. They can help you build the skills you need to help others without absorbing too much of the emotional burden yourself.

Finally, here are some "solutions" we suggest you avoid. While they seem like good answers on the surface, they often aren't as helpful as you'd think.

Just venting. While it's good to unburden yourself of your emotions—catharsis *can* reduce aggression—too much venting can actually increase stress levels. You want to move forward rather than dwell on problems. And this is as true for those confiding in you as it is for you. When people come to you to vent, consider saying something like, "I hear you! How about we think about what we can change to make this better?"

Going to your boss or HR. Sadly, the role of toxic handler is often under-recognized and underappreciated in organizations, despite its tremendous value. This means that while your boss may want to help, it can be risky for them in many organizational cultures. Similarly, many firms are unlikely to intervene in a toxic situation on behalf of the handler.

Yet toxic handlers are critical to the emotional well-being of organizations and the people in them. If you're a toxic handler, learn to monitor yourself for signs of emotional or physical fatigue—and know how to step away when you need to—so that you can keep doing what you do best.

SANDRA L. ROBINSON is a professor of organizational behavior at the University of British Columbia's Sauder School of Business. KIRA SCHABRAM is an assistant professor of organizational behavior at the University of Washington's Foster School of Business.

Adapted from content posted on hbr.org, November 30, 2016 (product #H03A8W).

11

Managing the Critical Voices Inside Your Head

By Peter Bregman

At 8:20 a.m., my 12-year-old daughter, Isabelle, was rushing to meet her ski group. She was 20 minutes late and stressed: She takes her skiing very seriously and was training for a race in a couple of days.

Near the competition center, she ran into one of her coaches, Joey. He looked at her, then his watch. "If this were a race day," he told her, with a disapproving scowl, "I would tell you to turn around and go home."

His words stung, and she burst into tears. A few moments later, she was greeted by another one of her coaches, Vicky, who saw how stressed she was.

"Honey, don't worry," she said. "This isn't a race. It's okay that you're running a little late. You'll just catch up with your group on top of the mountain."

Two vastly different coaches, two vastly different responses. Who's right? I bet you have an opinion.

But that's not the point.

My advice to Isabelle? You will have Joeys in your life, and you will have Vickys. They will show up as teachers, bosses, colleagues, and friends. So I said to her, "It's a good idea to get used to the different responses without getting thrown off balance. You can't control how people respond to you, but you can control how you take them in and how you respond to them."

But let's go one step further. The truth is, we all have a Joey and a Vicky inside, and they can both be useful. Joey might seem unkind, but his high expectations and low tolerance for failure can be helpful in driving us to be our best. On the other hand, sometimes we need empathetic support. To some, Vicky may appear soft. But her comfort and reassurance can be useful, especially during times of stress.

Here's the key: Be strategic and intentional about whom you listen to—and when—even if the voices are inside your head. In fact, *especially* if the voices are inside your head. Those can be the sneakiest. It's pretty easy to call Joey a jerk and ignore him; it's much harder to dismiss the voice inside your head because, well, it's you.

Try this tactic: When you hear the voices, give them names and personalities. Imagine a Joey on one side, a Vicky on the other.

1. Notice the voices in your head as voices. A lot of the time, most of us simply believe what we hear—either from other people or from ourselves. If your inner voice calls you lazy, it's hard not to think you're lazy. It helps if you imagine it's Joey calling you lazy instead.

2. Resist the urge to judge whether the voices in your head are right. It's impossible to know, and it doesn't matter anyway. Are you lazy? The truth is that you probably are, in some ways. And in other ways, you're not. But that's not the right question.

3. Instead, think about the outcome you want, and ask this question: Is what this voice is saying—and how it's saying it—useful right now? This is the same question you should be asking if you're confronted by an actual Joey or Vicky. Is this voice helpful to me in this particular moment? If you think it'll motivate you, listen to it. If it will demoralize you, don't.

This is an important skill: the ability to ignore critical voices when they're destructive, without discounting them entirely. They might be useful another time.

The goal is flexibility. Cultivate a varied group of critics and coaches, both internal and external. Be aware of whom is speaking and when you should listen.

Feeling comfortable with multiple voices is particularly important if you are a manager. You need to be able to be Joey or Vicky, depending on the situation. Sometimes people need to feel your high expectations and disapproval. Other times they need your gentleness and empathy. Don't default to one or the other. Pause to assess what's needed, and then make a choice.

"It's hard," Isabelle told me after we spoke about the different voices and messages they brought with them. "How do I stop from thinking Joey is just a jerk? Or that I'm lame for being late?"

"He might be a jerk, and you may be lame," I said, "but not because he said so. Here's the question: Will you be more likely to be on time tomorrow because of what he said?"

"Yes," she conceded. "But it felt terrible."

"And, when you feel terrible, can you hear Vicky's voice too?"

"Yes," she said, beginning to smile.

"Then it's a good thing you have two coaches," I told her.

Because sometimes, both voices are the perfect combination.

PETER BREGMAN is a Master Certified Coach and the CEO of Bregman Partners, where he leads a team of over 25 coaches, helping senior leaders and teams create positive behavioral change and work more effectively together to achieve the company's most critical business results. Peter is the best-selling author of *Leading with Emotional Courage* and hosts the *Bregman Leadership Podcast*.

Adapted from content posted on hbr.org,
April 6, 2015 (product #H01ZOW).

Index

How to be human at work.

HBR's Emotional Intelligence Series features smart, essential reading on the human side of professional life from the pages of *Harvard Business Review*. Each book in the series offers uplifting stories, practical advice, and research from leading experts on how to tend to our emotional well-being at work.

Harvard Business Review Emotional Intelligence Series

Available in paperback or ebook format. The specially priced six-volume set includes:

- Mindfulness
- Resilience
- Influence and Persuasion

- Authentic Leadership
- Happiness
- Empathy

HBR.ORG

Buy for your team, clients, or event.
Visit hbr.org/bulksales for quantity discount rates.

Confidence

HBR EMOTIONAL INTELLIGENCE SERIES

.

HBR Emotional Intelligence Series

How to be human at work

The HBR Emotional Intelligence Series features smart, essential reading on the human side of professional life from the pages of *Harvard Business Review*.

Authentic Leadership	*Leadership Presence*
Confidence	*Mindful Listening*
Dealing with Difficult People	*Mindfulness*
Empathy	*Power and Impact*
Focus	*Purpose, Meaning, and Passion*
Happiness	*Resilience*
Influence and Persuasion	*Self-Awareness*

Other books on emotional intelligence from *Harvard Business Review*:

HBR Everyday Emotional Intelligence

HBR Guide to Emotional Intelligence

HBR's 10 Must Reads on Emotional Intelligence

Confidence

HBR EMOTIONAL INTELLIGENCE SERIES

Harvard Business Review Press

Boston, Massachusetts

HBR Press Quantity Sales Discounts

Harvard Business Review Press titles are available at significant quantity discounts when purchased in bulk for client gifts, sales promotions, and premiums. Special editions, including books with corporate logos, customized covers, and letters from the company or CEO printed in the front matter, as well as excerpts of existing books, can also be created in large quantities for special needs.

For details and discount information for both print and ebook formats, contact booksales@harvardbusiness.org, tel. 800-988-0886, or www.hbr .org/bulksales.

Copyright 2019 Harvard Business School Publishing Corporation
All rights reserved
Printed in the United States of America

13

No part of this publication may be reproduced, stored in or introduced into a retrieval system, or transmitted, in any form, or by any means (electronic, mechanical, photocopying, recording, or otherwise), without the prior permission of the publisher. Requests for permission should be directed to permissions@hbsp.harvard.edu, or mailed to Permissions, Harvard Business School Publishing, 60 Harvard Way, Boston, Massachusetts 02163.

The web addresses referenced in this book were live and correct at the time of the book's publication but may be subject to change.

Library of Congress Cataloging-in-Publication Data

Title: Confidence.
Other titles: Confidence (2019) | HBR emotional intelligence series.
Description: Boston, Massachusetts : Harvard Business Review Press, [2019] |
    Series: HBR emotional intelligence series | Includes index.
Identifiers: LCCN 2018044756 | ISBN 9781633696648 (pbk.)
Subjects: LCSH: Self-confidence. | Success in business—Psychological
    aspects. | Attitude (Psychology) | Emotional intelligence.
Classification: LCC BF575.S39 C66 2019 | DDC 155.2—dc23
LC record available at https://lccn.loc.gov/2018044756

ISBN: 978-1-63369-664-8

eISBN: 978-1-63369-665-5

The paper used in this publication meets the requirements of the American National Standard for Permanence of Paper for Publications and Documents in Libraries and Archives Z39.48-1992.

Contents

Contents

Contents

Contents

Confidence

HBR EMOTIONAL INTELLIGENCE SERIES

1

How to Build Confidence

By Amy Gallo

Very few people succeed in business without a degree of confidence. Yet everyone, from young people in their first real jobs to seasoned leaders in the upper ranks of organizations, have moments—or days, months, or even years—when they are unsure of their ability to tackle challenges. No one is immune to these bouts of insecurity at work, but they don't have to hold you back.

What the experts say

"Confidence equals security equals positive emotion equals better performance," says Tony Schwartz, the president and CEO of The Energy Project and the author of *Be Excellent at Anything: The Four Keys to Transforming the Way We Work and Live*. And yet he concedes that "insecurity plagues consciously or subconsciously every human being I've met." Overcoming this self-doubt starts with honestly assessing your abilities (and your shortcomings) and then getting comfortable enough to capitalize on (and correct) them, adds Deborah H. Gruenfeld, the Moghadam Family Professor of Leadership and Organizational Behavior and Codirector of the Executive Program for Women Leaders at Stanford Graduate School of Business. Here's how to do that and get into the virtuous cycle that Schwartz describes.

Prepare

Your piano teacher was right: Practice does make perfect. "The best way to build confidence in a given area is to invest energy in it and work hard at it," says Schwartz. Many people give up when they think they're not good at a particular job or task, assuming the exertion is fruitless. But Schwartz argues that deliberate practice will almost always trump natural aptitude. If you are unsure about your ability to do something—speak in front of a large audience, negotiate with a tough customer—start by trying out the skills in a safe setting. "Practice can be very useful and is highly recommended because, in addition to building confidence, it also tends to improve quality. Actually deliver the big presentation more than once before the due date. Do a dry run before opening a new store," says Gruenfeld. Even people who are confident in their abilities can become more so with better preparation.

Get out of your own way

Confident people aren't only willing to practice, they're also willing to acknowledge that they don't—and can't—know everything. "It's better to know when you need help than not," says Gruenfeld. "A certain degree of confidence—specifically, confidence in your ability to learn—is required to be willing to admit that you need guidance or support."

On the flip side, don't let modesty hold you back. People often get too wrapped up in what others will think to focus on what they have to offer, says Katie Orenstein, founder and director of The OpEd Project, a nonprofit that empowers women to influence public policy by submitting opinion pieces to newspapers. "When you realize your value to others, confidence is no longer about self-promotion," she explains. "In fact, *confidence* is no longer the right word. It's about purpose." Instead of agonizing about what others might think of you or your work, concentrate on the unique perspective you bring.

Get feedback when you need it

While you don't want to completely rely on others' opinions to boost your ego, validation can also be very effective in building confidence. Gruenfeld suggests asking someone who cares about your development as well as the quality of your performance to tell you what she thinks. Be sure to pick people whose feedback will be entirely truthful; Gruenfeld notes that when performance appraisals are only positive, we stop trusting them. And then use any genuinely positive commentary you get as a talisman.

Also remember that some people need more support than others, so don't be shy about asking for it. "The White House Project finds, for example, that many women need to be told they should run for office before deciding to do so. Men do not show this pattern of needing others' validation or encouragement," says Gruenfeld. It's okay if you need praise.

Take risks

Playing to your strengths is a smart tactic but not if it means you hesitate to take on new challenges. Many people don't know what they are capable of until they are truly tested. "Try things you don't think you can do. Failure can be very useful for building confidence," says Gruenfeld. Of course, this is often easier said than done. "It feels bad to not be good at something. There's a leap of faith with getting better at anything," says Schwartz. But don't assume you should feel good all the time. In fact, stressing yourself is the only way to grow. Enlisting help from others can make this easier. Gruenfeld recommends asking supervisors to let you experiment with new initiatives or skills when the stakes are relatively low and then to support you as you tackle those challenges.

Principles to remember

Do:

- Be honest with yourself about what you know and what you still need to learn

- Practice doing the things you are unsure about

- Embrace new opportunities to prove you can do difficult things

Don't:

- Focus excessively on whether or not you have the ability—think instead about the value you provide

- Hesitate to ask for external validation if you need it

- Worry about what others think—focus on yourself, not a theoretical and judgmental audience

Case study #1: Get the knowledge and get out of your own way

In 2010, Mark Angelo was asked by the CEO of Hospital for Special Surgery in New York to create and implement a program to improve quality and efficiency. Mark was relatively new to the organization. He had worked as a business fellow for the previous year but had recently taken on the role of director of operations and service lines. Even though he had background in operations strategy from his days as a management consultant, he was not familiar with the Lean/Six Sigma principles he'd need to use for this project and didn't feel equipped to build the program from scratch. He was particularly concerned he wouldn't be able to gain the necessary support from the hospital's physicians and nurses. What would they think of a young administrator with no hospital experience telling them how to improve quality and increase efficiency?

For five months, Mark struggled to get the project on track, and his confidence suffered. He knew that his apprehension was in part due to his lack of knowledge of Six Sigma. He read a number of books and articles on the subject, talked to consultants who specialized in it, and spoke with hospitals that had been successful in developing and implementing similar programs. This helped, but he realized he still didn't know if he would be able to get the necessary people on board. "I was anxious and stressed because I had no idea how I was going to transform the organization. I knew I couldn't do it on my own. It was going to take a collective effort that included our management team and all of our staff," he said.

He talked with the CEO, who had supported him since the beginning. He also looked to his family for emotional support. Through these conversations, he realized that his anxiety stemmed from a desire to be liked by his colleagues and therefore to avoid conflict. "After many discussions with my CEO and observing how he handled these situations, I learned that it is better to strive to be well-respected than well-liked," he said.

This was a turning point for Mark. Instead of worrying so much about what others thought of him, he focused on doing what was best for the patient and the institution. In December, he presented the vision for the program to the entire medical staff. While he was nervous about how it would be received, he knew this was a critical moment. "I was able to get up in front of one of our toughest constituencies and present the vision that we had been developing over the past few months," he says. His presentation was met with applause. "In the end, my confidence grew by leaps and bounds and we were able to design a program that has since taken off with great success across the hospital. I was able to overcome my mental blocks and knowledge deficits to build a program that will truly help transform how we approach performance improvement and patient care," he says.

Case study #2: Know the value you bring

Julie Zhuo knew she had things to say, but she wasn't sure how to get heard. As a product design manager at Facebook, she had developed valuable expertise in the products she worked on. Yet she lacked the confidence to share her ideas. She was used to being one of very few women in the room. That had been the case when she was studying computer science at Stanford, and it was still true now that she was at Facebook. She knew this meant she needed to make a concerted effort to speak up. But being the minority voice wasn't the only reason she felt unsure of herself. She says that she also suffered from "imposter syndrome," feeling as if she hadn't earned a right to her ideas—that she had somehow ended up where she was accidently, not through hard work.

Julie was intrigued when someone in HR told her about a workshop offered at Stanford by the OpEd Project. After attending and getting positive feedback about her ideas, Julie tried something she had never thought to do before: write an op-ed.

In November 2010, she published a piece in the *New York Times* entitled "Where Anonymity Breeds Contempt" about the danger of anonymity in online discussions. "It was a matter of someone saying 'You can do it,'" she explains. "It had never occurred to me that I could be published. But it actually wasn't hard at all." The reaction she got in the workshop and afterward back at Facebook boosted her confidence. Since then, she's gotten a lot of support from colleagues, which has emboldened her to speak her mind. "Of course it's still a work in progress, but now I'm a much more confident speaker and writer," she says.

AMY GALLO is a contributing editor at *Harvard Business Review* and the author of the *HBR Guide to Dealing with Conflict*. She writes and speaks about workplace dynamics. Follow her on Twitter @amyegallo.

Adapted from content posted on hbr.org,
April 29, 2011 (product #H0076H).

2

Overcome the Eight Barriers to Confidence

By Rosabeth Moss Kanter

To get a more confident you—or a more confident company, community, family, or team—first know what gets in the way. The best resolutions will go nowhere without the confidence to stick with them.

Confidence is an expectation of a positive outcome. It is not a personality trait; it is an assessment of a situation that sparks motivation. If you have confidence, you're motivated to put in the effort, to invest the time and resources, and to persist in reaching the goal. It's not confidence itself that produces success; it's the investment and the effort. Without enough confidence, it's too easy to give up prematurely or not get started at all. Hopelessness and despair prevent positive action.

To muster the confidence to work toward your goals, avoid these eight traps:

Self-defeating assumptions. You think you can't, so you don't. A British Olympic runner is so rattled by a misstep that cost her a contest that she dropped out of the next event. A company team decides that a popular world leader is so far out of their league that they don't invite him to speak at their customer event. Talented women sometimes "leave before they leave," as Sheryl Sandberg puts it, assuming that they won't be promoted (or succeed when they have children) so they start behaving like they're departing years before departure, thus foreclosing their options. It's one thing to be realistic, it's another to behave like a loser before entering the game.

Goals that are too big or too distant. I know how often leaders say they want to tackle BHAGs—"big hairy audacious goals." But having only enormous goals can actually undermine confidence. The gap between a giant goal and today's reality can be depressing and demotivating. Confidence comes from small wins that occur repeatedly, with each small step moving you closer to the big goal. But the small steps must be valued and turned into goals themselves. Winners think small as well as big.

Declaring victory too soon. This is the dieter's dilemma: You lose the first few pounds and feel so good that you reward yourself with chocolate cake—then when the pounds go back on, you feel so discouraged that you have more cake to feel better. I saw this pattern in a college football team that was coming off a nine-year losing streak (yes, nine years!). After winning its first game in nearly a decade, a team member shouted, "Now we'll win the championship!" First, of course, they had to win the next game— which they didn't. Step-by-step discipline builds confidence.

Do-it-yourself-ing. It's a trap to think you can go it alone, without a support system and without supporting others. Losing teams have stars, but they focus on their own records, not how well the whole team does; the resulting resentments and inequalities provoke internal battles that drag everyone down. To build your confidence, think about building the confidence of others and creating a culture in which everyone is more likely to succeed, whether through mentoring them or recognizing their strengths. Giving to others boosts happiness and self-esteem, as numerous research studies show. Supporting them makes it easier to ensure that they support you.

Blaming someone else. Confidence rests on taking responsibility for one's own behavior. Even in difficult circumstances, we have choices about how to respond to adversity. Whining about past harms reduces confidence about future possibilities. When the blame game is carried out within companies, everyone loses confidence, including external stakeholders. Confidence is the art of moving on.

Defensiveness. It's one thing to listen and respond to critics; it's another to answer them before they've done anything. Don't defend yourself if you're not being attacked. Apologize for your mistakes, but don't apologize for who or what you are. Instead, take pride in where you've come from and lead with your strengths.

Neglecting to anticipate setbacks. Confidence involves a dose of reality. It is not blind optimism, thinking that everything will be fine no matter what. Confidence stems from knowing that there will be mistakes, problems, and small losses en route to big wins. After all, even winning sports teams are often behind at some point in the game. Confidence grows when you look at what can go wrong, think through alternatives, and feel you are prepared for whatever might happen.

Overconfidence. Confidence is a sweet spot between despair and arrogance. Don't let confidence slip over into the arrogant end. Overconfidence is the bane of economies (e.g., the irrational exuberance that preceded the global financial crisis), corrupt leaders (who assume they're so necessary that they won't get into trouble for a small expense account fudge), or individuals who swagger and feel entitled to success rather than working for it. Arrogance and complacency lead to neglect of the basics, deaf ears to critics, and blindness to the forces of change—a trap for companies as well as individuals. Sure enough, like the old proverb, "Pride goeth before a fall," the slide into a losing streak often begins with a winning streak. A little humility goes a long way to moderate arrogance and keep just the right amount of confidence.

———————

Remember, it's not enough just to *feel* confident. You have to do the work. But with an expectation of success, you can try new things, form new partnerships, contribute to shared success, and revel in small wins that move you toward bigger goals.

ROSABETH MOSS KANTER is a professor at Harvard Business School and chair and director of the Harvard Advanced Leadership Initiative. Her latest book is *MOVE: How to Rebuild and Reinvent America's Infrastructure.* Follow her on Facebook and Twitter @RosabethKanter.

Adapted from content posted on hbr.org, January 3, 2014 (product #H00M4Q).

3

Everyone Suffers from Impostor Syndrome— Here's How to Handle It

By Andy Molinsky

One of the greatest barriers to moving outside your comfort zone is the fear that you're a poser, that you're not worthy, that you couldn't possibly be qualified to do whatever you're aiming to do. It's a fear that strikes many of us: *impostor syndrome.*

I know I've certainly had those thoughts while publishing pieces of writing, whether it's blogs or books. I've had them while teaching my first university classes and giving speeches to corporate audiences. I appear confident on the outside but feel deeply insecure on the inside, wondering who I am to be stepping up to this stage. What could I possibly have to say that anyone would want to hear?

And I'm not alone. Actress (and Harvard alum) Natalie Portman described the self-doubt she experienced as a Harvard student in a poignant commencement speech several years ago. "I felt like there had been some mistake," she said, "that I wasn't smart enough to be in this company, and that every time I opened my mouth I would have to prove that I wasn't just a dumb actress." Howard Schultz, the former executive chairman and CEO of Starbucks, revealed that he and CEOs he knows feel the same way: "Very few people, whether you've been in that job before or not, get into the seat and believe today that they are now qualified to be the CEO. They're not going to tell you that, but it's true."[1]

What can you do to overcome these feelings of inadequacy that so many of us experience?

A first tip is something that Portman highlights in her Harvard address, which I've found quite helpful: Recognize the benefits of being a novice. You might not realize it, but there are great benefits to being new in your field. When you are not steeped in the conventional wisdom of a given profession, you can ask questions that haven't been asked before or approach problems in ways others haven't thought of.

It's no surprise, for example, that some of the best research ideas I get as a professor come from undergraduate students with little previous experience, people who can think with a fresh outsider's perspective. This is true in business as well. The pharmaceutical company Eli Lilly has created a crowdsourcing platform called InnoCentive, through which outside innovators are paid to solve vexing problems the company faces. And it works! In fact, according to a study by Karim Lakhani of Harvard Business School, many problems are solved by those from outside the field in question—physicists solving chemistry problems, for example.[2] So the next time you feel inadequate in a particular domain, remember that as an outsider to the role in question, you might have the most critical perspective of all.

A second tip for combating impostor syndrome is to focus more on what you're learning than on how you're performing. According to psychologist Carol Dweck, the feelings that impostor syndrome leaves you with are ones we might actually be able to control.[3] With a *performance mindset*, which people suffering from impostor syndrome often have, you tend to see your feelings of inadequacy or the mistakes you make as evidence of your underlying limitations. This mindset only fuels the concerns you have about being unfit for your job. But there's something you can work to cultivate instead: a *learning mindset*. From this perspective, your limitations are experienced quite differently. Your mistakes are seen as an inevitable part of the learning process rather than as more evidence of your underlying failings.

That brings us to the third tip: Understand the power of perspective. Those of us who experience impostor syndrome often feel like we're the only ones feeling this way, but reality is very different. Early in my career, when I walked into a networking event, I was convinced that I was the only one worried about making small talk with strangers. But over time, I've realized that practically everyone in the room shares that same concern. According to a recent survey by Vantage Hill Partners, being found incompetent is the number-one fear of executives worldwide.[4] So if you're feeling like an impostor, chances are that others in your situation feel the exact same way. Or, as Tina Fey once quipped, "I've realized that almost everyone is a fraud, so I try not to feel too bad about it."[5]

It may not be easy, but overcoming impostor syndrome is possible—you don't need to feel helpless or alone. Next time you're in a situation that feels completely outside your comfort zone, don't focus on your failures. Consider it your opportunity to learn from your missteps and to bring forth a new perspective that others may not have.

ANDY MOLINSKY is a Professor of Organizational Behavior at the Brandeis International Business School. He's the author of *Global Dexterity: How to Adapt Your Behavior Across Cultures Without Losing Yourself in the Process* and *Reach: A New*

Strategy to Help You Step Outside Your Comfort Zone, Rise to the Challenge, and Build Confidence.

Notes

1. Howard Schultz, "Good C.E.O.'s Are Insecure (and Know It)," interview by Adam Bryant, *New York Times*, October 9, 2010.
2. Karim R. Lakhani et al., "The Value of Openness in Scientific Problem Solving," working paper 07-050 (Boston: Harvard Business School, 2007), http://www.hbs.edu/faculty/Publication%20Files/07-050.pdf.
3. Carol Dweck, "The Power of Believing That You Can Improve," filmed November 2014 in Norrköping, Sweden, TED talk, https://www.ted.com/talks/carol_dweck_the_power_of_believing_that_you_can_improve.
4. Roger Jones, "What CEOS Are Afraid Of," hbr.org, February 24, 2015, https://hbr.org/2015/02/what-ceos-are-afraid-of.
5. "Tina Fey—From Spoofer to Movie Stardom," *The Independent*, March 19, 2010, https://www.independent.co.uk/arts-entertainment/films/features/tina-fey-from-spoofer-to-movie-stardom-1923552.html.

Adapted from content posted on hbr.org,
July 7, 2016 (product #H02ZSC).

4

Mental Preparation Secrets of Top Athletes

An interview with Daniel McGinn
by Sarah Green Carmichael

Sarah Green Carmichael: *Welcome to the HBR IdeaCast from* Harvard Business Review. *I'm Sarah Green Carmichael. To get psyched up for the big game, sports teammates give each other pep talks, listen to an exciting song during warm-ups, or follow a particular pregame routine. Then there's a locker-room speech, often dramatized in popular movies, where the coach inspires individuals to greatness:*

[Excerpt from *Miracle*]:

Herb Brooks: I'm sick and tired of hearing about what a great hockey team the Soviets have. Screw them. This is your time. Now go out there and take it.

But what's the business equivalent of the pep talk? When you have a big presentation, job interview, quarter-ending sales meeting, or situation where you really need to be on, how do you prepare for it? If you're like a lot of people, you probably think about what you're going to say and what you're going to wear, and then you just kind of, well, show up.

HBR's senior editor Dan McGinn thinks we can all do better than that by taking a cue from how the best athletes and performers prepare. He's the author of the article "The Science of Pep Talks" in the July–August 2017 issue of Harvard Business Review, *and he is also the author of the book* Psyched Up: How the Science of Mental Preparation Can Help You Succeed. *Dan, thank you for joining us today.*

Daniel McGinn: Thank you, Sarah.

So did you have to get psyched up to write this book?

I did, actually. Writing this book did change the way I get ready to perform my job as a writer every morning or many mornings. If you watch sports, you become pretty accustomed to seeing the athletes and what they do when they warm up. They tend to have headphones on, and you know that they're listening to a certain set of songs. It's not just up to chance. You're used to seeing locker-room speeches. You're used to seeing that gaze, that locked-in look that they have, and that focus.

And they're taught to do that. There are sports psychologists who teach them exactly what they should be thinking about before a game. The argument I have is that more of our jobs are like that these days. It's less like factory work where you're doing the same thing every day and more about the big pitch, the presentation, the sales call, and that we should learn to do what these athletes do to try to lock ourselves in.

I think about coming into my job every day and that maybe we should run through the halls and give every editor a high five and then chew a pen and then put the pen back in the bin or other crazy things. How feasible is it to do some of these things on a daily basis?

Yeah, obviously, if our boss Adi Ignatius gave us a speech like Knute Rockne did before we sat down to edit articles, we would all think it was kind of crazy. If you don't know who that is, Rockne was the legendary Notre Dame football coach from the 1920s.

So why do people have rituals? And why is there a lot of research that suggests that they work? Well, one theory is that they help us remember how much practice we've done. They help get our bodies and our minds into the groove. The other is that they give us something to focus on other than being nervous and anxious. Think of a funeral. Funerals are very awkward occasions, and there's this whole set of rituals about what we do when we go through it. That's because it's awkward, and we want something to do to not think about the nervousness.

So there's a distractive element to rituals. They just help your body get into the groove. I'm not suggesting that we should run out and chest bump every day before we go to our desks. But I am saying that if you have some quiet, maybe private, thing that you do to get your day started, you might be a little bit better at it.

So a lot of what athletes and performers do is about reducing their pregame jitters. But isn't some amount of anxiety supposed to help you amp up for a big moment?

Yeah, no question. I was not a very good high school athlete. And when I started this reporting, I thought a lot of this was about adrenaline and about getting yourself psyched up, amped up, highly energized. The more research I did, the more I found out that that's really a simplistic view.

Adrenaline is a physiological response. But it's much more about what you're feeling, and it's about reducing your anxiety, trying to boost your confidence, and trying to manage your energy level so that it's appropriate to what you're trying to do. If you're a WWE wrestler, that's a little bit different than giving a commencement address. So you need to calibrate the energy level to make sure it's right for what you're doing.

What about trying to increase your confidence, though? I mean, can these rituals and things really help with that? Or is it like the movie Dumbo, *where little Dumbo had that silly feather and thought that's how he could fly? Is it just that this helps me because I believe it helps me?*

Yeah, so the feather would be an example of a superstitious ritual because clearly the feather doesn't really help him fly. It's just a placebo effect. What can help you gain confidence is controlling your thought patterns and thinking about what I'd call your "greatest hits." So, Sarah, for the show, if you were going to get yourself psyched up, you should think about the best podcast interviews you've done. You might actually want to go back for five minutes at your desk and listen to a couple of them.

Before I walked in the room with you today, I went back and listened to the best interview I've had with you because it made me think, "Gosh, you're good at this." And that's what you want to be thinking before you go into these environments. It sounds cheesy. You may remember the Stuart Smalley self-affirmations from *Saturday Night Live* in the '90s: "I'm special . . . People like me." But it does work. The messages there are to be relentlessly upbeat and positive. Be confident. Remember your greatest hits. And basically talk yourself up and psych yourself up with the idea that you've done this before, and you can do it again.

Was there any organization you came across where they really do make you go back and actually listen to or watch your greatest hits?

At the U.S. Military Academy at West Point, I spent a day in what they call the Center for Enhanced Performance, which is a team of psychologists that work at West Point. And one of the things they do is take their athletes and their cadets and put them in these enclosed, almost egg-shaped chairs. And they play audio tracks that they've created for each cadet that talk about how great they are.

The one I watched was a lacrosse goalie, and there's a professional actor narrating along with music: "John, you're the best lacrosse goalie ever.

Remember the game against Shrewsbury High when you did this?" So it really is a greatest-hits kind of thing. That's probably the most tangible, visceral example I have found of that.

Could it ever work so well that you'd get to a point where you were insanely overconfident and then that would actually lead you to perform worse?

Sure. I think in a sports setting or in a business setting, we certainly see examples of organizations that become overconfident, too convinced of their dominance, too complacent. But I think for your average, everyday business performers thinking about a job interview, a pitch scenario, a big presentation, or a negotiation, probably the average person suffers a little bit too much from a lack of confidence or an imposter syndrome. On the whole, most people are going to benefit from trying to dial it up a little bit.

One of the things in the book that really surprised me was the part where you explain that golfers who used Tiger Woods's clubs or clubs they were told were Tiger Woods's clubs—I'm not sure he participated in the study—actually golfed better than players who were just using any old random club. How does something like that work?

They call that process "social contagion," and it's the theory that knowing that someone celebrated or highly accomplished has touched an object physically imbues some magical powers. I tried to test that out in the book. I reached out to Malcolm Gladwell, who's a very well-known and acclaimed nonfiction writer. I asked him if I could write the book on a keyboard that he had used. Knowing that such a great writer has typed on these same keys and struggled through it absolutely helped me. I don't know if Tiger Woods's club would help my golf game though. My golf game is really beyond help. [Laughter]

Yes, I've actually read about similar studies—I'm not sure how good they are—that show that when women wear heels, they feel more confident. I think in my case, the opposite is true, because I have a really hard time walking in heels. But that's something where if you are Stephen Colbert or David Ortiz or one of these big stars you talk about in the book, you can really control your environment so that you can perform the ritual. But I think for most of us in offices, it feels like we're not in control of our space. So how can those of us who are not David Ortiz or Stephen Colbert really carve out time for these rituals that are so powerful?

They don't have to be super-elaborate, and they don't have to be something that anyone else can even recognize you're doing. So I don't do this every day, but I'll put on a pair of noise-canceling headphones. That has a functional purpose because it blocks out noise, but also the feel of it on my head is a signal to myself that it's time to get to work here. Some of it is just this Pavlovian signal to our bodies that, "OK, it's time for me to get to work." So it doesn't need to be throwing chalk dust in the air or crazy hand gestures. It can be something as simple as putting something on.

DANIEL MCGINN is a senior editor at *Harvard Business Review* and the author of *Psyched Up: How the Science of Mental Preparation Can Help You Succeed.* Follow him on Twitter @danmcginn. SARAH GREEN CARMICHAEL was an executive editor at *Harvard Business Review*. Follow her on Twitter @skgreen.

Adapted from "Mental Preparation Secrets
of Top Athletes, Entertainers, and Surgeons" on
HBR IdeaCast (podcast), June 29, 2017.

5

Research:
Learning a Little
About Something
Makes Us
Overconfident

By Carmen Sanchez and David Dunning

As former baseball pitcher Vernon Law once put it, experience is a hard teacher because it gives the test first, and only then provides the lesson.

Perhaps this observation can explain the results of a survey sponsored by the Association of American Colleges & Universities. Among college students, 64% said they were well prepared to work in a team, 66% thought they had adequate critical thinking skills, and 65% said they were proficient in written communication. However, among employers who had recently hired college students, fewer than 40% agreed with any of those statements. The students thought they were much further along in the learning curve toward workplace success than their future employers did.[1]

Overconfidence among beginners

Our research focuses on overconfidence as people tackle new challenges and learn. To be a beginner is to be susceptible to undue optimism and confidence. Our work is devoted to exploring the exact shape and timeline of that overconfidence.

One common theory is that beginners start off overconfident. They start a new task or job as "unconscious incompetents," not knowing what they don't know. Their inevitable early mistakes and miscues prompt them to become conscious of their shortcomings.

Our work, however, suggests the opposite. Absolute beginners can be perfectly conscious and cautious about what they don't know; the unconscious incompetence is instead something they grow into. A little experience replaces their caution with a false sense of competence.

Specifically, our research focused on the common task of probabilistic learning in which people learn to read cues from the environment to predict some outcome.[2] For example, people must rely on multiple signals from the environment to predict which company's stock will rise, which applicant will do the best job, or which illness a patient is suffering from. These can be hard tasks—and even the most expert of experts will at times make the wrong prediction—but a decision is often essential in many settings.

In a laboratory study, we asked participants to imagine they were medical residents in a post-apocalyptic world that has been overrun by zombies. (We were confident that this would be a new scenario to all our participants, allowing them all to start as total novices.) Their job, over 60 repeated trials, was to review the symptoms of a patient, such as whether the patient had glossy eyes, an abscess, or brain inflammation, and diagnose whether the patient was healthy or infected with one of two zombie diseases. Participants needed to learn, by trial and error, which symptoms to rely on to identify zombie infections. Much as in a real-world medical diagnosis of a (non-zombie) condition, the symptoms were informative but fallible clues. There were certain symptoms that made one diagnosis more likely, but those symptoms were not always present. Other potential symptoms were simple red herrings. Participants diagnosed patients one at a time, receiving feedback after every diagnosis.

The beginner's bubble

We found that people slowly and gradually learned how to perform this task, though they found it quite challenging. Their performance incrementally improved with each patient.

Confidence, however, took quite a different journey. In each study, participants started out well-calibrated about how accurate their diagnoses would prove to be. They began thinking they were right 50% of the time, when their actual accuracy rate was 55%. However, after just a few patients, their confidence began skyrocketing, far ahead of any accuracy they achieved. Soon, participants estimated their accuracy rate was 73% when it had not hit even 60%. (See figure 1.)

It appears that Alexander Pope was right when he said that a little learning is a dangerous thing. In our studies, just a little learning was enough to make participants feel they had learned the task. After a few tries, they were as confident in their judgments as they were ever going to be throughout the entire experiment. They had, as we termed it, entered into a "beginner's bubble" of overconfidence.

FIGURE 1

Total novices lack confidence, but as their confidence grows, it outpaces accuracy

In a lab experiment, "doctors" quickly began to overestimate their diagnostic ability.

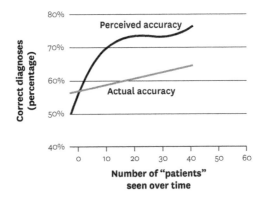

Source: "Overconfidence Among Beginners: Is a Little Learning a Dangerous Thing?" by Carmen Sanchez and David Dunning, *Journal of Personality and Social Psychology,* 2018.

What produced this quick inflation of confidence? In a follow-up study, we found that it arose because participants far too exuberantly formed quick, self-assured ideas about how to approach the medical diagnosis task based on only the slimmest amount of data. Small bits of data, however, are often filled with noise and misleading signs. It usually takes a large amount of data to strip away the chaos of the world, to finally see the worthwhile signal. However, classic research has shown that people do not have a feel for this fact.[3] They assume that every small sequence of data represents the world just as well as long sequences do.

But our studies suggested that people do eventually learn—somewhat. After participants formed their bubble, their overconfidence often leveled off and slightly declined. People soon learned that they had to correct their initial, frequently misguided theories, and they did. But after a correction phase, confidence began to rise again, with accuracy never rising enough to meet it. It is important to note that although we did not predict the second peak in confidence, it consistently appeared throughout all of our studies. (See figure 2.)

FIGURE 2

Overconfidence declines—slightly—with experience

But according to a lab experiment mimicking hospital visits, you can't keep it down for long.

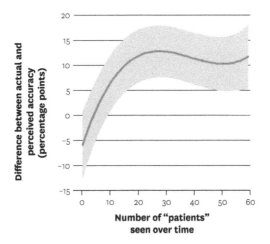

Source: "Overconfidence Among Beginners: Is a Little Learning a Dangerous Thing?" by Carmen Sanchez and David Dunning, *Journal of Personality and Social Psychology,* 2018.

A real-world bubble

The real world follows this pattern. Other research has found that doctors learning to do spinal surgery usually do not begin to make mistakes until their 15th iteration of the surgery.[4] Similarly, beginning pilots produce few accidents—but then their accident rate begins to rise until it peaks at about 800 flight hours, where it begins to drop again.[5]

We also found signs of the beginner's bubble outside of the laboratory. As with probabilistic learning, it has been shown that most people under the age of 18 have little knowledge of personal finance.[6] Most primary and secondary educational systems do not teach financial literacy. As such, personal finance is something most learn by trial and error.

We found echoes of our laboratory results across the life span in surveys on financial capability conducted by the Financial Industry Regulatory Authority.[7] Each survey comprised a nationally representative sample of 25,000 respondents who took a brief financial literacy test and reported how knowledgeable about personal finance they believed they were. Much like in the laboratory, both surveys showed that real financial literacy rose slowly, incrementally, and uniformly across age groups.

Self-confidence, however, surged between late adolescence and young adulthood, then leveled off among older respondents until late adulthood, where it began to rise again—a result perfectly consistent with our laboratory pattern.

It is important to note that our work has several limitations. In our experiments, participants received perfect feedback after each trial. In life, consistent feedback like this is often unavailable. Also, our tasks traced how confidence changed as people learned truly novel tasks. There are plenty of tasks people learn in which they can apply previous knowledge to the new task. We do not know how confidence would change in these situations. Relatedly, we cannot be certain what would happen to overconfidence after the 60th trial.

With that said, our studies suggest that the work of a beginner might be doubly hard. Of course, the beginner must struggle to learn—but the beginner must also guard against an illusion they have learned too quickly. Perhaps Alexander Pope suggested the best remedy for this beginner's bubble when he said that if a few shallow draughts of experience intoxicate the brain, the only cure was to continue drinking until we are sober again.

CARMEN SANCHEZ is a PhD candidate in Social and Personality Psychology at Cornell University. She studies how perceptions of abilities change as people learn, cultural differences in self-enhancement, and financial decision-making. DAVID DUNNING is a Professor of Psychology at the University of Michigan. His research focuses on the psychology of human misbelief, particularly false beliefs people hold about themselves.

Notes

1. Hart Research Associates, *Falling Short? College Learning and Career Success* (Washington, DC: Association of American Colleges and Universities, 2015), https://www.aacu.org/leap/public-opinion-research/2015-survey-results.

2. Carmen Sanchez and David Dunning, "Overconfidence Among Beginners: Is a Little Learning a Dangerous Thing?" *Journal of Personality and Social Psychology* 114, no. 1 (2018): 10–28.

3. Ibid.

4. Bawarjan Schatlo et al., "Unskilled Unawareness and the Learning Curve in Robotic Spine Surgery," *Acta Neurochirurgica*, 157, no. 10 (October 2015): 1819–1823.

5. William R. Knecht, "The 'Killing Zone' Revisited: Serial Nonlinearities Predict General Aviation Accident Rates from Pilot Total Flight Hours," *Accident Analysis & Prevention* 60 (November 2013): 50–56.

6. Stephen Avard et al., "The Financial Knowledge of College Freshmen," *College Student Journal* 39, no. 2 (June 2005): 321–339.

7. FINRA Investor Education Foundation, *Financial Capability in the United States 2016*, July 2016, http://www.usfinancialcapability.org/downloads/NFCS_2015_Report_Natl_Findings.pdf.

Adapted from content posted on hbr.org,
March 29, 2018 (product #H048R2).

6

To Ace Your Job Interview, Get into Character and Rehearse

By Cathy Salit

You've landed an interview for the job of your dreams. You're ideally suited for the position, and your resume is bulletproof. You've researched the company, the culture, the job, and the person who will be interviewing you. (Thank you, LinkedIn.) You've got your answers ready and selling points lined up. But when the interview starts, something's "off." You want to be commanding, but your nervousness gets in the way. Your voice sounds stiff. You hear yourself trying too hard, but you can't seem to stop yourself. As the minutes tick by, your answers sound more and more like canned monologues. And your interviewer isn't warming up—the job opportunity is slipping, slipping, slipping out of reach.

What went wrong?

As I see it, you probably prepared your content well, but—like many people—you didn't prepare something equally, if not more important: your *performance*. Yes, performance, the theatrical kind. Just as an actor prepares the character they will play on stage or screen, you can steal some tricks from the actor's toolbox to prepare the character you will play in the interview. For this kind of scene, you'll need to exude confidence, competence, likability, flexibility, and more. How to do this in a high-stakes situation? Tap into your natural ability to imagine and pretend—and craft your character.

"But wait a minute," you say. "Character? Pretend? What about being my authentic self?"

I get asked about that a lot, and it's a good question—many job coaches and experts extol authenticity, values-based behavior, and being "genuine" at work.

My company's own two decades of practice and research have focused on what we call the "Becoming Principle," in which the tools of theatrical performance give us the transformative power to become who we are not . . . yet. When we consciously use our capacity to pretend and perform, we can grow new—and genuine—parts of ourselves. (The Latin verb in the word pretend is *tendere*, literally to stretch, not to fake or wear a mask.) This idea resonates with the findings of Herminia Ibarra in her landmark HBR article, "The Authenticity Paradox." Ibarra writes that our adherence to one "true self" can hold us back as we take on new challenges and bigger roles. In other words, by sticking to "your story," you're limiting yourself.

In the job interview, you are literally *auditioning* for a new role. Developing your skills as a performer will help you not only to land the job, it will also help you grow and gain a new skill that is critical in the 21st-century workplace—navigating constant change that requires flexibility and new performances all the time.

Who do you want to be in this scene? That's where your "job interview character" comes in. Make a list of the qualities the successful candidate should convey. To some extent, these qualities will depend on the particular job you are applying for—a software engineer and a sales director will need to emphasize different leading attributes. And you'll want to convey in your performance that you have a feel for the company's culture—a laid-back dude vibe could be a turn-off in a formal environment, and vice versa.

Skilled interviewers will often be looking for the qualities that are known to correlate with success on the job, such as confidence, energy, and positive body language. How to physically act out these personal qualities? Much has been written about the body language of confidence and how specific gestures such as physical stance, tone, handshake, and eye contact instantly communicate both ease and authority. If you are not sure how to portray these qualities, look for others who seem to embody them, then observe, closely, how they do it. You're not looking to slavishly copy, but rather creatively imitate them. Try it on, try it out, and see what works for you.

Most important—rehearse! Like any good performer, you need to practice in advance. If you tend to be shy, expand your range of expression (and what you're comfortable doing) by practicing what might feel like an exaggerated performance, using hand gestures and passion. If you talk a lot using run-on sentences with no period at the end (a lot of us do this when we're nervous), practice pausing and breaking your thoughts into short sentences.

Even with practice and rehearsal, we can get overloaded and stressed in new situations, particularly when we're the center of attention and under scrutiny. That's why I suggest that—in addition to those outlined above—your job interview character have a special trait: Instead of performing as a person who is trying really hard to get the job, perform as someone who wants to have a *great conversation* with the human being across from you.

Your mindset is more like *I've done some cool and interesting things in my life and work that I'd love to share, and I'm really interested to hear about you and your company.* In other words, you'll play the role of a *good conversationalist.* Here's how:

- *Be curious.* Most people talk too much during an interview. Instead, perform curiosity—ask open-ended (not yes or no) questions that are connected to what you just heard. This will help you discover common ground with your interviewer, which is key to making a great first impression.

- *Accept every conversational offer.* Of course you need to prepare "talking points" for your interview. But being in a conversation (instead of delivering a rehearsed pitch) means creating back-and-forth repartee. That means you can do what improvisers do, and treat everything the interviewer says or does as an "offer"—which you should accept and build upon (rather than waiting for them to finish so that you can fire off another talking point). You can practice this kind of listening today, by starting every sentence with the words "yes, and . . . " Improv skills are now highly valued in the workplace. And in an interview, this fundamental improv technique will make you less focused on proving yourself and much more attuned to the other person.

- *Prepare to tell stories.* This may be one of the most powerful elements of a great conversationalist performance. The ancient art of storytelling has a powerful effect on stirring empathic emotions and boosting your own likeability. Prepare and practice yours in advance so that when the interviewer asks if you're experienced in leading projects, you can tell the story in a way that dramatizes the most recent project you led. Describe how the project began, what you did, the obstacles you faced and how you overcame them. Good stories have a beginning, middle, and end. Make them short, but pack a punch.

Some of these techniques won't feel like "you"—and that's the point. By making use of your natural ability to perform in new ways, you're expanding your comfort zone and increasing your repertoire of what feels natural. This is how you grow. It's how you become *who you are not yet*. It's also how you get the job.

CATHY SALIT is CEO of Performance of a Lifetime and the author of *Performance Breakthrough: A Radical Approach to Success at Work*.

Adapted from content posted on hbr.org, April 21, 2017 (product #H03M6K).

7

Six Ways to Look More Confident During a Presentation

By Kasia Wezowski

Several years ago, colleagues and I were invited to predict the results of a startup pitch contest in Vienna, where 2,500 tech entrepreneurs were competing to win thousands of euros in funds. We observed the presentations, but rather than paying attention to the ideas the entrepreneurs were pitching, we were watching the body language and microexpressions of the judges as they listened.

We gave our prediction of who would win before the winners were announced and, as we and the audience soon learned, we were spot on. We had spoiled the surprise.

Two years later, we were invited back to the same event, but this time, instead of watching the judges, we observed the contestants. Our task was not to guess the winners, but to determine how presenters' nonverbal communication contributed to their success or failure.

We evaluated each would-be entrepreneur on a scale from 0 to 15. People scored points for each sign of positive, confident body language, such as smiling, maintaining eye contact, and persuasive gesturing. They lost points for each negative signal, such as fidgeting, stiff hand movements, and averted eyes. We found that contestants whose pitches were rated in the top eight by competition judges scored an average of 8.3 on our 15-point scale, while those who did not place in that top tier had an average score of 5.5. Positive body language was strongly correlated with more successful outcomes.

We've found similar correlations in the political realm. During the 2012 U.S. Presidential election, we conducted an online study in which 1,000 participants—both Democrats and Republicans—watched two-minute video clips featuring Barack Obama and Mitt Romney at campaign events delivering both neutral and emotional content. Webcams recorded the viewers' facial expressions, and our team analyzed them for six key emotions identified in psychology research: happy, surprised, afraid, disgusted, angry, and sad. We coded for the tenor of the emotion (positive or negative) and how strongly it seemed to be expressed. This analysis showed that Obama sparked stronger emotional responses and fewer negative ones. Even a significant number of Republicans—16%—reacted negatively to Romney. And when we analyzed the candidates' body language, we found that the president's resembled those of our pitch contest winners. He displayed primarily open, positive, confident positions congruent with his speech. Romney, by contrast, often gave out negative signals, diminishing his message with contradictory and distracting facial expressions and movement.

Of course, the election didn't hinge on body language. Nor did the results of the startup competition. But the right kinds of nonverbal communication did correlate with success.

How can you send out the same signals—and hopefully generate the same success? At the Center for Body Language, we've studied successful leaders across a range of fields and identified several positions which are indicators of effective, persuasive body language.

The box

Early in Bill Clinton's political career, he would punctuate his speeches with big, wide gestures that made him appear untrustworthy. To help him keep his body language under control, his advisers taught him to imagine a box in front of his chest and belly and contain his hand movements within it. Since then, "the Clinton box" has become a popular term in the field.

The box: Trustworthy, truthful

Source: Center for Body Language.

Holding the ball: Commanding, dominant

Source: Center for Body Language.

Holding the ball

Gesturing as if you were holding a basketball between your hands is an indicator of confidence and control, as if you almost literally have the facts at your fingertips. Steve Jobs frequently used this position in his speeches.

Pyramid hands: Self-assured, relaxed

Source: Center for Body Language.

Pyramid hands

When people are nervous, their hands often flit about and fidget. When they're confident, they are still. One way to accomplish that is to clasp both hands together in a relaxed pyramid. Many business executives employ this gesture, though beware of overuse or pairing it with domineering or arrogant facial expressions. The idea is to show you're relaxed, not smug.

Wide stance: Confident, in control

Source: Center for Body Language.

Wide stance

How people stand is a strong indicator of their mindset. When you stand in this strong and steady position, with your feet about a shoulder width apart, it signals that you feel in control.

Palms up: Honest, accepting

Source: Center for Body Language.

Palms up

This gesture indicates openness and honesty. Oprah makes strong use of this during her speeches. She is a powerful, influential figure, but also appears willing to connect sincerely with the people she is speaking to, be it one person or a crowd of thousands.

Palms down: Strong, assertive

Source: Center for Body Language.

Palms down

The opposite movement can be viewed positively too—as a sign of strength, authority and assertiveness. Barack Obama has often used it to calm a crowd right after moments of rousing oration.

———————

The next time you give a presentation, try to have it recorded, then review the video with the sound off, watching only your body language. How did you stand and gesture? Did you use any of these positions? If not, think about how you might do so the next time you're in front of an audience, or even just speaking to your boss or a big client. Practice in front of a mirror, then with friends, until these positions feel natural.

Nonverbal communication won't necessarily make or break you as a leader, but it might help you achieve more successful outcomes.

KASIA WEZOWSKI is the founder of the Center for Body Language, the author of four books on the subject, and the producer and director of *Leap*, a documentary about the coaching profession.

Adapted from content posted on hbr.org,
April 6, 2017 (product #H03ETV).

8

You Don't Just Need One Leadership Voice—You Need Many

By Amy Jen Su

We often equate developing a leadership voice with finding ways to appear more confident. We assume that our success depends on mimicking someone else, increasing our self-promotion, or saying things more loudly than others. But rather than living with imposter's syndrome, or feeling exhausted by wearing your game face all day, you can build a truer confidence by more intentionally focusing on cultivating many different parts of your leadership voice each day. Ultimately, you should cultivate enough parts of your voice so that no matter the leadership situation or audience you find yourself facing, you can respond in an authentic, constructive, and effective way. So, what are the various voices to access within yourself and cultivate over time? And what are the situations that warrant each voice?

Your voice of character

First and foremost, consider the voice of your character. This is the part of your voice that is constant and consistent. It is grounded in fundamental principles about whom you choose to be and what guides and motivates your interactions with others. I've had leaders share that they hold key leadership principles in mind such as "Give the benefit of the doubt," "Don't take things personally," "Focus on what's best for the business," or "Be direct with respect" when walking into a difficult conversation, meeting, or potential conflict. Anchoring ourselves in the character we know we have keeps us from becoming chameleons, acting out of a fight-or-flight reaction, or only showing respect when there is a commercial gain or benefit—while being uncivil to others who we believe are of less value. A voice of character is ultimately about who you are and the intentions and motivations that guide your speech and actions.

Your voice of context

As you take on increasingly senior roles, your view and perspective of the business grow. You hold more of the big picture. Part of the job then becomes finding ways to express and communicate that bigger picture to others. Too often, in the race against time, we dive right into the details of a presentation, meeting, or conversation without taking an extra few minutes to appropriately set the stage and share critical context. Places where you can bring more of your voice of context include:

- Sharing vision, strategy, or upcoming organizational change with others

- Presenting to executives, and being clear on what you are there for and what you need

- Kicking off a meeting with your team and giving the bigger picture for the topic at hand

- Making your decision-making criteria or rationale transparent to others

Your voice of clarity

In a world of high-intensity workplaces, you have the opportunity to be the voice of clarity and help your team stay focused on the most important priorities. Leaders who envision new possibilities, muse aloud, or have knee-jerk reactions run the risk of teams trying to deliver on their every whim; these teams end up scattered, spread thin, and unfocused, falling short on delivering on the most important wins. Here are a few ways you can be the voice of clarity to help channel others' energies more productively:

- At the start of the year, sit down with each direct report to prioritize and clarify what the big wins are in each of their areas. One client of mine shared how she asks each team member: "If we were to publish this in a newspaper, what would you want the big headlines to be for you and your team at the end of the year?"

- Periodically come back to helping your direct reports reprioritize what's on their plates. You can do this in one-on-one meetings or with your entire team.

- Empower your team to say no.

Your voice of curiosity

As a leader, you have a responsibility to give direction, share information, and make important decisions. But you need to be sure that you're not approaching every situation as if you have all the answers or as if you need to advise on, problem-solve, or fix everything in front of you. In many cases, being the voice of curiosity is a better choice for the situation. As one of my clients once shared about facing pushback from others, "While I'm confident in my own business judgment and instincts, I know that my organization has hired really smart people. Therefore, if one of my peers or team members has a different perspective or pushes back, I don't take it personally. I get really curious to understand where they are coming from first so that we can get to the best solution." Some situations where bringing your voice of curiosity can help you and your colleagues move forward:

- When you're engaging in work that is inter-dependent, and a better solution will come from hearing all perspectives in the room before coming to a final decision

- When you're coaching a direct report, asking good questions to help them grow in new ways, explore issues they're facing, or support their career development

- When you're in a difficult conversation where hearing out the other person is an important part of defusing emotion, understanding each party's needs and views, and then figuring out the best way forward

Your voice of connection

As your span of control or influence grows, it can be-come increasingly more difficult to make a connection

with a broadening set of colleagues, strategic networks, and teams. We often have folks working for us
many layers deep into the organization, such that we
no longer know everyone in our area and still must find
ways to stay connected and visible. Being a voice of
connection can come in many forms. Some of the
ways I've seen others do this effectively:

- Increase your skill as a storyteller. Stories make
  our points more memorable and salient. They
  can enliven a keynote address or an all-hands
  meeting, drive home a point we're making in
  a presentation, or help to close a large deal or
  transaction.

- Thank and acknowledge. Our teams and colleagues often go to great lengths to ensure that
  deliverables are met, revenues are strong, and
  customers are satisfied. When we use our voice
  of connection, we remember to express gratitude to a team that worked through the holidays to close on the financials at the end of the

quarter, or we remember to loop back with a colleague who made a valuable introduction or referral for us.

- Making time for a few minutes of icebreaking or rapport building at the start of a conversation or meeting. So often, we want to get right down to business, so we skip the niceties or pleasantries that help to build relationships with others. Where possible, and especially with colleagues who value that kind of connection, spend a couple of minutes to connect before diving into the work. On days where you're crunched for time, state that up front and transparently, so as not to create any misunderstandings. You can say something like: "I'm a little crunched for time today, so it would be great if we could dive right in."

———————

Discovering and developing your voice as a leader is the work of a lifetime. The key is to stay open to an increasingly wide array of new situations and people. Use each situation as an opportunity to access more parts of your voice, rather than having a one-size-fits-all approach. Bring your voices of character, context, clarity, curiosity, and connection as the moment or situation warrants. Through this kind of learning and growth, not only will you increase your inner confidence and resilience, but you will also inspire the confidence of others around you in a more authentic and impactful way.

AMY JEN SU is a cofounder and managing partner of Paravis Partners, an executive coaching and leadership development firm. She is the author of the forthcoming book, *The Leader You Want to Be: Five Essential Principles for Bringing Out Your Best Self—Every Day,* and coauthor, with Muriel Maignan Wilkins, of *Own the Room: Discover Your Signature Voice to Master Your Leadership Presence.* Follow Amy on Twitter @amyjensu.

Adapted from content posted on hbr.org,
January 10, 2018 (product #H043HT).

9

Cultivate a Culture of Confidence

By Rosabeth Moss Kanter

One difference between winners and losers is how they handle losing.

Even for the best companies and most accomplished professionals, long track records of success are punctuated by slips, slides, and mini-turnarounds. Even the team that wins the game might make mistakes, fumble, and lag behind for part of it. That's why the ability to recover quickly and get back on course is so important.

Troubles are ubiquitous. Surprises can fall from the sky like volcanic ash and appear to change everything. New ventures can begin with great promise and still face unexpected obstacles, unanticipated delays, and critics that pop up at the wrong moment. That's why I coined Kanter's Law: "Anything can look like a failure in the middle."

Nothing succeeds for long without considerable effort and constant vigilance. Winning streaks end for predictable reasons: Strategies run their course. New competition emerges to take on the industry leader. Ideas get dusty. Technology marches on. Complacency sets in, making people feel entitled to success rather than motivated to work for it.

Thus, a key factor in high achievement is bouncing back from the low points. Long-term winners often face the same problems as long-term losers, but they respond differently, as I found in the research for my book *Confidence*. I compared companies and sports teams with long winning streaks and long losing streaks, and then looked at how leaders led turnarounds from low to high performance.

Consider first the pathologies of losing. Losing produces temptations to behave in ways that make it hard to recover fast enough—and could even make the situation worse. For example, panicking and throwing out the game plan. Scrambling for self-protection and abandoning the rest of the group. Hiding the facts and hoping that things will get better by themselves before anyone notices. Denying that there is anything to learn or change. Using decline as an excuse to let facilities or investments deteriorate.

The culture and support system that surrounds high performers helps them avoid these temptations. They can put troubles in perspective because they are ready for them. They rehearse through diligent practice and preparation; they remain disciplined and professional. Their leaders put facts on the table and review what went right or wrong in the last round in order to shore up strengths and pinpoint weaknesses and to encourage personal responsibility for actions. They stress collaboration and teamwork—common goals; commitment to a joint vision; respect and support for team members, so when someone drops the ball, someone else is there to pick it up—and responsibility for mentoring, so the best performers lift everyone's capabilities. They seek creative ideas for improvement and innovation, favoring widespread dialogue and brainstorming.

Resilience is not simply an individual characteristic or a psychological phenomenon. It is helped or hindered by the surrounding system. Teams that are immersed in a culture of accountability, collaboration, and initiative are more likely to believe that they can weather any storm. Self-confidence, combined with confidence in one another and in the organization, motivates winners to make the extra push that can provide the margin of victory.

The lesson for leaders is clear: Build the cornerstones of confidence—accountability, collaboration, and initiative—when times are good and achievement comes easily. Maintain a culture of confidence as insurance against the inevitable downturns. And while no one should deliberately seek failure, remember that performance under pressure—the ability to stay calm, learn, adapt, and keep on going—separates winners from losers.

ROSABETH MOSS KANTER is a professor at Harvard Business School and chair and director of the Harvard Advanced Leadership Initiative. Her latest book is *MOVE: How to Rebuild and Reinvent America's Infrastructure.* Follow her on Facebook and Twitter @RosabethKanter.

Reprinted from *Harvard Business Review*,
April 2011 (product #F1104E).

10

Great Leaders Are Confident, Connected, Committed, and Courageous

By Peter Bregman

B rad was leading a difficult turnaround of his company and had decided to fire his head of sales, who was a nice guy but wasn't performing.

Three months later, he still hadn't fired him.

I asked him why. His answer? "I'm a wimp!"

Brad (not his real name—I've changed some details to protect people's privacy) is the CEO of a financial services firm and is most definitely not a wimp. He's a normal human, just like you and me. And he's struggling to follow through on an important, strategic decision. Just like, at times, you and I do.

No matter your age, your role, your position, your title, your profession, or your status, to get your most important work done, you have to have hard conversations, create accountability, and inspire action.

In order to do that, you need to show up powerfully and magnetically in a way that attracts people to trust you, follow you, and commit to putting 100% of their effort into a larger purpose, something bigger than all of you. You need to care about others and connect with them in such a way that they feel your care. You need to speak persuasively—in a way that's clear, direct, and honest and that reflects your care—while listening with openness, compassion, and love. Even when being challenged.

And, of course, you need to follow through quickly and effectively.

In 25 years of working with leaders to do all of the above, I have found a pattern that I share in my book, *Leading with Emotional Courage*, consisting of four essential elements that all great leaders rely on to rally people to accomplish what's important to them. To lead effectively—really, to *live* effectively—you must be confident in yourself, connected to others, committed to purpose, and emotionally courageous.

Most of us are great at only one of the four. Maybe two. But to be a powerful presence—to inspire action—you need to excel at *all four simultaneously*.

If you're confident in yourself but disconnected from others, everything will be about you and you'll alienate the people around you. If you're connected to others but lack confidence in yourself, you will betray your own needs and perspectives in order to please everyone else. If you're not committed to a purpose, something bigger than yourself and others, you'll flounder, losing the respect of those around you as you act aimlessly, failing to make an impact on what matters most. And if you fail to act powerfully, decisively, and boldly—with emotional courage—your ideas will remain idle thoughts and your goals will remain unfulfilled fantasies.

Let's apply this to Brad and identify precisely where and how he was getting stuck.

Confident in yourself

Brad struggled with this element, which might feel surprising since he was so successful in his career. But this is not uncommon. He worked tremendously hard, but it came from some degree of insecurity— he wanted to prove himself and please those around him. He became unnerved in the face of potential failure and was not particularly gentle or compassionate with himself when he did fail. He did have important strengths in this element: He saw the person he wanted to become and he worked toward that future, putting aside distractions and investing his energy wisely and strategically.

Connected to others

This was Brad's greatest strength. He was well-loved and always took great care of his team. People clearly knew and felt that he trusted them, even when he disagreed with them. They appreciated his curiosity—

about people and problems—and were grateful that he did not draw quick conclusions about them. All that said, even in this element, he had room to grow: He was not always direct with people and tended to procrastinate on difficult conversations.

Committed to purpose

This was a mixed element for Brad. On the one hand, Brad was clear about what needed to get done to grow the firm, he engaged people in the early stages of work, and he was open and willing to ask for help. On the other hand, he was somewhat scattered. He wasn't clear enough about the small number of things that would move the needle, and he didn't have a reliable process for staying focused on the most important things, ensuring accountability and driving follow-through. Not firing his head of sales sent a mixed message to his team—was he really serious about the firm's success?

Emotionally courageous

Brad had room to grow here, and it turned out to be an important element for growing his strength in the other three elements. Risks, by definition, make us feel vulnerable, and Brad avoided that feeling. He resisted the unknown and intentionally avoided uncomfortable situations. This made it hard for him to tell people hard truths and make hard decisions quickly, which stalled his actions.

So Brad's strongest element was "connected to others," followed by "committed to purpose." He was weaker in "confident in yourself" and "emotionally courageous."

Which puts his challenge in perspective: His connection to his head of sales was at war with his commitment to the success of his team and company. Meanwhile, his confidence in himself and his emotional courage weren't strong enough to break the tie. That's a recipe for inaction and painful frustration.

Just knowing what was happening helped him immediately. We spent some time strengthening his emotional courage by taking small risks *while* feeling the emotions he had been trying to keep at bay. Each time he followed through, regardless of whether he succeeded, he obviously survived and also felt the accomplishment of addressing the risk itself. Which, of course, built his confidence. Which helped him take bigger risks.

In a short time, he felt prepared (even though he may never have felt "ready") to follow through on what he had known he needed to do for the past three months. With his natural care, compassion, and humanity, he fired his head of sales (who, by the way, and unsurprisingly, knew it was coming and said he felt "relieved").

Brad was extremely uncomfortable going into the conversation—that's almost always the feeling you'll have when you do anything that requires emotional courage.

But using emotional courage builds your emotional courage. Brad emerged from the conversation stronger in all four elements: He was more confident in himself, more connected to his team (and even, believe it or not, his head of sales), more committed to purpose, and more emotionally courageous.

PETER BREGMAN is CEO of Bregman Partners, a company that helps senior leaders create accountability and inspire collective action on their organization's most important work. He is the best-selling author of *18 Minutes*, and his latest book is *Leading with Emotional Courage*. He is also the host of the Bregman Leadership Podcast.

Adapted from content posted on hbr.org,
July 13, 2018 (product #H04FUI).

11

Helping an Employee Overcome Their Self-Doubt

By Tara Sophia Mohr

You want to give a member of your team a stretch assignment, but she tells you she's just "not ready yet"—she'd like to get more experience before taking it on.

You offer to make a valuable introduction for someone you mentor. He seems excited about it at first, but doesn't follow up. Later, you discover that he felt intimidated, like he'd have nothing to say.

As managers and mentors, we frequently encounter situations like these, when we come up against the limiting voices of self-doubt in the people we support.

The negative impact of that voice is tremendous. If someone on your team is hampered by a harsh inner critic, they're likely to talk themselves out of sharing their ideas and insights. Held back by self-doubt, some of your most talented people will shy away from leading projects or teams, or put off going for the big opportunities—new clients, new business lines, innovative moves—that could help your business grow.

As a manager or mentor, one of the most powerful ways you can unlock your people's potential is to give them a tool kit for managing self-doubt.

The manager's common mistake

Typically, managers and mentors make this mistake: They think their job is to encourage, compliment, or cheerlead when their people are struggling with self-doubt. They say things like, "You really *can* do this!" or "I have complete confidence in you. I wouldn't have given you this role if I didn't think you had the capability to do it."

In the coaching field, this is known as "arguing with the inner critic." It's the dialogue between someone's voice of self-doubt (*"I can't do that, I don't have what it takes, etc."*) and the affirming words of a supportive person who has a different perspective (*"Yes you can! You are great!"*).

Coaches-in-training are taught, "Never, never argue with the client's inner critic." It's understood that such arguments are usually a waste of everyone's time, for two reasons.

First, such reassurance rarely is convincing. The inner critic's view is not based in data but in instinctual, over-reactive fears of vulnerability and failure. Hearing another individual say something along the lines of "No, you're great at that!" often doesn't speak to those underlying fears. In fact, it can *add* to the stressful feelings of being an imposter, as in, "No one around me realizes that I *really* don't know what I'm doing, and they are all counting on me, thinking I can pull this off—but I can't!"

Second, if you help team members and mentees through their self-doubt by giving them compliments or reassurances, the solution requires your presence or the presence of someone like you. You're giving your people fish, but you aren't teaching them *how* to fish. You haven't given them tools to navigate self-doubt on their own. That's what they really need, because they will make most of their inner-critic-driven decisions quickly, in their own heads, without talking to anyone.

An alternative approach

The alternative is to take the conversation up a level. Instead of arguing with your team members' inner critics, you can introduce a conversation *about* self-doubt—what it is, why it shows up for each of us, and how it can impact what you achieve as a team. You can start to do this with a couple of steps.

1. *Introduce the idea of the "inner critic."* You might choose to call it imposter syndrome, the voice of self-doubt, monkey mind, or another term you feel is appropriate for your work context.

   What's key is to introduce the concept of a voice in all of our heads that does not reflect realistic thinking, and that anxiously and irrationally underestimates our own capabilities. There are common qualities of the inner critic's voice you can use to help your people identify their critics: a voice that critiques harshly, is irrational or untrue, sounds like a broken record, or makes arguments about what's in your best interest, for instance.[1] You can also use the table "Get to know your inner critic" to talk about the difference between the inner critic and more realistic thinking.

2. *Ask your team members to start developing the skill of managing their inner critics.* Clarify

Get to know your inner critic

How the voice in your head compares with realistic thinking.

Inner critic	Realistic thinking
• Very sure it knows the truth of the situation	• Curious and conscious of the many unknowns in the situation
• Asks yes/no questions: *"Is it possible?"*	• Asks open-ended questions: *"How might this be possible?" "What part is possible?"*
• Focuses on problems	• Seeks solutions
• Sounds anxious and pessimistic in tone	• Sounds calmer and generative in tone
• Thinks in extreme, black-and-white terms	• Able to see subtlety and gray
• Is repetitive	• Is forward-moving

that you understand that fears and self-doubts will naturally come up when your team members or mentees grow into new roles, take on greater responsibility, or speak up. The goal you want them to work toward is not unfailing confidence but more-skillful management of their own limiting beliefs and self-doubts.

In doing this, you are introducing a powerful new idea: that readiness for advancement and leadership does not depend on an innate quality of confidence but rather on building the skill of managing one's own self-doubts.

To do this, they should practice noticing when they're hearing their critic, and to name the critic's thoughts as such when they occur. That's as simple as noting to oneself, "I'm hearing my inner critic's worries about this again."

Typically, once someone understands the fear-based roots of the critic's voice and is conscious of when it's speaking up, they can choose to not take direction from it and to take direction from more resourceful and rational parts of themselves instead.

One woman in my course, a manager at a telecommunications company, brought a small group of her colleagues together for this conversation. One colleague told her afterward, "I knew I had a little, mean, nagging voice inside my head, but until now I hadn't really appreciated how much impact it had on the choices I make." Another realized she was not applying for an available promotion largely because of her inner critic. After the discussion, she applied for the job—and got it.

Grace, an executive at a professional services firm, worked with a manager who was dealing with major changes in the scope of her role, activating the manager's inner critic. "In addition to encouraging her," Grace said, "we spent time digging through how the changes had triggered her inner critic. We made a clear plan for what she needed to accomplish. Many milestones were reached (and celebrated), but when things didn't go to plan, we explored whether/how the manager's inner critic was factoring in. As time went on, the manager learned to better predict when her inner critic might kick in and how it could be quieted. She gained a tool she can rely on and navigated challenging times of change with flying colors."

You want your people to do all that they are capable of—to keep saying "yes" to being on their growing edge. That means they'll frequently feel self-doubt.

You can empower them by addressing the inner critic head-on, and you can give them tools to become skillful responders to their own self-doubt.

TARA SOPHIA MOHR is an expert on women's leadership and the author of *Playing Big: Practical Wisdom for Women Who Want to Speak Up, Create, and Lead*, named a best book of the year by Apple's iBooks. She is the creator of the Playing Big leadership programs for women, which now have more than 2,000 graduates worldwide. Connect with her at taramohr.com.

Note

1. Tara Mohr, "7 Ways to Recognize Your Inner Critic," https://www.taramohr.com/inspiration/7-ways-to -recognize-your-inner-critic/.

Adapted from content posted on hbr.org, October 1, 2015 (product #H02DB8).

12

To Seem Confident, Women Have to Be Seen as Warm

By Margarita Mayo

Why are there so few women in leadership roles? My research collaborators (Laura Guillén of ESMT and Natalia Karelaia of INSEAD) and I believe we have shed some new light on this conundrum. But first, some background.

One frequently cited reason has to do with confidence. In a previous study, my colleagues and I found that women tend to rate their abilities accurately, while men tend to be overconfident about theirs.[1] Thus, one argument goes, women are less confident than men, which hurts their chances of promotion.

Previous research has measured how women see themselves, but we wanted to know how outside perceivers—bosses, subordinates, colleagues—rate women's confidence, and what influences those ratings.

Susan Fiske and her colleagues have shown that people seem to universally use two dimensions to judge others: competence and warmth.[2] We decided to test for both of those in addition to confidence. As a proxy for the likelihood of being promoted, we also tested for influence, on the theory that people who are seen as influential are more likely to be promoted to leadership roles.

We conducted a study analyzing the judgments that colleagues made regarding the competence and warmth of 236 engineers working in project teams at a multinational software development company.[3] As part of their performance evaluation, the engineers were evaluated online by their supervisor, peers, and collaborators on competence and warmth. A total of 810 raters provided this confidential evaluation. A year later, we collected a second wave of data on the same 236 engineers about their apparent confidence at work and their influence in the organization. This time, a total of 1,236 raters provided information.

Our study shows that men are seen as confident if they are seen as competent, but women are seen as confident only if they come across as both competent and warm. Women must be seen as warm in order to capitalize on their competence and be seen as confident and influential at work; competent men are seen as confident and influential whether they are warm or not.

In other words, for male engineers, competence and perceived confidence go hand in hand. The more competent male engineers are, the more confident they are seen as being (and vice versa). The more confident they are seen as being, the more influence they have in the organization, regardless of whether others like them. It seems that warmth is irrelevant to men appearing confident and influential, at least when they are performing a typically male job like engineering.

For women, in the absence of warmth there was virtually no relationship between competence and confidence ratings. When women were seen as both warm and competent, they were also seen as more confident—and thus more influential. Competent but less-affable female engineers were evaluated by their colleagues as less confident in their professional roles. These female engineers were, in turn, less influential within the organization. In sum, women's professional performance is not evaluated independently from their personal warmth.

Personal experience and empirical research suggest that it's not enough for women to be merely *as* gregarious, easygoing, sociable, and helpful as men. To get credit for being warm—and to have their other strengths recognized—they might need to be even more so.

I still remember my first performance evaluation as an assistant lecturer: I was told to be more "nurturing." I had gone to just as many social events as the men had, had been just as gregarious with my students. But women simply are expected to show more warmth. Studies show, for example, that women's performance reviews contain nearly twice as much language about being warm, empathetic, helpful, and dedicated to others.[4]

To us, this study suggests that if women are to succeed in a biased world, encouraging them to be more confident is not enough. To get credit for having confidence and competence, and to have the influence in their organizations that they would like to have, women must go out of their way to be seen as warm.

We wish this were not the case. We wish women and men could be evaluated according to the same meritocratic standards. But as our research shows, we seem to be a long way off from those days.

MARGARITA MAYO is Professor of Leadership and Organizational Behavior at IE Business School in Madrid. She was featured on the Thinkers50 Radar as one of 30 thought leaders to watch in 2017. She is the author of *Yours Truly: Staying Authentic in Leadership and Life.*

Notes

1. Margarita Mayo et al., "Aligning or Inflating Your Leadership Self-Image? A Longitudinal Study of Responses to Peer Feedback in MBA Teams," *Academy of Management Learning and Education* 11, no. 4 (2012): 631–652.
2. Susan T. Fiske et al., "Universal Dimensions of Social Cognition: Warmth and Competence," *Trends in Cognitive Sciences* 11, no. 2 (2006): 77–83.
3. Laura Guillén et al., "The Competence-Confidence Gender Gap: Being Competent Is Not Always Enough for Women to Appear Confident," working paper (Berlin: ESMT, 2016), https://margaritamayo.com/wp-content/uploads/2016/07/The-competence-confidence-gender-gap.pdf.
4. Shelley Correll and Caroline Simard, "Research: Vague Feedback Is Holding Women Back," hbr.org, April 29, 2016, https://hbr.org/2016/04/research-vague-feedback-is-holding-women-back.

Adapted from content posted on hbr.org,
July 8, 2016 (product #H03036).

13

Why Do So Many Incompetent Men Become Leaders?

By Tomas Chamorro-Premuzic

There are three popular explanations for the clear underrepresentation of women in management: They are not capable; they are not interested; or they are both interested and capable, but they are unable to break the glass ceiling, an invisible career barrier based on prejudiced stereotypes that prevents women from accessing the ranks of power. Conservatives and chauvinists tend to endorse the first; liberals and feminists prefer the third; and those somewhere in the middle are usually drawn to the second. But what if they have all missed the big picture?

In my view, the main reason for the unbalanced gender ratio in management is our inability to discern between confidence and competence. That is, because we (people in general) commonly misinterpret displays of confidence as a sign of competence, we are fooled into believing that men are better leaders than women. In other words, when it comes to leadership, the only advantage that men have over women (from Argentina to Norway and the USA to Japan) is the fact that manifestations of hubris—often masked as charisma or charm—are commonly mistaken for leadership potential and that these occur much more frequently in men than in women.[1]

This is consistent with the finding that leaderless groups have a natural tendency to elect self-centered, overconfident, and narcissistic individuals as leaders and that these personality characteristics are not equally common in men and women.[2] In line with this, Freud argued that the psychological process of leadership occurs because a group of people—the followers—have replaced their own narcissistic tendencies with those of the leader, such that their love for the leader is a disguised form of self-love or a substitute for their inability to love themselves. "Another person's narcissism," he said, "has a great attraction for those who have renounced part of their own . . . as if we envied them for maintaining a blissful state of mind."

The truth of the matter is that pretty much anywhere in the world, men tend to *think* that they are much smarter than women.[3] Yet arrogance and overconfidence are inversely related to leadership talent—the ability to build and maintain high-performing teams and to inspire followers to set aside their selfish agendas in order to work for the common interest of the group. Indeed, whether in sports, politics, or business, the best leaders are usually humble—and whether through nature or nurture, humility is a much more common feature in women than men. For example, women outperform men on emotional intelligence, which is a strong driver of modest behaviors.[4] Furthermore, a quantitative review of gender differences in personality involving more than 23,000 participants in 26 cultures indicated that women are more sensitive, considerate, and humble than men, which is arguably one of the least counter-intuitive findings in the social sciences.[5] An even clearer picture emerges when one examines the dark side of personality: For instance, our normative data, which includes thousands of managers from across all industry sectors and 40 countries, shows that men are consistently more arrogant, manipulative, and risk-prone than women.[6]

The paradoxical implication is that the same psychological characteristics that enable male managers to rise to the top of the corporate or political ladder are actually responsible for their downfall. In other words, what it takes to *get* the job is not just different from, but also the reverse of, what it takes to *do the job well*. As a result, too many incompetent people are promoted to management jobs, and promoted over more competent people.

Unsurprisingly, the mythical image of a "leader" embodies many of the characteristics commonly found in personality disorders, such as narcissism (Steve Jobs or Vladimir Putin), psychopathy (fill in the name of your favorite despot here), histrionic tendencies (Richard Branson or Steve Ballmer), or a Machiavellian personality (nearly any federal-level politician). The sad thing is not that these mythical figures are unrepresentative of the average manager, but that the average manager will fail precisely for having these characteristics.

In fact, most leaders—whether in politics or business—fail. That has always been the case: The majority of nations, companies, societies, and organizations are poorly managed, as indicated by their longevity, revenues, and approval ratings, or by the effects they have on their citizens, employees, subordinates, or members. Good leadership has always been the exception, not the norm.

So it struck me as a little odd that so much of the recent debate over getting women to "lean in" has focused on getting them to adopt more of these dysfunctional leadership traits. Yes, these are the people we often choose as our leaders—but should they be?

Most of the character traits that are truly advantageous for effective leadership are predominantly found in those who fail to impress others with their talent for management. This is especially true for women. There is now compelling scientific evidence supporting the notion that women are more likely to adopt more-effective leadership strategies than are men. Most notably, in a comprehensive review of studies, Alice Eagly and colleagues showed that female managers are more likely to elicit respect and pride from their followers, communicate their vision effectively, empower and mentor subordinates, and approach problem solving in a more flexible and creative way (all characteristics of "transformational leadership"), as well as fairly reward direct reports.[7] In contrast, male managers are statistically less likely to bond or connect with their subordinates, and they are relatively less adept at rewarding them for their actual performance. Although these findings may reflect a sampling bias that requires women to be more qualified and competent than men in order to be chosen as leaders, there is no way of really knowing until this bias is eliminated.

In sum, there is no denying that women's path to leadership positions is paved with many barriers, including a very thick glass ceiling. But a much bigger problem is the lack of career obstacles for incompetent men, and the fact that we tend to equate leadership with the very psychological features that make the average man a more inept leader than the average woman.[8] The result is a pathological system that rewards men for their incompetence while punishing women for their competence, to everybody's detriment.

TOMAS CHAMORRO-PREMUZIC is the Chief Talent Scientist at ManpowerGroup, a professor of business psychology at University College London and at Columbia University, and an associate at Harvard's Entrepreneurial Finance Lab. He's the author of *Why Do So Many Incompetent Men Become Leaders? (And How to Fix It)* (Harvard Business Review Press, 2019). Find him on Twitter @drtcp or at www.drtomascp.com.

Notes

1. Adrian Furnham et al., "Male Hubris and Female Humility? A Cross-Cultural Study of Ratings of Self, Parental, and Sibling Multiple Intelligence in America, Britain, and Japan," *Intelligence* 30, no. 1 (January–February 2001): 101–115; Amanda S. Shipman and Michael D. Mumford, "When Confidence Is Detrimental: Influence of Overconfidence on Leadership Effectiveness," *The Leadership Quarterly* 22, no. 4 (2011): 649–655; and Ernesto Reuben et al., "The Emergence of Male Leadership in Competitive Environments," *Journal of Economic Behavior & Organization* 83, no. 1 (June 2012): 111–117.

2. The Ohio State University, "Narcissistic People Most Likely to Emerge as Leaders," Newswise, October 7, 2008, https://newswise.com/articles/view/545089/.

3. Sophie von Stumm et al., "Decomposing Self-Estimates of Intelligence: Structure and Sex Differences Across

12 Nations," *British Journal of Psychology* 100, no. 2 (May 2009): 429–442.

4. S. Y. H. Hur et al., "Transformational Leadership as a Mediator Between Emotional Intelligence and Team Outcomes," *The Leadership Quarterly* 22, no. 4 (August 2011): 591–603.

5. Paul T. Costa, Jr., et al., "Gender Differences in Personality Traits Across Cultures: Robust and Surprising Findings," *Journal of Personality and Social Psychology* 81, no. 2 (2001): 322–331.

6. Blaine H. Gladdis and Jeff L. Foster, "Meta-Analysis of Dark Side Personality Characteristics and Critical Work Behaviors Among Leaders Across the Globe: Findings and Implications for Leadership Development and Executive Coaching," *Applied Psychology* 64, no. 1 (August 27, 2013).

7. Alice H. Eagly and Blair T. Johnson, "Gender and Leadership Style: A Meta-Analysis," *Psychological Bulletin* 108, no. 2 (1990), 233–256.

8. A. M. Koenig et al., "Are Leader Stereotypes Masculine? A Meta-Analysis of Three Research Paradigms," *Psychological Bulletin* 137, no. 4 (July 2011): 616–642.

Adapted from content posted on hbr.org,
August 22, 2013 (product #H00B50).

14

Less Confident People Are More Successful

By Tomas Chamorro-Premuzic

There is no bigger cliché in business psychology than the idea that high self-confidence is key to career success. It is time to debunk this myth. In fact, *low* self-confidence is more likely to make you successful.

After many years of researching and consulting on talent, I've come to the conclusion that self-confidence is only helpful when it's low. Sure, *extremely* low confidence is not helpful: It inhibits performance by inducing fear, worry, and stress, which may drive people to give up sooner or later. But just-low-enough confidence can help you recalibrate your goals so they are (a) more realistic and (b) attainable. Is that really a problem? Not everyone can be CEO of Coca-Cola or the next Steve Jobs.

If your confidence is low, rather than extremely low, you stand a better chance of succeeding than if you have high self-confidence. There are three main reasons for this:

Lower self-confidence makes you pay attention to negative feedback and be self-critical. Most people get trapped in their optimistic biases, so they tend to listen to positive feedback and ignore negative feedback. Although this may help them come across as confident to others, in any area of competence (e.g., education, business, sports, or performing arts) achievement is 10% performance and 90% preparation. Thus, the more aware you are of your soft spots and weaknesses, the better prepared you will be.

Low self-confidence may turn you into a pessimist, but when pessimism teams up with ambition it often produces outstanding performance. To be the very best at anything, you will need to be your own harshest critic, and that is almost impossible when your starting point is high self-confidence. Exceptional achievers always experience low levels of confidence and self-confidence, but they train hard and practice continually until they reach an acceptable level of competence. Indeed, success is the best medicine for your insecurities.

Lower self-confidence can motivate you to work harder and prepare more. If you are serious about your goals, you will have more incentive to work hard when you lack confidence in your abilities. In fact, low confidence is only demotivating when you are not serious about your goals.

Most people like the idea of being exceptional but not enough to do what it takes to achieve it. Most people want to be slim, healthy, attractive, and successful, but few people are willing to do what it takes to achieve it—which suggests that they don't really want these things as much as they think. As the legendary Paul Arden (former executive creative director at Saatchi & Saatchi) noted: "*I want* means: [I]f I want it enough I will get it. Getting what you want means making the decisions you need to make to get what you want." If you really want what you say you want, then your low confidence will only make you work harder to achieve it—because it will indicate a discrepancy between your desired goal and your current state.

Lower self-confidence reduces the chances of coming across as arrogant or being deluded. Although we live in a world that worships those who worship themselves—from Donald Trump to Lady Gaga to the latest reality TV "star"—the consequences of hubris are now beyond debate. According to Gallup, more than 60% of employees either dislike or hate their jobs, and the most common reason is that they have narcissistic bosses. If managers were less arrogant, fewer employees would be spending their working hours on Facebook, productivity rates would go up, and turnover rates would go down.

Lower self-confidence reduces the chances not only of coming across as arrogant but also of being deluded. Indeed, people with low self-confidence are more likely to admit their mistakes—instead of blaming others—and rarely take credit for others' accomplishments. This is arguably the most important benefit of low self-confidence because it points to the fact that low self-confidence can bring success, not just to individuals but also to organizations and society.

In brief, if you are serious about your goals, low self-confidence can be your biggest ally in achieving them. It will motivate you to work hard, help you work on your limitations, and stop you from being a jerk, deluded, or both. It is therefore time debunk the myth: High self-confidence isn't a blessing, and low self-confidence is not a curse—in fact, it is the other way around.

TOMAS CHAMORRO-PREMUZIC is the Chief Talent Scientist at ManpowerGroup, a professor of business psychology at University College London and at Columbia University, and an associate at Harvard's Entrepreneurial Finance Lab. He's the author of *Why Do So Many Incompetent Men Become Leaders? (And How to Fix It)* (Harvard Business Review Press, 2019). Find him on Twitter @drtcp or at www.drtomascp.com.

Adapted from content posted on hbr.org,
July 6, 2012 (product #H0092K).

Index

How to be human at work.

HBR's Emotional Intelligence Series features smart, essential reading on the human side of professional life from the pages of *Harvard Business Review*. Each book in the series offers uplifting stories, practical advice, and research from leading experts on how to tend to our emotional well-being at work.

Harvard Business Review Emotional Intelligence Series

Available in paperback or ebook format. The specially priced six-volume set includes:

- Mindfulness
- Resilience
- Influence and Persuasion

- Authentic Leadership
- Happiness
- Empathy

HBR.ORG

Buy for your team, clients, or event.
Visit hbr.org/bulksales for quantity discount rates.

Power and
Impact

HBR Emotional Intelligence Series

How to be human at work

The HBR Emotional Intelligence Series features smart, essential reading on the human side of professional life from the pages of *Harvard Business Review*.

Authentic Leadership	*Leadership Presence*
Confidence	*Mindful Listening*
Dealing with Difficult People	*Mindfulness*
Empathy	*Power and Impact*
Focus	*Purpose, Meaning, and Passion*
Happiness	*Resilience*
Influence and Persuasion	*Self-Awareness*

Other books on emotional intelligence from *Harvard Business Review*:

HBR Everyday Emotional Intelligence

HBR Guide to Emotional Intelligence

HBR's 10 Must Reads on Emotional Intelligence

Power and Impact

HBR EMOTIONAL INTELLIGENCE SERIES

Harvard Business Review Press

Boston, Massachusetts

HBR Press Quantity Sales Discounts

Harvard Business Review Press titles are available at significant quantity discounts when purchased in bulk for client gifts, sales promotions, and premiums. Special editions, including books with corporate logos, customized covers, and letters from the company or CEO printed in the front matter, as well as excerpts of existing books, can also be created in large quantities for special needs.

For details and discount information for both print and ebook formats, contact booksales@harvardbusiness.org, tel. 800-988-0886, or www.hbr.org/bulksales.

Copyright 2020 Harvard Business School Publishing Corporation
All rights reserved
Printed in the United States of America

10 9 8 7

No part of this publication may be reproduced, stored in or introduced into a retrieval system, or transmitted, in any form, or by any means (electronic, mechanical, photocopying, recording, or otherwise), without the prior permission of the publisher. Requests for permission should be directed to permissions@harvardbusiness.org, or mailed to Permissions, Harvard Business School Publishing, 60 Harvard Way, Boston, Massachusetts 02163.

The web addresses referenced in this book were live and correct at the time of the book's publication but may be subject to change.

Library of Congress Cataloging-in-Publication Data

Title: Power and impact / Harvard Business Review.
Other titles: HBR emotional intelligence series.
Description: Boston, Massachusetts : Harvard Business Review Press, [2020]
    | Series: HBR emotional intelligence series | Includes index. |
Identifiers: LCCN 2019030885 | ISBN 9781633697942 (paperback)
Subjects: LCSH: Power (Social sciences) | Power (Philosophy) | Influence
    (Psychology) | Leadership. | Abuse of administrative power.
Classification: LCC HN49.P6 P6838 2020 | DDC 303.3—dc23
LC record available at https://lccn.loc.gov/2019030885

The paper used in this publication meets the requirements of the American National Standard for Permanence of Paper for Publications and Documents in Libraries and Archives Z39.48-1992.

Contents

Contents

Contents

Power and Impact

HBR EMOTIONAL INTELLIGENCE SERIES

1

Don't Let Power Corrupt You

By Dacher Keltner

n the behavioral research I've conducted over the past 20 years, I've uncovered a disturbing pattern: While people usually gain power through traits and actions that advance the interests of others, such as empathy, collaboration, openness, fairness, and sharing, when they start to feel powerful or enjoy a position of privilege, those qualities begin to fade. The powerful are more likely than other people to engage in rude, selfish, and unethical behavior. The 19th-century historian and politician Lord Acton got it right: Power *does* tend to corrupt.

I call this phenomenon "the power paradox," and I've studied it in numerous settings: colleges, the U.S.

Senate, pro sports teams, and a variety of other professional workplaces. In each I've observed that people rise on the basis of their good qualities, but their behavior grows increasingly worse as they move up the ladder. This shift can happen surprisingly quickly. In one of my experiments, known as "the cookie monster" study, I brought people into a lab in groups of three, randomly assigned one to a position of leadership, and then gave them a group writing task. A half hour into their work, I placed a plate of freshly baked cookies—one for each team member, plus an extra—in front of everyone. In all groups each person took one and, out of politeness, left the extra cookie. The question was: Who would take a second treat, knowing that it would deprive others of the same? It was nearly always the person who'd been named the leader. In addition, the leaders were more likely to eat with their mouths open, lips smacking, and crumbs falling onto their clothes.

Studies show that wealth and credentials can have a similar effect. In another experiment, Paul Piff of UC Irvine and I found that whereas drivers of the least expensive vehicles—Dodge Colts, Plymouth Satellites—*always* ceded the right-of-way to pedestrians in a crosswalk, people driving luxury cars such as BMWs and Mercedes yielded only 54% of the time; nearly half the time they ignored the pedestrian and the law. Surveys of employees in 27 countries have revealed that wealthy individuals are more likely to say it's acceptable to engage in unethical behavior, such as taking bribes or cheating on taxes. And recent research led by Danny Miller at HEC Montréal demonstrated that CEOs with MBAs are more likely than those without MBAs to engage in self-serving behavior that increases their personal compensation but causes their companies' value to decline.

These findings suggest that iconic abuses of power —Jeffrey Skilling's fraudulent accounting at Enron,

Tyco CEO Dennis Kozlowski's illegal bonuses, Silvio Berlusconi's bunga bunga parties, Leona Helmsley's tax evasion—are extreme examples of the kinds of misbehavior to which all leaders, at any level, are susceptible. Studies show that people in positions of corporate power are three times as likely as those at the lower rungs of the ladder to interrupt coworkers, multitask during meetings, raise their voices, and say insulting things at the office. And people who've just moved into senior roles are particularly vulnerable to losing their virtues, my research and other studies indicate.

The consequences can be far-reaching. The abuse of power ultimately tarnishes the reputations of executives, undermining their opportunities for influence. It also creates stress and anxiety among their colleagues, diminishing rigor and creativity in the group and dragging down team members' engagement and performance. In a recent poll of 800 managers and employees in 17 industries, about half the respondents who reported being treated rudely at work said they deliberately decreased their effort or lowered the quality of their work in response.

So how can you avoid succumbing to the power paradox? Through awareness and action.

A need for reflection

A first step is developing greater self-awareness. When you take on a senior role, you need to be attentive to the feelings that accompany your newfound power and to any changes in your behavior. My research has shown that power puts us into something like a manic state, making us feel expansive, energized, omnipotent, hungry for rewards, and immune to risk—which opens us up to rash, rude, and unethical actions. But new studies in neuroscience find that simply by reflecting on those thoughts and emotions—"Hey, I'm feeling as if I should rule the world right now"—we can engage regions of our frontal lobes that help us keep our worst impulses in check. When we recognize and label feelings of joy and confidence, we're less likely to make irrational decisions inspired by them. When we acknowledge feelings of frustration (perhaps because subordinates aren't behaving the way we want), we're less likely to respond in adversarial or confrontational ways.

You can build this kind of self-awareness through everyday mindfulness practices. One approach starts with sitting in a comfortable and quiet place, breathing deeply, and concentrating on the feeling of inhaling and exhaling, physical sensations, or sounds or sights in your environment. Studies show that spending just a few minutes a day on such exercises gives people greater focus and calm, and for that reason techniques for them are now taught in training programs at companies like Google, Facebook, Aetna, General Mills, Ford, and Goldman Sachs.

It's also important to reflect on your demeanor and actions. Are you interrupting people? Do you check your phone when others are talking? Have you told a joke or story that embarrassed or humiliated someone else? Do you swear at the office? Have you ever taken sole credit for a group effort? Do you forget colleagues' names? Are you spending a lot more money than in the past or taking unusual physical risks?

If you answered yes to at least a few of these questions, take it as an early warning sign that you're being tempted into problematic, arrogant displays of power. What may seem innocuous to you probably doesn't to your subordinates. Consider a story I recently heard about a needlessly hierarchical lunch delivery protocol on a cable television writing team. Each day when the team's sandwiches arrived, they were doled out to the writers in order of seniority. In failing to correct this behavior, the group's leaders were almost certainly diminishing its collaborative and creative potential. For a contrast, consider U.S. military mess halls, where the practice is the reverse, as the ethnographer and author Simon Sinek notes in the title of his book, *Leaders Eat Last*. Officers adhere to the policy not to cede authority but to show respect for their troops.

Practicing graciousness

Whether you've already begun to succumb to the power paradox or not, you must work to remember and repeat the virtuous behaviors that helped you rise in the first place. When teaching executives and others in positions of power, I focus on three essential practices—empathy, gratitude, and generosity—that have been shown to sustain benevolent leadership, even in the most cutthroat environments.

For example, Leanne ten Brinke, Chris Liu, Sameer Srivastava, and I found that U.S. senators who used empathetic facial expressions and tones of voice when speaking to the floor got more bills passed than those who used domineering, threatening gestures and tones in their speeches. Research by Anita Woolley of Carnegie Mellon and Thomas Malone of MIT has likewise shown that when teammates subtly signal understanding, engagement, interest, and concern for one another, the team is more effective at tackling hard analytical problems.

Small expressions of gratitude also yield positive results. Studies show that romantic partners who acknowledge each other's value in casual conversation are less likely to break up, that students who receive a pat on the back from their teachers are more likely to take on difficult problems, and that people who express appreciation to others in a newly formed group feel stronger ties to the group months later. Adam Grant of Wharton has found that when managers take the time to thank their employees, those workers are more engaged and productive. And my own research on NBA teams with Michael Kraus of Yale University shows that players who physically display their appreciation—through head raps, bear hugs, and hip and chest bumps—inspire their teammates to play better and win nearly two more games per season (which is both statistically significant and often the difference between making the playoffs and not).

Simple acts of generosity can be equally powerful. Studies show that individuals who share with others in a group—for example, by contributing new ideas or directly assisting on projects not their own—are deemed more worthy of respect and influence and more suitable for leadership. Mike Norton at Harvard Business School has found that when organizations provide an opportunity to donate to charities at work, employees feel more satisfied and productive.

It might seem difficult to constantly follow the ethics of "good power" when you're the boss and responsible for making sure things get done. Not so. Your capacity for empathy, gratitude, and generosity can be cultivated by engaging in simple social behaviors whenever the opportunity presents itself: a team meeting, a client pitch or negotiation, a 360-degree feedback session. Here are a few suggestions.

To practice empathy:

- Ask a great question or two in every interaction, and paraphrase important points that others make.

- Listen with gusto. Orient your body and eyes toward the person speaking, and convey interest and engagement vocally.

- When someone comes to you with a problem, signal concern with phrases such as "I'm sorry" and "That's really tough." Avoid rushing to judgment and advice.

- Before meetings, take a moment to think about the person you'll be with and what is happening in his or her life.

Arturo Bejar, Facebook's director of engineering, is one executive I've seen make empathy a priority as he guides his teams of designers, coders, data specialists, and writers. Watching him at work, I've noticed that his meetings all tend to be structured around a cascade of open-ended questions and that he never fails to listen thoughtfully. He leans toward whoever is speaking and carefully writes down everyone's ideas on a notepad. These small expressions of empathy signal to his team that he understands their concerns and wants them to succeed together.

To practice gratitude:

- Make thoughtful thank-yous a part of how you communicate with others.

- Send colleagues specific and timely emails or notes of appreciation for jobs done well.

- Publicly acknowledge the value that each person contributes to your team, including the support staff.

- Use the right kind of touch—pats on the back, fist bumps, or high fives—to celebrate successes.

When Douglas Conant was CEO of the Campbell Soup Company, he emphasized a culture of gratitude across the organization. Each day he and his executive assistants would spend up to an hour scanning his email and the company intranet for news of employees who were "making a difference." Conant would then personally thank them—everyone from senior executives to maintenance people—for their contributions, usually with handwritten notes. He estimates that he wrote at least 10 a day, for a total of about 30,000 during his decade-long tenure, and says he would often find them pinned up in employees' workspaces. Leaders I've taught have shared other tactics: giving small gifts to employees, taking them out to nice lunches or dinners, hosting employee-of-the-month celebrations, and setting up real or virtual "gratitude walls," on which coworkers can thank one another for specific contributions.

To practice generosity:

- Seek opportunities to spend a little one-on-one time with the people you lead.

- Delegate some important and high-profile responsibilities.

- Give praise generously.

- Share the limelight. Give credit to all who contribute to the success of your team and your organization.

Pixar director Pete Docter is a master of this last practice. When I first started working with him on the movie *Inside Out*, I was curious about a cinematic marvel he'd created five years before: the montage at the start of the film *Up*, which shows the protagonist, Carl, meeting and falling in love with a girl, Ellie; enjoying a long married life with her; and then watching her succumb to illness. When I asked how he'd accomplished it, his answer was an exhaustive list of the 250 writers, animators, actors, story artists, designers, sculptors, editors, programmers, and computer modelers who had worked on it with him. When people ask about the box-office success of *Inside Out*, he gives a similar response. Another Facebook executive I've worked with, product manager Kelly Winters, shares credit in a similar way. When she does PowerPoint presentations or talks to reporters about the success of her Compassion team, she always lists or talks about the data analysts, engineers, and content specialists who made it happen.

———————

You can outsmart the power paradox by practicing the ethics of empathy, gratitude, and generosity. It will bring out the best work and collaborative spirit of those around you. And you, too, will benefit, with a burnished reputation, long-lasting leadership, and the dopamine-rich delights of advancing the interests of others.

DACHER KELTNER is a professor of psychology at the University of California, Berkeley, and the faculty director of the Greater Good Science Center. He is also the author of *The Power Paradox: How We Gain and Lose Influence.*

Reprinted from *Harvard Business Review,*
October 2016 (product #R1610K).

2

What's Your Power Style?

By Maggie Craddock

Have you ever wondered if a person's childhood experiences influence the way they operate as a professional later in life? Did that boardroom bully who intimidates others in order to make a point shove people around on the playground as a kid?

Whether you are trying to get ahead at your existing firm or land a job in a new organization, it's helpful to understand that many of your instincts for giving and taking power stem from ways you were conditioned in the first system you experienced in life—your family system. Through my research for my book *Power Genes*, I discovered that the building blocks of anyone's signature power style are rooted in the ways they have been conditioned to respond emotionally and behaviorally to the first authority figures they encountered in life, namely, their caregivers.

To get a sense of how you may be emotionally conditioned to respond to power in the workplace, reflect for a moment on the predominant way that your caregivers exerted authority in your family system. Did they motivate you by considering your feelings, or did they issue orders they expected to be promptly obeyed? If you were raised by caregivers who asked your opinion when making important family decisions, you probably react positively to colleagues who take the time to connect with you at a human level. This type of reaction indicates that the emotional dimension of your signature power style may be trust-based.

In contrast, people who were raised by caregivers who were either rigidly authoritarian or highly permissive often find that the emotional dimension of their power style can be fear-based. They may react negatively to consensus building on the job and gravitate toward leaders who operate independently and exude an aura of confidence.

But there is another level of your power style that needs exploring. The behavioral dimension of your power style stems from the way you learned to deal with your caregivers as a unit to get what you wanted in childhood. Did a more informal approach win the day, or did you learn to operate more formally with them?

If your childhood experience taught you that you could sometimes get one parent to agree to a request that had been refused by the other, the behavioral dimension of your signature power style may be predominantly informal. People with a strong informal dimension to their power style prefer one-on-one interactions on the job when they are trying to influence others. For example, even when they know they will need to present an idea or proposal to a group, they will tend to run their ideas by key individuals privately before the group meets.

In contrast, clients who report that their caregivers stuck together when disciplining or rewarding them often exhibit a preference for dealing with groups to further a professional agenda later in life. People whose behavioral preferences indicate a formal dimension to their signature power style prefer to orchestrate an open debate around contentious issues with a group than negotiate individual agreements in private.

Comparing the ways my clients learned to adapt to get their needs met in childhood with the challenges these same clients were facing in their current jobs unearthed some important trends. For example, Jeff, a senior executive in the advertising industry, was about to be passed over for promotion because his tendency to talk over others in meetings made him appear too anxious to lead a creative team. Jeff had worked with presentation coaches, but his urgent need to be heard held sway.

Jeff grew up in the shadow of an older sister who was a champion figure skater. His parents, who loved and supported him, had been so preoccupied with his sister's athletic career that they had inadvertently left Jeff feeling ignored. Jeff longed to capture and hold his parents' attention. This longing drove Jeff to create advertising campaigns that successfully grabbed the attention of families around the world. As Jeff began to understand the way that his fear of being overlooked as a child was undermining the tone he set internally on the job, he was able to become a more powerful listener and land the promotion he deserved.

The first step in making change is to identify your own power style. You can evaluate your signature power style by examining your dominant emotional triggers and behavioral patterns. Most people find that their signature power style is a blend of at least two of these four core power styles:

- *The Pleaser.* Due to outside stressors, Pleasers often didn't get the attention they craved from their caretakers early in life. Pleasers often grow up hungry for validation and are hardwired to take care of others. Pleasers often wield power by attempting to connect with others at a personal level.

- *The Charmer.* Charmers were often required to soothe an emotionally needy parent early in life. As a result, they sometimes have little respect for formal authority and may manipulate others in order to get their needs met. The Charmer power style is exemplified by people with an intensity of focus that both intimidates and seduces others into compliance.

- *The Commander.* Often, a Commander has grown up in a family system devoted to sports, religion, the military, or any larger system that reinforces discipline and a strict code of conduct. Commanders operate with a results orientation and tend to foster a sense of urgency in others.

- *The Inspirer.* The family systems that foster Inspirers often value self-expression over conformity, and the caregivers in such systems are often willing to make personal sacrifices to achieve excellence in areas such as artistic expression or scientific inquiry. Inspirers tend to be innovative thinkers and operate with a consistent commitment to the greater good.

Each style has inherent strengths and challenges, and each presents us with important lessons about power in the workplace. Jeff discovered that his approach to wielding power reflected a blend of the Pleaser and the Commander, and he was able to use that knowledge to adjust his habits and behavior.

As you identify your own power style, it's important to bear in mind that there are no good or bad power styles, and remember not to make snap judgments about others or about yourself. Most of us employ more than one power style, and you may even switch styles depending upon the situation.

MAGGIE CRADDOCK is the president and founder of Workplace Relationships. She is the author of *Power Genes: Understanding Your Power Persona—and How to Wield It at Work* (Harvard Business Review Press, 2011).

Adapted from content posted on hbr.org, May 9, 2011.

3

How to Figure Out How Much Influence You Have at Work

By Maxim Sytch

A banker in Southeast Asia wanted to allow employees of a car rental agency to buy used cars from the employer. But not a single business unit was able to put together that product. Different departments were stopped by the existing product portfolio, the underlying risk, or regulatory guidelines. One of the banker's colleagues, however, was able to facilitate valuable introductions across the company. That led to the solution being code-signed and jointly offered by two business units.

Credit the success of this new financial product to the banker's informal power. Informal power—which is unrelated to your formal title—can enable you to mobilize resources, drive change, and create value for the organization as well as yourself. And in the modern workplace, informal power is increasingly pivotal and can secure your place within your organization.

Why? Nowadays, workflow is migrating from specialized verticals to the white spaces between them, as companies respond more precisely to customer needs. This trend matters in organizations with cross-functional teams, account managers, or a matrix structure. Even smaller organizations are increasingly project driven.

And more and more, work is done outside the organization in collaboration with suppliers, distributors, and customers. Companies are crowdsourcing ideas and work. We engage with freelancers and third parties. Sometimes we even collaborate with competitors.

The fact is, your formal title, direct reports, and formally granted authority do not always carry you far when working across your own organization and with outside stakeholders.

Do you have the informal power to generate value and get things done? Here's how to do a power audit:

- *Step 1:* List your top 10 contacts that enable you to get work done. These contacts can be either internal or external to your organization.

- *Step 2:* For each contact, assign a score from 1 to 10 indicating how much you depend on them. If a contact provides a lot of value and is also difficult to replace, assign a high score. Think broadly about the value your contacts offer. This includes career advice, emotional backing, support with daily activities, information, and access to resources or stakeholders.

- *Step 3:* Do the same in reverse. Assign a score to yourself from others' perspectives.

Approximate how much value you offer your contacts and how difficult it would be to replace you. Be honest.

Next, look for red flags in your power audit. These could indicate that you lack informal power and are replaceable.

Do all of your contacts work in one team, function, product unit, or office building? This could indicate a limited ability to generate value beyond the basic requirements of your job description.

Do your contacts provide you with more value than you return? Such relationships are difficult to sustain in the long run. Asymmetries in dependence indicate others hold the power in a relationship.

Are your dependence scores low throughout? This could indicate the prevalence of transactional relationships, ones often driven by quid pro quo. In contrast, high-dependence relationships can be imbued with values and relational dynamics that are not simply calculated.[1]

Is all of the value you give or receive concentrated in a couple of contacts? You could be vulnerable if you lose these contacts or your relationship changes. One senior executive shared with me that two key contacts drove the value in his network. Unfortunately, one passed away and the other moved to a different region. This executive's informal power shut down overnight.

———————

So, now that you've conducted your informal power audit, how can you improve your standing?

First of all, a prime way to rectify unfavorable power audit scores is to earn relationships by delivering value to your contacts. Ask yourself: What value can you deliver to them? One way is to develop and continuously improve upon a skill set that leads others to value your contributions. Then proactively use your skills to help others, well beyond the demands of your formal role. You don't want to be the expert whom nobody knows.

Second, let your job help you. Manage your job description so that you can contribute to the workflows of multiple functions inside the organization as well as customers, outside partners, or regulators. Volunteer for cross-functional initiatives. View lateral transfers as a move up. By positioning yourself at the intersection of workflows, you set yourself up to meet, learn from, and deliver value to a variety of diverse groups in the organization.

Third, get to know your stakeholders and collaborators better as individuals. You may be surprised how something that is rather easy for you to do carries significant value for them. Sometimes we freeze because we believe that we have to offer really significant contributions or do massive favors for others. Knowing others well can present us with helpful alternatives. And don't limit yourself to the professional domain.

Outside of work, join social associations as well as professional ones. Shared activities have an underestimated impact on expanding our networks beyond an insular group of immediate coworkers. A friend of mine, an entrepreneur, first learned from his swim club partner about venture capital firms' criteria for selecting and funding life science companies. That partner ended up being his first investor.

Your value should not be defined solely by your ability to perform a formal organizational role. If it is, you are likely in trouble—sooner or later, a cheaper, younger, and smarter competitor will join the company. By creating value for diverse stakeholders and making yourself irreplaceable, you open possibilities for yourself within the organization and beyond. And, by doing so, you add value to your company.

MAXIM SYTCH is an associate professor of management and organizations at the University of Michigan's Stephen M. Ross School of Business. His research focuses on networks of social relationships and the dynamics of influence within and between organizations.

Note

1. R. Gulati and M. Sytch, "Dependence Asymmetry and Joint Dependence in Interorganizational Relationships: Effects of Embeddedness on a Manufacturer's Performance in Procurement Relationships," *Administrative Science Quarterly* 52, no. 1 (2007): 32–69.

Adapted from content posted on hbr.org, February 18, 2019 (product #H04SSW).

4

Four Ways Leaders Fritter Their Power Away

By Ron Carucci

The last thing I want is to be perceived as a power-monger." That was what one high-ranking executive recently told me, and the sentiment among top leaders is common. The executive who embezzles money, curries favor with bribes, or gets caught in sordid affairs makes headlines and is justly derided. But our 10-year longitudinal study revealed that the paralyzed executive is just as dangerous and likely more common.

We conducted more than 2,700 interviews with more than 100 newly transitioned executives, and while the data warned against the allure of using power for self-interest, we saw the greater challenge of power wasn't exploiting it, but abdicating it.

In an effort to create egalitarianism, to make direct reports feel valued and included, and to avoid risks associated with making tough calls, these leaders struggled to exercise power. Of those interviewed, 57% found decisions more complicated and risky than they expected, while 61% said people wanted more of their time than they could give, yet felt guilty saying no because they didn't want to appear inaccessible. Frozen in a need to please or be liked, or in fearful avoidance of catastrophic error, these leaders effectively felt powerless: An astounding 60% of our participants struggled with the fact that people ascribed more power to them than they actually believed they had. Nearly half our respondents indicated believing the power accompanying their jobs was insufficient to execute the objectives with which they were charged.

At some point, probably every executive has lamented, "How is it I have all these resources, and I still can't make anything happen?" We frequently hear this from new executives. And yet such leaders are often guilty of abdicating the power that they do have. Of the many abdications of power we isolated, we identified four particularly recurring and destructive ones:

Paralysis. This is one of the most widespread forms of abdication, and can have crippling effects on an organization. One executive bore the nickname "the waffle" because of his inability to stick to a decision. He was frequently susceptible to the "last one in" phenomenon—the last person in his office swayed him toward their views. Regardless of the data or support he amassed, he never declared a final choice, leaving behind confusion about whether a decision had been made. The team quickly learned this lack of clarity worked to their advantage. Absent any evidence a decision had been finalized, they could interpret meeting outcomes consistent with their views. The risk was minimal because they could always claim it was what they understood "his" decision to be.

Over-inclusion. Including too many people also inhibits leaders' decisiveness. Fearful leaders delude themselves in thinking that the way to disperse risk is by getting lots of people involved. While including those who must live with a decision's consequences is important, over-including people at the expense of action isn't consensus building; it's hiding. Many respondents pointed with exasperation to this challenge among executive ranks. One complained, "The number of people who expect to have a say in decisions is ridiculous. I spend more time building false consensus than increasing the quality of the decision. I thought I would have more authority than I do." Newly appointed executives must have thick skin to withstand the inevitable hostility that comes with unpopular decisions. Avoiding it doesn't disperse risk. It heightens it.

Accommodation. Pandering to the agendas of others at the expense of a greater good also abdicates power. Yes, people feel deep ownership when they have greater control over the direction of their projects, but that kind of empowerment should never come at the expense of a broader organizational agenda. Senior leaders can shape that strategic direction while still leaving plenty of room for others to make choices that translate the vision into action. Doling out yeses to resource requests for individuals' agendas "so they feel ownership" is not empowerment; it's abandonment. Narrowing priorities and focus to strengthen execution is one of an executive's greatest unifying contributions. When the need to say yes overpowers the courage to say no, it fragments organizations and results in the final form of abdication.

Tolerating poor performance. This is the final major pattern we noticed, and unfortunately, in organizations where people are confused by too many competing priorities and grappling with poorly allocated resources, there's a lot of poor performance to observe. Once people conclude the plan can't be taken seriously because the priorities change by the day, their commitment to drive the strategy is diluted, and results falter. To avoid exposing their own hypocrisy, executives who set the mayhem in motion can't call the question on the performance free fall, so must tolerate it. Paradoxically, doling out too many yeses serves to exterminate the very ownership executives sought to strengthen and leads the splintered organization into the performance pitfall these leaders so desperately believed they were avoiding.

Power is an essential asset of executive roles. It is the currency that ensures a leader's legacy. It can right organizational injustices, nurture promising talent, and drive great achievements. It requires careful stewardship, yes, but the way to make good things happen is by embracing your influence, not fearing it.

RON CARUCCI is cofounder and managing partner at Navalent, working with CEOs and executives pursuing transformational change for their organizations, leaders, and industries. He is the bestselling author of eight books, including *Rising to Power*. Follow him on Twitter @RonCarucci.

Adapted from content posted on hbr.org, October 29, 2015
(product #H02FZY).

5

Make Your Team Feel Powerful

By Harrison Monarth

Research has shown that helping others feel more powerful can boost productivity, improve performance, and leave employees feeling more satisfied on the job. A study conducted by Yona Kifer of Tel Aviv University and published in *Psychological Science* found that employees were 26% more satisfied in their roles when they had positions of power.[1]

Feelings of power also translated to more authenticity and feelings of well-being, the researchers found. Power made the subjects feel more "true to themselves," enabling them to engage in actions that authentically reflected values they hold dear.

This subjective sense of authenticity in turn created a higher sense of well-being and happiness.

Yet Gallup research has found that an astonishing 70% of American workers aren't engaged or committed to their employers. Gallup estimates the cost of their apathy at between $450 billion and $550 billion in lost productivity per year.[2] I'm guessing those workers aren't feeling all that powerful.

While it would be great to think we could just repeat a mantra each morning to facilitate these well-being-enhancing feelings of power, another global study conducted by Gallup found that among some 600,000 workers across several industries, leadership support, recognition, constant communication, and trust were essential to creating a thriving environment where frontline employees felt they had the autonomy to make a real difference in the organization.[3] In other words, to instill a sense of power in people for sustained engagement, you need the support of the entire system.

In contrast, overly structured management-driven empowerment programs that are coupled with continuous improvement initiatives don't work, according to researchers from the University of Illinois, as employees tend to feel such programs are often forced upon them without their input on the initiatives' usefulness.[4]

Instead, the researchers found that even the least powerful employees will commit to finding ways to make their organization more efficient if given the autonomy to make decisions and execute the improvement measures they find most useful. Managers are advised to act more as coaches, giving direction and support, and trusting that frontline employees, who are the experts on the ground, know better which improvements ultimately work in the best interest of the organization. The study, by Gopesh Anand, Dilip Chhajed, and Luis Delfin, shows that employees will be most committed to the organization when they feel their day-to-day work environment is autonomous and when they trust leaders to have their back. These feelings of power and the reciprocal trust in leadership in turn lead to proactive behaviors by frontline employees, as they're likely to take charge in continuously seeking ways to improve their daily work practices that lead to organizational efficiency.

While a companywide effort of making employees feel autonomous and trusted yields the greatest benefit in employee commitment, managers can start with their own team members. Encouraging others to share their unvarnished views on important issues, delegating and sharing leadership, assigning managerial tasks, communicating frequently, and allowing for mistakes to serve as learning opportunities can all empower employees and develop them into independent thinkers who aren't afraid to take risks and actively contribute in moving the organization forward.

It isn't necessary, or indeed possible, to elevate every member of staff to a leadership position. But a good manager can offer choices that lead to empowerment, no title required. While we know that people instinctively crave higher status, M. Ena Inesi of London Business School discovered that agency is just as important. She primed study participants to feel either powerful or powerless. They then had to choose whether to shop at a nearby store with fewer options, or a store that was farther away but which offered considerably more options. When participants felt powerless, they craved more choices. The participants who felt powerful, however, were content to have fewer choices. "You can imagine a person at an organization who's in a low-level job," Inesi said at the time.[5] "You can make that seemingly powerless person feel better about their job and their duties by giving them some choice, in the way they do the work or what project they work on."

People need to believe they have a sense of control over their situation, particularly in times of change and uncertainty, or they may adopt what psychologist Martin Seligman at the University of Pennsylvania termed "learned helplessness," where they basically stop trying. In a similar vein, Harvard psychology professor Ellen Langer conducted research on mindfulness and choice and found that giving people choices over their environment actually extended life by years, according to her studies conducted among the elderly in nursing homes.

Tom Peters once said, "Leaders don't create followers; they create more leaders." Giving your employees real autonomy and helping them feel more powerful is not only your best chance to buck the trend of disengagement and apathy, it is at the heart of competitive strategy.

HARRISON MONARTH is an executive coach, and the *New York Times* bestselling author of *The Confident Speaker* and the international bestseller *Executive Presence*. Harrison works with leaders and organizations on positive behavior change, authentic leadership, and effective communication. His latest book is *Breakthrough Communication*. Follow him on Twitter @HarrisonMonarth.

Notes

1. Y. Kifer et al., "The Good Life of the Powerful: The Experience of Power and Authenticity Enhances Subjective Well-Being," *Psychological Science* 24, no. 3 (2013): 280–288.
2. Susan Sorenson and Keri Garman, "How to Tackle U.S. Employees' Stagnating Engagement," Gallup, June 11, 2013, https://news.gallup.com/businessjournal/162953/tackle-employees-stagnating-engagement.aspx.
3. Peter Flade, Jim Harter, and Jim Asplund, "Seven Things Great Employers Do (That Others Don't)," Gallup, April 15, 2014, https://news.gallup.com/businessjournal/168407/seven-things-great-employers-others-don.aspx.
4. Phil Ciciora, "Study: Job Autonomy, Trust in Leadership Keys to Improvement Initiatives," Illinois News Bureau, November 14, 2012, https://news.illinois.edu/view/6367/204937.
5. "It's All About Control," Association for Psychological Science, https://www.psychologicalscience.org/news/releases/its-all-about-control.html.

Adapted from content posted on hbr.org, May 7, 2014
(product #H00SOU).

6

How to Use Your Superpower for Good

By Peter Bregman

folded my bike and carried it into the lobby of the office building in midtown Manhattan. The security guard behind the desk looked up at me, grimaced, then looked down again, and growled something indecipherable.

"Excuse me?" I asked.

He sighed loudly and didn't say anything for a moment. Then, without bothering to look at me, he said, "You're not coming in here with that."

I was already jittery because of a near miss with a taxi on the ride over, and this deflated me even more. It wasn't his message—I've faced many security guards who don't like to permit bicycles into their buildings—it was his cold, disdainful tone.

I tried to stay calm and upbeat. I showed him how small it was when folded. I told him I had a bag I could put it in. He repeated the same line.

Finally, after citing the Bicycle Access to Office Buildings Law, which requires New York City buildings with freight elevators to admit bicycles, he let me in.

When I made it to the freight elevator, I smiled at the operator who was joking with some construction workers. He looked at me, then looked back at his friends and kept talking. I waited uncomfortably for several minutes and then asked him if he would take me to the 19th floor. He said something rude to his friends about tenants, took me up in silence, and left me in a small vestibule with a locked door but no clear way to enter.

He shut his door as I was asking him how to get in. "Try pushing the button," he barked through the closed elevator door. I saw the button he meant and pushed. At this point I was feeling lower than low.

Then, like magic, my morning changed.

"Hi! You must be Peter. Welcome!" Lisa (names have been changed), the receptionist, sang as she opened the door. She smiled, and then looked worried. "Why did you come up in the freight?"

I explained my morning and she frowned empathetically. "I'm so sorry. That's terrible. Here, let me take your bike."

I could have cried from happiness. In one second, Lisa turned my emotions around, from the negative spiral of anger, frustration, and despair to the positive spiral of relief, appreciation, and happiness.

And that's when I realized: We all have superpowers.

We can make people feel good or bad by as simple a thing as a gesture, an expression, a word, or a tone of voice.

But wait. Can I really blame my grumpiness on you? Isn't each person responsible for his or her own mood?

Here's what we know: Like the common cold, emotions are contagious. Caroline Bartel at New York

University and Richard Saavedra at the University of Michigan studied 70 work groups across a variety of industries and found that people who worked together ended up sharing moods, good and bad.[1] Moods converge.

This is particularly important to understand for people in positions of authority because leaders, more than anyone, set and spread the mood. If you've ever worked in an office, you know this from experience. If the boss is in a bad mood, conflicts increase. If she's in a good mood, people lighten up.

Does that mean we aren't responsible if we snap at someone in the hallway? That it's really the fault of the guy who bumped into us on the subway and didn't apologize?

Look at it this way: If you catch a cold from someone, does that mean you can go around sneezing on everyone else? You might be able to blame your mood on someone else, but you're still responsible for what you pass to others.

Nevertheless, it's hard to completely avoid infecting others when you have a cold. Several years ago I was asked to coach Renée, a senior manager in a retail company, who was receiving feedback that she was too harsh with her employees. She often raised her voice, criticized them mercilessly for mistakes, and humiliated them for not knowing things.

When I spoke to others in the office, I found out that the CEO to whom Renée reported treated his direct reports the same way. He was short-tempered, yelled a lot, and demanded perfection from others.

That didn't make it okay for Renée to treat her direct reports that way; it just made it harder for her not to.

Which is a problem for the business because mood affects performance. According to research done by Sigal Barsade at Yale University, positive moods improved cooperation, decreased conflict, and increased performance.

So what's the solution?

Know your emotions, be in touch with your moods, and think of them like the common cold. If you feel infected by bad cheer, take a deep breath, recognize how you're feeling, and choose not to pass it on.

Instead, treat people with the empathy, care, and good humor that will make them feel happier, more connected, and more productive.

Here's the good news: Barsade's research found that positive moods are just as contagious as negative moods.

Is it really a choice though? If you're in a bad mood, can you decide to be happy? I find it hard, inauthentic, even dishonest, to feign happiness.

But I have found a pretty simple solution to turning it all around: kindness.

No matter how bad a mood I'm in, I've found it pretty straightforward to treat others with kindness. And that, invariably, has a positive effect on those around me, which, as we've seen, has a positive effect on me. And, voilà, my mood changes for the better.

When Lisa brought me to my client's office, I told him how my ugly morning had been turned around by his delightful receptionist. He responded with a story of his own. Once, when Lisa was sick and couldn't come to work, a quiet and reserved man named Frank acted as receptionist for the day. Frank was not the sing-song type.

But Frank was used to Lisa's good cheer. Each morning, like everyone else in the office, he received her buoyant emails welcoming people to the office. And, on this particular day, when he was asked to fill in for Lisa, the mere memory of her lighthearted emotions was enough to influence him.

First thing that morning, on his own initiative, Frank wrote an email to the whole office that read: "It's pizzaaaaaaa for lunch! I hope everybody has a happy day!!!!!!"

PETER BREGMAN is the CEO of Bregman Partners, a company that helps successful people become better leaders, create more-effective teams, and inspire their organizations to produce great results. Bestselling author of *18 Minutes*, his most recent book is *Leading with Emotional Courage*. He is also the host of the Bregman Leadership Podcast.

Note

1. C. A. Bartel and R. Saavedra, "The Collective Construction of Work Group Moods," *Administrative Science Quarterly* 45, no. 2 (2000): 197–231.

Adapted from content posted on hbr.org, February 15, 2011 (product #H006U3).

7

Feeling Powerful at Work Makes Us Feel Worse When We Get Home

By Trevor A. Foulk and Klodiana Lanaj

ave you ever interacted with a supervisor who was on a power trip and come away feeling disrespected, hurt, or upset? You're far from alone. Abundant research shows that when people feel powerful, they tend to abuse others, supporting the notion that "power tends to corrupt, and absolute power corrupts absolutely."[1] Many studies show that abused employees suffer distress, perform worse, are less creative, and are more likely to quit their jobs.[2] Abusive power holders, on the other hand, seem immune to their own negative behaviors: Research suggests that they continue about their day as if nothing has happened.

But what if this isn't the entire story? What if power comes at a cost for powerful leaders, too?

We investigate this possibility in a study of 108 managers, whom we surveyed for 10 consecutive workdays.[3] These managers worked in different organizations in industries including health care, engineering, education, and banking. Although the leaders had some degree of structural power, research suggests that one's sense of power fluctuates daily and can be triggered by certain events (for example, reminders of being in charge, attending a meeting for management, or making a hiring or firing decision). To manipulate daily power, we randomly assigned participants to five "power days" and five control days. On power days managers were asked to think and write about a time when they had power over someone else and to complete several short word exercises (such as "Complete the following word fragment with the first real word that comes to mind: p_w_r"). Research shows that both of these techniques activate a sense of power. On control days managers completed similar exercises that did not prime power. For example, they described their commute to work that day and completed neutral sentences ("Complete the following word fragment with the first real word that comes to mind: i_la_d").

Participants interacted with their coworkers, managers, and customers over the course of the study, which gave us ample opportunities to assess the leaders' behaviors multiple times each day, both at work and at home. We emailed survey links to participants three times each day: We manipulated power with the morning survey, which participants completed at approximately 8:28 a.m.; we assessed daily abuse and perceived incivility from others at the end of the workday, at approximately 5:23 p.m.; we measured relaxation and need fulfillment at home at approximately 8:24 p.m.

Consistent with literature supporting the corrupting nature of power, we found that on days when participants felt powerful, they reported having more negative interactions with others. These negative interactions came in two forms: Participants reported engaging in more abusive behaviors toward others (they yelled or swore more, behaved in a rude manner, or made fun of coworkers), but they also perceived more incivility *from* others (they felt that coworkers addressed them more unprofessionally, talked to them in a condescending tone, and paid little attention to their statements and opinions). These findings are well aligned with prior research on the effects of psychological power. Power causes us to view others as psychologically distant, inconsequential, and as a means to our ends, all of which explain why power enhances abuse. At the same time, psychological power makes us feel special and more deserving of others' attention, respect, and favor. These inflated expectations often are not met, which may explain why power holders experience more incivility from others.

Although our findings depict a rather bleak picture for the effects that power has on leaders, there are several silver linings. First, not everyone was affected by psychological power to the same degree. For example, using a personality survey, we measured leaders' trait-level agreeableness and found that agreeable leaders abused others less when experiencing power. Agreeable people care about others' well-being and make it a priority to maintain positive relationships with coworkers. Their innate desire to maintain social harmony may explain why agreeable leaders do not engage in as much abuse when they experience power. The absolute corrupting nature of power, therefore, may not be as absolute as we have come to believe.

Second, power holders were hurt by their own bad behaviors. When we surveyed leaders in the evening, at home, we noticed that powerful leaders who engaged in abuse and who perceived more incivility from others reported feeling less fulfilled by their workday—they felt less competent, less able to relate to others, and less autonomous. Additionally, abusive power holders were less able to kick back and relax at home. These findings suggest a "power hangover"— the effects of power experienced during the workday reduced leaders' well-being in the evening at home. Overall, our power manipulation accounted for 15% of a manager's daily variability in need fulfillment and 2% of their variability in relaxation, suggesting that even a minor manipulation of power in the morning can have noticeable effects on well-being that last until the evening.

Why does power hurt leaders' well-being, even at home? One reason might be that power-induced negative interactions threaten leaders' ability to maintain power over others at work; abused followers may retaliate or may not comply with abusive leaders' demands in the future. It is also possible that powerful leaders who reflect on their negative behaviors at home may feel guilty because they recognize that they violated social norms for proper work conduct.

Although many people would prefer to have more power and influence, our study shows that power not only prompts us to do bad things but can also make us feel worse at home. It is prudent, therefore, to temper our rosy view of power and to start considering its costs as well.

It is important for people in positions of power to become aware of the negative influence that power can have on our interactions with others, as well as on our own well-being. It may help to ask trusted mentors and colleagues to keep us accountable for how we behave at work. From an organizational perspective, it could be helpful to assign agreeable employees to powerful roles, because agreeable leaders are less susceptible to power-induced abuse.

It's often said that "with great power comes great responsibility." As we show in this study, greater power also seems to come with greater suffering.

TREVOR A. FOULK is an assistant professor at Robert H. Smith School of Business at the University of Maryland. KLODIANA LANAJ is the Walter J. Matherly Professor at Warrington College of Business at the University of Florida.

Notes

1. C. Anderson and S. Brion, "Perspectives on Power in Organizations," *Annual Review of Organizational Psychology and Organizational Behavior* 1 (2014): 67–97.
2. E. X. M. Wee et al., "Moving from Abuse to Reconciliation: A Power-Dependence Perspective on When and How a Follower Can Break the Spiral on Abuse," *Academy of Management Journal* 60, no. 6 (2017): 2352–2380; S. Aryee et al., "Abusive Supervision and Contextual Performance: The Mediating Role of Emotional Exhaustion and the Moderating Role of Work Unit Structure," *Management and Organization Review* 4, no. 3 (2008): 393–411; D. Liu, H. Liao, and R. Loi, "The Dark Side of Leadership: A Three-Level Investigation of the Cascading Effect of Abusive Supervision on Employee Creativity," *Academy of Management Journal* 55, no. 5 (2012): 1187–1212; C. I. C. Farh and Z. Chen, "Beyond the Individual Victim: Multilevel Consequences of Abusive Supervision in Teams," *Journal of Applied Psychology* 99, no. 6 (2014): 1074–1095.

3. T. A. Foulk et al., "Heavy Is the Head That Wears the Crown: An Actor-centric Approach to Daily Psychological Power, Abusive Leader Behavior, and Perceived Incivility," *Academy of Management Journal* 61, no. 2 (2018): 661–684.

Adapted from content posted on hbr.org, June 13, 2017 (product #H03PQ2).

8

How to Work with a Manipulative Person

By Liz Kislik

Almost everyone who's ever gone to work has had to deal with an office manipulator. Unfortunately, most employees hesitate to go public with their concerns. And with good reason: Even if they do, typical corporate responses range from wary or dismissive to actually retaliating against the victim, rather than the wrongdoer.

Unfortunately, many workplaces promote manipulators because they appear to be effective at getting things done, despite the significant costs their abuse can inflict on productivity and people over time.[1] Particularly when you can't get the hierarchy or other authorities to intervene on your behalf, it helps to have your own approaches for coping, short of legal action.

Over almost 30 years of consulting, I've encountered countless examples of manipulation, bullying, and inappropriate use of power. Three kinds of responses have proven to be consistently effective for confronting most garden-variety manipulators, even if you have less rank, power, or status. At a minimum, they'll help you assert yourself and regain a sense of control rather than suffering in silence while you figure out your long-term plan.

First, be skeptical about receiving too much special attention

Manipulators don't usually show their true colors at the beginning of a relationship. In fact, they often present themselves as allies or confidantes, because they need to draw you close to size up where your soft spots are and how much they can get from you.

They're skilled at assessing which employees are sophisticated and confident enough to stand on their own and which ones are eager to please or easy to shame.

It's exciting if a powerful colleague or superior seems interested in you, but if you've heard scary things about them, it's sensible to proceed with caution. In particular, note if someone treats you as their favorite—but includes little digs that make you feel bad about yourself, puts you down when talking with others, or pressures you to act against your own interests to stay on their good side.

One C-level executive I worked with was hurt by a colleague who claimed to be her supporter and good friend but constantly pointed out imperfections and mistakes in a way that seemed helpful at first but eventually undercut her confidence. Over time, she began to doubt her own instincts and started acting like the manipulative colleague's sidekick rather than championing her own causes.

By the time the weaker executive recognized what was going on, she had trouble separating herself from her colleague and lost a significant amount of status and clout with her peers. Her credibility and self-image were shaken, and she was not able to regain her footing or influence until she left the company.

Second, be willing to risk small public confrontations

Sometimes the only way to expose a manipulator's maneuverings is by confronting them in the moment. It can be hard to do this if you're the junior party. Even senior people can be stunned into disbelief, or might be unable to think of what to say when someone is subverting normal standards of behavior and fair play, despite the organizational damage they know is being done. So when someone has both the moxie and the wit to intervene, it puts the manipulator on notice that their behavior has been detected, and it shows observers that it's possible to intervene and keep others safe while moving the business forward.

During one client meeting I attended, an executive was making a report by phone while the rest of the leadership team was physically present. At one point, a vice president who had an extremely self-serving and manipulative reputation raised his eyebrows in apparent surprise, shook his head repeatedly, and at the end shrugged, as if to indicate to his peers in the room that he either didn't agree with what his colleague was saying or didn't understand why he was saying it—all without him saying a word.

The vice president on the phone had no idea that his credibility and content were being disparaged. I asked the manipulator directly, "Was there something you wanted to add? You looked like you disagreed strongly with what we just heard. Did you want to counter either the conclusion or any of the specifics, or are you comfortable with the report?"

The vice president in the room denied having any disagreement, but he was clearly uncomfortable at being put on the spot and could no longer lord it over or cast aspersions on his colleague. And his colleague was tipped off to the possibility that he had been undermined.

Third, refuse to keep secrets or to act as interpreter in ways that normalize underhanded behavior

Instead, be direct and straightforward and hold your ground. These schemers may treat you like a trusted insider, feeding you tidbits about other people's inadequacies and failures, as if only you have the perspective and discretion to understand what's important. Don't be taken in by the implied flattery. Ask for details and specifics to flush out their intent: "I'm not sure I understand what you mean. Why are you telling me this? What is it you're asking me to do?"

In another client company, I worked with a leader who was uncomfortable with direct conflict and who tried to get other people—including me—to convey messages that she was afraid to deliver. Rather than letting her hide her criticisms behind others, I would say things like, "You've been clear that you don't like how James handled his team's conflict. I'll be happy to meet with you and James so that you can explain your concern, and then I can work with him on managing his team." Now that she understands her own behavior pattern and has received support to change, she's far less likely to offload uncomfortable situations to others.

If your position is senior to the manipulator's, the most effective thing is to begin a rigorous plan of corrective action promptly, using approaches such as these and providing concrete behavioral feedback until either they drop their inappropriate habits or you remove them. And if you hold less power or influence, these three approaches will help you protect yourself and minimize their negative impact both on you and on the rest of the organization, for as long as you're willing to stay in the game.

LIZ KISLIK helps organizations from the *Fortune* 500 to national nonprofits and family-run businesses solve their thorniest problems. She has taught at NYU and Hofstra University, and spoken at TEDxBaylorSchool.

Note

1. Christine Porath and Christine Pearson, "The Price of Incivility," *Harvard Business Review*, January–February 2013.

Adapted from content posted on hbr.org, November 6, 2017 (product #H03ZQ5).

9

Sex, Power, and the Systems That Enable Men Like Harvey Weinstein

By Dacher Keltner

When I first heard accounts of film producer Harvey Weinstein's predatory behavior, my mind devised punishments fitting for Renaissance Europe or the film *A Clockwork Orange*: Cover his face with a shame mask widely used centuries ago in Germany; shock his frontal lobes so that he'd start empathizing with the women he's preyed on. When we learn of injustice, it's only human to focus on how to eliminate or punish the person responsible.

But my research into the social psychology of power suggests that—without exculpating corrupt individuals—we also need to take a hard look at the social systems in which they commit their abuses.

For 25 years, I and other social scientists have documented how feeling powerful can change the behavior of ordinary citizens—what might be called the banality of the abuses of power. In experiments in which one group of people is randomly assigned to a condition of power, those in the "powerful" group are prone to two shortcomings: They develop empathy deficits and are less able to read others' emotions and take others' perspectives.[1] And they behave in an impulsive fashion—they violate the ethics of the workplace. In one experiment, participants in power took candy from children without blinking an eye.[2]

Our research also shows that these two tendencies manifest in inappropriate sexual behavior in male-dominated contexts, echoing the accounts of the women assaulted by Weinstein. Powerful men, studies show, overestimate the sexual interest of others and erroneously believe that the women around them are more attracted to them than is actually the case.[3] Powerful men also sexualize their work, looking for opportunities for sexual trysts and affairs, and along the way leer inappropriately, stand too close, and touch for too long on a daily basis, thus crossing the lines of decorum—and worse.[4]

These findings from laboratory studies tell us that abuses of power are predictable and recurring. So, too, does a quick reflection on history. While I've been studying power, each year there's been a new example of a powerful man sexually abusing others, and in every imaginable context—religious organizations, the military, Capitol Hill, Wall Street, fraternities, sports, the popular media, tech, labs, and universities.

We should also take a lesson from the now-canonical studies of Stanley Milgram on obedience to authority. Those studies, inspired by Milgram's quest to understand the conditions that gave rise to Nazi Germany, showed that authoritarian contexts can prompt ordinary, well-meaning citizens to give near-lethal shocks to strangers off the street. In a similar fashion, contexts of unchecked power make many of us vulnerable to, and complicit in, the abuse of power. We may not like what's going on, but many of us wouldn't do anything to stop it. This doesn't excuse the rest of us any more than it excuses the powerful for their crimes, but it should prevent us from telling ourselves the comforting lie that we'd behave better than the people in The Weinstein Company who reportedly knew what Weinstein was doing and failed to put a stop to it.

The challenge, then, is to change social systems in which the abuses of power arise and continue unchecked. And on this, the social psychology of power offers some insights.

First, we need to hear tales from those abused by the powerful, as difficult and unsettling as it can be to share these stories. Kudos to the brave people who are calling out the bullying and sexual abuse of Weinstein and others. These tales galvanize social change. For example, when English citizens started to hear the stories about the treatment of slaves on slave ships in the 1700s, the moral calculus of the slave trade started shifting, and antislavery laws followed. Telling such stories also functions as a means by which those with less power construct the reputations of those in power and constrain their impulsive tendencies.

We are also learning of the many benefits of women rising to positions of power, from lower rates of corruption to more-profitable bottom lines.[5] Hollywood is one of the most male-dominated sectors, where only 4% of directors are female; more female directors and producers would change the balance of power in filmmaking. Studies show this kind of systemic change will reduce the likelihood of sexual abuse. For example, ethnic minorities are more likely to be targeted in hate crimes as the numerical advantage enjoyed by whites increases.[6] Greater numerical balance between people of different groups constrains the abuses of power: Those from less powerful groups have more allies, they are more likely to be watchfully present in the contexts in which the powerful abuse power, and they are more likely to feel empowered to speak truth to power.

Finally, we need to take on the myths that sustain the abuses of power. Social scientists have documented how coercive power structures sustain themselves through social myths, which most typically justify the standing and unfettered action of those at the top. We've heard them before: "Women aren't biologically equipped to lead." "African Americans aren't worthy of the vote." "He may scream at people and cross some lines, but he's a genius." And a favorite in Hollywood: "Women are turned on by men with power like Weinstein." Actual scientific studies find something quite different: When women (and men) are placed into positions of less power, their anxiety, self-consciousness, and worry rise dramatically, and their pleasure and delight, including sexual, are turned off.[7]

This moment has the potential to become a tipping point in the fight against systemic sexual assault. For it to live up to the promise of this billing, we have to recognize the banality of Harvey Weinstein, and turn our attention to changing the social context in ways that make the human tendency to abuse power a thing of the past.

DACHER KELTNER is a professor of psychology at the University of California, Berkeley, and the faculty director of the Greater Good Science Center. He is also the author of *The Power Paradox: How We Gain and Lose Influence*.

Notes

1. A. D. Galinsky et al., "Power and Perspectives Not Taken," *Psychological Science* 17, no. 12 (2006): 1068–1074.
2. P. K. Piff et al., "Higher Social Class Predicts Increased Unethical Behavior," *PNAS* 109, no. 11 (2012): 4086–4091.
3. J. W. Kunstman and J. K. Maner, "Sexual Overperception: Power, Mating Motives, and Biases in Social Judgment," *Journal of Personality and Social Psychology* 100, no. 2 (2011): 282–294.

4. D. Keltner, D. H. Gruenfeld, and C. Anderson, "Power, Approach, and Inhibition," *Psychological Review* 110, no. 2 (2003): 265–284.

5. Matthew Swayne, "Women Still Less Likely to Commit Corporate Fraud," *Penn State News*, August 13, 2013, https://news.psu.edu/story/284069/2013/08/13/research/women-still-less-likely-commit-corporate-fraud.

6. D. P. Green, D. Z. Strolovitch, and J. S. Wong, "Defended Neighborhoods, Integration, and Racially Motivated Crime," *American Journal of Sociology* 104, no. 2 (1998): 372–403.

7. C. Langner and D. Keltner, "Social Power and Emotional Experience: Actor and Partner Effects Within Dyadic Interactions," *Journal of Experimental Social Psychology* 44, no. 3 (2008): 848–856.

Adapted from content posted on hbr.org, October 13, 2017 (product #H03YL9).

10

Use Your Everyday Privilege to Help Others

By Dolly Chugh

often forget I am straight. I just don't think about it much. When asked what I did this weekend, or when setting family photos on my desk at work, I have no reason to wonder if what I say will make someone uncomfortable, or lead to a joke at my expense, or cause a coworker to suddenly think I am attracted to them. Our culture is set up for straight people like me to be ourselves with very little thought. But for some gay colleagues, a simple question about the weekend or a decision of how to decorate the workspace carries significant stress—how to act, who to trust, what to share. A recent study found that 46% of LGBTQ employees are closeted in the workplace, for reasons ranging from fear of losing their job to being stereotyped.[1] Unlike me, a non-straight person lacks the privilege of going an entire day without remembering their sexual orientation.

This privilege of being able to forget part of who you are is not unique to straight people. Each of us has some part of our identity that requires little attention to protecting ourselves from danger, discrimination, or doltish humor. For example, in America, if you are white or Christian or able-bodied or straight or English-speaking, these particular identities are easy to forget. It is just an "ordinary" way of being. *Ordinary privilege* is ordinary because it blends in with the norms and people around us and, thus, is easily forgotten.

Just about every person in America has one form or another of this ordinary privilege. This is nothing to be ashamed of, or deny, even though it can often feel like an accusation. Ordinary privilege is actually an opportunity. Research repeatedly confirms that those with ordinary privilege have the power to speak up on behalf of those without it, and have particularly effective influence when they do. For so many of us looking for an opportunity to fight bigotry and bias in the workplace or in our broader culture, we may be missing the opportunity staring back at us in the mirror: using the ordinary nature of who we are as a source of extraordinary power.

For example, psychologists Heather Rasinski and Alexander Czopp looked at how people perceive confrontations about a racially biased comment.[2] They found white observers were more persuaded by white confronters than by black confronters and rated the black confronters as more rude. Whiteness gave the person more legitimacy than blackness when speaking up on racial bias.

Similarly, scholars David Hekman, Stefanie Johnson, Maw-Der Foo, and Wei Yang studied what happens to people who try to advocate for diversity in the workplace.[3] Those who were female and nonwhite were rated worse by their bosses than their nondiversity-advocating female and nonwhite counterparts. White and male executives saw no difference in their ratings, whether or not they advocated for diversity. They found the same pattern with hiring decisions. If a white male manager hired someone who looked like him (or someone who did not), it had no impact either way on his performance ratings. But, if a nonwhite male manager hired someone who looked like him, he took a hit for it. In other words, ordinary privilege—that part of our identities which we think less about—is also the place where we wield outsized influence on behalf of others.

This influence even exists online, as political scientist Kevin Munger showed through a clever experiment on Twitter, focused on people using the n-word in a harassing way toward others online.[4] Using bots with either black or white identities, he tweeted at the harassers, "Hey man, just remember that there are real people who are hurt when you harass them with that kind of language." This mild tweet from a "white" bot who appeared to have 500 followers led to a reduction in the racist online harassment in the seven-day period following the tweet, whereas the same tweet from a "black" bot with the same number of followers had little effect (interestingly, only anonymous n-word users were affected; those using what appeared to be a real name and photo were unaffected by the confrontation). If this is the effect a mild tweet from a stranger can have, we have to wonder about the potential impact of our own ordinary privilege.

To use your ordinary privilege, here are some things you can do:

- First, figure out the parts of your identity that you think about least. Once you've pinpointed them, you've identified your ordinary privilege.

- Second, start learning what people who lack that ordinary privilege encounter as challenges at work, at school, and in their communities.

You can use the internet as a good starting point for first-person accounts.

- Third, look for opportunities to speak and act. Confronting people is only one of many ways we can use our ordinary privilege. Instead, we can ask questions, raise issues, and add perspectives that are not organically emerging in discussions at work. We can introduce data, invite people into conversations, and create buzz around ideas. We can amplify the views of people not being heard at meetings, and bring back conversations when someone is interrupted. We can give credit for people's work and spread the word about their talent. We can notice when bias is playing out around us, and name it when it happens.

- Fourth, be thoughtful about moments when you may inadvertently speak over the group you mean to support. It is not unusual to accidentally center ourselves instead of the people to whom we are trying to be an ally, but it is costly. When it happens, step aside or step back, and learn from those whose lives are directly affected by the issue, rather than presenting yourself as the expert. Take *their* lead while using *your* ordinary privilege.

What we think about least may be the place from which we can do the most good. Each of us has some form of ordinary privilege, and that's good news, because that means almost all of us have more influence than we may realize.

DOLLY CHUGH is an associate professor at New York University Stern School of Business and author of *The Person You Mean to Be: How Good People Fight Bias*.

Notes

1. Human Rights Campaign, "A Workplace Divided: Understanding the Climate for LGBTQ Workers Nationwide," https://www.hrc.org/resources/a-workplace-divided -understanding-the-climate-for-lgbtq-workers-nationwide.

2. H. M. Rasinski and A. M. Czopp, "The Effect of Target Status on Witnesses' Reactions to Confrontations of Bias," *Basic and Applied Social Psychology* 32, no. 1 (2010): 8–16.

3. D. R. Hekman et al., "Does Diversity-Valuing Behavior Result in Diminished Performance Ratings for Non-White and Female Leaders?" *Academy of Management Journal* 60, no. 2 (2016): 771–797.

4. K. Munger, "Tweetment Effects on the Tweeted: Experimentally Reducing Racist Harassment," *Political Behavior* 39, no. 3 (2017): 629–649.

Adapted from content posted on hbr.org, September 18, 2018.

11

To Create Change, Leadership Is More Important Than Authority

By Greg Satell

Aspiring junior executives dream of climbing the ladder to gain more authority. Then they can make things happen and create the change that they believe in. Senior executives, on the other hand, are often frustrated by how little power they actually have.

The problem is that, while authority can compel action, it does little to inspire belief. It's not enough to get people to do what you want, they also have to *want* what you want—or any change is bound to be short-lived.

That's why change management efforts commonly fail. All too often, they are designed to carry out initiatives that come from the top. When you get right down to it, that's really just the same thing as telling people to do what you want, albeit in slightly more artful way. To make change really happen, it doesn't need to be managed, but empowered. That's the difference between authority and leadership.

In the 1850s, Ignaz Semmelweis was the head physician at the obstetric ward of a small hospital in Pest, Hungary. Having done extensive research into how sanitary conditions could limit infections, he instituted a strict regime of hand washing and virtually eliminated the childbed fever that was endemic at the time.

In 2005, John Antioco was the eminently successful CEO of Blockbuster, the 800-pound gorilla of the video rental industry. Yet, despite the firm's dominance, he saw a mortal threat coming in the form of online streaming video and nimble competitors like Netflix. He initiated an aggressive program to cancel late fees and invest in an online platform.

Things ended poorly for both men. Semmelweis was castigated by the medical community and died in an insane asylum, ironically of an infection he contracted while under medical care. Antioco was fired by his company's board, and his successor reversed his reforms. Blockbuster filed for bankruptcy in 2010.

While today the insights of Semmelweis and Antioco seem obvious, they did not at the time. In the former case, it was believed that illness was caused by an imbalance of humors, and in the latter, the threat of online video seemed too distant to justify forsaking short-term profits. Even given their positions of authority, neither was able to overcome the majority view.

We tend to overestimate the power of influence. It always seems that if we had a little bit more authority, had more data to back us up, or were able to make our case more forcefully, we could drive our ideas forward. Yet Semmelweis and Antioco not only had authority, but also had the facts on their side and were willing to risk their careers. They failed nonetheless.

In the 1950s, the eminent psychologist Solomon Asch performed a series of famous experiments that help explain why. He showed the following chart to a group of people and asked which line on the right matched the line on the left.

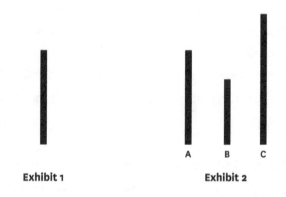

Exhibit 1   Exhibit 2

It seems like a fairly simple task, and it should be, but Asch, renowned for his ingenuity, added a twist. All of the people in the room, except one, were confederates who gave the wrong answer. By the time he got to the last person, who was the true subject, almost everyone who participated conformed to the majority view, even though it was obviously wrong.

While we like to think of ourselves as independent and freethinking, the truth is that we are greatly affected by the views of those around us. If you are in an office where people watch silly cat videos, you'll find yourself doing the same and laughing along. Yet often you'll find that they're not nearly as funny when viewed in different company.

Conformity is never absolute. Even in Asch's experiments, there were some who held out, much like Semmelweis and Antioco. We all have our points of conviction on which we are unlikely to be swayed, other areas in which we need more convincing, and still others that we really don't care enough about to form much of an opinion at all.

That essentially is what the threshold model of collective behavior predicts: Ideas take hold in small local majorities; many stop there and never go any further, but some saturate those local clusters and move on to more reluctant groups through weak ties. Eventually, a cascading effect ensues.

The best-known example of the threshold model at work is the diffusion of innovations model developed by Everett Rogers, in which a small group of innovators gets hold of an idea and indoctrinates a somewhat more reluctant group of early adopters to form local majorities. The reticent denizens of those clusters find themselves outnumbered and begin to conform, just as in Asch's study. Before long, the new converts find themselves passing the idea on to other social groups they belong to. The process continues until the idea has grown far beyond its original niche. Eventually, even the most skeptical laggards join in.

Now we can see the failure of Semmelweis and Antioco—and the folly of so many aspiring executives—for what it is. Rather than seeking to lead a passionate band of willing innovators and build a movement, they leaned on their authority to create wholesale change by forcing the unconvinced against their will. Instead of painstakingly building local majorities, they attempted to compel entire populations.

Control is an illusion and always has been an illusion. It is a Hobbesian paradox that we cannot enforce change unless change has already occurred. Higher status—or even a persuasive presentation full of facts—is of limited utility. The lunatics run the asylum; the best we can do as leaders is empower them to run it right.

And that's why change always requires leadership rather than authority. Respectable people always prefer incumbency to disruption. Only misfits are threatened by the status quo. So if you want to create real change, it is not power and influence that you need, but those who seek to overthrow them.

GREG SATELL is an international keynote speaker, adviser, and bestselling author of *Cascades: How to Create a Movement That Drives Transformational Change.* His previous effort, *Mapping Innovation*, was selected as one of the best business books of 2017. You can learn more about Greg on his website, GregSatell.com. Follow him on Twitter @DigitalTonto.

Adapted from content posted on hbr.org, April 21, 2014
(product #H00RV4).

12

How to Think About Building Your Legacy

By Kimberly Wade-Benzoni

As a leader, leaving a great legacy is arguably the most powerful thing you can do in your career and life because it enables you to have influence well into the future—even after you are out of the picture yourself. It's key to optimizing your impact on your organization and its people. Legacy building in business contexts can take the form of working to ensure the long-term viability of the organization and leaving it stronger, more productive, and more valuable than it was before. Or, in more dramatic scenarios led by entrepreneurs, creating an entirely new organization. Thinking about your legacy is also a great way to ensure that you are taking into account the long-term perspective of your organization and resisting the temptation to make myopic decisions that are overly focused on short-term gain.

So then, how can you keep your legacy in mind as you go about your everyday decisions? Fortunately, more than a decade of research on how people make decisions that involve future generations provides some specific strategies for helping you to keep legacy building in mind and leverage those thoughts to maximize your impact on the world.[1]

Think about what the previous generation did for you

Recall your predecessors and how their actions affected you. What resources did they leave behind for you and your contemporaries? How did they change the organization to provide you with opportunities? How did they shape your organization's culture?

While you can't always reciprocate the deeds of prior generations because they are no longer part of the organization, you can pay it forward by behaving similarly to the next generation of organizational actors. When you take the long-term perspective and think about your organization in terms of multiple generations, reciprocity is not direct, but rather it takes on a more generalized form. Research shows that when we know we have benefited from the legacy of the prior generation, that gets us thinking about the positive legacy we want to leave for future generations and we tend to make better long-term-oriented decisions.[2]

Focus on the burdens rather than the benefits

When making decisions about the future, leaders may be allocating desirable benefits such as profit or natural resources or they may be distributing burdens that they and others wish to avoid, such as debt or hazardous waste. Research shows that whether a resource is a benefit or a burden matters when it comes to allocation decisions and legacies.[3] People are more concerned with avoiding leaving a negative legacy than with creating a positive one. Compared to leaving benefits to future others, leaving burdens leads individuals to feel a greater sense of responsibility toward and affinity with those in the future as well as more moral emotions, such as shame and guilt.

Highlighting the burdensome aspects of long-range decisions can help leaders to recognize the negative legacies that such choices can create. Further, it is strategic for organizations to intentionally connect decisions about benefits and burdens so that managers must make them simultaneously. The increased focus on ethical considerations that accompanies the allocation of burdens can help attenuate the short-sighted and self-interested behavior that often guides the allocation of benefits.

Consider the responsibility that comes with your power

Most research on power suggests that the experience of power tends to make people more self-focused and self-interested. This research primarily considers the effect of power in limited time frames. However, recent research on intergenerational decisions involving longer time frames reveals that power can lead decision makers to be more concerned with the interests of others in the future.[4] When intergenerational decisions are combined with an enhanced experience of power, people feel more social responsibility and are more focused on their legacy, compared to when their power is not prominent. The result is that they are more generous to future generations, which naturally helps them to build a positive legacy. When it is clear that we are in a position to determine outcomes for powerless and voiceless others, our decisions are ethically charged and we consider the moral implications of our actions more seriously.

Remember that you will die someday

One day in 1888, a wealthy and successful man was reading what was supposed to be his brother's obituary in a French newspaper. As he read, he realized that the editor had confused the two brothers and had written an obituary for *him* instead. The headline proclaimed, "The merchant of death is dead," and then described a man who had gained his wealth by helping people to kill one another. Not surprisingly, he was deeply troubled by this glimpse of what his legacy might have been had he actually died on that day. It is believed that this incident was pivotal in motivating him to leave nearly his entire fortune following his actual death eight years later to fund awards each year to give to those whose work most benefited humanity. This is, of course, the true story of Alfred Nobel, the inventor of dynamite and the founder of the Nobel Prize.

Yes, we all die. When we are reminded of our deaths, we remember that we don't want to die—we want to live! But we understand death's inevitability, and that fact creates an existential dilemma in light of our deeply rooted survival instinct. One of the most effective things we can do to buffer our anxiety about death is to attempt to transcend death by finding meaning in our lives. Central to this meaning is that we have impact that persists beyond our physical existence.

Research shows that reminding people of death motivates them to consider their legacy and causes them to act in ways that benefit future generations, thus improving the overall quality of their long-term decisions.[5] People feel better in the face of death if they are a part of something that will live on after them. Having a positive impact on future generations can help fulfill that need. Nobel lives on through his legacy, and receiving a shocking reminder of the inevitability of his death helped him to get there. His story also illustrates how avoiding a negative legacy can be more motivating than simply wanting to build a positive one.

In sum, the epitome of power is to leave a great legacy that lives on after you are gone. This is how you can maximize your influence and ensure you are keeping the long-term success of the organization in mind. And as a bonus you get a little bit of (symbolic) immortality.

Ultimately, your legacy is all you've got. Think about how you want to be remembered by other people and act on those thoughts. Give the grim reaper a run for his money by creating something meaningful that will outlive you.

KIMBERLY WADE-BENZONI is an associate professor of business administration and Center of Leadership and Ethics Scholar at the Fuqua School of Business at Duke University. She is an internationally recognized, leading scholar in the area of intergenerational decisions and has received numerous competitive awards for her research from the International Association for Conflict Management, State Farm Companies Foundation, the U.S. Environmental Protection Agency, and the National Science Foundation.

Notes

1. K. A. Wade-Benzoni and L. P. Tost, "The Egoism and Altruism of Intergenerational Behavior," *Personality and Social Psychology Review* 13, no. 3 (2009): 165–193.
2. K. A. Wade-Benzoni, "A Golden Rule Over Time: Reciprocity in Intergenerational Allocation Decisions," *Academy of Management Journal* 45, no. 5 (2017): 1011–1028.
3. K. A. Wade-Benzoni, H. Sondak, and A. D. Galinsky, "Leaving a Legacy: Intergenerational Allocations of Benefits and Burdens," *Business Ethics Quarterly* 20, no. 1 (2010): 7–34.
4. L. P. Tost, K. A. Wade-Benzoni, and H. H. Johnson, "Noblesse Oblige Emerges (with Time): Power Enhances Intergenerational Beneficence," *Organizational Behavior and Human Decision Processes* 128 (2015): 61–73.
5. K. A. Wade-Benzoni et al., "It's Only a Matter of Time: Death, Legacies, and Intergenerational Decisions," *Psychological Science* 23, no. 7 (2012): 704–709.

Adapted from content posted on hbr.org, December 15, 2016
(product #H03CE6).

13

How Humble Leadership Really Works

By Dan Cable

When you're a leader—no matter how long you've been in your role or how hard the journey was to get there—you are merely overhead unless you're bringing out the best in your employees. Unfortunately, many leaders lose sight of this.

Power, as my colleague Ena Inesi has studied, can cause leaders to become overly obsessed with outcomes and control and, therefore, treat their employees as means to an end. As I've discovered in my own research, this ramps up people's fear—fear of not hitting targets, fear of losing bonuses, fear of failing. As a consequence, people stop feeling positive emotions, and their drive to experiment and learn is stifled.[1]

Take, for example, a UK food-delivery service that I've studied. The engagement of its drivers, who deliver milk and bread to millions of customers each day, was dipping while management was becoming increasingly metric-driven in an effort to reduce costs and improve delivery times. Each week, managers held weekly performance debriefs with drivers and went through a list of problems, complaints, and errors with a clipboard and pen. This was not inspiring on any level, for either party. And, eventually, the drivers, many of whom had worked for the company for decades, became resentful.

This type of top-down leadership is outdated and, more importantly, counterproductive. By focusing too much on control and end goals, and not enough on their people, leaders are making it more difficult to achieve their own desired outcomes.

The key, then, is to help people feel purposeful, motivated, and energized so they can bring their best selves to work.

There are a number of ways to do this, as I outline in my book *Alive at Work*. But one of the best ways is to adopt the humble mind-set of a servant leader. Servant leaders view their key role as serving employees as they explore and grow, providing tangible and emotional support as they do so.

To put it bluntly, servant leaders have the humility, courage, and insight to admit that they can benefit from the expertise of others who have less power than them. They actively seek the ideas and unique contributions of the employees that they serve. This is how servant leaders create a culture of learning and an atmosphere that encourages followers to become the very best they can be.

Humility and servant leadership do not imply that leaders have low self-esteem or take on an attitude of servility. Instead, servant leadership emphasizes that the responsibility of a leader is to increase the ownership, autonomy, and responsibility of followers—to encourage them to think for themselves and try out their own ideas.

Here's how to do it.

Ask how you can help employees do their jobs better—and then listen

It sounds deceptively simple: Rather than telling employees how to do their jobs better, start by asking them how you can help them do their jobs better. But the effects of this approach can be powerful.

Consider the food-delivery business I previously mentioned. Once its traditional model was disrupted by newer delivery companies, the management team decided that things needed to change. The company needed to compete on great customer service, but in order to do so, the team needed the support of their employees who provided the service. And, they needed ideas that could make the company more competitive.

After meeting with consultants at Pricewater-houseCoopers and some training, the management team tried a new format for its weekly performance meetings with the drivers.

The new approach? Instead of nit-picking problems, each manager was trained to simply ask the drivers, "How can I help you deliver excellent service?" As shown in the research of Bradley Owens and David Hekman, leaders need to model these types of servant-minded behaviors to employees so that employees will better serve customers.[2]

There was huge skepticism at the beginning, as you can imagine. Drivers' dislike of the managers was high, and trust was low. But as depot managers kept asking, "How can I help you deliver excellent service?" some drivers started to offer suggestions.

For example, one driver suggested new products like Gogurts and fun string cheese that parents could get delivered early and pop into their kids' lunches before school. Another driver thought of a way to report stock shortages more quickly so that customers were not left without the groceries they ordered.

Small changes created a virtuous cycle. As the drivers got credit for their ideas and saw them put into place, they grew more willing to offer more ideas, which made the depot managers more impressed and more respectful, which increased the delivery people's willingness to give ideas, and so on. And, depot managers learned that some of the so-called "mistakes" that drivers were making were actually innovations they had created to streamline processes and still deliver everything on time. These innovations helped the company deliver better customer service.

What it comes down to is this: Employees who do the actual work of your organization often know better than you how to do a great job. Respecting their ideas, and encouraging them to try new approaches to improve work, motivates employees to bring more of themselves to work.

As one area manager summarized: "We really thought that we knew our delivery people inside out, but we've realized that there was a lot we were missing. Our weekly customer conversation meetings are now more interactive and the conversations are more honest and adult in their approach. It's hard to put into words the changes we are seeing."

Create low-risk spaces for employees to think of new ideas

Sometimes the best way for leaders to serve employees—and their organization—is to create a low-risk space for employees to experiment with their ideas. By doing so, leaders encourage their people to push on the boundaries of what they already know.

For example, when Jungkiu Choi moved from Singapore to China to start his gig as head of consumer banking at Standard Chartered, he learned that one of the cultural expectations of his new job was to visit the branches and put pressure on branch managers to cut costs. Branch staff would spend weeks anxiously preparing for the visit.

Jungkiu changed the nature of these visits. Instead of emphasizing his formal power, he started showing up at branches unannounced, starting his visit by serving breakfast to the branch employees. Then, Jungkiu would hold "huddles" and ask how he could help them improve their branches. Many branch employees were very surprised and initially did not know how to react. But Jungkiu's approach tamped down their anxiety and encouraged ideation and innovative ideas.

Over the course of one year, Jungkiu visited over 80 branches in 25 cities. His consistency and willingness to help convinced employees who were skeptical at first. The huddles exposed many simple "pain points" that he could easily help solve (for example, training for the new bank systems, or making upgrades to computer memory so that the old computers could handle the new software).

Other employee innovation ideas were larger. For example, one of the Shanghai branches was inside a shopping mall. In the huddle, employees asked Jungkiu if they could open and close at the same time as the mall's operating hours (rather than the typical branch operating hours). The team wanted to experiment with working on the weekends. Within a few months, this branch's weekend income generation surpassed its entire weekday income. This was not an idea that Jungkiu had even imagined.

These experiments paid off in terms of company performance. Customer satisfaction increased by 54% during the two-year period of Jungkiu's humble leadership. Complaints from customers were reduced by 29% during the same period. The employee attrition ratio, which had been the highest among all of the foreign banks in China, was reduced to the lowest among all foreign banks in China.

Be humble

Leaders often do not see the true value of their charges, especially lower-level workers. But when leaders are humble, show respect, and ask how they can serve employees as they improve the organization, the outcomes can be outstanding. And perhaps even more important than better company results, servant leaders get to act like better human beings.

DAN CABLE is professor of organizational behavior at London Business School. He is the author of *Alive at Work: The Neuroscience of Helping Your People Love What They Do* (Harvard Business Review Press, 2018).

Notes

1. Dan Cable, "Why People Lose Motivation—and What Managers Can Do to Help," hbr.org, March 12, 2018, https://hbr.org/2018/03/why-people-lose-motivation-and-what-managers-can-do-to-help.
2. B. P. Owens and D. R. Hekman, "Modeling How to Grow: An Inductive Examination of Humble Leader Behaviors, Contingencies, and Outcomes," *Academy of Management Journal* 55, no. 4 (2012): 787–818.

Adapted from content posted on hbr.org, April 23, 2018 (product #H04AJO) and *Alive at Work* (product #10184), by Dan Cable, Harvard Business Review Press, 2018.

Index

How to be human at work.

HBR's Emotional Intelligence Series features smart, essential reading on the human side of professional life from the pages of *Harvard Business Review*. Each book in the series offers uplifting stories, practical advice, and research from leading experts on how to tend to our emotional well-being at work.

Harvard Business Review Emotional Intelligence Series

Available in paperback or ebook format. The specially priced six-volume set includes:

- Mindfulness
- Resilience
- Influence and Persuasion

- Authentic Leadership
- Happiness
- Empathy

HBR.ORG

Buy for your team, clients, or event.
Visit hbr.org/bulksales for quantity discount rates.

Self-Awareness

HBR EMOTIONAL INTELLIGENCE SERIES

HBR Emotional Intelligence Series

How to be human at work

The HBR Emotional Intelligence Series features smart, essential reading on the human side of professional life from the pages of *Harvard Business Review*.

Authentic Leadership	Leadership Presence
Confidence	Mindful Listening
Dealing with Difficult People	Mindfulness
Empathy	Purpose, Meaning, and Passion
Focus	Resilience
Happiness	Self-Awareness
Influence and Persuasion	

Other books on emotional intelligence from *Harvard Business Review*:

HBR Everyday Emotional Intelligence

HBR Guide to Emotional Intelligence

HBR's 10 Must Reads on Emotional Intelligence

Self-Awareness

HBR EMOTIONAL INTELLIGENCE SERIES

Harvard Business Review Press

Boston, Massachusetts

HBR Press Quantity Sales Discounts

Harvard Business Review Press titles are available at significant quantity discounts when purchased in bulk for client gifts, sales promotions, and premiums. Special editions, including books with corporate logos, customized covers, and letters from the company or CEO printed in the front matter, as well as excerpts of existing books, can also be created in large quantities for special needs.

For details and discount information for both print and ebook formats, contact booksales@harvardbusiness.org, tel 800-988-0886, or www.hbr.org/bulksales.

Copyright 2019 Harvard Business School Publishing Corporation
All rights reserved
Printed in the United States of America

10 9

No part of this publication may be reproduced, stored in or introduced into a retrieval system, or transmitted, in any form, or by any means (electronic, mechanical, photocopying, recording, or otherwise), without the prior permission of the publisher. Requests for permission should be directed to permissions@hbsp.harvard.edu, or mailed to Permissions, Harvard Business School Publishing, 60 Harvard Way, Boston, Massachusetts 02163.

The web addresses referenced in this book were live and correct at the time of the book's publication but may be subject to change.

Library of Congress Cataloging-in-Publication Data

Title: Self-awareness.
Other titles: HBR emotional intelligence series.
Description: Boston, Massachusetts : Harvard Business Review Press, [2018]
    Series: HBR emotional intelligence series
Identifiers: LCCN 2018022311 | ISBN 9781633696617 (pbk. : alk. paper)
Subjects: LCSH: Self-consciousness (Awareness) | Employees—Psychology. |
    Management. | Emotional intelligence.
Classification: LCC BF311 .S4345 2018 | DDC 153—dc23
LC record available at https://lccn.loc.gov/2018022311

ISBN: 978-1-63369-661-7
eISBN: 978-1-63369-662-4

The paper used in this publication meets the requirements of the American National Standard for Permanence of Paper for Publications and Documents in Libraries and Archives Z39.48-1992.

Contents

Contents

Contents

Self-Awareness

HBR EMOTIONAL INTELLIGENCE SERIES

1

The First Component of Emotional Intelligence

By Daniel Goleman

elf-awareness is the first component of emotional intelligence—which makes sense when one considers that the Delphic oracle gave the advice to "know thyself" thousands of years ago. Self-awareness means having a deep understanding of one's emotions, strengths, weaknesses, needs, and drives. People with strong self-awareness are neither overly critical nor unrealistically hopeful. Rather, they are honest—with themselves and with others.

People who have a high degree of self-awareness recognize how their feelings affect them, other people, and their job performance. Thus, a self-aware person who knows that tight deadlines bring out the worst in him plans his time carefully and gets his work done well in advance. Another person with high self-awareness will be able to work with a demanding client. She will understand the client's impact on her moods and the deeper reasons for her frustration. "Their trivial demands take us away from the real work that needs to be done," she might explain. And she will go one step further and turn her anger into something constructive.

Self-awareness extends to a person's understanding of his or her values and goals. Someone who is highly self-aware knows where he is headed and why; so, for example, he will be able to be firm in turning down a job offer that is tempting financially but does not fit with his principles or long-term goals. A person who lacks self-awareness is apt to make decisions that bring on inner turmoil by treading on buried values. "The money looked good so I signed on," someone might say two years into a job, "but the work means so little to me that I'm constantly bored." The decisions of self-aware people mesh with their values; consequently, they often find work to be energizing.

How can one recognize self-awareness? First and foremost, it shows itself as candor and an ability to assess oneself realistically. People with high self-awareness are able to speak accurately and openly—although not necessarily effusively or confession-ally—about their emotions and the impact they have on their work. For instance, one manager I know of was skeptical about a new personal-shopper service that her company, a major department-store chain, was about to introduce. Without prompting from her team or her boss, she offered them an explanation: "It's hard for me to get behind the rollout of this ser-vice," she admitted, "because I really wanted to run the project, but I wasn't selected. Bear with me while I deal with that." The manager did indeed examine her feelings; a week later, she was supporting the project fully.

Such self-knowledge often shows itself in the hiring process. Ask a candidate to describe a time he got carried away by his feelings and did something he later regretted. Self-aware candidates will be frank in admitting to failure—and will often tell their tales with a smile. One of the hallmarks of self-awareness is a self-deprecating sense of humor.

Self-awareness can also be identified during performance reviews. Self-aware people know—and are comfortable talking about—their limitations and strengths, and they often demonstrate a thirst for constructive criticism. By contrast, people with low self-awareness interpret the message that they need to improve as a threat or a sign of failure.

Self-aware people can also be recognized by their self-confidence. They have a firm grasp of their capabilities and are less likely to set themselves up to fail by, for example, overstretching on assignments. They know, too, when to ask for help. And the risks they take on the job are calculated. They won't ask for a challenge that they know they can't handle alone. They'll play to their strengths.

Consider the actions of a midlevel employee who was invited to sit in on a strategy meeting with her company's top executives. Although she was the most junior person in the room, she did not sit there quietly, listening in awestruck or fearful silence. She knew she had a head for clear logic and the skill to present ideas persuasively, and she offered cogent suggestions about the company's strategy. At the same time, her self-awareness stopped her from wandering into territory where she knew she was weak.

Despite the value of having self-aware people in the workplace, my research indicates that senior executives don't often give self-awareness the credit it deserves when they look for potential leaders. Many executives mistake candor about feelings for "wimpiness" and fail to give due respect to employees who openly acknowledge their shortcomings. Such people

WHAT MAKES A LEADER?

What distinguishes great leaders from merely good ones? It isn't IQ or technical skills, says Daniel Goleman. It's emotional intelligence: a group of five skills that enable the best leaders to maximize their own *and* their followers' performance. When senior managers at one company had a critical mass of emotional intelligence (EI) capabilities, their divisions outperformed yearly earnings goals by 20%.

The EI skills are:

- *Self-awareness:* knowing one's strengths, weaknesses, drives, values, and impact on others

---

are too readily dismissed as "not tough enough" to lead others.

In fact, the opposite is true. In the first place, people generally admire and respect candor. Furthermore, leaders are constantly required to make judgment

- *Self-regulation:* controlling or redirecting disruptive impulses and moods
- *Motivation:* relishing achievement for its own sake
- *Empathy:* understanding other people's emotional makeup
- *Social skill:* building rapport with others to move them in desired directions

We're each born with certain levels of EI skills. But we can strengthen these abilities through persistence, practice, and feedback from colleagues or coaches.

---

calls that require a candid assessment of capabilities—their own and those of others. Do we have the management expertise to acquire a competitor? Can we launch a new product within six months? People who assess themselves honestly—that is, self-aware people—are well suited to do the same for the organizations they run.

DANIEL GOLEMAN is codirector of the Consortium for Research on Emotional Intelligence in Organizations at Rutgers University, coauthor of *Primal Leadership: Unleashing the Power of Emotional Intelligence*, and author of *The Brain and Emotional Intelligence: New Insights*, *Leadership: Selected Writings* and *A Force for Good: The Dalai Lama's Vision for Our World*. His latest book is *Altered Traits: Science Reveals How Meditation Changes Your Mind, Brain, and Body*.

Excerpted from "What Makes a Leader?" in *Harvard Business Review*, January 2004 (product #RO401H).

2

What Self-Awareness Really Is (and How to Cultivate It)

By Tasha Eurich

elf-awareness seems to have become the latest management buzzword—and for good reason. Research suggests that when we see ourselves clearly, we are more confident and more creative.[1] We make sounder decisions, build stronger relationships, and communicate more effectively.[2] We're less likely to lie, cheat, and steal.[3] We are better workers who get more promotions.[4] And we're more effective leaders with more satisfied employees and more profitable companies.[5]

As an organizational psychologist and executive coach, I've had a ringside seat to the power of leadership self-awareness for nearly 15 years. I've also seen how attainable this skill is. Yet, when I first began to delve into the research on self-awareness, I was surprised by the striking gap between the science and the practice of self-awareness. All things considered, we knew surprisingly little about improving this critical skill.

Four years ago, my team of researchers and I embarked on a large-scale scientific study of self-awareness. In 10 separate investigations with nearly 5,000 participants, we examined what self-awareness really is, why we need it, and how we can increase it.

Our research revealed many surprising roadblocks, myths, and truths about what self-awareness is and what it takes to improve it. We've found that even though most people *believe* they are self-aware, self-awareness is a truly rare quality: We estimate that only 10%–15% of the people we studied actually fit the criteria. Three findings in particular stood out, and are helping us develop practical guidance for how leaders can learn to see themselves more clearly.

ABOUT OUR RESEARCH

The major components of our research included:

- Analyzing the results of nearly 800 existing scientific studies to understand how previous researchers defined self-awareness, unearthing themes and trends, and identifying the limitations of these investigations.

- Surveying thousands of people across countries and industries to explore the relationship between self-awareness and several key attitudes and behaviors, like job satisfaction, empathy, happiness, and stress. We also surveyed those who knew these people well to determine the relationship between self ratings and other ratings of self-awareness.

- Developing and validating a *seven-factor, multi-rater assessment of self-awareness*, because our review of the research didn't identify

(Continued)

ABOUT OUR RESEARCH

any strong, well-validated, comprehensive measures.

- Conducting in-depth interviews with 50 people who had dramatically improved their self-awareness to learn about the key actions that helped them get there, as well as their beliefs and practices. Our interviewees included entrepreneurs, professionals, executives, and even a *Fortune* 100 CEO. (To be included in our study, participants had to clear four hurdles: (1) they had to see themselves as highly self-aware, which we measured using our validated assessment, (2) using that same assessment, someone who knew them well had to agree, (3) they had to believe they'd experienced an upward trend of self-awareness over the course of their life. Each participant was asked to recall their level of self-awareness at different stages of their life up to their current (for example, early adulthood: ages 19–24, adulthood: ages 25–34, midlife: ages 35–49, mature adulthood: ages 50–80), and (4) the person rating them had to agree with the participants' recollections.)

- Surveying hundreds of managers and their employees to learn more about the relationship between leadership self-awareness and employee attitudes like commitment, leadership effectiveness, and job satisfaction.

Coauthors of this work are Haley M. Woznyj, Longwood University; Phoenix Van Wagoner, Leeds School of Business, University of Colorado; Eric D. Heggestad, University of North Carolina, Charlotte; and Apryl Brodersen, Metropolitan State University of Denver. We want to thank Dr. Stefanie Johnson for her contributions to our study as well.

#1: There are two types of self-awareness

For the last 50 years, researchers have used varying definitions of self-awareness. For example, some see it as the ability to monitor our inner world, whereas others label it as a temporary state of self-consciousness.[6] Still others describe it as the difference between how we see ourselves and how others see us.[7]

So before we could focus on how to improve self-awareness, we needed to synthesize these findings and create an overarching definition.

Across the studies we examined, two broad categories of self-awareness kept emerging. The first, which we dubbed *internal self-awareness*, represents how clearly we see our own values, passions, aspirations, fit with our environment, reactions (including thoughts, feelings, behaviors, strengths, and weaknesses), and impact on others. We've found that internal self-awareness is associated with higher job and relationship satisfaction, personal and social control, and happiness; it is negatively related to anxiety, stress, and depression.

The second category, *external self-awareness*, means understanding how other people view us, in terms of those same factors listed above. Our research shows that people who know how others see them are more skilled at showing empathy and taking others' perspectives. For leaders who see themselves as their employees do, their employees tend to have a better relationship with them, feel more satisfied with them, and see them as more effective in general.

It's easy to assume that being high on one type of awareness would mean being high on the other. But our research has found virtually no relationship between them. As a result, we identify four leadership archetypes, each with a different set of opportunities to improve, as seen in figure 1.

FIGURE 1

The four self-awareness archetypes

This 2 × 2 maps internal self-awareness (how well you know yourself) against external self-awareness (how well you understand how others see you).

	Low external self-awareness	High external self-awareness
High internal self-awareness	**INTROSPECTORS** They're clear on who they are but don't challenge their own views or search for blind spots by getting feedback from others. This can harm their relationships and limit their success.	**AWARE** They know who they are, what they want to accomplish, and seek out and value others' opinions. This is where leaders begin to fully realize the true benefits of self-awareness.
Low internal self-awareness	**SEEKERS** They don't yet know who they are, what they stand for, or how their teams see them. As a result, they might feel stuck or frustrated with their performance and relationships.	**PLEASERS** They can be so focused on appearing a certain way to others that they could be overlooking what matters to them. Over time, they tend to make choices that aren't in service of their own success and fulfillment.

When it comes to internal and external self-awareness, it's tempting to value one over the other. But leaders must actively work on both seeing themselves clearly *and* getting feedback to understand how others see them. The highly self-aware people we interviewed were actively focused on balancing the scale.

Take Jeremiah, a marketing manager. Early in his career, he focused primarily on internal self-awareness—for example, deciding to leave his career in accounting to pursue his passion for marketing. But when he had the chance to get candid feedback during a company training, he realized that he wasn't focused enough on how he was showing up. Jeremiah has since placed an equal importance on both types of self-awareness, which he believes has helped him reach a new level of success and fulfillment.

The bottom line is that self-awareness isn't one truth. It's a delicate balance of two distinct, even competing, viewpoints. (If you're interested in learning where you stand in each category, you can take a free shortened version of our multi-rater self-awareness assessment at insight-quiz.com).

#2: Experience and power hinder self-awareness

Contrary to popular belief, studies have shown that people do not always learn from experience, that expertise does not help people root out false information, and that seeing ourselves as highly experienced can keep us from doing our homework, seeking disconfirming evidence, and questioning our assumptions.[8]

And just as experience can lead to a false sense of confidence about our performance, it can also make us overconfident about our level of self-knowledge. For example, one study found that more experienced managers were less accurate in assessing their leadership effectiveness compared with less experienced managers.[9]

Similarly, the more power a leader holds, the more likely they are to overestimate their skills and abilities. One study of more than 3,600 leaders across a variety of roles and industries found that, relative to lower-level leaders, higher-level leaders more significantly overvalued their skills (compared with others' perceptions).[10] In fact, this pattern existed for 19 out of the 20 competencies the researchers measured, including emotional self-awareness, accurate self-assessment, empathy, trustworthiness, and leadership performance.

Researchers have proposed two primary explanations for this phenomenon.[11] First, by virtue of their level, senior leaders simply have fewer people above them who can provide candid feedback. Second, the more power a leader wields, the less comfortable people will be to give them constructive feedback, for fear it will hurt their careers. Business professor James O'Toole has added that, as one's power grows, one's willingness to listen shrinks, either because they think they know more than their employees or because seeking feedback will come at a cost.[12]

But this doesn't have to be the case. One analysis showed that the most successful leaders, as rated by 360-degree reviews of leadership effectiveness, counteract this tendency by seeking frequent critical feedback (from bosses, peers, employees, their board, and so on).[13] They become more self-aware in the process and come to be seen as more effective by others.[14]

Likewise, in our interviews, we found that people who improved their external self-awareness did so by seeking out feedback from *loving critics*—that is, people who have their best interests in mind *and* are willing to tell them the truth. To ensure they don't overreact or overcorrect based on one person's opinion, they also gut-check difficult or surprising feedback with others.

#3: Introspection doesn't always improve self-awareness

It is also widely assumed that introspection—examining the causes of our own thoughts, feelings, and behaviors—improves self-awareness. After all, what better way to know ourselves than by reflecting on why we are the way we are?

Yet one of the most surprising findings of our research is that people who introspect are *less* self-aware and report worse job satisfaction and well-being. Other research has shown similar patterns.[15]

The problem with introspection isn't that it is categorically ineffective—it's that most people are doing it incorrectly. To understand this, let's look at arguably the most common introspective question: "Why?" We ask this when trying to understand our emotions (*Why do I like employee A so much more than employee B?*), or our behavior (*Why did I fly off the handle with that employee?*), or our attitudes (*Why am I so against this deal?*).

As it turns out, "why" is a surprisingly ineffective self-awareness question. Research has shown that we simply do not have access to many of the unconscious thoughts, feelings, and motives we're searching for.[16] And because so much is trapped outside of our conscious awareness, we tend to invent answers that *feel* true but are often wrong.[17] For example, after an uncharacteristic outburst at an employee, a new manager may jump to the conclusion that it happened because she isn't cut out for management, when the real reason was a bad case of low blood sugar.

Consequently, the problem with asking *why* isn't just how wrong we are, but how confident we are that we are right.[18] The human mind rarely operates in a rational fashion, and our judgments are seldom free from bias. We tend to pounce on whatever insights we find without questioning their validity or value, we ignore contradictory evidence, and we force our thoughts to conform to our initial explanations.

Another negative consequence of asking *why*—especially when trying to explain an undesired outcome—is that it invites unproductive negative thoughts.[19] In our research, we've found that people who are very introspective are also more likely to get caught in ruminative patterns. For example, if an employee who receives a bad performance review asks *Why did I get such a bad rating?*, they're likely to land on an explanation focused on their fears, shortcomings, or insecurities, rather than a rational assessment of their strengths and weaknesses. (For this reason, frequent self-analyzers are more depressed and anxious and experience poorer well-being.[20])

So if *why* isn't the right introspective question, is there a better one? My research team scoured hundreds of pages of interview transcripts with highly self-aware people to see if they approached introspection differently. Indeed, there was a clear pattern: Although the word "why" appeared fewer than 150 times, the word "what" appeared more than 1,000 times.

Therefore, to increase productive self-insight and decrease unproductive rumination, we should ask *what*, not *why*.[21] "What" questions help us stay objective, future-focused, and empowered to act on our new insights.

For example, consider Jose, an entertainment industry veteran we interviewed, who hated his job. Where many would have gotten stuck thinking "Why do I feel so terrible?" he asked, "What are the situations that make me feel terrible, and what do they have in common?" He realized that he'd never be happy in that career, and it gave him the courage to pursue a new and far more fulfilling one in wealth management.

Similarly, Robin, a customer service leader who was new to her job, needed to understand a piece of negative feedback she'd gotten from an employee. Instead of asking "Why did you say this about me?" Robin inquired, "What are the steps I need to take in the future to do a better job?" This helped them move to solutions rather than focusing on the unproductive patterns of the past.

A final case is Paul, who told us about learning that the business he'd recently purchased was no longer profitable. At first, all he could ask himself was "Why wasn't I able to turn things around?" But he quickly realized that he didn't have the time or energy to beat himself up—he had to figure out what to do next. He started asking, "What do I need to do to move forward in a way that minimizes the impact to our customers and employees?" He created a plan and was able to find creative ways to do as much good for others as possible while winding down the business. When all that was over, he challenged himself to articulate what he learned from the experience— his answer both helped him avoid similar mistakes in the future and helped others learn from them, too.[22]

These qualitative findings have been bolstered by others' quantitative research. In one study, psychologists J. Gregory Hixon and William Swann gave a group of undergraduates negative feedback on a test of their "sociability, likability, and interestingness."[23] Some were given time to think about *why* they were the kind of person they were, while others were asked to think about *what* kind of person they were. When the researchers had them evaluate the accuracy of the feedback, the "why" students spent their energy rationalizing and denying what they'd learned, and the "what" students were more open to this new information and how they might learn from it. Hixon and Swann's rather bold conclusion was that "thinking about why one is the way one is may be no better than not thinking about one's self at all."

All of this brings us to conclude: Leaders who focus on building both internal and external self-awareness, who seek honest feedback from loving critics, and who ask *what* instead of *why* can learn to see themselves more clearly—and reap the many rewards that increased self-knowledge delivers. And no matter how much progress we make, there's always more to learn. That's one of the things that makes the journey to self-awareness so exciting.

TASHA EURICH, PhD, is an organizational psychologist, researcher, and *New York Times*–bestselling author. She is the principal of The Eurich Group, a boutique executive development firm that helps companies—from startups to the *Fortune* 100—succeed by improving the effectiveness of their leaders and teams. Her newest book, *Insight*, delves into the connection between self-awareness and success in the workplace.

Notes

1. Paul J. Silvia and Maureen O'Brien, "Self-Awareness and Constructive Functioning: Revisiting 'the Human Dilemma,'" *Journal of Social and Clinical Psychology* 23, no. 4 (August 2004): 475–489.
2. D. Scott Ridley, Paul A. Schutz, Robert S. Glanz, and Claire E. Weinstein, "Self-Regulated Learning: The Interactive Influence of Metacognitive Awareness and Goal-Setting," *Journal of Experimental Education* 60, no. 4 (Summer 1992): 293–306; Clive Fletcher and Caroline Bailey, "Assessing Self-Awareness: Some Issues and Methods," *Journal of Managerial Psychology* 18, no. 5 (2003): 395–404; Anna Sutton, Helen M. Williams, and Christopher W. Allinson, "A Longitudinal, Mixed Method

Evaluation of Self-Awareness Training in the Workplace,"
European Journal of Training and Development 39, no. 7
(2015): 610–627.

3. Silvia and O'Brien, "Self-Awareness and Constructive
   Functioning."

4. Allan H. Church, "Managerial Self-Awareness in High-
   Performing Individuals in Organizations," *Journal of
   Applied Psychology* 82, no. 2 (April 1997): 281–292;
   Bernard M. Bass and Francis J. Yammarino, "Congruence
   of Self and Others' Leadership Ratings of Naval Officers
   for Understanding Successful Performance," *Applied Psychology* 40, no. 4 (October 1991): 437–454.

5. Bass and Yammarino, "Congruence of Self and Others'
   Leadership Ratings of Naval Officers for Understanding
   Successful Performance"; Kenneth N. Wexley, Ralph A.
   Alexander, James Greenawalt, and Michael A. Couch, "At-
   titudinal Congruence and Similarity as Related to Inter-
   personal Evaluations in Manager-Subordinate Dyads,"
   Academy of Management Journal 23, no. 2 (June 1980):
   320–330; Atuma Okpara and Agwu M. Edwin, "Self-
   Awareness and Organizational Performance in the Nige-
   rian Banking Sector," *European Journal of Research and
   Reflection in Management Sciences* 3, no. 1 (2015): 53–70.

6. Daniel Goleman, blog, November 15, 2012, http://www
   .danielgoleman.info/on-self-awareness/; Shelley Duval
   and Robert A. Wicklund, "Effects of Objective Self-
   Awareness on Attribution of Causality," *Journal of Experimental Social Psychology* 9, no. 1 (January 1973): 17–31.

7. Erich C. Dierdorff and Robert S. Rubin, "Research: We're Not Very Self-Aware, Especially at Work," *Harvard Business Review*, March 12, 2015.

8. Berndt Brehmer, "In One Word: Not from Experience," *Acta Psychologica* 45, nos. 1–3 (August 1980): 223–241; Stav Atir, Emily Rosenzweig, and David Dunning, "When Knowledge Knows No Bounds: Self-Perceived Expertise Predicts Claims of Impossible Knowledge," *Psychological Science* 26, no. 8 (July 2015); Philip E. Tetlock, *Expert Political Judgment: How Good Is It? How Can We Know?* rev. ed. (Princeton, NJ: Princeton University Press, 2017).

9. Cheri Ostroff, Leanne E. Atwater, and Barbara J. Feinberg, "Understanding Self-Other Agreement: A Look at Rater and Ratee Characteristics, Context, and Outcomes," *Personnel Psychology* 57, no. 2 (June 2004): 333–375.

10. Fabio Sala, "Executive Blind Spots: Discrepancies Between Self- and Other-Ratings," *Consulting Psychology Journal: Practices and Research* 55, no. 4 (September 2003): 222–229.

11. Ibid.

12. Jennifer Pittman, "Speaking Truth to Power: The Role of the Executive," Markkula Center for Applied Ethics, February 1, 2007, https://www.scu.edu/ethics/focus-areas/business-ethics/resources/speaking-truth-to-power-the-role-of-the-executive/.

13. Joseph Folkman, "Top-Ranked Leaders Know This Secret: Ask for Feedback," *Forbes*, January 8, 2015.

14. Susan J. Ashford and Anne S. Tsui, "Self-Regulation for Managerial Effectiveness: The Role of Active Feedback Seeking," *Academy of Management Journal* 34, no. 2 (June 1991): 251–280.

15. Anthony M. Grant, John Franklin, and Peter Langford, "The Self-Reflection and Insight Scale: A New Measure of Private Self-Consciousness," *Social Behavior and Personality* 30, no. 8 (December 2002): 821–836.

16. Richard E. Nisbett and Timothy DeCamp Wilson, "Telling More Than We Can Know: Verbal Reports on Mental Processes," *Psychological Review* 84, no. 3 (May 1977): 231–259.

17. Ibid.

18. Timothy D. Wilson, Dana S. Dunn, Delores Kraft, and Douglas J. Lisle, "Introspection, Attitude Change, and Attitude-Behavior Consistency: The Disruptive Effects of Explaining Why We Feel the Way We Do," *Advances in Experimental Social Psychology* 22 (1989): 287–343.

19. Ethan Kross, Ozlem Ayduk, and Walter Mischel, "When Asking 'Why' Does Not Hurt. Distinguishing Rumination from Reflective Processing of Negative Emotions," *Psychological Science* 16, no. 9 (September 2005): 709–715.

20. Susan Nolen-Hoeksema, Angela McBride, and Judith Larson, "Rumination and Psychological Distress Among Bereaved Partners," *Journal of Personality and Social Psychology* 72, no. 4 (April 1997): 855–862; John B. Nezlek, "Day-to-Day Relationships Between Self-Awareness, Daily Events, and Anxiety," *Journal of Personality* 70,

no. 2 (November 2002): 249–276; Grant et al., "The Self-Reflection and Insight Scale."

21. Tasha Eurich, "Increase Your Self-Awareness with One Simple Fix," TEDxMileHigh video, 17:17, December 19, 2017, https://www.youtube.com/watch?v=tGdsOXZpyWE.

22. Paul Brothe, "Eight Lessons I Learned from Buying a Small Business," LinkedIn, July 13, 2015.

23. J. Gregory Hixon and William B. Swann Jr., "When Does Introspection Bear Fruit? Self-Reflection, Self-Insight, and Interpersonal Choices," *Journal of Personality and Social Psychology* 64, no. 1 (January 1993): 3–43.

Reprinted from hbr.org, originally published January 4, 2018 (product #H042DK).

3

Successful Leaders Know What Made Them Who They Are

By Bernie Swain

Can you identify the one person, event, or influence that made you who you are as a leader and a person? Over the past 10 years, I've put that question to 100 of the eminent people I represented as chairman of the Washington Speakers Bureau: Madeleine Albright, Tom Brokaw, Colin Powell, Terry Bradshaw, Condoleezza Rice, and many others. I was curious to find out what they felt were the turning points in their lives—the defining moments and influences from which they draw motivation and inspiration.

Identifying the foundational moments of our success allows us to maximize our potential, uncover our own passions, and become better leaders. In my case, the defining moment in my life was the realization that I was never going to enjoy working for other people—a recognition that paradoxically came to me right at the moment when I was on the verge of being offered my dream job (which I eventually turned down to become an entrepreneur). The realization helped fuel me even during periods of uncertainty by reinforcing my will to succeed and comforting me that I was on the right trajectory. Everyone has such an event and can usually identify it after some reflection. Among my interviewees, turning points fell into three broad categories.

People

Forty-five of those interviewees identified a person as the single most enduring influence on their lives. For Madeleine Albright, the former U.S. secretary of state, it was her father, a serious man with far-ranging intellect whose career as a Czechoslovak diplomat was short-circuited twice: by the German occupation in World War II and by the Communist takeover after the war. After the family moved to the United States, he became a professor living in cramped faculty housing—quite a step down from an ambassador's residence—but worked at his job cheerfully and diligently. She says that being secretary of state was challenging, but she never had any trouble staying focused: "I just had to picture my father in his flooded basement study, working away with his feet up on bricks."

For Tom Brokaw, who had been student body president and a three-sport athlete in high school, but who then dropped out of college twice, it was a strict and caring political science professor. For legendary basketball coach Mike Krzyzewski, it was his mother, who had only an eighth-grade education. Her homespun advice to always "get on the right bus . . . filled with good people" became the moral cornerstone of "Coach K's" life and career.

Events

Forty of my one hundred interviewees identified an event—a failure, an injury, a death, or the like—as the turning point in their lives.

What defined former secretary of labor Robert Reich, at first, was his height. "I am 4'11" and have always been short," said Reich. Starting in kindergarten, he was teased and bullied, and he learned to find someone bigger who could act as a protector. One of those who watched out for him was an older kid named Michael Schwerner. Years later, in 1964, Mickey Schwerner and two other young civil rights workers were brutally murdered in Neshoba County, Mississippi, by the Ku Klux Klan—a crime that shocked the country and horrified Reich, who had just graduated from high school. The event galvanized Reich, setting him on a lifelong course of public service and commitment to social justice. "Mickey protected me," said Reich, now a professor at UC Berkeley. "I, in turn, feel a responsibility to protect others."

For Tony Blair, a rebellious troublemaker in school, it was his father's stroke, cutting short the elder Blair's promising political career and evoking in Tony the discipline and diligence that would eventually make him prime minister of Great Britain.

Debbi Fields, founder of Mrs. Fields Cookies, found the drive and passion to succeed as her unpretentious self when a boorish social superior threw a dictionary in her lap because she had misused a word in conversation.

Environments

Fifteen of my interviewees considered environments—such as a place, a time, or an enveloping experience—as the most powerful influence in their lives. For Condoleezza Rice, it was the love of reading and education that was passed down through her family, beginning with her paternal great-grandmother, Julia Head, who learned to read as a slave on an Alabama cotton plantation. Rice's grandfather, born in 1892 to Julia and her sharecropper husband, was determined to go to college and went on to become a Presbyterian minister. One day he brought home nine leather-bound, gold-embossed books—the works of Shakespeare, Hugo, and others—which cost $90, a huge sum at the time.

"My grandfather believed in having books in the home," Rice told me, "and, more important, he believed in having his children read them." Rice's father earned two master's degrees, and her aunt Theresa got a PhD in Victorian literature. In 1981, when Rice received her PhD in political science, her father gave her the five remaining books from her grandfather's set. They sit now on her mantelpiece.

For Chris Matthews, it was his stint in the Peace Corps in Swaziland that took him off his path to academia and sent him toward a life of engagement in politics and journalism.

Colin Powell's enduring influence comes from a neighborhood in the South Bronx called Banana Kelley, where he grew up among caring family members and a multilingual, nurturing community of hardworking people. "I owe whatever success I've had to . . . Banana Kelley," he says.

Successful leaders are self-aware. That's the overriding lesson I've learned from working and talking with some the world's most accomplished people over the past 36 years. For some, like Powell or Albright, identifying and owning the turning points in their lives comes easily. But for many people, it can be difficult. It took three increasingly painful conversations for Terry Bradshaw to fully get at his: As the number-one pick in the NFL draft by the Pittsburgh Steelers, he paid little heed to his coaches, goofed off in practice, and exhibited a bravado that masked his deep insecurity as a southern country boy in a big northern city. But as the losses piled up on the field and the boos rained down from the stands, he could no longer sustain his devil-may-care façade. One night he broke down crying in his apartment, prayed, and heard a gentle voice telling him to get real. "I went to practice the next day," he said to me, "and I set out cultivating a new attitude." He went on to become one of only three quarterbacks to have won four Super Bowls.

Highly accomplished people have an inner voice and pay attention to it. They understand the defining moments of their lives and thereby better understand their own strengths, biases, and weaknesses as leaders. And that understanding provides them with a deep well of energy and passion that they draw on throughout their lives. We may not all have careers that match the 100 people I interviewed, but we can all share their ability to grasp—and harness—the turning points of our lives and careers.

BERNIE SWAIN is the founder and chairman of Washington Speakers Bureau and the author of the book *What Made Me Who I Am*. Follow him on Twitter @swain_bernie.

Reprinted from hbr.org, originally published September 5, 2016 (product #H033OD).

4

Two Ways to Clarify Your Professional Passions

By Robert Steven Kaplan

ave you ever noticed that highly effective people almost always say they love what they
do? If you ask them about their good career
fortune, they're likely to advise that you have to love
what you do in order to perform at a high level of effectiveness. They will talk about the critical importance of having a long-term perspective and real passion in pursuing a career. Numerous studies of highly
effective people point to a strong correlation between
believing in the mission, enjoying the job, and performing at a high level.

So why is it that people are often skeptical of the
notion that passion and career should be integrally

linked? Why do people often struggle to discern their passions and then connect those passions to a viable career path? When people hear the testimony of a seemingly happy and fulfilled person, they often say, "That's easy for them to say *now*. They've made it. It's not so easy to follow this advice when you're sitting where I'm sitting!" What they don't fully realize is that connecting their passions to their work was a big part of how these people eventually made it.

Passion is about excitement. It has more to do with your heart than your head. It's critical because reaching your full potential requires a combination of your heart *and* your head. In my experience, your intellectual capability and skills will take you only so far.

Regardless of your talent, you will have rough days, months, and years. You may get stuck with a lousy boss. You may get discouraged and feel like giving up. What pulls you through these difficult periods? The answer is *your passion*: It is the essential rocket fuel that helps you overcome difficulties and work through dark times. Passion emanates from a belief in a cause or the enjoyment you feel from performing certain tasks. It helps you hang in there so that you can improve your skills, overcome adversity, and find meaning in your work and in your life.

In talking to more experienced people, I often have to get them to mentally set aside their financial obligations, their role in the community, and the expectations of friends, family, and loved ones. It can be particularly difficult for midcareer professionals to understand their passions because, in many cases, the breakage cost of changing jobs or careers feels so huge to them that it's not even worth considering. As a result, they try not to think too deeply about whether they like what they're doing.

The problem for many midcareer people is that they're experiencing a plateau that is beginning to alarm them and diminish their career prospects. This plateau is often a by-product of lack of passion for the job. It may be that the nature of the job has changed or the world has changed, and the mission and tasks of their career no longer arouse their passions. In other cases, nothing has changed except the people themselves. They simply want more meaning from their lives and professional careers.

Of course, these questions are never fully resolved. Why? It's because there are many variables in play, and we can't control all of them. The challenge is to be self-aware.

That's difficult, because most of our professional days are chaotic. In fact, life is chaotic, and, sadly, we can't usually predict the future. It feels as if there's no time to reflect. So how are you supposed to get perspective on these questions?

I suggest that you try several exercises. These exercises may help you increase your self-awareness and develop your abilities to better understand your passions. They also encourage you to pay closer attention to and be more aware of the tasks and subjects you truly find interesting and enjoyable.

Your best self

This exercise involves thinking back to a time when you were at your best. You were great! You did a superb job, and you really enjoyed it. You loved what you were doing while you were doing it, and you received substantial positive reinforcement.

Remember the situation. Write down the details. What were you doing? What tasks were you performing? What were the key elements of the environment, the mission, and the nature of the impact you were making? Did you have a boss, or were you self-directed? Sketch out the complete picture. What did you love about it? What were the factors that made it enjoyable and helped you shine?

If you're like most people, it may take you some time to recall such a situation. It's not that you haven't had these experiences; rather, you have gotten out of the habit of thinking about a time when you were at your best and enjoying what you were doing.

After sketching out the situation, think about what you can learn from this recollection. What are your insights regarding the nature of your enjoyment, the critical environmental factors, the types of tasks you took pleasure in performing, and so on? What does this recollection tell you about what you might enjoy now? Write down your thoughts.

Mental models

Another approach to helping you think about your desires and passions is to use mental models. That is, assume xyz, and then tell me what you would do—and why. Here are examples of these models:

- If you had one year left to live, how would you spend it? What does that tell you about what you enjoy and what you have a passion for?

- If you had enough money to do whatever you wanted, what job or career would you pursue?

- If you knew you were going to be highly successful in your career, what job would you pursue today?

- What would you like to tell your children and grandchildren about what you accomplished in your career? How will you explain to them what career you chose?

- If you were a third party giving advice to yourself, what would you suggest regarding a career choice?

Although these mental models may seem a bit silly or whimsical, I urge you to take the time to try them, consider your answers, and write them down. You're likely to be surprised by what you learn. Each of them attempts to help you let go of fears, insecurities, and worries about the opinions of others—and focus on what you truly believe and desire.

Passion is critical in reaching your potential. Getting in touch with your passions may require you to give your fears and insecurities a rest and focus more on your hopes and dreams. You don't need to immediately decide what action to take or assess whether your dream is realistic. There is an element of brainstorming in this effort: You don't want to kill ideas before you've considered them. Again, allow yourself to focus on the *what* before you worry about the *how*. These exercises are about self-awareness, first and foremost. It is uncanny how much more likely you are to recognize opportunities if you're aware of what you're looking for.

ROBERT STEVEN KAPLAN is president and chief executive of the Federal Reserve Bank of Dallas. Previously, he was the senior associate dean for external relations and Martin Marshall Professor of Management Practice in Business Administration at Harvard Business School. He is the author of three books: *What You Really Need to Lead*, *What You're Really Meant to Do*, and *What to Ask the Person in the Mirror*.

Adapted from *What You're Really Meant to Do: A Road Map for Reaching Your Unique Potential* (product #11370), by Robert Steven Kaplan, Harvard Business Review Press, 2013.

5

Emotional Agility

By Susan David and Christina Congleton

Sixteen thousand—that's how many words we speak, on average, each day. So imagine how many unspoken ones course through our minds. Most of them are not facts but evaluations and judgments entwined with emotions—some positive and helpful (*I've worked hard and I can ace this presentation; This issue is worth speaking up about; The new VP seems approachable*), others negative and less so (*He's purposely ignoring me; I'm going to make a fool of myself; I'm a fake*).

The prevailing wisdom says that difficult thoughts and feelings have no place at the office: Executives, and particularly leaders, should be either stoic or cheerful; they must project confidence and damp down any negativity bubbling up inside them. But that goes against basic biology. All healthy human beings have an inner stream of thoughts and feelings that include criticism, doubt, and fear. That's just our minds doing the job they were designed to do: trying to anticipate and solve problems and avoid potential pitfalls.

In our people-strategy consulting practice advising companies around the world, we see leaders stumble not because they *have* undesirable thoughts and feelings—that's inevitable—but because they get *hooked* by them, like fish caught on a line. This happens in one of two ways. They buy into the thoughts, treating them like facts (*It was the same in my last job . . . I've been a failure my whole career*), and avoid situations that evoke them (*I'm not going to take on that new challenge*). Or, usually at the behest of their supporters, they challenge the existence of the thoughts and try to rationalize them away (*I shouldn't have thoughts like this ... I know I'm not a total fail-ure*), and perhaps force themselves into similar situations, even when those go against their core values and goals (*Take on that new assignment—you've got to get over this*). In either case, they are paying too much attention to their internal chatter and allowing it to sap important cognitive resources that could be put to better use.

This is a common problem, often perpetuated by popular self-management strategies. We regularly see executives with recurring emotional challenges at work—anxiety about priorities, jealousy of others' success, fear of rejection, distress over perceived slights—who have devised techniques to "fix" them: positive affirmations, prioritized to-do lists, immersion in certain tasks. But when we ask how long the challenges have persisted, the answer might be 10 years, 20 years, or since childhood.

Clearly, those techniques don't work—in fact, ample research shows that attempting to minimize or ignore thoughts and emotions serves only to amplify them. In a famous study led by the late Daniel Wegner, a Harvard professor, participants who were told to avoid thinking about white bears had trouble doing so; later, when the ban was lifted, they thought about white bears much more than the control group did. Anyone who has dreamed of chocolate cake and french fries while following a strict diet understands this phenomenon.

Effective leaders don't buy into *or* try to suppress their inner experiences. Instead they approach them in a mindful, values-driven, and productive way—developing what we call *emotional agility.* In our complex, fast-changing knowledge economy, this ability to manage one's thoughts and feelings is essential to business success. Numerous studies, from the University of London professor Frank Bond and others, show that emotional agility can help people alleviate stress, reduce errors, become more innovative, and improve job performance.

We've worked with leaders in various industries to build this critical skill, and here we offer four practices—adapted from Acceptance and Commitment Therapy (ACT), originally developed by the University of Nevada psychologist Steven C. Hayes—that are designed to help you do the same: Recognize your patterns; label your thoughts and emotions; accept them; and act on your values.

Fish on a line

Let's start with two case studies. Cynthia is a senior corporate lawyer with two young children. She used to feel intense guilt about missed opportunities—both at the office, where her peers worked 80 hours a week while she worked 50, and at home, where she was often too distracted or tired to fully engage with her husband and children. One nagging voice in her head told her she'd have to be a better employee or risk career failure; another told her to be a better mother or risk neglecting her family. Cynthia wished that at least one of the voices would shut up. But neither would, and in response she failed to put up her hand for exciting new prospects at the office and compulsively checked messages on her phone during family dinners.

Jeffrey, a rising-star executive at a leading consumer goods company, had a different problem. Intelligent, talented, and ambitious, he was often angry—at bosses who disregarded his views, subordinates who didn't follow orders, or colleagues who didn't pull their weight. He had lost his temper several times at work and been warned to get it under control. But when he tried, he felt that he was shutting off a core part of his personality, and he became even angrier and more upset.

These smart, successful leaders were hooked by their negative thoughts and emotions. Cynthia was absorbed by guilt; Jeffrey was exploding with anger.

Cynthia told the voices to go away; Jeffrey bottled his frustration. Both were trying to avoid the discomfort they felt. They were being controlled by their inner experience, attempting to control it, or switching between the two.

Getting unhooked

Fortunately, both Cynthia and Jeffrey realized that they couldn't go on—at least not successfully and happily—without more-effective inner strategies. We coached them to adopt the four practices:

Recognize your patterns

The first step in developing emotional agility is to notice when you've been hooked by your thoughts and feelings. That's hard to do, but there are certain telltale signs. One is that your thinking becomes rigid and repetitive. For example, Cynthia began to see that her self-recriminations played like a broken record, repeating the same messages over and over again. Another is that the story your mind is telling seems old, like a rerun of some past experience. Jeffrey noticed that his attitude toward certain colleagues (*He's incompetent; There's no way I'm letting anyone speak to me like that*) was quite familiar. In fact, he had experienced something similar in his previous job—and in the one before that. The source of trouble was not just Jeffrey's environment but his own patterns of thought and feeling. You have to realize that you're stuck before you can initiate change.

Label your thoughts and emotions

When you're hooked, the attention you give your thoughts and feelings crowds your mind; there's no room to examine them. One strategy that may help you consider your situation more objectively is the simple act of labeling. Just as you call a spade a spade, call a thought a thought and an emotion an emotion. *I'm not doing enough at work or at home* becomes *I'm having the thought that I'm not doing enough at work or at home.* Similarly, *My coworker is wrong—he makes me so angry* becomes *I'm having the thought that my coworker is wrong, and I'm feeling anger.* Labeling allows you to see your thoughts and feelings for what they are: transient sources of data that may or may not prove helpful. Humans are psychologically able to take this helicopter view of private experiences, and mounting scientific evidence shows that simple, straightforward mindfulness practice like this not only improves behavior and well-being but also promotes beneficial biological changes in the brain and at the cellular level. As Cynthia started to slow down and label her thoughts, the criticisms that had once pressed in on her like a dense fog became more like clouds passing through a blue sky.

Accept them

The opposite of control is acceptance: not acting on every thought or resigning yourself to negativity but responding to your ideas and emotions with an open attitude, paying attention to them and letting yourself experience them. Take 10 deep breaths, and notice what's happening in the moment. This can bring relief, but it won't necessarily make you feel good. In fact, you may realize just how upset you really are. The important thing is to show yourself (and others) some compassion and examine the reality of the situation. What's going on—both internally and externally? When Jeffrey acknowledged and made room for his feelings of frustration and anger rather than rejecting them, quashing them, or taking them out on others, he began to notice their energetic quality. They were a signal that something important was at stake and that he needed to take productive action. Instead of yelling at people, he could make a clear request of a colleague or move swiftly on a pressing issue. The more Jeffrey accepted his anger and brought his curiosity to it, the more it seemed to support rather than undermine his leadership.

Act on your values

When you unhook yourself from your difficult thoughts and emotions, you expand your choices. You can decide to act in a way that aligns with your values. We encourage leaders to focus on the concept of *workability*: Is your response going to serve you and your organization in the long term as well as the short term? Will it help you steer others in a direction that furthers your collective purpose? Are you taking a step toward being the leader you most want to be and living the life you most want to live? The mind's thought stream flows endlessly, and emotions change like the weather, but values can be called on at any time, in any situation.

When Cynthia considered her values, she recognized how deeply committed she was to both her

WHAT ARE YOUR VALUES?

This list is drawn from the Personal Values Card Sort (2001), developed by W. R. Miller, J. C'de Baca, D. B. Matthews, and P. L. Wilbourne, of the University of New Mexico. You can use it to quickly identify the values you hold that might inform a challenging situation at work. When you next make a decision, ask yourself whether it is consistent with these values.

Accuracy	Duty	Justice	Realism
Achievement	Family	Knowledge	Responsibility
Authority	Forgiveness	Leisure	Risk
Autonomy	Friendship	Mastery	Safety
Caring	Fun	Moderation	Self-knowledge
Challenge	Generosity	Nonconformity	Service
Comfort	Genuineness	Openness	Simplicity
Compassion	Growth	Order	Stability
Contribution	Health	Passion	Tolerance
Cooperation	Helpfulness	Popularity	Tradition
Courtesy	Honesty	Power	Wealth
Creativity	Humility	Purpose	
Dependability	Humor	Rationality	

family and her work. She loved being with her children, but she also cared passionately about the pursuit of justice. Unhooked from her distracting and discouraging feelings of guilt, she resolved to be guided by her principles. She recognized how important it was to get home for dinner with her family every evening and to resist work interruptions during that time. But she also undertook to make a number of important business trips, some of which coincided with school events that she would have preferred to attend. Confident that her values—not solely her emotions—were guiding her, Cynthia finally found peace and fulfillment.

———————

It's impossible to block out difficult thoughts and emotions. Effective leaders are mindful of their inner experiences but not caught in them. They know how to free up their internal resources and commit to actions that align with their values. Developing emotional agility is no quick fix. Even those who, like Cynthia and Jeffrey, regularly practice the steps we've outlined here will often find themselves hooked. But over time, leaders who become increasingly adept at it are the ones most likely to thrive.

SUSAN DAVID is a founder of the Harvard/McLean Institute of Coaching, is on faculty at Harvard Medical School, and is recognized as one of the world's leading management thinkers. She is author of the number-one *Wall Street Journal* bestseller *Emotional Agility* (Avery) based on the concept named by HBR as a Management Idea of the Year. A speaker and adviser in wide demand, David has worked with the senior leadership of hundreds of major organizations, including the United Nations, Ernst & Young, and the World Economic Forum. You can take her free Emotional Agility assessment at susandavid.com/learn. CHRISTINA CONGLETON is a leadership and change consultant at Axon Coaching, and researches stress and the brain at the University of Denver. She holds a master's in human development and psychology from Harvard University.

Reprinted from *Harvard Business Review*, November 2013 (product #R1311L).

6

Why You Should Make Time for Self-Reflection (Even if You Hate Doing It)

By Jennifer Porter

When people find out I'm an executive coach, they often ask who my toughest clients are. Inexperienced leaders? Senior leaders who think they know everything? Leaders who bully and belittle others? Leaders who shirk responsibility?

The answer is none of the above. The hardest leaders to coach are those who won't reflect—particularly leaders who won't reflect on *themselves*.

At its simplest, reflection is about careful thought. But the kind of reflection that is really valuable to leaders is more nuanced than that. The most useful reflection involves the conscious consideration and analysis of beliefs and actions for the purpose of learning. Reflection gives the brain an opportunity to pause amid the chaos, untangle and sort through observations and experiences, consider multiple possible interpretations, and create meaning. This meaning becomes learning, which can then inform future mind-sets and actions. For leaders, this "meaning making" is crucial to their ongoing growth and development.

Research by Giada Di Stefano, Francesca Gino, Gary Pisano, and Bradley Staats in call centers demonstrated that employees who spent 15 minutes at the end of the day reflecting about lessons learned performed 23% better after 10 days than those who did not reflect.[1] A study of U.K. commuters found a similar result when those who were prompted to use their commute to think about and plan for their day were happier, more productive, and less burned-out than people who didn't.[2]

So, if reflection is so helpful, why don't many leaders do it? Leaders often:

- *Don't understand the process.* Many leaders don't know how to reflect. One executive I work with, Ken, shared recently that he had yet again not met his commitment to spend an hour on Sunday mornings reflecting. To help him get over this barrier, I suggested he take the next 30 minutes of our two-hour session and just quietly reflect and then we'd debrief it. After five minutes of silence, he said, "I guess I don't really know what you want me to do. Maybe that's why I haven't been doing it."

- *Don't like the process.* Reflection requires leaders to do a number of things they typically don't like to do: slow down, adopt a mind-set of not knowing and curiosity, tolerate messiness and inefficiency, and take personal responsibility. The process can lead to valuable insights and even breakthroughs—and it can also lead to feelings of discomfort, vulnerability, defensiveness, and irritation.

- *Don't like the results.* When a leader takes time to reflect, she typically sees ways she was effective as well as things she could have done better. Most leaders quickly dismiss the noted strengths and dislike the noted weaknesses. Some become so defensive in the process that they don't learn anything, so the results are not helpful.

- *Have a bias toward action.* Like soccer goalies, many leaders have a bias toward action. A study of professional soccer goalies defending penalty kicks found that goalies who stay in the center of the goal, instead of lunging left or right, have a 33% chance of stopping the goal, and yet these goalies only stay in the center 6% of the time. The goalies just feel better when they "do something." The same is true of many leaders. Reflection can feel like staying in the center of the goal and missing the action.

- *Can't see a good ROI.* From early roles, leaders are taught to invest where they can generate a positive ROI—results that indicate the contribution of time, talent, or money paid off. Sometimes it's hard to see an immediate ROI on reflection, particularly when compared with other uses of a leader's time.

If you have found yourself making these same excuses, you can become more reflective by practicing a few simple steps.

- *Identify some important questions.* But don't answer them yet. Here are some possibilities:

  - What are you avoiding?

  - How are you helping your colleagues achieve their goals?

- How are you *not* helping or even hindering their progress?

- How might you be contributing to your least enjoyable relationship at work?

- How could you have been more effective in a recent meeting?

- *Select a reflection process that matches your preferences.* Many people reflect by writing in a journal. If that sounds terrible but talking with a colleague sounds better consider that. As long as you're reflecting and not just chatting about the latest sporting event or complaining about a colleague, your approach is up to you. You can sit, walk, bike, or stand, alone or with a partner, writing, talking, or thinking.

- *Schedule time.* Most leaders are driven by their calendars. So, schedule your reflection time and then commit to keep it. And if you find yourself trying to skip it or avoid it, reflect on that!

- *Start small.* If an hour of reflection seems like too much, try 10 minutes. Teresa Amabile and her colleagues found that the most significant driver of positive emotions and motivation at work was making progress on the tasks at hand. Set yourself up to make progress, even if it feels small.[3]

- *Do it.* Go back to your list of questions and explore them. Be still. Think. Consider multiple perspectives. Look at the opposite of what you initially believe. Brainstorm. You don't have to like or agree with all of your thoughts—just think and examine your thinking.

- *Ask for help.* For most leaders, a lack of desire, time, experience, or skill can get in the way of reflection. Consider working with a colleague, therapist, or coach to help you make the time, listen carefully, be a thought partner, and hold you accountable.

Despite the challenges to reflection, the impact is clear. As Peter Drucker said: "Follow effective action with quiet reflection. From the quiet reflection will come even more effective action."

JENNIFER PORTER is the managing partner of The Boda Group, a leadership and team development firm. She is a graduate of Bates College and the Stanford Graduate School of Business, an experienced operations executive, and an executive and team coach.

Notes

1. Giada Di Stefano, Francesca Gino, Gary P. Pisano, and Bradley R. Staats, "Making Experience Count: The Role of Reflection in Individual Learning," working paper 14-093, Harvard Business School, 2014.
2. Jon M. Jachimowicz et al., "Commuting as Role Transitions: How Trait Self-Control and Work-Related Prospec-

tion Offset Negative Effects of Lengthy Commutes," working paper 16-077, Harvard Business School, 2016.
3. Teresa Amabile and Steven J. Kramer, "The Power of Small Wins," *Harvard Business Review*, May 2011.

Reprinted from hbr.org, originally published
March 21, 2017 (product #H03JNJ).

7

You, By the Numbers

By H. James Wilson

A few years ago entrepreneur and scientist Stephen Wolfram wrote a blog post titled "The Personal Analytics of My Life."[1] In it, he mapped data about his email usage, time spent in meetings, even the number of keystrokes he's logged—*for 22 years*. The resulting charts and graphs are mesmerizing, and somewhat instructive. Wolfram has documented that he's a man of routine who likes to work alone late at night. He knows that although his scheduled telephone calls usually start on time, his in-person meetings are less predictable—and that he's hitting the backspace key 7% of the time he's on the keyboard.

This "effort at self-awareness," as Wolfram described it, makes him a trailblazer in the growing discipline of *auto-analytics*—the practice of voluntarily collecting and analyzing data about oneself in order to improve. Athletes have long used visual and advanced statistical analysis to ratchet up their performance. Now auto-analytics is flourishing in the workplace, too. With wearables, mobile devices and apps, sophisticated data visualization, and AI, it has become fairly easy to monitor our office activity—and any factors that might affect it—and to use that information to make better choices about where to focus our time and energy.

This heralds an important shift in how we think about tracking work performance and even career planning. Employees have long been measured, but managers have traditionally chosen the tools and the metrics—and, more important, decided how to interpret the findings. With auto-analytics, individuals take control. They can run autonomous experiments to pinpoint which tasks and techniques make them most productive and satisfied—and then implement changes accordingly.

Wolfram's insight was that his "shockingly regular" routine liberated him to be "energetic—and spontaneous—about intellectual and other things." But he did not use the data to discover ways to improve his performance, and in that way his blog post is as much cautionary as it is pioneering, for it highlights the pitfalls of embracing auto-analytics without first adopting a plan. Lacking a clear goal at the outset, Wolfram took two decades to synthesize his vast collection of data. Even then he stopped at observation rather than progressing to analysis and intervention. What improvements could he have made on the basis of his findings? Would it have been more useful to map, say, project time lines against stress levels— or, given that he runs his company remotely, moods against time spent with others?

If these kinds of questions are not tackled up front, auto-analytics runs the risk of becoming a promising concept that's poorly applied and then dismissed as just another tech fad. To do it right, you need to understand the tools and develop an approach. The aim is not merely to increase self-awareness but to become better at your job and more satisfied with your life.

The tools

There are two broad types of auto-analytics tools. The first are *trackers*, which reveal patterns and help you set goals. They allow you to document routines and physical responses such as sleep hours, heart rate, and food consumed or calories burned—information you can use to learn, for example, how your caffeine and sugar consumption affects your work output or which office interactions spike your blood pressure. Trackers are best used longitudinally (over days, weeks, or longer) and iteratively, to test interventions and their results until the right balance is struck. You gather a baseline of personal data and then run cycles of data collection and analysis.

That analysis readies you for the second type of tools, *nudgers*, which guide you toward your goals by asking questions or prompting action on the basis of the data they've received. Nudgers are often apps or online tools that might tell you to work out, to stop drinking coffee, or to slow down during a presentation. They usually require some up-front investment to make the algorithms "know" how and when to ping you.

The analysis

What exactly can you measure? Using successful cases and research, I have developed a framework that includes three arenas where auto-analytics can be useful: the physical self, the thinking self, and the emotional self (body, mind, and spirit).

The physical self

Your physical condition affects your work. We've known this roughly since the Industrial Revolution, when Frederick Taylor's famous time and motion studies showed that an iron-plant worker's movements, such as shoveling pig iron into a cart, could be measured and improved. Likewise, the sleep patterns, stress levels, and exercise regimens of knowledge workers have been shown to affect productivity, creativity, and overall job performance. Today these workers can choose from a variety of mobile apps, wearable sensors, or desktop tools that autonomously collect rich data about their bodies' movements and physiological systems.

Business consultant Sacha Chua wanted to understand the relationship between her sleep schedule and achieving her professional priorities, so she has tested several tools for this purpose. Using a sleep-tracking app, she monitored her bedtimes, wake-up times,

SELF-MEASUREMENT AT A GLANCE

Tools in the field of auto-analytics often employ behavior-based algorithms to make recommendations to users. The analyzed data may be collected by wearable devices with sensors and visualized on mobile devices or computers. Most tools focus on one of three personal domains.

The physical self

Tools that measure and monitor physical movements and body functions help you make better decisions about professional effectiveness and well-being. Sleep trackers may gather data on sleep quantity and quality, enabling you to understand why you feel alert (or lethargic) on certain workdays and how to optimize the relationship between rest and performance. Movement or fitness trackers may count the

(Continued)

SELF-MEASUREMENT AT A GLANCE

number of steps you've taken or nudge you to get up when you've been sitting still for too long.

The thinking self

Tools focused on the thinking self gather data related to the routines, habits, and productivity of knowledge work. Browser-based attention trackers visualize patterns that reflect where and how much your attention flows across categories while on the web during a workday.

---

amount of sleep per night, and sleep quality over several weeks. (See the sidebar "Self-Measurement at a Glance.") With this baseline and a hypothesis that she was sleeping later than she should, she then tried waking up earlier—at 5:40 rather than 8:30 a.m.

Chua discovered, to her surprise, that she was getting *more* and better sleep with the new wake-up

The emotional self

Tools that measure emotions increase users' awareness of how professional decisions, situations, and actions correlate with mood. A mood-tracking app may prompt you with occasional simple questions to track your state of mind over time. Then it can make recommendations, derived from clinical practice insights and research data, about how you can improve job performance and satisfaction.

time, which improved her engagement and performance at work. It seemed to be forcing her to eschew unimportant late-night activities, such as browsing the web, so that she could go to bed earlier. Instead of squandering much of her morning in low-quality sleep while hitting the snooze button over and over, she could spend the time writing and programming.

This exercise was nominally about sleep, but the data provided a more rigorous way for Chua to explore, prioritize, and act on what really mattered to her personally and professionally.

The thinking self

In the 1960s Peter Drucker legitimized quantifying the thinking self into units of knowledge work. Although knowledge work has remained notoriously tough to measure rigorously or directly while it is being performed, its output is still tracked with approximations like billable hours, reports filed, or lines of code written. Such measures can inform managers and financial systems, but they do little to guide individuals who want to learn how to get better at their jobs. Auto-analytics can help by gathering data as you perform cognitive tasks, such as client research on your smartphone or statistical analysis in Excel.

Google engineer Bob Evans used both trackers and nudgers to investigate the relationship between his attention and his productivity. He explains, "As engineers, we load up our heads with all these variables, the intellectual pieces of the systems we are building. If we get distracted, we lose that thread in our heads."

With a tool that interacts with online calendars, Evans analyzed how frequently he was shifting between solitary thinking and collegial interaction across his days and weeks—and then mapped that against his work output. The data showed him that he needs about four straight hours to get anything ambitious done, so he's now focusing on his most challenging tasks when he has that kind of time, not during days when lots of meetings disrupt his mental flow.

Evans also uses a mobile app that randomly pings him three times a day, asking, "Have you been working in the past two hours?" If he hasn't, he's prodded to refocus. If he clicks yes, the app asks more questions: "What was your primary work activity?" and "What was your secondary work activity?" This data-gathering approach, developed by psychologist

Mihaly Csikszentmihalyi, is called the experience sampling method, or ESM. Just over a week into Evans's three-week experiment, the ESM data began to show that he was responding to work emails too frequently, which distracted him from more important tasks. So he began to answer email just twice a day to see whether that increased his productivity. It did. In the third week, every time the app pinged him, he was in the midst of his core programming work. (Notably, one of Evans's colleagues set the app to check in with him *eight* times a day. He grew so frustrated that he abandoned the experiment.)

The emotional self

Daniel Goleman famously asserted that nearly 90% of the difference between outstanding and average leaders is attributable to emotional factors, not intellectual acumen. Indeed, many professionals are intrigued by the role emotions play in their careers, and they aspire to become more aware of their own emotional states and their ability to manage them. Yet assessment tools and coaches focusing on emotional intelligence are expensive, intrusive, and often reserved for select members of the C-suite.

Auto-analytics tools don't measure emotional intelligence per se, but they provide an easier way to gain insight into emotions and use data to enhance our predictions of what will make us happy in our daily work and careers. Many apps and tools track moods by prompting the user: "How do you feel right now?" If you use one on a GPS-enabled mobile phone, you can discover correlations between your emotions and your location. Are you happiest working at home, at Starbucks, or at the office? Are you less happy at certain client sites or when you travel? Or, using a tool that crunches textual data—such as the types of words in your email communications or journal entries—you can quantify feelings about a particular assignment or job opportunity.

These tools are no substitute for personal reflection, but they can facilitate the process. A case in point is that of Marie Dupuch, a branding strategist who had long envied people who "could recognize their mood and know exactly what put them in it." Realizing she wasn't that intuitive, she instead tried a quantitative approach to understanding her emotions.

With college graduation looming, and the pressure to "reflect and figure things out" before entering the job market, she began tracking her moods. During her three-month final semester, she used a beta version of a tracker app that asked her to rate her mood on a five-point scale three times a day. At first, the findings were predictable: Talking to friends and family on Skype enhanced her mood; riding on public transportation depressed it. But one data point stood out: Thursdays were her happiest days, which surprised her given that they were also her busiest.

On Thursdays Dupuch drove from her college campus to the city for a course on advertising that featured guest lecturers and required interaction with advertising executives and other creative types. She hypothesized that it was the exposure to the advertising world in an urban location that made her hardest day her happiest. So she decided to test her theory: She scheduled six informational interviews over five days with ad agencies in Manhattan and measured her mood the whole time. She reflects, "Through this test I was able to see with real data that advertising was a good bet, that this was the kind of career that would make me happy." Today she is working happily and productively in the advertising industry in New York.

Of course, effectively tracking your emotions presupposes that you can take an analytical—even a clinical—view of your mood when data are being gathered. That's quite different from tracking hours of sleep or number of emails sent. Dupuch is among many I've spoken to who say that the process is unnatural at first but that it gets easier with practice and eventually improves your ability to sense and react to how you're feeling.

The future

It's still early days for auto-analytics. Nevertheless, important new streams of research, based in cognitive and behavioral science, are currently being conducted at universities and by private enterprises. A project called Quantified Self is hosting opportunities for individuals to try out auto-analytics tools and experimental methods. In addition, new field-based insights on data visualization and algorithm innovation from the field of business analytics have direct application for auto-analytics practitioners and toolmakers.

Two other trends are also emerging. First, the tools will become more sophisticated. Some will be smarter, with machine-learning algorithms that make the nudging function more nuanced so that, for example, the technology knows better when and how to ping you. They may also allow for more accuracy, gathering more types of data related to diet and physical activity at a faster rate. Some tools will become less visible—woven into clothing to capture physical data, for instance, or embedded in professional tools such as spreadsheets and word processing apps. Second, a more holistic approach to auto-analytics will develop. Applications will consolidate many kinds of measurements in a single dashboard and allow us to analyze ourselves across ever more complex dimensions.

Some tools already combine tracking and nudging—and can add a social dimension. They ask you to create a goal, such as increasing your number of sales calls or conversations with direct reports each week, and then use digital displays to help you analyze your daily progress toward achieving it. To increase your motivation, they use nudges or even levy small financial penalties when you veer off track. And they can be used socially so that people—even strangers—working toward the same goal can share data and encourage one another, as people do in a weight-loss club.

Tech entrepreneur Nick Winter has used this methodology to great success. When he felt he was on a productivity plateau and sensed that his new business was in jeopardy, he began gathering data on his work activities and output. Over a 10-month period, Winter tested four distinct approaches to being more productive, from spreadsheet tracking to nudger tools. He settled on an auto-analytics technique called "percentile feedback graphing" to help him see trends clearly. He has now assembled an online group of like-minded colleagues who compare—and compete on—their metrics.

Another example of data consolidation is Personal Analytics Companion (PACO), an open-source mobile app designed by Google's Bob Evans, whose story appeared earlier. "Instead of having all these vertical apps, from mood trackers to meeting trackers, this is one place where you . . . can mash all your data together and compare," Evans says. "You can see trends, distributions, relationships."

Imagine the auto-analytics app that helps a manager reschedule his innovation session because it knows he didn't sleep well, his extra-long commute created stress, and he has a dull budget meeting right before the session. Or consider the knowledge worker who arms herself before a performance review with personal benchmark data that will support or counter her manager's assessment.

That's where auto-analytics is heading. When analysis reveals higher performance on noncore tasks, auto-analytics can even become the impetus for a full-on career switch. Think of how much less anxiety that life-altering decision would cause if you had data to support it.

Applied the right way, auto-analytics can provide hard evidence in situations where traditionally we've relied on intuition and anecdotal feedback. Quantifying yourself is a revelatory experience—and perhaps the best thing you can do to improve your career and your life.

H. JAMES WILSON is a managing director of Information Technology and Business Research at Accenture Research. Follow him on Twitter @hjameswilson. Wilson is coauthor with Paul Daugherty of *Human + Machine: Reimagining Work in the Age of AI* (Harvard Business Review Press, 2018).

Note

1. Stephen Wolfram, "The Personal Analytics of My Life" (blog post), March 8, 2012, http://blog.stephenwolfram.com/2012/03/the-personal-analytics-of-my-life/.

Adapted from *Harvard Business Review*, September 2012 (reprint #R1209K).

8

How Are You Perceived at Work? Here's an Exercise to Find Out

By Kristi Hedges

I t's not easy to understand how other people perceive us. We are often uncertain, confused, or even completely unaware of what we project. And this lack of self-awareness can be career-limiting.

Consider a former client of mine who was angling for the C-suite but had received feedback that his colleagues considered him negative and difficult. He was stunned; he thought of himself as analytical and thorough and assumed everyone understood that he pushed back in order to get to the best answer. He was also unaware that he had a habit of grimacing while processing information, which looked to others like annoyance.

My client was suffering from what psychologists call the *transparency illusion*—the belief that we're all open books and that what we intend is what people see. But there can be a wide gap between intent and impact. People are often unaware of their facial expressions, especially when deep in thought. (As a colleague of mine says, "Thinking faces aren't pretty.") And particular emotions can be confusing to interpret. Frustration and slight discomfort, for example, can easily be mistaken for each another.

Knowing that most of us don't clearly project what we intend doesn't stop us from confidently forming impressions based on the *impact* we feel. And in organizations, these impressions are often crowdsourced (a kind of offline Yelp for people) and a common narrative can emerge. These narratives get shared as advice (*Just started reporting to Ana? Here's the best way to work with her*) or spread as malicious gossip (*Claude's jockeying for power again*).

Tapping into this collective impression can give us valuable information on what's working for us and where we may need to adjust our style. Even if we get frequent feedback at work, it's typically about our functional performance. You may be told that your sales skills need sharpening, but not that people see you as self-interested. Which one has more of an impact on your career?

In *The Power of Presence*, I outline a straightforward presence audit to determine how others perceive you. It only takes a couple well-worded questions to a few key people to get the information you need. (If you've ever conducted a 360-degree evaluation, you've seen how quickly impressions start repeating.)

While this exercise won't take a lot of time, it may be psychically intensive. So keep in mind that there's never a comfortable time to do this and assume now is the exact right time.

Use this process as a guide:

- *Select five people.* Choose colleagues who see you repeatedly in relevant work situations:

bosses, executives, direct reports, peers, or even former colleagues. Influential coworkers who have their ears to the ground make great sources. If they know you in more than one aspect of your work or life, even better. While it's important that you have trusted people in your group, make sure to choose people who will tell it to you straight.

- *Ask for a face-to-face meeting.* Be clear that you'll keep whatever the person tells you confidential, which will encourage honesty, and that you'll be collecting feedback from several people to find themes, which lessens the burden for any one individual. Make the request in person if you can. People are more likely to consent to participate if they can see you. A phone call can work too if you can't be physically in front of someone. If you have to make the request via email, offer to answer any questions ahead of the meeting.

- *Ask two questions.* In the meeting, ask these two simple questions designed to tap into the collective wisdom:

  1. *What's the general perception of me?*

  2. *What could I do differently that would have the greatest impact on my success?*

  Depending on the person, you'll hear responses ranging from eye-opening and helpful to vague and confusing. If the person is uncomfortable, they may rely on job- or project-specific feedback. In that case, clarify:

  > *I appreciate that feedback. May I go up a level now and ask about the general perception of me as a leader/colleague/person?*

- *Manage your reaction.* Resist the temptation to explain yourself, defend your actions, or reveal disappointment. Your interviewees will be looking to see what effect their feedback has on you in real time. The quality of your feedback will only be as good as your ability to remain comfortable while receiving it. Ask for details or examples if you need them. And end with a sincere thank-you.

When you've finished the interviews, look for themes and repetitive points (it's OK to shed outliers as long as you're sure they don't contain valuable information). If the perceptions of you are in line with what you intend, great. If not, it's time to change your behaviors and begin to shift perception.

Many times clients have come back to me after completing this exercise and said, "Why didn't anyone tell me this before? I can easily change that!"

This is precisely what happened with my client who was perceived as negative and difficult. After realizing that he was being misinterpreted, he made a commitment to state his intentions up front to foster transparency. He adjusted his style in meetings to ask open-ended questions to make clear he was interested in understanding the other person's position. And he worked hard to control his tendency to grimace and keep a neutral facial expression that connoted openness. Gradually he was able to change perceptions, and allow people to know the empathetic and caring person that he knew himself to be.

The transparency illusion is a common trap for managers at all levels. Fortunately, it's possible to close the gap between how people perceive you and how you want to be perceived. Gather reliable information and then make a commitment to change.

KRISTI HEDGES is a senior leadership coach who specializes in executive communications and the author of *The Inspiration Code: How the Best Leaders Energize People Every Day* and *The Power of Presence: Unlock Your Potential to Influence and Engage Others.* She's the president of The Hedges Company and a faculty member in Georgetown University's Institute for Transformational Leadership.

Reprinted from hbr.org, originally published
December 19, 2017 (product #H04316).

9

How to Solicit Negative Feedback When Your Manager Doesn't Want to Give It

By Deborah Grayson Riegel

I n my role as a leadership coach, I consistently hear my clients say that they crave negative feedback from their managers in order to improve in their jobs, grow their careers, and achieve better business results. However, when it comes to soliciting negative feedback, they find that their managers would rather dismiss, deny, or delay it rather than speak directly, truthfully, and immediately about what isn't working and what needs to change.

That makes sense when you consider what may be at risk when giving (and receiving) negative feedback. In her article, "How to Give Negative Feedback When Your Organization Is 'Nice,'" my colleague Jennifer

Porter cites barriers to giving negative feedback that include hurt feelings; a desire to maintain professionalism (rather than having things get "messy"); a lack of role models for giving negative feedback; the prospect of an emotional outburst; and not wanting to jeopardize the "nice" culture.[1]

Additional research from University of California professors Naomi Eisenberger and Matthew Lieberman, and Purdue University professor Kipling D. Williams, shows that negative feedback can be experienced as a form a social rejection ("You're telling me I'm not good enough and that I don't belong here" is one frequent interpretation), and that social rejection hurts emotionally *and* physically.[2] Few managers want to cause their direct reports pain and potentially risk an emotional outburst, loss of commitment, or even retaliation.

Nevertheless, when people don't receive useful negative feedback, they can't grow. According to authors Jack Zenger and Joseph Folkman in their article, "Your Employees Want the Negative Feedback You Hate to Give," when asked what was most helpful in their careers, 72% of respondents attributed performance improvement to getting negative feedback from their managers.[3] The same study also showed that managers were reluctant to give negative feedback.

Bill Gates agrees: "We all need people who will give us feedback. That's how we improve."[4]

So what do you do if you know that negative feedback is what you need to succeed—and nobody's talking? Stop asking for negative feedback (you've already tried that, right?) and try one of these creative approaches instead:

- *Give yourself negative feedback first.* According to Wharton professor and author Adam Grant, "When people shy away from giving constructive feedback, it's often because they're afraid of hurting your feelings. But if they hear you talk

about what you did wrong, the fear melts away."
Start by saying something like, "I know that
I tend to work quickly and sometimes overlook important details. I'd like to get better at
that. Do you have any thoughts on how I could
improve?" And then, once you have them talking, you can ask, "And is there anything else I
could be working to improve right now?"[5]

- *Make self-improvement a personal commitment—and ask for help.* If directly soliciting
  negative feedback isn't working, tell your manager that you've made a commitment to yourself to improve in three areas this year, and that
  you'd like her feedback on what one or more of
  those should be. Ask, "Would you please help
  me keep the commitment I've made to myself?"
  That way, she can view her feedback as more
  about helping you make good on a promise and
  less about hurting your feelings.

- *Reframe negative feedback as a learning opportunity.* If your manager, colleague, or client is reticent to offer negative feedback directly, ask, "What is something you think I could learn from you?" It gives the other person a chance to reflect on their own talents and skills (which makes most people feel good), and share their thinking about where they could help you grow—in a nonthreatening context. (If you're really lucky, they might even ask you, "And what is something you think I could learn from you?" and then you get to give some gentle negative feedback, too.)

- *Preemptively minimize the impact of the negative feedback.* When people are willing to give negative feedback, they often couch it as "just one little thing—it's not a big deal" to minimize the impact. You can do that yourself by asking, "If I could change just one small habit, what should it be?" That signals to the other person that they don't have to minimize, apologize, or put negative feedback in context to make it palatable for you—you've done it already.

Managers should be able to give negative feedback, but even if they don't, you need to learn how to solicit it so that you get the information you need to grow in your job and career.

DEBORAH GRAYSON RIEGEL is a principal at The Boda Group, a leadership and team development firm. She also teaches management communication at the University of Pennsylvania's Wharton School of Business.

Notes

1. Jennifer Porter, "How to Give Negative Feedback When Your Organization Is 'Nice,'" *Harvard Business Review*, March 14, 1016; Amy Jen Su, "How to Give Negative Feedback to People Who Cry, Yell, or Get Defensive," *Harvard Business Review*, September 21, 2016.

2. Naomi I. Eisenberger, Matthew D. Lieberman, and Kipling D. Williams, "Does Rejection Hurt? An fMRI Study of Social Exclusion," *Science* 302, no. 5643 (October 2003): 290–292.

3. Jack Zenger and Joseph Folkman, "Your Employees Want the Negative Feedback You Hate to Give," *Harvard Business Review*, January 15, 2014.

4. Jana Kasperkevic, "Bill Gates: Good Feedback Is the Key to Improvement," *Inc.*, May 17, 2013.

5. Adam Grant, "Wondering" (blog), January 2018, http://www.adamgrant.net/wondering.

Reprinted from hbr.org, originally published
March 5, 2018 (product #H046U4).

10

Find the Coaching in Criticism

By Sheila Heen and Douglas Stone

Feedback is crucial. That's obvious: It improves performance, develops talent, aligns expectations, solves problems, guides promotion and pay, and boosts the bottom line.

But it's equally obvious that in many organizations, feedback doesn't work. A glance at the stats tells the story: Only 36% of managers complete appraisals thoroughly and on time. In one recent survey, 55% of employees said their most recent performance review had been unfair or inaccurate, and one in four said they dread such evaluations more than anything else in their working lives. When senior HR executives were asked about their biggest performance management challenge, 63% cited managers' inability or unwillingness to have difficult feedback discussions. Coaching and mentoring? Uneven at best.

Most companies try to address these problems by training leaders to give feedback more effectively and more often. That's fine as far as it goes; everyone benefits when managers are better communicators. But improving the skills of the feedback giver won't accomplish much if the receiver isn't able to absorb what is said. It is the receiver who controls whether feedback is let in or kept out, who has to make sense of what he or she is hearing, and who decides whether or not to change. People need to stop treating feedback only as something that must be pushed and instead improve their ability to pull.

For the past 20 years we've coached executives on difficult conversations, and we've found that almost everyone, from new hires to C-suite veterans, struggles with receiving feedback. A critical performance review, a well-intended suggestion, or an oblique comment that may or may not even be feedback ("Well, your presentation was certainly interesting") can spark an emotional reaction, inject tension into the relationship, and bring communication to a halt. But there's good news, too: The skills needed to receive feedback well are distinct and learnable. They include being able to identify and manage the emotions triggered by the feedback and extract value from criticism even when it's poorly delivered.

Why feedback doesn't register

What makes receiving feedback so hard? The process strikes at the tension between two core human needs—the need to learn and grow, and the need to be accepted just the way you are. As a result, even a seemingly benign suggestion can leave you feeling angry, anxious, badly treated, or profoundly threatened. A hedge such as "Don't take this personally" does nothing to soften the blow.

Getting better at receiving feedback starts with understanding and managing those feelings. You might think there are a thousand ways in which feedback can push your buttons, but in fact there are only three.

Truth triggers are set off by the content of the feedback. When assessments or advice seem off base, unhelpful, or simply untrue, you feel indignant, wronged, and exasperated.

Relationship triggers are tripped by the person providing the feedback. Exchanges are often colored by what you believe about the giver (He's got no credibility on this topic!) and how you feel about your previous interactions (After all I've done for you, I get this petty criticism?). So you might reject coaching that you would accept on its merits if it came from someone else.

Identity triggers are all about your relationship with yourself. Whether the feedback is right or wrong, wise or witless, it can be devastating if it causes your sense of who you are to come undone. In such moments you'll struggle with feeling overwhelmed, defensive, or off balance.

All these responses are natural and reasonable; in some cases they are unavoidable. The solution isn't to pretend you don't have them. It's to recognize what's happening and learn how to derive benefit from feedback even when it sets off one or more of your triggers.

Six steps to becoming a better receiver

Taking feedback well is a process of sorting and filtering. You need to understand the other person's point of view, try on ideas that may at first seem a poor fit, and experiment with different ways of doing things. You also need to discard or shelve critiques that are genuinely misdirected or are not helpful right away.

But it's nearly impossible to do any of those things from inside a triggered response. Instead of ushering you into a nuanced conversation that will help you learn, your triggers prime you to reject, counterattack, or withdraw.

The six steps below will keep you from throwing valuable feedback onto the discard pile or—just as damaging—accepting and acting on comments that you would be better off disregarding. They are presented as advice to the receiver. But, of course, understanding the challenges of receiving feedback helps the giver be more effective, too.

1. Know your tendencies

You've been getting feedback all your life, so there are no doubt patterns in how you respond. Do you defend yourself on the facts ("This is plain wrong"), argue about the method of delivery ("You're really doing this by email?"), or strike back ("You, of all people?")? Do you smile on the outside but seethe on the inside? Do you get teary or filled with righteous indignation? And what role does the passage of time play? Do you tend to reject feedback in the moment and then step back and consider it over time? Do you accept it all immediately but later decide it's not valid? Do you agree with it intellectually but have trouble changing your behavior?

When Michael, an advertising executive, hears his boss make an offhand joke about his lack of professionalism, it hits him like a sledgehammer. "I'm flooded with shame," he told us, "and all my failings rush to mind, as if I'm Googling 'things wrong with me' and getting 1.2 million hits, with sponsored ads from my father and my ex. In this state it's hard to see the feedback at 'actual size.'" But now that Michael understands his standard operating procedure, he's able to make better choices about where to go from there: "I can reassure myself that I'm exaggerating, and usually after I sleep on it, I'm in a better place to figure out whether there's something I can learn."

2. Disentangle the "what" from the "who"

If the feedback is on target and the advice is wise, it shouldn't matter who delivers it. But it does. When a relationship trigger is activated, entwining the content of comments with your feelings about the giver (or about how, when, or where she delivered the comments), learning is short-circuited. To keep that from happening, you have to work to separate the message from the messenger, and then consider both.

Janet, a chemist and a team leader at a pharmaceutical company, received glowing comments from her peers and superiors during her 360-degree review but was surprised by the negative feedback she got from her direct reports. She immediately concluded that the problem was theirs: "I have high standards, and some of them can't handle that," she remembers thinking. "They aren't used to someone holding their feet to the fire." In this way, she changed the subject from her management style to her subordinates' competence, preventing her from learning something important about the impact she had on others.

Eventually the penny dropped, Janet says. "I came to see that whether it was their performance problem or my leadership problem, those were not mutually exclusive issues, and both were worth solving." She was able to disentangle the issues and talk to her team about both. Wisely, she began the conversation with their feedback to her, asking, "What am I doing that's making things tough? What would improve the situation?"

3. Sort toward coaching

Some feedback is evaluative ("Your rating is a 4"); some is coaching ("Here's how you can improve").

Everyone needs both. Evaluations tell you where you stand, what to expect, and what is expected of you. Coaching allows you to learn and improve and helps you play at a higher level.

It's not always easy to distinguish one from the other. When a board member phoned James to suggest that he start the next quarter's CFO presentation with analyst predictions rather than internal projections, was that intended as a helpful suggestion, or was it a veiled criticism of his usual approach? When in doubt, people tend to assume the worst and to put even well-intentioned coaching into the evaluation bin. Feeling judged is likely to set off your identity triggers, and the resulting anxiety can drown out the opportunity to learn. So whenever possible, sort toward coaching. Work to hear feedback as potentially valuable advice from a fresh perspective rather than as an indictment of how you've done things in the past. When James took that approach, "the suggestion became less emotionally loaded," he says. "I decided to hear it as simply an indication of how that board member might more easily digest quarterly information."

4. Unpack the feedback

Often it's not immediately clear whether feedback is valid and useful. So before you accept or reject it, do some analysis to better understand it.

Here's a hypothetical example. Kara, who's in sales, is told by Johann, an experienced colleague, that she needs to "be more assertive." Her reaction might be to reject his advice ("I think I'm pretty assertive already"). Or she might acquiesce ("I really do need to step it up"). But before she decides what to do, she needs to understand what he really means. Does he think she should speak up more often, or just with greater conviction? Should she smile more or less? Have the confidence to admit she doesn't know something or the confidence to pretend she does?

Even the simple advice to "be more assertive" comes from a complex set of observations and judgments that Johann has made while watching Kara in meetings and with customers. Kara needs to dig into the general suggestion and find out what in particular prompted it. What did Johann see her do or fail to do? What did he expect, and what is he worried about? In other words, where is the feedback coming from?

Kara also needs to know where the feedback is going—exactly what Johann wants her to do differently and why. After a clarifying discussion, she might agree that she is less assertive than others on the sales floor but disagree with the idea that she should change. If all her sales heroes are quiet, humble, and deeply curious about customers' needs, Kara's view of what it means to be good at sales might look and sound very different from Johann's *Glengarry Glen Ross* ideal.

When you set aside snap judgments and take time to explore where feedback is coming from and where it's going, you can enter into a rich, informative conversation about perceived best practices—whether you decide to take the advice or not.

5. Ask for just one thing

Feedback is less likely to set off your emotional triggers if you request it and direct it. So don't wait until your annual performance review. Find opportunities to get bite-size pieces of coaching from a variety of people throughout the year. Don't invite criticism with a big, unfocused question like "Do you have any feedback for me?" Make the process more manageable by asking a colleague, a boss, or a direct report, "What's one thing you see me doing (or failing to do) that holds me back?" That person may name the first behavior that comes to mind or the most important one on his or her list. Either way, you'll get concrete information and can tease out more specifics at your own pace.

Roberto, a fund manager at a financial services firm, found his 360-degree review process overwhelming and confusing. "Eighteen pages of charts and graphs and no ability to have follow-up conversations to clarify the feedback was frustrating," he says, adding that it also left him feeling awkward around his colleagues.

Now Roberto taps two or three people each quarter to ask for one thing he might work on. "They don't offer the same things, but over time I hear themes, and that gives me a good sense of where my growth edge lies," he says. "And I have really good conversations—with my boss, with my team, even with peers where there's some friction in the relationship. They're happy to tell me one thing to change, and often they're right. It does help us work more smoothly together."

Research has shown that those who explicitly seek critical feedback (that is, who are not just fishing for praise) tend to get higher performance ratings. Why?

Mainly, we think, because someone who's asking for coaching is more likely to take what is said to heart and genuinely improve. But also because when you ask for feedback, you not only find out how others see you, you also *influence* how they see you. Soliciting constructive criticism communicates humility, respect, passion for excellence, and confidence, all in one go.

6. Engage in small experiments

After you've worked to solicit and understand feedback, it may still be hard to discern which bits of advice will help you and which ones won't. We suggest designing small experiments to find out. Even though you may doubt that a suggestion will be useful, if the downside risk is small and the upside potential is large, it's worth a try. James, the CFO we discussed earlier, decided to take the board member's advice for the next presentation and see what happened. Some directors were pleased with the change, but the shift in format prompted others to offer suggestions of their own. Today James reverse-engineers his presentations to meet board members' current top-of-mind concerns. He sends out an email a week beforehand asking for any burning questions and either front-loads his talk with answers to them or signals at the start that he will get to them later on. "It's a little more challenging to prepare for but actually much easier to give," he says. "I spend less time fielding unexpected questions, which was the hardest part of the job."

That's an example worth following. When someone gives you advice, test it out. If it works, great. If it doesn't, you can try again, tweak your approach, or decide to end the experiment. Criticism is never easy to take. Even when you know that it's essential to your development and you trust that the person delivering it wants you to succeed, it can activate psychological triggers. You might feel misjudged, ill-used, and sometimes threatened to your very core.

Your growth depends on your ability to pull value from criticism in spite of your natural responses and on your willingness to seek out even more advice and coaching from bosses, peers, and subordinates. They may be good or bad at providing it, or they may have little time for it—but you are the most important factor in your own development. If you're determined to learn from whatever feedback you get, no one can stop you.

SHEILA HEEN and DOUGLAS STONE are cofounders of Triad Consulting Group and teach negotiation at Harvard Law School. They are coauthors of *Thanks for the Feedback: The Science and Art of Receiving Feedback Well*, from which this article is adapted.

Reprinted from *Harvard Business Review,*
January–February 2014 (product #R1401K).

11

Shakespeare's Characters Show Us How Personal Growth Should Happen

By Declan Fitzsimons

Norman Mailer once wrote that there is a cruel but just law of life that says we must change or pay an increasing cost for remaining the same.

As a leadership scholar teaching in a business school, I encounter leaders daily for whom this "law" is a very real and disquieting one. They know what will happen if they don't make the changes to their businesses, but they are not so sure what *they* should do to support those changes. Is it about learning how to run more effective team meetings? Or how to be better listeners? Or adopting a different leadership style to bring about a shift in organizational culture?

While there is no formulaic answer to these questions, there are some fundamentals without which no amount of skills development is ever going to work. One source of insight into what these fundamentals might look like is the work of an author whose work has never been out of print for over 400 years: William Shakespeare.

In the opening chapter of his book *Shakespeare: The Invention of the Human*, Harold Bloom, who has taught Shakespeare at Yale for 30 years, suggests that before Shakespeare, characters in plays would *unfold* but not necessarily *develop*.

If a character merely unfolds, we intuit correctly that we already know all there is to know about them when they first appear onstage. Their authors have robbed them of the one quality that would make them interesting: the capacity for self-inquiry that might reveal something unexpected not only to us but also to themselves. They teach us little because they cannot surprise us, essentially because they cannot surprise themselves. This is the real-world equivalent of the manager who comes out of a feedback session and thinks, "Nothing new—the same feedback as I have heard before," and then says to themselves, "I guess I am what I am!" or "I have my way of doing things, and some people like it and some people don't."

Shakespeare does not let us off the hook so easily. He shows us that we are not simply who we say we are, but instead are made up of many conflicting and unknown parts. As Bloom puts it, Shakespeare's characters develop because they have the ability to *overhear* themselves talk, either to themselves or to others, and are thus able to *reconceive* themselves. By endowing his characters with complex inner worlds, Shakespeare treats us, 400 years before Freud, to virtuoso displays of what to the modern ear sounds very much like self-discovery. There is not one Hamlet but many. After learning of his father's murder, he discovers in soliloquies of stunning intensity that he cannot bear to remain as he is. So tortured is he by his inner conflicts that he considers, in perhaps the most famous soliloquy in all literature, the pros and cons of suicide ("to be or not to be").

We are mesmerized—not simply through the beauty of the language, but because we realize that he is hearing these things *for the first time.* And no matter how many times we see the play, we never tire of it, because it is at such moments that Hamlet, while in real danger of unraveling, is at the same time exquisitely vulnerable and thus truly human.

Shakespeare shows us through Hamlet and other characters not only the *sine qua non* of human development—that in order to change ourselves, we must first discover ourselves—but also what that development sounds like, looks like, and feels like. He shows us that it is the moment when Hamlet is so close to falling apart that he is able to fall together. In like fashion, the young Prince Hal, in *Henry IV, Part 2*, on becoming king, shuns his former companions ("Presume not that I am the thing I was") and begins his extraordinary transformation from profligate prince to King Henry V, hero of Agincourt.

For us, far away from the dramatic intensity of fictional characters, the point is not that we can change only if we contemplate killing ourselves or turn our backs on our friends; change is rather about moving toward, rather than away from, the anxieties that powerful external challenges provoke in our internal worlds. Hamlet was able to face his own inertia and cowardice; Hal was able to confront and thus transcend his dissolute lifestyle and embrace a new identity fit for a king. But both were possible only after the characters became willing to discover what lay within.

Shakespeare teaches us moderns that in the face of an uncertain world, self-awareness—that much-vaunted leadership quality—is only worthy of the name when it is revelatory. And it can only be revelatory when we are willing to concede that we know ourselves only partially.

Development, then, is less about changing ourselves by learning new skills than about discovering ourselves by giving something up—including some of our most cherished notions of the person we think we are—in order to discover the person we could become.

DECLAN FITZSIMONS is adjunct professor of organizational behavior at INSEAD. He researches and consults to companies planning and implementing shared leadership.

Reprinted from hbr.org, originally published January 30, 2017 (product #H03F8L).

Index

How to be human at work.

HBR's Emotional Intelligence Series features smart, essential reading on the human side of professional life from the pages of *Harvard Business Review*. Each book in the series offers uplifting stories, practical advice, and research from leading experts on how to tend to our emotional well-being at work.

Harvard Business Review Emotional Intelligence Series

Available in paperback or ebook format. The specially priced six-volume set includes:

- Mindfulness
- Resilience
- Influence and Persuasion
- Authentic Leadership
- Happiness
- Empathy

HBR.ORG

Buy for your team, clients, or event.
Visit hbr.org/bulksales for quantity discount rates.